WILLIAM STYRON, A LIFE

WILLIAM STYRON, A LIFE

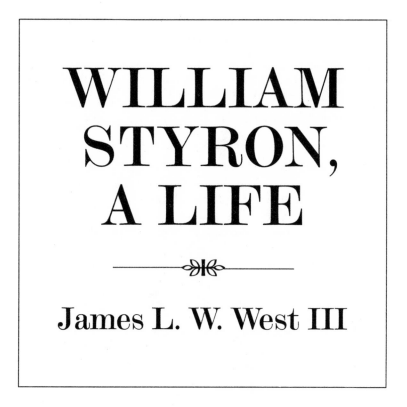

James L. W. West III

RANDOM HOUSE
NEW YORK

4/99 Gift

Grateful acknowledgment is made to Random House, Inc., for permission to reprint
two lines from a letter from Bennett Cerf to William Styron dated March 17, 1959, and
to reprint various excerpts from *This Quiet Dust* by William Styron. *This Quiet Dust*
copyright © 1953, 1961, 1962, 1963, 1964, 1965, 1968, 1972, 1974, 1975, 1976, 1977, 1980,
1981, 1982, by William Styron. All material reprinted by permission of Random House, Inc.

Portions of this book appeared in earlier form as the following:

"Styron in Paris," *Sewanee Review*, 103 (Spring 1995), 231–46.

"William Styron at Duke, 1943–44," *Southern Literary Journal*, 28
(Fall 1995): 5–18. Special Styron issue.

Introduction (by JLWW) to William Styron, *Inheritance of Night: Early
Drafts of* Lie Down in Darkness. Durham: Duke University Press,
1993. xx, 140 pp.

"Voices Interior and Exterior: William Styron's Narrative Personae,"
in *Traditions, Voices, and Dreams: The American Novel since the 1960s,*
ed. Melvin J. Friedman and Ben Siegel. Newark:
Univ. of Delaware Press, 1995, pp. 48–61.

Library of Congress Cataloging-in-Publication Data

West, James L. W.
William Styron : a life / James L.W. West III. — 1st ed.
p.   cm.
Includes bibliographical references and index.
ISBN 0-679-41054-6 (hard cover)
1. Styron, William, 1925– —Biography. 2. Novelists,
American—20th century—Biography. I. Styron, William, 1925–
II. Title.
PS3569.T9Z94   1998   97-27969
813' .54—dc21

Random House website address: www.randomhouse.com

Printed in the United States of America on acid-free paper

24689753

FIRST EDITION

For my sons
JAMES · THOMAS · WILLIAM

And I gave my heart to know wisdom,
   and to know madness and folly:
   I perceived that this also
   is vexation of spirit.
For in much wisdom is much grief:
   and he that increaseth knowledge
   increaseth sorrow.

        —ECCLESIASTES 1:17–18

PREAMBLE

If one wishes to know William Styron, one must walk with him. That is to say, one must go with him on his daily walk for exercise. It is a ritual that he rarely misses; usually he takes the walk alone, though sometimes he goes with his wife or a friend or visitor. The walk covers between four and five miles unless the weather is bad, in which case it is abbreviated.

Preparations for the walk begin around three o'clock with the calling of the dogs. There are two dogs just now, both females—a golden retriever named Tashmoo and a black Labrador named Dinah. Tashmoo is sweet-tempered and shy; Dinah is brash and adventurous. Styron is devoted to them both but is especially fond of Dinah, who amuses and exasperates him. He summons the dogs by hooting at them: *"Baby! Hooo! Come to Daddy! Hooo! Come on!"* The dogs, attuned to the schedule, are ready. Dinah appears, dirty and panting; Tashmoo, who has been resting, trots over to Styron and waits. An old coat is spread over the backseat of the car, and the dogs jump in. Styron and his guest settle into the front seats; Styron starts the engine and puts the car into motion.

Styron almost always drives to the beginning point of a walk. He has explored and measured off many walking paths near his two homes, and he rarely takes the same walk two days in a row. The paths themselves are far from automobile traffic, but one must drive through traffic to reach them. Styron operates the car skillfully; he drives impatiently and a little too fast. On the way he announces the location and direction of our walk for the day, then talks baby talk to Dinah, who licks the back of his head and bites his ears while he is driving.

Styron arrives at the starting point, sets the dogs loose, and begins the walk. He takes the first half-mile at a relaxed amble, to loosen the muscles; then he settles into a steady pace that accelerates the heartbeat and gives the lungs a workout. Though seventy-two years old, Styron can outwalk many men twenty or thirty years his junior. He walks with a spraddle-legged gait, slightly slew-footed, and leans forward from the waist. The exercise is good for his bronchial troubles; he clears his throat and blows his nose frequently on these walks, especially during the winter.

The conversation on the walks is good. Sometimes Styron talks about something he has been reading—an editorial from *The New York Times,* perhaps, or a memoir written by a friend. At other times he mentions critics of his own work, clearing his throat and spitting out the names of unsympathetic book reviewers with great vehemence. Sometimes he discusses politics; during the Reagan and Bush administrations he would do wonderfully profane riffs on the Republicans, venting his irritations over their dastardly behavior. Styron does most of the talking during these walks. It is satisfying to listen, for he is a good talker.

The dogs provide diversion. Tashmoo, the golden retriever, stays close by Styron, her head at his knee. Occasionally she leaves to sniff a bush or lap water from a pool; then she returns and falls back into step with Styron. Dinah, the Lab, is a canine pinball, tearing through the woods after squirrels and rabbits, seeming to bounce off trees and stone fences. If Styron cannot hear her he becomes worried and begins to hoot for her. If she does not come he grows angry and calls her harshly: *"Dinah! Come here!"* She returns when it suits her, muddy and grinning, then sets off again in a few moments.

The walks vary according to the seasons. From early October until June of each year, Styron and his wife, Rose, live near Roxbury, Connecticut. This is rolling, hilly, wooded country, sparsely populated and quiet. The walks here are best during the fall, when the leaves are turning and the southbound geese pass overhead, honking and beating their wings. Styron often takes his walks along the Shepaug River, a tributary of the Housatonic. Unless he has a guest, he frequently sees no other human being on these walks.

The Styrons spend June through September of every year at Vineyard Haven, a town on the island of Martha's Vineyard, and here the walks are more lively. Styron must dodge tourists on bicycles and motor scooters as he drives to the starting point of the walk. He curses as he accelerates and swings the car to avoid them. Some of the paths around Vineyard Haven lead through quiet, leafy woods, but other walks take us through Republican territory—enclaves of well-to-do stockbrokers and attorneys from New York and Boston who have weekend places on the island. One of the walks, up through an area called West Chop, leads through a tennis compound for the wealthy; the courts are usually filled in the afternoons with middle-aged women playing doubles. Often a cocktail party is about to get under way, and we pass plump, sunburned men in brightly colored golf pants escorting thin women with carefully made-up faces. Styron is a strange figure among these well-turned-out professional people. He wears rumpled khakis and a nondescript shirt; his hair, now almost white, is long and windblown; his shoes are dusty. Many of these people seem to know who he is, but they do not speak to him or greet him.

Styron does not pause as we move through this area, though he does glance at the tennis courts and the clubhouse. Dinah, however, causes trouble. She barks at well-behaved dogs and tries to make them chase her. She runs after tennis balls that are hit outside the courts, and if she gets a ball she will not return it. She rushes up to strangers and seems about to jump on them with muddy paws, only to veer away at the last moment. Styron does not discipline her.

The walk is sometimes circular, but more often it leads to a halfway point where we turn and retrace our steps to the car. The dogs, now wet and tired, are told to get into the backseat. Tashmoo cooperates, but Dinah refuses to get in until she has made Styron angry and caused him to shout at her. The drive back is pleasant: our chests and backs are sweaty, and our legs tingle from the exercise. The rest of the day will be laid out on the return drive. There will be a period now when Styron will go into his study to write; then he will reappear around seven-thirty or eight. Dinner will be ready at around nine o'clock; one is free until then to read or take a nap.

At times during these walks Styron speaks about himself—about his upbringing in Tidewater Virginia, his education in prep school and college, and his stints in the Marine Corps. Often he talks about his father, who died in 1978. Sometimes he tells stories of his travels—to France or India or Russia or Mexico—or he talks of academic life and says how glad he is to have avoided it. One listens carefully, for Styron is articulate, perceptive, and witty. One adds a comment occasionally and sometimes carries the conversation for a hundred yards or so, but Styron does most of the talking.

If one has taken these walks over many years and has listened to these talks before, one knows by now that Styron will have revealed very little about himself in what he has said. His words will have been sharp and penetrating, but he will have given no real glimpse of himself—his ambitions and desires, his obsessions and fears, his fantasies and dreams. To someone accustomed to the talk of literary people, this was at first surprising. Often such people are free with their inner feelings and almost confessional in what they say in conversation, even to virtual strangers. Styron does not show himself in this way. He is among the most private of authors: on a few occasions there has seemed to be a hint of fear or a note of longing in his voice, but perhaps one has only imagined these things. Perhaps, after all, our walks have only been for exercise.

William Styron can be apprehended and understood best through what he has written. His novels and other fictions are immensely and painfully self-revealing, and it has always been a curious relief to turn to them in the weeks and months between the walks. Perhaps Styron is too private a man to be approached directly. Still, one can undertake the task; one can go on the walk, observe, and listen.

CONTENTS

Preamble   *ix*

1. Ancestors   *3*
2. Youth   *18*
3. Newport News   *27*
4. Pauline's Death   *39*
5. Fourteenth Year   *54*
6. Christchurch   *63*
7. Davidson   *79*
8. Duke and William Blackburn   *93*
9. Marines, First Stint   *109*
10. After the War   *129*
11. McGraw-Hill   *142*
12. Durham and Flatbush   *159*
13. Valley Cottage and West Eighty-eighth Street   *172*
14. Marines, Second Stint   *189*
15. *Lie Down in Darkness*   *202*
16. Paris, 1952   *214*
17. *The Long March*   *224*
18. Rome   *237*
19. Marriage and Ravello   *252*
20. New York and Roxbury   *266*

21. Mailer and Others   278
22. Completion   297
23. *Set This House on Fire*   306
24. Reentry   315
25. Preparations   331
26. Composition   344
27. *The Confessions of Nat Turner*   362
28. Aftermath   380
29. Interlude   396
30. *Sophie's Choice*   411
31. Breakdown   428
32. "A Tidewater Morning"   447
    Coda   456

    Sources and Notes   457
    Acknowledgments   485
    Index   489

WILLIAM STYRON, A LIFE

1

❦

Ancestors

WILLIAM STYRON'S ROOTS in the South are deep. His family in North America traces its lineage to two brothers, John Stireing and George Styring, who were living in Virginia by the early 1700s. It is from George, the younger of these two brothers, who relocated in North Carolina around 1720, that the author is descended. The family line, however, can be traced back a good deal further—through Barbados and Yorkshire to Sweden and Denmark. The Styr clan in Scandinavia is an ancient one, beginning in Uppsala around A.D. 700 with the Viking warrior Styr the Strong. Through its various travels and conquests, the clan left its name throughout Europe—in an Austrian province called Styria; in Stiring-Wendel in Germany; in Styra, a town in the Ukraine; and with the Styr River in Poland. The descendants of Styr the Strong were related by birth or marriage to various Scandinavians of picturesque sobriquet, including King Harald Bluetooth of Denmark and Svein Forkbeard, father of Canute, who ruled England from 1016 to 1035. Other connections included Richard I, duke of Normandy, from whom William the Conqueror and Edward the Confessor traced their lineage, and Edmund Ironside, grandfather of Edgar the Atheling.

During the period of Danish rule in England, members of the Styr clan settled in Yorkshire and became warriors and landholders. Some of their property is recorded in the Domesday Book of 1086, and one of their number became a progenitor of the McDougal clan in Scotland. Members of Styr families intermarried with local clans in Yorkshire; thus in England the Styrs developed into an amalgamation of Swedes, Norwegians, Danes, Normans, and Anglo-Saxons. By the 1500s the surname had evolved into Styring, spelled in a variety of ways.

Some of the Yorkshire Styrings were among the first Englishmen to emigrate to the West Indies island of Barbados during the seventeenth century. They arrived there around 1635 and established themselves successfully. Family members left detailed wills and are mentioned in various documents and transactions of the period. Like most of the early settlers on Barbados, these Styrings were small landowners and farmers who cultivated tobacco, cotton, and indigo. During this period the island was an open, frontier society; slavery had not yet come to dominate the economy.

In the 1640s and 1650s, however, Barbados changed. The English Civil War drove prominent Royalist and Roundhead families from their estates, and many of them emigrated to the New World—to the Virginia and Carolina colonies especially, and to Barbados. These families, with capital and financial connections, brought about the Sugar Revolution on the island during the second half of the seventeenth century. They bought up tracts of land from small freeholders and established huge sugar plantations. African slaves were imported in great numbers to cultivate the sugar cane; small landholders, including the Styrings, were forced out.

Thousands of these former landholders on Barbados, unwilling to labor for wages on the big sugar plantations, left the island for the Cape Fear region of North Carolina or for Tidewater Virginia. Two of these migrants were the brothers John Stireing and George Styring, who abandoned Barbados sometime after 1710 and settled in Princess Anne County, Virginia. Their wills show that they were brothers, though they spelled their surnames differently. John Stireing remained in Virginia, but the other brother, George Styring, moved with his wife, Mary Cason, to the Outer Banks of North Carolina. He spent the years between 1720 and 1740 following the sea, then took up livestock raising on six hundred acres of land awarded to him by the governor of the colony. At his passing in 1745 he left a substantial estate; his sons and daughters (John, Henry, Elizabeth, George, Adonijah, Cason, and

Joyce) continued to live on or near the Outer Banks and to produce off-spring. The name Styron, as a consequence, is fairly common today on the Outer Banks and in eastern North Carolina.

One of George Styring's sons, also named George, took root on Portsmouth, one of the most beautiful of the islands in the Outer Banks chain. This George, who spelled the surname Stiron, married Mary Salter, one of a large clan of Salters on Portsmouth Island, and they produced five children. Their descendants for the next three generations lived and worked on the island. One of their great-grandsons, Thomas Wahab Styron, is the great-grandfather of the subject of this biography. Most of these early Styrons made a living from the sea. They fished and dug oysters; at least two were channel pilots; others gave their occupation to the census taker as "seaman." A few were small farmers, but none of these owned slaves. The 1850 Slave Schedules for eastern North Carolina, in fact, list only one member of the family who was a slaveholder—Benjamin F. Stiron, a forty-year-old sailmaker who owned thirteen slaves, four of them adults.

Alpheus Whitehurst Styron, William Styron's paternal grandfather, was born on Portsmouth Island on January 21, 1848, to Thomas Wahab Styron and Rebecca Whitehurst. William Styron never knew this grandfather (Alpheus died in 1920, five years before the author was born), but he heard a great deal about him—about his service as a Confederate courier and about his career as a steamboat captain and tobacco manufacturer. Surviving photographs show a marked physical resemblance between the two men. William Styron is also said within the family to have inherited his temperament, and much of his story-telling ability, from his grandfather Alpheus.

The island on which Alpheus Styron grew up—Portsmouth Island—was an important southern antebellum trading center. Almost five hundred people lived there, and the local economy was active and strong. Only five miles long, the island had white beaches with wild ponies grazing among the dunes. Game was plentiful, and excellent oyster beds were nearby. The town itself, also called Portsmouth, was a thriving seaport where sailing vessels stopped to off-load cargo or sometimes picked up pilots who would guide them across the treacherous Pamlico Sound to the mouths of the North Carolina rivers. Portsmouth boasted a grammar school, an academy, and two churches; the Styrons attended the Methodist Episcopal church, where Alpheus's father was a trustee.

Portsmouth Island was important enough to be among the first targets for Union troops in the early months of the Civil War. They occupied the island early in 1862 and established a hospital there. The island was important because it commanded the main inlet to the Pamlico Sound and thus controlled access by water to much of central North Carolina. Alpheus Styron was a youth of fourteen when a garrison of Yankee soldiers occupied his town. His brother David, twelve years older, was on the mainland fighting in the Confederate army; Alpheus, too young to enlist, hoped that the war would not end before he could manage to get into it somehow.

In April 1864 he got his wish. A Confederate force under General Robert F. Hoke made a surprise attack on Portsmouth Island and captured the Union troops and supplies there. Alpheus Styron, then sixteen, was put to work immediately as a courier. He was still too young to enlist officially, but he managed to persuade General Hoke to take him to the mainland for the action that was to follow. Alpheus Styron left Portsmouth and served as a messenger boy during the last year of the war. As an old man he told lively tales of dodging in and out of the Confederate and Union lines in eastern North Carolina, carrying messages and orders, usually under cover of darkness. The Civil War years were a time of adventure for him: he was only seventeen when Lee surrendered at Appomattox, and he came out of the conflict unharmed, with his youth and health intact.

Soon after the war ended, Alpheus settled in Washington, a small commercial town on the Pamlico River in North Carolina. Little Washington, as it was known, had been vandalized and burned by Federal troops in 1864, but now it was being rebuilt, and opportunities looked good for a young man with energy and drive. Alpheus Styron found work in the steamboat trade that moved along the local rivers and the inland waterways. He rose quickly in the business; he had become a captain by his early twenties and regularly took paddle-wheelers from Little Washington down the Pamlico River, up the Pungo, and on to Norfolk, Washington, D.C., and Baltimore. His vessels carried lumber, shingles, cotton, corn, and other products on the trips north and brought back manufactured goods and machinery. There was also some passenger trade.

One of the stops along the Pungo River was the dock at Caleb F. Clark's large plantation, just opposite Leechville. It was almost surely there that Alpheus Styron met Marianna Clark, the petite, dark-haired daughter of Caleb Clark. Perhaps he courted her at her father's plantation; the romance blossomed in any case, and the two were married in 1875, when he was twenty-seven and she twenty-four.

Marianna Clark (1851–1938), William Styron's grandmother, was from one of the most prominent families in nineteenth-century North Carolina. The Clarks traced their lineage to early English settlers in North Carolina, who sometimes spelled the name Clarke. Less is known of their Old World origins than of those of the Styron family, but it is clear that they prospered after they came to the colonies. They were planters and slaveholders; their wills survive and list numerous acres and many slaves, some of whose names (Clow, Ret, Big Morning, Little Samuel, Prude, Clarissa, Heziak, Fair, and Love) would one day appear in *The Confessions of Nat Turner.*

Marianna Styron's father was Caleb Foreman Clark (1819–1890). He owned around eleven thousand acres in eastern North Carolina and was one of Hyde County's largest taxpayers. His name appears throughout the Washington Courthouse registry books, and in the 1850 census he is listed as the owner of thirty-four slaves. In the mid-1850s, two little black girls were born on his plantation and given the names Drusilla and Lucinda. Caleb gave these slaves to his daughter Marianna to be her playmates and friends; in later years she would tell of nursing them through childhood illnesses, plaiting their hair with ribbons, and knitting woolen socks for them.

Like many southerners, the Clarks and their slaves went through hardships during the Civil War. Their plantation was ransacked by a detachment of Ambrose Burnside's men in 1862: these soldiers did not burn the house (it was still early in the war, before Sherman's March), but they did take all of the livestock and provisions. As an old lady, Marianna Styron would recall that the troops came from Ohio and that they were surly and profane. They cleaned out the storerooms and smokehouses: she told her grandson Billy stories of how the Union soldiers formed a bucket brigade and tossed hams and bags of meal up the cellar stairs, out of the windows, and into the supply wagons. Because of this pillaging, the Clarks—white and black—suffered for a long period from hunger. They ate roots and acorns from the woods, and they killed and ate rats.

• • •

Soon after their marriage in 1875, Alpheus Styron and Marianna Clark became parents. By 1880 they had three children; by 1889 there were two others, the younger of whom was William Clark Styron, the father of the author. Marianna Styron would bear eight children in all, six of whom would survive infancy. Finances were tight, so Marianna's father, Caleb Clark, lent a hand in March 1889. Now seventy years old and only a few months from his own death, he paid fifteen hundred dollars for a two-story frame house on the northwest corner of Main and Bonner Streets in Little Washington. He conveyed the house and some land adjoining it to his daughter, and she and her husband and children occupied it in April 1889. The house remains in the Styron family today.

Success must have seemed imminent to Alpheus Styron in 1889. He did not lack energy and determination, nor did he fear hard work. He was venturesome and imaginative but tended to overreach himself and attempt too many things at once. As a result, he never really made his strike. He always lacked capital, pursuing his projects on shoestring financing, and he was impatient for success—too impatient to pursue any line of business over a long period. Twice he fell victim to big-business interests—once to the railroads, which all but wiped out inland steamboat shipping, and a second time to the American Tobacco Company, which undercut small tobacco manufacturers near the end of the century.

At first, after his marriage to Marianna, Alpheus Styron was a shipbuilder. His finances were precarious: according to one account he began "with a blind mule and ten gallons of honey and built the steamer *Edgecombe.*" He launched at least four more vessels in the late 1870s and 1880s, and in 1889 he laid the keel for a four-hundred-ton steamer, the largest ever built up to that time in North Carolina. Eventually he was involved in the building and operation of over twenty river steamers.

The boom in railroad building, however, eventually caused the demand for river steamers to dry up. When the trade began to dwindle, Alpheus Styron found himself without an occupation. He was inventive, though: he converted a local side-wheeler, the *Aurora,* into a weekend excursion boat for romantic moonlight cruises to the Outer Banks. The local undertaker was his ticket agent, selling passes from his funeral parlor. This venture, however, did not prosper, and the cruises were discontinued. Alpheus Styron tried other moneymaking schemes:

he was an agent for Farmer's Co-Operative Oil Mills in Tarboro and brokered lots of cotton seed, lime, and meal; for a time he also operated a lime kiln on Castle Island, near Washington. Like his other attempts in business, however, these two failed.

Alpheus Styron's most successful stint in commerce came in the early 1890s as a tobacco manufacturer. He and a man named E. W. Ayers began to process cigarette tobacco and bag it in the small sacks that were then carried by roll-your-own cigarette smokers. (Machine-made cigarettes had not yet come to dominate the market.) Styron and Ayers began making their product, called Mocking Bird Smoking Tobacco, in a shed on the back lot behind Alpheus Styron's house. Their little sacks sold for five cents apiece, and business was good at first. The company expanded and moved to a building in downtown Washington; at its peak it employed almost one hundred people.

Fairly quickly, however, Alpheus ran afoul of the Duke brothers—Benjamin N. Duke and James B. Duke—and their huge trust, the American Tobacco Company. In a ruthlessly competitive national business, the Dukes had, by the late 1880s, fought their way nearly to the top. In 1890 they consolidated their gains by launching the American Tobacco Company, a stock-issuing organization that subsumed five competing firms and brought order to what was then a chaotic, speculative business. James Buchanan Duke, the younger brother, known in North Carolina as Buck Duke, won his victories by bypassing small operators like Alpheus Styron and driving them out of business. Buck Duke also worked behind the scenes to prevent the newly invented Bonsack cigarette-maker from being used by any but the major competitors, thus shutting out minor operators, like Alpheus Styron, who might have acquired one or two of the machines.

A nationwide business panic in 1893 drove tobacco prices down and wiped out many small manufacturers, including Alpheus Styron. Exactly how this happened is not clear, but Alpheus believed to the end of his days that the Duke brothers had brought about his ruin. He called them rapscallions and piratical devils and professed special contempt for Buck Duke, the sharper businessman of the two. James Buchanan Duke had been born with slightly misshapen feet; Alpheus Styron, as an old man, invariably referred to him as "that club-footed son-of-a-bitch Buck Duke"—the syllables rolling out as if the entire epithet were one long name.

Despite his failures in business, Alpheus Styron was respected and admired in Little Washington. He was called Captain Styron; tall, erect, and handsome, he wore whiskers and carried a mahogany cane. He was known locally as a fine raconteur; one of his sons, many years later, recalled that he possessed "much native writing ability," had "a vivid imagination," and was a "persuasive talker." He also had a good singing voice and was a stalwart of the Methodist choir. When he died on November 4, 1920, at the age of seventy-two, all stores in Washington closed the next afternoon in tribute to him.

Though his family was pinched for money, William Clark Styron, the author's father, passed a pleasant boyhood. Much of Little Washington had been rebuilt by the time he was born in 1889, and commerce in the town was reviving. The area nearby had its own peculiar beauty and charm. Then as now, the flat, sandy fields stretched away from the narrow roads toward a distant line of pine forest. Here and there were the cabins of farmers, black and white, and tobacco-curing sheds stood near the roads. The climate was mild in winter, hot in summer, and the growing season was long. Little Washington was cooled by breezes from the Pamlico River; the fishing was good. The town docks were always fascinating: there a boy might buy fresh oysters or see a big raft of chained logs float down the river from a backwoods sawmill. He might also watch a cargo ship from the West Indies sail up the Pamlico and dock at the wharf. Young W. C. Styron had a special advantage because his father was a steamship captain. As a boy he would sail with his father down the Pamlico River, across the northwest corner of Pamlico Sound, up the Pungo River past his mother's girlhood home, and on up the inland waterway to Norfolk or Baltimore, then back again in a day or two.

W. C. Styron grew into a good-looking man. He was tall, with straight brown hair, piercing eyes, thin lips, a prominent nose, and flat cheekbones. He had a gift for language: he read Shakespeare, Tennyson, and the Bible, and in his youth he wrote flowery compositions for his teachers. He was a good student, and, in the fall of 1906, at the age of seventeen, he left home for college. He wanted to pursue a course in the liberal arts but was compelled by inadequate finances to attend a technical school—North Carolina College of Agriculture and Mechanic Arts (later North Carolina State University) in Raleigh. He won a scholarship to study there and held the grant for all four of his years in school. Without the scholarship he could not have attended college.

The A.&M., as it was then called, provided practical, applied education. When W. C. Styron arrived there in the autumn of 1906, the institution was small and offered a heavily technical curriculum. The course work concentrated on engineering, agriculture, and the mechanic arts. He majored in mechanical engineering and took courses in descriptive geometry, forge-work, physics, electricity and magnetism, steam engines, valve gears, and dynamo machinery. The liberal arts were scantily represented in his course work, though he did manage to take four full years of English, taught to him by Thomas P. Harrison, a cousin of the southern poet Sidney Lanier.

After taking his degree in 1910, W. C. Styron indulged a romantic streak and went to sea, spending nine months as an oiler and deck engineer on the transatlantic freighter *Kansan*. He docked in Mexico, then crossed the Atlantic to see the Netherlands, Germany, and Wales. He seems, however, to have decided that he was unsuited for life at sea, and in 1911 he took a job as a mechanical draftsman at the Newport News Shipbuilding and Drydock Company in Newport News, Virginia, about a hundred miles north of Little Washington.

A year or so after he came to Newport News, W. C. Styron began to think of marriage. He had fallen in love with Eunice Edmundson, a petite, curly-haired young woman from Goldsboro, North Carolina. He courted her for two years, visiting her in Goldsboro when he could. He asked her to marry him, but there were other suitors. One of these was Greene S. Johnston III, who came from a family of means in Statesboro, Georgia. With a law degree in hand from Emory University, Johnston had excellent prospects. W. C. Styron's prospects were not as good, and his marriage proposal was rejected. In October 1914 he learned that Eunice was to marry Johnston. He did the gentlemanly thing, bowing out and sending her a moving letter of farewell. He was sad, he told her, but hoped "that sometime between the rising and setting of some sun" he would find "a sweet joy and consolation in the knowledge that all things turned out for good and perfect peace." He would hold her image "in the shrine of memory" and would try to think of "a land of to-morrow where there is nothing but everlasting friendship and where there are no blighted hopes." He finished the letter with a quotation from Tennyson's "Tears, Idle Tears." Eunice kept the letter all her life. Almost sixty years later, she and W. C. Styron would discover each other again and would finally marry. For the present, though, he was heartbroken.

W. C. Styron continued to work in Newport News and to think about his future. He probably did not plan to spend the rest of his life in Newport News, but that is what happened. He worked at the shipyard for over forty years, retiring in 1955 at the age of sixty-five. He seems always to have felt, however, that he was miscast in life. He performed creditably at the shipyard, working as a fitter in the structural department and finishing his career as a cost estimator, but his career did not flourish. People who knew him recalled that he was not typical in personality and behavior for his job. He seemed better educated and more highly cultivated than his fellow workers, though there was nothing about him to suggest that he felt superior to them.

W. C. Styron's belief that he had been miscast in life is important. It helped him to recognize his son's literary bent and to sympathize with his desire to be a writer. It allowed him to endure young William Styron's rebelliousness and lack of academic discipline. W. C. Styron was indulgent through mediocre performances in high school and at two colleges, and he provided financial and moral support for his son while he was finding his feet and producing his first novel. That support was crucial: without it William Styron would almost surely not have become a writer.

William Styron also has roots in the North. His mother, Pauline Margaret Abraham, of Uniontown, Pennsylvania, was descended from Welsh, Scottish, Irish, and Swiss immigrants who came to Pennsylvania during the seventeenth and eighteenth centuries. Many of these ancestors were adventurers and religious dissenters. Pauline Abraham's earliest known forebear in the colonies was Thomas Wynne, who helped William Penn plan his colony in London and then came to Pennsylvania in 1682 aboard the ship *Welcome*. Thomas Wynne was a staunch Quaker from North Wales who resettled in the colonies to escape religious persecution and imprisonment. He was a physician by training; he became a civil judge and was prominent in the early affairs of Penn's new colony.

One of Thomas Wynne's granddaughters, named Mary Wynne, married into the Abraham family in 1729 and is the great-great-great-great-grandmother of William Styron. She and her husband, a Welshman named Noah Abraham, established themselves on a farm in Nantmeal Township, about fifty miles west of Philadelphia. Their son Enoch, born in 1738, took the Abraham line into western Pennsylvania. He was a soldier there in 1759, serving near Pittsburg (as the name was then spelled) during the last year of the French and Indian Wars. He returned to Chester County, married a woman named Jean Hamilton, and fathered four children, but he grew restless and in 1775 took his family west to a place called Turkey Foot, near the headwaters of the Youghiogheny River. There he lived during the Revolutionary War, serving in the Pennsylvania militia. Then in 1778 he moved farther west to a tract of over three hundred acres in what is now Westmoreland County, not far from Uniontown. He named his new holdings (rather whimsically) Vegetability. Perhaps after the wanderings of his early years he looked forward to a period of consolidation and repose. Enoch realized his aim: he lived to be eighty-five and founded a line that remained on Vegetability for four generations.

One of his great-great-grandsons, Enoch Hamilton Abraham, born at Vegetability in December 1854, would be the father of Pauline Margaret Abraham, William Styron's mother. Three of this Enoch's brothers—Isaac, James, and William—fought for the Union in the Civil War, William losing his life in the Wilderness campaign. Enoch was too young to serve in the war. He was a good student and in the 1870s became a schoolteacher; he resigned after a few years, however, in order to enter business. During the early 1880s he was the proprietor of the Summit House, a summer resort near Uniontown; perhaps he tried other ventures as well, but he surely knew that if he were to make a significant mark in Uniontown, he needed to enter the coke business. This he did at some point in the late 1880s.

Uniontown sits directly atop the famous Nine-foot Pittsburgh Seam, the richest and most volatile bed of bituminous coal in the world. Coal-mining and coke production had been carried on in the Uniontown area since the early 1800s, but the post–Civil War boom had given enormous impetus to the steel industry in Pittsburgh and the Ohio Valley, and this in turn had caused a huge increase in coke production in Uniontown.

Enoch Abraham was canny enough to ally himself initially with Henry Clay Frick, the industrial baron who dominated the coke trade. Enoch became a superintendent for Frick, managing one of the largest coke-producing operations in Uniontown (called Continental No. 1) during the late 1880s and early 1890s. This was well-rewarded work, and Enoch saw his income and status rise. He married a local beauty named Annabelle (or Belle) Rush; they took up residence in Uniontown and brought up their four children there—two sons, Harold and Clyde, and two daughters, Edith and Pauline. Pauline Abraham, William Styron's mother, was reared in comfortable circumstances. By 1900, when she was thirteen, her father had gathered enough capital to leave Frick and strike out on his own in an operation that he called the Newcomer Coke Company. He earned substantial profits from this business during the last decade of his life, and when he died of cancer in 1911, at the age of fifty-six, he was a wealthy man.

Enoch Abraham, however, was required throughout his career in the coke business to defend his money and position against the labor unions. The coke ovens were tended by immigrant laborers—Italians, Poles, Romanians, Czechs, and Hungarians. Strikes and violence over pay scales, working hours, and safety conditions were frequent during the 1890s and early 1900s, and Enoch was involved in them. He modeled his position after that of Henry Clay Frick, his former employer, who was staunchly anti-labor and refused to compromise or even to negotiate with workers' organizations.

William Styron learned about these matters during his visits to Uniontown as a boy during the 1930s. His grandfather Enoch was dead by then, but the labor strife had continued. There had been several long, bitter strikes in and around Uniontown—one in 1922, another in 1927, and a third in 1933—and the difficulties between management and labor were always a topic of discussion there. As a youngster visiting his northern relatives, William Styron often heard accounts of labor violence and of other local unrest. He also witnessed dinner-table arguments between his father, who was pro-labor, and his Uniontown relatives, who sided with management. W. C. Styron occupied a spot near the middle of the hierarchy at the Newport News shipyards and sympathized with the problems of industrial workers. He had inherited a dislike for big-money barons from his father: to W. C. Styron there was little difference between Buck Duke and Henry Clay Frick. Pauline

Styron's relatives, on the other hand, sided with management and regarded the laborers as troublesome and lawless. The battles at the dinner table were always heated and sometimes became ugly. Finally Pauline and her sister banned all talk of unions and strikes from dinnertime discussions.

Prejudice against the laboring classes in Uniontown also had racial overtones. The strikebreakers, or scabs, were mostly southern Negroes, brought north by management and protected by the thuggish Coal and Iron Police, who were recruited and armed by the mine owners. Much of the violence during the 1922 and 1927 strikes was racial. There were frequent intimidations, beatings, riots, and even murders as the white immigrants attacked the Negro strikebreakers and tried to drive them from the region. People from the managerial classes, such as the Abrahams, had little sympathy for either group, considering both to be violent and degraded. Thus William Styron learned some of his earliest lessons about racial and ethnic prejudice in the North, not in the South.

As a young woman Pauline Abraham was slim and pretty, with long brown hair, which she wore upswept in a bun. She had a strong nose and mouth and a graceful neck, which she accentuated by wearing high collars. She had weak eyesight and even as a teenager wore glasses. Pauline enjoyed a privileged upbringing in Uniontown, but there was little educational opportunity or cultural stimulation for her there, or for her brothers and her sister. Her two brothers chose military life: Clyde, the older, entered West Point in 1900 and made a considerable success. He was an all-American lineman for the football team and stayed in the service as a career officer, rising eventually to the rank of brigadier general. Harold, the younger boy, attempted to emulate this success: he enlisted in the U.S. Army as a teenager and fought with the American infantry in Europe during World War I, but he returned a victim of shell shock and chronic depression, and he spent much of the rest of his life in the Veterans Hospital at Perry Point, Maryland, where he died in 1953.

The Abraham daughters found their escape through music. Edith, the older of the two, was a good pianist; Pauline had a beautiful contralto voice. The two girls took what education they could in Uniontown during their teenage years, both attending a local private school called Mount Pleasant Institute. Their father, however, possessed the means to do more for them—to send them to Europe for serious training. Both young women spent lengthy periods in Vienna between 1905 and 1907 studying piano and voice and attending concerts and operas. These stays were preceded and followed by tours through various European cities: Pauline's postcards and letters home, which survive, were sent from Liverpool (where she landed), London, Paris, Anvers, Amsterdam, Brussels, Rome, and Florence; they mention museums, restaurants, art galleries, and shopping districts in those cities.

In Vienna, Pauline and Edith lived in a pension with several other American girls from well-to-do families; these young women were studying music or being tutored in drawing and painting. Pauline's letters to her family speak of homesickness but also of much excitement—nights at the opera, delicious Viennese food, and an impromptu Halloween party with apple-bobbing and dancing. Pauline took her first voice lessons from a Frau Gianpietro but graduated soon to tutelage under Theodor Leschetizky, a master pianist, teacher, composer, and conductor (his piano compositions are still sometimes performed today). For Pauline this was a golden period, and she remembered it, eventually with great longing, for the rest of her life. She kept a framed photograph of Maestro Leschetizky, bearing his affectionate inscription to her, in her home. The photograph shows a thickset, white-bearded man of benign expression and bearing; he is standing in his ornately decorated studio, leaning against a grand piano and surrounded by busts of Mozart, Beethoven, Bach, and other composers. As a boy William Styron would study this photograph and ask his mother to tell about her times in Vienna and to identify the composers in the picture. Over fifty years later he would re-create the photograph and the busts in a story called "A Tidewater Morning."

By 1908 Pauline had returned to Uniontown from Vienna. She was now twenty-one years old and, in the normal course of things, would have married and settled down. But this did not happen: she seems to have stayed close to home during her father's final illness and for the years just after he died in 1911, perhaps to look after her mother. Her sister, Edith, was married by then, and the young women with whom she had roomed at the pension in Vienna were finding husbands and writing letters to her about their weddings, letters that she saved. Her friends were inquisitive: "Pauline, you sinner, what has become of you?" asks one. "How's your voice?" inquires another. "Are you never coming over again to Europe?—I suppose you are awaiting your honeymoon!" Pauline, though, had found no suitable young man. She continued to live at home, performing as a soloist in the Presbyterian church and giving voice lessons to a few pupils, but she must have seen little future for herself in Uniontown. Probably she felt lonely and isolated there, wondering what direction her life would now take.

Very likely that is why, in 1914, she enrolled in a two-year course in public-school music at the University of Pittsburgh. Though older (at twenty-seven) than most of her classmates, she joined in the college activities: she sang in the Girls' Glee Club and was a member of the Dramatic Club; she also signed up for the YWCA. After earning a Certificate in Education in 1916 she taught public-school music in Pittsburgh for a year but grew restless and took a job for the next year quite far away, as director of public-school music in Pueblo, Colorado—very much an adventure for a young single woman in 1917. Pauline traveled on her own during this period, visiting California and living through a frightening earthquake in Long Beach, which she described in a letter home. She seems to have been determined to break away from western Pennsylvania and to live elsewhere. Perhaps that is why in 1918, with the United States involved in World War I, she took a position with the YWCA and went to Newport News, Virginia, to help with the war effort. When she arrived there she was thirty years old.

2

❦

Youth

NEWPORT NEWS was buzzing with activity when Pauline Abraham arrived there. Triple shifts of workers labored in the big shipyard, building battleships and destroyers to escort convoys to Europe. Troop embarkations were frequent, and the city was flooded with wives, mothers, and sweethearts who had come to say farewell to the soldiers. Hostess Houses had been established by the YWCA to accommodate these women; it was here that Pauline did much of her work, helping worried women find their men and telling them where to eat and sleep for a few days until the troopships sailed.

Not long after she came to Newport News, Pauline met a first lieutenant in the army who was stationed at one of the troop depots nearby. He was handsome and eligible, and he fell in love with her. She did not think that she really loved him, but he courted her with commitment, and by the summer of 1918 she had told him that she would marry him. Her mother, accompanied by her brother Clyde, came to Newport News to meet the young man. They checked into the Chamberlain Hotel at Old Point Comfort and arranged to meet Pauline and her lieutenant for dinner that evening. At the appointed hour Belle and Clyde Abraham came down the staircase at the Chamberlain and walked over to Pauline, who was standing in the lobby with her suitor. Pauline turned and began the formalities of introduction. Then a bizarre thing happened: she found that she could not say the lieutenant's name. It was not that she had forgotten it; she simply could not bring herself to utter the name.

Pauline became flustered, then apologetic. Everyone laughed and tried to smooth over the awkward moment, but it was plain that something more than nervousness was behind this behavior. The foursome managed to get through dinner; afterward Pauline had a long talk with her suitor and confessed that she did not want to marry him. The engagement was broken that night, and Pauline's mother and brother went back to Uniontown. In later years Pauline told the story frequently, always emphasizing the Freudian nature of her gaffe. She insisted on her unconscious knowledge that the marriage would have been a mistake.

Late in the fall of 1918 Pauline met W. C. Styron. The YWCA was serving hot meals to shipyard workers, and W. C. Styron met her one day when he came by for lunch. They liked each other and found a mutual interest in music. He took her to church, and she learned that he had an excellent tenor voice. He was tall and gentlemanly, a native North Carolinian, an engineer at the shipyard, and only slightly younger than she. (Pauline had turned thirty-one the previous December; W. C. Styron had turned twenty-nine that October.) His age, in fact, was one of his attractions. At twenty-nine, he was past the prime age for military service and was fixed at the shipyard in a defense job. He was calm and mature, and though he was sometimes a little embarrassed by not being in uniform, he knew that he was contributing honorably to the war effort by helping to build ships.

Pauline Abraham and W. C. Styron became engaged. In those days engagements were often quite extended, and they did not marry until the fall of 1921. There was much to delay them. The Armistice had been signed in November 1918, shortly after they had met, but work at the shipyard had continued. There were contracts worth $80 million to be fulfilled and thousands of troops to be brought back. At Twenty-seventh Street and West Avenue the city had thrown up a wooden victory arch, painted to resemble marble; the returning soldiers marched off their ships and passed under it. (Later the temporary arch was replaced by a permanent one of stone.) Pauline now did her work at the YWCA in reverse, helping women find their returning soldiers and make arrangements to take them home.

Pauline Margaret Abraham was wed to William Clark Styron on

September 20, 1921, in her home in Uniontown. She was given away by her brother Clyde and wore a dress of blue Caton crepe. It was a small wedding—only about thirty guests were invited—and after the ceremony everyone went to a luncheon given by Pauline's sister. The couple went on a short honeymoon, then returned to Newport News and began living in the Perkins Court Apartments on Thirty-fifth Street. Pauline continued at the YWCA, where she was now general secretary, and her husband took up his work at the shipyard again.

In the fall of 1924, three years after her marriage, Pauline Styron discovered that she was pregnant. This was likely a surprise: she was now thirty-six and had probably thought that she would not have a child. *I was born two days later.* Her pregnancy went smoothly. She gave birth on June 11, 1925: the baby, a boy, was named William Clark Styron, Jr., after his father. He was born on the second floor of the Buxton Hospital on Chesapeake Avenue and was delivered by Dr. Joseph T. Buxton, who had built the hospital in 1906.

They called the child Billy, and they doted on him. He was frequently weighed, measured, and photographed. At four months he weighed fourteen and a half pounds; a short time later his parents had a droll photograph taken of him reclining in a dishpan. He was a good-looking blond child with brown eyes and an animated face. He babbled constantly and talked early. Billy was imaginative: by the time he was three he had two invisible friends named Scubishay and Scaramouche who slept in the bleachers at an athletic field behind the apartment in which they lived. Each night before bed, Billy would have the back window of his room opened and would shout "Goodnight, Scubishay! Goodnight, Scaramouche!" into the void.

Over the next few years the child was watched carefully. He endured measles, chickenpox, and whooping cough. The health of children was monitored anxiously in those days, before antibiotics and other miracle drugs. There were frequent polio scares in Newport News; Billy would be kept inside during these times, and he would also stay indoors for several days if there were reports of diphtheria or scarlet fever. Billy's most serious medical problem was a tendency to develop earaches. Typically he would catch a cold early in the winter, develop a clogged Eustachian tube, and find himself with a throbbing earache. These were his first experiences with severe pain. The cure was to have his eardrum punctured, a gruesome procedure executed by a lugubrious family physician named Dr. Poindexter. Two neighbors would be called in to hold Billy's arms and legs, and his father would hold his head. His mother would have to leave the apartment because she could not stand hearing Billy's screams. Then the eardrum would be ruptured and allowed to drain. The pain would vanish, almost magically. The Styrons would apply codeine drops when it began to return, but these never worked especially well. Billy would catch other colds and develop other infections later in the winter, and the eardrum would sometimes have to be repunctured two or three more times. Eventually, when Billy was ten, he had a particularly bad infection that invaded the mastoid bone on the right side of his head. This was so near the brain that the physician feared meningitis, so part of Billy's mastoid bone was removed in surgery. Even this procedure did not put a stop to the ear infections; Billy outgrew them only after he entered college.

By the time he was five, Billy Styron had begun to show unusual verbal ability. He had such a keen interest in words that a neighbor upstairs volunteered to teach him to read. She was Sally Cox Hayes, a former grade-school teacher; she had a son about Billy's age, named Buddy, who sometimes played with him. Billy Styron was an eager pupil; he read easily and liked to show off his ability. One day he went downtown with his father to get a haircut. While the elder Styron was in the chair, Billy wandered about the place. He knelt beside an empty barber's chair and, with his forefinger, traced out the letters cast in the metal footrest. H-E-R-C-U-L-E-S. He stood and announced loudly: "HERCULES!" The customers smiled, and the barbers guffawed. The child liked the reaction.

His parents were pleased with him and often gave him chances to show off. They would give him a book far advanced in difficulty for a child of his age, and he would read from it for visitors or relatives. This became, very early, his way of attracting attention and praise. One of his older cousins in Little Washington remembered seeing him at about the age of six sitting on a bed and reading aloud from a novel. Suddenly he stopped, and his face grew dark. He stared at the page in vexation and then announced: "I can't read that damn French word!"

Billy Styron entered first grade at the John W. Daniel Grammar School in the fall of 1931, at the age of six. Along with the other children he was put to work on the Baby Ray texts—forerunners of the Dick and Jane readers of the 1950s. But these texts were so easy that he became bored and inattentive—a tendency he would show throughout his school career. Baby Ray was beneath him; he read at home every night from bigger and harder books. Reading was his favorite thing to do: his father would later say that his interest in words was "almost an obsession." One day at school he showed off for his teacher by spelling the word *formaldehyde,* and a few days later she took him to the principal's office, where he read aloud from the seventh-grade text.

Near the end of Billy Styron's first year in school, his parents decided to leave the apartment in Perkins Court and buy a house at 56 Hopkins Street in Hilton Village, a few miles beyond what were then the Newport News city limits. The Styrons had talked from time to time of leaving Newport News and making a start elsewhere. W. C. Styron was not altogether happy at the shipyard, and Pauline longed to return to music teaching and to live in a less heavily industrialized area. The Depression had begun, however, and work was not easy to find elsewhere. W. C. Styron, now forty-three, had some seniority at the shipyard (he had been there for over twenty years), and his job was secure, even with the economy in its low state. The Styrons therefore decided to buy a home and settle down.

They were buying a house in the first planned community built by the United States government for wartime defense workers. Hilton Village had been erected in 1918 and 1919 to house Newport News shipyard laborers and their families. The architects who designed Hilton Village had been influenced by Ebenezer Howard's Garden City Movement, launched several years earlier in the North. Howard's idea was to surround an urban center with small garden suburbs, each of which would have residences, stores, schools, and churches. Hilton Village was such a suburb.

The houses in the development were designed in a Cottage Style, with solid shapes, smooth walls, high-pitched slate roofs, and small casement windows. The entire community—which included a shopping district, two parks, an elementary school, and four churches—had a quaint, picturesque look. It had been carved from a heavily wooded farm on the banks of the James River, and most of the trees had been left standing. Small wooded areas were scattered throughout the village, and the trees were tall and beautiful. The houses were of modest size: the Styrons' two-story stucco home had six small rooms and a bath. It was located on the southeastern edge of Hilton Village and backed up to a wooded area where Billy and the neighborhood children could play.

Most of the fathers in Hilton Village were skilled laborers or low-level managers at the shipyard. Many were from Virginia or North Carolina, but a surprisingly large number were shipfitters who had emigrated from England, Wales, and Scotland. On Hopkins Street alone, for example, there were Scottish families named McPherson, Watson, and Knox, and elsewhere in the village there were McDonnoughs, Bells, Rogers, Pollocks, Sloans, and McDonalds. One of Billy Styron's best friends, Aleck Watson, had been born in Glasgow.

To the southwest, Hilton Village sidled up to the majestic James River, the enormous, brackish estuary that had figured so importantly in early American history. To the southeast lay Hampton Roads, and on beyond, toward the north, were the broad waters of the Chesapeake Bay. To the northeast of Hilton Village, just across Warwick Boulevard, were the Chesapeake & Ohio tracks, which bisected Newport News on its long axis and ran between the white and black sections of town. When the Styrons moved to Hilton Village in 1932, the area around the tracks was thickly wooded. As teenagers Billy and his friends camped overnight there and hunted rabbits around the tracks.

A few blocks away from the Styron home was the Hilton Village shopping area, which included an A&P, a variety store, another food store called Seward's Grocery, a post office, a barbershop, and a pharmacy run by Dr. Francis, who had a wooden leg and was known as Dr. Buzzard. A few years after the Styrons moved to Hilton Village, a small movie theater, Art Deco in style, was added to the shopping area; Billy got his first job there as an usher when he was fourteen.

The people who lived in Hilton Village were all white, but each morning many black women walked across the C&O tracks to work as domestics in the houses. On weekends and during the summers they would bring their sons and daughters to play with the white children. The Styrons usually had a black woman to help cook and clean. These women would come and go as better jobs beckoned or as problems at home took them away. The servant William Styron remembered best was Annie Swan, already in her seventies when the Styrons moved to Hilton Village. Annie—one of a large family of Swans who lived near Jefferson Avenue—had been born a slave in the 1860s but remembered very little about it. She was paid standard wages of three dollars a week plus "totin' privileges," which meant that she could carry home odds and ends for her own use—leftovers, old clothes, used appliances, and cleaning supplies. William Styron would later give her last name to Ella and La Ruth Swan in *Lie Down in Darkness*.

The fall after the Styrons moved in, Billy entered the second grade at Hilton Village Elementary School. The principal there was Miss Alice M. Menin, a spinster who had devoted her life to schoolteaching. The school bore her stamp: she believed devoutly in high standards but was not an especially strict disciplinarian. Behavior in the school was relaxed, almost laissez-faire. Miss Menin did very little punishing; she was better at rewards and praise. Billy Styron thrived in her school.

Students recalled in later years the Music Memory Contests and Famous Painting Pageants that Miss Menin organized. These exercises exposed the children to classical music and well-known art works. Miss Menin was best known, however, for staging May Day pageants. These events, held in the front yard of the school, were the climax of the academic year. The flagpole became a Maypole, and the school steps were transformed into the May Queen's courtroom. Each pageant had a theme. One year, for example, the celebration was staged as a Colonial garden party. Older children dressed as Mistress Betsy Randolph, Mistress Anne Jefferson, James Madison, Thomas Jefferson, George Washington, and the Marquis de Lafayette. Other children were Minuet Dancers, Colonial Militiamen, and Flowers of various kinds: Tulips, Pansies, and Roses. There were Dryads, Butterflies, Frogs, and Birds, all of whom flew, danced, or hopped. There was also a Friendly Neighboring Tribe of Indians and a large group of Plantation Pickaninnies in blackface, headed by a grizzled old house servant named Pompey. No one thought anything of it; blackface characters were included almost every year in the events.

Billy Styron took part in these pageants and, like the other boys, hated the costumes he had to wear. He was especially embarrassed the year that the theme was the story of Cinderella. Pretty Greig Campbell, whom Billy liked, took the part of Cinderella; he wanted to be the prince but instead was given the role of the page boy who carried the glass slipper. He was mortified by the white tights he was obliged to wear, which showed his skinny legs to disadvantage. Many years later he would include a fictionalized version of the ordeal in "Inheritance of Night," an early version of *Lie Down in Darkness*.

More to Billy's liking were events like Talent Night. He, Aleck Watson, and another boy named Carl Roy—all of whom played harmonicas—got up a blackface minstrel-show routine and went to the auditions but could not make it past the tryout judges. Billy had more success a few years later in a production of Dickens's *A Christmas Carol* in which he played Marley's Ghost. He was painted with ghastly white makeup and draped with rattling chains. Almost fifty years later he could recall the horror on the faces of the small children in the audience as he dragged himself across the front of the stage, moaning and grinding his teeth.

Billy Styron was happy and secure at Miss Menin's school. He excelled at reading, was adequate at arithmetic, and especially liked history. He did so well in reading and writing that he was allowed to skip a grade. (He cannot today remember which grade but thinks it was the third.) This was a common practice for bright children during those years. In his small elementary school, it made for no great change in his life. He often played with the older children in the neighborhood; it felt only slightly different now to go to classes with them. Grade levels were confused for many of the children. Several of them had the opposite problem: they were behind in school because they had lost time during quarantines. Billy's friend Aleck Watson, for example, lost two full years when he and his family were quarantined during epidemics of diphtheria. A few years later, however, Billy Styron's precocity worked against him. In high school he was a year younger than his classmates; this, combined with a late physical maturation, made his early teenage years difficult.

Outside school Billy's best friends were three boys named Dick Osborne, Jimmy Cochran, and Leon Edwards. They were in and out of one another's houses constantly; no one locked doors in Hilton Village, and children came and went freely through the back entrances. Billy was also friendly with Buddy Hayes, whose mother had taught him to read at Perkins Court and whose family had moved to Hilton Village at about the same time as the Styrons. These boys played at sports and games and gathered during the spring and summer at a long wooden pier behind the elementary school. This pier was a meeting place for children and teenagers during the hot months. The heat in Tidewater Virginia during the summers was fierce and smothering, but the pier caught a few breezes from the river, and the water was cool. Often the children arrived at the pier early in the day, swam and fished all morning, went home for lunch, returned to laze about in the afternoon, and hurried home for supper at six or six-thirty. After dark, when the temperature dropped a little, they would congregate again. Older children were allowed to spend the night on the pier in sleeping bags and to go swimming by moonlight. The water they swam in, however, was none too clean; the sewage treatment plant for Hilton Village dumped its effluent into the James River only a short distance away. The children learned to swim only at high tide, when the waste was carried upstream, and to dodge any unidentified matter that drifted by.

Between the pier and the school was a wooded area where the children played. Running through it was a ditch filled with stagnant water; the boys liked to leap the ditch or swing over it on vines. One Saturday morning when he was ten, Billy was playing in this area. He was to go to downtown Newport News later that day to compete in a statewide elocution contest, and he was killing time until his ride came. He and some friends were swinging across the ditch together on a vine. Someone fell and tripped Billy, and someone else landed on his head. He went home feeling dizzy, but his head cleared and he went to the contest as planned. There he won first prize in his age group. He brought his blue ribbon home, where it was properly admired, and he hung it in his room. Later that night, however, he began to feel disoriented and sick, and the doctor was summoned. It turned out that Billy had sustained a fairly serious concussion. He recovered in a few days, though, and came to feel that the injury added lustre to his victory. It was an event that he remembered proudly from his pleasant, secure childhood.

3

Newport News

THE NEWPORT NEWS of William Styron's boyhood was very much a city of the New South. Industrial and urban, noisy and commercial, it had a great deal more in common with Atlanta or Birmingham than it did with Thomas Wolfe's Asheville or William Faulkner's Oxford. The South, then as now, was a large and varied region—far from monolithic in social organization and cultural demography. Cities such as Newport News were certainly southern but hardly represented the moonlight-and-magnolias South of movies and popular fiction. Newport News was a sprawling, bustling, vital community with a large population of transients and almost no real history, in the conventional sense, to speak of.

Newport News is not itself considered a historic city, but there is a great deal of history nearby. The city is located in Virginia at the tip of the peninsula formed by the York River on the north and the James River on the south. Its special advantage—and the defining factor in what history it does possess—is the large, deepwater harbor that lies directly off its banks, just at the mouth of the James. This huge natural harbor was recognized by the first explorers in the New World as being of immense potential importance, and so it has proved to be.

The earliest settlers named the waters around the tip of the peninsula in curious fashion. The broad expanse just north of the mouth of the James was called The Earl of Southampton's Roadstead after one of the sponsors of the Virginia colony. This cumbersome name was short-ened over time to Hampton Roads, and the city at the end of the "Peninsula" (as local people call it) was called Hampton. The begin-nings of the name Newport News are more difficult to trace. The first explorer to land on the spot was Captain Christopher Newport, who stopped there in the late spring of 1607 with his three ships—*Susan Constant, Godspeed,* and *Discovery.* His men rested and drank from a freshwater spring and then proceeded upriver to the tiny settlement at Jamestown. Christopher Newport left one hundred colonists there and returned to England. In four later voyages he brought provisions and news to the colony; probably that is why the southern bank of the Peninsula, where his ships were met by the eager, news-hungry colonists, was designated on early nautical charts as Newportes Newes, later shortened to Newport News. For roughly the first 250 years of its existence, however, Newport News was little more than a name on a map. Some captains stopped for water from the spring; other vessels, to-bacco ships mostly, laid over there, waiting to form convoys to sail to England. A few shacks and a pier were built, but nothing marked the spot as a location of much importance.

Much eighteenth- and nineteenth-century American history was played out very near Newport News: political and social events of great moment occurred at Jamestown, Williamsburg, Yorktown, and Rich-mond, but none of these involved Newport News. Only with the begin-nings of the Civil War did the spot assume importance. The North, recognizing the strategic value of the harbor, occupied and fortified the end of the Peninsula in May and June of 1861. General Benjamin F. Butler—later known as Spoon Butler for his habit of appropriating chests of family silver from southern plantations—had his men dig trenches, erect a palisade, and mount four pieces of artillery at Newport News to guard the mouth of the James. These fortifications were part of an overall plan to secure the Peninsula tip, then to march north-west to capture Richmond. The Confederates, under General John Bankhead Magruder (a name that young William Styron liked to pro-nounce for its solid sound), anticipated the strategy and met the ad-vancing Federals at a spot called Big Bethel on the night of June 10. The Yankee forces were routed and were checked in subsequent battles; the Peninsular Campaign eventually failed, largely because of the vac-illations of the Union general, George B. McClellan. Newport News remained in federal hands for the rest of the war and was used as a staging area for other campaigns.

In the spring of 1862, a major event did occur near Newport News: the encounter between two ironclads, the *Monitor* and the *Merrimac.* On March 8, 1862, the Confederate ship *Merrimac,* invulnerable to cannon shot, sank the Union sloop *Cumberland* and destroyed the frigate *Congress* just off the banks of Newport News. The next morning the *Merrimac* met the Union's own ironclad, the *Monitor,* in Hampton Roads. The four-hour contest ended in a draw. The *Merrimac* might have changed the course of the war, breaking blockades and opening supply lines, but the ship's home base at Norfolk was captured in May and the *Merrimac* was scuttled by the Confederates to prevent her capture. The *Monitor* sank seven months later in a storm off Cape Hatteras.

As a child William Styron was very much aware of these bits and pieces of history. Sitting in the fifth-grade classroom in Hilton Village School, he could look out the back window and see the James River flowing by a short distance away. Over yonder, he was told—just a little way out from the banks—Captain John Smith had sailed by in 1607. And just there, a few years later in 1619, a Dutch trader had moved upriver with her melancholy burden, the first African slaves brought to the New World. In Southside Virginia on the opposite bank one could still visit Bacon's Castle, the peculiar-looking demesne of the hotheaded Nathaniel Bacon, whose rebellion in 1676 had been put down by Governor Berkeley. Newport News might have been lacking in historical distinction, but it could certainly claim historical proximity.

After Appomattox, the Union breastworks in Newport News were abandoned. Except for a small Confederate cemetery, little was left to remind one of the late conflict. Newport News lay dormant during the Reconstruction years. In 1880, however, railroad magnate Collis P. Huntington took the initial steps toward extending the Chesapeake & Ohio line eastward from Richmond to the sea. As the terminating point he chose Newport News, and the commercial history of the city began at that moment.

Collis P. Huntington was a Connecticut native and a self-made man. He had pushed through the first transcontinental railroad in the late 1860s; he had then taken over the Chesapeake & Ohio and had advanced the line westward through the Virginia mountains to the Ohio

River. He had rehabilitated the older sections of the line, many of which had been untended since the end of the Civil War. An important part of his plan was to make Newport News a major port for deep-draft ocean steamers. Before 1880, the only coaling stop in Virginia had been near Richmond, where coal had been trundled to the ships in wheelbarrows. Newport News, with its fine natural harbor, was Huntington's choice as a place to build a modern, efficient coaling operation. Civil War earthworks and palisades were leveled, and wharves, piers, and railroad tracks were constructed. Two hotels were built; the railway line was finished in May 1882; the loading docks went into operation soon after. Coal began to move from the rich Appalachian coalfields across Virginia to the sea. Huntington now built a second facility—a shipyard at Newport News to handle repairs for the cargo vessels that stopped there. He chartered this company in 1886 and had it in operation by 1889, the year William Styron's father was born. Shipbuilding was added in 1890, and the company was named the Newport News Shipbuilding and Dry Dock Company.

The commercial health of Newport News was (and still is) directly tied to U.S. agriculture and mining. But the city is even more tightly linked to the nation's defense industry. This has been a fortunate association, helping to rescue the local economy more than once and influencing its identity up to the present day. In January 1894 the U.S. Navy awarded contracts for the construction of three gunboats to the Newport News shipyard and two years later assigned the company two more contracts, these for the *Kearsage* and the *Kentucky,* the first modern battleships in the United States arsenal. Thereafter Newport News and the nearby cities of Norfolk, Portsmouth, and Hampton grew into centers for the construction and maintenance of engines of warfare. The pattern began with the Spanish-American War in 1898 and held through the Vietnam War in the 1960s and 1970s. Wartime was always boomtime for Newport News, both for shipbuilding and troop embarkation.

The shipyard expanded rapidly in the first decade of the new century, and by the time W. C. Styron signed on there in 1912 the company occupied ten city blocks along the James, with huge overhead cranes and drydocks standing along the riverbanks. During World War I there was an enormous increase in activity as the workers built battleships, cruisers, destroyers, submarines, gunboats, and patrol craft. The most acute problem for the city was lack of proper housing; many blocks of drab apartments and strings of jerry-built houses were thrown up for immediate habitation.

No effort was made in those days to mask troop embarkations, and regiment after regiment paraded through the streets to the docks. Three military camps sprang up north of the city, and Camp Stuart, a sprawling facility, was built along Hampton Roads. The shipyard expanded, employing over 12,500 workers and pumping a weekly payroll of $400,000 into the municipal economy. Many of the workers lived in barracks and tent colonies or slept in hot beds—so called because they were shared by two or three men on different shifts. Workers came to Newport News from all over the country—especially from Southside Virginia and eastern North Carolina. Wages were high, and the demand for labor was steady.

This large, temporary population of workers created many problems. "Essentially the city was raw, clamorous, industrial, and unsightly," William Styron would recall, "with a big, drab white slum and an even drabber and bigger black slum, a part of which, even in those days before cocaine or crack had been heard of, was prey to such unceasing violence that it bore the lurid name Blood Fields." Such a city did not inspire much affection, even among its permanent residents: "It was hard to love a place where much of the population was transient, shifting, faceless: swarms of country boys, black and white, seeking railroad or shipyard jobs, an endless invasion of seamen from merchant ships, and a horde of soldiers and sailors from every base in the swollen military encampment which the lower Tidewater was becoming."

Much of the undistinguished appearance of Newport News can be traced to this rapid development. There was no indigenous aristocracy of property owners to slow the rush of commerce. But if Newport News boomed during World War I, it fell into stagnation with equal rapidity during the late 1920s and the 1930s. The Great Depression began when William Styron was four, and its effect on Newport News was drastic. The shipyard, anticipating lean times, had begun to repair locomotives and construct turbines, but this work could not sustain the local economy. By 1933 the laborers who remained were on a four-day week, and the city was in the doldrums. This was the Newport News of William Styron's boyhood, a place in which his father was glad to have a modest but secure position at the shipyard.

There were labor problems during these years, and young William

Styron heard much debate over whether the shipyard workers should unionize. It was difficult to organize laborers in the South, however, because of racial divisions. Whites and blacks were reluctant to join the same unions. A few of the shipyard men did so; an independent, racially mixed group called the Peninsula Shipbuilders Association existed at the shipyard, but its membership was not large nor was its influence especially strong. William Styron's father did not belong to the PSA, as it was called, though he always spoke in favor of it. (The union was founded in 1939, a year that was enormously difficult for W. C. Styron, as we shall see. Union membership was surely the last thing on his mind in 1939.) True unionization did not come to the shipyard until 1980.

The defense industry eventually rescued Newport News from the Depression, this time with a contract to construct the first aircraft carrier. This enormous vessel, the *Ranger,* was launched in June 1934, and contracts followed for three more carriers—the *Yorktown* (1937), the *Enterprise* (1938), and the *Hornet* (1941). The entire Peninsula began to hum again during the late 1930s and early 1940s; many years later Styron remembered the scenes vividly:

> Certainly no landscape in the United States was more imbued with the sense of bristling martial affairs than this part of Tidewater Virginia. We woke up daily to the lumbering drone of the new Flying Fortresses from Langley Field. Hampton Roads itself was ceaselessly dotted with blue silhouettes of monster warships. Navy fighter planes from the Norfolk air station joined the racket, shoals of sailors and masses of soldiers from Fort Eustis and Fortress Monroe jammed the streets of Newport News; and there seemed to be always an intermittent faraway cannonade from artillery practice and bombing runs, grumbling and flashing from all points of the compass. In my native Newport News itself all life was dominated by the biggest shipyard in America—where my father worked—and by the outlines of such naval behemoths as *Ranger* and *Yorktown* and *Enterprise,* each of which as a boy I witnessed slithering majestically down ways larded with tons of sheep tallow into the muddy James, which parted at the prodigious impact like the Red Sea making way for Moses. It was an incredibly busy, deafening, dynamic world I grew up in—all technology and energy revving up for the greatest clash of arms in history.

• • •

William Styron spent the first fifteen years of his life in Newport News. It was a long, narrow municipality, bisected by the C&O tracks, which ran the length of the city before making a sweeping turn to the right and terminating at the river. To the north of that spot, across Hampton Roads, were Old Point Comfort and Fortress Monroe (where Jefferson Davis had been imprisoned after the Civil War). Near the train terminals were warehouses, grain elevators, and stock pens—these last occupied by restless cattle or sometimes by broken-down nags headed for the bullrings of Spain, where they would be ridden by the picadors.

Hilton Village, where the Styrons lived, was a good distance upriver from the train terminals, stock pens, and shipyards. It was linked to the downtown area by a trolley line that ran all the way over to Buckroe Beach on the Chesapeake Bay. From Hilton Village one could look downriver and see the James River Bridge, an enormous six-mile span stretching over to Southside Virginia. Farther downriver were the ship-yards themselves, with their huge derricks and piers. Clustered around the shipyards, on Washington Avenue, were pawnshops and theaters and stores that sold cheap clothing and work shoes. During the day, lunch wagons parked around the entrance to the shipyards, selling pork sandwiches, deviled crabs, and bowls of ham hocks and beans.

Upriver from Hilton Village was the better part of town. A Mariners' Museum had been built there by Archer M. Huntington, the adopted son of Collis Huntington; it housed a collection of marine artifacts—ship models, paintings, charts, maps, globes, figureheads, anchors, and even a few small vessels. William Styron often went there on school trips as a boy. Not far away from the museum were some of the most handsome houses in Newport News, occupied mostly by shipyard ex-ecutives, and a bit farther upriver was the James River Country Club, to which the more prosperous families belonged.

This club would one day make an appearance in *Lie Down in Dark-ness.* The clubhouse was a handsome white-brick structure with a big party room and a locker area downstairs where boys and girls some-times went to kiss and touch. One wing housed a golf museum with a collection of antique putters and mashies, a library of books on golf, and a scale model of the original course at St. Andrews in Scotland. Club members were proud of the museum, though its four large sky-lights leaked. Outside and down the hill toward the river was a new swimming pool; near that was a huge live-oak tree. The Styrons did not belong to this country club; they had no interest in golf or tennis, and the yearly dues were high. But rules about visitors were relaxed, and young William Styron went there sometimes with friends for swimming and parties.

Because Newport News had no true aristocracy, it created its own. These were white-collar professionals and successful businessmen, mostly Protestant and fully conventional. Styron described this ersatz gentry in an early draft of *Lie Down in Darkness:*

> These last—"middle class" by ordinary American standards—were the new, or rather original, aristocracy, and it was in this manner—in assuming a patrician status that was gratuitous and synthetic but unquestioned, in appropriating a way of life which was not their inheritance, but certainly no one else's—that they divested themselves, at least locally, of the "middle class" stamp, and became Southern gentlemen. They built nice modern houses near the water where there was air stirring and a view. They raised well-mannered children, sent them to church, either Episcopal or Presbyterian, and to dancing school, and made sure that the transition from the perambulator to the convertible was accomplished with ease and dispatch.

Below this local gentry was the white working class, farm-bred men from Virginia and North Carolina who had migrated to Newport News, found wives and fathered families, and taken up residence in rows of small clapboard houses. "They were poor but not impoverished," Styron remembered. "They had large families, and some of them had Fords and Chevrolets in which they drove to the movies faithfully on Saturday night and just as faithfully to church on Sunday." As a boy William Styron observed these people at only a small remove. His own family did not belong to the country-club set, but neither was it working-class. His father and mother were both college-educated, and his father wore a coat and tie to work. His friends' fathers in Hilton Village were mostly foremen or skilled artisans just a little lower than the Styrons on the social scale. Lower still were families whose fathers were welders, joiners, riveters, and painters, but these stratifications were not well defined or especially strong. The in-between status of the Styrons allowed their son to mix easily with several levels of society.

The Styrons attended the First Presbyterian Church in downtown Newport News. William Styron went to Sunday school there and, in his early teens, after he had been confirmed as a church member, attended the services for the full congregation. His religious instruction was conventional and, in the manner of most Presbyterian churches of the time, quite straightforward and rational in presentation. There was little ceremony in Presbyterian services; the church struck him, even as a boy, as offering little that appealed to his emotions or his spirit. As an adult he would recall his boredom as he sat through the Sunday services, especially during the hot months. He also remembered resenting the pastor of the church, who had an unctuous manner and was inordinately proud of his long, snow-white hair, which he wore in an elaborately sculpted style. A great many years later Styron would base a character in his story "A Tidewater Morning" on this clergyman.

The great mystery to William Styron in Newport News was the large population of black people. They were everywhere, working in white people's homes as domestics, laboring at the shipyard, walking on the downtown streets or sitting in the backs of buses and trolleys—for this was the era of Jim Crow. Styron remembered this clearly as an adult:

> Even now I marvel at the outward appurtenances of segregation, which in retrospect have an unreal, almost nightmarish quality: the lily-white grammar and high schools, the separate eating facilities and rest rooms and drinking fountains, the buses at shipyard quitting time parading down Washington Avenue, their posterior space jammed with black workers while the front remained ludicrously vacant. Even the ferry boats which used to steam across Hampton Roads were victims of this schizophrenia—with portside for blacks and starboard for whites—and as a young child this provoked me into a weird speculation: suppose going to some event in Norfolk, a baptism or a church gathering, suddenly hundreds of black people were to get on board. Wouldn't the ferry list to port so fearfully that it might just capsize?

The most obvious sign of Negro accomplishment on the Peninsula was Hampton Institute. This college, founded in 1868 by the American Missionary Association, was a strong force for black education and progress. One of its graduates was Booker T. Washington, who would found Tuskegee Institute. For the most part Hampton Institute offered practical job training for African Americans, though it had a reasonably full range of offerings in the arts and sciences and trained many teachers. About a thousand students were enrolled there. The college had a large endowment, most of it contributed by northerners, a fact that caused some resentment among white Virginians but also gave the institute much freedom in determining its own course. Hampton existed in a kind of precarious harmony with the surrounding white society, many of whose members were wary of its aspirations.

Hampton Institute was famous for its vocal groups, some of which preserved and sang Negro spirituals. Young William Styron went to some of these performances; as a grown man he could remember feeling chills when he heard the black choirs at Hampton sing "Every Time I Feel the Spirit" or "Go Tell It on the Mountain." But even as a boy he was aware that these were modernized, synthetic versions of black music. Later he learned that some of the students at Hampton had resented having to sing them, believing that they perpetuated ideas about docile darkies on antebellum plantations.

Genuine, uncosmeticized Negro religion was also to be found throughout Newport News, and young William Styron observed it with fascination. He was especially aware of two messianic leaders on the Peninsula: Bishop Charles Emmanuel Grace, known as Daddy Grace, and Elder Solomon Lightfoot Michaux, called The Happy Am I Evangelist and The Colored Billy Sunday. (Both men would serve as models for Daddy Faith in Lie Down in Darkness.) Elder Michaux was an early evangelist of the airwaves. Energetic and charismatic, he attracted followers for his Church of God Movement from all over eastern Virginia. William Styron listened regularly to his services on the radio, catching the rhythms and inflections of the preaching, and hearing in the background the shouts and amens of the parishioners. Elder Michaux was famous in the region: during the 1930s and 1940s his influence spread to Washington, D.C., where he held mass baptisms in the baseball park, immersing converts in water said to have been brought over from the River Jordan. Though a showman, Elder Michaux was also a leader of serious purpose: his church took care of derelicts and evicted families, and his followers operated farms, schools, hotels, orphanages, housing projects, and homes for old people.

Daddy Grace, Elder Michaux's chief rival, was flamboyant in a different way. Of mixed African and Portuguese descent, he was bronze in color, had long flowing hair, and cultivated three-inch fingernails that he painted red, white, and blue. His United House of Prayer boasted a chain of more than twenty churches up and down the eastern seaboard. His services, also heard on black radio stations, were full of passion, with frequent moaning, fainting, and speaking in tongues. Energy filled the airwaves: cries of "Sweet Daddy!" "Daddy, you feel so good!" and "Come to me, Daddy!" rang out. Services were punctuated by fund-raising breaks and by sales of Daddy Grace's line of products— toothpaste, hair pomade, face powder, soap, stationery, shoe polish, and cookies.

During the hot months Daddy Grace held mass baptisms in Newport News. Followers in robes and turbans, carrying watermelons and layer cakes and baskets of fried chicken, paraded through the downtown streets. These baptisms took place at the tip of the Peninsula near the Little Boat Harbor, a man-made basin not far from the C&O train terminal. Daddy Grace's followers, sometimes as many as twenty thousand of them, would throng the streets beforehand, shouting hallelujah, slowing traffic, and straining for a glimpse of Sweet Daddy in his limousine. He would preside at the actual baptisms in magnificent robes, standing on an offshore platform set just an inch or so beneath the water to give the illusion that he was walking upon the surface. William Styron and his friends would go downtown on Sundays and witness these spectacles from a little distance. Later they would see film clips of them in the Fox Movietone newsreels in local theaters.

Yet for all this exposure to black people, young William Styron could not say that he knew the Negro. Black men and women, though part of his surroundings, remained mysterious and unknowable. His own childhood feelings about Negroes, he later admitted, were "confused and blurred, tinged with sentimentality, colored by a great deal of folklore, and wobbling always between a patronizing affection, fostered by my elders, and downright hostility." Most baffling was the way that Negroes, if observed closely, seemed to vanish: "To my bemused and attentive eye, as a boy, Negroes were participants in a bewildering magic trick, appearing and disappearing at the whim of some prestidigitator, who caused them to throng the stage of the city by the thousands—especially at four o'clock, the shipyard quitting time—but who then made them vanish in a puff, so that at night the same main street would be occupied only by Caucasians, not a single black soul in sight."

This disappearing act, so baffling, kindled in him an enormous curiosity: "My awareness of Negroes was honed to an exquisite receptivity not by their presence so much as by their absence. I was still quite young when I began to wonder at this absence. Why weren't they in school with me? Why didn't they belong to the Presbyterian church, like I did? Why weren't they in the movie theaters, at the baseball games? Why were Florence, the cook, whom I was so fond of, and old William, who mowed the lawn and told me funny stories, finally such strangers, disappearing at night into a world of utter mystery? Because they were absent, even though constantly visible and present, Negroes exacted a powerful and curiously exotic hold on my boyhood; their lives, their peculiarity, their difference, their frustrating untouchability all fascinated me, and finally comprised a kind of obsession."

Young William Styron, surrounded by the energy and clamor of the New South, did not have a typically southern upbringing. His early years in Newport News marked him strongly but did little to tie him to the city or to the South. Newport News, he later said, was a "rootless and synthetic town," a place to which he felt only lightly bound. It was "a strangely soulless community," he remembered, "and despite what I still reckon to have been a relatively happy childhood spent in and around the place, I never discovered its center, its identity." Still, from his childhood in the city he took and retained a sense of the nearness of history, a feeling for the irresistible power of a wartime economy, a familiarity with several levels of white society, and a powerful curiosity about the black man.

4

Pauline's Death

TWO YEARS AFTER William Styron's birth, his mother discovered that she had breast cancer. Billy was kept in the dark about her condition until he was ten or eleven, when it became obvious that she was not well. The neighbors were told very little. People with cancer endured a social stigma; breast cancer, in particular, was "the sort of thing you didn't talk about." Pauline had a double mastectomy in 1927, and for a time the cancer was arrested. Eventually it returned, however, and reached other parts of her body. It invaded her bones and the lining of her scalp; her bones were weakened, and her hair began to fall out. By the time Billy was twelve, Pauline and her husband knew that she would not live much longer.

The disease sapped her strength and affected her sense of balance. One Thursday evening as she was leaving the house with her husband and son to go out to a local restaurant for dinner, she fell and broke her leg. Normally she would have walked on the narrow sidewalk from the front door to the street, but on this evening she tried to negotiate a small terrace down to the curb. Her sense of balance was defective, and the tiny incline proved too much for her. She fell and broke the major bone in her right leg—the tibia. An ambulance had to be summoned to take her to the hospital. There the broken leg was set and put in a cast, but in the weeks that followed the cancer-riddled bones refused to mend fully. For what remained of her life, she had to wear a heavy metal leg brace and walk with a cane.

Pauline was now confined to the house almost entirely and was often in pain. She spent most of her days sitting on the living-room sofa with her leg extended in front of her on an ottoman. She had been a steady reader for most of her life; now her appetite for books became voracious. Fiction occupied her mind and helped to take her thoughts away from her predicament. It was one of Billy's duties now to ride his bicycle to the lending library and check out books for her. She asked for the novels of Willa Cather and Thomas Wolfe, he later remembered; she also read popular best-sellers for distraction and escape.

Billy's other important duty, during the short cold season, was to hurry home after school and build up the blaze in the small fireplace before which his mother sat all day in the living room. Like most houses in the Tidewater region, the Styrons' home did not have much of a heating system. There was really no need for one: the weather was cold only a few days out of the year, and most families made do with small furnaces, or with stoves and fireplaces. The Styrons had a tiny coal-burning furnace in one corner of the kitchen (there was no basement), but this furnace did not produce enough heat to keep Pauline warm when the weather turned chilly in the afternoons. Billy's task was to run home after school, carry in logs from the woodshed out back, and kindle a fire in the living-room fireplace.

One cold afternoon in the winter of his thirteenth year, Billy neglected to go home and stoke the fire. A classmate had offered him the chance to go riding with an older brother in the family's new Packard. Billy forgot his duty to his mother and went off on a joyride through the frosty fields around Newport News. Late that afternoon it dawned on him what he had done, and he begged to be taken home. By the time he arrived, his father had returned from work and had found Pauline, badly frightened and blue from the cold, huddled on the sofa under the worn afghan with which she covered her useless leg. Billy was sick with shame and guilt; he never forgot the reproach he saw in his mother's eyes as he came through the front door.

By way of punishment Billy's father made him sit for almost two hours in the freezing woodshed out back. It was a proper penance: his mother had sat shivering on the sofa for two hours. Billy realized even then that his father's sentence was just—that it was more appropriate than a lecture or a blow. The punishment, however, failed to rid him of guilt and remorse. Later, after Pauline's death, he came to fear illogically that his forgetfulness that day had somehow accelerated her sickness and hastened her passing.

Pauline's medical treatments, supervised by Dr. Russell Buxton, were expensive and put great strain on the family's finances. W. C. Styron was also helping to support one of his sisters in Little Washington. She had given birth to a houseful of children and had then been widowed. "She just couldn't stop procreating!" the elder Styron would say in dismay. The Styrons had to count pennies. They were never in desperate straits and never lacked for essentials, but they had to make compromises. They did not have a good car and made do with an aged, secondhand model—until, by great good luck, the senior Styron won an Oldsmobile in a shipyard lottery. There was little money for treats or amusements, and Billy's allowance was small. Some of the boys in the village had their own sailboats and took them out onto the James River in the spring and summer. Billy wanted a secondhand sailboat of his own, but his father told him that they could not afford one. New clothes were a luxury, as were books and phonograph records. A full-time domestic became necessary, and this was expensive. The Styrons hired a melancholy black woman named Florence, who was steady and dependable, but whose glumness and taciturnity irritated Pauline.

Billy Styron was aware that his mother was sick, but he was still too young, even at twelve and thirteen, to realize the full gravity of her condition. She explained very little about her illness to him; it was thought best to keep him uninformed. He continued to go to school and to play with his friends as he had always done. Occasionally something would remind him of her illness—one night he saw her smile curiously and tell his father to watch out for a gay divorcée down the street, once he was eligible again—but for the most part Billy tried not to think of these things. "I knew she was dying—I knew," he later remembered. "I didn't want to accept it, though. I didn't want to absorb that fact."

He spent as much time as he could with his father. Sometimes they went swimming together or talked about the Civil War. They discussed articles from the newspaper or talked about local sports teams or navy vessels under construction at the shipyard. Billy especially liked the evenings when he and his father went downtown together to William Morgenstern's gift shop on Washington Avenue. Morgenstern, a Jew of Levantine aspect, had come to America in 1912. He had lived in Arizona for ten years and then had moved to Newport News, where he had opened the China Palace Gift Shop. He specialized in imported china, glassware, and costume jewelry; there was also a hobby section in his store, filled with airplane models, electric trains, jars of paint, and racks of balsa wood. Morgenstern had a good layman's knowledge of literature, art, and music. He and W. C. Styron liked each other and enjoyed conversation in the evenings. They sat and discussed books and composers while Billy wandered through the shop or simply sat and listened to the talk. The rhythms of adult conversation were interesting. Much of the discussion was above him, but he liked to hear Morgenstern's heavily accented English and to look at his dark skin and eyes, his black hair, and his sparkling white teeth. Billy also sensed the pleasure his father took from these evenings and the distraction they provided from his worries.

The Styrons socialized very little, but they did have a few friends, among them a local couple named Tom and Thérèse Skinner who sometimes came over after dinner. Tom Skinner was an artist, a painter who had lived in Paris as a young man. There he had met and married Thérèse, a native Parisian. Tom's sister was the wife of the president of the shipyard, and work had been found for him there: he did paintings of navy and commercial vessels as they were completed or repaired, and these were presented as a bit of lagniappe at the launching ceremonies. Tom and Thérèse were likable, sophisticated, and broad-minded. Tom often became tipsy on these visits. He would upset glasses and ashtrays or stumble over the furniture, but no one seemed to mind. He would smile, shrug apologetically, and say with a flourish: *"C'est la vie!"*

Whenever the Skinners came for a visit, Billy was allowed to sit up for an hour or so and listen to their stories about Paris or hear their comments about art and music. This gave him his first sense of what French culture might be like. On these evenings his mother talked about her months in Vienna and other European cities, and this awakened in him a desire to travel and see. Later, after he had been put to bed by his father, Billy would creep out on the landing above the living room and listen to the risqué, slightly off-color stories that the adults told and chuckled over.

Pauline was willing to go out in public occasionally, especially if there was a concert. Newport News had a local series sponsored by the Community Concert Association; it was patronized entirely by white people, and the Styrons nearly always went. W. C. Styron was treasurer of the group and had some say in selecting the artists who would come each year. The Styrons saw famous performers and groups on tour: Arthur Rubinstein, Lily Pons, the Philadelphia Orchestra under Eugene Ormandy, the Vienna Boys Choir. There was also a similar series, with artists and groups of comparable quality, at Hampton Institute, the black college. The Styrons and many other white people attended these concerts. They were given in Ogden Hall, on the Hampton Institute campus, and the audience was fully integrated, with whites and blacks sitting together, though this was technically a violation of a Jim Crow statute called the Massenburg Law, which had been passed in the state legislature in 1926. Hampton avoided the law by declaring its concerts to be private gatherings and issuing guest cards to white friends of the college. The Styrons had such a card.

These evenings made a strong impression on Billy Styron; as an adult he nearly always mentioned them when he talked about his childhood. They were an adventure: black people were everywhere in the city, of course, but whites almost never went to large gatherings of Negroes—to their church services or dances or social events. The concerts at Hampton Institute were an anomaly, and Billy liked them. The auditorium was small and cozy, the music was beautiful, and there were black people all around him. Sitting next to his mother, he could feel her pleasure as the music of Mendelssohn or Mozart or Beethoven washed over her, acting as a narcotic, easing her pain.

Music was a part of the Styron home too, though there was no piano and Billy was never trained to play an instrument. The harmonica was his only accomplishment in that line; he taught himself to play a chromatic harmonica, and he was good at it. His showpiece was "Roll Out the Barrel," which he executed with trills, runs, and grace notes. Pauline's instrument was her own voice. She often sang around the house, without accompaniment. She loved Bach and Wagner; one of her favorite pieces was Brahms's "Alto Rhapsody," of which they had a scratchy recording. Sound quality on the Victrola was poor in the 1930s, but music could be reproduced fairly well on a radio set. The Styrons listened faithfully to the Metropolitan Opera broadcasts on Saturdays and to the NBC Symphony conducted by Arturo Toscanini on Sunday afternoons at five o'clock.

Pauline was still able to travel, and sometimes on Saturday mornings the small family headed south in their automobile to Little Washington for an overnight stay. It was a short trip, taking only a little over two hours. The house on Main Street in Washington, in which Grandmother Marianna still lived, was too crowded to accommodate visitors. W. C. Styron's sister (the one he helped to support) lived there with her children, so Billy and his parents stayed downtown in a hotel.

The drive down to Little Washington took the Styrons across the James River Bridge, south through the peanut fields near Suffolk in Southside Virginia, and on into the flat, desolate counties of eastern North Carolina—Gates, Hertford, Bertie, Martin, and Beaufort. This was a strange region, isolated and sparsely inhabited. In Styron's memory it was "the South of pine forests and unpainted farm shacks, Bull Durham signs and coffee-brown sluggish streams winding through swamps, mule teams off in the distance and shabby little Negro churches in a stand of ancient oak trees." The speech of the white locals was rapid and slurred—difficult to understand even for someone accustomed to southern diction—and the accents of the black people in the region were impenetrable. Some of the territory that the Styrons passed through seemed godforsaken. One spring evening they drove over a stretch of road near a swamp in which the frogs were breeding. These creatures, wet and sluggish, had hopped onto the road by the hundreds. They were engaged in a loud mating ritual and refused to move. Billy's father had to drive over them, very slowly. Billy got goose bumps listening to the frogs pop beneath the wheels of the car.

The visits to Little Washington, though, were fun. Billy was much younger than his cousins there, and they petted and humored him. He would be brought in to see his tiny grandmother and hug her, but very gently, since she was now past eighty and quite frail. Her hands were warm, but her skin was so pale and translucent that it felt like tissue paper. She would tell him her stories—of life on the Clark plantation as a girl; of Drusilla and Lucinda, her two little slave girls; of the perfidious Yankees who had ransacked the Clark homestead and burned Little Washington; and of Grandfather Alpheus's steamboats and his tobacco business. She had only a few stories to tell now, but Billy liked to hear them. He would ask her to tell her familiar narratives, and she would oblige him, repeating the details so predictably that he came to know them by heart.

Marianna Clark Styron was deeply loyal to her region and never really forgave the North for what had happened to southern civilians during the war. She was polite to northerners, but it was difficult for her to be warm. Pauline Styron, a Pennsylvanian, felt uncomfortable around her, and there was some strain in their conversations, however cordial things seemed to be on the surface. "She has never really liked me, has she?" Pauline said to her husband late one afternoon on the way back to Newport News. W. C. Styron tried to soothe his wife and to deflect her question, but it was plain to both of them that she was right.

In truth, Pauline herself had never felt entirely at home in the South. Though outgoing and amiable, she could never quite understand how southerners dealt with one another, nor could she get used to their garrulous pokiness. She was not on easy terms with black people. The few blacks in her hometown of Uniontown had been scab laborers; she had never come into close contact with them. Perhaps as a result she was a bit intimidated by the sheer number of black people in Newport News. She could not entirely accommodate herself to the constant presence of Negroes, nor could she understand the elaborate, complicated relationships that existed across color lines, despite the laws that mandated segregation. It was she who taught her son not to use the term "colored lady" but always to say "colored woman." Certainly she was not bigoted or prejudiced, as we understand those terms today, and if she had lived longer she might eventually have felt more at ease with black people, but as her disease worsened she was increasingly cut off from the society around her, black and white, and she never really adjusted.

The Styrons sometimes took trips to Uniontown to visit with Pauline's family. This was a long journey, but they made it as often as they could, especially as Pauline's time grew shorter. The trip took all day. Billy and his parents would start early in the morning and drive to Fredericksburg, angle across northern Virginia to Middleburg in the Shenandoah Valley, then head up through the West Virginia panhandle and drive across the northwest corner of Maryland into southwest Pennsylvania. Uniontown was situated in the Allegheny Mountains, close to the state border, and it was cool there—a welcome escape from the heat in Newport News when the Styrons visited during the summer. They usually stayed with Pauline's sister, Edith, and her husband, a physician named Arthur Crow. The Crows had a large, handsome home in the mountains near Uniontown.

W. C. Styron, as we have seen, was not at ease on these trips. He and Dr. Crow did not see eye to eye on labor unions or social class, and there had been some unpleasant scenes during previous visits. Billy, sitting in the backseat during the long drives up to Uniontown, would hear his mother caution his father. "Now, we're not going to get into politics!" she would say, again and again. For Billy, however, the trips to Pennsylvania were fine. He liked the long car rides into the green mountains near Uniontown. He had a cousin there of about his age named Juddy Abraham, and the two boys played together amicably when the Styrons visited. Juddy, slightly older, gave lectures on what he understood to be the mechanics of sexual intercourse. Sometimes the two boys examined the illustrations in Dr. Crow's medical encyclopedias and would speculate on the functions of this or that part of the human anatomy. One of their adventures took a bad turn, though: an older friend of Juddy's who had a driver's license took the two boys to a morgue in Pittsburgh, where Billy saw a corpse. The experience frightened him and caused bad dreams for months afterward.

By the summer of 1938, when Billy turned thirteen, Pauline's cancer was far advanced. She would linger for another year, but both traveling and concert-going became more difficult for her and were finally abandoned. She began radium treatments, which helped for a time, but the aftereffects were severe. "I still have to go on and on and on (so it seems) with the X-ray," she wrote to a friend, "hoping they or it will keep the sleeping beast in leash." This was a time of great strain in the Styron household. Try as they might, Billy's parents had little time for him; they were preoccupied with drugs and treatments, and the atmosphere in the home was medicinal and melancholy. Sometimes Pauline tried to talk with her son about his schoolwork or his friends, but the conversations were strained and brief. She was so distracted by her pain that it was hard for her to show affection to him; he felt distant from her and powerless to help.

Billy's parents decided that it would be better if he could move out of the house for a time. They asked for aid from an old friend, Sally Cox Hayes, the neighbor who had taught Billy to read in her living room. He went to stay with the Hayes family, who now lived only a few blocks from the Styrons in Hilton Village. He slept and ate his meals there and checked in with his mother and father in the afternoons or evenings. Mrs. Hayes mothered him and looked out for him; he chafed a little under her discipline, but it was as good a temporary arrangement as might have been hoped for. Billy liked the Hayeses' tall son, Buddy, and there was an empty bedroom for him now that Buddy's older sister was out and on her own. Sometimes the two boys played outdoors or hung around the pier, but Buddy remembered in later years that Billy spent many hours alone upstairs in his room reading. Billy had some talent for drawing, and he and his friend Aleck Watson, who could also draw, often spent afternoons upstairs doing their own illustrations for books like *Treasure Island* or *The Count of Monte Cristo.*

In the fall of 1938 Billy Styron began his freshman year at Morrison High School. The problems caused by his having skipped a grade in elementary school now began to be apparent, and he had difficulty in adjusting. He was too small and light for athletics, and he was oppressed by the school hazing system. Freshmen, known as rats, were required to sit on benches in the aisles of the school buses where they were poked and harassed by sophomores. The abuse continued in the halls between classes. Billy did find a way to shine, however: he had been reading Joseph Conrad and decided to try his hand at fiction for the Morrison High School newspaper, *The Sponge.* "I wrote an imitation Conrad thing," he later remembered. " 'Typhoon and the Tor Bay' it was called—you know, a ship's hold swarming with crazy Chinks. I think I had some sharks in there too. I gave it the full treatment." He liked seeing his words in print, and his classmates praised him, but for the time being he was not moved to further composition.

Billy had something else to distract him that fall—stamp collecting. One of Pauline's friends from her music-teaching days was Mrs. Lynwood R. Holmes, who now lived in Philadelphia. Mrs. Holmes, a Virginia native from Lexington, had been given the name Elmer by her father, who had wanted a boy. She had married late in life and had had no children of her own. She and her husband, an agent for Furness/Withy, a tour company that operated cruise boats to Bermuda, lived in the Society Hill section of Philadelphia. They often took young boys and girls who were talented in art or music under their supervision and encouraged them. Billy Styron was in Newport News, too far away for them to have much contact with him, but Elmer—probably at Pauline's suggestion—adopted Billy as a correspondent and started him on stamp collecting. She sent him first-day covers, bags of foreign stamps, albums, tweezers, and a magnifying glass. Billy loved the stamps and the paraphernalia of philately. He responded with a poem:

> A connoseur of stamps am I,
> Upon philately I rely.
> I make Ma go into fits,
> When on Russia she sedately sits.
> Pa relapses into deep recessions,
> When he flops on the British Possessions.
> Watch out! Don't breathe a breath.
> Blow THEM stamps away. . . . .
> AND SUDDEN DEATH
> I know my stamps; boy can I LICK 'em!?
> And I know sweet girls. . . . . . . I sho can PICK 'em!

Elmer Holmes became Auntie Elmer to him, and they kept up a correspondence for the next four years. In July 1938, in fact, the Styrons decided that Billy might travel by himself to Philadelphia to visit for a week. He had just turned thirteen; this was to be his first trip alone. Pauline prepared the way with a letter to Elmer. Billy was terribly excited, she said, and had checked out some books about Philadelphia from the local library. Pauline was sure that his manners would be exemplary but was less certain about his bathing habits. "Make him *scrub*," she wrote to Elmer. "He will go in and throw the water in his face and let it go at that if not watched." Billy, who was learning to type, pecked out his itinerary on a small sheet of paper and sent it ahead to Auntie Elmer. His father would drive him to Old Point Comfort in Hampton, where he would catch the 10:40 Bay Line Steamer for Cape Charles, just across the mouth of the Chesapeake Bay. There he would take a day coach up the Delmarva Peninsula to Philadelphia and arrive at Broad Street Station at 6:56 P.M. The trip came off on schedule, and Billy spent six days with the Holmeses. It was his first experience of a big northeastern city.

When he returned to Newport News the next week, Billy gave his parents a full account of the trip. In a letter to Elmer, Pauline wrote: "I was amazed how he remembered every detail and *proud* that he could express himself so well and entertainingly—He took out his 'list' and we heard it all from beginning to end." Billy had visited Independence Hall and seen the Liberty Bell and the old market section. He had also spent a fascinating afternoon at the planetarium and had passed several hours in the guest bedroom reading a dictionary—something he liked very much to do. "In some ways he is so child-like," Pauline wrote to Elmer, "and then again I am struck by his—shall I say intelligence?"

Pauline's letter to Elmer continues on another matter: "I am feeling *much* better than I did several weeks ago, but both Bill and I were a little washed out for a day or so after his accident." W. C. Styron had hurt his shoulder at the shipyard and was having his upper body strapped every day before going to work. Pauline, as before, had to put on her heavy leg brace each morning. "We are a scream when we start out together," she wrote to Elmer, "one armless and the other legless! Ho-hum."

What Pauline did not mention—and what she might not have known—was the true cause of her husband's injury. He had told Billy, and probably Pauline as well, that a chain on an aircraft carrier had snapped and struck him while he was inspecting some repairs. Years later W. C. Styron told his son the real story: he had been involved in a fistfight with another worker at the shipyard. His adversary, whose name was Burke, was a left-leaning Irishman from New York City who was voluble in his criticisms of the South—especially its treatment of Negroes. Though W. C. Styron agreed with much of what Burke said, he disliked listening to lectures on the South's shortcomings from an outsider, and he could not abide Burke's self-righteous manner. Usually he tried to ignore the man, but one day Burke came into his office and began to bait him about mistreatment of blacks in the shipyard. The argument veered out of control, and the two men came to blows. This was a serious fight, not just a shoving match. Desks were overturned and office machinery upset onto the floor. W. C. Styron dislocated his shoulder in the fracas.

That the senior Styron, now almost fifty years old and normally an even-tempered, dignified man, could have allowed himself to become involved in a fistfight at his place of work is an indication of the enormous strain he was under. He was immensely frustrated and angry, unable to do much more than make payments on his multitudinous medical bills and attempt to comfort his wife as she inched toward death. W. C. Styron's worries, though not expressed openly to his son, must have communicated themselves to the boy all the same.

Billy had other problems. A year or more younger than most of his classmates, he stood only a little over five feet tall and weighed only about ninety pounds. Most of the boys in his classes were much larger. They were sprouting hair on their upper lips and bodies, and their voices were changing. None of these things had begun to happen to him yet, and he sometimes worried whether he would ever reach full physical development. He also worried, irrationally, that he might be becoming a woman—developing breasts and female sex organs. His friends were more curious about sexual matters than he was. The year before, several of the boys had organized a circle jerk in the woods, where they kept a tent, but Billy had not been able to participate. "I was not mature enough," he remembered years later with a smile. "I hadn't gotten my hormones. I remember feeling kind of out of it." There were inflammatory tales from classmates of boy-girl trysts at parties or in the balcony of the theater, but the girls in Billy's classes were not interested in him. "They considered me a little dwarf," he recalled. "They wanted these big bastards at the roller rink who could skate backwards."

As a way of drawing attention and establishing an identity, Billy Styron developed his wit. He learned to be quick and funny, cutting and sarcastic. Ridicule—if delivered with the proper timing—could be as effective as physical size in keeping people at bay, and humor, if keen and original, could win their approval. Billy did not have size or athletic ability, but he had words. He practiced with them, rehearsing sarcastic routines in front of the mirror. He collected obscure words and learned to use them correctly; if one dropped a big word in front of one's peers with a certain élan, one could develop a reputation for braininess. Billy also knew which classmates could hurt his feelings or his ego if they tried, and he developed verbal barbs to keep them off-balance.

Billy Styron might have employed his ability with words in the classroom, but he found the high school curriculum stultifying, and his performance was mediocre. Only history interested him; here he made his only good grades. Much of what he learned about was the proud past of his native state. Virginia history was near at hand: with his father he visited Jamestown and Yorktown and went several times to Williamsburg, which had been restored a few years before by the Rockefellers. What he loved above all else, though, were trips to the stately plantation houses along the James River—Westover, Berkeley, Carter's Grove, and the exquisite Shirley. The other historical sites were disappointing in comparison. Jamestown, then unrestored, was a melancholy spot with a ruined church and some illegible tombstones. Yorktown was a river beach where the soupy water was infested with jellyfish. Williamsburg, though tidy and bright, was contrived and artificial. The mansions along the James, however, captivated the boy's imagination with their grace and originality. Especially Shirley, with its eighteenth-century balance and its carved-pineapple finials, signifying hospitality, seemed to embody the best traditions of Virginia. These mansions belonged just where they were—in harmonious connection with the surrounding gardens and fields, and with the majestic James River in the distance.

Virginia history, as young William Styron learned it, was freighted heavily with romanticism and hero worship. That year, for example, the history text was decorated on its front cover with a photograph of General Robert E. Lee. This was reasonable enough, but the text for the following year was similarly decorated—with a photograph of Lee's faithful horse Traveller. More incongruous still was the fact that this was a photo of Traveller's carcass, stuffed and standing on display in the chapel at Washington and Lee University in Lexington. Perhaps Traveller's remains were an appropriate symbol after all. Like the noble old steed, much of Virginia's past now smelled faintly of the taxidermist's chemicals.

Billy also knew, even at thirteen, that large areas of Virginia history were skimmed over or ignored in his textbooks. He knew that there had been black slaves at Williamsburg, tending stock and cooking and making beds in the taverns. These people were not mentioned in the set speeches delivered by the smiling guides in Colonial Williamsburg garb. Billy also knew that his beloved James River plantations had been built and maintained by black labor, and that vast human chattel had been essential to such Virginia families as the Byrds, Carters, and Harrisons. Sometimes on a tour of Shirley or Westover, a guide might point out the foundations of a "servant" cabin, but that was all. What had these black people done? How had they lived? Did they have a history? Had they all been happy darkies singing in the fields, or cute pickaninnies playing around the cabins, or officious old uncles like Pompey in Miss Menin's May Day Pageant? Surely there was more to be known, but where could he learn it? Apparently not in his history texts. Could his Grandmother Marianna in Little Washington tell him? Probably not. Her memories were now cloudy: she was bedridden and would die that summer. Perhaps one could find out about slave life from books and lectures and historical records. Someday, he thought, he would learn more.

When his freshman year ended in the spring of 1939, Billy Styron went to live for three weeks with his cousin Frances Welch and her family in Ahoskie, North Carolina, a small cotton and peanut town in Hertford County, about forty miles north of Little Washington. His cousin's husband, whose name was Arthur Welch, was a sergeant in the state troopers, a job that had put him in the way of some violence. A few years before, he had been shot in the face by a Negro bootlegger and had lost part of his mouth and lower jaw. The population around Ahoskie was heavily black; Arthur Welch's main duty was to keep them in line. Sometimes he let Billy ride with him in his cruiser as he drove around the county. Billy would watch the faces of the black people. Years later he recalled how the Negroes rolled their eyes and looked carefully away as the cruiser moved by. Rides in the police car were all right, but much of the time Billy wanted to be alone. His cousin remembered that he spent most of his visit to Ahoskie in his room, drawing or fiddling with his stamps or playing solitaire.

Billy's mother was never far from his mind. He wrote letters home to her and his father but avoided the subject of her illness in them. When he returned to Newport News, he saw that things were much worse for her. It was now obvious that she did not have much time to live. He no longer knew how to answer questions about her health. Mercifully, word of her condition had spread through Hilton Village, and everyone knew not to ask him how his mother was feeling. She had become emaciated, almost cadaverous, and was now bedridden. She received injections of morphine, but her pain was still excruciating. There were nights near the end when her beautiful voice could be heard throughout the house, lifted up in an aria of pain. Billy was shielded from most of these scenes because he was again staying with the Hayes family, but he witnessed some of them, and he knew that his mother would soon be gone.

On the evening of July 20, 1939, Pauline Styron died in her bedroom. Her last weeks had been cruelly painful: because her body had built up a tolerance for morphine, the drug no longer helped to ease her agony. Her passing was merciful. Billy was at the Hayeses' house when she died, reading a book alone in an upstairs bedroom. It fell to Mrs. Hayes to tell him of his mother's death. She came to the door and said to him, "Billy, your mother is no longer with us."

William Styron, as an adult, could not remember his reaction. He was certain only that he had not been able to weep. He recalled a feeling of numbness but could not remember whether he felt actual grief, then or later. Almost surely he never let his sorrow show or experienced the catharsis of tears. He had only just turned fourteen and was still too young to grasp the reality of death as an adult would. And too, grief was tightly restrained at that time and place among members of his social class. The Styrons were a dignified family; this was Tidewater Virginia; the year was 1939. People expressed personal sorrow in private or kept their grief inside and did not express it at all. Billy Styron must have been stunned. Probably he did not know what was expected of him, either just after his mother's death or during her burial several days later in Uniontown. Wit and sarcasm, his usual resources, were not called for. Words of any kind seemed inadequate. The adults in Newport News and Uniontown probably did not know how to help him grieve. They seem to have conspired unwittingly, and from the best of intentions, to prevent him from coming to terms with his mother's death. They must have felt that as a child he did not need the purgation of sorrow. Instead he needed distraction and entertainment—things to amuse him and take his mind off his mother's passing.

Perhaps as a result William Styron was never able fully to rid himself of an immense subconscious burden of sorrow over his mother's death or of an illogical feeling of guilt. Had he been a good son to her? Had he been dutiful toward her? Might he have helped more during her final months? Had he really loved her? Had she loved him? He would never know the answers to these questions. He was too young to ask them in the months that followed her death, and as he grew older he buried them. They became internal, unexpressed preoccupations that had much to do with the formation of his adult personality.

5

Fourteenth Year

I N THE FALL OF 1939 William Styron began his sophomore year at Morrison High School. German forces invaded Poland that same autumn. Billy, then fourteen, followed the war in a desultory way in the newspapers and on the radio, and he heard speculation from neighbors about possible U.S. involvement. Such matters were watched closely in Newport News because the shipyard was tied so intimately to the national defense industry. Wartime meant prosperity, money, contracts, and jobs. Some of the men in Hilton Village said privately that American involvement in this war would not be such a bad thing: certainly it would help the city's economy. But the fighting in Europe seemed far away to Billy Styron—remote from his own concerns and worries. It did not occur to him that this war would ever involve him or his friends.

The fall of 1939 began well for young William Styron. He was elected president of his class in September and later won the title of "Wittiest" in a class election. He was still too small and light to go out for sports, but he did serve as manager of the football team, keeping up with towels and tape and riding on the team bus to games at other schools. He was self-conscious about his size, but the boys on the football team liked him and protected him from the worst of the razzing and abuse in the halls. Billy earned a school monogram for managing that fall and had it sewn on a white pullover sweater. In class photos the broad M covers his entire chest.

That October, on a football trip, William Styron had an experience that was to stay with him for many years. Several of the teams that Morrison played were located in Southside Virginia, in Isle of Wight and Southampton counties, not far from the Great Dismal Swamp. As the team bus drove south through the flat, sandy country, Billy would look out the windows at the peanut fields or read the roadside ads for snuff and chewing tobacco. He also tried to decipher the Virginia state historical markers, though usually the bus moved by too quickly for him to read more than the first few lines. These metal markers, painted silver with raised black lettering, were scattered throughout the Old Dominion. Most of them told of Civil War battles or pointed out the birthplaces of statesmen or generals. One afternoon, however, Billy spotted a marker unlike any that he had seen before. He was traveling on Virginia Route 58, about two miles west of Courtland. He made the bus driver stop so that he could get out and read the entire sign. The wording was as follows:

SOUTHAMPTON

INSURRECTION

SEVEN MILES SOUTHWEST NAT TURNER, A NEGRO, INAUGURATED, AUGUST 21, 1831, A SLAVE INSURRECTION THAT LASTED TWO DAYS AND COST THE LIVES OF ABOUT SIXTY WHITES. THE SLAVES BEGAN THE MASSACRE NEAR CROSS KEYS AND MOVED EASTWARD TOWARDS COURTLAND (JERUSALEM). ON MEETING RESISTANCE, THE INSURRECTION SPEEDILY COLLAPSED.

This marker rang a faint bell. In his sixth-grade history text, Billy had come across a brief reference to this rebellion. Nat Turner had led an uprising in which many whites had been slain; the insurrection had been put down quickly and its leaders hanged. The historian had said nothing more. Nat Turner's Rebellion, Billy now realized, had happened only a few miles from where he lived, yet he knew virtually nothing of it. He had been taught a great deal about Jamestown and Williamsburg, about the Peninsular Campaign, and about the *Monitor* and the *Merrimac,* but no one had taught him about Nat Turner's Rebellion. Obviously it had been more than a minor event. Almost sixty white people had been killed in the uprising; many black people had probably died as well. Why did no one talk about this rebellion? Billy climbed back into the bus and rode on to the football game.

Someday, he thought, he would learn more about this particular piece of history.

For Christmas 1939, Auntie Elmer gave Billy a Wanamaker Diary for 1940. He kept it faithfully from January 1 until August 24, writing in it each night before going to bed. The diary is essentially a log of his activities: there is almost nothing self-revelatory in it. If young William Styron had private thoughts, he did not confide them to his diary. The entries do give a good picture of his daily life that winter and spring, however. He was now an usher at the Hilton Village movie theater and saw a great many films—*Judge Hardy and Son* with Mickey Rooney, *The Hunchback of Notre Dame* with Charles Laughton, *Blackmail* with Edward G. Robinson, *The Grapes of Wrath* with Henry Fonda, *My Little Chickadee* with W. C. Fields, and *The Man They Could Not Hang* with Boris Karloff. He also watched some war films—*The Marines Fly High* and *Torpedo Raider*—and one afternoon he and Leon Edwards rode the train to Richmond and saw *Gone With the Wind* at a matinee. Billy played chess and cards with friends and read *Boy's Life, True Detective,* and *Crimefile.* In the evenings he listened to *Amos 'n' Andy* and *Fibber McGee and Molly* on the radio.

Often his father worked late at the shipyard. That fall and winter they would go together to the Bide-a-Wee Cafe in downtown Newport News for supper; then his father would return to his office for more work at night, sometimes taking Billy, who would read or fool around with the typewriters and adding machines. W. C. Styron, still under great strain, was attempting to bury himself in work. Melancholy and depressed, he was under a doctor's care, but the treatments were having little effect.

Billy, only fourteen, was not fully aware of the stress his father was under. An incident that winter, however, made him much more conscious of his father's condition. One cold Sunday afternoon, W. C. Styron had tuned in to the regular five o'clock radio broadcast of the NBC Symphony. The orchestra was playing Ravel's *Bolero;* Billy, reading on his bed in his room upstairs, could hear the music clearly from the first floor. He listened to the monotonous, insistent rhythms of the piece. Suddenly he heard a shouted curse followed by a crash from the kitchen below. He ran down the steps and found his father in his shirtsleeves, shaking with anger. On the floor was their tiny radio set, its plastic case chipped and cracked. His father, angered by the repetitiveness of the music, had struck the radio from the counter. This was the small radio set on which Billy and his father and mother had listened to the Sunday-afternoon symphony broadcasts in past years. Not much was said: W. C. Styron composed himself and put the set back where it belonged. He apologized to his son and told him to go back upstairs. In the weeks that followed, though, Billy was more than ever aware of the toll that his mother's death had taken on his father.

On February 21, 1940, W. C. Styron entered the hospital for three weeks of rest. Billy stayed with the Hayes family. W. C. Styron was partly restored by his time in the hospital; then, on March 13, he left on a ship for Puerto Rico, where he rested for three more weeks with Pauline's brother Clyde, who was still in the army and was stationed at San Juan. The treatment seems to have worked well enough; W. C. Styron returned in early April, resumed work at the shipyard, and brought Billy back to the house to live.

In his father's absence Billy had begun a new job, an afternoon paper route. He wanted to earn money to buy a sailboat. In order to deliver his papers, Billy had to go every afternoon to an establishment just outside Hilton Village called Adams Place—but known facetiously to the locals as the Hilton Country Club. It was a beer joint just across Warwick Boulevard, operated by a couple named Adams, whose two sons, Milton and Raymond, went to high school with Billy. Adams *père* held the concession for the Newport News afternoon newspaper, the *Times-Herald,* and the paperboys worked for him. Adams Place was popular with some of the parents in the village; they would go there in the evenings and would often take their children along. The parents sat at tables in the back and drank beer; children sat in booths up front swilling pop, reading comic books, and contemplating the aged candy bars and dusty gimcracks in a glass display case.

Billy's parents had never gone to Adams Place, so it was new territory for him. What he chiefly recollected about it years later was a huge glass jar that sat on the counter and was filled with pickled sausages swimming in a moldy-looking brine. He also remembered Mrs. Adams, who smoked Lucky Strikes and cursed the patrons in a good-natured way. Billy rather liked the atmosphere at Adams Place, but he hated his newspaper job, partly because the boys with afternoon routes had to get up early on Sundays and deliver the heavy Sunday morning editions, and partly because he was drinking up most of his weekly wage in pop, for which he was docked a nickel a bottle by the eagle-eyed Mr. Adams. Billy did not last long at the job: he quit on April 1, 1940, the Monday before his father returned from Puerto Rico.

That spring and summer Billy Styron had several other concerns. During his mother's final illness, his father had become friendly with a woman named Elizabeth Buxton. Now it looked as if they might marry. Billy was not sure about Lizzy Buxton, as he called her in his diary. Did he like her? Did she like him? Did he want her as his stepmother? Though she seemed friendly, she had to make an effort to smile, and she never laughed at his witticisms. Still his father seemed to like her, and he trusted his father's judgment.

If his father and Elizabeth Buxton did marry, Billy knew that he would find himself connected with one of the most prominent families in Newport News. The Buxton name in the city was synonymous with medicine. Dr. Joseph T. Buxton, a North Carolina native, had come to Newport News in 1899 after interning in Philadelphia. He had become a general practitioner and surgeon; in 1906 he had built the Buxton Hospital on Chesapeake Avenue, where he had delivered Billy Styron in 1925. Joseph Buxton's son, Russell, had followed his father's example and become a physician, taking over most of the elder Buxton's duties after the doctor fell ill with cancer in 1937. It was Russell Buxton, in fact, who had treated Pauline Styron during her final illness.

Elizabeth Buxton, his sister, had also entered medicine; she was a nurse and had been trained in the nursing school established by her father in the city in 1907. She was prominent in her profession and now trained nurses herself; she was head of the Virginia State Board of Nurse Examiners and frequently attended meetings in Richmond. She was devoted to her father and was helping to care for him in his final illness. She had never married; instead she had spent her life working with her father and serving in the hospital. The Buxtons followed lofty ideals of public service and worked with great energy. Elizabeth believed in self-sacrifice and unstinting labor, and she disliked carelessness and indolence.

She and W. C. Styron must have been drawn together by their common dilemma. His wife had died of cancer, as would her father. Elizabeth, who had recently turned forty, was a tall woman, serious in demeanor and proper in behavior, almost never appearing in public without white gloves and a hat. W. C. Styron was gentlemanly and well spoken, and he admired her father and brother. Outwardly the two seemed a good match. When the senior Styron returned from Puerto Rico, he began to visit Elizabeth Buxton at her home and to take her out occasionally, often bringing Billy along.

Sometimes these outings would include Elizabeth's sister, Helen Buxton. Helen had been a problem for the Buxton family. She was mentally retarded, and though her retardation was slight, she was undisciplined and rebellious. She was also accident-prone: several years earlier she had fallen under a trolley car, and a leg had been severed from her body. Now she wore a wooden prosthesis. This odd foursome—W. C. Styron, Elizabeth Buxton, Billy Styron, and Helen Buxton—went to movies together or to the Bide-a-Wee for supper. Elizabeth and Billy tried to get on friendly terms; he attempted to be funny and talkative, and she made an effort to unbend. Her attempts (and her nerve) were in many ways admirable: Billy now had his learner's permit, and one day she let him drive her to Richmond in her LaSalle automobile. He liked the power and smoothness of the heavy vehicle. "Boy, does that car drive!" he wrote in his diary.

Young William Styron's consuming interest that spring was his sailboat. It was an aging, dried-out Snipe that his father had bought for ten dollars from a friend. The boat had been stored for many years in a shed and needed much work. All through that spring Billy sanded, caulked, varnished, and painted the little craft—sometimes noting his exhaustion in his diary. Reading the entries now, one can see that there was something obsessive about this work. Certainly Billy saw the sailboat as a potential social advantage: he must have dreamed about sailing excursions on the river with pretty girls or friends. But he seems also to have done the labor for its own sake, to occupy his mind and tire his body. Working on the sailboat must have kept him from thinking about his mother's death and his father's possible marriage to Elizabeth Buxton.

That same spring his first cousin Hugh Styron, whose father had died in the flu epidemic of 1918, came to live with Billy and his father. Hugh, in his mid-twenties, was working at the shipyard. Brash and overbearing, he sometimes made life miserable for Billy, but he was willing to help with the Snipe. Hugh was handy with tools and was a good carpenter; he and one of his friends pitched in and did the more difficult repairs on the sailboat. By early June the vessel was pronounced sea-worthy.

Billy took his Snipe out on the James River for the first time on June 8. He got in a few more days of sailing in mid-June, but later that month he had problems with the centerboard. The boat swamped and had to be paddled in. Billy went sailing in rough weather on the twenty-seventh of June but turned the boat over; a month later, after a trip with his father to Uniontown to visit his mother's grave, he took the Snipe out again, but Milton Adams swam alongside and pulled it over. Young William Styron was persistent with the sailboat, as he tended to be throughout his life when something appealed to his imagination or his desires, but his bad luck continued. Late in July he lost the tiller and had to ask Hugh to make a new one. He sailed a few more times after that but decided to concentrate on tennis and swimming for the rest of the summer.

W. C. Styron had decided that his son should go away to prep school for the remainder of his high school career. Billy had done poorly in his classwork as a sophomore, earning mostly C's and D's. He had also become disobedient in school, managing one day to have himself thrown out of history class for cutting up. During the spring he had begun dating a little, riding around in cars with his older classmates and drinking beer when he could get it. He would not always account for his whereabouts: one day in May he skipped school to go swimming, and later that month he left the senior prom (which he had attended stag) and rode to Williamsburg with a friend and a sack of beer to hear Glenn Miller's orchestra, which was playing at William and Mary that night.

Such behavior was predictable enough for a boy now almost fifteen, but to W. C. Styron it must have suggested more serious problems. Billy was unfocused and undisciplined. He had worked obsessively on his sailboat, for example, but had not stuck with his paper route. Perhaps Billy needed more order than was available at home. W. C. Styron had by now spoken to Elizabeth Buxton of marriage, and they had an understanding, but she would not marry him until her father had passed away. The immediate future for Billy in Newport News promised only more meals at the Bide-a-Wee and nights spent in friends' homes.

There was another good reason to go away to prep school. Billy needed to be channeled toward subjects that suited him. Most of the college-bound boys in the city followed a pattern: they finished high school, took a year of prep school, often at a military academy, then went to Virginia Polytechnic Institute in the mountains of southwest Virginia to be in the cadet corps there and study engineering. Later they returned to work at the shipyard, often for life. Other boys stayed in the city after high school and attended the Newport News Apprentice School, where they trained for specific jobs at the shipyard. Obviously these patterns would not suit young William Styron; he was imaginative and verbal, much more inclined toward the liberal arts than toward the practical sciences. W. C. Styron was determined that his son would not repeat his own mistake: Billy would not attend a technical college and be miscast in life. The right college for him would be Washington and Lee or Hampden-Sydney or perhaps the University of Virginia. He therefore needed a prep school that would make him ready for one of those institutions. Fortunately such a place was near at hand: Christchurch, a small Episcopal boys' school not far to the north of Newport News, near a paper-mill town called West Point. Billy and his father visited the school in July, and Billy liked it. Christchurch had sailboats and a dock, and its location was beautiful. They agreed that he would go there in September.

First, however, Billy was going to travel to New York City to see the 1939 World's Fair, still in operation in Flushing Meadows. He and the Edwards brothers from Hilton Village—Holland and Leon—got permission to take the Edwards family car and drive north to New York for a few days. They planned to stay with an Edwards uncle who had an apartment on Fifth Avenue near Ninety-sixth Street. The boys left one morning in late August and drove all day. Leon began by teasing Billy about his voice, which was changing now to a deeper register, but fairly quickly Leon became carsick and threw up in the backseat. They opened the windows, held their noses, and pressed on. According to Billy's diary they crossed over Newcastle Ferry at 1:30 in the morning and entered New York City via the Holland Tunnel at 4:00 A.M.

The next day they took the subway to the fair and stayed all day. They visited the Bell Telephone building and the Westinghouse pavilion, where Billy appeared on a gadget called television. They played with an indexing machine at an IBM exhibit and saw the fair's twin symbols, the Trylon and Perisphere. They listened to a band concert and went to an amusement park, where they watched a couple get married at the parachute ride. Later they took the subway to Times Square and had doughnuts and coffee at 10:00 P.M. Afterward they walked around, looking at people and watching the lighted signs. Back home in Newport News a week later, Billy took up his Wanamaker Diary and printed "MY TRIP TO N.Y. (in story form)" at the top of an entry, but he never wrote the account and, in fact, never returned to the diary. There was too much else to do—school clothes to buy and a trunk to be packed. In September he and his father drove to Christchurch. There he would begin his final two years of preparation for college.

6

Christchurch

CHRISTCHURCH had been founded in 1921 by the Right Reverend William Cabell Brown, seventh bishop of Virginia. It was tiny initially, operating during its first year with only one instructor and seven boys; by the autumn of 1940, when Bill Styron began his first year there, it was still small, with only its headmaster, five teachers, and around sixty students. Christchurch was underfunded and threadbare but was magnificently located on a broad, wooded hill overlooking the Rappahannock River, fourteen miles inland from the Chesapeake Bay, just across Urbanna Creek from the small town of Urbanna. The red-brick buildings of the school were arranged around two huge oak trees, the highest points in Middlesex County, often used by sailors and fishermen on the Rappahannock as reckoning points. The main building, in which the boys attended their classes, slept, and ate, was called Bishop Brown Hall after the school's founder. There was also a gymnasium, an infirmary, a laboratory building, a headmaster's house, a chapel, and a bell tower. Student life revolved around Rec Hall, an old train depot that had been dismantled and re-erected behind Brown Hall. There the boys picked up mail, bought soft drinks and candy, and smoked if they were at least fifteen years old and had a letter of permission from home.

Christchurch was headed by William Smith, a strong-willed administrator who had managed to keep the school afloat through the worst years of the Depression. Smith was what was then known as an attitude developer. Many of the students at Christchurch were there because they were academically lazy, and he preached an Arnoldian doctrine of diligent study, vigorous sports, and muscular Christianity. At least once a week he would lecture in chapel on good habits and self-discipline. His favorite piece of advice was: "A journey of a thousand miles begins with the first step."

Despite such admonitions Christchurch was a relaxed, cheerful place. The schedule was not very demanding, and the pace was slow. The school was Episcopalian in its religious affiliation, but the curriculum did not contain a heavy religious element. Subjects for the older boys were standard for the time: English, Latin, French, history, science, and math. A normal day began with a study hall, followed by classes until noon, lunch and a few more classes, sports and activities, chapel (with coat and tie required), then supper, and then another study hall afterward.

Boarding students, of whom there were around fifty, lived on the top two floors of Bishop Brown Hall in individual cubicles measuring about six by eleven feet, each with a bed, desk, closet, and dormer window. Privacy was minimal: there were no doors to the cubicles, and the partitions that divided them reached only part of the way to the ceiling. A bachelor teacher lived in a large corner room on each floor and kept the behavior more or less orderly. During his first year at Christchurch, Bill Styron had one of the less desirable cubicles on the southwest side of Brown Hall, but in his second year he arrived early and claimed one of the choice corner cubicles on the northeast side, with windows on both outside walls. One of his windows looked out over the slate roof of the headmaster's house; the other commanded a view of the bell tower, the woods near the school, and the broad Rappahannock in the distance.

Christchurch had two special attractions: its emphasis on sailing and its excellent food. The school owned eight Hampton I sailing sloops— old, leaky, and often in need of repair, but maneuverable and graceful out in the broad river. And the food was wonderful. The kitchen was run by a large, paternal black man named Joseph Cameron, a gifted cook who somehow managed with limited funds to provide delicious meals for the students and faculty. Joe Cameron's chief advantage was his proximity to the Chesapeake Bay, and he regularly loaded his tables with bluefish, mackerel, and soft-shelled crab. The beef, pork, potatoes, and green beans came fresh from nearby farms. Often there was fried chicken; occasionally there were platters of ham and cornbread. At the midmorning break from classes, Joe Cameron would set out big plates of fresh biscuits and bowls of apple butter, and he always had pitchers of fresh lemonade in the kitchen if a boy wanted a drink. The milk at mealtimes struck the only sour note: it was purchased from a local dairy farm where wild onions had invaded the pastures. The cows now produced milk that tasted faintly leeky. Still, Styron remembered the victuals as superb: "While my Ivy League friends still complain thinly and bitterly of soggy Swiss steaks and glutinous mashed potatoes, I recall cheese biscuits and pastries and delicately grilled fish, fresh from the river or the bay, which would have caused a French chef to salivate with envy."

Bill Styron would spend two years at Christchurch, and by his own account they were happy and satisfying. For a boy of his disposition, Christchurch was in most ways ideal. Academic pressure was not severe, the food was good, and there was plenty to do. The school was isolated and protected; he felt as if he were a member of a large, chaotic family—a good experience for an only child. Christchurch was surrounded by thick woods of maple, elm, and oak, and a student could sometimes sneak off there in the afternoon to read. Bill did so many times. One afternoon he took a copy of a Victor Hugo novel with him and became so lost in the story that he missed chapel. At Christchurch one was always conscious of the natural beauty of the Virginia countryside—of the Rappahannock River, majestic and lazy, flowing away toward the east, and of the sounds of birds and the beauty of the magnolia trees scattered across the grounds. The climate was mild, and even on the hottest days there was usually a breeze from the river.

Most of the boys were from middle-class Virginia families, and many of them spoke with the soft Tidewater accent, difficult to mimic, that transforms *house* into something resembling *hoose* and *out* into a sound like *oot*. Jimmy Davenport was from the Northern Neck of Virginia; Tommy Peyton was from Crozet, near Charlottesville; Langley Wood was originally from Lynchburg, in the Shenandoah Valley. Hugh Dischinger was from nearby Gloucester, and Carroll and Randolph Chowning were day students from Urbanna. Not all of the students were from Virginia, however. Bill Bowman, known as Mick, had somehow come south from New York City to attend the school, and Lewis

Collins, nicknamed Zeke, had grown up as the child of a diplomat and had lived all over the world.

As soon as classes began in September, Bill Styron settled into a routine. A typical day for him started with breakfast in the basement dining hall, followed by a morning study period. Bill and Mick Bowman always sat together in the back of the study hall, where they began by working on the crossword puzzle from the *Richmond Times-Dispatch.* Then Bill would pursue what had become a passion for him—the study of geography. He had liberated the tattered Rand-McNally atlas from the school library, and he spent each morning poring over it, memorizing countries, regions, cities, rivers, mountain ranges, and bodies of water. (As an adult he would attribute this passion to his wish to travel, to see, to move away from his conventional upbringing.) He would learn not only the names but also the positions of geographical features, and he would show off for his friends by drawing, freehand and from memory, the details of particular coastlines and island chains. Near the end of study hall each morning, he would have Bowman quiz him on the continent or hemisphere he had studied that day. "He was always letter-perfect," Bowman remembered. "I could never stump him."

Bill Styron's attention in the classroom did not match his absorption in geography. At Christchurch, as throughout his academic career, he was an indifferent student, working only when it suited him and studying only the subjects that caught his fancy. He liked history, was mildly interested in languages, disliked science, and detested math. English was taught by Colgate Bryan, a stickler for proper grammar and a devotee of Elizabethan literature. Bryan's mimeographed "Outline of English Grammar" was treasured by his students, many of whom kept it and used it through four years of college. Bryan's particular passion was Shakespeare, and the yearly syllabus was heavy with the great tragedies and history plays. The students were required to memorize passages from Shakespeare, and all seniors had to be able to write out Hamlet's soliloquy from beginning to end, with the correct punctuation. During the week preceding the quiz, the top floor of Brown Hall would echo with the lines and pointing. "To be or not to be— semicolon—that is the question." Bill Styron's marks in history and English were good during both of his years at Christchurch, but in the other subjects his work was mediocre and in math his performance was abysmal. Only some crash tutoring from his friend Tom Peyton, in the spring of his senior year, kept him from failing solid geometry.

Classes were over by midafternoon; after that the students were expected to participate in activities or sports. Athletic pursuits at Christchurch were relaxed. There were numerous teams, and one was supposed to participate in something, but no one worried much about won-and-lost records. Bill Styron sailed in the fall and played basketball in the winter. He also belonged to the rifle team and joined the chess club and the choir. His deepest interests, however, were reading and writing. In the fall of his second year at Christchurch he was elected president of the Literary Society and supervised their activities—reading, declamation, and discussions of current events. With his knack for memorization and elocution he shone here, delivering Kipling's "Gunga Din" and "A Code of Morals" at evening chapel.

Styron's fellow students remember him today as a slight, pale boy who resented authority and liked to gripe about school regulations. During his first year he had still not reached full physical development, so he continued to compensate for his small size by his wit and sarcasm. "He had a tongue like a double-edged razor," recalled one classmate. "He could make you bleed. I can remember wanting to strangle him." By now Bill Styron had developed an instinct for finding the chinks in adolescent armor, and he kept many of the students at a distance. Words were his weapon, along with a talent for mimicry and for imitating accents. He adopted an irritated, impatient manner: in school pictures he always looks away from the camera and wears a bored, introspective expression. The inscriptions that he wrote in his classmates' yearbooks were not always friendly. "Go away, little man," reads one.

Bill Styron put his verbal gifts to use on the *Stingaree,* a mimeographed and stapled school newspaper filled with gossip and humor. During his first year at Christchurch, he co-edited the paper with Vincent Canby, a scholarship student from Lake Forest, Illinois, who later became the lead movie critic for *The New York Times.* Bill continued to work on the paper during his second year at the school, and it was not unusual for him and the other boys to produce an entire issue overnight. Most of the writing was schoolboyish, and the humor was so local and specific that it is today incomprehensible.

Bill Styron also shone at dramatics. The productions were mounted at old Christ Church itself, a small nineteenth-century Episcopal chapel not far from the school. In Bill's first year, the boys produced *The Ghost Train,* Arnold Ridley's mystery/melodrama involving drug-smuggling and false identities. Because he could manage a good British accent, Bill played the role of an eccentric Englishman, wearing knickers for the part. Scenery for the production was minimal, and sound effects were chancy. At a climactic moment on opening night, the audience was meant to hear, offstage, the sounds of a train pulling into a station. Someone had found a recording of train noises, and this was played at the appropriate time. The recording was to be followed by the sound of two pistol shots, and Styron had been pressed into service to fire two blanks from the track team's starting pistol. At the appointed moment, however, the gun misfired. Two loud clicks were heard from the wings, followed by Styron's anguished whisper: "Mr. Smith! Mr. Smith! The goddamn gun won't fire!" Improvising, Styron stuck his head around the edge of the curtain, waved the pistol, and shouted, "Bang! Bang!" It brought down the house.

During his second year at Christchurch, Bill had a leading role in the school production of *Brother Orchid,* a play about an ex-convict who reforms and joins a monastery. (The play had already been made into a movie starring Edward G. Robinson.) Bill played Frecks, a henchman described in the script as "a tall, slim, extremely nervous man of forty, who is constantly smoking cigarettes." In later years Styron would remember that the requirement to smoke began a tobacco habit that persisted with him into his late thirties.

Some things about Christchurch irritated young William Styron. Most of his classmates admired the headmaster, William Smith, but he did not. Partly this dislike stemmed from a kind of natural antipathy to authority, evident already in his personality, but it was also a reaction against Smith's tedious moralizing. During Bill's senior year, for example, he decorated his corner cubicle in Brown Hall with Vargas girls from the pages of *Esquire.* These were colored drawings by the artist Alberto Vargas of beautiful, scantily clad young women; the pictures were popular and could be found on bulletin boards in many college dorm rooms of the 1940s. (Later they were plastered on the walls of GI barracks during World War II.) William Smith found the Vargas pinups immoral and called Styron on the carpet for having them in his room. Styron remembered years later that Smith delivered a long lecture to him, telling him repeatedly that he had an unhealthy attitude toward sex. Smith criticized the Vargas girls for their unnaturalness. By way of example he pointed to his dog, Lady, a female German shepherd who was sprawled on the floor of his study. "Look at Lady!" Smith said, gesturing toward the dog. "She's *natural*! Sex is a *natural* thing for her!"

Styron's revenge was to invent a nickname for the headmaster that stuck. He became Smut Smith. Styron's classmates remembered that he had an evil genius for nicknames. The sobriquet was often the opposite of the target's personality. Smut Smith was moralistic and puritanical, for example, and Tom Peyton, who usually behaved himself, was dubbed Satan Peyton. A dull teacher was christened The Sog. Other boys were nicknamed Gleek, Mole, Hump, and Zombie. Styron himself was known as Sty.

Most of the social life at Christchurch revolved around a group of girls in Urbanna known as the Urb girls. The relationship was symbiotic: Christchurch was a boys' school, and the Urb girls were nearby; Urbanna was sleepy and slow, and the girls there enjoyed dating across the river. On Friday nights the Christchurch boys would walk or hitchhike to Urbanna, where they would often check in first with Dorothy Groome, called Nutt, who was two years older than they and was already working at Virginia Electric and Power Company. She would telephone around town and locate dates for them. The fun was charmingly innocent: the boys and girls would go to the drugstore for ice cream or to the local roller rink to skate and drink frosted mugs of root beer. Sometimes they would pool their money, buy hot dogs and soft drinks, and go to Urbanna Beach for a cookout. They sang popular songs on the beach or while sitting together on the curb outside the drugstore. Like his father and grandfather, Bill Styron had a good tenor voice and often led the group in Presbyterian hymns. Sometimes he, Tom Peyton, and two of the other boys would have a go at barbershop harmony.

Little in the way of romance went on at these gatherings. Most of the Christchurch boys had serious girlfriends back home, and it was usually these girls who were invited to the school for dance weekends. Bill's favorite partner among the Urbanna girls was Rebecca Chappell. During his second year at the school he was much absorbed by Frances Taylor Hayward, known as Fan Tay, a brunette from Newport News whom he later dated a few times in college. He idealized both girls and brooded much about love and the opposite sex, but nothing came of either romance. By the spring of his second year, however, he had at least got his growth. In one long spurt he had shot up to almost six feet in height. Despite Joe Cameron's cooking he was still thin, weighing not quite 120 pounds, but at least he was taller now than the girls he dated. This helped him at dances and parties.

Learning to drink was part of the education at Christchurch. It was easy for boys from the school to get beer—or even whiskey, which was available from a woman bootlegger outside the Urbanna town limits for seventy-five cents a pint. Beer was often brought along on the beach cookouts or when the girls and boys went sailing in the school boats. Alcohol and amusement were available closer to Christchurch in a dive called Cooks Corners, only a quarter mile or so from the school grounds. Cooks Corners was run by a large Negro man named Harlan Jackson, who rode a black motorcycle and was not much worried about the ages or colors of his customers. Blacks and whites mingled harmoniously enough in the place, but it was still known to be rough and dangerous. "Girls wouldn't step a foot in it," remembered Dorothy Groome years later. The beer of choice for the Christchurch boys was called Atlantic; it cost a dime a bottle. This concoction was so crudely brewed that one could see gobbets of yeast floating in it. Bill Styron, Mick Bowman, and their friends would spend hours in Cooks Corners, swilling the foul brew, playing the jukebox, and singing along with the tunes.

Much of the fun at Christchurch came from attempts to hoodwink the schoolmasters and sneak off the grounds, either for visits to Cooks Corners or for trips to Urbanna to go to the movies. A favorite dorm activity was penny-ante poker—usually seven-card stud, five-card draw, or blackjack. A more solitary pursuit was masturbation, about which there was much joking and badinage. There was little privacy in the cubicles, and one had to be furtive in order to indulge. Occasionally a boy would be caught masturbating in the shower; the penalty for the onanist, in one instance at least, was to have his private parts encircled by a looped belt and to be led down to study hall in the nude, there to have his secret made public and his character assailed.

A fair amount of energy went into pranks, some of them aimed at parents. During the last few weeks before graduation Bill's senior year, Jimmy Davenport and Randolph Chowning distilled a quart of grain alcohol in the school lab. On graduation day there were to be two punchbowls—one with alcohol for the parents, and the other with lemonade for the boys and for those who did not imbibe. Davenport and Chowning double-spiked the parents' punch but watched in disappointment for the expected effects. These were sturdy Episcopalian parents, veterans of many wet receptions. The double ration of alcohol had no effect on them at all.

Bill Styron participated in most of these pranks and was in on much of the other fun. He was not retiring, but there was something remote and private about him. He liked to tell outlandish stories, but always about other people. He would sometimes talk about his girlfriends and about sex, but what he said was impersonal and ironic. Sometimes he would mention Newport News, but only in general terms. He sat in on bull sessions and listened to his classmates as they analyzed their friends and families, but he revealed nothing about himself or his own family. No one who knew him at Christchurch ever heard him mention his mother's death.

Part of his silence about family matters had to do with developments back in Newport News. It seemed that he was indeed to have a stepmother: Elizabeth Buxton and his father had announced their plans to marry. Bill had come to know Elizabeth better during the summer after his first year at Christchurch, when he had been home on vacation, and what he had learned was not reassuring. She had criticized him for sleeping late and being messy. His grades had been a little better at Christchurch than at Morrison High, but there had been no great improvement. Elizabeth scolded him for not working up to capacity, often mentioning the financial strain that his father was undergoing to send him to Christchurch. She told him that he was disorganized and lazy, and she frowned on his carousing and beer drinking with teenaged friends that summer. Bill's response was a mixture of rebellion and apprehension. He resented Elizabeth's assumption of authority but felt powerless to prevent her marriage to his father. She was to be his stepmother; that now seemed certain. The question was whether they could learn to get along.

W.C. Styron married Elizabeth Buxton on October 18, 1941, during his son's second year at Christchurch. Elizabeth's father had died earlier that year; now she was free to wed. Bill, however, was given little part in the wedding or the later festivities, and the exclusion rankled him. "Pop doesn't want me to have the whole week-end," he wrote to

Auntie Elmer, "so Mr. Smith, the headmaster, is going to drive me down that Saturday at about 1:00 and bring me back the same afternoon, after the reception. Ain't that something?!"

Soon after marrying Elizabeth Buxton, W. C. Styron sold the house in Hilton Village and moved with his new wife to 139 Chesapeake Avenue, an impressive stone dwelling with a large front porch overlooking Hampton Roads. Bill found, however, that he had little affection for the place. Emotionally he still thought of home as the small house on Hopkins Street in which his mother had died. He felt that he had been evicted from that house and that his father had been taken from him. Bill made weekend visits from Christchurch to 139 Chesapeake Avenue and spent a few holidays there as well, but these times were tense and strained. The house quickly became Elizabeth's territory: much of the furniture and many of the possessions were hers, and Bill felt like a visitor. His relationship with Elizabeth deteriorated quickly after her marriage to his father. He found that he had little to say to her; conversations were brief, and mealtimes were filled with silences. At issue were the same matters that had surfaced the summer before—Bill's tendency to stay up late and to sleep until noon the next day, his messiness, his mediocre grades and poor study habits, and his late-night carousing with friends.

Bill Styron's dislike for Elizabeth Buxton was in part the natural antipathy of any stepchild toward a new stepparent. He resented her elevation to a position of authority over him. He had managed well enough on his own during his first year at Christchurch and did not feel that he needed her supervision now. He saw no particular reason why he should conform to her house rules or to her standards of hygiene or conduct. He must also have wanted to test her authority by deliberate disobedience.

From Elizabeth's point of view her new stepson must have seemed moody, perverse, and touchy. He could be charming and mannerly if so inclined, but he was also capable of truculence and sarcasm. She had no experience with such a person and little inclination to put up with his moods. Elizabeth was accustomed to regularity and neatness at home and in the hospital. She was also used to having her orders obeyed quickly, and to the letter, by her house servants and by the nurses she trained. The medical world was a world of hierarchies, which Elizabeth accepted without question. She had idolized her father and now felt the same respect for her brother. Elizabeth admired most doctors, in fact, and was deferential to them. By the same token, she expected attention and respect from nurses, orderlies, and others beneath her in the pecking order. She was not accustomed to rebelliousness from a thin, sarcastic, sixteen-year-old boy.

It was clear to Bill Styron that Elizabeth Buxton had little affection for him. He also came to believe that she had only nominal respect for his father. He saw that music, art, history, and literature—the things that mattered to him and his father, and that had been of such importance to his mother—did not rank high in Elizabeth's estimation. Serious people, she believed, devoted their lives to medicine or law or the ministry. She often told him that he should aspire to be an Episcopal clergyman.

W. C. Styron was sweet-tempered, mild, and reluctant to quarrel. He had been worn down by his first wife's long illness: he was over fifty years old now, and he badly wanted a second marriage that would be serene and peaceful. Elizabeth quickly established her dominance over him; Bill, in fact, saw that his father wanted things this way. He wanted a woman who would take charge. Elizabeth's family, her possessions, and her unyielding personality gave her leverage and strength, and the senior Styron was unable to stand up to her or to defend his son against her. She was too formidable, too convinced of the correctness of her own standards.

After a few weekend visits to the house on Chesapeake Avenue and a miserable Thanksgiving dinner there, Bill grew reluctant to go back to Newport News at all. Instead his father would drive up and visit him at Christchurch, and Bill, to avoid trouble, would spend weekends and holidays with friends. These were pleasant occasions at least, and though he missed his father badly, he enjoyed being in his classmates' homes. There were new places to see, different families to get to know, and new girls to date.

Over Christmas break in 1941, for example, he had a good visit with Mick Bowman and his family in New York City. The two boys barhopped in the Village, saw the movie *Babes on Broadway* with Mickey Rooney and Judy Garland, and visited Chinatown. On New Year's Eve they walked from Mott Street over to the Bowery and up to Astor Place, then caught the bus to Times Square to see the new year come in. It was Bill's first experience in such a huge throng of people; in the crush he had his pocket picked. Bill spent other holidays and school breaks with Tom Peyton and his family in Crozet. He liked it there and became a kind of adjunct member of the Peyton family. He was especially fond of Mrs. Peyton, who mothered him. (He kept up a correspondence with her in later years, much as he did with Auntie Elmer.) In Crozet he and Tom would date the local girls or make french fries in a can of grease on the family's old wood-burning kitchen stove. Tom was a good wing shot, and sometimes the boys would have quail for breakfast. Tom attempted to get Bill to go hunting, but Bill nearly always refused, preferring to stay home and read.

Back at Christchurch, Bill and Tom Peyton were frequently together. The friendship also included a slightly younger boy—a small, handsome, irreverent student named Jack Bennett. On Saturday afternoons in the spring, the three boys would take one of the school's sailboats over to Urbanna, recruit female passengers, and head out on the river for several hours of sailing. Tom did not drink, but Bill and Jack brought beer along. Toward the end of a long, warm afternoon of sailing, the pressure on one's bladder became strong. At first Styron would suffer in silence, too shy to relieve himself in the presence of the girls, but Bennett would not hesitate. He would perch on the stern of the boat and, with much mugging and groaning, add a little volume to the mighty Rappahannock. In a day of much restraint in boy-girl relations this was a daring move, but Bennett brought it off with easy, innocent merriment. Eventually Bill Styron learned to do it too. The antics of the boys would make the girls scream with laughter.

Not far from Christchurch was a post office and general store owned by a black man named James Wright, who was also pastor of a small church nearby. The Christchurch boys bought candy and pop from Reverend Wright and chatted with him and his daughter Naomi, who helped run the store. One Sunday Bill Styron, Chet Porter, Jimmy Davenport, and Mick Bowman went to the evening service at Reverend Wright's little A.M.E. Zion church. They wanted to hear the black people sing. After the service Reverend Wright, an imposing man, confronted the boys. They had come, he assumed, to laugh at the emotionalism of his service. Bowman told him that they had not—that they only wanted to listen. Reverend Wright was skeptical. The boys persisted, though, and returned in later weeks to the Sunday evening services. Bill Styron was especially regular in his attendance. He liked to sit in the small church, surrounded by black people, listening to the sounds of their voices. These services were quite different from the Episcopalian services he attended at Christchurch, which were restrained and ascetic, and altogether unlike the Presbyterian services he had gone to in Newport News, which were cold and austere. Styron and his friends continued to go to Reverend Wright's services, and eventually they were accepted. If they missed a Sunday evening, Reverend Wright would scold them when they came to his store the next week. "Come back," he would say. "It's all right. We used to you now."

Bill Styron returned frequently. Something about the experience seems to have had private meaning for him. Perhaps it reminded him of the occasions, only a few years before, when he and his father and mother had gone to Ogden Hall at Hampton Institute to hear the concerts there. His small family had been intact then, sitting together, surrounded by black people and enveloped by the music of Mozart or Haydn or Brahms. Negro people had sat in front of him and behind him, very close, close enough for him to study their clothing, their hair, their skin, their hands and fingernails. Often they would smile at him, and he would smile back, but they would avoid touching him or his parents, even when they brushed against one another as they filed out at the end of the concert. Could one come to *know* these Negro people? They were all around in Tidewater Virginia, yet they remained hidden and mysterious. Could one touch them, make contact with them?

During this same year, 1941–42, his second at Christchurch, Bill Styron tried his hand at fiction. In December he was required to write a short story for English class, and he turned out a good one, which he later sent to Auntie Elmer. Set in wartime Germany, it was called "A Chance in a Million." The story begins this way:

> Haarmann's methodical brain worked with lightning-like rapidity. Cool, calculating, with fiendish design, his criminally trained mind, steeled to all outside distraction, was working out every detail and angle in this plan, this magnificent and glorious pattern of crime, which was to be the crowning achievement of his twisted career.

The principal character in this yarn is Karl von Haarmann, heir to the Wessel-Platzmüller fortune and scion of the Haarmann family of Bremen. The crafty von Haarmann pulls off the greatest bank robbery in European history and heads for the Austrian border with three million Reichmarks in negotiable bonds. He wants to escape to the Bavarian Alps but is apprehended at the last minute by a Gestapo officer, who recognizes him as a draft dodger. (His draft card is No. 1,000,000— hence the title of the story.) Coincidental plotting aside, this was an impressive piece of writing for someone of Styron's age. The dialogue was rendered in a patois of German and English, reminiscent of many movies of the early 1940s, and the characters, though stock figures, were deftly portrayed. Mr. Bryan, the English teacher, awarded an A. His only comment: "Watch your too frequent use of adjectives."

"A Chance in a Million" is dated December 8, 1941—a Monday. Bill Styron must have copied out the final draft of the story the night before, Sunday evening, December 7, 1941, only a few hours after news of the Japanese bombing of Pearl Harbor reached the United States. Surely young William Styron was excited and distracted by the broadcasts, but he could not yet have known what this war would mean to him and his friends.

Many years later Styron recalled how he first learned of the Japanese attack. On Saturday night, December 6, he and Mick Bowman bought a bag of beer at Cooks Corners. They consumed half of the supply and hid the rest. The next afternoon they retrieved the beer and hitchhiked to Urbanna, where they looked up Carroll Chowning, a day student from the town. They talked him into lending them his car—a 1932 Ford V-8, painted green and the envy of the school. Next they picked up two of the Urb girls and cruised out of town toward West Point, the paper-mill town nearby where even on Sunday one could smell the ripe stench of hydrogen sulfide. Bowman, who was driving, pulled into a seedy café; they all went inside and ordered hamburgers. As they sat in the booth, eating and swilling the beer surreptitiously, a waitress approached with the news. "I'll never forget her homely face," recalled Styron many years later, "nor her voice, which had all the sad languor of the upper Pamunkey River." " 'The Japanese, they done bombed Pearl Harbor,' " she told them. Then she added, in a puzzled tone, " 'Pearl Harbor . . . That's down in South Carolina, ain't it?' "

The effects of the Japanese attack on Pearl Harbor would soon be felt by every boy at Christchurch. Later that afternoon they all gathered at the headmaster's house to listen to the radio and to wonder how the coming conflict would affect them. The next day, Monday, December 8, the United States declared war on Japan. Virtually all of the students at Christchurch ended up serving in World War II, and many saw combat. Hugh Dischinger was a fighter pilot at Iwo Jima and in the Philippines. Mick Bowman joined the army and was badly wounded at the Battle of the Bulge. Carroll Chowning and Langley Wood became navy officers in the Pacific, and Wood was wounded in a kamikaze attack. Tom Peyton, like Styron, became a marine officer. Jack Bennett, their friend who had so amused the Urb girls by peeing in the Rappahannock, died on a beachhead in the Pacific.

During the spring of 1942 most of the talk among the seniors was about the war. The next most popular topic of conversation, however, was colleges. Nearly all of the Christchurch boys planned to go to college for several terms before they entered the service, and there was much discussion of the merits of various institutions. Bill Styron's first choice was Washington and Lee, but he could not persuade his father to send him there. W&L, like the University of Virginia, had a reputation as a drinking school. W. C. Styron feared that Bill was too young to withstand such temptations. He therefore took his son to visit Hampden-Sydney College, a Presbyterian school with a quieter reputation, but Bill did not like the place. He stood with his father on the edge of the football stadium (nicknamed Death Valley) and pleaded tearfully not to be sent to the school. Finally they compromised on Davidson College, another Presbyterian institution, which was located in North Carolina, just above Charlotte. Davidson had a good academic reputation, and drinking was strictly forbidden there. Bill accepted his father's decision with as much grace as he could muster. After a visit to Davidson in late March, he wrote Auntie Elmer that he had misgivings about the school but then added, without much conviction, "I reckon I'll like it a lot after I go there for a while."

As graduation from Christchurch approached, William Styron found himself with mixed feelings. He was still young; he would turn seventeen that June. He considered staying at Christchurch for an extra year (a common practice if one was young for one's grade or was deficient academically), but he seems to have realized that he was capable of doing college-level work. Christchurch had been a place of refuge for him. He had been unhappy in Newport News and had become alienated from his stepmother. Christchurch had allowed him to escape. It prepared him well enough for college and put him in the company of boys who were mischievous but decent and well brought up. He matured physically and emotionally at Christchurch and began to learn a few of the mysteries of dating and courtship. Christchurch did not provide a polished preparatory-school experience; it was not Andover or Choate or Saint Paul's. It was more relaxed, less pressured—perhaps even a little seedy. Styron would remember it that way in later years: "Christchurch may not have been in those days a well-heeled place," he would recall, "but it had a warm and golden ambience, and life was sweet, and we ate like kings."

7

Davidson

WILLIAM STYRON arrived at Davidson College in June 1942, only a few days after graduating from Christchurch. He had seen Davidson only once before, when his father had brought him there for a short visit; now he explored the grounds more thoroughly. He found a school that was small, tidy, and conventionally collegiate. Brick buildings of Georgian design were arranged around the campus; magnolias, oaks, and maples shaded the lawns, and squirrels and chipmunks were everywhere. The street opposite the college grounds was lined with shops, many of which catered to the students. The weather was hot and promised to get hotter. The college was slow and sleepy; everyone seemed to know everyone else, and no one was in much of a hurry.

Davidson had been founded in 1837 by Presbyterians who wanted to establish "a Christian college of high rank." The institution was named for General William Lee Davidson, a hero of the Revolutionary War. It survived early financial difficulties and a long period of privation after the Civil War to emerge, in the 1930s, as a liberal arts college of good repute. Davidson was homogeneous, conservative, and insular. Most of the faculty had earned their undergraduate degrees there, had gone on for graduate work, often in Ivy League schools, and had returned to take up permanent teaching positions at the college. There were about fifty faculty members and, during the normal fall and spring semesters, around 650 students, all male. Many of the students were from North Carolina or Virginia, a few others from South Carolina, Kentucky, Tennessee, or Alabama, and a scattering from New York or New Jersey.

Bill Styron had come to Davidson immediately after graduation that June because of the war. Many American colleges had altered their schedules and were operating on a trimester system for the full twelve months of the year. Under this streamlined approach one could begin college the summer after finishing high school and complete a full two years' worth of academic work by the end of the next summer. A student could thus finish four years of classwork much more quickly and could enter the military, usually as an officer candidate, by June of the third year in college. Styron, who had only just turned seventeen, had not yet decided what branch of the service he would join, but he knew that he was going to be in the war. If nothing else, he would be drafted as soon as he turned eighteen in June 1943. He therefore enrolled in the accelerated program at Davidson and began to think about enlisting— probably in the Marine Corps, though he was not sure.

That summer at Davidson, on this accelerated program, Bill Styron took two semesters' worth of both English and history. The pace was grueling. Each class met for two hours a day, Saturdays included, and writing exercises were due in English almost every time the class met. William P. Cumming taught English to Styron that summer; forty-six years later he could still remember the blistering weather and the experience of marking some 550 freshman papers in one four-week period. Cumming, a careful scholar and a supremely methodical man, saved all of his students' papers over the years. After William Styron had become well known, Cumming was able to donate Styron's freshman themes to the Davidson College Library. They are written on predictable topics: there are autobiographical sketches, business letters, a "hobby" theme (Styron wrote on sailing), a library exercise, a theme on one's favorite magazine (Styron chose *Time*), a descriptive paragraph (Styron's is entitled "Fog on the River"), a series of short themes on Hardy's *The Return of the Native,* and a lengthy term paper (Styron's was written on "Volcanism in the East Indies"). Perhaps the best of these papers is an attack on tabloid journalism: "The appeal to the masses," writes freshman Styron, "lies wholly in the presentation of sensational stories, reeking with sadism, vice, and crime." In most ways these themes are unremarkable. The style is competent, and there is a good vocabulary in evidence, but one searches in vain for hints of nascent literary genius. The few opinions offered seem to be those a student was expected to express. Styron got through summer school respectably, with grades of B or B+ in his subjects.

That fall he had his real introduction to life at Davidson. During orientation week, he listened with his fellow freshmen to talks on the war effort and on budgeting time and money. He learned that there were hall prayer meetings in the dorms, and it was reemphasized to him that chapel was compulsory and that drinking was not tolerated. He met his roommate, a boy named Herman Walker from Greenville, South Carolina, and he tacked up maps of the world on the walls of their room. Styron told everyone that his ambition was to join the foreign service, and, as he had done at Christchurch, he impressed his classmates by his ability to locate virtually any city, province, or river on the globe.

Freshman hazing was still part of the Davidson system in 1942. At orientation Bill Styron was handed a red freshman cap and told to wear it. He also received a copy of the *Wildcat Handbook* and was instructed to memorize the rules for first-year students. (He saved the handbook; today it is among his papers at Duke.) As a freshman Styron had to wear his cap at all times, to show respect to upperclassmen, to know school songs and football yells, to avoid walking on the grass, to remain in his chapel seat until all upperclassmen had cleared the room, to go to all pep meetings, to attend all major athletic events, to wear his YMCA nameplate, to pick up and deliver laundry for upperclassmen, and to tip his cap to all faculty members.

Freshman rules at Davidson were enforced by a Court of Control, an eight-man, black-robed tribunal composed mostly (in Styron's memory) of beefy members of the football team. That fall the court was headed by "Judge" Joe McCoy, who spoke to the freshman class during orientation week on Frosh Laws. He told them that the court held weekly sessions at which it tried malefactors and handed out punishments. The court had a good deal of power: it could pass elaborate, irritating sentences on first-year men and could confine them to campus on weekends for offensive behavior.

Not surprisingly Styron soon ran afoul of the Court of Control. He was found guilty of "disrespect to upperclassmen" in early October and had his name published in the campus newspaper on a list of "Noxious Freshmen." The next month he was brought before the court again, this time for refusing to wear his freshman cap. For this second offense he was made to write a fifteen-hundred-word theme entitled "Why Freshmen Should Obey Freshmen Rules" and to report to one of the members of the court every morning at seven-thirty for a week. Other freshmen earned similar penalties, but apparently these sentences did little to bring them into line. The next month, as a farewell punitive gesture, just before its authority expired, the Court of Control confined the entire freshman class to campus for two weeks. This was a bad start for Bill Styron. The freshman hazing, which struck him as adolescent and silly, awakened his rebelliousness and resentment.

Once the orientation period was over, Styron found a few things to divert him at Davidson. There were several concerts and a Stunt Night. *Arsenic and Old Lace* was staged by the college dramatic society, and tryouts were held for a production of *H.M.S. Pinafore.* There were YMCA mixers and get-acquainted events; Styron got to know and like the campus YMCA leader, a friendly, goateed man named Shaw Smith who put on magic shows in his spare time. Styron also made friends with a boy named Manly C. Sanders—known as "Slimy"—who had a Victrola and a collection of records in his dorm room. Sanders introduced Styron not only to some of the works of Mozart and Beethoven but also to the country songs of Roy Acuff and Hank Williams.

The war generated some excitement that semester: in October the students crouched in their dormitory basements for an air-raid blackout drill; a few days later the college organized a patriotic parade through town, and students went from door to door collecting scrap for the war effort. They followed news of the battles on the radio and in the newspapers: some of the boys had older brothers who were serving in Europe or North Africa, and there was discussion of Hitler's invasion of Soviet Russia and of Rommel's retreat in North Africa. The news from the Pacific theater had been bad initially but now was better. The long, bloody battle for Guadalcanal was still in progress, but by late October the last Japanese counteroffensive had been turned back, and an American victory seemed certain.

The war was important, of course, but it was half a world away. Battles in such places as Rostov, El Alamein, and Buna-Gona seemed impossibly remote. Of greater importance that fall to the Davidson freshmen, absurdly, was fraternity rush. The college was so small and isolated that failure to receive a bid to a fraternity amounted to social ostracism. There was much earnest conversation in dorm rooms that October about the merits of Kappa Alpha versus those of Sigma Phi Epsilon or Phi Gamma Delta and much speculation about which of the nine fraternity chapters on campus would pursue which freshmen. Because he was bright, witty, Presbyterian, and Anglo-Saxon, Styron found himself a desirable property. So anxious were the brothers of Phi Delta Theta to annex him to their membership that four of them hot-boxed him as he sat one autumn night under a big elm tree near the center of campus. Hot-boxing was a technique by which four or five brothers surrounded the undecided freshman, flattered him and told him amusing stories of fraternity antics, and extracted from him a promise to accept a bid should one be extended. Years later Styron could recall quite clearly the moment at which the Phi Delt president, sitting on the grass beside him, laid a large, warm hand on his knee and said with quiet earnestness, "You know, Bill, once you pledge Phi Delt, you're our brother for life!" Styron remembered his reaction with a smile: "I keeled over like a three-dollar whore. From then on it was Phi Delt or nothing for me." The bid was duly issued; Styron made good on his promise; he became a Phi Delt pledge in October.

Other freshmen, however, were not so lucky. One of Styron's roommates from that summer, a homely country boy from the backwoods of North Carolina, received no bids. He was miserable for most of the remainder of his freshman year until, during a second rush period in the spring, he was belatedly tapped by one of the campus chapters. A second boy whom Styron knew and liked was not even this fortunate. Styron remembered him as bright and funny but with a fatal social flaw—unmanliness. "I mean really unmanly, he was *effeminate.* And I remember seeing him—on that great final day when you discover whether you are pledged or not—standing alone there thumbing a ride to Charlotte, with that silly little freshman cap on his head, and he was weeping. And after the end of the semester he did not come back. At a larger school with fraternities—a university, say—he might have been able to forget about it, immerse himself in the great swim; but at Davidson he was an outcast, marked, a pariah, and he knew it, and so he never came back."

Life at Davidson was almost entirely monastic. Sometimes girls from Salem and Queens Colleges would be brought over for weekend YMCA gatherings, but it was unusual to see females on campus during the week. One had to endure long bus trips if one wanted to enjoy the company of young women. Boys traveled south to date at Agnes Scott, Converse, or Winthrop, or rode north to Hollins or Sweet Briar or Randolph-Macon Women's College. The all-male atmosphere produced some curious behavior. Table manners deteriorated, and bathing was often dispensed with. Styron took to the habit and earned the sobriquet Stinky Styron.

So rare was it to see a woman on the Davidson campus that an informal system of alert was developed whenever a sighting occurred. If an attractive young faculty wife, for example, began to walk across the college grounds, a window in the first dormitory she passed would fly up, and a boy would shout, "Fire!" Immediately, windows in adjacent buildings would clatter open, and the alarm would be spread from dorm to dorm—"Fire! Fire!" There was nothing subtle about the practice, and pretty town girls, to amuse themselves, would sometimes go out of their way to stroll through the college, just to cause a commotion.

Styron's awareness of the complexity of racial matters was not yet fully developed, but he must have noticed inconsistencies and contradictions at Davidson. There were many reminders of old attitudes toward Negroes. An ancient black janitor, known simply as Enoch, born in slavery and now well into his eighties, shuffled around the dormitory, pushing a broom, grinning, and bobbing his head to the students. A blackface minstrel show was staged on campus with the usual foolishness by Mr. Interlocutor and his sidemen. On December 1 of Styron's freshman year, Sigma Upsilon, the honorary literary fraternity at Davidson, heard a reading of a story entitled "Deputy Sheriff," which had been written by a member of the Davidson faculty. According to the college newspaper, the story concerned a young southern aristocrat who was saved from the clutches of an escaped convict by a faithful Negro servant. The old darky was killed defending the white man but died content "in the knowledge that his former mistress and favorite 'massah' were to get married." This short story was followed by a paper, read by a Davidson alumnus, entitled "They Also Serve." The paper was an account of "some of the experiences, humorous and otherwise," that the alumnus had undergone "while serving with negro troops at Ft. Benning."

There were efforts on campus to counteract such thinking, however. The YMCA raised money for a local Negro community center and sponsored a black Boy Scout troop, which met on campus and was led by Davidson students. The college paper carried liberal editorials on race, and Davidson organized a visit in December by Reverend Charles Tyler, a black Presbyterian clergyman from Alabama who spoke in chapel about his work in depressed areas of Birmingham. The college president, John R. Cunningham, made a speech in April on the position of the Negro in southern society and criticized the Church quite sharply for its failure to help the black man.

These inconsistencies would have been found almost anywhere in the United States in 1942. The Negro was at once a figure of fun and a human being whose problems needed attention. What William Styron was witnessing at Davidson College was a microcosm of a struggle over race that was beginning to gather momentum. Many years later he would play a controversial role in that struggle, but in 1942 he could laugh at the malapropisms of Tambo and Bones in the minstrel show and applaud the speech by Reverend Tyler at chapel, not especially aware of the contradictions in his behavior.

When he was with his friends he heard jokes about clownish black figures named Leroy and Tyrone, and he listened to boys speculate about what it would be like to sample poontang. By himself he watched black people and listened to them. He saw that they were intriguingly complex—often touchy, proud, and wary of whites. He used the word "nigger" now and then but, like most southerners of his upbringing, knew that it was an offensive, ugly word. Occasionally he would refer to black people as Negroes, but usually he would employ the term "colored people," the polite locution during the 1940s. Always he would be conscious of black people and curious about them, and he would wish to understand them better, but it would be many years before he would embark seriously on that effort.

Racial matters were a gray area at Davidson, but there was no confusion about alcohol. Drinking was forbidden for Davidson students, even off-campus. The penalty, if one was caught, was expulsion. For Bill Styron's father this policy had been one of the institution's attractions. Styron later said, however, that his father had underestimated his resourcefulness. One could buy beer in the nearby town of Mooresville; many years later Styron could recall sitting in a grimy café there, smoking cigarettes and drinking the appalling wartime brew. Mooresville seemed "as wicked and exciting as Marrakesh," he remembered. He felt "incredibly daring and adventurous" just to be there.

It was also possible to ride the bus to Charlotte, about fifteen miles south of Davidson, and do one's imbibing there. One weekday afternoon in December 1942, near the end of Styron's first semester in Davidson, he and a friend from Mississippi were drinking beer in the bar of the Barringer Hotel in Charlotte. After an hour or so, the friend ("a worldly fellow," in Styron's recollection) had a suggestion. "Why don't we go get laid?" he said. Styron did not want to admit that he was a virgin—that in fact he had only a little knowledge about sexual intercourse and that he certainly had no idea of how one might go about finding a prostitute. He was a bit afraid but was also curious and anxious to shed his virginal status. He agreed to go along, so his friend, who was slightly older and considerably more experienced, led the way to the nearby Green Hotel.

They found a bellboy, who was black, and learned that he did have a woman available. The price was three dollars, to be paid in advance. The boys handed over the money and ascended to the second floor. Styron, worried and scared, let his friend go in first. "I sat out in the hall reading *Life* magazine upside down," he remembered. To make matters worse, his friend took an agonizingly long time. "Forty minutes must have passed," Styron recalled. Finally the friend came out, and it was Styron's turn. Just before he went in, the friend pressed a foil-wrapped prophylactic into his hand. Styron, however, was already prepared: for months he had carried a rubber in his wallet as a sort of talisman, hoping that sometime he might have an opportunity to use it. Thus he entered the prostitute's chamber fully prepared—with his friend's gift prophylactic in his hand and his own treasured rubber tucked inside his wallet.

The woman inside, who was white, looked to be in her late thirties. She had on only a slip, and Styron noticed her sagging figure and bad skin. By way of preliminaries, he asked her where she was from. She told him, in her slow drawl, that she had grown up on a farm in South Carolina. After a few more lines of conversation she took charge—helping him disrobe and don one of his protective devices. At the last moment, in a rush of safety-mindedness, he put on the second prophylactic as well and thus approached his task doubly sheathed. Then the woman began to practice her profession, but Styron, twice encased, could feel scarcely a thing. After a lengthy period of effort, the woman paused and sighed. "C'mon, honey," she said. "You're taking longer than that other boy." Eventually, by a supreme effort of concentration, Styron completed the act. He mumbled his thanks and made his way out. Later, riding the bus back to Davidson, he felt simultaneously elated and let down. He had gone through this particular *rite de passage,* but the experience had hardly been erotic.

Styron would later say that during his one year at Davidson he had been "the most miserable freshman in the state of North Carolina." Part of the trouble, he correctly divined, was that his "innate sinfulness was in constant conflict with the prevailing official piety." But a more compelling reason was that Davidson was academically quite rigorous. Styron was a lazy student, content to get by with the gentleman's C. In later years he would remember three teachers as having been especially fine—Chalmers Davidson in history, William P. Cumming in English, and Henry T. Lilly, also in English. He would regret that he had not been more conscientious in his work for them since all three, in his recollection, were "brilliant and classy."

What stuck in Styron's craw, though, was Bible class—two semesters' worth—which all freshmen had to take. The classes were taught by two superannuated faculty members whom Styron remembered as "stern, dreadful, horrifying old men." Years later he set down his recollections in a letter to Chalmers Davidson: "My memory of these two old fossils (and I have no doubt that, privately, they were decent, kindly men) is freighted with such abject *meanness* and *dreariness* that I still find it difficult to confront the Good Book without thinking of it as a swamp of Abijahs and Ephraims instead of the supremely great revelation that it is. . . . Let ministers of the gospel learn the name of Aaron's wife, or people who want to win TV quiz shows; but not college freshmen, even in a church school." One of these teachers was so inflexible in his execution of the rules that, toward the middle of the second semester, he dropped Styron's grade on an important test from a D to a D– for having been forty-five seconds late to class one morning. Styron had managed a C in Bible his first semester, but after this incident he gave up the struggle and took an F in the subject for the second term. By that time he knew he was going to transfer to another university and did not care about an odd three credits in Bible. Styron's other grades during his freshman year were mostly C's. He passed the majority of his work, but it is fair to say that he was not academically engaged. "I was a rotten student," he later admitted.

One activity on campus that did catch Styron's interest was writing for Davidson's school publications. He fancied himself a creator of comic verse and made his debut in the December issue of *Scripts 'n Pranks,* the campus humor magazine, with an effort entitled "The Terrible Case of Theodore Twaddle's Hiccups." The best that can be said for this long, sprawling poem is that it fills almost two full pages of an otherwise thin number. A better effort followed in the May issue. Entitled "Get All You Can," it is a verse parody of Coleridge, Shakespeare, Shelley, Kipling, and Tennyson. The title of the poem refers to the advice being given to students who had enlisted in the military and who were now awaiting orders. "Stay in school and get all the education you can," they were being told. "You'll be called away to the war soon enough." Herewith Styron's rendering of that counsel into Tennysonian dactyls:

> Half a year, half a year,
> Half a year onward,
> Into the E. R. C.
> Went the Six Hundred;
> "Stay here, get all you can,
> We're with you, man for man,
> You'll never see Japan!"
> Blissful Six Hundred.

The war was transforming many aspects of life at Davidson. In February and March there was great confusion as approximately two hundred Army Air Corps cadets were brought to campus for temporary training. (This same scene was being played out at colleges throughout the country as institutions everywhere were mobilizing for the war effort.) East Dormitory at Davidson was vacated; its residents were squeezed into other dormitories or quartered in houses in town to make room for the military trainees. Styron published an account of the dorm evacuation in the college newspaper: "The exodus of the boys from East makes the flight of the Children of Israel look like a parchesi game," he wrote. "East is bare and deserted, looking more like a Philadelphia sugar warehouse than an ex-breeding place of corruption."

Most of the incoming air cadets were from the North, and their presence on campus was disturbing. There was genuine apprehension over what their behavior might be like. Styron investigated the matter for the newspaper: "Although the large majority of the fledglings are Yankees," he reported with mock seriousness, "they are not radicals, and from all appearances the time-honored Blue vs Grey feud has been suspended." Still, the reserved atmosphere at Davidson College had received a shock.

William Cumming recalled many years later that during the 1930s and early 1940s fully 90 percent of a typical entering class at Davidson would be made up of southern boys, and at least a quarter of these would bear Scots Presbyterian surnames. Many of these transitory air cadets, by contrast, were of Irish, Jewish, Italian, and East European extraction. They had been assigned to Davidson alphabetically from a long master list in an office somewhere in Washington. Cumming remembered that the college was sent all of the boys whose surnames began with H, I, J, and K. There was apparently one spot left open, and it was filled by the top L on the list, a northern boy with a lovely, liquid, Italian name that ordinarily would never have been seen on a Davidson class roll.

That fall, when Bill Styron went home to Newport News for Thanksgiving, he saw that the war was transforming the city. The shipyard now hummed around the clock. Contracts had been let for cruisers, battleships, and landing craft; laborers were also beginning work on the first of eight huge aircraft carriers that would be completed, at an average of one every fifteen weeks, between January 1943 and April 1945. The shipyard was expanding enormously; there were over thirty thousand new workers on its payroll. Trailer camps were springing up, and the government was erecting two huge dormitory facilities for unmarried male and female laborers. The harbor was now patrolled—U-boat attacks were feared—and troop shipments to Europe were veiled in secrecy. Styron saw soldiers transported through downtown Newport News at night in darkened troop trains, and he sat at home with his father and Elizabeth Buxton through blackout drills.

Styron himself took his first step toward entering the war that February. He knew that when he turned eighteen in June, he would immediately be drafted—probably into the army, unless he had already committed to another branch of the military. He thought that his chances for an officer's commission were best in the Marine Corps, so he enlisted in the Marine Corps Reserves, Class IIId, Officer's Candidate Class. He was apprehensive, though, fearing that he would not pass the physical examination because he was so thin. One had to weigh at least 125 pounds; Styron weighed about 120. He spent the week before his physical exam gorging himself at meals and had some success, but on the appointed day he was still about three pounds underweight. On the advice of friends he went to the grocery store and bought a dozen bananas, which he choked down during the bus ride to the induction center in Raleigh. Once there, Styron and the others had to strip to their skivvies and line up for examination. Years later he could recall the sneer on the face of the burly recruiting sergeant who looked him over. The sneer, he thought, was probably justified: before the sergeant stood a tall, pale, skinny college boy with a suspiciously protruding belly. Still, the tactic worked: Styron weighed in at a shade over 125 pounds.

Styron had another physical problem as well. He had been born with a congenital cataract (or lenticular opacity) in his right eye. His vision in that eye was bad—blurry and unfocused, especially at distances. The condition could not be corrected with eyeglasses, so Styron had adjusted and learned to use his left eye for nearly everything. He knew, though, that this defect in his vision might keep him out of the Marines, since his right eye was his shooting eye, the one he would use to aim a rifle. He badly wanted to be in the war; a medical deferment was unthinkable. He therefore memorized the test chart with his left eye as he stood in line at the induction center. Then, when his turn came, he stepped up and recited the line for 20/20 vision. (Over fifty years later he could still remember the sequence of letters: A-E-L-T-Y-P-H-E-A-L-T.) He was pronounced physically fit, signed the papers, took the oath, and returned to Davidson to wait for his orders.

The initial word was that he would go straight to Parris Island for boot camp on July 1, then be sent to West Virginia University or to the University of Virginia for advanced training. Later that spring, however, Styron learned that he was instead being transferred to Duke University, where he would join the Marine Corps V-12 program and would continue going to classes until he was called up. Styron seems to have been happy enough with these orders. At least he would be leaving Davidson. The college, by now, was in turmoil. Over one hundred of the Air Corps trainees were shipped out in late March, and another dormitory was vacated for an additional 250 new cadets who came in early April. "People are being drafted right and left," Styron reported in a letter to his father. "At present there are only about 225 boys left in school, which is quite a decimation, what? The morale is really quite awful. No one is studying much, and activities are at a minimum." In this fashion Styron's freshman year limped to its close.

Styron's accomplishments during his one year at Davidson were few. He managed to pass thirty-six hours of academic work with approximately a C average. He joined a fraternity and wrote a few pieces for the humor magazine and the college newspaper. He drank a fair amount of beer, began to smoke cigarettes regularly, lost his virginity, and joined the Marine Corps. Through a classmate he was introduced to some good music, classical and country. He made a few friends and had a few dates, but none of the friendships endured and none of the dates was serious. He was ready now to close this chapter of his academic career and move on to Duke. There, he suspected, it would be easier to find a place for himself in the large, heterogeneous student body.

William Styron and Davidson College had suffered from a case of acute incompatibility. Davidson had not been among the schools he had wanted to attend; it had been chosen for him by his father. Davidson was not Christchurch: it was larger, more conservative, and more academically rigorous. The college was isolated, and the kinds of amusement that were available were not really to Styron's taste. The pervasive presence of religion—the compulsory chapel and Bible classes and dorm prayer meetings—did not go down well with him.

Had Styron entered Davidson a few years later, after the war, he would have come to a different college. Davidson emerged from the war years as a more open institution. It retained its basic identity but shed many of the rules and customs that had so irritated young William Styron, and it eventually became one of the most selective, prestigious undergraduate colleges in the country. Styron might have flourished at Davidson, had he been a freshman there in 1950, and had he developed better academic self-discipline.

It must be said too that William Styron, in 1942, would probably have been unhappy at any school he attended. He had not entirely recovered from the loss of his mother. He was continuing to have difficulties with his stepmother and knew that he was not welcome in Newport News. He was still immature, emotionally and physically, and he had little idea of what he wanted to do in life. For most American boys of his age it was pointless to think about such matters in any case: they were heading into the war. Nothing had yet caught Styron's fancy or stimulated his intellect. He needed to catch fire. Perhaps he would do so at Duke.

8

Duke and
William Blackburn

WILLIAM STYRON arrived at Duke University near the end of
June 1943, a few days after his eighteenth birthday. A local bus
deposited him late at night on the West Campus of the university, just
at the foot of the statue of James Buchanan Duke (with cigar in hand)
that stands in front of Duke Chapel. The statue, Styron later remembered, "appeared to regard my arrival with some self-satisfaction. After
all, it was he and his father Washington who had run my grandfather
out of the tobacco business in Beaufort County, North Carolina, in the
last century. I supposed he could afford to look smug; it was that
sculpted cigar that created the effect."

Styron was not entirely happy to be coming to Duke. Its academic
reputation, though respectable, was not as high as it would later become. Duke was then known as a good private university that catered
to well-heeled northerners unable to get into Ivy League colleges.
(Campus wags, in consequence, sometimes referred to Duke as the University of New Jersey in Durham.) Duke's location was not altogether
attractive either. The city of Durham—called Durms by the students—
was then still a tobacco town with warehouses and cigarette factories
but with little in the way of cultural diversion. Durham was much like
Newport News—a raw, ugly, fast-growing industrial city of the New
South. All things considered, Styron would rather have gone to the
University of North Carolina in nearby Chapel Hill, a more typically

southern school in a quiet college town, but the machinery of military bureaucracy had instead shuttled him to Duke. Still, Styron was not entirely disappointed with his lot. Among other things he noticed how handsome the university was. As he stepped off the bus on West Campus that first evening, he paused to look around. "Dark as they were," he recalled, "the Gothic outlines of the campus loomed in the shadows most attractively and impressively, and the Chapel tower rose up against the night with formidable majesty and grace. I remember thinking that there were worse-*looking* places to end up."

Duke University in 1943 was a well-endowed, rapidly emerging private institution that traced its lines of descent to Trinity College, a small Methodist school founded in Randolph County, North Carolina, in 1839. Trinity College had moved to Durham in 1892 and, in 1924, had been chosen by the Duke family to receive a large endowment that would transform it into a major national institution. The college had been renamed Duke University, and new facilities and programs had been added. Some of the old Trinity College buildings had become the core of a large adjunct campus, called East Campus, principally for women students. A handsome new main campus had been erected in West Durham, with gray limestone and granite buildings in the Collegiate Gothic style. Schools of divinity, law, medicine, nursing, and engineering had been established, so that by the time Styron arrived there in 1943 Duke had completed its transformation into a true university.

Styron noticed the differences between Duke and Davidson immediately. Though Duke had carried over its Methodist affiliation from Trinity College, there was no compulsory chapel and no Bible-class requirement. Duke was large and bustling, with a diverse, cosmopolitan mixture of undergraduate, graduate, and professional-school students. The medical school was a dominating presence, and, for the first time since his sophomore year in high school, there were females in his classes. Most of the nonmilitary undergraduates were from conventional, middle- to upper-class families; many of them wore expensive clothes and had ready spending money. Fraternities were much in evidence, but one could have a social life without joining; Styron could have affiliated with the Phi Delta Thetas (he had been initiated to the Davidson chapter the previous spring), but he decided not to belong. He had lost interest in fraternities while at Davidson, never having developed a taste for their style of socializing. Besides, as a V-12 trainee he was in a different orbit from the fraternity boys. He wore a uniform every day and was kept almost constantly busy with military indoctrination and training.

The war had caused great changes in student and faculty life at Duke. The V-12 program had brought in almost one thousand new male students and had altered the curriculum and academic calendar. The V-12 program was designed to hold young U.S. Navy and Marine Corps officer candidates in college for several semesters; there they could mature a little while studying subjects that were supposed to be useful once they went on active duty. Duke, like Davidson, was following a trimester system during the wartime years in order to crowd as much learning as possible into each twelve-month cycle. This system, however, applied only to military trainees. Regular male students and all co-eds continued to follow a traditional nine-month two-semester system, a situation that created much confusion, especially for faculty members who taught on both calendars.

Most of the V-12 students knew that they were at Duke only temporarily; they would be shipped out to basic training camp after three or four terms. Thus they felt little loyalty or affection for the university, and many of them felt genuinely unwelcome there. They came from all parts of the country, and many of them were decidedly not Duke types. (The university placed special restrictions on its women students, in fact, to shield them from these outsiders.) The usual college social events—mixers, dances, and rush parties—could not accommodate the numerous V-12 boys, and campus hangouts like the Dope Shop in the student union were always overcrowded with uniformed V-12's, smoking cigarettes and talking in military slang.

It was an odd atmosphere—nervous and hectic, temporary and artificial. The campus newspaper carried stories about alumni in uniform in almost every issue. They were serving everywhere, it seemed: England, India, North Africa, Europe, Australia, New Guinea, and on the various Pacific islands. Articles describing their bravery appeared regularly, and alumni on leave from the war came back to campus to give inspirational talks and to show off their battlefield decorations. Duke students mounted paper and scrap-metal drives; co-eds in white dresses—wearing sashes that read ANY BONDS TODAY?—walked about the tobacco-fragrant streets of downtown Durham selling war bonds. The movie stars John Payne and Jane Wyman visited the campus to boost the war effort, and Margaret Bourke-White, the photojournalist, came and described the Allied barrage at Cassino, which she had photographed for *Life*. The V-12 trainees pitched their tents on the school baseball diamond and drilled on the grassy mall leading away from the chapel. In one of the quads on West Campus, trainees set up a mock graveyard, surrounded by a white picket fence. The tombstones bore these admonitory legends:

> "I blabbed my sailing date."
> "I stood up to investigate."
> "I didn't finish a wounded Jap."

Styron registered for his first semester of course work a few days after arriving at Duke. If he had been a navy recruit, he would have been made to take what amounted to a pre-engineering curriculum, with courses in mathematical analysis, physics, engineering drawing, navigation and nautical astronomy, chemistry, elementary heat power, and calculus. Styron would almost surely not have survived such a spate of technical requirements. He might well have washed out and been sent to the Pacific. Fortunately, though, the curriculum for the Marine V-12's was not nearly so practical and technical. Marine trainees were free to take a good many more electives than were their navy opposite numbers. What is more, Styron was classed as an irregular V-12 marine, which meant that he had already finished at least one semester of college elsewhere. These irregular students could continue to sign up for classes in their major areas. Styron was therefore able to take most of his work in English, French, history, philosophy, political science, and psychology. The only technical course he could not duck was elementary physics—a requirement that, as we shall see, would leave some indelible marks on his academic record.

At the beginning of his first semester at Duke, Styron signed up for English 103, Literary Composition, taught by a professor named William Blackburn. This course was one of the first offered at a large southern university in a field that would later be called creative writing. Styron's desire to be an author was at this point still "vagrant" and "nubile," he remembered, "so fuzzy, really, as to border on a whim." Still, he thought that he might like to give this writing course a try. It seemed "attractively undemanding, vaguely educative and entertaining," so he decided to sign up for it.

He was soon to learn that the course was not a schedule filler. A week or so into the term he composed his first paper for Professor Blackburn, a two-page exercise in descriptive writing. "I chose a Tidewater river scene, the mudflats at low tide; attempting to grapple with the drab beauty of the view, groping for detail, I wrote of the fishnet stakes standing in the gray water, 'looking stark and mute.' A pretty conceit, I had thought, until the theme came back from Blackburn covered with red corrections, including the scathing comment on my attempt at imagery: *Mute? Did those stakes ever say anything?*" Styron received a D– on this first theme and learned, by discreet inquiry, that his was the lowest mark in class. He had discovered that he would not be able to skate by on his verbal facility. "A certain precision, you see, was what the professor was after and I was lucky to be made to toe the line early," he later recalled. Styron's vanity had also been stung: he had always thought of language as his métier; it surprised him that Blackburn had not been much impressed by his maiden effort.

In consequence, and for almost the first time in his life, Styron found himself eager to meet the standards of a demanding teacher. He worked hard on his next composition for Blackburn, a sketch entitled "Where the Spirit Is," which was based on his first experiences with alcohol. It was an ambitious piece, with much dialogue and with a long stream-of-consciousness passage on the last few pages. Styron was apprehensive when he typed the final copy of the story. Beneath the title on the first page he put, "Dubiously Submitted: Bill Styron." This time, however, Blackburn responded much more favorably: "A sincere and beautiful story, ably told," he wrote on the front of the theme. "You have got to the inwardness of your subject & that is poetry."

Styron was elated but not yet satisfied. He was intrigued by Blackburn, who was formal and remote, and wanted to see whether he could break through this professor's forbidding exterior. "I sweated like a coolie over my essays, themes and fledgling short stories until my splintered syntax and humpbacked prose achieved a measure of clarity and grace," Styron recalled in later years. "Blackburn in turn warmed to my efforts—beginning to sprinkle the pages with such invigorating phrases as 'Nice!' and 'Fine touch!'—and before the term was half through I had begun to acquire a clutch of Bs and As. More importantly, I began to know Blackburn, the great-hearted, humane, tragicomical sufferer who dwelt behind the hulking and lugubrious facade."

William Blackburn had come to the Duke English department as an instructor in 1926. A Rhodes Scholar with a B.A. and an M.A. from Oxford, Blackburn had quickly begun to distinguish himself as a teacher. He developed a local reputation as a pedagogue, but he was initially without a Ph.D. and showed little interest in academic scholarship. As a result his achievements as a teacher were overshadowed by the presence on the Duke faculty of several high-powered literary scholars—Newman Ivey White, whose biography of Shelley had been much praised; Paull F. Baum, a well-known editor and critic of Chaucer and the Victorians; Lewis Leary, a talented scholar in American literature; Jay B. Hubbell, whose seminal work on the authors of the American South was highly regarded; and Clarence Gohdes, a rigorous historian and bibliographer of American literature. In such company Blackburn did not stand out in the same way that he might have in a smaller, less prestigious department. At the urging of his dean he had uprooted his wife and children and had gone back to graduate school for a doctorate, taking a Ph.D. at Yale in 1943 with a dissertation on Matthew Arnold. He had published a scattering of journal articles on Arnold and Thomas Carlyle, but his academic career had not flourished. Still an associate professor, he had watched others of his generation be promoted and rewarded while he languished in the middle ranks.

Perhaps as a consequence Blackburn tended to be melancholy and withdrawn around the university. Styron later remembered him as reserved and distant:

> A large, bulky, rather rumpled man (at least in dress), he tended to slump at his desk and to sag while walking; all this gave the impression of a man harboring great unhappiness, if not despair. Nor did he smile effortlessly. There was something distinctly cranky and dour about him, after so many teachers I had known with their Ipana smiles and dauntless cheer. He was ill at ease with strangers, including students, and this is why my first impression of Blackburn was one of remoteness and bearish gloom. Only a remarkably gentle South Carolina voice softened my initial feeling that he was filled with bone-hard melancholy and quiet desperation.

In the classroom, however, Blackburn was magical. Styron eventually took Blackburn's two classes in creative writing and his course in Elizabethan and seventeenth-century literature as well. Blackburn, he learned, was in possession of an uncanny ability to reveal a work of literature to the young people under his tutelage. He did not use the Socratic method: for the most part he lectured on biography and literary history and commented on style and meaning. There was little class participation; Blackburn usually held the floor. Often he simply read to his pupils from the text they were studying. Styron remembered:

> Reading aloud from Spenser's *Epithalamion* with its ravishing praise, or the sonorous meditation on death of Sir Thomas Browne, his voice would become so infused with feeling that we would sit transfixed, and not a breath could be heard in the room. . . . The sweetness and the longing and erotic fever of the lines would bring to his saturnine face an expression of focused aesthetic bliss; a glistening tear, forthright, unashamed, would appear at the corner of his eye. . . . It would be too facile a description to call him a spellbinder, though he had in him much of the actor *manqué;* this very rare ability to make his students *feel,* to fall in love with a poem or poet, came from his own real depth of feeling and, perhaps, from his own unrequited love, for I am sure he was an unfulfilled writer or poet too.

As Styron's performance on his papers improved, Blackburn began to pay more attention to him. One day, to Styron's great surprise, Blackburn invited him to lunch. "We went to an East Durham restaurant," Styron remembered. "The beer was good, the food atrocious." At first Blackburn was awkward and remote, but as soon as the conversation turned to books and reading he relaxed a little. He asked Styron what books he had read, and Styron had to confess that, really, he had read very little—*Huckleberry Finn,* some novels by Sinclair Lewis, and *The Good Earth* by Pearl S. Buck. "Most gently he then informed me that one could not become a writer without a great deal of reading," Styron recalled. "Read Thomas Mann and Proust, he said, the Russians, Conrad, Shakespeare, the Elizabethans." Styron listened and nodded and made mental notes of titles and authors. " 'To write one must read,' " repeated Blackburn, " '*read.* . . .' "

Styron embarked immediately on what he later remembered as a "one-man rampage through the libraries of both campuses." He read poetry and prose of various styles and periods—works by Housman, Swinburne, FitzGerald, Donne, George Eliot, Whitman, Joyce, Conrad,

Dickinson, Melville, Cather. He became so single-minded about reading that he quickly came to resent the V-12 regulations that compelled him to take other courses, especially those in physics and math. To express his displeasure he began to read novels openly in the classroom while his professors demonstrated the principles of the fulcrum or lectured on the sine and cosine. One morning he was thrown out of physics class for reading André Gide instead of paying attention to the lesson. Another day he was put on report by his math teacher for reading Dos Passos's *U.S.A.* in class, and he took the opportunity to engage the instructor, a young woman named Bonnie Cone, in a friendly, spirited debate about the relative merits of mathematics versus literature. "I'm going to write a novel someday, and I'll send it to you," he said to her. "I hope you do that," she replied.*

Styron's letters home to his father during this period are full of the names of books and writers. He reported reading an eclectic mix of authors: "Hemingway, Wolfe, Faulkner, Dos Passos and short stories by Balzac, Thurber, de Maupassant, Joyce, Poe, and others." He was so enthralled by Thomas Wolfe that he went on a binge, plowing through Wolfe's novels and stories one after another in an extended orgy of reading. ("I think he's the greatest writer of our time," he confessed in a letter to his father.) Years later he could still remember the effect on him of *Look Homeward, Angel,* Wolfe's first novel, with its "lyrical torrent and raw, ingenuous feeling." The book, he recalled, matched exactly his own feelings of "youthful ache and promise and hunger and ecstasy." It mattered little to Styron, at eighteen, that Wolfe's writing was windy and verbose: "I gobbled it all up, forsaking my classes, hurting my eyes, and digesting the entire large Wolfe *oeuvre*—the four massive novels, plus the short stories and novellas, and the several plays, even then practically unreadable—in something less than two weeks, emerging from the incredible encounter pounds lighter, and with a buoyant serenity of one whose life has been forever altered."

Styron's grades suffered. During his initial term he made his first F in physics and managed only a D in French; he earned C's in political science and psychology, a B+ in Blackburn's English class, and an A (of

___

*Many years later Styron noticed, in a newspaper announcement, that Bonnie Cone had been named the acting chancellor of the University of North Carolina at Charlotte. He wrote to her, congratulating her on her success, and sent her a copy of *Lie Down in Darkness.*

which he was proud) in history. During his second term he did even less well, earning D's in math, general engineering, and political science, and another F in physics. The sole bright spot that semester was an A from Professor Blackburn. These grades were typical, by and large, of Styron's performance during his first stint at Duke. To his credit he dutifully reported his marks, high and low, to his father back home. "My work, while far from Phi Beta Kappaish, is being maintained with mediocrity and fair promise of passing," he wrote. "I'm afraid that scholastically I'm pretty much of a border-line case."

The only classes he really anticipated with pleasure were Blackburn's. The classroom, long and narrow, was tucked alongside a concert hall on the third floor of the East Duke Building. The room doubled as Blackburn's office and contained his cluttered desk, battered bookcases, and a tea-making apparatus—for he would often serve a cup of tea to a student during an office conference. Styron was quiet and attentive in Blackburn's classes. Usually he sat by the window and smoked, and occasionally he would offer a comment, but that was all.

Though paternal and generally benign, Blackburn remained formal with most of his students, always addressing them as Mr. and Miss. With Styron, though, he made an exception, beginning now to take the young man gently under his wing. Almost certainly he saw in Styron a good deal of promise and a need for guidance. This student was obviously unsure of his direction and out of place at Duke. Blackburn encouraged him to be a writer and complimented him on his work. In his assessment of Styron's second-semester performance he wrote: "I take great pride in your progress this term. While I don't usually urge undergraduates to make writing their livelihood, you are definitely one to be encouraged." This soupçon of praise was enough to drive Styron to even greater efforts at reading and writing. In Blackburn he saw a paternal, authoritative figure who told him that it was good, even admirable, to devote one's life to the written word. In the busy wartime atmosphere at Duke, where all activity was organized and utilitarian, this was an important confirmation of Styron's own instincts and desires.

Blackburn came to Styron at the right moment and turned him in the direction he needed to go. Though the relationship remained formal, there was surely more than a little affection between the two men, partly because each must have recognized in the other much of his own personality. Both were solitary, sensitive, and melancholy; both were desirous of praise but not truly able to enjoy it; both were inclined to overreact to negative criticism. Like Blackburn, young William Styron could be prickly and withdrawn, and like his professor he responded deeply to fine music and good writing. For Styron, William Blackburn was his great discovery at Duke.

The other parts of Styron's life at Duke were conventional enough. He shared a dormitory room with two V-12 trainees and developed a reputation for slovenliness. "I used to try to get him to change his socks at least once a week," remembered one roommate, "but it was a hard sell." Styron spent as much time as possible in his bunk, smoking and reading, and would tidy up his part of the room only for an inspection. He found, however, that he could not stay up late reading and talking because the Marine V-12's had to hit the deck every morning at six o'clock for calisthenics. The physical training was rough and demanding: it included running, swimming, boxing, wrestling, and jujitsu. ("I am continually being thrown on my can," he reported to his father.) The trainees also studied map-reading and listened to lectures on military leadership.

There were a few things Styron liked about the V-12 program: he enjoyed wearing the marine uniform, especially the dress greens, and he rather liked close-order drill, with its rhythmical movements and cadences. He also appreciated the fact that his tuition, room, and board were paid for by the federal government, and he was glad to have the pocket money that V-12 trainees received—fifty dollars a month, which covered his beer, cigarettes, and dating expenses. With this money he could also buy an occasional meal in a local restaurant—a virtual necessity because the food in the college dining halls was so wretched. Hygiene there was bad too, so lax that Styron was one among a large number of V-12 trainees who came down with roaring cases of trench mouth—an infection that would have unpleasant consequences for him later on.

What rankled Styron about the V-12 program, however, were its curfews and restrictions. He liked to go into downtown Durham with his fellow trainees to drink and carouse. He was especially fond of a working-class bar called Mayola's, where he and his friends would sit in booths, drinking beer and listening to country tunes on the jukebox. Trips into town were permitted so long as a trainee had a pass from one of the noncommissioned officers who ran the V-12 program, but passes were not always forthcoming, especially on weeknights, and the curfew was absurdly early—10:00 P.M. As a result Styron took to leaving campus without permission, drinking for several hours downtown, and then sneaking back to his dorm.

Soon enough he was caught. A chief petty officer snagged him at half-past eleven on the night of Tuesday, October 5, as he was returning to campus. The chief demanded his name, and Styron, half in insolence and half in jest, identified himself as Ben Franklin. Styron watched in amusement as the chief, without thinking, wrote down the name. Disciplinary action was promised, and Styron was sent on his way. The next day the chief discovered the deception—there was no Ben Franklin on the roll of V-12 trainees—and word went out in the dorms that this chief was searching for the trainee who had falsely identified himself. Locating the malefactor was easy enough: the chief simply walked up and down the ranks at evening formation, peering into the faces of the recruits one by one until he recognized "Ben Franklin." Styron, now identified, was turned over for punishment to the warrant officer in charge of the Marine V-12 wing.

This man, Gunner Joseph Blanchard, was a career marine—a member of the Old Breed. A strict disciplinarian, he had little patience with the antics of college boys, and he was regarded with a good deal of trepidation by the Marine V-12's at Duke. Over forty years later Styron could still recall his own nervousness as he faced Blanchard. He could remember particularly the glare in the man's eyes. Styron was reamed out and threatened with immediate deportation to boot camp at San Diego—a punishment that would have put him on a Pacific beachhead in a few months. Blanchard withheld that sentence for the time being, though, and instead put Styron on restriction for twenty-five days. Styron behaved himself for a week or two but then again broke curfew, was caught, and was confined to campus for the remainder of the fall term and denied permission to go home for Christmas. Styron stayed in Durham over the shortened Christmas break in 1943 and was saved from a lonely holiday only by the kindly intervention of Professor Blackburn, who invited him over for Christmas dinner.

Styron had reached his full height by now, a little over six feet, and had filled out in the shoulders and upper body. He was not movie-star handsome, but his features were strong—especially the nose and chin, which he had inherited from his father and grandfather. He had a good smile, when he chose to show it, but the smile rarely reached his eyes. His hands and feet were small for a man of his height; he wore his hair in a military brush cut; his carriage was erect and his gaze direct and penetrating. Most young women were attracted to him, though they sometimes found him remote and abstracted, not interested in the usual games of courtship.

Before his confinement to campus, Styron had managed a little in the way of social life. He had begun to date a few of the co-eds from East Campus, but the restrictions on their dress and behavior were so severe that the possibilities for fun were limited. Curfews were mercilessly early, and dates were meant to be formal affairs. Duke girls in those wartime years were compelled to wear stockings, hats, and white gloves whenever they ventured off-campus with a boy. "I'll never forget the purity of those intimidating white gloves which usually, for some reason, went up to the elbows and, quite literally, kept at arm's length all of our desires, laden with such impurity," Styron recalled many years later. Sexual contact was minimal, and heavy necking was usually as much as one could hope for. Styron did manage, however, to be treated to the expert manipulations of one co-ed who had learned to satisfy her dates with just her hands. So skillful was she (operating on Styron in the dark under a tree on East Campus) that she kept her soft white gloves on through the whole procedure—an erotic touch that he still remembered with pleasure almost fifty years later.

Styron also dated at other campuses, and he made a connection with a sexually adventurous girl at a college not far from Durham. He visited her on several spring weekends, and they experimented with sex in hotel rooms and on a golf course under the stars. He also had an amorous romp in a graveyard one warm spring night with a fortyish woman who identified herself only as Mrs. Cole. He had picked her up in a Durham bar earlier that evening. By contrast to later decades the 1940s were an "erotic ice age," Styron later said, but with persistence he was managing to widen his sexual experience a little.

The 1940s were a time when sharp distinctions were made between girls who were nice and girls who were not nice. One might attempt to take liberties with young women in the second category, but nice girls were idealized and treated with hands-off respect. Styron met such a girl in Blackburn's class during his second term at Duke, and he soon began to date her steadily. She was Barbara Taeusch, known as Bobbie—a lovely young woman with dark green eyes, long brunette hair, and a friendly, open smile. She had grown up in Cambridge, where her father had been a professor in the Harvard Business School. During the thirties he had been drawn to Washington, D.C., to work in FDR's New Deal administration, and her family now lived just outside the city. Bobbie had attended Vassar for one year but hadn't much liked it, so she had come south to Duke, arriving there in the spring of 1943. She was a botany major but had literary leanings and, like Styron, had fallen under William Blackburn's spell. "I adored him," she remembered, recalling especially the times when he would read aloud to the class, his voice trembling and breaking with emotion.

The attraction between Bobbie Taeusch and Bill Styron was strong. She found him "charming, considerate, and gentle," and she loved his sense of humor. He found her intelligent, idealistic, bighearted, and fun to be with. "She was my dreamboat," he later said. Neither of them had much interest in frat parties or other campus activities. Usually they would walk and talk during their evenings together, occasionally going out for a cheap meal or a movie. Their only arguments came when she scolded him for his cynicism or grew weary of his diatribes about V-12 training or about the uselessness of math and physics to a would-be writer.

Styron's authorial ambitions at this point centered on Duke's literary magazine, the *Archive*. He began to submit his fiction there and managed to have five short stories published during his first period at the university. He also landed one poem in the *Archive,* but under a pseudonym—Martin Kostler. The stories demonstrate promise: they show Styron using his gift for language and searching through his earlier experiences for situations and emotions. Two of the stories, "Where the Spirit Is" and "Autumn," draw on experiences from Christchurch. The first story is the composition about adolescent drinking that had impressed Blackburn in the fall of 1943; the second is a perceptive picture of an introverted English teacher at a boys' school very much like Christchurch. The paragraph below from "Autumn," though slightly overcooked, shows what Styron was capable of at the age of eighteen:

> He gazed out of the window toward the darkening river, lying calm and wide, like a misty shadow, in the last fading gold of the sun. Far over on the other shore, dotted with tiny white farmhouses, a pale rind of moon was rising behind a hazy pall of autumnal smoke. As he gazed at the river, once more he was impressed with its flowing, somnolent beauty, its weary, everlasting strength, running out like a man's life to the sea.

A third narrative, entitled "A Story about Christmas," is an unsure attempt at handling alternating points of view—interesting, however, because it includes a short section narrated through the consciousness of a black man. And the pseudonymous poem, called "October Sorrow," is a four-stanza effort in rhymed quatrains, melancholy and grieving though a little shaky in scansion.

The two remaining stories are quite good. The first, entitled "The Long Dark Road," concerns the lynching of a Negro man in the Deep South. The story is filtered through the consciousness of Dewey Lassiter, a young white boy whose loutish older brother is one of the leaders of the lynch mob. Dewey is terrified and flees into the hot summer night, appalled at the barbarism he has seen. Most of the characters in the story are stereotypes, but Dewey is sharply delineated and his moral dilemma is acutely rendered. The second notable effort, entitled "Sun on the River," is set in a community that closely resembles Hilton Village, Styron's hometown on the banks of the James River. This brief sketch describes a young boy's first encounter with death—in this case the death of a neighborhood girl thrown from a horse. The boy, uncomfortable and unsure of how he should behave, wanders off by himself to come to terms with his grief:

> "This day is so strange," he thought. "Where is she now, and the oak tree? Are all of these gone now, and will they ever return? This is Sunday afternoon. This thing, and all my thoughts now, are here—and they will go and never return. The gulched earth is yellow and raw in March, and the wind wrestles with the sycamores along the streets.

This is Sunday afternoon, the days are changing, and they will never come back."

Taken together these early efforts in the *Archive* are promising. They show some verbal straining and artificiality of emotion, but by and large they are impressive work. They reveal an obvious gift for description and a natural sense of how the rhythms and sounds of language fit together. The writings are muted and melancholy in tone: they concern unhappiness, frustration, loneliness, and loss, but they avoid the mawkishness typical of most undergraduate writing. A precocious maturity of voice and feeling is evident; when reading these stories, one must remind oneself from time to time that William Styron was only eighteen and nineteen when he wrote them.

Styron shone in the *Archive,* but in most other ways his record during his first stint at Duke was dismal. He made a few A's and B's, but the majority of his marks were C's and D's. He managed to fail physics yet again, giving him three black F's in the same course. Only a sympathetic instructor, probably weary of seeing Styron's inattentive face in the class, saved him from a fourth failure: on a final try during the July–October term of 1944, he managed to squeeze through with a courtesy D. Styron's poor showing at Duke, though, was consistent with his general attitude toward academic work. Throughout his prep-school and college years he was easily bored, indifferent to grades, and unwilling to study any subject that did not stimulate his imagination. He seems to have understood from the beginning that his destiny would not involve academia, that he would make his way through life in some other fashion. What he did learn to do was to ease along and do the bare minimum in order to stay in school where he could use his time, in what was obviously a calculated way, to prepare himself to be a writer.

Styron did not waste his time at Duke: he invested his energies in listening, observing, writing, and reading. His lack of interest in matters academic grew out of his uncertainty about his future. Like all V-12's at Duke he knew that he was in a holding pattern. The military bureaucracy was keeping him in college until he was old enough to be trained as an officer and sent into battle. His future, for the time being, was not going to involve the classroom: it was instead to involve putting his life on the line in a war that he might well not live through. In October

1944, near the end of his fourth term at Duke, Styron received his call-up. He was ordered to report to boot camp at the end of the grading period. He took his exams, collected his marks, and said good-bye to Professor Blackburn and Bobbie Taeusch. In late October he left Raleigh on a troop train bound for the Marine Corps base at Parris Island, South Carolina.

9

Marines, First Stint

PARRIS ISLAND lies in a hot, boggy region just off the southern coast of South Carolina. Fortunately Styron had not come there during the summer, when temperatures regularly topped 100 degrees and recruits were attacked by swarms of sand fleas and mosquitoes. Temperatures were bearable in November, and insects were not so much in evidence, though the training base itself was still remote and desolate. Spanish moss hung from the trees, the swamps were full of alligators, and the woods were infested by snakes. Many of the buildings at Parris Island were of World War I vintage; others had only recently been erected, very quickly, for the new war. At the center of the base was the drill field, known on all Marine Corps bases as the Grinder. The drill field at Parris Island was forty-four acres of solid pavement on which the recruits endlessly practiced close-order drill and learned the mysteries of the manual of arms.

Styron settled into his unit and within a few days began to think of himself as Pvt. W. C. Styron, Jr., 542307, USMCR. His first few weeks were taken up with marching and with learning to fire the M1 rifle. From the beginning Styron was uncomfortable with the weapon. A fellow recruit remembered seeing him sitting on his bunk, holding his M1 in his hands and cursing it. "This goddamn low-life Army rifle," he muttered, over and over. Part of Styron's frustration had to do with his antipathy toward all mechanical devices, but he was also angry with the

M1 because he could not fire it accurately. Styron's congenital cataract in his right eye—the condition he had hidden at his induction exam by memorizing the eye chart—now made him an extremely erratic marksman. He could have been discharged with a defective shooting eye, but he wanted to join his generation in this war. He therefore set about learning how to fire the M1 left-handed. The procedure was awkward: the M1, when fired, automatically ejected a spent shell almost into the face of a left-handed shooter. (Natural lefties, as a consequence, usually learned to fire right-handed.) Styron practiced, though, and somehow he managed to come up to the minimum standard for new recruits on the rifle range—probably, he wrote to his father, because "the boys pulling the targets" gave him "enough extra points to qualify."

The recruits learned to fieldstrip and reassemble the M1 and to name its various parts. They went through the inevitable exercise of crawling on their bellies under live machine-gun fire, and they endured obstacle courses, running, hiking, and instruction in hand-to-hand combat with bayonets and Ka-Bar knives. There was endless cleaning and polishing of rifles, boots, uniforms, and living quarters. Predictably there was a constant round of goading, browbeating, and tongue-lashing from the drill instructors and sergeants. It was the time-honored way in which the Marine Corps molded its recruits into fighting men. Years later Styron remembered the process clearly: "the remorseless close-order drill hour after hour in the burning sun, the mental and physical abuse, the humiliations, the frequent sadism at the hands of drill sergeants, all the claustrophobic and terrifying insults to the spirit that can make an outpost like Quantico or Parris Island one of the closest things in the free world to a concentration camp."

Amid the abuse, Styron found a friend and kindred spirit in Bob Snider, a cheerfully cynical twenty-year-old from North Dakota. According to Snider, he and Styron both had a thoroughly dim view of the military and liked to gripe about incompetent instructors and chickenshit regulations. Both young men were rebellious, and both had literary inclinations. What free time they had was usually spent in the enlisted men's recreational club, known on Marine Corps bases as the Slop Chute. Both Snider and Styron had committed long passages of A. E. Housman to memory; they would sit over beers and try to put one of the measured, mournful stanzas from *A Shropshire Lad* to jukebox music or, sometimes, to a Protestant hymn. Styron's favorite, according to Snider, was the poem designated L in Housman's volume. "Bill sang it to some kind of a (Southern) episcopal dirge," Snider remembered:

> *Clunton and Clunbury*
> *Clungunford and Clun,*
> *Are the quietest places*
> *Under the sun.*
> In valleys of springs of rivers,
> By Ony and Teme and Clun,
> The country for easy livers,
> The quietest under the sun.

Despite their rebellious attitudes, Styron and Snider were attracted, at least a little, to the rituals and hero worship in the Marine Corps. The highest-ranking enlisted men were first sergeants, and most of them were old leathernecks—grizzled, crusty, and tough. There was one sergeant at Parris Island named Lou Diamond who was already a legend. Over fifty years old, with a paunch and a goatee, Diamond had fought his way through some of the bloodiest battles at Guadalcanal. He was a mortar specialist and was said to have sunk a Japanese cruiser by putting an 81mm round down her stack. That story was a fabrication, but it was true that Diamond had tried to mount his mortar piece on a Higgins boat and go after a Japanese sub he had spotted offshore at Guadalcanal. He had had to be restrained from the chase by a superior officer. Now he was out to pasture, running the delousing plant at Parris Island. He had plenty of business: the louse was as indigenous to the place as the sand flea. Styron and Snider would see Diamond when they hauled bedding and clothes over to be deloused or when they were compelled to take the treatment themselves. Styron, in fact, served as Diamond's assistant for a week or so and listened to some of his tales, for Diamond fancied himself a raconteur. To Styron and Snider, Lou Diamond was the personification of the Old Corps.

There were other marines on the base who had also seen combat. One, a corporal who taught the use of the flamethrower, had already used the ghastly device on one of the Pacific islands to fry Japanese soldiers in their bunkers. "They sizzle like a bunch of roaches," he told Private Styron. Other veterans exhibited items that they had stripped from Japanese bodies—pistols, knives, and battle insignia. Some of the trophies were grisly. One gunnery sergeant, for example, kept some partic-

ularly intimate mementos on his person. Styron wrote about them years
later:

> He carried in his dungaree pocket two small shriveled dark objects
> about the size of peach pits. When I asked him what they were he told
> me they were "Jap's nuts." I was struck nearly dumb with a queasy
> horror, but managed to ask him how he had obtained such a pair of
> souvenirs. Simple, he explained; he had removed them with a bayonet
> from an enemy corpse on Tarawa—that most hellish of battles—and
> had set them out at the end of a dock under the blazing sun where
> they quickly became dried like prunes. The sergeant was highly re-
> garded in the company and I soon got used to seeing him fondle his
> keepsakes whenever he got nervous or pissed off, stroking them like
> worry beads.

One afternoon in mid-November, while the platoon was drilling, a
messenger came with an order for Private Styron to fall out and report
to the regimental dispensary. A medical corpsman there drew a blood
sample from his arm; then Styron went back to his unit. No explanation was given, and Styron assumed that this was a routine matter.
Probably a lab technician had dropped the blood sample they had taken
from him a week or so earlier. Styron had almost forgotten the incident
when, two days later, the same messenger came to find him again. It was
just after lunch, and Styron's platoon was cleaning its gear. Styron reported back to the dispensary and was sent in immediately to see a doctor. The physician was direct: "We think you have syphilis," he said.

Styron was stunned. He had had no chancre and no mucous skin le-
sions—the most common symptoms of syphilis. The evidence from the
lab, however, seemed incontrovertible: his count on the Kahn test was
stratospheric. Styron was immediately pulled from his unit and placed
in the urological ward of the base hospital. Because most of the patients in that ward had picked up gonorrhea, the place was known as
the Clap Shack. The marines in Styron's platoon, according to Bob
Snider, treated the matter with great levity. Styron was in the Clap
Shack? But how had he picked up VD? Life at Parris Island was rigor-
ously monastic. If Styron was getting laid, would he please share? It
seemed a great joke to them.

To Styron, of course, his predicament was not funny. In 1944 gonorrhea was usually a curable disease, but syphilis, which he was suspected of having, often was not. Penicillin, then thought of as a new wonder drug, was beginning to be used to treat bacteriological infections. Penicillin could cure syphilis in its early stages, but not if the disease was far advanced. Being told in the mid-1940s that one was infected with syphilis was not unlike being told today that one is HIV-positive. The consequences of unchecked syphilis were grave—locomotor ataxia, which attacks the spinal cord and brings eventual paralysis, and paresis, which affects the brain, causing insanity and death. The consequences of syphilis for Styron's military career, though not as important, were still quite serious and also bothered him. When an officer candidate was found beyond question to have venereal disease, he was labeled unfit for command and was washed out of his unit. If he was cured, he went back into the enlisted ranks. In addition, he lost all back pay for the time spent in the VD ward.

Styron stayed in the Clap Shack for a little over two weeks. His case puzzled the doctors there, since they never determined positively that he had syphilis. His Kahn test remained sky-high, but he showed none of the common symptoms of syphilis—not an unusual circumstance, since syphilis is a clever disease that often mimics the symptoms of other maladies. The physicians, uncertain of the diagnosis, chose simply to keep Styron in limbo. They isolated him from the other troops and ran tests from time to time on his blood. They tied a tag to the foot of his bed; it read, "DU (Syphilis)"—meaning "Diagnosis Undetermined: Syphilis Suspected." The doctors did not treat Styron with penicillin or with any other drug. Instead they kept him "under observation." No one discussed his condition with him or offered him any hope that his case was curable, nor did the doctors make it clear that he might not have syphilis at all. Styron was left in the dark to worry and brood. He feared, understandably, that he did have syphilis and that his case was so far advanced as to be untreatable.

To be pulled from the ranks, just as he was moving into the momentum of basic training, was difficult for Styron. He felt as if he had been shanghaied into the Clap Shack. The action on the training grounds was noisy and sometimes dangerous; the routine in the urological ward, by contrast, was enervating and the atmosphere colossally dull. Each day began with roll call and short-arm inspection. Patients were forbidden to urinate until they had lined up and exhibited their penises.

Then a medical corpsman would call out: "Skin it back! Squeeze it! Milk it down!" The tip of each penis was inspected for the mucous discharge known as "gleet." This fluid was a symptom of gonorrhea rather than syphilis, but Styron still had to undergo the inspection each morning since syphilitics in the course of their adventures often picked up the clap as well. Because he was thought to have syphilis, Styron possessed a certain reverse cachet on the ward. He had to use the washbasin and toilet set aside for syphilitics, and he was given a special tag to wear on his wrist. His tray and flatware were segregated and had to be sterilized after each use. He felt like a leper.

The daily routine on the ward was depressing beyond words. For most of the day, the patients sat around in robes or khaki Marine Corps underwear. Most of them played cards, listened to the radio, speculated about their symptoms, or traded stories about their sexual escapades. Some read paperbacks or comic books, others simply stared at the walls. A few of the patients had viral VD and were dying. Years later Styron recalled the "charnel-house atmosphere of draining buboes, gonorrhea, prostate massages, daily short-arm inspections, locomotor ataxia, and the howls of poor sinners in the clutch of terminal paresis." The only excitement was an occasional visitor or the latest Kahn-Wassermann result.

Styron was idle and troubled, and this gave him much time to think. He was puzzled by the diagnosis and the lack of symptoms. His sexual experience had been limited. There had been the prostitute in Charlotte, but that had been over three years earlier, and he had worn two rubbers. Still, he might have contracted syphilis from her. If so, had he had the disease for three years? Had the spirochetes been secretly multiplying in his body for all those weeks and months? Were they continuing to multiply as he sat idle and untreated in the ward? After the prostitute in Charlotte, his only sexual experiences had been with the college girl in Virginia and his encounter with "Mrs. Cole" in the Durham graveyard. Surely he had not picked up the disease from the college girl. Had he then *given* the disease to her? Styron had been required to tell the details of his sexual history to the urologist in charge of the ward—a cold-eyed doctor named Klotz who pried into Styron's past and shamed him for his fornications. If Styron indeed did have syphilis, he would be required to write to his college girlfriend and tell her of his condition—now, presumably, her condition as well. The possibility was nightmarish.

Styron also had to tell his father about his predicament. He wrote a letter home saying only that he had been confined in the infirmary with a "blood problem." Elizabeth Buxton read the letter and, with her medical background, immediately divined that the problem was venereal disease. She wrote a letter to her stepson that he remembered for the rest of his life. The letter does not survive (Styron destroyed it), but in later years he remembered it as judgmental and hateful. He had engaged in sexual misconduct? Then he had got what was coming to him. It was his own fault and a proper punishment for his self-indulgence. "That cheered me up," Styron recalled.

Deliverance was imminent, however. Shortly before he had left Duke, Styron had contracted trench mouth. Hygiene at the mess halls for the V-12 trainees had been slipshod, and many of them had picked up the disease. Trench mouth, a bacteriological infection, is contagious and uncomfortable. Caused by the spiral microorganism *Borrelia vincentii,* it results in bleeding gums, fetid breath, and soreness in the mouth. Styron's symptoms at Duke had disappeared in a few days, but the bacteria had not been banished from his system. These same bacteria will often produce a false positive reaction for syphilis on the Kahn test. This is what had happened to Styron. It takes a practiced medical technician to distinguish trench mouth from syphilis under the microscope. Both are spirochetes, and the corpsman who had analyzed Styron's blood samples—and who, presumably, was inspecting hundreds of samples each day—had not recognized the difference. This was a fairly common error for the time: the kinds of antigens necessary to perform accurate identification of *Treponema pallidum* (the bacterium that causes syphilis) had not yet been developed. *B. vincentii* was still in Styron's blood, and the corpsman mistook it for *T. pallidum.*

Trench mouth has a psychosomatic component; if it is latent in the system it will flare back up under stress. Styron, very much worried over his condition, now had a recurrence of the symptoms. The trench mouth bacteria latent in his system became active and multiplied, causing his mouth to become ulcerated and his gums to bleed. Styron was issued a pass to visit one of the base dentists. This dentist swabbed his gums liberally with gentian violet, a strong bactericide, and repeated the treatment a few days later. The gentian violet almost magically cleared up Styron's gums. But infinitely more miraculous was the fact that his Kahn test now plummeted to zero. His blood samples were now examined more closely, and the mystery was cleared up. Styron had had trench mouth. Toward the end of November he was called in by a chief pharmacist's mate and was told that his condition had been misdiagnosed. He had not had syphilis after all. He had had trench mouth, for which he had been treated and cured. Now he could return to his unit. Styron later recalled that he was released "with no more ceremony than if I were being turned out of a veterinary clinic."

His immediate reaction was ecstatic. "My life was restored," he recalled. He could contact his father and announce his deliverance, and he could look up his buddies and tell about his ordeal over beers in the Slop Chute. He could cut the tag from his wrist and stop using the toilet for syphilitics. Everything was back to normal, or so it seemed. The two-week stint in the Clap Shack, however, left marks on Styron. The impersonal treatment had rankled him, as had his segregation from the other patients. The snafu in the lab was perhaps understandable, but the doctors had not seemed to care about the absence of the proper symptoms. No hope had been extended and little explanation given either of the nature of syphilis or of the treatments available for it. "Cruel bastards!" Styron said years later when telling about the experience. "Ignoramuses!"

Medical treatment, often impersonal even when given by a family physician, would have been especially perfunctory in a wartime boot camp. Probably Styron was treated no more inhumanely than were the other men on the ward. There were rules for syphilitics: they were applied to him. But Styron did take the experience personally. It had been his private parts and his blood samples that they had treated mechanically. It had been his sexual history that they had poked about in. He would never forgive them, and the experience would confirm his dislike, then already strong, of the dehumanization that routinely occurs in the military, or in any bureaucracy.

During his days in the Clap Shack, Styron had also had a chance to think about and clarify some of his youthful rebelliousness. He had made no resolutions about sexual abstinence or upright behavior. Instead he had thought seriously about religion and morality and had decided that a conventional approach to these matters was impossible for him. He set down his position in a long letter to his father a few days after leaving the VD ward. The letter—which shows very few touches of the sophomoric—is a remarkable testament for a nineteen-year-old to have written:

> Last night when I first started to write this letter, I wrote a couple of pages attempting to explain my views on the idea of morality. After rereading it, I tore it up because it really makes no difference to you or anyone else what my moral philosophy is. I'm probably not old enough to have such a philosophy. I know this for a fact, though— that the morality which we have in a so-called "moral" society is the weakest leg that civilization has to stand upon. The religion of the Church, which is the basis for morality, is a religion of hypocrisy, and each man should realize that the good life is a life of *Good Will,* a life of Love and Loneliness (as Thomas Wolfe would say), and not the fanatical adherence to a Book, most of which is a gruesome melange of cruelty and pagan cosmology. The Bible begins with the fantastic story of Adam and Eve, continues through countless bloody anecdotes of "religious" warfare, torture, and human sacrifice, and ends with St. John's laudanum dream of an absurd and impossible Apocalypse. In parts the Bible is a literary masterpiece. Nothing finer has been written than the story of Job and the sermon of Ecclesiastes, and I believe that if Christ was not the son of God, he approached such a divine kinship as nearly as any man ever born. But it is impossible for me to cling to a Faith which attempts, and succeeds in too many cases, in foisting upon the multitude a belief in so much which is utter fantasy. And it is such a religion which, throughout its history of corruption and strife, has promulgated its own standard for morality behind a thin veil of cant and hypocrisy. I have my own personal religion, *and* I believe that I am as steadfast in it as any one of our Baptist Fundamentalists. I am far from believing with George Santayana that religion is the "opiate of the poor;" but I do believe that an overdose of religious activity, in which people tend to take the syrupy tenets of the preacher and the vindictive dogmatisms of the Old Testament at face value, both deadens the mind and makes life a pretty sterile and joyless affair.

> I have probably not made myself very clear (which makes little difference), and I imagine you are not a little disappointed in knowing that your boy, after all those years of Sunday School, has not "turned out right;" but please don't think that I have sunk into the slough of degeneracy. I have never as yet done anything which I was really ashamed of. After the war I'm going to write a book and tell people

what I think. Carlyle, I think it was, said that the real preachers are not those who stand behind the pulpit, but who sit behind a writing desk. In the meantime I'm going to keep on thinking, loving Life as much as I can in a world where the value of life is only the value of the lead in a .30 calibre bullet, and loving my fellow man (which the greatest Preacher said was the finest virtue of all).

To write to his father in this way took courage. The senior Styron was in many ways conventionally religious, though fortunately he was not doctrinaire or rigid about what he believed. He was willing to accept his son's rebelliousness and misbehavior, and he was not by nature a judgmental man. Surely young William Styron, sitting in the barracks at Parris Island, knew these things about his father, and it is difficult to see why he should have felt it necessary to explain himself at such length in this letter. One concludes that the letter—with its pointed references to love and goodwill—was not addressed entirely to his father. It was written at least as much for the eyes of Elizabeth Buxton Styron, his stepmother.

Styron returned briefly to his old platoon, but he was now out of sync with their training schedule and had to be transferred to Casual Company, the group of recruits who, owing to sickness or injury or some other cause, were behind in their progress. These recruits were eventually placed in other units, but for the present there was no spot open for Styron elsewhere. He was therefore given some training as a drill instructor and put to work for several weeks as a DI. He drew a platoon of brand-new recruits, most of them backwoods boys from the mountains of North Carolina and Virginia. Many of them, according to Styron, were seeing the larger world for the first time. They had never read a newspaper, never seen a movie, never really been far from the mountains and hollows in which they had grown up. Many of them were in the grip of a kind of fierce culture shock. Styron thought it best to keep them busy, so he marched them up and down the Grinder, calling out commands and making them sing the chants and responses that all marines learn to march to.

After several weeks as a DI, Styron was assigned to another platoon. His original group had been made up of V-12 trainees from Duke and Emory, most of them middle-class boys from Virginia, North Carolina, South Carolina, and Georgia. They had liked one another and had begun to form an esprit in which Styron had shared, but he had been pulled from this platoon and now felt as if he did not belong to any unit. To his great displeasure he was reassigned to a platoon from California—"hotshot Stanford and Berkeley assholes," he later called them. Here he was a misfit. The other recruits in this platoon knew that Styron had been in the Clap Shack. His story was that he had had a case of trench mouth, but who could be sure? And too, this new man had a bad eye and had to fire the M1 left-handed. He was hopeless on the rifle range. "I had a terrible score, I didn't qualify, and the Californians all hated me because my low score brought down the platoon average," Styron remembered. "They thought I was a malingerer." Styron persevered, though, and eventually did manage to get a passing score on the rifle range and complete boot camp. Despite his problems with his eyesight, he was approved as an officer candidate. This was a great relief, a victory. Now he knew that he would eventually be sent to Quantico for Platoon Commander School.

First, however, Styron and his fellow candidates had to go through a preparatory round of physical training at Camp Lejeune, North Carolina, and they were transferred there in February. The regimen at Lejeune was difficult, and Styron's bad luck continued. For his platoon leader he drew a scrawny second lieutenant, fresh out of Quantico and much enamored of his new authority. Styron later described him as a "frog-faced fellow with hornrims, and a soul and spirit that would shame a jackal." This man threw tantrums over minor irregularities and was obsessed with orderliness, making the trainees clean their rifles and put out their gear for inspection again and again. He was sadistic during training exercises, running the men around the barracks repeatedly and denying them water breaks. Styron stayed at Lejeune for only a few weeks, so his problems with this officer did not last long, but he remembered the man for many years afterward. "Did you ever put a tracer on that bastard?" he wrote to Bob Snider in 1958. "He could not possibly survive in civilized society, except behind bars, and I've often yearned to know what institution he was eventually committed to. . . . Sometimes I still dream about him and wake up screaming, rigid with outrage."

Toward the end the training at Lejeune became more interesting. Styron and the other officer candidates were learning the fundamentals of command and studying tactics they would use in the assault on mainland Japan—for that, as they were beginning to suspect, was the offensive they were slated for. After the disaster at Pearl Harbor and the loss of the Marshall and Gilbert Islands and the Philippines, the United States had regrouped, mobilized, and moved inexorably back across the Pacific, retaking the island strongholds of the Japanese in assault after bloody assault. The navy had won the Battle of Midway in June 1942; the Solomon Islands had fallen in a series of campaigns in 1942 and 1943; the Gilbert Islands were secured late in 1943; the Marshalls, New Guinea, and the Marianas were recaptured in 1944; and the Philippines were back in Allied hands by March 1945. Styron and the other trainees knew the roll call of beachhead assaults and island battles: Guadalcanal, Bougainville, Tarawa, Saipan, Guam, Corregidor, Iwo Jima. Now only Okinawa and mainland Japan itself were left. In this war of attrition the United States, with superior industrial power, more men, and more materials, would probably prevail, but there was no sign that the Japanese would surrender. Emperor Hirohito had promised a stubborn, bloody defense of the home islands, to the last Japanese man or woman. Landing beaches on the islands were being heavily fortified; the Japanese were constructing a system of caves and tunnels and were massing their artillery for coastal defense. Styron and his fellow officer candidates knew that they would be the ones to attack these fortifications.

Styron and the other trainees anticipated no rescue, no deus ex machina. They expected instead sometime soon to charge onto a Japanese beachhead in southern Kyushu and to go into a fight to the death with a well-armed, determined foe. "You can figure that four out of five of you will get your asses shot off," a marine colonel told them offhandedly one day in a lecture. There was every reason to believe that he was right. Styron had the examples of thousands of American boys a year or two older than he to judge by. "The class just ahead of me in college was virtually wiped out," he later recalled. "Beautiful fellows who had won basketball championships and Phi Beta Kappa keys died like ants in the Normandy invasion. Others only slightly older than I— like myself young Marine Corps platoon leaders, primest cannon fodder of the Pacific war—stormed ashore at Tarawa and Iwo Jima and met ugly and horrible deaths on the hot coral and sands."

• • •

Most of what had happened to Styron in the Marine Corps so far had been grim. He had begun to believe that he was snakebitten. Boot camp at Parris Island had included the weeks in the Clap Shack, and the time at Lejeune had been made nearly intolerable by the gung-ho lieutenant. In May, as Styron headed to Platoon Commander School at Quantico, on the Potomac outside Washington, D.C., he must have felt that he was due for a shift in luck—and that is what happened. Almost the first person Styron met at Quantico was Charles H. Sullivan, a tall, impressive marine corporal from California. Charlie Sullivan had enlisted in the Corps in 1942 after five semesters in college. He had passed through boot camp in San Diego and four months later had been in the Solomon Islands during the first great offensive of the Pacific war. He had fought as an enlisted man at Guadalcanal in the fall and winter of 1942–43 and later had been in the Bougainville campaign. He had distinguished himself in action. His group was preparing to ship out for Guam when his commander tapped him as officer material. Sullivan was shipped back to the States and put into the V-12 program at Penn State for a semester, then sent to Princeton for more training. Eventually he, like Styron, was transferred to Quantico.

Because he had seen combat, Sullivan was the old man of Styron's group. Sullivan was only a year or two older than most of the other trainees, but his experience and his ability to lead set him apart. By the accident of alphabetical order, Styron and Sullivan were bunkmates—Styron on the top rack and Sullivan on the bottom. The two quickly became friends. "He was a great big commanding fellow," Styron remembered. "Plainly he was going to be the leading candidate in OCS. Everyone was in awe of him. He had already been to the Pacific, had been shot at, and had tremendous command presence. He also happened to be very bright."

Sullivan, like Styron, was a reader. College had been delayed for him by the war, but he was self-disciplined and curious intellectually. Sullivan's tastes leaned toward philosophy and economics; at Quantico he was reading Plato, Schopenhauer, and Marx. Styron's inclination was to read fiction. The two talked and argued and compared ideas in their free time, either in the Slop Chute or barhopping in Washington. (Their beer of choice, Sullivan remembered, was National Bohemian.) They developed much respect for each other, and Sullivan began to look out for Styron in the training exercises. Styron remembered the friendship as a "Mutt-and-Jeff relationship"—Sullivan clearly the better military man, but Styron with enough intelligence and potential to hold his own.

Quantico was arduous and challenging, but Styron liked it. He was in the best physical condition of his life: he had gained eight or ten pounds, most of it muscle, and he felt strong and fit. The food was at least tolerable, and he had earned the respect of the top trainee in his class. There was good esprit in his unit, and he was surviving the training exercises. To judge from his letters, he seems also to have liked the noise and power of the weapons. Often he mentions the ordnance he is firing—the Browning Automatic Rifle (the BAR) and the .50-caliber machine gun. He seems especially to have liked the 60mm and 81mm mortars. With these weapons his bad eye was no handicap. If he were to get into action, he thought, it would probably be at the head of a mortar platoon.

Bob Snider, Styron's friend from boot camp, was also at Quantico, and he and Styron spent some weekends in Washington together. The city was mobbed with troops on leave, and women were scarce, so sometimes they simply rounded up a few other trainees, took a hotel room, and got drunk. One night, in one such room, high in a downtown hotel, Styron's inebriated companions began to tease him, threatening to grab him and dangle him out of the window by his heels. The kidding grew more serious, and they began to wrestle him toward the window. They stopped the game after a few minutes, but not before Styron had become frightened. He remembered the experience and used it, a few years later, in *The Long March.*

Occasionally Styron and Snider did manage to line up dates. Styron reminisced about one pair of female companions in a letter to Snider: "I recall that you had a luscious little blonde creature, very acquiescent, whose name I forget, while I was stuck with a WAC radio operator, a skinny redheaded Mormon from Utah. . . . I've always held that against you, Snider." Some weekends the trainees were confined to the base at Quantico; other times Styron visited his father in Newport News. Bob Snider went along on one of those trips and, in later years, remembered the imperious manner of Elizabeth Buxton and the uneasy atmosphere at the dinner table.

Bobbie Taeusch had graduated from Duke and was working for Union Carbide in New York City. She would sometimes come down to visit Styron. She would stay with her parents, who lived near Washington, and he would arrive from Quantico bearing gifts—often recordings of classical music that they both liked. Their attraction to each other had remained strong, but Bobbie was ambivalent about the possibility of marriage. She was quite idealistic in her vision of what marriage should be, and she was not sure that she and William Styron were well matched. Styron's feelings were the same: he had not yet finished college and had no idea whether he had the talent to become a full-time writer who could support a family. For now he simply enjoyed Bobbie's company. He liked to go to concerts and museums with her, and to talk with her.

Styron finished officer training and was commissioned a second lieutenant in the Marine Corps in late July. Now it was time to go to war. Both Bob Snider and Charlie Sullivan were kept behind at Quantico for a time as drill instructors, but most of the other new officers, including Styron, boarded a troop train for San Francisco. Okinawa had fallen to U.S. forces in June; the enormous American war machine was now preparing for the assault on the Japanese mainland. Styron believed that he would be a platoon leader in that attack. He and his friends talked a good deal about what they might expect—some of the young officers wishing aloud for a "Hollywood wound," one serious enough to incapacitate a man but not grave enough to cause lasting disability. All of them knew that many would die, but no one talked much about the odds or possibilities. For the most part they simply tried to imagine what combat was going to be like.

On August 6, 1945, however, while Styron and thousands of other marines waited in San Francisco to be ordered onto troopships, the *Enola Gay* flew over Hiroshima and dropped the first atomic bomb. On August 9 the second A-bomb fell on Nagasaki, and five days later the Japanese surrendered. Styron and the other new second lieutenants were jubilant. There was no ambivalence over the morality of the bomb; for now the war had ended, and they were going to survive it. At first they were told that the fighting might not yet be over: Styron remembered, "I thought that the momentum was so great that we'd all be in for the next three years, mopping up, going to islands and shooting Japs who weren't going to surrender. But that wasn't it at all. It turned out that when the Japanese surrendered, by god, they *surrendered.*"

Within a few weeks after the end of the war, Styron and the other officers were told that they would be mustered out in another three to four months. In the meantime they were given a choice of temporary duty postings at military bases all over the globe. "I remember being given a list—a most amazing list—of posts," Styron recalled. "They wanted you to serve *some* time to give them a chance to move you into discharge status. I could have gone to California, Hawaii, Japan, the Canal Zone, Alaska—practically any place I wanted where there was a Naval station." The assignment that caught Styron's eye was at the Naval Disciplinary Barracks on Harts Island in Long Island Sound. Bobbie Taeusch was working in New York City, and Styron wanted to be near her. He wanted also to be close to the city itself, near its literary and artistic centers, its publishers and editors, its museums and concert halls and restaurants and bars.

Styron signed up for the Harts Island billet and was transferred there in October. He spent a little over a month at this naval prison and later remembered it as relatively good duty. The accommodations were adequate, and the work was not difficult. He was commander of the First Guard Platoon and of the First Prisoner Regiment; he also served as recreation officer. Downtown Manhattan and Bobbie Taeusch were not as close as he might have liked: to see her he had to catch the ferry, take a bus through the Bronx, then make a long subway ride to the city. But he was on the East Coast, and he had only a little longer in the Marine Corps before returning to college. He and Bobbie had some good times in the city, going to concerts and exploring the Greenwich Village bookstores and bars.

Harts Island was Styron's first experience with imprisonment—a subject that fascinated him later. The impressions that he stored up at this prison would help him to understand institutions as diverse as American Negro slavery and the Nazi concentration camps. In 1953 he attempted to write a novella about Harts Island. He never completed it, but he did produce a seven-thousand-word beginning. What Styron remembered was the "time-exhausted drabness" of the prison, its "air of melancholy and erosion of the spirit." There were about two thousand prisoners on the island. Few of them were major criminals—no one had committed murder or high treason—but they were not exactly minor offenders either. "They had thieved and raped and deserted and had been caught committing buggery and had been drunk or asleep, or both, while on duty and had been, almost to a man at one time or another, away without leave," Styron wrote. The marine enlisted men who guarded them ruled "with a piratical swagger and a fine grip on the principles of intimidation." It was a court-martial offense to strike a prisoner, but physical violence was hardly necessary. Harts Island gave Styron a good chance to observe the psychology of subservience and domination:

> To slap a man about invites rebellion, while a tyranny of simple scorn cows the will and ulcerates the soul. Armed only with short billy-clubs of hickory, the Marines sauntered safe and serene and with a wisecracking arrogance among the fidgety horde, poking ribs and facetiously whacking behinds. The prisoners were gray with the grayness of men who seldom are exposed to light, and suffer the sick, constant ache of loneliness. It was the peculiar grayness somehow stamped only upon the perpetually browbeaten—a lack-luster and forlorn complexion, the hue of smoke. . . . Then there was an enormous siren, mounted atop a water tower. It was this machine, like an intransigent apocalyptic voice, which seemed to dominate the island and the proceedings of each day. Like an archangel's horn, too, it was apt to blow at any hour. It had the impact of a smack across the mouth, and at its shocking, pitiless wail the prisoners fled galloping across the island like panicked sheep, egged on by the Marines' rowdy cries.

Styron also saw the effects of imprisonment on those who wielded authority. The officers, of whom he was one, enjoyed considerable power; within the prison their word was never challenged. "At their approach the prisoners scrambled erect, removed their caps (being forbidden to salute), and stood in alarmed and rigid silence. Such were the rules, and thus even the meanest lieutenant might feel that same spinal thrill and hot flush of privilege that a cardinal must feel, or a general at parade, and sense chill little ecstasies of dominion."

Styron became friendly with a marine captain named R. O. Culver, an older man and a fellow southerner who had been a federal prison officer in civilian life. Just before the war, in fact, Culver had been in command of the guard at Alcatraz. "He was an amiable Alabamian," Styron remembered, "not at all the mean, tough sadist you expect to find in that sort of job. He knew how to handle these convicts, was very compassionate toward them really." Styron learned lessons about the privileges of rank from Culver, and at the end of his time at Harts Island he thought that he had acquitted himself decently and employed his authority circumspectly. Six years later, as a gesture of thanks, he gave the name Thomas Culver to one of the two central characters in *The Long March.*

Styron completed his stint at the Harts Island prison in November and was sent south for discharge to Portsmouth, Virginia, just across Hampton Roads from Newport News. The discharge procedure was anticlimactic. Styron stayed with his father and stepmother at the house on Chesapeake Avenue; each morning for more than a week he rode the bus to Portsmouth and sat in offices and waiting rooms at the naval depot, reading magazines and waiting for signatures on release forms. Finally the business was accomplished, and in early December he became a civilian again. There was nothing to do now but wait until he could return to Duke for the spring term.

The wait was unpleasant: his relations with Elizabeth Buxton Styron were now more hostile than ever. Styron felt that he had come into his manhood; he had finished almost three years of college and had been commissioned as an officer in the Marine Corps. Elizabeth, however, seemed unimpressed by these accomplishments. She made light of his military service because he had not seen combat or shot at the enemy. She also belittled his literary ambitions. "Billy *thinks* he can write," she would say to her friends in his presence. Things were not helped by his sexual involvement with a nurse trainee, one of Elizabeth's charges, whom he kept out several times well past her curfew at the training school. He stayed up late at night, writing and typing, and slept until noon or one o'clock the next day. Often he would spend the rest of the day lying on a sofa downstairs, reading, and some nights he and his boyhood friend Leon Edwards would go out and drink beer. One day he found an encyclopedia of psychiatry lying on the sofa arm, opened to the entry for Paranoid Sociopath. The parts of the entry describing loneliness, brooding, irregular hours, and excessive drinking had been underlined in red. Styron did not need to ask who had left the book there, or who had done the underlining.

• • •

Styron's experience as a marine ended ambiguously. He had been part of the great event of his generation, but aside from his experiences in training camps, nothing much had happened to him. He had not seen combat, nor had he even been to a war zone. He had been whipped into shape by the Marine Corps and had been prepared to fight, but like thousands of other servicemen he had been saved by the A-bomb. He was in love, he thought, with Bobbie Taeusch, but their relationship was chaste and unresolved. He knew that the Marine Corps had probably changed him, but he was unsure what those changes were. For the present there was nothing to do but loaf around until he could return to Duke.

In retrospect, though, Styron would come to realize that his first stint in the Marine Corps had changed him greatly. Despite his contempt for the stupidities of military routine, he remained proud throughout his life of his performance as a marine. For most of his boyhood and adolescence he had been thin and undersized, not especially good in athletics and mediocre in his schoolwork. The Marine Corps had been a considerable victory. He had been taken by the toughest branch of the U.S. military service and had survived its training regimen. He had made close friends and earned respect from a man who had seen combat. He had overcome the Clap Shack and a bad shooting eye at Parris Island, and he had endured an abusive officer at Camp Lejeune. He had gone on to Quantico and had won his officers' bars. Certainly he had not been blinded to the shortcomings of the military. Later he wrote almost eloquently about the absurdities of Marine Corps life, with its "training manuals and twenty-mile hikes, stupefying lectures on platoon tactics and terrain and the use of the Lister bag, mountains of administrative paperwork, compulsive neatness and hideous barracks in Missouri and Texas, sexual deprivation, hot asphalt drill fields and deafening rifle ranges, daily tedium unparalleled in its ferocity, awful food, bad pay, ignorant people and a ritualistic demand for ass-kissing almost unique in the quality of its humiliation."

Styron could also recognize, though, that he had been improved and transformed by what he had been through. "It is for me a touchstone of the Marine Corps' fatal glamour," he later wrote, "that there is no ex-Marine of my acquaintance, regardless of what direction he may have taken spiritually or politically after those callow gung-ho days, who does not view the training as a crucible out of which he emerged in some way more resilient, simply *braver* and better for the wear." During his stint with the Marines, Styron had seen impersonality, physical and mental cruelty, institutional bungling and stupidity, imprisonment and abuse of authority. He had also seen camaraderie, endurance, self-discipline, and pride. His wartime experiences had matured him and shaped him. Almost forty years later he would say: "In many ways the onrushing war made me what I became."

10

After the War

STYRON RETURNED to Duke for the spring term of 1946, but he was not altogether happy to be coming back. He felt little kinship with most Duke undergraduates, few of whom shared his concerns or ambitions. Bobbie Taeusch was working in New York, and though he managed to visit her there once or twice, their future plans remained unresolved. He had dates with a few co-eds at Duke but found no one who interested him.

Somehow the entire collegiate scene in Durham was typified for Styron by two Duke undergraduates named Buffa and Bubba. Bertha (Buffa) Garrett was a tall, striking blonde from Rockingham, North Carolina, the Sweetheart of Alpha Delta Pi and one of the best-looking women at the university. Her steady beau was John (Bubba) Seward, a handsome, square-jawed basketball star and junior-class president from Styron's hometown of Newport News. These two seemed to fit smoothly into Duke undergraduate life and to ascend almost effortlessly to the top by virtue of their good looks and talents. Styron did not dislike them: in fact, he had a kind of sneaking admiration for this collegiate queen and her prince consort. Things seemed to come easily and naturally to them. Styron knew that he, by contrast, did not fit into the mainstream at Duke and that the world of the Buffas and Bubbas was not for him. He did see, though, that he might carve out a niche for himself in the circle that revolved around Blackburn and the *Archive*.

Styron made a few new friends that spring. He had some good times with a New Jersey native named Pershing G. Smith, a returning veteran who liked to go with him on drinking expeditions into downtown Durham. And Styron found, oddly enough, that he was doing better in his academic work without necessarily trying harder. He was now free of the onerous V-12 requirements and could take most of his courses in literature and history. His marks improved, and he surprised his father by almost making the dean's list in the spring semester of 1946.

Styron decided to take a holiday from school that summer. He had either been enrolled in college or on active military duty for almost the entire period since June 1942, and he wanted a break. He knew, though, that it would not be a good idea for him to spend more than a few days in Newport News. He could not endure Elizabeth Buxton's complaints about his messiness and laziness and late hours, so he began to look around for something else to do. His desire to be a writer was as strong as ever, so he decided to apply to the Bread Loaf writers' conference in Vermont, then already the best-known summer writing program in the country. He mailed in his application and was accepted for a two-week stint in August, but that still left the intervening period empty. Perhaps, he thought, he might do some seafaring. He knew that Newport News was a major embarkation point for grain and livestock, so just after he came home in June he scouted around and located a cattle boat bound for Trieste. On impulse he filled out the application papers and signed on as a deckhand for the voyage.

The ship on which Styron was to sail was a merchant vessel called the *Cedar Rapids Victory,* a 440-foot cargo ship that had been built the previous year. The ship was bound on a postwar relief mission to Yugoslavia, sponsored by a religious group that Styron knew only as The Brethren. The *Cedar Rapids* was to carry some fifteen hundred cattle and two hundred horses to the Yugoslavs; these animals were breeding stock, sent over to help repopulate the supply of farm animals in the war-damaged country.

Styron shipped out on the *Cedar Rapids* in early July. Soon he had made friends with one of the veterinarians on board, a young midwesterner with whom he got along well. He became this man's assistant and helped him inspect the animals and give them vaccinations and wormings. Most of the cattle were springing heifers—that is, cows scheduled to give birth soon after they reached Yugoslavia. About halfway through the voyage, though, many of these cows began to drop their calves early. Styron was kept in constant motion, hustling around belowdecks, pulling the newborn calves from their mothers, clearing their noses and mouths of mucus, and getting them on their feet in the cramped, smelly pens. Styron also had to collect the bloody afterbirths and toss them into buckets that were swung out from the ship on booms and emptied into the ocean. As an older man Styron could recall the parade of sharks that followed the ship. He would watch, appalled, as they went into feeding frenzies whenever the buckets were dumped.

The *Cedar Rapids* sailed past Gibraltar and through the Straits of Messina, then steamed up the Adriatic to Trieste. That multinational city was in limbo: it had been in Italian hands during the war and had been heavily bombed in 1944; now it was being operated as a free territory, under a temporary Anglo-American administration. The city was still recovering from wartime damage, and its economy was in disarray. Many of the docks and warehouses had been destroyed, and the harbor, crowded with British warships at anchor, was functioning only at a fraction of its normal capacity. Several Italian ships, scuttled during the last days of the war, sat on the bottom of the harbor. Only their funnels were visible; Styron's ship had to be maneuvered carefully around them to its docking position.

Just as the *Cedar Rapids* arrived, a strike broke out among the dockhands in Trieste, and they refused to unload the cattle and horses. This was a serious problem; the summer weather was sweltering, and the animals would perish if left on board. The dockworkers were finally persuaded to unload the cattle and horses but still refused to take off the straw and manure—important by-products meant to be spread on local fields. This was fine with Styron; now he would be able to stay in Trieste until the strike was over. The *Cedar Rapids* had been scheduled for a quick turnaround, but now it would have to sit in the harbor, reeking of manure and urine, until the labor dispute was settled.

Styron's veterinarian friend had made the voyage to Trieste before, and he knew that there was a flourishing postwar black market there. The most valuable commodity on that market was American cigarettes. He had come prepared, with a sea chest full of Camels, Chesterfields, and Lucky Strikes. He and Styron smuggled the cartons of cigarettes into Trieste in pillowcases and realized a tidy profit.

They also managed to hook up with two young women who worked on the black market and to spend several days with them in a hotel. Styron's companion was Italian and the vet's was German: neither spoke much English, but the foursome was compatible. They walked around the narrow streets of the old section of the city together, visiting the Roman ruins and the castle on San Giusto Hill. Styron found an odd mix of buildings in Trieste—Mediterranean stucco side by side with Austrian gingerbread. On the outskirts of the city, near the Yugoslavian border, the houses were gray and weatherbeaten and the atmosphere lugubrious and menacing. The words VIVA TITO were painted on stone walls there, alongside mysterious slogans in Serbian. Anti-American sentiment was strong in these parts of the city; Styron, the veterinarian, and their girlfriends narrowly avoided an incident in an open-air café there one night and did not go back to the Yugoslav quarter again. Instead they drank in the cafés around the Piazza Garibaldi or diverted themselves in their hotel rooms.

But this idyll could not last. The strike by the dockworkers was settled, and they prepared to clean out the livestock pens on the *Cedar Rapids*. The ship had sat cooking for so long in the sun, however, that it was filled with poisonous methane gas from the cow manure. Styron later remembered that the dockhands had to wear gas masks while they mucked out the ship. Once that work was done, the *Cedar Rapids* sailed for home. If it had been an ordinary merchant vessel, it would have carried a return cargo, but it was on a relief mission and sailed back empty. Styron and the others, with almost no real work to do, lay about and read or played cards and talked for the entire return passage. Styron had a go at growing a beard, in emulation of some of the hirsute Brethren who had come along on the trip. He liked the way his whiskers looked, but his neck itched so fiercely that he shaved off the beard just before the ship docked in Newport News.

In August, Styron made his way to Middlebury College in Vermont for two weeks at Bread Loaf. This annual conference had been held every summer since 1926 at the Bread Loaf Inn and in some surrounding buildings and grounds—all situated near the village of Ripton in the Green Mountains. The summer of 1946 produced a bumper postwar crop of 130 enrollees for the conference, the largest class ever. The staff that year included the publisher William Sloane, who taught the fiction workshops, and Louis Untermeyer, who handled the poetry writers. Graeme Lorimer from *The Saturday Evening Post* was there, along with Wallace Stegner, who sang folk songs in the evenings in the barn recreation room. The dominant presence was Robert Frost, who had been associated with the conference off and on since its founding.

Styron did very little during his two weeks at Bread Loaf. He had no special goals and did not work very hard to make connections with editors and publishers. Mostly he wanted to be in the company of writers and watch their behavior. What did they look like? What did they talk about? How did they dress? How did the real writers differ from the pretenders and hangers-on? Could he fit in and function well in this atmosphere? Styron had known very few published writers: no one in Newport News could claim to be a real author, and in Durham the only writer he knew was Frances Gray Patton, who wrote for *The New Yorker.*

Styron participated in the workshops and heard Sloane utter such dicta as "Begin where the action becomes inevitable." Styron skipped a good many of the evening activities, but he did go to a lecture by Frost and hear the eminent poet make his famous declaration "I would as soon play tennis without a net as write free verse." During the afternoons he saw Frost and Untermeyer actually playing tennis on the Bread Loaf courts and heard Frost curse with abandon whenever he double-faulted.

Styron met some of the other novice writers and found himself smitten by an ethereal-looking poetess named Lois Schnabel, but she did not return his attentions. For the most part he put in his time working on short-story manuscripts, reading, and walking through the woods near the inn. He enjoyed many things about the conference, but for the first time in his life he was conscious of the undercurrent of tension and hope—the enormous "strain of aspiration," in Frost's phrase—that filled the air at such places as Bread Loaf. That atmosphere made him uncomfortable, probably because he knew that he was beginning to contribute to it himself.

Back at Duke that September, Styron signed up for courses in English, history, and philosophy. He went to visit Professor Blackburn and told him about his voyage to Trieste and his stay at Bread Loaf. He saw Blackburn now fairly frequently, walking over to the professor's home occasionally in the evenings for conversation and advice. Sometimes he would come with a group of students for a spaghetti dinner. (Blackburn would fuss endlessly with the sauce, one student remembered, until the whole group begged him to stop and allow the food to be served.) Afterward Blackburn would play records for the students on his Magnavox hi-fi. Frequently they listened to Mozart and Beethoven, or sometimes to early blues discs. Blackburn liked the gritty songs of Leadbelly and Bessie Smith and would hum along with the tunes.

Styron had come to know Blackburn reasonably well by now, simply by observing him and listening to him. Styron could see that Blackburn was uncomfortable in his marriage; his wife, Tris Cheney, was a silk-mill heiress from Manchester, Connecticut, intelligent and charming but unhappy herself. Styron could feel tension whenever he visited the Blackburn home, and he could sense that the marriage might not survive. He knew, from a dropped remark or two, that Blackburn felt uneasy about his wife's money, which enabled them to live more comfortably than would have been possible on his associate professor's salary alone. Styron also knew that Blackburn was frustrated professionally and that he carried much of this anger home with him from the university.

Styron was also beginning to have some understanding of Blackburn's difficulties in the English department at Duke. Blackburn believed that his teaching was not highly valued there. His courses in creative writing were snickered at by his colleagues—or at least so he thought. Academic criticism, published in scholarly journals or issued in book form by university presses, was the ticket to advancement and success in the profession, not teaching the great hits of Elizabethan poetry and prose in an emotional style. Styron sided with Blackburn: he knew that dispassionate critical exegesis was sometimes illuminating and useful, but he was also savvy enough to recognize that much academic criticism was reductive and pedestrian. His own inclinations toward creative work, coupled with his great affection for his mentor, caused him to empathize entirely with Blackburn.

He found himself irritated by the pedantic approach to literature that some of his professors used in the classroom, and he rebelled against it.

On his Chaucer exam that fall he did not address the questions that his professor, Paull F. Baum, had posed on the mimeographed sheet. Instead he wrote a long, cranky essay attacking what he felt to be Baum's mechanical approach to *The Canterbury Tales*. It was a nervy tactic, but Styron was so impassioned and articulate in the essay—and so obviously appreciative of Chaucer's work in a general way—that Baum gave him a B. "You've got to allow for that point-of-view, too," Baum said to a colleague.

The matter is of some significance because Styron's later attitude toward academic criticism—especially toward the attentions of college professors to his own writings—appears to have had its beginnings in his undergraduate years at Duke. Throughout his own career he remained on the side of the Blackburns, appreciative of attentive teaching and wary of published academic criticism. This would put him in a difficult position sometimes in later years: he would usually be pleased to see his work explicated and analyzed in scholarly journals and books, but he remained suspicious of formalist criticism, put off by its condescending tone and contemptuous of its jargonish, lumpy style. What he sought and appreciated (and could write himself, as a matter of fact) was a broader, more discursive type of literary criticism aimed at the informed lay reader. These attitudes and preferences Styron absorbed initially from William Blackburn.

Over on West Campus, Styron occasionally spent some time on Pub Row, a string of offices for the editors and staffs of the various student publications. He got to know Mac Hyman, Peter Maas, and Guy Davenport, students in Blackburn's classes who would go on to have successes later as writers. He also met Ashbel Brice, a young instructor in the English department. He became friendly with an Ohio native named Bob Loomis, whom he met in the Toddle House near the East Campus one evening; over ten years later Loomis would become his editor at Random House. And he talked occasionally with Clay Felker, who would go on to become the editor of *Esquire* and would help to found *New York* magazine. Felker's girlfriend caught Styron's eye: she was a trim, flirtatious beauty from Bronxville, New York, named Leslie Blatt. She and Felker were involved in a campus scandal: they drove off to Pinehurst, North Carolina, and spent the night there together; both were expelled from Duke as a result. They got married, but the marriage did not last. Leslie Blatt would turn up in Styron's life again in the 1950s.

During his second stint at Duke, Styron produced two stories for the *Archive*. The first, entitled "The Ducks," is a narrative about duck-hunting that oddly anticipates Hemingway's *Across the River and into the Trees*—which would not appear until 1950. The story is told through the consciousness of Frank Thornton, an overweight coffee salesman who hunts on weekends. As the story opens, Thornton sits shivering in a duck blind, musing on the failures and disappointments of his life. He is melancholy and suffers from a kind of post–World War II ennui. At the end of the story he dies of a heart attack, much as Hemingway's Colonel Cantwell does in *Across the River*. The other *Archive* story from this period, entitled "This Is My Daughter," is a first-person account by a young man who tells of an encounter with a strange two-some—a handsome, bored young woman and her talkative, protective mother. The narrative is a study of alcoholism, failed marriage, and the desperate pretenses that human beings use to deny their faults. "The Ducks" and "This Is My Daughter" mark an advance over the earlier *Archive* material; they are better constructed and are psychologically more penetrating. Styron was finding his natural material in these stories and learning to handle narrative voice more confidently.

Styron wrote a few other items for the *Archive* during his second period at Duke—a book review, a column of campus chat, and two sketches about Duke faculty members—but he was beginning to want a wider audience. He submitted some work to the *Virginia Quarterly Review* without success, and he cast about for a good plot for a novel, asking his father to send down some suggestions. By now he had seen some of his writing appear between hard covers, in a collection called *One and Twenty*. Claire Leighton, a wood engraver and book designer, had been a visiting lecturer in the Art Department at Duke during the 1943 and 1944 terms. She and her pupils had worked with Blackburn and his students on a clothbound collection of writing, selected from past issues of the *Archive*. The book had been published in November 1945 by Duke University Press. Leighton's students had supplied the design and decorations; Blackburn had selected the contents, choosing Styron's story "The Long, Dark Road" for inclusion. Blackburn sent a copy of *One and Twenty* to John Selby, a book editor at Rinehart who had earlier come down to Duke to talk to the students in the fiction-writing classes. Selby wrote to Styron from New York, praising "The Long, Dark Road" and offering to look at a novel manuscript, should Styron have one to show.

Blackburn's efforts had also brought Styron a letter from Hiram Haydn, then an editor at Crown. Blackburn had become friendly with Haydn during Haydn's two-year stint as a teacher at the Women's College in Greensboro. Blackburn had written to Haydn, suggesting that Styron's work might have promise. Remarkably enough, these two contacts, both arranged by Blackburn, would have pivotal influences on Styron's professional life. Selby would help Styron get a start in the publishing business at McGraw-Hill in the spring of 1947, an experience from which the early chapters of *Sophie's Choice* eventually grew. And Haydn would bring Styron's first novel, *Lie Down in Darkness,* into print in the fall of 1951.

Blackburn was active on other fronts as well. He had been a Rhodes Scholar in the mid-1920s before coming to Duke; in the fall of 1946 he found himself a member of the selection committee for Rhodes Scholar candidates from the state of North Carolina. The typical aspirant was an excellent student, a campus leader, and an athlete—someone destined for success in government, business, or the law. But the requirements had been adjusted just after the war to admit candidates who had less conventional profiles—young men who were talented in literature and the arts, for example. Styron seemed an obvious possibility, despite his sub-par academic record, so Blackburn got him to apply—giving him the proper forms to fill out and prodding him to have letters of recommendation sent in. Along with his application materials, Styron submitted some of his writing from the *Archive.*

Styron seems initially to have gone along with the idea only to please Blackburn. He had no real hope of success against the Phi Beta Kappas, class presidents, and tennis stars who were arrayed against him. To his great surprise, though, he was chosen as one of three finalists from North Carolina colleges. (Blackburn's presence on the selection committee, Styron thought, surely had something to do with his being picked.) Styron was to go to the regional competition in Atlanta on a Saturday in early December 1946. On the Thursday before the competition, Blackburn loaned Styron forty dollars and gave him a book to read and a clean white shirt. That evening Styron took a flight to Atlanta from the Raleigh-Durham airport, the first time in his life that he had flown on a commercial aircraft. (The one-way ticket cost twenty dollars.) Styron was put up in Atlanta at the Biltmore Hotel on Peachtree Street, where the interviews with the selection committee were to take place on Saturday. He slept all day Friday, arose on Saturday, donned Professor Blackburn's white shirt, and prepared to make a good impression on the committee.

The Rhodes Scholar program, first instituted in 1902, was designed to send promising young college graduates from the countries of the old British Commonwealth to Oxford University for a period of postgraduate study. The award carried much prestige, and it promised good times in the cloistered halls of one of the world's great universities. Styron knew that he was a long shot to win, but he knew too that the writings he had submitted were good and that he would probably do well in the interview with the committee. Still, he felt doubtful: he had never expected to be a finalist and, deep down, was not sure that he wanted to go to Oxford. Things had moved so quickly that he had not had time to contemplate what the actual winning of a Rhodes scholarship might mean.

Styron went through the competition that Saturday and then settled down to wait, lounging around the hotel lobby and chatting with the other candidates. The committee delayed and delayed, leaving the young men to dangle in boredom and tension. Finally, long after suppertime, a weary-looking committee member emerged from the conference room and read the names of the winners. Styron's name was not among them. Almost immediately (he later recalled) he felt a blissful sense of relief. He who hated academic work so thoroughly—what would he have done if he had managed to bluff his way into Oxford? He wanted to be a writer, not a scholar.

As the candidates began to drift away, Styron was called aside by a distinguished-looking committee member who was just emerging from the conference room. The man was Harvie Branscomb, D.D., chancellor of Vanderbilt University. Dr. Branscomb shook hands with Styron and offered condolences, then revealed why the committee had taken so long. "It was because of you," he confessed. "We argued and argued about you for at least an hour. You see—your writing, those stories—they really were very impressive. . . . We did want a creative person, but . . ."

Styron, in a later re-creation of the conversation, guessed the next line: "Yes," said Branscomb, "to flunk Physics not just once but *three* times in a row. . . . One of the committee members said that you seemed to demonstrate a 'pertinacity in the desire to fail.' We had to consider how such a trait might appear to the people at Oxford. . . ."

Styron nodded, and Branscomb, after a pause, continued to speak. Perhaps it was better that Styron had not won, he said. "I've watched hundreds of Rhodes Scholars come back to America and begin their careers and I'll be dogged if I can name a single writer—a single poet or playwright or short story writer or novelist—that came out of the entire huge crowd," he told Styron. "If you really want to know the truth, I believe that if we had chosen you it may have been the end, once and for all, of your ambitions to be a writer. Most probably, you would have become a teacher—a doggone good teacher, you understand, but not a writer."

Styron thanked Dr. Branscomb and headed for his room. He packed his bag, paid his bill, and walked to the train station. On the way he bought a half-pint bottle of bourbon—the first hard liquor he had ever purchased, for until then his libation had always been beer. On the way back to Durham that night he pondered his deliverance, thankful to the avuncular Dr. Branscomb for taking the sting out of the defeat. Between surreptitious pulls on the bottle of bourbon he realized how grateful he was that he would not be going to Oxford. Somewhere in North Carolina he drifted off into an alcoholic slumber and missed his stop at Durham. He slept through the night and woke up on Sunday morning as the train pulled into Norlina, a little town almost on the Virginia border. Styron caught a southbound train back to Durham later that day, arriving with a hangover but with lightened spirits. He had made a narrow escape from *la vie académique.*

Styron's impatience with his studies had by now become acute. He had even begun to chafe in English classes, especially when the readings were not to his taste. He enrolled in a survey of early American literature taught by Clarence Gohdes that fall, and though he liked Gohdes he was colossally bored by the material. One day, in supreme exasperation, he barked out "Oh, for Christ's sake!" in the middle of a lecture on some dull colonial figure. Later that semester he vented his spleen in a letter to his father:

> I've come to the stage when I know what I want to do with my future. I want to write, and that's all, and I need no study of such quaint American writers as Cotton Mather or Philip Freneau—both of whom we are studying in American Lit.—to increase my perception or outlook on literature and life. For a person whose sole, burning ambition is to write—like myself—college is useless beyond the Sophomore year. By that time he knows that further *wisdom* comes from reading men like Plato + Montaigne—*not* Cotton Mather—and from getting out in the world and *living.* All of the rest of the scholarship in English literature is for pallid, prim and vapid young men who will end up teaching and devoting 30 years of their sterile lives in investigating some miserably obscure facet of the life of a minor Renaissance poet. Sure, scholarship is necessary, but it's not for me. I'm going to write, and I'll spend the rest of my days on a cattle-boat or jerking sodas before I'll teach.

Despite such pronouncements Styron managed to earn straight B's that fall semester. These marks allowed him to slip onto the tail end of the dean's list. His father must have been flabbergasted.

Styron completed his requirements for graduation that spring, earning an appropriate grade of "Out" for each of his four classes. This was an exam-free option available to graduating seniors: one almost feels that the registrar should have recorded an exclamation point after each of those grades on Styron's transcript. "Out!" He now set his sights on New York City. Bobbie Taeusch was there, working for Union Carbide, and he had letters of encouragement from John Selby at Rinehart and Hiram Haydn at Crown. With these slim assets he decided to head north.

As was often the case with him during these years, though, he first had to explain his decision to his father in a long, soberly worded letter. "There is, I think, little need for rationalization," he wrote to the senior Styron. "I am doing nothing here now but boring myself, drinking beer, and wasting time better wasted somewhere else." Styron knew that it was time to change his surroundings: "This move I am making—though I perhaps, egotistically, exaggerate its import—is not conventional and is, at the same time, an important decision. But it is not impetuous. I have given it good thought." He knew where his future lay: "I mean *writing,* a field in which I know I can become supreme if I can only develop the discipline and strength and love." At the end of the letter he added one last thought: "I'll see Dr. Blackburn tomorrow, who I'm sure will greet my decision with some dismay, and equivocal mumblings, and who will give me his dear and always cherished benediction."

11

McGraw-Hill

WHEN STYRON ARRIVED in New York City in the spring of 1947, he went to see John Selby, the editor at Rinehart who had written to him while he was at Duke. Styron told Selby that he was looking for something in publishing—an entry-level job that would earn him a little money and give him time to write some short stories. Selby did in fact know of such a position at Whittlesey House, the trade-book division of McGraw-Hill. He sent Styron to see William Poole, the editorial director there, and Poole proved to be personable and friendly. Yes, he told Styron, he did have a job for a beginning assistant editor. Yes, Styron could have it. He could begin work the next week.

Styron could scarcely believe his luck. Jobs in publishing were difficult to find, and he had landed one almost immediately. He had been staying in a cheap hotel room; now he would look around for more permanent quarters. After some searching he found a single room—a tiny cell, really—in a "residence club" on West Eleventh Street in the Village. The place was grim and dreary, inhabited mostly by older men who were down on their luck and by a few younger fellows who, like Styron, stayed there because the accommodations were cheap—ten dollars a week for the room, with access to a bath down the hall. It was a depressing place, but it was all he could afford. He moved in, unpacked his bags, walked about the Village a little, and waited for his job to begin.

The building to which Styron reported for work a few days later was one of the most unusual-looking structures in New York City. Certainly it stood in enormous contrast to the dingy residence club on Eleventh Street. McGraw-Hill had erected a green-brick skyscraper at 330 West Forty-second Street in 1930–31. It had been designed in a variation of Art Deco style and dated from the same era as the Chrysler Building and the Empire State Building. Metallic bands of green, silver, and gold encircled the ground floor outside and continued indoors into an ornate lobby. Rows of bluish-green terra-cotta bands echoed the motif on the façade above. The building was striking enough to be pictured in many Manhattan guidebooks, and there were always tourists outside gawking up at the windows. Unfortunately the offices within were drab and institutional, more genuinely reflective of the firm's conservatism than were the stylish exterior ornaments.

Whittlesey House, where Styron now worked, was one of the smallest operations in the building. It was supposed to publish respectable trade books if it could, but Styron quickly learned that other divisions at McGraw-Hill were more important. The firm owed its financial success to technical manuals, industrial journals, scientific reports, and textbooks—all of which were predictable earners with good profit margins. Most of the books published by Whittlesey House, by contrast, lost money—but at least McGraw-Hill could claim to be putting out something other than trade journals and business manuals.

Styron found his duties at Whittlesey House dull and tiring. As the lowliest worker in the office hierarchy, he had to wade through the slush pile—the collection of manuscripts that comes unsolicited to every publisher. Nearly all of these manuscripts had already been turned down by other houses, usually for good reason. Styron found himself slogging through stacks of smudged Hammermill Bond and assessing material that ranged from the undistinguished to the truly wretched. He tried to put a good face on his duties in a letter to his father: "The work is about the same," he wrote, "much manuscript reading, brightened up occasionally by interviews with prospective authors and now and then a few letters to write." If nothing else, he could take perverse pleasure in the low quality of what came across his desk. "The novels I read still remain uniformly bad or, at most, mediocre," he wrote to his father, "and I am gaining comfort at least from the slightly invidious fact that I can do so much better than the majority of these *opera.*"

Things did not improve when he went home to his room on Eleventh Street. His only escape from the dreariness there was through books and beer. He was deep into a reading of William Faulkner's works— initially in Malcolm Cowley's Viking Portable edition, an anthology that presented the Yoknapatawpha tales as a cycle or saga. "I have often thought I might do the same thing with a North Carolina or Pennsylvania family," he wrote to his father. But his reading and imbibing could not shut out the unpleasant surroundings. "I don't think I'm a complete sybarite," he wrote in another letter home, "but I believe that even a Jesuit would find it gloomy business living in the box I live in. Imagine a room the size of the big bathroom upstairs at home, ill-lighted, decorated with muddy wall-paper, and subjected to a ninety degree temperature all summer, and you'll get an idea of my nocturnal mode of living."

To make matters worse he came down with hepatitis. He never knew how he had picked it up—probably from bad hygiene at one of the cheap restaurants he frequented—but he knew that hepatitis was serious and could be life-threatening. He went to the emergency ward of the French Hospital on West Thirtieth Street and spent several hours lying on a gurney in a crowded hallway, waiting for treatment. He was finally admitted and placed in a large public ward, where he stayed for almost two weeks. Some of the patients in the ward were terminally ill, and several died while Styron was there—one in the bed just beside his. Bobbie Taeusch visited him when she could, bringing a portable phonograph and some Beethoven records. He was allowed to play these at low volume, to ease his boredom and discomfort. When he was let go from the hospital, Bobbie made him convalesce in her apartment. He wrote to his father that he was getting back on his feet: "The doctor informs me that I was lucky to have a very mild case, because the convalescence period for the average case is usually two or three months—enough to make anyone lose their job! As it is, the people at Whittlesey House have been very nice in telling me to stay in bed until I was completely well, and in bringing manuscripts every other day or so up to Bobbie's apartment for me to read."

His spirits were beginning to lift when, out of the blue, he received a long letter from Elizabeth Buxton. The letter does not survive, but Styron's recollection of it suggests that his relationship with his stepmother had not improved. "The gist of her letter was this," he recalled many years later: "while she was happy that I had recovered, she hoped from her heart that I realized that I had *brought the illness on myself,* that by the loose and debauched life I had been living—drinking, irregular habits, etc—I had no one to blame but myself for my close call with oblivion. I was still very weak when I read her words, barely able to get out of bed, and they made—to say the least—a bleak impression on my spirit." To add to his problems, he was now suffering through a bout of jaundice—one of the side effects of hepatitis—and his skin had turned a dark yellow.

At least things seemed to be looking up at McGraw-Hill. Early in September, the firm brought in Edward C. Aswell as editor in chief of Whittlesey House. Aswell was a southerner, a native of Nashville who had started in publishing as an assistant editor at *Forum* magazine and later had worked at the *Atlantic Monthly.* From there he had moved on to Harper & Brothers as a book editor. The high point of his career had come in the late 1930s when he had been Thomas Wolfe's last editor. After his breakup with editor Maxwell Perkins at Scribner's in 1937, Wolfe had signed on with Harper and had been given Aswell, then only thirty-seven, as his editor. Aswell had been helping Wolfe give birth to a new novel when Wolfe had died suddenly. Aswell had sifted through Wolfe's fabled trunk of manuscripts and had cobbled together three books for posthumous publication—*The Web and the Rock, You Can't Go Home Again,* and *The Hills Beyond.*

Those days were well in the past now, but Aswell's name still had a little cachet in the New York publishing world. McGraw-Hill expected Aswell to bring a more elevated tone to Whittlesey House. Styron was at first happy to learn that he would work under Aswell, imagining that the older man might take an interest in him and share a few anecdotes about his times with Wolfe. More experienced hands at the publishing game could have told Styron that he should instead be wary—that the appointment of a new boss usually meant a shake-up, and that some people at Whittlesey House were likely to be cut loose.

As it turned out, Styron was one of the first to go. He took an almost immediate dislike to Aswell, finding him remote and pompous. Styron did not help the situation by coming to work late or by drowsing through Aswell's editorial conferences. Styron was not interested in his job and made no particular effort to hide his boredom. He was doing competent enough work, but Aswell could see that he had no real interest in publishing.

Styron also managed to irritate Aswell by cutting up around the office. Early one afternoon a fellow worker named Dorothy Parker presented Styron with a gag gift she had purchased on her lunch hour—a kit for blowing plastic bubbles. Styron inflated six or eight of these iridescent, bluish-green spheres and set them adrift from the window of his office. They were caught by the updraft from the street below and remained suspended, floating in the air, just outside the building. Secretaries from the other offices saw them and rushed to their windows, squealing and giggling. Styron invented a word on the spot: he dubbed his creations "bubbleoons." A report of this foolishness made its way to Aswell, and Styron's stock at McGraw-Hill dropped another notch. Not long after, Aswell called Styron into his office and gave him his release. Aswell did not criticize his work; he only said that Styron did not fit into the plans drawn up by "management." Aswell wanted someone with more experience and wider contacts, and that was that. Styron was told to draw his last paycheck and clean out his desk.

Styron was not surprised by his dismissal. In fact, he began immediately to feel a curious elation. "When I left the McGraw-Hill Building for the last time," he later recalled, "I felt the exultancy of a man just released from slavery." More time at Whittlesey House, he sensed, would blunt his desire to write; the dispiriting effect of the slush pile, the numbing hours spent in editorial meetings, the dull coffee breaks and unpleasant office politics—all of this would finally make him cynical about the publishing process and perhaps about literature itself.

It remained only for him to write and tell his father of his status as a member of the newly unemployed. In this letter, which he wrote on October 10, 1947, Styron blamed his dismissal on plans for expansion at McGraw-Hill: "Aswell obviously has his mind on someone whom he has worked with, and who is older, more experienced, and has all sorts of 'contacts' with agents, authors, and so forth." Aswell's attitude still rankled him, however, and Styron was not prepared to be charitable. "I still bear a half-hearted resentment against the cold, pudgy little man who so abruptly dismissed me," he wrote, "and I'm sure *he'll* never publish any of Styron's immortal and lucrative prose." Styron knew, though, that he was lucky to have escaped from the world of publishing. "All the editors, friends of mine at Whittlesey House, wished me godspeed and were frankly and sincerely rather envious," he wrote to his father. "They too, when they were my age, wanted to write but got enmeshed in publishing, which is only a counterfeit, a reflection, of really creative work."

There was a little good news to write home about: Styron had found a better place to live and was no longer in his cell on Eleventh Street. He had hooked up with a friend from Duke named Ed Hatcher, and the two were sharing a basement apartment at 1453 Lexington Avenue, near Ninety-fourth Street. (Later they would move to a second-floor apartment next door.) Hatcher was a tall, laconic North Carolinian with a good sense of humor, and he and Styron hit it off well. Bobbie Taeusch had taken leave from her job at Union Carbide to go on a trip through New England with a girlfriend and to think seriously about where her relationship with Bill Styron was heading. Ed Hatcher took over her job at Union Carbide as a temporary replacement, and he and Styron settled into the apartment.

Styron's first acquisition was a dog, a cocker spaniel named Mr. Chips. Styron doted on the animal, talking baby talk to it and allowing it to lick his face. He took the dog along whenever he and Hatcher went barhopping, and he got into the habit of asking for a saucer at each watering hole they visited. This he would fill with beer for Mr. Chips, who had developed a taste for hops. The dog would become drunk after the fifth or sixth saucer and would have colossal hangovers in the mornings.

Styron and Hatcher were both impecunious, but in the late 1940s New York City was not a bad place in which to be young and poor. A ride on the bus or subway cost only a nickel, and there was plenty of cheap entertainment. Most of the museums were free or charged only small admissions fees, and there were free concerts in Lewisohn Stadium or Washington Square or Central Park. And the city was safe: Styron and Hatcher could walk the streets without fear; years later Styron recalled that he and Bobbie Taeusch had sometimes taken a blanket to Central Park at night and had lain there in perfect safety until the early morning hours, only watching the stars and talking.

Styron, free from McGraw-Hill, now considered his possibilities. Under the GI Bill he could collect twenty dollars a week from the Veterans Administration while he prepared himself for a career—even if he only claimed to be "self-employed." But twenty dollars a week was not enough for rent and food. Fortunately, at this juncture, Styron had a windfall: his father wrote and told him that he had inherited approximately one thousand dollars from the estate of Belle Abraham,

Pauline's mother. Styron asked his father to begin doling out the money to him at a rate of sixty dollars a month. He could add this sum to his VA benefits for a total of $140—about the same as his monthly salary had been at McGraw-Hill. By economizing he could feed himself and pay his rent without having to take another job.

Another advantage of the GI Bill was that it would pay for college courses. Styron had already enrolled, earlier that fall, in a seminar in fiction-writing at the New School for Social Research, located just a short distance from his former room on Eleventh Street. The New School had been founded in 1918 by a group of dissident academics, most of them associated with *The New Republic*. In 1935 the school had become affiliated with the University in Exile, a group of European scholars who had fled Hitler and Mussolini. By 1947, when Styron came there, the New School had evolved into a lively, energetic haven for maverick writers, scholars, and artists. It ran a popular series of public lectures and offered classes at night on a great array of subjects—from political thought to advanced sculpture to phenomenology to comparative religion to urban gardening to the philosophy of education. The New School was supported by its lecture series and by gifts from wealthy liberals, for it was egalitarian, cosmopolitan, and left-leaning. It occupied a handsome building, designed in the International Style, at 66 West Twelfth Street.

The leader of the fiction-writing seminar at the New School was Hiram Haydn. While Styron had still been at Duke, Blackburn had written to Haydn, praising Styron's potential. Haydn had responded with a get-acquainted letter to Styron. Now Haydn, again alerted by Blackburn, had made contact with Styron again, sending a letter to him while he was still at Whittlesey House. Would Styron like to join his novel workshop at the New School? If so, he should send over some work in progress. Admission to the workshop was competitive: there were only twelve spaces.

Haydn, then about to turn forty, was not exactly an academic, but he had academic connections. He had earned a Ph.D. in English from Columbia in 1942 but, after the two years of teaching in Greensboro, had left the classroom to become editor of *The American Scholar*. He was supplementing his income by working as an editor for Crown Publishers and teaching at the New School. Haydn was a large, paternal man— not unlike Blackburn in appearance and demeanor. Both men were melancholy and "conflicted," and both could absorb alcohol without showing much effect from it. Both men were also inclined to look after their protégés.

Styron's work in progress—a short story he had been writing that summer—earned him admittance into Haydn's workshop. He showed Haydn two other stories as well: one of them, entitled "The Enormous Window," dealt with Christchurch, and the other, called "A Moment in Trieste," was based on his cattle-boat experiences. (Both were eventually published in *American Vanguard,* a clothbound series that brought together short writings by promising apprentice authors.) Styron reported Haydn's reaction to these stories in a letter to his father:

> [He] liked them so well that he has offered me an advance of a substantial sum of money if I write a novel. Of course, since I haven't written anything on the novel he can't offer me a contract right now. But he was so enthusiastic over the stories that he called me down to his office at Crown and told me that he had informed the publishing director (the big shot) at Crown that he had so much faith in my potentialities that he suggested that they break their rule (against giving advance-on-royalties to unknown writers) in my case. The publishing director finally agreed, after a lot of rhetoric by Haydn, so now all I have to do is write the damn novel.

Styron was poised to begin his first effort at a long work of fiction. He was well situated, and his various supports were in place. He had enough money to get by and a fairly comfortable place to live. He had Blackburn's blessings from afar, expressed in occasional letters, and he had Haydn's approval and influence nearby in the weekly seminar. He would soon have a contract from Crown Publishers and a $250 advance. His relationship with Bobbie was his only worry: he thought he wanted to marry her, but her reluctance and skittishness had caused her to leave New York. At least this postponed the time when he and she would have to make a decision about marriage. He was only twenty-two; he had no way of supporting a wife and no wish to go back to a steady job. For now he would live the bohemian life and work on his book.

It is important to realize, however, that Styron did not drift into literature. He made a calculated decision to invest his small capital in preparing himself to be a professional author. His financial supports included his weekly dole from the GI Bill plus the small inheritance from his grandmother. He also had some valuable intangibles: his belief in the dignity and seriousness of a life devoted to literature and his faith in his own talent and drive. These two things he had inherited most directly from William Blackburn, who, for all his melancholy grumpiness, had believed implicitly in the high importance of great literature and in the potential of his most promising student.

Also crucial to Styron was his father's support. Styron knew that his father was no literary critic and that his confidence in his son's talent was based more on emotion and hearsay than on rational calculation. This did not really matter, though, since there was praise enough from qualified judges like Blackburn and Haydn. What was important to Styron was his father's love, spontaneously and freely expressed. The monthly checks, Styron knew, would arrive regularly from home, accompanied by garrulous, well-meaning letters full of faintly sententious advice. Styron took his cue and responded in kind. His letters back to his father are seasoned with literary allusions and filled with not insincere ruminations about the literary vocation. The paragraph below, from a letter to the senior Styron, is typical of many that would appear in these epistles during the months to come:

> I'm very glad that you see eye to eye with me about my present attitude concerning my attempts at writing, and about the loss of my job. I realize that I've finally come to grips with myself, and that the job was in reality merely a delaying action. Writing for me is the hardest thing in the world, but also a thing which, once completed, is the most satisfying. I have been reading the letters of Joseph Conrad, and really feel a kinship—if nothing but in spirit—with the late master, for one discovers in the letters that writing, for Conrad, was the most despairing, painful job in the world. It most definitely is that way for me. But someone—I think it was Henry James—said that only through monstrous travail and agonizing effort can great art be brought forth from those who, like himself (James), are not prodigies or, like Shelley, spontaneous founts of genius. Anything less than unceasing toil will produce nothing or, at best, facility. I am no prodigy but, Fate willing, I think I can produce art. For me it takes much girding up of loins and an almost imbecile faith in my potentials—but I suppose that's part of the satisfaction.

Styron wrote letters like these, in an elevated rhetorical style, because that was what his father expected. But the letters also gave him a chance to express his hopes and ideals in language that his friends might have smiled at. Surviving letters written to others during this same period are much more ironic and self-deprecatory. With the senior Styron, though, the young man knew that he could unbutton himself and speak without embarrassment about his ambitions and dreams.

Styron's immediate task in the fall of 1947 was to get his novel under way. Its central figure was to be a young woman named Peyton Loftis. Styron already had a working title—"Inheritance of Night," adapted from Matthew Arnold's elegy "Requiescat," the final line of which reads: "Tonight it doth inherit the vasty hall of Death." He had a narrative strategy in mind, and he set it down on a separate sheet of paper for Haydn and the administrators at Crown. "I intend for this novel to be divided into three books of from ten to fifteen sections apiece," he wrote. "Each book is to be preceded by a monologue, direct or interior, which is intended to throw light upon Peyton and her story."

A model for interior monologue was ready to hand in Faulkner's *The Sound and the Fury,* with its opening section narrated from the mind of Benjy Compson, a thirty-three-year-old idiot. Styron decided to try something similar: he would begin "Inheritance of Night" with a passage of interior monologue from the point of view of Maudie Loftis, a simpleminded woman in her late twenties who has been placed in the Mordecai Clinic in Richmond by her father, Milton Loftis. Maudie here is very different from the character she will become in the published version of *Lie Down in Darkness.* In that book she will be profoundly retarded and almost mute. Here, however, she is only "slow" and speaks in an idiom that suggests lack of education rather than feeblemindedness. In "Inheritance of Night," Maudie delivers her monologue in September 1945, just after being institutionalized. She is angry over her father's treatment of her and resents the fact that her father favors her younger sister, Peyton:

> Papa would come up the steps with sweat on his face and pat me on the back and say "Hello, Maudie, honey," and run right into the house hollering, "Peyton, Peyton." And Peyton would be hid somewhere in the house and he'd rush all over inside, I could hear him inside whistling and then she'd come out from wherever she was hid and if they were near to the window I could see him pick her up and kiss her, him laughing and her laughing just like that. Oh I reckon she

was his favorite, all right. He'd call her his little glamour girl and then Mama would holler out from the sunporch in the back. I could hear her say, "Milton, Milton, please try to be quiet, my migraine is so bad today," and they'd hush up, Papa and Peyton, and then they'd come out of the house real quiet, whispering together like he wasn't any older than her, and go up to Powhatan Road and get some ice cream and bring me back some. Lord, it was hot that summer.

Maudie believes that only her injured leg—maimed in a trolley-car accident—has held her back in life and that otherwise she is normal. She reveals various things about her family: her father drinks too much, for example, and her mother is a hypochondriac. Maudie talks about her first menstrual period and reminisces about her only lover, a married man named Harvey who worked as the family gardener. She resents her incarceration in the clinic and ends her monologue, "I want to do things like other people and I think it's a shame that Papa put me in this place. I just want to be happy, I tell you."

Maudie is reminiscent in some ways of Benjy Compson. Though not nearly so backward mentally, she has, like Benjy, been brought up by an alcoholic father and a neurotic mother, and she has been sent to a mental institution, just as Benjy was sent to the state sanitarium in Jackson, Mississippi. There the similarities largely cease, probably because the real model for Maudie was Elizabeth Buxton's slightly retarded sister, Helen Buxton, who used to accompany Billy Styron, his father, and Elizabeth to movies or to the Bide-a-Wee Cafe in downtown Newport News during the year following Pauline Styron's death. Helen, who was only a little backward, had had her leg severed from her body in a trolley-car accident. Styron was thus beginning with a familiar model. It must have seemed a lucky accident that his own extended southern family included, like the Compsons, a slow child who could become a character in his book.

Styron finished Maudie's section just before Christmas and showed it to Haydn, who seemed pleased. The question now was what to write next. On December 25 he took the subway over to Brooklyn and discussed the problem over Christmas dinner with another of Blackburn's pupils who had come north to make a start. This was Mac Hyman, a Georgia native whom Styron had met during his most recent stint in Durham. Hyman had arrived in the city that fall with his wife, Gwen, and was now making the rounds of publishing houses, talking to editors and showing them samples of his work. Hyman was a veteran of the Army Air Corps. He had been an aerial photonavigator and had flown numerous combat missions over Saipan, Guam, and Japan. It had been his task to photograph the damage to Hiroshima shortly after the *Enola Gay* had dropped its atomic bomb on the city. The annihilation that Hyman had witnessed had shaken him badly; some of his friends believed that he had still not recovered from the experience. He was working on a comic novel called "The Recruits," written from the point of view of a draftee from the Georgia backwoods. Eventually he would finish the book and publish it successfully, under the title *No Time for Sergeants,* but for now he was an unknown. Styron liked Hyman and his wife and had been visiting them in Brooklyn when he could.

Hyman, he later remembered, was thoroughly unhappy in the North. His Georgia accent was pronounced, and he was touchy when anyone commented on it. He was reckless, inclined to get into fights in bars with people who spoke slightingly of the South. Styron could sympathize in a general way with Hyman's dilemma; he was only now beginning to come to terms with the casual bigotry of many northerners toward southerners, their unthinking tendency to regard a southern accent as certain evidence of backwardness, ignorance, and racial prejudice. One day that fall, shortly after he had begun taking Haydn's seminar at the New School, Styron had become involved in a nasty shouting match over just this sort of thing. Another student, someone he had just met, had snickered at his Tidewater accent and disparaged his southern background. An ugly argument had followed, and Styron had come close to striking the man. Finally he had screamed, directly into this person's face, "*You're* the bigot, you bastard! *You're* the bigoted one!" Styron had rushed from the building and had fumed over the incident for two or three days.

By now Styron had taught himself to ignore such attitudes, or at least not to be drawn into arguments about the South. Hyman had not yet reached this point: he still brooded about whispered comments and imagined slights, and he was constantly on the defensive in public. One night he sat down at the piano in his apartment and began playing "Three Little Fishes in an Itty-Bitty Pool." He played it over and over, seeming to pass into a trance. Gwen, his wife, tried to make him stop, but he would not. She called Styron for help, and he took the subway over to Brooklyn. Together they got Hyman to their car and put him into the backseat. Then they began to drive south. Gwen wanted to take Hyman all the way to Cordele, Georgia, his hometown. Styron drove them to Durham—as far as he could go. Gwen drove the rest of the way to Cordele. Many years later Styron remembered that Hyman stayed in the backseat during the first several hours of the trip, lying on his side in a fetal position, wrapped in a blanket. Only when they had crossed the Potomac River Bridge into Virginia and were literally in the South would he consent to uncurl and sit up.

Styron, in his basement apartment the day after Christmas, continued to puzzle over the next section of his novel. Early that morning a blizzard had descended on New York, dumping almost twenty-six inches of snow on the city and paralyzing its businesses and bus systems. There was nothing for Styron to do but stay inside and read. He picked up Robert Penn Warren's novel *All the King's Men* and began to work his way through the story of Willie Stark and his rise to power, as narrated by the character Jack Burden. Styron was enthralled by the book: as an older man he recalled in a memoir the experience of being buried in his basement, with snow piling up against the windows, reading chapter after chapter of *All the King's Men.* "No work since that of Faulkner had so impressed me," he remembered, "impressed by its sheer marvelousness of language, its vivid characters, its narrative authority, and the sense of truly felt and realized life. It was a book that thrilled me, challenged me and filled me with hope for my own possibilities as a writer." As he read, he felt the outlines of his own novel begin to take shape in his mind: "I would write about a young girl of twenty-two who committed suicide. I would begin the story as the family in Virginia assembled for the funeral, awaiting the train that returned her body from the scene of her death in New York City. The locale of the book, a small city of the Virginia Tidewater, was my own birthplace, a community so familiar to me that it was like part of my bloodstream."

A day or two later he began to set down a few paragraphs of descriptive writing. As his model he used the opening pages of *All the King's Men,* an introductory section in which the reader is addressed in the second person, as "you," and is drawn smoothly into the world of the novel. Styron's attempt, in manuscript, was similar to what Warren had done:

Riding down to Port Warwick from Richmond the train begins to pick up speed on the outskirts of the city, past the tobacco factories with their ever-present, hovering haze of faintly acrid dust and past the rows of uniformly-brown, clapboard houses which stretch down the hilly streets for miles, it seems, the hundreds of rooftops all reflecting the pale light of dawn; past the suburban roads still sluggish and sleepy with early-morning traffic, and rattling swiftly now over the long bridge which separates the last two hills where in the valley below you can see the James River winding beneath its acid-green, malignant crust of scum out past the chemical plants and more rows of uniformly-brown, clapboard houses and into the woods beyond.

The words continued to flow, appearing almost without effort on the page. Styron described the interior of the train and the "guttural and negroid" accent of its white conductor; he borrowed two black field hands from Warren's Louisiana cotton fields and put them to sawing timber in the eastern Virginia pineywoods; he pictured the "mist lifting off the fields" and the "solitary cabins" of the Negroes, just as Warren had done. He used the second-person "you" throughout. When he had finished the section and reread it several times, he was as pleased with it as with anything he had ever written. Here at least were three pages that he would be proud to publish.

Styron knew that his novel would center on Maudie's sister, Peyton. Styron took this name from a girl named Peyton Voorhees, a cousin of his Christchurch friend Tom Peyton whom he had met a few years before on a trip with Tom to North Carolina. Peyton Voorhees had been younger than Styron; he and Tom had been fond of her and had thought of her as a cute, vivacious kid sister. She had died less than a year later in a terrible automobile accident. Her death had badly shaken both Tom Peyton and Styron. Peyton Voorhees had not been unhappy or rebellious, as Styron's heroine would be, but she had been bright and promising. Her passing had taught him something about how sudden and brutal death could be.

Styron kept writing in the weeks that followed, fashioning now a scene in which Peyton's body arrives at the train station in Port Warwick—his fictional name for Newport News. (The name combines elements from the names of Portsmouth, the Virginia city just across Hampton Roads from Newport News, and Warwick, a town just north of Newport News on the same side of the James River.) At the train station, Peyton's body is met by the grieving father, Milton Loftis, and his mistress, Dolly Bonner. Also in attendance is an undertaker, Mr. Casper, and an old black family retainer named Ella Swan. Styron even put a version of himself into the narrative, calling the character Marcus Bonner and making him an ineffectual, Prufrockian young man who lives "alone in a furnished room in a residence club" and reads manuscripts for a large New York publishing house. Marcus, we learn, has tracked down Peyton's body after her suicide and has had it exhumed from its pauper's grave. He is now riding with the body on the train down to Port Warwick.

Styron paused in February long enough to write a letter home. In it he tried to explain to his father how important his manuscript was becoming to him:

> I can't tell you how much this novel means to me. The process of sitting down and writing is pure torture to me, but at the same time I think about the book all the time and am in more or less a suspended state of worry and anxiety if I'm *not* writing. I worry, too, about the sincerity of my effort; if whether what I'm writing is not so much rhetoric, and it is only in my most now-self-critical mood that I can even come vaguely to realize that what I write does, in truth, have an element of truth in it and is, after all, a more faithful rendering of life than I believe it to be in my moments of doubt.

Styron continued to push ahead through the rest of the winter and the early spring of 1948. The plot of his novel was beginning to reveal itself: the story would hinge on a revelation of incest, or perhaps near incest, between Peyton and her father. And there would be a wretchedly destructive relationship between Milton and Helen Loftis, Peyton's father and mother. Thus many of the major elements of *Lie Down in Darkness* were already in Styron's mind as he was writing "Inheritance of Night."

That spring Styron put together a summary of the rest of the novel for the executives at Crown Publishers. This five-page synopsis describes the major characters one by one and introduces a plot element of misdirected inheritance—hence the working title of the book. In form, this summary closely resembles William Faulkner's "Compson Appendix" to *The Sound and the Fury.* Faulkner had done this piece of writing at Malcolm Cowley's request, and Cowley had published it in the Viking Portable collection, the volume Styron had been reading. In Styron's synopsis of "Inheritance of Night," he reveals that his novel, like Faulkner's, will be filled with melancholy elements—alcoholism, adultery, marital discord, failed love, suicide, and family dissolution—and that he will set this tale against the background of the modern South. There was to be little in the way of redemption for Styron's characters: only Ella Swan, the aged black servant, would finally understand and endure—much as Faulkner's Dilsey had done in *The Sound and the Fury.*

By June of 1948 Styron had produced around fifty pages of typescript, but other than the three-page opening he was not especially pleased with what he had written. He could see that the style was fairly good and that some of the characters were coming to life, but he could also see that the plot was disjointed and that the novel was not really going anywhere. Marcus Bonner, his alter ego, was neither sympathetic nor compelling. And there was some imitativeness. The cribbing from Warren in the first three pages would probably go unnoticed, but the imitation of Faulkner was readily apparent. Faulkner's influence was present throughout the typescript, not just in the appendix-like synopsis but in the language of the chapters themselves. There were echoes of F. Scott Fitzgerald as well: the hints of incestuous feeling between father and daughter bring to mind *Tender Is the Night,* and at one point Peyton's voice is said to have in it "the sound of silver coins clinking together"—surely an allusion to Daisy Buchanan's voice in *The Great Gatsby.*

Styron could probably have pushed ahead and finished "Inheritance of Night" in another year or so. If his writing had held to the level of what he had produced already, then his novel would have been fairly good, well above the average for first novels. "Inheritance of Night" would probably not have attracted much attention, though, and would have been only a beginning, immature and derivative. Styron would have had to produce a second and better effort to earn the praise and high reputation he wanted. He knew these things: perhaps that is why he now stopped working on the manuscript. He was already beginning to show a capacity for rigorous (and sometimes crippling) self-criticism that would be typical of him throughout his career. He was ambitious, persistent, and not afraid of work, but he was also unwilling to let mediocre writing pass into print.

Many of these things he said to Haydn in a long personal conference early in July. Haydn was sympathetic: perhaps a change of scene would help? Young novelists did not necessarily have to live in New York City. Why not go back to his circle of friends in Durham? Styron jumped at the suggestion. A few months earlier, in fact, he had written about the possibility of living elsewhere in a literary letter to his father:

> New York is beginning to wear on my nerves, and now that spring is coming I want to leave. The novelty has worn off; the city, with all its excitement and grandeur, is a terrible place. The tide swarms on; how people manage the pretense of humanity in such a jostling, surly ant-heap is beyond me. The eye bends down from the jutting skyscraper—man's material achievement—to gaze in horror on the pawing mess of Broadway at lunchtime and the greasy, muttering squalor of the interior of a subway car—surely the symbol of man's spiritual decay. *I thought it was wonderful.*

He decided to go back to Durham, where his money would stretch farther. He could find a cheap place to live and could socialize with a crowd of people there whom he had come to know through Blackburn. (They referred to themselves jokingly as the West Durham Literary Society.) He would be near Blackburn, who would offer counsel and support, and he would be reasonably close to his father in Newport News. Accordingly, in early July, Styron packed his belongings, enclosed Mr. Chips in an orange crate, and headed for the train station. But Chips panicked and chewed his way out of the crate before Styron could board the train, and Styron had to catch the dog, find a taxi, and take him to a friend's apartment. He left the dog there and, upset, headed south alone. (Eventually Chips, properly caged, followed him to Durham.) Sitting on the train, Styron went over his plans. He meant to live for a while in Durham, renew some old friendships, turn out some short stories that would sell, and make some headway on his novel. Perhaps, with work, he could write something that he would be satisfied to publish.

12

Durham
and Flatbush

STYRON ARRIVED in Durham in early July 1948. He spent the first few nights sleeping on the sofa at Ashbel Brice's apartment on Sixth Street. Brice had been an instructor in the English department at Duke during Styron's last year in college, and they had become friendly then. Now Brice was working at Duke University Press, of which he would eventually become director. Brice had a circle of young friends, whom he frequently invited over for informal dinners and parties, and Styron became a member of this group.

Styron found a three-room apartment at 901 East Fifth Street, very close to the East Campus of Duke, where the women's dormitories were located. He persuaded another friend from the previous spring, a young man named Bill Snitger, to share the apartment with him. Snitger worked at a local radio station and often came to Brice's gatherings. The immediate problem was that Styron and Snitger had no furniture. Styron appealed to his father for help, and the elder Styron shipped down some chairs, lampshades, and other odds and ends. For the rest, Styron and Snitger went to secondhand stores in Durham or borrowed things from acquaintances.

Styron soon felt comfortably a part of Brice's crowd. Besides himself and Snitger, the group included Bill Canine, Bob Loomis, Ellen Mordecai, the Lewis Learys, Sandy Limouze and his fiancée, and a young student from the university named Guy Davenport. Many of these people were academics or people who worked with Brice at Duke University Press, and most of them had connections with William Blackburn. Blackburn, however, rarely appeared at the gatherings: he and his wife had decided to divorce, and he had moved out of their house into separate quarters. Styron saw him at the West Campus of the university and sometimes had lunch with him downtown. Styron was no longer a student now, and Blackburn could be more open with him, unburdening himself sometimes of private frustrations and griefs.

Styron began working on his novel as soon as he had settled into his apartment. He had decided that he needed a new title—"Inheritance of Night" no longer suited him—but all he could think of was "The Death of Peyton Loftis." He had decided to scrap the opening interior monologue by Maudie Loftis and begin the novel with the passage he had patterned after *All the King's Men.* He set about revising and expanding the remaining pages of "Inheritance of Night," trying (with considerable success) to purge them of Faulkner's rhythms and vocabulary.

Early in September he contacted a literary agent in New York and asked her to handle his magazine work. Her name was Elizabeth McKee; she had been recommended to him by Dorothy Parker, his friend at Whittlesey House who had purchased the bubbleoon kit for him. McKee, then in the early years of her career, would eventually become quite successful in the New York literary marketplace, handling the work of Flannery O'Connor among others. In Styron's first letter to McKee, dated September 9, he mentions that he is working on a novel for Hiram Haydn at Crown. He notes that "only a small part" has been written. "I ain't no speedball," he admits. His plan, he tells her, is also to turn out some short stories, which he hopes she can place for him in paying magazines.

This was a sensible strategy for a young author in 1948. Many American magazines still published short fiction regularly, and it was possible for a beginning writer to make some money by appearing in the ·"slicks"—magazines of large circulation such as *The Saturday Evening Post, Collier's,* and *Redbook,* all of which were printed on slick, glossy paper. Styron knew, of course, that he hadn't the inclination or the knack for truly commercial writing, but he did hope that with McKee's help he might break into some respectable mid-circulation periodicals— *Harper's,* perhaps, or even *The New Yorker.* He enclosed a short story with his letter to McKee and told her a little about himself:

I'm twenty-three years old, and for some dreary and inexplicable reason I guess I'll keep at this writing business for a long time. Maybe it's because it's the only thing I know how to do with even a faint degree of competence. As you may see from the enclosed story, I don't try to write for the slicks. It's not pride, and Lord knows I could use the money. It's just that I don't think I know *how* to write a slick story. If you think it would be worth while for both you and me, however, I'd appreciate your trying to find a market for my work.

McKee wrote back, agreeing to take Styron on as a client and asking to see what he had written of the novel. In mid-October he sent her the revised material from "Inheritance of Night" along with a description of what the rest of the book would be like:

The story, in short, is nothing but that of a modern upper South middle-class family, and the daughter of the family, named Peyton Loftis. I've got no drum to beat, political or otherwise. I just want to give a picture of a way of life that I have known, and of the people therein. I probably have a moral purpose—the late Bliss Perry said that you *had* to have one—but it hasn't quite yet emerged. Anyway, Peyton, who is twenty-four and something of a bitch, has just died violently and I must say horribly in New York and is being returned to her home town for a hasty and unpublicized interment. What transpires on the one day of her burial is the burden of the novel. Gradually, through their memories, you get a picture of Peyton and, I hope, of the "way of life" of which I was speaking. If the story seems morbid it's because I'm probably morbid myself, although I've got some good ghastly humor later on.

Some of Styron's energy that fall went into playing the role of bohemian author. Brice hosted noisy, convivial suppers at his apartment; the usual fare was pressure-cooker spaghetti, washed down by martinis that Brice served in jelly glasses. Styron almost always attended, usually bringing along Mr. Chips, who had now arrived from New York and established himself in Styron's apartment. When introduced to new people as a "writer-in-training," Styron would often pull a long face and intone, semiseriously, "I have *annnngst!*" His personal habits became lax, and he would sometimes go for several days without bathing. He had read somewhere that a side effect of chlorophyll was to kill odor, so he acquired a supply of tiny green chlorophyll pills and carried them about in his trousers pocket. At Brice's parties, he would place seven or eight of these in his palm, toss them into his mouth, chew on them vigorously, and announce: "Ahh! The writer's bath!"

The conversation at Brice's was sometimes literary. Brice later recalled that members of the group that year were discussing Evelyn Waugh, Conrad, and the Russian novelists, and that no one liked Ezra Pound. Styron had recently finished Malcolm Lowry's *Under the Volcano* and was recommending it to everyone. Some members of the group read aloud from work in progress. Styron read the parts of his novel that most pleased him, and afterward everyone sat around and tried to come up with a title for the book.

In truth, Styron's writing was not going especially well, and this was causing him some problems with the Veterans Administration. He was still drawing twenty dollars a week from the VA, but in order to remain in good standing with the agency he had to report to a petty bureaucrat at the local VA office once a month and show that he was making progress in the writing game. This meant that Styron had to produce actual manuscripts and typescripts that this functionary could examine. The bureaucrat, Styron later remembered, was skeptical from the first of anyone's using VA money to become a writer and suspected that this particular ex-marine was simply a sponger on the dole. The situation was not helped by the fact that Styron had little manuscript material to show. A slow worker even in the most productive of periods, he could bring in only a small stack of new pages at the first two or three appointments. The bureaucrat seemed displeased: he carefully logged in the titles, page counts, and first and last sentences of Styron's manuscripts so that Styron would not be able to submit them again for credit in later months. Styron was worried until someone suggested that he go over to the Duke campus and plunder the filing cabinets of the *Archive*. There, blessedly, he found the typescripts of all of his undergraduate work—seven short stories, plus other odds and ends. These he could now bring with him, one or two at a time, when he went for his interviews at the VA. His productivity was thus increased, and the bureaucrat was mollified.

Styron was trying to write, but on most days he seemed to be spinning his wheels. Every afternoon he put a disk on his phonograph—often Bill Canine's record of Mozart's Piano Concerto no. 20. He then set up a wobbly card table and went to work, but often the sentences would not come. He was avoiding the novel for the moment, unsure of how to proceed with it, and was trying to write short stories instead. Most of these efforts he later destroyed, but one manuscript does survive—an eight-page narrative called "The Brothers." If it is typical of what he was writing during the fall of 1948, then one can see why he was frustrated: the story, about two redneck brothers from Mississippi named Leroy and Monroe, is essentially plotless and without discernible point. The two boys, flush with money from selling their father's cotton crop, are driving home to their backcountry farm from the cotton market in Memphis. The first few lines of the story are typical of the entire manuscript:

> The old slat-sided truck rolled south through the outskirts of Memphis, past the streets of old broken-down shanties along the river, and then out along the highway. It was late in the afternoon. Twilight was setting in smokily over the grey meadows and the brown stubble fields of picked cotton.
>
> Monroe held the wheel while Leroy tried to light a cigarette, but the wind blew in through the broken window and put out the match. Leroy cussed loudly.
>
> "Why in hell don't Paw fix that pane?"
>
> "Gimme a weed," Monroe demanded.
>
> Leroy lit the cigarette and snuffled contemptuously.
>
> "You're too young, son, you're too young."

The brothers stop at a roadhouse to drink beer and fall into the company of two women, one named Dorleen and the other without apparent name, though we learn that she has a harelip and talks "like the words were coming out of her nose." The narrator adds: "She was ugly as home-made sin, but she was built." Leroy and Monroe become thoroughly drunk and prepare to leave with the women, but Leroy, who is older and more experienced, senses that the two women are in cahoots with local rowdies who mean to rob them of their cotton money. Leroy comes to his senses and drags Monroe away from the girls. The two brothers drive off in their truck at the end of the story, and that is that. The narrative is so ineptly executed that one almost wonders whether Styron wrote it as a parody of some southern regionalist of the 1940s— Erskine Caldwell at his worst, perhaps. Magazine editors agreed: a cover sheet from Elizabeth McKee's agency shows that the manuscript was rejected by *The New Yorker, Harper's Bazaar, Esquire, Story,* and *The American Mercury.*

Styron tried to get back to his novel in November but found it difficult to make progress. "The novel is coming along at about its usual slow but steady turtle's pace," he wrote to his father. "It's a tedious and agonizing process and I loathe writing with almost a panic hatred, but as I've said before I'm always restless when I'm not working at it. If ever I become well-known because of my writing, it may honestly be said by whatever person that chooses to tell about me: 'he wrote in spite of himself.' " In another letter to his father, written a month later, he notes: "I write and write and it's amazing what I've written. And it's probably a commentary on my lack of discipline to note that the more I write the further the end of the book seems to be within sight."

Discouraged, Styron decided to go to New York City just after Christmas to see Haydn. He also wanted to talk with Elizabeth McKee, who was having no luck selling his stories, and see whether she might give him some advice about writing for the magazines. He made the trip and enjoyed himself, visiting with friends from the New School and going to several movies alone. He was bucked up by his conference with Haydn, who looked over the reworked material from "Inheritance of Night" and pronounced it much improved. Styron also broached the idea with Haydn of putting the novel aside for the time being and beginning a new project—a short story or perhaps a novella based on his experiences as a prison guard at Harts Island. Haydn liked the idea but urged Styron to stick with the novel for a little longer. He set a deadline of March 1: on that date Styron was to mail a substantial installment of new material to him in New York.

Back in Durham, Styron set himself doggedly to the task and managed, in January and February of 1949, to turn out approximately twenty pages of new writing. A little of this eventually made its way into *Lie Down in Darkness,* but most of it did not. There is a well-written five-page passage in which Styron traces the history of Port Warwick from coaling stop to shipbuilding center, but the material is so transparently expository and informative that it sticks out awkwardly from the surrounding narrative. There is also an attempt, after the manner of Carson McCullers, to develop the character of Dolly Bonner, Milton Loftis's mistress. Dolly, we learn, is a native of Port Warwick. Her father died when she was fourteen, leaving her and her mother in straitened circumstances. Her mother had to take in boarders in order to make ends meet, and Dolly married one of these people, "a fleshy, asthmatic man of about forty with soft hands and spectacles and a look of vague alarm." The boarder, whose name is Albert Brokenborough, is an early version of Pookie Bonner, Dolly's husband in the published version of *Lie Down in Darkness*. Albert has a lung ailment and has come to Port Warwick for the sea air. He misrepresents himself to Dolly as a person of independent financial means; he and Dolly have intercourse before marriage (both for the first time), but after the ceremony the union lapses into celibacy. Albert's lung trouble worsens and he becomes an invalid. Near the end he confesses to Dolly that "he had slept in the same bed with his mother until he was past thirty, first as a little child, to protect her from the bears, and then during his adolescence— after his father died—to ward off and keep her secure against thieves, and finally for no reason at all: out of habit he had crept into bed with the old woman until the night she died." Albert himself passes away about a year after marrying Dolly, and she is left alone.

Styron was displeased with this writing. At the bottom of the final page, he wrote several notes to Haydn about upcoming scenes:

> A paragraph or so on Dolly's second, more genteel marriage
> Her developing sophistication, another paragraph: the "common"
>   girl who makes good
> Meets Loftis at dance for Peyton at country club
> First glimpse of Peyton—abrupt, mutual jealousy
>   betw. P. + Dolly
> Portrait of Peyton
> Or am I too far gone? Would like to write a war novel:
>   These people give me the creeps.

A few days after mailing off this new material, Styron sat down and wrote a troubled letter to Haydn. The letter does not survive, but apparently it revealed some genuine angst. "That was quite a letter," Haydn replied. "I think I will keep it for posterity." He and Styron agreed that things might go better if Styron moved back north. Perhaps he should set aside his novel for a while and try to work on the prison novella. Haydn offered guidance: "I feel confident that between us we can map out a project that you can really go to town on," he wrote.

The period in Durham had been largely a bust. Styron had spent some time with William Blackburn, but his old teacher had been glum over his marital problems and more irritated than ever about the politics in the English department. There had been a few good evenings at Brice's apartment, and he had had some fun with two nurse trainees, who had helped keep his bed warm at night, but his writing had gone nowhere. The revision and expansion of the "Inheritance of Night" material had improved it, but most of the new writing, he sensed, would have to be junked. None of his short stories had sold, and he had no particular inclination to work further on them. To top things off, his landlady had complained about Mr. Chips, who was becoming neurotic, and Styron had had to give the dog away to a professor in the philosophy department at Duke. Perhaps, Styron wrote to his father, Chips would become "very profound and stoical about a dog's life," now that he had "Plato and Spinoza to sustain him" in his new home.

By mid-April, Styron had a line on a furnished fifth-story walk-up in an artsy neighborhood on the East Side. He had become friendly with Bob Loomis, who was editing the *Archive* that year and wanted to go to New York to make a start in publishing. Loomis was graduating in June and planned to come to New York after commencement. He agreed to share quarters with Styron in the city. "That will cut down substantially on the rent problem," Styron wrote to his father. "I'm pretty healthy now," he added, "drinking less beer and eating three square meals a day. Given the help of you and Hiram Haydn and God, I don't think I'll fail."

W hen Styron arrived in Manhattan in May, he found that the walk-up had been rented. He stayed in a cheap hotel for a night or two, then drifted over to the New School to see whether he might locate someone who would put him up until he could find somewhere to live. Almost the first person he ran into was Agnes de Lima, an attractive, capable woman, then in her early fifties, who was publicity director at the New School. Aggie de Lima had a daughter named Sigrid who was about the same age as Styron. Sigrid had been a student in Hiram Haydn's novel workshop with Styron; he and she had become friendly while he was living in the Lexington Avenue apartment. She was a writer of considerable promise, working then on a novel entitled *Captain's Beach*, which Scribner's would publish in 1950. Eventually she published four more novels. She was tall and slender, articulate and very gentle, and she liked Styron, as did her mother. When they heard his story, they offered him the sofa at their apartment on West Fourth Street, and he accepted.

A day or two later, Styron and Aggie de Lima sat down and went through the classified sections in the Manhattan newspapers, looking for rental rooms that he could afford. The postwar housing crunch was still on in the city, though, and there was almost nothing available in Styron's price range. He decided to check listings for the boroughs, where housing was cheaper, and found something that might do—a room and bath on the ground floor of a house located at 1506 Caton Avenue, in the Flatbush section of Brooklyn. Styron took the subway over and found the place. It was a big, rambling frame house, formerly a residence but now divided into small flats and individual rooms. The landlady was Jewish, friendly and loquacious, and the room and bath were spotless. Styron decided to take the room and left a down payment. He returned for one more night with Sigrid and her mother, then moved his gear into the Brooklyn room the next day.

The location on Caton Avenue, he found, was quite pleasant. He described the neighborhood in a letter to his father written a few days after he had moved in: "The house where I live directly overlooks Prospect Park, and often, if I imagine it hard enough, the place seems about as big-cityfied as High Point, North Carolina. The street is lined with sycamores and elms, the houses all have green lawns, and sometimes—along with the scent of mown grass and burning leaves—I seem not to have ever left Hilton Village. Especially the suburban sort of smells—grass, food cooking, smoke; these are so evocative of memory. At any rate, it's quite pleasant, if a bit far out from the City itself."

Styron's ground-floor room was comfortable, but it lacked privacy. It was separated from the adjacent flat by a set of double sliding doors that would not close fully, so that there was always a narrow gap through to the room next door. To make matters worse, the couple directly overhead was prone to engage in loud, gymnastic lovemaking at almost any hour of the day or night. They seemed wholly uninhibited and more than a little exhibitionistic: certainly they made no effort to muffle their grunts and cries, which were audible through the ceiling. Styron, who was attempting to write a short story based on some Christchurch material, found that he was apt to be interrupted during his writing hours by the sounds of enthusiastic copulation from above.

The distraction was maddening and impossible to ignore. Should he complain to the landlady? Should he bang on the ceiling and tell his fellow roomers to quiet down? Or should he simply abandon his writing desk for a walk around the park or a beer at a restaurant down the street?

This was a serious dilemma: Styron found himself so aroused by the sounds upstairs that it was impossible to concentrate on his writing. Sometimes the activities became so spirited that the furniture in his room shook and the light fixture on the ceiling rattled. Styron felt, though, that he could not complain too loudly because he was entertaining a female friend in his own bed from time to time—a young woman with whom he had been casually involved while living on Lexington Avenue during the winter and spring of 1947–48. Soon after returning to New York he had looked her up and rekindled their affair. His landlady in Flatbush was lenient about visitors of the opposite sex—an unusual policy during the late 1940s. Styron's friend could come over for visits and even spend the night if she was circumspect about it.

After a short while in his new quarters, Styron began to realize that he was living in a heavily Jewish section of Brooklyn. A majority of the roomers at 1506 Caton Avenue had recognizably Jewish names; most of the residents in the surrounding neighborhood had Semitic features; many of them spoke with East European accents. He saw men and boys wearing yarmulkes, and he had to ask what they were. Styron had encountered Jews before—there were a few Jewish families in Newport News, and a great many of the students at the New School had been Jewish—but he had never lived in a neighborhood that was predominantly Jewish. Actually he knew very little about Jews and was mostly ignorant of their religion and customs. The roomers and neighbors who were Jewish seemed to like him well enough and not to hold his southernness against him. That, at least, was a relief. (Many of his neighbors, he later came to realize, had learned English only recently and so did not recognize his accent as southern.) He found himself comfortable and essentially invisible among these Jews, and he enjoyed studying them in an idle way, listening to them speak, watching them at stores and restaurants, and observing them with their children.

Like many other American Gentiles, Styron was more than normally curious about European Jews during the summer of 1949. The horror of the Nazi concentration camps was now being fully exposed. The national press had downplayed the Holocaust during the war; the average American had not been aware of the Nazi final solution until the spring of 1945, when Allied troops had pushed across Germany and liberated the extermination camps at Majdanek, Treblinka, and Auschwitz-Birkenau. The enormity of the Holocaust—the extent of the cruelty and the sheer numbers of the dead—had by now been revealed. Styron knew a little about it: during his last year at Duke he had read a memoir by a survivor of Auschwitz named Olga Lengyel. The book, entitled *Five Chimneys,* had troubled and haunted him.

One morning Styron met a survivor of one of the death camps. She was a fellow roomer at 1506 Caton Avenue: he met her on the doorstep of the rooming house as he was going out for breakfast. She had blond hair and was quite handsome, with high cheekbones and a lovely voice. He talked with her briefly; her English was good, but she spoke it hesitantly and with an accent he could not identify. Her first name, he learned, was Sophie. She told him her last name, but it was a complicated mixture of consonants, and he forgot it. He noticed that she had a number tattooed on her wrist, but he did not yet ask about it. They chatted several more times over the next few days, and she went out with him once or twice on his walks around the neighborhood. During these walks he learned that she had acquired her tattoo at Auschwitz and that she was a survivor of the internment camp there, but that she was Catholic, not Jewish. The difficult last name and the accent were Polish; though she was not a Jew, she had been imprisoned by the Nazis all the same, as had thousands of other Polish Gentiles. After she had been set free from Auschwitz, she had recuperated in a hospital and had emigrated to the United States. She was now living with her cat in a single room upstairs at 1506 Caton Avenue; her boyfriend lived there too, in a single room next door to hers. Styron did a little discreet reconnoitering and discovered that it was Sophie who occupied the room above his and that she and her boyfriend were the noisy lovers. Styron saw the boyfriend from time to time on the stairs or on the walkway outside and nodded to him, but that was all. He seemed innocuous and undistinguished. Styron was intrigued by Sophie, however: she was a little older than he, perhaps in her late twenties, and seemed exotic and mysterious.

Had he lived in Brooklyn for a longer time, Styron might have come to know Sophie more fully and might have learned more about her past.

But his writing was going badly, and he sensed that he would make no progress on his novel in Flatbush. Money was beginning to be a problem as well. Bob Loomis was scheduled to share the room with him and had in fact been already contributing toward the rent, but Loomis had been delayed in coming north, and the rent was high—sixteen dollars a week. Styron's GI benefits would end in another few months, and the money from his windfall legacy was almost exhausted. He decided that he would probably have to take a job and save some money before he could return to his novel. He wrote his father that he had decided to look for "a handyman's job in some publishing house"—a temporary, fill-in position for someone on vacation. "I don't want to get a full-time job," he added, "but I've got to get something."

He took the subway into Manhattan one day to look for work and dropped in on Aggie and Sigrid de Lima. He told them about his difficulties, and they astonished him with an extraordinary offer: he could come and live rent-free, if he wished, in their country residence near Nyack, New York, just up the Hudson River from the city. Aggie de Lima owned a beautiful old stone house there in a village called Valley Cottage. During the week she stayed in New York at the apartment on Fourth Street, but she spent weekends and most vacations at Valley Cottage. Sigrid spent time there too, and she told him that it was an excellent place to work. There was a vegetable garden already planted there that needed weeding and a bedroom that he could have for his own. Was he interested?

Styron accepted. This offer unburdened him of much anxiety over his finances and promised him deliverance from the noisy lovers out in Flatbush. And a few days later he received a gift from his father, who had been alarmed by his son's plan to seek work. The elder Styron had sent a check for one hundred dollars, along with admonishments to keep working on the novel. He promised to stake his son at the rate of one hundred dollars a month until the novel was completed. This was a substantial sum of money in 1949. Styron's father seems to have supplied it freely and gladly, however, remembering the circumstances that had made it necessary for him to become an engineer and spend his working life in a profession that held no real interest for him.

Styron was relieved and grateful. With his father's money each month he could help out respectably with groceries at Valley Cottage and still have pocket money for beer and cigarettes. He returned to Brooklyn, gave notice for the end of the week, and endured one or two more bouts of loud lovemaking by his amorous neighbors upstairs. Then, on a weekend in late June, he gathered his manuscripts and other belongings and departed for Valley Cottage.

13

Valley Cottage and West Eighty-eighth Street

S TYRON KNEW that he must not waste the chance that the de Limas were giving him. He had been marking time for too long on his novel; it had been almost twenty months since he had left McGraw-Hill, and he had produced only a few pages of usable manuscript. "It just wouldn't come," he later remembered. "I realized that something was going on in my unconscious that was valuable, but the book was not getting together, and I was rather unhappy." He could identify his troubles in a general way—they had to do with structure and narrative voice—but only after he had moved to the de Limas' house in Valley Cottage was he able to face his problems squarely and solve them. "I had to sit down and consider, very painfully and clearly, an architecture," he recalled. "And I did."

To some extent the solution involved distancing himself yet further from William Faulkner's work. From the beginning, in the earliest drafts of "Inheritance of Night," Styron had conceived of his novel as multivoiced, but he could not decide how to let these voices speak. Should some of his characters be allowed to address the reader directly, as Faulkner's characters had done in *As I Lay Dying*? Or should there be a traditional omniscient voice, a narrative persona with access to the minds of all of the characters? If so, then how would Styron present his own ideas? Should a character speak with his voice, or should an all-knowing narrator represent him? There were things that *he* wanted to say, but the character Marcus Bonner, weak and indecisive, was not a satisfactory alter ego. And what of Peyton: should she be heard? If so, at what point in the novel should she speak?

Styron's solution was to drop Marcus Bonner as a character altogether and create for himself a transparently omniscient authorial voice. This strategy, in the end, would have much to do with making *Lie Down in Darkness* the profoundly disturbing novel that it is—a story in which many voices alternate, mingle, and compete with one another for attention. There is a central narrative persona, an apparently objective voice that speaks from the first lines of the book. Very little of the story, however, is told neutrally, through the consciousness of this persona. The bulk of the narrative comes instead through the minds of major characters—Milton Loftis, Helen Loftis, Dolly Bonner, and Carey Carr. The viewpoint alternates among these characters, and a few others, and the reader's sympathies shift as the perspective changes. The narrative takes on color and bias from each consciousness, and because most of these characters are obsessive and unforgiving, the coloration is strong.

One finds oneself on an old domestic battleground, listening to combatants who have had many years to work up their arguments and self-justifications. Their voices are alternately plaintive and argumentative, defensive and accusatory. Styron's uncanny ability to listen to these voices and to reproduce their moralizing and defensiveness makes the experience of reading *Lie Down in Darkness* quite unsettling. One's sympathies change section by section and even page by page as one hears Milton's side of the story, then Helen's, then Dolly's—and as the voice of the Episcopal priest, Carey Carr, is heard from its peculiar perspective. The central narrative voice is almost never didactic: instead it is chameleon-like, taking its coloration from the character who has the floor.

The technique is entirely appropriate for a novel about guilt and the failure to forgive. On this particular day, while the hearse bearing Peyton's body makes its slow progress from the railroad station to the graveyard, it is natural for the minds of the stunned survivors to range back and forth across the past in search of motives, explanations, and excuses. Styron decided that Peyton's voice would be withheld until very nearly the end of the novel. Then she would be given a long section of interior monologue showing her intelligence and sensitivity and reveal-

ing the damage done to her by her father's fawning and her mother's hatred. The reader would follow her tortured thoughts up until the moment of her suicidal leap. The novel would end with a coda, narrated by
the authorial voice.

As Styron worked he created a center of morality in his novel, a perspective that is never truly identified but that is constantly present beneath the narrative. This perspective is not exactly Peyton's: for most
of the narrative she is a shadowy character, beautiful and charming,
but, for all the reader can tell, vacuous and materialistic. The perspective is instead Styron's own. He is present throughout, listening and
judging, holding up Milton and Helen Loftis and the society in which
they live for examination and judgment. The implied perspective is
that of a talented youth in need of love and discipline but lost to the
self-centeredness of adults and the meretriciousness of their world.
This perspective is the author's: he is Peyton's advocate and chief
mourner in the novel. In a larger sense the perspective is that of Styron's generation—confused, neglected, and more hopelessly lost than
the postwar generation of the 1920s had ever been with its public self-
indulgence and stagy disillusionment.

In developing this architecture and narrative method, Styron did not
entirely abandon his models. There is still much of William Faulkner in
the novel and not a little of James Joyce. The progress of the funeral
cortege across Port Warwick from the train terminal to the graveyard is
reminiscent of the trek of the Bundren family, in *As I Lay Dying,* from
their farm in the Mississippi backcountry to the cemetery in Jefferson
where they bury Addie. The time scheme of the book (a single day, with
flashbacks to the past) calls to mind both *Ulysses* and *The Sound and
the Fury,* and perhaps *Under the Volcano* as well. Styron's decision to
cast Peyton as the central female figure around whom the thoughts of
the other characters revolve is similar to Faulkner's decision to center
The Sound and the Fury on Caddy Compson and *As I Lay Dying* on
Addie Bundren. Like Addie, Peyton will speak from the grave, but in a
lengthy passage of interior monologue that is most immediately suggestive of Molly Bloom's stream-of-consciousness monologue at the
end of *Ulysses.*

There is even more in *Lie Down in Darkness* that is suggestive of *The
Sound and the Fury.* Helen Loftis is as neurotic and destructive as Car-
oline Bascomb Compson; she functions as a cold, negative weight that

burdens and finally destroys the Loftis family. Milton Loftis, like the elder Jason Compson, drinks more than he should and, like Quentin Compson, is bothered by quasi-incestuous longings. But there are many differences as well: Mrs. Compson is a more passive villainess than is Helen Loftis, and Mr. Compson is stronger and more dignified than Milton. Faulkner's Reverend Shegog, in Dilsey's section of *The Sound and the Fury,* brings comfort and strength to his black congregation; Styron's Daddy Faith is essentially a charlatan. Faulkner's Dilsey is a magnificently complex character, while Ella Swan, in *Lie Down in Darkness,* is flat and lacks definition. Jefferson, Mississippi, is a closely knit town of the Old South; Port Warwick, Virginia, is a sprawling commercial city in the New South, without internal cohesion or identity. For all its pessimism, *The Sound and the Fury* exhibits some sense of order and some hope for redemption at the end. *Lie Down in Darkness* holds out no such hope: it is bleak and finally almost nihilistic. Styron was attempting to go beyond Faulkner and to present his own ideas and his own dark and very different vision.

Styron was following one other model—Thomas Wolfe—in writing a novel based on the private lives of some of the people in his hometown. The central situation in *Lie Down in Darkness* was based on a marriage in Newport News between a prominent local businessman and a woman from a well-to-do family. This man, dark-haired and handsome, was a snappy dresser who was aware of his good looks and had an eye for other women. In a superficial way he was the model for Milton Loftis. His wife, on the other hand, was in no way the model for Helen Loftis. This wife was an active, energetic society woman who doted on her children and supervised their behavior and education closely. During Styron's adolescence and his teenage years in Newport News, it was generally known that this marriage was unhappy. House servants reported that the couple never spoke to each other at home; they exchanged a few words at entertainments and public occasions, but that was all. The main issue was apparently infidelity: the man was involved in a visible affair with a woman who worked with him. This woman served as an approximate model for Dolly Bonner in the published version of *Lie Down in Darkness,* but Dolly, weak and dependent, does not very much resemble the original, who was strong-minded and independent, just as Milton and Helen Loftis do not actually have much in common with the businessman and his wife.

For Milton Loftis's personality, Styron drew more heavily on what he knew of a handful of other men, all of whom had problems in their marriages and most of whom drank. Some of what he knew of marital discord came from observing his own father, who was not entirely happy in his marriage to Elizabeth Buxton. Other models for marital strife were William Blackburn and his first wife, Tris, and Hiram Haydn and his second wife, Mary. One of the strengths of *Lie Down in Darkness* is the accuracy with which Milton Loftis's alcoholism is anatomized. Here Styron could draw on his observations of several men, among them Blackburn and Haydn—though these two held their liquor more successfully than did Milton. Some of the details and much of the psychology of Milton Loftis as an alcoholic can also be traced to Styron's reading of *Under the Volcano* and to the harrowing portrait in that book of the alcoholic diplomat Geoffrey Firmin.

Helen Loftis was based on Elizabeth Buxton. Helen's neurotic self-righteousness, her anger, her religiosity, her inability to forgive, her intolerance for weakness, and her failure to understand the workings of human love were all taken from the personality of Elizabeth Buxton, as Styron assessed it. Helen Loftis is a brilliant characterization, a classic study in evil and self-destructiveness; she is also, more privately, William Styron's portrait of the stepmother who he believed had driven him from home and taken his father from him.

The models for Peyton Loftis's character are multiple and complex. Her name, as we have seen, was taken from Tom Peyton's cousin, Peyton Vorhees. Her life, however, was based on the life of a good-looking young woman from Newport News who had displeased her parents by going to Greenwich Village to study art and drama, and by marrying a Jewish man there. For Peyton's behavior and manner, Styron also drew on this woman's younger sister, a daring and rebellious girl whom Styron had dated once or twice during his prep-school years. He had been frustrated over her lack of interest in him and her rejection of his advances.

Neither of these sisters, though, was a tragic figure. Certainly neither was suicidal; both seemed psychologically stable. For this element of Peyton Loftis's personality, Styron drew on what he knew about a young woman from Hilton Village whose life was taking a genuinely tragic course, even while he was writing his novel. This young woman—whom we shall call Anna—had lovely brownish-auburn curls and sparkling blue eyes. Styron had been enamored of her, hopelessly, when he was fifteen. Anna was over a year younger than he, but she was so much in demand at parties that he could not bring himself to approach her. He watched from a distance as she danced and talked with other boys. Anna was popular, he knew, but she was also rumored to be unhappy. She was a product of a "mixed marriage," which in those years meant that one parent was Catholic and the other Protestant. There were religious difficulties in the marriage, and, more seriously, severe mental problems with Anna's mother, who had been hospitalized several times at the state sanitarium. Anna's father operated a prosperous business in Newport News, and Anna had pretty clothes and other advantages, but her mother was said to put severe pressure on her to excel. Styron knew from his friends that the mother was irrationally suspicious of her daughter and accused her of bad behavior with the boys she dated.

Anna's parents had divorced a year or two earlier, and her father had remarried. During the war Anna had married a young naval officer. She had given birth to a baby while her husband was in the Pacific, and she was living with her father and her stepmother in a house in Newport News. Anna was suffering terribly from postpartum depression, and her baby was going through a prolonged siege of colic. The child screamed constantly. Anna begged her father to take the baby from her, but he would not. One afternoon Anna took the baby into the bathroom and locked the door. She filled the bathtub with water and tried to drown her child in it. Anna's father, hearing the running water and the baby's gurgling cries, broke down the door to the bathroom and rescued the child. Anna was committed the next day to Eastern State Sanitarium in Williamsburg, the same institution at which her mother had been confined.

William Styron knew most of this story at second hand, from friends back home and from his father. Anna stayed in Eastern State for well over a year; her husband divorced her during this period, and their child was legally taken from her to be raised by his family. During much of the time that Styron was writing *Lie Down in Darkness,* Anna was under observation and treatment at Eastern State. He knew that she was there and seems to have understood something of her plight. She, like him, had endured great sadness and turmoil in her young life, and his heart went out to her. Much of the psychological imbalance in Peyton

Loftis's character can probably be traced to what Styron knew or intuited of Anna's tragic history, a story that still had one final chapter to be played out.

Once he had moved into the de Limas' house and had decided on a narrative strategy and voice for his novel, Styron found that the actual writing went smoothly. The tone of his letters to his father changed almost immediately: instead of self-doubt and frustration one senses confidence and certainty of purpose. Much of the literary language disappears as well from the letters. "I'm hard at work," he wrote to his father in late July 1949, "and now that I've established a 'plan of attack,' as it were, it promises to go awfully well. Writing itself, as usual, is very difficult—except for those rare fine moments when it all begins to *pour*—but, inching along, I can manage now and then to see how the whole thing *will* end, and in a point of time, I hope, not too far away."

From the window of his room he could see the foothills of the Ramapo Mountains, covered with an "ocean of trees . . . wonderfully green." He reported that the de Limas had "a gorgeous radio-phonograph full of Mozart and Beethoven," and that he could listen to full-length opera performances on WABF, a New York FM station. The situation, he told his father, seemed almost sinfully comfortable:

> I've begun to wonder what I've done to deserve this nice way of life. I feel really *healthy* for a change—physically and mentally. I've become confident of my powers, and I'm ready to put my whole heart into the accomplishment of writing at least good fiction and, I hope, someday great fiction. Is that hoping too much?

He followed a writing regimen that would be typical of him for many years to come. Everything in the day was calculated either to prepare him for his stint at the worktable or to reward him for putting in that stint. The writing was central: all else was subordinate. He rose in the late morning and had lunch around one o'clock. He then tended the vegetable garden or ran errands or took a long walk—alone usually, though sometimes with Sigrid. At four o'clock or so, he began to compose and normally put in a period of between four and five hours at his table. He was using a large old adjustable tilting desk that had once belonged to the radical journalist Randolph Bourne, who had been a friend of Aggie de Lima's during the thirties. Styron wrote in his bedroom; Sigrid was usually working on her own novel at the same time, elsewhere in the house.

In the late evenings they cooked together: often Styron prepared fried chicken, his specialty, about which he had fixed ideas (fresh young broiler parts, coated with seasoned flour, not batter, and fried slowly in an uncovered pan in bacon fat, not oil, with frequent turning of the pieces). He allowed himself to drink only after the day's writing was finished, and he limited himself to beer—quart bottles of Shaeffer, procured from a local distributor. The food and beer were plentiful, and he found his weight edging up. After supper he and Sigrid played word games or chess or listened to music. Sometimes they discussed their novels and read to each other from their manuscripts. Styron usually stayed up late, often until one or two o'clock in the morning, reading, smoking, and listening to the phonograph.

He and Sigrid were good friends. There was only a little romance involved: chiefly they seem to have felt affection and respect for each other and to have been quite companionable. The weeks went by smoothly through the fall and into the winter. Aggie de Lima came out from the city on weekends, and there were visits from both his father and William Blackburn. When it snowed later that winter, he and Sigrid went on treks through the woods and once or twice went sledding. Occasionally there were expeditions to New York: "Sigrid and I were down in the city last Saturday night to Hiram Haydn's house, a sort of soirée," he wrote to his father. "Haydn's still waiting, apparently anxiously, for the next installment. Also at the party were Aldous Huxley's son and Clifton Fadiman's nephew. Celebrities."

The pile of manuscript for his novel continued to grow; by mid-November 1949 Styron had written around fifty thousand words, and by December 12 he estimated that he had completed at least one half of the novel. He began to hope that he could finish by the summer of 1950. "For private and gratuitous reasons," he wrote to his father, "I'd like to complete it before my twenty-fifth birthday. However, I'm not going to strain myself in that direction." He could see clearly where his narrative was taking him, and he had the scenes roughly blocked out in his mind for the rest of the book. The characters were very much alive in his imagination, and the writing went ahead steadily, though almost as slowly as ever. "I've learned to write with greater ease and poise and rhythm than I did when I started out," he reported in another letter home. "The book has a lot of flaws," he added, "but I think a lot of very good things, too, and nothing whatsoever that I can be actually ashamed of." His most irritating problem was that he could not think of a good title. For the time being he was still using "The Death of Peyton Loftis." He wrote down a few alternate possibilities on a sheet of notes that he kept with the manuscript, but none of them seemed satisfactory: "I Die at Dawning," "How Brief Is My Time," "Brief Beauty, Brief Time," "Sleep, Brief Beauty."

In February, Sigrid published her novel *Captain's Beach,* and Scribner's gave a cocktail party in her honor. Styron sent this account to his father:

> The cocktail party was very successful and gay. About 150 people were there, including such stellar characters as William Rose Benét, John Hall Wheelock, Ridgely Torrence, Jean Starr Untermeyer, Freda Kirchwey (editor of *The Nation*), Horace Kallen, Alvin Johnson (president emeritus of the New School), and a horde of lesser luminaries. Afterwards Haydn and his wife and Sigrid and I and another couple all went to a very chi-chi bistro on Waverley Place named Ricky's and had lamb chops and brandy, and proceeded homeward in quite a glow. As a sad sort of postscript, a friend of ours drove all the way down from Boston to the party—*the next day.*

Styron's reading that winter and spring was eclectic: a new translation of *Don Quixote,* Sinclair Lewis's *Babbitt,* Sandburg's *Lincoln: The War Years,* and Dreiser's *An American Tragedy*—which he pronounced "the 'G.A.N.,' if any novel is." Most of his energy went into composing his manuscript. By mid-May 1950 he estimated that he was "well along into what I guess is the backstretch of the novel," writing the section in which Milton becomes drunk in Charlottesville, at a fraternity party, while Maudie lies near death in the hospital at the University of Virginia medical school. He could now see the end of the novel and seems to have felt that it was a good time to pause and take stock.

The situation at the de Limas' house, though comfortable, was beginning to weigh heavily on him. He felt indebted to Sigrid and her mother and knew that there was no way he could ever repay them. Marriage to Sigrid was not a possibility: they were friendly and affectionate, but there was no spark of love between them. Styron knew that it was time for him to move along, to disengage himself and return to the city, where he could finish the final chapters of his novel. He had in fact begun to miss the noise and friction of life in New York and felt that he needed a change.

On a bulletin board at the New School, he spotted a hand-lettered advertisement seeking a roommate to share a one-and-a-half-room apartment at 314 West Eighty-eighth Street, between Riverside Drive and West End Avenue. He went to the address and met the man who had pinned up the ad—a Jewish painter and sculptor named Howard Hoffman, who was taking classes at the New School. The lodgings looked comfortable enough, and the price was right—$8.25 per week. Styron agreed to move into the apartment on the first day of June 1950. He stayed out in Valley Cottage long enough to put in a garden for Sigrid and her mother and promised to return during the summer to weed the corn and pick the tomatoes. Then he moved to the city and settled into his new quarters. "I think I'm all set up until I finish the novel," he reported to his father, "at which time I intend to move to Sussex County, Va., and raise peanuts, with writing as an avocation."

In early July he learned that Haydn had left Crown to become editor in chief of the trade list at Bobbs-Merrill in Indianapolis. This was an odd professional move: Bobbs-Merrill was known mostly as a Midwest lawbook and textbook firm and had never made much of a showing in fiction and belles lettres. But the president of the firm, David Laurance Chambers, had decided to enter trade publishing vigorously, and Bobbs-Merrill had made a good offer to Haydn. He was to have much influence on shaping the list, he thought, and he could exercise the contacts he had built up while editing *The American Scholar.* Most attractive, from Haydn's point of view, was the fact that he could continue to live in the East and communicate with the parent company in Indianapolis via telephone and the mails.

Styron had a contract at Crown, but he felt so closely bound to Haydn that he decided to follow him to Bobbs-Merrill. The move was not as easy as he had anticipated, but with coaching from Haydn and from Mavis McIntosh—the literary agent who was in partnership with Elizabeth McKee—Styron managed to secure a release from Crown. By late July he had signed with Bobbs-Merrill: they had paid back his $250 advance from Crown and had given him an additional $250, with $500 more due on delivery of the finished manuscript.

Howard Hoffman, his new roommate, proved to be an estimable fellow, and he and Styron struck up a good friendship. Together they did battle against cockroaches and schemed against the landlady, who was cranky. They shared the cooking chores and food bills: once they thought that they had struck a bonanza when they discovered in a package of frozen green beans the equally frozen corpse of a caterpillar. Styron spent one evening composing an outraged letter to the packaging company, with hints of possible legal action. He and Hoffman were sure that the letter would yield a substantial offer of money if they would agree to waive their complaint, but all that came back in the mail were coupons for two more packages of green beans.

Styron and Hoffman made evening jaunts to the Village; they usually wore T-shirts and dungarees and once disrupted a party by shooting at the guests with water pistols. Parties in the Village were mixed gatherings: there were painters from India and sculptors from Mexico, novelists from the Midwest and playwrights from the Bronx, African American dancers and British poets, young women from Hunter and Sarah Lawrence, professors from Columbia and NYU. Often Styron and Hoffman went to the San Remo Bar together in the Village and talked to the odd characters there, including a scrawny little man named Joe Gould, a kind of professional bohemian-cum-panhandler, who claimed to be writing a massive manuscript entitled "An Oral History of Our Time." Styron and Hoffman bought him beers, and he entertained them with bizarre stories told to him by the vagrants who passed through the Village and slept in the park there.

Howard Hoffman was a veteran who had seen much action in the war. He had joined the army just out of high school and had become a mortarman. His infantry unit had landed at Cassino in 1944 and had fought its way to Rome. Later Hoffman had been in the Allied assault on southern France. In all he had endured almost three hundred days of combat. He and Styron talked only a little of their military experiences, but Hoffman learned that Styron had hated life in the Marine Corps and now dreaded the possibility of being recalled for the Korean Conflict, which was beginning to escalate.

Styron talked to Hoffman occasionally about the novel in progress, but for a long time Hoffman read none of the drafts and had no idea whether Styron had any particular promise as a writer. For all he knew, Styron was only another would-be novelist of large ambition and small talent. One afternoon, though—probably after Styron had decided that he liked Hoffman and could trust him—he read a passage aloud to him from his manuscript. It was a description of Abraham Lincoln visiting Richmond shortly after the surrender at Appomattox—an eerie, sorrowful passage, beautifully measured and phrased. Hoffman realized then that Styron had genuine talent and that the novel, when finished, would likely be a good one. He said these things to Styron, and thereafter, from time to time, Styron would read other passages aloud in the evenings. He also talked about his characters—about Peyton and Daddy Faith especially. One afternoon he showed Hoffman some notes and other materials he had been collecting about Nat Turner; he meant someday to write a novel about the rebel slave, he said.

In the mornings, to pick up extra money, Hoffman worked in a children's day-care center. That left his afternoons free, and he was often in the apartment, painting or sculpting, while Styron was putting in his daily stint of composition. Hoffman observed Styron's writing habits and could recall them clearly forty years later. Styron worked always on long yellow legal pads and wrote with no. 2 black-lead pencils. He wrote a line or two, then paced about the apartment for a time. Occasionally he stopped and chatted briefly with Hoffman before returning to the writing table and writing another few lines. "I never saw him erase a line or change a word," Hoffman recalled. The surviving holograph of *Lie Down in Darkness* shows that Hoffman's impression is not literally correct, but the manuscript is remarkable all the same for its very few revisions and erasures. (This habit of slow, painstaking composition, followed by only a little revision, has remained constant throughout Styron's career.) Usually Styron played music on a small phonograph while he wrote—Vivaldi, Bach, Beethoven, Brahms, and endlessly, it seemed, Handel's *Messiah*. Hoffman heard the line "We like sheep have gone astray" so frequently that it became mixed up in his mind with an advertising jingle for mozzarella cheese.

Styron kept in touch with the de Limas through the summer and fall of 1950, writing newsy, affectionate letters to Sigrid and visiting sometimes at the Valley Cottage house on the weekends. He had a new romantic interest—Wanda Malinowska Montemora, a divorced former fashion model who was living in an apartment on Sixth Avenue, near MacDougal Street. Wanda was the daughter of the pioneering anthropologist Bronislaw Malinowski, a Polish exile, and Elise Masson, an

Australian. Malinowski was famous for his work with primitive tribes in New Guinea, Melanesia, East Africa, and Mexico. Wanda had been born in France and educated in Europe, and she spoke English with an upper-class London accent, acquired during several years in the city as a teenager.

Wanda's childhood had been unhappy in ways that were familiar to Styron: her mother had died when she was thirteen, after a long and painful battle with multiple sclerosis, and her father had remarried soon after. Wanda and her stepmother had been at serious odds, and Wanda had been shunted off to boarding school. In her late teens she had begun to work as a fashion model in New York, first for Harry Conover and later for the Ford Agency. Her professional name was Wanda Delafield, but she disliked it because her agent had culled it from the New York social register as a substitute for the ethnic-sounding Malinowska. In her private life she always pronounced her first name Vonda, as it would have been pronounced in Poland, and she tried to model under her real last name but was not allowed to. She was versatile: layouts in issues of *Vogue* and *Vanity Fair* from the 1940s show that she could be photographed with equal success either as an all-American girl, in casual, sporty clothes, or as a sophisticated woman with a European air, modeling haute-couture gowns and jewelry. Wanda had eventually wearied of modeling and had married a handsome Italian named Vincent (Nicky) Montemora. She had given birth to three children in quick succession, but the marriage had failed. Now Wanda was on her own with one child; the other two were staying for the time being with their father, who had remarried.

Wanda met William Styron at a party in the Village given by her sister, who was friendly with Hiram Haydn and his wife. The Haydns had brought Styron along that afternoon, and he and Wanda met in the garden behind her sister's house. They began to see each other regularly and after a time became lovers. They went to movies and parties or took walks together; he sometimes slept over at her apartment, though when he did he was often awakened at an unconscionably early hour by Wanda's youngest child, who was sometimes visiting there. Occasionally he worked on his novel on her kitchen table. The relationship was casual but satisfying for them both. They did not expect it to become permanent, and they never talked of marriage. They had only one serious quarrel during the time they knew each other: Wanda became so angry that she threw an empty teapot at Styron, but it missed him, and they both immediately began laughing. (Neither could remember in later years what the argument was about.) The affair lasted only through the spring of 1951, when Styron finished his novel, but the friendship continued into the 1950s. Styron remembered Wanda Malinowska as beautiful, sensitive, intelligent, and uninhibited: years later he would incorporate many things about her into the character of Sophie Zawistowska in *Sophie's Choice.*

By December of 1950 Styron was closing in on the end of his novel. He was writing every afternoon now and sometimes in the evenings as well. His urgency was caused by the escalation of the Korean War during the final months of 1950 and by his fear that he would be recalled for active duty. "I almost faint with fright every time I see a brown envelope in the mailbox," he wrote to Bill Canine, a friend from the West Durham Literary Society. Styron had been fully discharged from the Marine Corps in December 1945, but in April 1947, just before taking his degree from Duke, he had decided to reenlist in the reserves. The plan that persuaded him to reenter did not require him to wear a uniform or attend weekend meetings, features that he liked. Its only real advantage, though, was that if he was recalled he would automatically go in as an officer. In the spring of 1947 this had somehow seemed important; three years later Styron knew that he had made a boneheaded decision by entering the reserves. A great many men were being called up for active duty in Korea, and Styron suspected that he was about to be tapped. His nervousness shows in a letter to his father, written that December: "I don't know what's going to happen, and I try—in order to keep my wits about me—not to think about it, and proceed about my work in an orderly fashion. The Marines . . . will probably not make me join up for a while yet—unless there's a real war—because reserve officers are called up by serial number, and my number is a relatively low one. So that's some temporary consolation, at least."

Styron tried to increase his speed of composition. He had been giving the novel to Hiram Haydn piecemeal as he finished it; Haydn praised these sections, but Styron still found the going difficult. He tried to describe his state of mind in the same letter to Bill Canine: "So close to the end of the book, I have a feeling that it will never be completed.

It's not any sense of doom, especially, but merely the feeling that, after having spent such a painfully long time on it, I will be totally unable to accept the fact that it's all over and done with."

Styron was close to finishing the manuscript when the bottom dropped out. In late January he was contacted by the Marine Corps and ordered to report to Camp Lejeune by March 3. "It was a great shock to me," he wrote to his father, "and I've been walking around like a zombie for the past few days." He went to the Brooklyn Navy Yard for his physical, hoping that his bad vision would disqualify him. He went out of his way to point out the cataract in his right eye to the physician in charge, and the eye itself tested 20/70 on the vision examination, but the physician laughed and told him that he could get through the war with no trouble. A bum eye wouldn't be too bad a thing in Korea, he said. "I could have strolled in there with no arms and a case of leukemia and they still would have taken me," Styron wrote to Canine.

Styron now asked Haydn for help, and Haydn responded. Through a friend in publishing, he contacted a high-ranking officer in the Pentagon and by March had secured a deferment for Styron until early May. Styron now set to work to finish the last part of his book. He wrote the final one hundred pages of the manuscript in a single, sustained drive: most of this effort went into Peyton Loftis's interior monologue, which he composed in an extended, feverish two-week stint. Styron lost fifteen pounds during this final push and was drained, physically and psychologically, at the end.

He had the last pages of the manuscript typed and took the train out to Haydn's house in Westport, Connecticut, to deliver them and to go over some proposed revisions. Styron had finally settled on a title: "Lie Down in Darkness," taken from Sir Thomas Browne's "Urn Burial," a piece of writing from which William Blackburn had sometimes read aloud to his classes at Duke. As a final gesture of thanks, almost the only one he could make, Styron added a dedication page; it read: "For Sigrid." He and Haydn agreed on the revisions—for the time being these involved only some stylistic polishing—and Styron left the final section of the manuscript in his editor's hands. He had expected to feel elated, but he did not; instead he felt drained and depressed.

He took the train back to the city, and, at Grand Central Station, transferred to the subway uptown. At Fiftieth Street, almost forty blocks short of his stop, he became so upset that he left the subway car. He found that he could not complete the journey alone. He called Howard Hoffman on a pay telephone and asked for help. Hoffman took a cab to the subway station and located Styron: years later Hoffman could recall his shock at Styron's condition. He had never seen this side of his roommate's personality. Throughout their months together, Styron had seemed focused, methodical, and stable. The difficulty of disengaging himself from the manuscript, however, coupled with the knowledge that he was headed into another war, had brought Styron to his knees. Hoffman got him home and put him to bed. Over the next few days Styron reassembled himself. His father had shipped his old officer's uniforms to him, and he found that they still fit, more or less. All that remained was to say good-bye to Wanda and a few friends.

One of these was Elizabeth McKee, his literary agent. On April 20 Styron met with her for farewell drinks at the bar of the Sherry-Netherland. McKee tried to discuss some writing that Styron might do during his military service, but he seemed distracted and could talk only of the war in Korea. He downed several drinks and became a little woozy, then said good-bye to McKee, left the bar, and passed through the front door of the hotel onto Fifth Avenue. Styron tried to cross to the west side of the street but found his way blocked by the police, who had set up barriers for a parade. That day, April 20, had been declared Douglas MacArthur Day in New York City. MacArthur had been relieved of his command in Korea by Harry Truman nine days earlier, and there had been a widespread outpouring of bellicose public sentiment in his behalf—a feeling that Styron certainly did not share. MacArthur had criticized Truman before a joint session of Congress on the nineteenth, during which he had advocated the invasion of Communist China and further escalation of the war. Now he was being honored with a huge parade in New York. Styron's eye was caught by a front-page banner headline, in red ink, on copies of the New York *Journal-American* that people in the crowd were carrying. "God Bless Gen. MacArthur!" it read. Over seven million people had turned out to cheer MacArthur, and more than 2,800 tons of ticker tape had been showered over the parade route. As Styron stood on the sidewalk, the motorcade began to pass. Many years later, in a work of fiction, Styron described the brief glimpse he had of MacArthur, who was riding in an open limousine:

Flanked by shoals of motorcycle outriders, the ornate headpiece half an inch atilt as he saluted the mob with his corncob pipe, he fleetingly grimaced, gazing straight at me, and behind the raspberry-tinted sunglasses his eyes appeared as glassily opaque and mysterious as those of an old, sated lion pensively digesting a wildebeest or, more exactly, like those of a man whose thoughts had turned inward upon some Caesarean dream magnificent beyond compare. His glory worked like acid on my own sense of vulnerability. I was gripped by a feeling of doom and lonesomeness, and I think I stifled the urge to clout somebody when I heard a nearby voice say: "Hang that bastard Harry Truman!"

These were the images and sounds that Styron held in his mind as, later that day, he boarded a train in Penn Station and headed south to spend a few days with his father before reporting to Camp Lejeune.

14

Marines, Second Stint

S TYRON REPORTED to Camp LeJeune early in May 1951. He was assigned a room in the Bachelor Officers' Quarters (the BOQ) along with many of the other reservists. Most of them, he quickly learned, were as bitter as he about their forced reentry into the service. They had begun families and careers and businesses in the years just after World War II; now they were being uprooted and taken away, often at great personal and financial loss, to fight in a new war that most of them did not understand or believe in.

Lejeune had changed little since Styron's stay there in 1945. There were the same broad asphalt streets, the same anonymous brick barracks, and the same administration buildings topped with fake cupolas. The BOQ was bland and functional-looking, though it did have a commodious bar where Styron and the other reservists could go after hours to drink. Most of them stayed away from the officers' club, patronized by the regular officers and their wives. There was little fraternization between the regulars and the reservists. They were not actively hostile to one another, but there was wariness and restraint on both sides.

Camp Lejeune was already mercilessly hot and muggy in May. It sat adjacent to a North Carolina swamp filled with cypress, scrub oak, and longleaf pine. Ticks and chiggers were there in abundance, and the sluggish, muddy streams were filled with frogs and water moccasins. Training was made difficult by the temperatures; men often had to be carried to the infirmary to be treated for dehydration and heatstroke.

Styron and the other reservists began a two-part training regimen. In the mornings they went to Staff Command School and listened to lectures on communications or amphibious tactics or new weaponry. Often these talks were followed by training films, which Styron and his compatriots dozed through. In the afternoons they tackled field problems outdoors in the swamps, mounting mock assaults or relearning forgotten map-reading and troop-deployment skills. Styron found that he recalled almost nothing from his earlier stint in the Marine Corps, and he felt inept and out of place. In a letter to his Christchurch friend Tom Peyton, he wrote: "I've forgotten how to salute, to take a BAR apart, or even how to lick the anus of a brigadier-general."

The most obvious sign of Styron's passage from civilian to military life was the shift in language. He had spent the years since 1945 in college or around literary people, and he had just finished sweating out a novel that relied heavily on diction and style. Now he found himself trying to readjust to Marine Corps usages and crudities, hearing terms that he had not encountered since Quantico. Floors were decks, walls were bulkheads, and the bathroom was the head. The men were never called soldiers; they were marines. One o'clock in the afternoon was thirteen hundred hours, and dinnertime was chow. Candy was pogey bait, and search and reconnaissance missions were poopin' and snoopin'. Most Marine Corps profanity was monotonous and heavily dependent on the all-purpose shit and fuck. Some of it could be colorful, though: a recruit's scrotum was his stacking swivel, and women were known as split-tails or slot-bottoms. At the other end of the language spectrum was the bloodless bureaucratese of official dispatches and orders. The imaginary opponent in a field exercise was "Aggressor Enemy"; the objective was to "render him neutral." Even more debased was the witless gibberish used to communicate over the field radio.

Styron sought escape from the banality of Marine Corps life by writing letters. He had time on his hands and used much of it to write to his father and his friends. He seems to have realized that this was a turning point for him: he had completed his literary apprenticeship, finished his first novel, and moved into a new phase. He had many people to be grateful to, but the most important of these was his father. He had thanked the elder Styron from time to time over the years—for money, for moral support, and simply for believing in him—but he seems now to have wanted to render a more formal thanks, perhaps because he was not sure that he would survive this new war. He tried to set down his gratitude in a letter one Friday afternoon:

> Of course you must know what you've done for me. If it hadn't been for your faith in me, and your gentle and constant encouragement, the novel would never have been written. There are few enough artists who have gotten encouragement from people at large, much less their parents—toward whom the very fact that they create usually represents a tacit antipathy. But you have been faithful to the very end of my first endeavor, and I appreciate it to the bottom of my heart. . . . The very fact that you and I have worked together, no matter with what unspoken understanding, represents a partnership of the spirit, and if that is love, it will prevail—forever and ever.

Blessedly, Styron had the galley proofs of *Lie Down in Darkness* to divert him. These arrived piecemeal, and he spent hours with them, happy with the way his sentences looked in type. It pleased him to show the proofs to his fellow reservists; they proved that he was a real writer, one with prospects. There were irritations, however. The first reader at Bobbs-Merrill, Herman Ziegner, had praised *Lie Down in Darkness* enthusiastically but had been nervous about its sexual content, especially about some of the graphic language in Peyton Loftis's final monologue. Another in-house reader had gone over this monologue and discussed it with Ziegner, and the two men had made a list of the passages in the typescript that they felt needed to be toned down. They filed this memo:

> We were in complete agreement. We both felt, and feel, that we have recommended all the changes that should be made and only those that should be made. The precise wording of the changes is of course up to the author. If all or most of these changes are made, this passage should not receive an undue amount of attention from the critics and should not cause any shock to the moral sense or good taste of intelligent readers. This does not mean that we have asked the author to make the passage sterile. It may still be a little strong for the lower order of Mrs. Grundy's daughters.

The position at Bobbs-Merrill, stated by its president, David Laurance Chambers, and passed on to Styron by Haydn, was that *Lie Down in Darkness* should not draw notice because of sexually explicit language. It should not become a notorious novel—as *Ulysses* had remained for over a decade after its first publication, diverting attention from its artistic merit. *Lie Down in Darkness* should instead make its way on the basis of its manifest literary excellences.

Styron saw the logic of the argument, though he was not especially happy about giving in. He made the cuts and expurgations, realizing that he was blunting the sexual edge of Peyton's monologue. Excised were references to her lovers' sex organs, to menstruation, and to her underwear. A mention of "dog shit" on the streets of New York was taken out; also expunged were references to a "cowboy belt" and a "tube of jelly," ready for use in a sexual encounter. Styron felt that he had gone as far as he could in appeasing Bobbs-Merrill. To his dismay, however, a request for additional textual bleaching arrived. Readers in Indianapolis had ferreted out a handful of other offensive readings and were now asking that these too be done away with. At issue was another reference to Peyton's menstrual bleeding, one to vaginal penetration, one to a feminine napkin, one to an erection, and one to a failed erection. Irritated by this prissiness, Styron balked. Haydn, however, was insistent. "Bill, you certainly know me well enough to know that I am nobody's Aunt Dora," he wrote. "But it really does seem to me that it is a relatively foolish distinction you are making here. . . . If you have any confidence at all in my judgment on this stuff, please be assured that I am whole-heartedly, but only after long thought, in favor of your making these further, consistent changes." Styron reluctantly allowed the last few alterations to be made. Now there would be nothing explicit in his novel to offend those of a censorious temperament.

Styron was watching another first novel enjoy a smashing success during his stint at Lejeune. This was James Jones's *From Here to Eternity,* which he had read at Valley Cottage earlier that spring. Jones, a veteran who had fought on Guadalcanal, had written a long, blunt, powerful novel about life in the peacetime army. His mentor had been Maxwell Perkins at Scribner's, the famous editor who had handled Fitzgerald's, Hemingway's, and Wolfe's books in the twenties and thirties. Jones had been Perkins's last discovery: the editor had died when *Eternity* was in progress. Styron knew that there had been problems with the profanity Jones had wanted to use in his novel and that Jones had had to compromise with Scribner's. Perhaps the compromise had worked: he was a celebrity now, the subject of a long photo-essay that appeared in the May 7 issue of *Life.* The article described Jones's odd literary apprenticeship, served under a married woman named Lowney

Handy in his hometown of Robinson, Illinois. She and Jones had now set up a writers' colony of sorts at her home and were putting would-be novelists through a peculiar training regimen that included a spartan diet and long periods of simply copying out, word for word, entire short stories by Faulkner, Fitzgerald, Katherine Anne Porter, and Hemingway.

Styron could only hope that his novel would enjoy a fraction of the success that had come to *From Here to Eternity.* The early reports filtering down to him were favorable: Bobbs-Merrill, for all its squeamishness about language, was promoting the book strongly, and initial reactions were good. Haydn passed along the comment of an experienced Bobbs-Merrill book salesman who had been taking advance orders: "I think that Mr. Styron will—like Byron—go to sleep and wake up famous." The poet and critic Louis Simpson, then a junior editor at Bobbs-Merrill, wrote to tell him that "outside of Faulkner, and probably with Faulkner too, it is, in my opinion, the finest novel in English written in a long long time. And I, Sir, am a publisher's reader, whose innermost core is suspicion and dislike."

Perhaps the most satisfying report came from Dorothy Parker, the co-worker from his days at McGraw-Hill who had given him the bubble-blowing kit there. She was still an editor at Whittlesey House and saw a good deal of Edward Aswell. One day she was outside Aswell's office and heard him talking with John W. Aldridge, a young critic who was to publish his first book, *After the Lost Generation,* with McGraw-Hill that fall. Dorothy Parker sent down this account of the overheard conversation to Styron:

> Jack Aldridge had gone in to chat with Aswell, and during the course of the conversation up-coming books that people had heard of must have come up, whereupon Jack asked ECA if he'd heard about this brilliant new novelist of Hiram Haydn's. Ed Kuhn, who couldn't remember your last name, spoke up and said, "Oh yes, he used to work here." Then there was much surprise and calling of Joan Adams to find out the name of "that sallow-complexioned young man," etc. (You had jaundice.) Bubbleoon did not come up. I thought you'd want to know.

Such gossip helped Styron tolerate the boredom at Camp Lejeune. He also began to hear gossip of a very different kind—Marine Corps scuttlebutt about some of the officer candidates he had trained with six years before. Of greatest interest was what he learned about Charlie Sullivan, his friend from Quantico. Charlie had stayed in the Marine Corps after the war and was now a first lieutenant in Korea. He had served in China for three years and had then returned to the States for a year before being sent to Korea. Early in the war he had been cut off with his detachment in the northern part of the country but had fought his way out to safety. Sullivan had also been involved in the action around Chosin Reservoir in December 1950. He had been given the almost comic task of transforming a 102-piece military marching band into a fighting unit. He had done the job well, turning the trumpeters and clarinetists into squads of machine gunners and riflemen. "They are the fightingest damn band in the world," he told one newspaper reporter.

On the road between Hagaru and Koto-ri on December 6, 1950, Sullivan and his musicians were attacked by Chinese Communist troops and pinned down for seven hours. The Chinese used tracer bullets to set fire to the trucks and jeeps of the American unit and then attacked with tommyguns and hand grenades. Sullivan was trapped behind a burning vehicle and ran out of ammunition. A Chinese soldier with a tommygun charged him, firing wildly. Sullivan had already affixed his bayonet to his rifle; now he stood up, seized the carbine like a javelin, and hurled it ten yards straight into the stomach of the advancing soldier. A captain who was there described the feat in a newspaper account: "Hit him in the gut, dead center. The gun just went through and waved there for a minute. The Gook fell right there." Sullivan's kill quickly became famous in the Marines—a small, tightly knit branch of the military with an active, efficient grapevine. Eventually the exploit made its way into several histories of the Korean War.

Sullivan had survived that battle and was now stationed behind the lines as assistant headquarters commandant for the First Marine Division. He had access to the names of the reservists who were being recalled, and one day, scanning those lists, he spotted Styron's name. He immediately told his adjutant that he wanted Styron on his staff when Styron got to Korea. A billet was kept open: if Styron had made it through Lejeune and on to Korea, he would have served as Sullivan's assistant in division headquarters—but that was not to happen.

At Camp Lejeune, Styron listened to the tales of Charlie Sullivan's exploits with a kind of head-shaking awe. All of his life he would see Sullivan as a superb warrior, a man of action who could also read and think. Styron would later try to write about Sullivan in his fiction, but for now he seems only to have realized that his own role in the Korean War would be quite different from Sullivan's. This war, he felt, was futile and pernicious, with no clear moral issues and no eventual good purpose. Politicians, he knew, were largely to blame for the mess in Korea, and his irritation showed in a letter he wrote to Tom Peyton: "If the lunatic fringe of both the Republican and Democratic parties would for Christ's sake just get *killed* and the sane members get *together,* and quick, there might be a way to finish off Korea and work for a lasting, final peace. But I doubt it. If we are destroyed, remember that we are destroyed by evil, ignorant, criminal men, not only in Russia but in D.C. A man would be justified using a BAR on about half of Congress."

These matters came to a head for Styron during one twenty-four-hour period on June 20 and 21 of that summer. His regiment was on bivouac in the woods, wet and weary from two days and nights of steady rain. Just after lunch on June 20, a ghastly accident occurred. Two mortar rounds, fired as part of the field exercise, fell short among troops in the regiment just adjacent to Styron's. The men in that regiment, many of them reservists, had been advancing through the woods in a mock attack. Eight marines were blown apart and twenty-three wounded, some seriously. One of these men died the next day, bringing the death count to nine. Styron's regiment sent doctors and ambulances over immediately; Styron drove the regimental surgeon to the area in a jeep. He saw the confusion and a little of the carnage—the only time he ever saw men wounded by military firepower. Stunned by what he had observed, Styron returned to his regiment. The rumor, quickly circulated, was that the short rounds had been defective shells from World War II that had lost their full trajectory power. This did eventually prove to be the official explanation.

The colonel in command of Styron's regiment at Camp Lejeune was James M. Masters, a career officer who had just turned forty. He had been at Pearl Harbor for the Japanese attack and had served in several of the Pacific campaigns—the Solomons, Cape Gloucester, Guam, Saipan, the Marianas, and Okinawa. He had distinguished himself especially in the ground fighting at Cape Gloucester, where he had been nicknamed Jungle Jim. Masters was a fit, confident officer who stood ramrod-straight and always packed a sidearm. He had been told to whip Styron's regiment (the Eighth Marines, Second Marine Division) into condition for Korea. A member of the Old Breed and a career military man, Masters had little patience with the malingering and flaccidity of the reservists. He decided, just hours after the incident of the short mortar rounds, to have his regiment march all the way back to base camp, a distance of thirty-three miles, that very night. This would have been a demanding march even for young, well-conditioned troops, men who had worked themselves into shape with a series of shorter eight- or ten-mile hikes. But for overage reservists, many of them in their late twenties or thirties and all of them still flabby from civilian life, it was a cruelly long distance. One or two of the junior officers suggested as much to Masters, but he went ahead and issued the order. He must have thought that an all-night, thirty-three-mile march would separate the tough marines from the weak ones, scare most of the low-grade insubordination out of the reservists, and establish his reputation for toughness and rigidity.

The regiment set out at eight-thirty that night. At first the men bore up relatively well, but soon the least well-conditioned ones began to drop off the pace. There was much bitching but no outright insubordination or disobedience. Each man simply marched ahead until he could no longer walk. Masters strode along with the troops, periodically moving up and down the column in a jeep but always dismounting and resuming the hike, sometimes at the head of the regiment and sometimes at the rear. Halfway through the ordeal men began to collapse. Some were tongue-lashed back on their feet by the sergeants and managed to walk a few more miles, but eventually over one third of the men dropped out and had to be driven back to the base in trucks. Styron, however, was one of those who made it all the way. He was proud that his stamina had held out, though he could not say why he had completed the absurd march. A few days later he described it all—the defective mortar rounds and the long march—in a letter to Sigrid de Lima:

> We marched and marched and marched, from 8:30 P.M. until 7:00 the following morning, and it was sheer hell. I don't believe anyone has the slightest idea of how far 33 miles are, until one has hiked them, at

a set pace (2½ miles per hour) and in 85° heat and with a ten-minute break every hour. Even for the marines this hike was something of a record and only 65% of the regiment made it and I made it all the way in, with blisters on both feet the size of pingpong balls—though why I stuck it out I don't know. I—who have not walked 200 consecutive yards in the last five years. Now if you will add, to the simple fact of the hike, the blisters, the drugged, dead, plodding exhaustion after the no-sleep for the two preceding nights, the memory of the slain marines I'd just seen, the heat and, above all, the futility of it all—you can imagine what a state I, and all the others, was in at the end of the trail.

Though he probably could not have said it at the time, these two experiences—the short mortar rounds and the all-night march—came to epitomize for Styron much of his ambivalence about the Marine Corps. Even at the age of twenty-six he was still susceptible, just a little, to the glamour of the Marine Corps—to its uniforms and traditions, its swagger and polish. He liked the weaponry and the massed power of the men and equipment. The strutting machismo was more than a little seductive as well. Styron could legitimately fit into this world: he was not the best officer on the base, but he was not the worst either. He had survived Jungle Jim Masters's thirty-three-mile march and could survive worse if he had to. Gung-ho bravado was useful on the battlefield, he knew, but so were his own assets—brains and judgment. He felt that if he did end up in Korea, he would acquit himself as well as the next man.

What was beginning to trouble him (and what would make its way into his next extended work of fiction, *The Long March*) was that all of this force and firepower around him was only barely under control. Despite a carefully managed appearance of discipline and regimentation, the entire military apparatus, with its enormous potential for destruction, could be thrown into chaos by a round or two of defective ammunition or by the whimsical order of a senior officer. There was no deliberative, mature judgment behind the deployment of this force, either in the individual units or in the larger arena of politics. Much of what happened simply happened by accident.

Styron was not a romantic, then or later, about the need for a military establishment in a popular democracy. He knew that large, prosperous countries like the United States had to maintain military forces in order to protect their citizens and interests. But he also knew that the existence of huge military establishments almost guaranteed that sooner or later they would be put into the field—in wars and quasi-wars—by ignorant, shortsighted politicians. That was a fearsome prospect for men like Styron, who could easily be dragged into these illogical, bloody conflicts. Now Styron had learned firsthand just how quickly the whole apparatus of military force could swing out of control. He was beginning to realize too that a part of his role in society, should he survive Korea, would be to testify to the danger and absurdity inherent in any large military establishment. He would be a critic—querulous, attentive, and persistent—who would examine the morality and the aims of those who controlled military force. Weary and footsore from his thirty-three-mile march and numb from the shock of the carnage he had seen, Styron probably could not have framed these ideas in language, but they were surely present in his mind.

Styron had not yet resigned himself to service in Korea, however. He still had one trump card to play—the cataract in his right eye. Several days after the march, Styron's unit was taken to the firing range to test out on the M1 rifle. Styron proved to be as hopeless a marksman as ever: shooting right-handed, he failed to hit the target a single time. He played dumb, telling his captain that he was having difficulty with his eyesight but that he did not know why. The captain sent him to the regimental dispensary to have his eyes tested.

It was Styron's good fortune to be examined by a young reservist who was just as bitter as he about having been recalled. The physician's name was C. P. Kimbal; he was an ophthalmologist from Chicago who had been called back into the Marine Corps, thus wrecking his budding practice back home. He was vocal about his displeasure, telling Styron his story while conducting the eye exam and listening to Styron's gripes in return. Lieutenant Kimbal discovered the cataract in Styron's eye immediately and, without hesitating, typed out this recommendation:

> Patient has small central opacity at the Rt. lens at posterior pole i.e. Congenital cataract. . . . Suggest that patient be released to Inactive Duty according to SR 615 360 40 as condition is E.P.T.S. Patient does not meet physical requirements according to A.R. 40-115 and he has been recalled for less than 6 months.
>
> S/ C.P. KIMBAL
> LTJG   MC   USN

Styron's case went before the Physical Evaluation Board at Camp Lejeune. About a week later, he was recommended by the chief medical officer for discharge. He had escaped.

Styron felt no guilt over his good fortune. He had originally hidden his eye defect in order to get into the Marine Corps, cheating by memorizing the test charts with his good eye. He had served in World War II and had taken his chances with the rest in what he believed to be a just, moral war. He had been saved by the A-bomb and by the accident of his birth date. Now he had been dragooned into a foolish, immoral war and, again by chance, had been saved—this time by an irate ophthalmologist. ("I owe that guy," Styron said years later. "I owe him a lot.") His salvation, in its way, was just as absurd as his other experiences in the Marine Corps—the false positive test for syphilis, the stint in the Clap Shack, the short mortar rounds, the long march. Styron asked no questions: he lay low and waited around the base, serving temporarily as a regimental public information officer, writing press releases about the reservists for their local newspapers back home.

Just before he was discharged from the Marines, however, he received a shock. As he opened a letter from his father, he noticed a newspaper clipping inside the envelope. He looked at it and saw a picture of "Anna," the young woman from Newport News on whom he had partly based the character of Peyton Loftis. When he had last heard of Anna, she had been in the state sanitarium in Williamsburg, attempting to recover from the postpartum depression that had caused her to try to drown her child. She had eventually been released and had returned to Newport News. There she had attempted to reassemble her life but had failed. Now, Styron learned from the clipping, she had killed herself.

Anna had been dating a local man and had accepted his proposal of marriage, though she was terrified of the possibility of having another child. She was seeing a few of her old friends and had reestablished contact with her ex-husband, who had returned from the war. He had agreed to let her visit their child, who was living with his family, so long as a chaperon was present. He had been prepared to sign legal papers giving Anna this permission, and she had been elated at the prospect of seeing the child. Then, out of the blue, she learned that her former husband had drowned in a swimming-pool accident. This meant that she could not see her child, perhaps ever, and that she could never hope to explain herself to her ex-husband. To worsen matters, Anna's own mother, who had a history of mental instability, had suffered another breakdown and was back in the state asylum in Williamsburg, the institution from which Anna herself had only recently been discharged. Anna confessed her great fear to her friends: that her mental problems were inherited and that her own life would follow the pattern of her mother's, with periodic and inevitable incarceration for mental illness.

Anna visited her mother in Williamsburg on an afternoon late in July. She then drove back to Newport News and phoned several girlfriends, hoping to find someone who would go swimming with her that evening at the Chamberlin Hotel pool. All of her friends were busy, though, so Anna decided to go swimming alone. She put on a bathing suit. What happened next is not clear; what is known is that Anna took a single sheet of paper and wrote on it these words: "There's no answer." She placed it on her desk and, still in her bathing suit, got into her car and drove to the dock at Old Point Comfort. Onlookers later said that she stopped the car for a moment, then rolled up the windows and gunned the motor. The automobile swerved onto the dock, scattering people who were standing there, and raced toward the edge. Anna aimed the car between two piles and drove it directly into the dark waters of Hampton Roads. The car sank immediately. People who were there told the newspaper reporters that Anna's screams could be heard through the closed car windows as her automobile sped across the dock.

It took almost three days for divers, working with a dredging derrick, to locate the car in the deep, muddy, swirling waters off Old Point Comfort. During those three days, crowds of as many as six hundred people gathered to watch. Until the automobile was brought to the surface, no one knew for certain who was in it—though the police suspected that Anna was inside, since friends had reported her missing and had found the note on her desk. Styron's father, not knowing of Anna's connection to the heroine of *Lie Down in Darkness,* had clipped the story from the local paper and sent it to his son.

Anna's bizarre suicide was enormously troubling to Styron. He had loved this young woman from afar as a teenager and had felt sympathy for her as he had heard from friends about the tragedies of her life. Though he had not known her well, he had felt secretly connected to her. She had been alive during the time he was writing *Lie Down in Darkness,* which concluded with the suicide of the fictional character

based on her. Now she had killed herself. Had he predicted, in writing
the novel, that Anna would take her own life? Or worse, had he somehow caused her to kill herself? Logic and common sense told him that
this was not so—that Anna had been unstable and a high risk for suicide. But her death by drowning, in a public and symbolic way, was
eerily similar to the symbolic death that he had devised for Peyton
Loftis. Anna, who had tried to drown her child and whose ex-husband
had died by drowning, had drowned herself. Peyton, whose spirit is
earthbound, dies by attempting to fly: she throws herself from a fourth-
story window and falls to her death. Anna's suicide, coming on the very
eve of the publication of *Lie Down in Darkness,* was immensely unsettling to Styron. Over forty years later he could still remember the details
from the newspaper clipping that his father had sent to him at Camp
Lejeune.

On August 10, 1951, Styron was released from the Marine Corps. He
packed his gear and headed for Newport News to spend a few days at
139 Chesapeake Avenue. During this stay, a package arrived from
Bobbs-Merrill. It was a bright new copy of *Lie Down in Darkness,*
bound in brown cloth and encased in a brown-and-blue dust jacket designed by the artist George Salter. A few days later Styron took the
train to New York, with this copy of his book packed carefully in his
suitcase. He was now a published novelist, prepared to read his first reviews.

15

Lie Down in Darkness

WHEN STYRON RETURNED to New York in late August 1951, he moved in with John Maloney and his wife in their apartment on Thirteenth Street. Maloney was a friend from New School days and a protégé of Hiram Haydn's; talented but erratic, Maloney was working on a first novel that, as it turned out, he would never complete. After a few weeks with the Maloneys, Styron found a one-bedroom sublet at 48 Greenwich Avenue and rented it for the fall and winter. Moving in was simple: he had only a few clothes plus his library—several cardboard cartons of paperbacks that he had left behind when he went south to Camp Lejeune. He had retrieved the boxes and now kept them stored under his cot. He was working in a desultory way on some short stories but was mostly letting his pen run fallow. He had enough cash to get by for the time being and could see, as the weeks passed, that more money was going to come his way from *Lie Down in Darkness*.

Much of his attention and emotion during this period was absorbed by an *affaire de coeur* with a young married woman. He had written almost daily to this woman (whom we shall call Betty) from Camp Lejeune. Now he saw her several times a week, for lunch or for walks in the city parks. Styron sent lengthy, heartfelt letters to her at the office where she worked, and she responded with long letters of her own. Though Betty was a little older than Styron and already had a child, his feelings for her were strong enough for him to think seriously of marriage, despite the obstacles to divorce during the 1950s. He and she had long talks about what marriage would mean for him and his career, and about how it would change her child's life. Once she came very near to telling her husband about the affair and asking for a separation, but she lost heart at the last moment. For the time being the relationship drifted.

Lie Down in Darkness was officially published on September 10, and the initial reviews were as good as Styron could have hoped for. Orville Prescott, writing for *The New York Times,* spoke of the novel's "blazing power" and predicted that the book would "stir up a fine controversy." Martha MacGregor wrote in the *New York Post* that *Lie Down in Darkness* was an "impressive creative achievement"; Max Lerner, writing also in the *Post,* complained of overliterariness but concluded that "the fellow can write like an angel." One of the best early notices came from Howard Mumford Jones in *The Herald-Tribune Book Review:* he called *Lie Down in Darkness* a "rich, full and moving story" and praised Styron's insight and strong moral stance. "Few recent writers have had the courage of this affirmation," wrote Jones, "and few have had the capacity to mingle beauty, wisdom and narrative art as he has done." Maxwell Geismar was even more laudatory in the *Saturday Review of Literature,* naming *Lie Down in Darkness* as "the best novel of the year by my standards—and one of the few completely human and mature novels published since the Second World War."

Interviews with Styron appeared in *The New York Times Book Review, The Herald-Tribune Book Review,* the *Chicago Tribune,* and the *Saturday Review of Literature;* favorable notices were published in such newspapers as *The Washington Post, The Boston Sunday Globe,* the Los Angeles *Daily News,* and *The Kansas City Star.* A second wave of positive reviews appeared in major periodicals: there was praise from Harvey Breit in the *Atlantic Monthly,* Harvey Swados in *The Nation,* Robert Gorham Davis in *The American Scholar,* and Elizabeth Janeway in *The New Leader.* An especially discerning review was written by Malcolm Cowley for *The New Republic:* though recognizing Styron's debt to Faulkner, Cowley believed that "the example of Faulkner seems to have had a liberating effect on Styron's imagination" and that, in Peyton's final soliloquy, Styron had gone beyond Quentin Compson's section in *The Sound and the Fury.*

There were some sour notes. *Newsweek* was blunt in criticizing Styron: "Purple prose holds no terrors for him. When the intensity of his story drops, it collapses." *The New Yorker* was no kinder: "Mr. Styron describes with a characteristic outpouring of emotion. . . . Perhaps even he, somewhere in the enthusiastic wilderness of his vision, was uneasily aware that he had made the coffin too big for what is, when all is said and done, only a very young, slight, overwrought body." *Time,* then known for cheerful hatchet jobs, placed Styron in the "dread-despair-and-decay camp of U.S. letters" and called his characters "spiritual leeches" and "moral pygmies." Other reviewers fretted over Styron's morbidity and complained that his characters were pathetic, not tragic; Styron was charged with "theatricalism and tawdriness" by one reviewer and accused of creating "monumental foolishness" by another.

Much attention was devoted to *Lie Down in Darkness* in local newspapers across the country; in all, something over a hundred reviews appeared, most of them reasonably favorable and some of them quite laudatory. Many book critics called Styron a spokesman for the postwar period, often quoting Peyton's bitter comment about the Lost Generation of the 1920s: "They weren't lost. What they were doing was losing us." Many reviewers also mentioned Styron's southern background and suggested that he was Faulkner's heir apparent—a title that he would work hard to avoid in later years.

This kind of extended treatment in the national press—positive, negative, and mixed—was crucial in establishing William Styron as a serious author whose work was going to be watched. If one is to understand Styron's later career, it is important to recognize that after *Lie Down in Darkness* he was a marked man. In certain ways this was an advantage: though sometimes treated roughly by the literary press in later years, he was never neglected or ignored, and he never had to labor in the shadows. He did not have to publish a second or third novel before he drew wide attention; his fiction was read and discussed from the first. Even in the middle stages of his career, when there were long periods of silence between his novels, the literary world never lost interest in him. The disadvantage, of course, was that after *Lie Down in Darkness* Styron could never again work in obscurity and privacy.

Almost as interesting to Styron as the reviews of *Lie Down in Darkness* in the national press were the reactions that filtered up from Newport

News and the Peninsula. Alexander C. Brown, writing in the September 9 *Newport News Daily Press,* must have piqued the curiosity of the city with this paragraph:

> Although the customary disclaimer is not included in the fore part of the book, we can assume that all characters are imaginary, resemblance to persons living or dead being coincidental, etc. Despite this, undoubtedly rare and rewarding sport will be provided for those who enjoy exploring the not unreasonable possibility that they may contrive to discover that the seamier sides of some of their Peninsula acquaintances have gotten into the book.

A lengthy, positive notice was published in *The Norfolk Virginian-Pilot* for September 9, along with an interview with Styron's father. Summaries of the major New York reviews appeared in the Peninsula papers, and the mothers of Styron's boyhood friends wrote him that he was being much gossiped about in their book clubs. Many years later, residents of Newport News could still remember the great stir caused by *Lie Down in Darkness* in 1951 and the busy speculation among the locals about which characters were based on whom. "Almost every girl I knew claimed that she was Peyton," confided one lifelong resident of the city a few years ago. " 'How did he know all of those things about me?' they would say."

Elizabeth Buxton Styron wrote her stepson a letter of guarded praise. From hints in the letter it seems clear that she recognized herself as the model for Helen Loftis, but she did not pursue the matter further. (Nor did she later bring it up directly, either in writing or conversation. She died without ever discussing with her stepson his depiction of her as Helen.) Reports of his father's behavior made their way up to New York as well. The elder Styron was so excited that he began to corner coworkers at the shipyard and buttonhole people on the street in order to discuss his son's novel with them. He brandished sheaves of positive reviews or, in other moods, railed against the naysayers from *Time* and *Newsweek.* His lecturing became so hectic that friends called in the evenings and inquired anxiously after his health.

From Durham came a long letter from William Blackburn, full of generous praise. "Truly I'm proud—and amazed at the magnificent development of your powers," wrote the good professor. "God bless you—which is another way of saying, I suppose, that you have a great gift in trust. And a great achievement in hand: a work of art, a piece of literature." From Manchester, Connecticut, where she was now living, came a carefully worded letter from Blackburn's former wife, Tris, which suggested that she saw something of her former husband's melancholy and nihilism in the character of Milton Loftis. Ashbel Brice sent a six-page scrawl, filled with truculent compliments; other ex-members of the West Durham Literary Society simply sent their straightforward congratulations.

At several points during the initial reception of *Lie Down in Darkness,* Styron was asked to make statements about himself. These help to fill out a picture of him at this moment in his career. In a short autobiographical piece that he had written for *The Herald-Tribune Book Review* while still at Camp Lejeune, Styron commented on his future plans:

> I would like to go to Europe, and to read a lot more than I've been doing lately. I would like to discover the moral and political roots of our trouble, and to learn why it has come about that young men, like my friends at Lejeune and, more particularly, in places like Korea, have to suffer so endlessly in our time. If I found out why all this has come about I'd be able to write intelligently and without so much of the self-conscious whimper that characterized a lot of the writing of the '20s, and consequently perhaps I'd be able to commemorate not a lost generation but a generation that never was even found.

When the *Saturday Review of Literature* asked about his politics, he said this:

> I'm wildly interested in a way and wildly ignorant. I think I share qualities of both left and right but tend to become an intuitive liberal. I hate intolerance of any sort, but I'd never take any active part or fight for a political cause. I'm no fighter anyway.

And to another interviewer he had these things to say about writing as a vocation:

> I don't think I have ever burned to write, and I still don't know if I want to. I was never overwhelmed by this fury to pour things out. It's painful when I'm doing it, but I recognize all the compensations you get from it. And you reach a point where you figure it's a pretty worthwhile profession. You can't be lazy and write, but it's for a man who wants his own type of leisure.

From such statements, and from personal letters of the period, a picture emerges of a young writer who as yet has no fixed political or philosophical orientation. Styron seems naturally skeptical in his thinking, mistrustful of authority and of institutions generally, but not yet ready to become an activist. He is also intellectually curious, eager to read and learn more, conscious of how much he does not know. Some self-doubt is in evidence (a bad review could knock him off-stride for several days), but one senses a core of confidence and even cockiness. Ambition is present as well, as are self-discipline and drive.

For someone who, only a short while before, had been trudging through the North Carolina backwoods on a forced march, the rewards of this current success were pleasantly distracting. He was invited to literary cocktail parties and introduced to writers and publishers—John Hersey, Norman Mailer, E. E. Cummings, and Bennett Cerf among them. Profiles of him appeared in *Mademoiselle* and *Glamour.* He was on a panel at the PEN Club with Herman Wouk, Gore Vidal, and John P. Marquand, Jr. (a young Harvard graduate, son of the famous novelist of the same name, and an aspiring writer himself). Styron and Marquand hit it off well and began to go barhopping together in the Village, often ending up at a place called the Cedar Tavern. Marquand, who belonged to the Knickerbocker Club, used to visit Styron in his Greenwich Avenue sublet, often bringing along a friend named John Appleton. Marquand and Appleton would arrive in uptown attire— suits and Chesterfield overcoats, Marquand remembered—and would slum around in the Village with Styron, who wore khakis and T-shirts.

Styron appeared at a Columbia University forum that fall with Vidal, Malcolm Cowley, and John W. Aldridge. Marquand introduced him to James Jones, whom he immediately liked, and Styron spent an evening touring the cafés with Jones, Mailer, and the actor Montgomery Clift, who was to play a leading role in the movie version of *From Here to Eternity.* Clift and Mailer eventually retired for the night, but Styron and Jones stayed up until morning talking about books and women and the military. They liked each other and began a friendship on that occasion that would grow and mature in future years.

At another party, hosted by Leo Lerman, he met theater people: Laurence Olivier and Vivien Leigh, Tennessee Williams, and Marlene Dietrich. He reported on the evening to his aunt Edith in Uniontown: "The Oliviers were very frostily, Britishly pleasant, 'hedn't hed the pleasuah of ridding my book,' but hoped to soon. Tennessee Williams had read it, though, and said he liked it very much, but you could have knocked me over with a pin when Leo took me over to meet *la Dietrich* and she took my cold clammy hand in hers and said she had not only 'rad' LDID, but 'lawved' it! It was pure Elysium, I can tell you that, and the young Stendhals and Flauberts and de Maupassants who pined for the salons of Paris back in the 1850's couldn't have asked for more."

Late that fall there arrived, from Baltimore, one of the first invitations Styron ever received to appear on a college campus. It came from Louis D. Rubin, Jr., then a young instructor and Ph.D. candidate at Johns Hopkins, just beginning his long career as a critic and interpreter of southern letters. Rubin, an admirer of *Lie Down in Darkness,* had reviewed the novel positively in *The Richmond News Leader* and had followed with an expanded notice in *The Hopkins Review.* Now he wanted Styron to come to a graduate seminar at Johns Hopkins and talk to the students about writing and literature. Styron declined at first: he was having too much fun in New York and did not want to reenter academe, even as a visitor. But Rubin was persistent. He sent Styron a second letter, full of praise and promising that he could make a quick down-and-back trip. Baltimore was only a short train ride to the south; all Styron needed to do was to spend a pleasant afternoon with a roomful of admiring graduate students. Wouldn't he reconsider?

In what would turn out to be one of the most important decisions of his life, Styron decided to go. He appeared at the seminar on the appointed day, read some passages from his novel, and answered a few questions from the graduate students (one of whom was John Barth). After class, several of the students stayed behind to chat. One of them caught his eye—a small, dark-haired beauty who introduced herself as Rose Burgunder. They exchanged a few pleasantries, but that was all: he had to hurry away to dinner. That night, in the Belvedere Hotel in Baltimore, he could not sleep because he could not stop thinking about Rose Burgunder. He had met the woman he would marry two years later.

Back in New York, the reports from Bobbs-Merrill were heartening. The clothbound edition of *Lie Down in Darkness* had gone into its fourth trade impression and was climbing toward the thirty thousand mark in sales. The novel was holding steady toward the middle of the best-seller lists, usually in the company of Jones's *From Here to Eternity* and J. D. Salinger's *The Catcher in the Rye,* another publishing sensation of that year. Much fan mail arrived from readers, and in a *Saturday Review* poll of literary critics, *Lie Down in Darkness* tied with Faulkner's *Requiem for a Nun* for second place among Current Books Worth Reading. The subsidiary money from the novel was apparently going to be good: Signet had agreed to purchase the paperback rights for fifteen thousand dollars (half of which was to go to Styron) and had promised an edition of two hundred thousand copies for the spring; *Omnibook Best-Seller Magazine* was bringing out an abridgment of the novel in its January issue; British rights had been sold to the firm of Hamish Hamilton, a quite reputable house; and there would be translations into French, Spanish, Portuguese, Danish, Swedish, and Norwegian.

Perhaps most exciting to Styron was a rumor that *Lie Down in Darkness* might win the National Book Award. This did not come to pass (the nod went to *From Here to Eternity*), but *Lie Down in Darkness* was mentioned for other awards, among them the Prix de Rome of the American Academy of Arts and Letters. This was a new award, only a year old at the time. It was meant for young writers whose early work showed much promise. The selection committee that year was composed of Malcolm Cowley, John Hersey, Van Wyck Brooks, W. H. Auden, and Allen Tate. At a cocktail party in February, Styron ran into a jovial Cowley who informed him, sub rosa, that he had won the prize. Official word came a week later, and Styron learned that the Prix de Rome was a very fine award indeed. He was to spend a year in Rome, with free residence and meals at the American Academy there; he was also to receive a stipend of $1,250, reimbursement for his transportation over and back, and allowances for books and travel.

Styron was jubilant. He had been thinking of going to Europe for a stretch but had made no firm plans. The Prix de Rome brought matters to a head. His yearlong fellowship was to begin in October 1952, and during that period he would be expected to spend most of his time in Italy. He realized that if he meant to see other parts of Europe, he had better go over early and do his touring during the spring and summer. He therefore booked passage for England on the *Île de France* for March 5, 1952, planning to spend a month or so initially in London, where the British edition of *Lie Down in Darkness* was scheduled for publication on March 21. Then he would travel to some other parts of

Europe—surely to France and perhaps to Scandinavia as well—before reporting to Rome in October. "I'm of course looking forward to this trip with a lot of excitement—and some trepidation," he wrote to his father. "If you have any advice to a prospective *voyageur,* please send it along because I'm a mighty green continental character . . . and I don't spik French."

He found someone to take up the sublet for his flat on Greenwich Avenue. Then he collected some letters of introduction to people in London and Paris. All that remained was to bring his romance with Betty to a close. They had continued to see each other through that fall and winter, but their ardor had cooled, and their letters were now less intense. She had rejoiced in his successes but had gone no further toward breaking off her marriage. When the news came that Styron had won the Prix de Rome and she learned that he would be sailing for Europe in March, she seemed relieved. Her letters began to take on a big-sisterly tone, and she seemed resigned to the fact that their time together would end. Betty knew well enough the opportunities that would come to a successful young writer on the loose in Europe. In a last letter she wished him a "mamselle from Armentières," granting him his freedom. "Gather ye rosebuds. . . ." she said.

The voyage to Southampton on the *Île de France* was calm and pleasant. Styron traveled in cabin class and spent most of his time with a New York friend, the screenwriter Arthur Laurents. Singer Lena Horne and her husband, Lennie Hayton, were in first class; she knew Laurents and invited him and Styron up for drinks. "Lena sang for the assembled company," Styron reported to his aunt Edith in Uniontown, "and afterwards for a couple of nights Art & Lena & I managed to get paralyzed together in the First Class bar, up in God's country. . . . I wasn't precisely carried off the ship at Southampton, but I'm still rolling, rather than walking, around London."

Styron's editor at Hamish Hamilton, Roger Machell, took charge of him in London, booking him into the Stafford, a hotel in Piccadilly, and taking him about to restaurants and the cinema. They went to a few parties, and Styron met some London book critics and publishing-house employees. One night he went to a gathering at the flat of Michael Canfield, the half brother of Cass Canfield, whom Styron had known in New York. Both Canfields were involved in publishing; they were of the Canfield family associated with the house of Harper. At Michael Canfield's party Styron was introduced to a tall, engaging postgraduate student from King's College, Cambridge, named George Plimpton. They chatted briefly: Styron could not place Plimpton's accent and simply assumed that it was a British variant. Several months later Styron learned that Plimpton was an American and that he spoke with a classic upper-class Manhattan WASP accent, slightly anglicized.

Postwar food shortages persisted in London, and the restaurant fare was grim: "The British are admirable people in their uncomplaining acceptance of leathery shad and brussels sprouts steamed to the consistency of a green, wet floormop," he wrote to Aunt Edith. He had possessed the foresight, however, to bring along three bottles of American whiskey and ten pounds of Hormel ham; these commodities made him popular among his new acquaintances. He found no Styrons in the London phone book but did discover one Styran, two Styrins, and one Styring. "I guess they all missed the boat," he wrote to his father.

Lie Down in Darkness was published in London on March 21, and the reviews were mostly mixed or negative. *The Times Literary Supplement* complained of gloominess and unclear motivation; the daily *Times* notice included some favorable bits but was condescending; *The Sunday Times* was dismissive; *The New Statesman and Nation* was complimentary but noted "how little there is that is original about Mr. Styron's performance." The best review appeared in *Punch* ("warmly recommended"), the worst in The *Manchester Guardian* ("pretty sickening stuff"). These book notices were the beginning, for Styron, of what grew into a highly developed case of Anglophobia later in his life. The British, he felt, were not so much unappreciative of his work as they were uncomprehending of what he was trying to do. Perhaps the gap between the two cultures was too wide. The mixed reviews of *Lie Down in Darkness,* coupled with some snooty behavior by certain of the book critics at the cocktail parties, left Styron with a sour reaction to British literary culture.

Late in March, he made a getaway from London with two theater people he had met there—Bryan Forbes, an English actor and screenwriter who later gained much fame as a film director, and his wife, Constance Smith, an Irish actress. They toured in a hired Austin, stopping first in Cambridge to see King's College Chapel and to stroll along the river Cam. They drove on to visit the huge cathedral in Ely, traveled up through Lincolnshire, then dropped back down briefly again to London. A trip through the south of England followed; it included an all-night drive through Dorset and Devon, where wild ponies galloped along in the headlights of the Austin. Finally they reached St. Ives and Land's End, at the very southwesternmost point of England. Styron was much impressed by the spectacular cliffs and the "groaning, crashing sea" in Cornwall. In Porthleven they put up for a night with the vicar there, an old friend of Forbes's, and spent the evening chatting with him and his "insane, bird-like little wife." Styron found the place to be typically British: "It was the sort of vicarage you might visualize as being a *part* of England—huge and rambling, crammed with junk, but surrounded by chickens and lovely trees and gardens," he wrote his father. On the way back to London they stopped for lunch with Daphne du Maurier, another friend of Forbes's, at her estate near St. Austell. Her latest book, *My Cousin Rachel,* was then at the top of the *New York Times* best-seller list, but she spent much of the luncheon complaining about the high cost of things and about her relative poverty.

Styron was ready to move on from England to France, but he decided first to make a short trip to Denmark. In London he had met a young American novelist from Georgia named Calder Willingham, who had just published a collection of stories called *The Gates of Hell* in America. Styron and Willingham decided to travel together to Copenhagen and booked passage on a Danish ferryboat for early April. Years later, Styron remembered that he and Willingham were both thoroughly weary of English food and that they traded horror stories, before they boarded the ferry, of wretched meals in London restaurants. It therefore came to them as a wonderful surprise when almost the first thing they encountered on the Danish vessel was an enormous smorgasbord, free for the passengers. There were meats and cheeses and salads and fruits and breads and pickles and garnishes, so various and tempting as to make both young writers almost weep with pleasure. They attacked the table and gorged themselves for the better part of an hour.

Willingham stayed briefly in Copenhagen but left fairly soon to join a girlfriend elsewhere. Styron spent almost a week in Copenhagen, seeing the sights and hanging around the cafés. He was anxious by now to get to France, though, and bought a ticket in mid-April on a night train for Paris. It was a slow journey: the trip took almost a full day, largely because the train had to traverse numerous island channels in Denmark by means of railroad ferries. Styron passed through Germany and Belgium, both still recovering from wartime damage, and rolled on to France. He arrived in Paris twenty-two hours after departing Copenhagen, weary but excited. The weather was warm, and though it was nighttime when he walked out of the train station, he saw that the trees and flowers along the boulevards were already in bloom. He had arrived in Paris for the first time in his life, and it was April.

16

Paris, 1952

STYRON CHECKED INTO the Hôtel Washington, a plain-looking Right Bank tourist establishment just off the Champs-Elysées, a few streets down from the Arc de Triomphe. In later years he could remember little about the place—only the fact, puzzling to him at the time, that a bidet was situated squarely in his bedroom while the toilet was far down the hall. Styron spent his first day or so studying a Paris guidebook and trying to gather his nerve to use what little French he remembered from college. Only hunger or the need of cigarettes could make him enter a restaurant or a *tabac* to experiment with the few phrases he could recollect.

Friends in New York and London had given Styron letters of introduction to Peter Matthiessen, a young American writer then living in Montparnasse. On his second day in Paris, Styron made his way across the River Seine to Matthiessen's apartment on the Rue Perceval, a quiet little street behind the old Gare Montparnasse. There Styron met Matthiessen, a tall New York City native with a degree from Yale, and his wife, Patsy (née Southgate), who had graduated from Smith two years earlier. Peter was writing his first novel, *Race Rock,* and Patsy was translating French texts into English and thinking about having a go at fiction herself. Their apartment, three flights up, consisted of a big, high-ceilinged studio with a large skylight wall. Vines of ivy crawled across the outside of the skylight and cast dappled shadows on a red-tiled floor.

The Matthiessens found Styron good company, and the threesome talked and drank into the early evening. Then Peter led the way to a small Breton restaurant called Ti-Jos, where they all ordered oysters. Styron, inebriated by now, became melancholy toward the end of the meal. Perhaps it was the oysters, reminiscent of Tidewater Virginia, or the relief of relaxed, bookish conversation conducted in English after two days of faltering attempts at French with hoteliers and waiters. Whatever the cause, Styron became sentimental and lachrymose about home. Boozy and culture-shocked, he downed his last oyster, paused, and then said in a southern accent made heavier than usual by alcohol: "I'm goin' home to the James River to farm peanuts! I ain't got no more resistance to change than a snowflake!"

Over the next few days, the Matthiessens introduced Styron to others of their group—all young writers and artists who were enjoying the postwar expatriate life in Paris. The crowd included Thomas Guinzburg, the son of one of the founders of the Viking Press; William Pène du Bois, a writer and book illustrator; Jane du Bois, his wife; Terry Southern, a young writer from Texas; and Southern's friend Aram (Al) Avakian, a somber Armenian who later gained notice as a movie director. The oddest member of the crowd was Harold L. (Doc) Humes, a stocky, eccentric character who wore a cape and beret and carried a silver-headed cane. He was in publishing, he said, and had plans to write fiction. He had a girlfriend, Mary Lee, who was known to the crowd as Moose.

Much of the talk among this group was about a literary quarterly that they wanted to publish. Humes had bought a local magazine called *Kiosk* for six hundred dollars and had changed its name to the *Paris News-Post*. He had persuaded Matthiessen to serve as fiction editor, and they had put together one issue, which contained a good story by Terry Southern. Matthiessen, however, wanted to publish a real literary quarterly. He talked Humes into letting the *News-Post* expire and helping him found an expatriate journal that would publish fiction, poetry, and interviews. Humes was supposed to be the managing editor, but he proved so difficult to work with that Matthiessen asked his boyhood friend George Plimpton, whom Styron had met the previous month in London, to come across the Channel and take over the editorial chores. Plimpton, an affable young man who was a little eccentric himself, accepted the invitation and came to Paris after finishing the spring term at Cambridge. Styron and Plimpton became better acquainted now, and Styron was made to understand that Plimpton's accent was not British.

The question during that spring and summer was what kind of magazine these young expatriates wanted to publish and what its title should be. Styron was in on a few of the discussions, and his word carried some weight. He was not a central member of the group, but he had come to Paris with a widely reviewed first novel to his credit and with the Prix de Rome in hand. None of the others was quite this far along, so they listened to what he had to say. Styron's preferences, they found, were in line with theirs. He advocated a quarterly that would emphasize fiction and poetry, not criticism. His belief in the primacy of creative work over criticism, unchanged since his days at Duke, had been intensified by the recent reviews of *Lie Down in Darkness*. Some of those notices, even the positive ones, had irritated him by an obtuseness and condescension that he thought endemic to literary criticism. Many of the quarterlies of that period were heavy with exegetical and critical writing. Matthiessen, Plimpton, Styron, and the others agreed that the new journal should take a different direction. It should eschew criticism and be a showcase for the best creative work they could find.

Other ideas were discussed in the weeks that followed. There was considerable disagreement over whether the magazine should have a political stance and whether it should concentrate on avant-garde writing. The competition in Paris—the two English-language journals *Points* and *Merlin*—published work that was consciously experimental and politically engaged. These were major considerations for the new magazine, and there was much argument back and forth. One afternoon Matthiessen, Styron, Guinzburg, Humes, and du Bois were sitting unhappily in Matthiessen's apartment. They had reached an impasse about editorial policy and had decided to tackle an easier problem for the time being: the title of the quarterly. Should it be *Promises? Manuscript? Ascent? Tides? Weathercock?* At that juncture (as Styron later remembered it) a cheerful Plimpton arrived with two green and sinister-looking bottles of absinthe. Once these had been opened and some of their contents consumed, the discussion proceeded with much greater *amitié*.

The quarterly, it was decided that day, would have no overt political stance, nor would it be limited to avant-garde writing. Fiction and poetry would dominate the issues, with an occasional personal essay. There would be no book reviews, and all contributions would be in English. A staple feature (in every issue, it was hoped) would be an interview with a well-known author. The magazine would also print artwork—sketches, line drawings, photographs, and reproductions of paintings and sculptures. For the name of the quarterly, Matthiessen came up with the obvious choice: *The Paris Review*. Plimpton would serve as editor, and the others would accept various titles and duties. Matthiessen would be the fiction editor, Guinzburg the managing editor, and du Bois the art editor. (The poetry editor, appointed later, was Donald Hall, who had won the Newdigate Prize for Poetry at Oxford.) John Train, a college friend of Plimpton's, would serve as nonfiction editor. Styron, not eager to read manuscripts, would be listed as an advisory editor.

The disputatiousness, energy, and optimism that accompanied the founding of *The Paris Review* spilled over into the Left Bank cafés. Often the group gathered in a small, smoky *boîte* called the Chapelain on a little dogleg street near the Dôme; there was a grand piano there, and customers sometimes gave impromptu recitals. The group also spent time at the famous expatriate hangouts—the Rotonde, Brasserie Lipp, the Coupole, the Sélect, and Deux Magôts. They drank, talked, argued, gossiped, and played word games (the Matthiessens were particularly keen on a contest called Ghost). One drunken evening they burned the ends of their wine corks and drew odd masks on each other; at first the *patron* and the other customers were amused, but soon the antics became boisterous, with eyeglasses jerked from faces and flung into the street. The revelers were told to behave themselves or go elsewhere. "I was wrong about my life being clean and ordered," Styron wrote to his agent, Elizabeth McKee. "It is now slightly fingerprinted around the edges and distinctly disordered, but *très gai.*"

That spring and summer Styron also came to know another kind of nightlife—the haute monde of the Right Bank. His guide was the bluff, vigorous American writer Irwin Shaw, who was a kind of paterfamilias to the "tall young men" (as he called them) of the *Paris Review* set. Shaw, then at the height of his fame, was living a very different kind of expatriate life in Paris. This was the life of chic restaurants and expensive hotels, movie stars and Hollywood moguls. Through Shaw, Styron met Sam Goldwyn, Jr., John Huston, Gene Kelly, Harry Kurnitz, and others from the entertainment world. One night Darryl Zanuck hosted a birthday party for Goldwyn, and Styron was invited. He recalled the evening many years later: "The party was at a restaurant—I still remember the name, Chez Joseph, on the Right Bank, somewhere near the Étoile. I just had never thought of wine as being much of anything, you know. I had been drinking a little dago red in New York. But this must have been a prewar Château Margaux. And it was a revelation to me, to be in this splendid, small, chic restaurant drinking this magnificent wine, with Irwin and everyone else, and Darryl Zanuck paying for it all."

Styron admired Shaw's work, especially his early stories in *The New Yorker*. In fact, Styron had something of a fixation on Shaw. He had hoped he might meet him the previous fall in New York, just after *Lie Down in Darkness* had been published; sometimes during those months he had thought he was seeing Shaw in a bar or a restaurant. "One night, I sat in the Blue Mill Tavern in Greenwich Village and saw a big burly guy with powerful shoulders edging his way toward a table where not one but two girls awaited, fresh-faced and with adoring eyes. I was certain this was Irwin Shaw—perhaps the eager girls reinforced the idea. I had been seeing Shaw from time to time in the city streets ever since my arrival in New York. Almost any heavyset athletic man in his thirties with radiantly good-looking Jewish features was someone I suspected of being the author of 'The Girls in Their Summer Dresses' and 'The Eighty-Yard Run' and 'Act of Faith.' "

Now Styron was in Paris and had Shaw as a friend. The older writer was generous, bighearted, and ostentatious. He drove an enormous green Ford convertible that was almost as wide as some of the narrow streets down which he piloted it. The car drew attention wherever he took it in Paris. Shaw was enjoying a lucrative career as a screenwriter and a best-selling novelist, and he had money and connections. He also had women: he and his wife, Marian, often fought in public about his philandering. All of this was fascinating to Styron, though he could see that it might eventually affect Shaw's work.

Styron's days and nights on the Left Bank were lived on a more modest scale. He had by now moved to a better room in a more comfortable hotel—the Libéria, on the Rue de la Grande Chaumière, near the Dôme. There he had a large, sunny chamber for only ten thousand francs a month, the equivalent in those years of about forty American dollars. Food was also inexpensive; a good meal with a glass or two of wine cost less than two dollars in most Montparnasse restaurants.

Styron also cadged a few meals. He heard from Plimpton that Billy du Bois and his wife had been given the use of a large house in the middle of Paris through December. The place had been occupied by some friends of theirs, U.S. State Department employees who had been transferred to another country. The house, fully furnished and with the rent paid, was turned over to du Bois and his wife for the rest of the lease period. Plimpton was living in the toolshed, which was cluttered with gardening implements and inhabited by a tribe of street cats. Plimpton told Styron that the main house, where du Bois and his wife lived, had come equipped with a freezer full of frankfurters and a cupboard stacked with tins of baked beans—emergency supplies in the event of a Communist coup. Styron came by to investigate. Many years later, du Bois made a funny story of it:

> He appeared one morning and reached in his suit coat pocket from which he extracted an egg and said, "I have here a very fresh egg. Could not the three of us make it into a lunch?" This literary query had an Arabian Nights ring to it. "I have here seven grains of semolina. Let the three of us now sit to a feast of couscous!" The three of us sat to plates of hot dogs and baked beans. William Styron came to our house six days in a row, each time with a very fresh egg in his suit coat pocket. Each time we gave him hot dogs and baked beans. Then on the seventh day he came empty-handed so we made an omelette.

Paris was so seductive in her springtime beauty that Styron found himself content to loaf during his first month or so there. The trees and flowers blossomed, pigeons wheeled aloft against the sky, and cats sat in open windows or prowled along the rooftops. In these years just after the war, there were almost no automobiles in Paris, and it was pleasant and quiet to sit outside the cafés, even on the major thoroughfares. (The only sour notes were the "U.S. Go Home!" slogans, painted on walls here and there by the French Communists.) Styron and his new friends made excursions during the day to Saint-Germain-en-Laye or took picnic lunches of bread, saucissons, and brie to the banks of the Marne. "Paris is just about all they say it is," he wrote to his father. "I must say that the atmosphere here, however, is treacherous—so lulling and lazy that one is content to sit for hours and hours drinking a beer in a café, and to do nothing more, no work, just sit." He told Elizabeth McKee much the same thing: "I would be perfectly contented to stay here a long long time," he said in a letter to her, "were it not for the fact that the climate and what seems to be a perpetual *joie de vivre* in the air precludes the writing of long, tragic novels."

As pleasant as these days were, they were also lonely. Styron could spend only so many hours with the *Paris Review* crowd, talking and drinking. His new lodgings were across a big courtyard from Reed Hall, the building in which the junior-year-abroad contingent from Smith College was housed, and he sometimes watched from his window as the college girls entered and left. He tried to chat up two or three of them but found them self-absorbed, interested only in their own odds and ids—for they all seemed to have undergone psychoanalysis. Just to see what might happen, Styron put his name in the "Who is Where" lonely-hearts column in the Paris *Herald-Tribune.* He received about a dozen responses, but all were from "people whom I haven't the vaguest desire to meet," he reported to McKee. He filled the empty time by reading and by writing letters. He also studied his Paris guidebook and map, much as he had pored over the Rand-McNally atlas ten years before at Christchurch. He committed the layout and parts of the street plan of the city to memory, learning the locations of museums and monuments, the addresses of cafés and bistros, the locations of Metro stops and railroad stations. He also took walks, sometimes along the Boulevard Saint-Michel or over to the Luxembourg Gardens but more often with no particular destination in mind, simply to study the city and absorb its atmosphere—and of course to look at the Parisian women, many of whom he found lovely, but to whom he was reluctant to speak in his crippled French.

Styron was beginning to think about his next novel. He knew that he had made a good beginning with *Lie Down in Darkness* and was determined to follow it with a second effort that was even better. Mulling over the possibilities, he decided tentatively to write about Nat Turner and his 1831 slave rebellion, a subject that had been prodding at the edges of his consciousness for years. Styron had read a good bit about the history of American slavery, but he had made no focused attempt to educate himself on the subject. Now he proposed to do so. He was in

Paris, however, far from a comprehensive American library, and he was scheduled to go to Rome in October for his fellowship year at the American Academy. If he were to learn about the Nat Turner Rebellion, he would need help. On May Day, 1951, he included this paragraph in a letter to his father:

> I've finally pretty much decided what to write next—a novel based on Nat Turner's rebellion. The subject fascinates me, and I think I could make a real character out of old Nat. It'll probably take a bit of research, though, and I've written to people in the U.S.—among them Prof. Saunders Redding (whom I saw Christmas, you remember) of Hampton Institute—asking them to pass on any reference material they might have. Perhaps you know of a book or something on Nat Turner and would be willing to get it sent to me somehow. Actually, I'd be extremely interested in anything on life around the Southside-Carolina Border country of Virginia in the 1820–1850 period. If you can get your hands on something on that order without too much trouble I'd appreciate your letting me know. I don't know but whether I'm plunging into something over my depth, but I'm fascinated anyway.

The Hampton Institute faculty member mentioned by Styron in this letter was J. Saunders Redding, then a professor of English at the college. Redding, who held his degrees from Brown, had become friendly with Hiram Haydn through the *American Scholar* and had published his first book, *On Being Negro in America,* with Bobbs-Merrill in 1950. Thus he and Styron shared an editor and a publisher. Redding helped Styron by sending over a packet of materials, including a copy of William S. Drewry's *The Southampton Insurrection* (1900), the only book-length historical account of the rebellion then available. Redding sent two other books as well—Frederick Law Olmsted's *A Journey in the Seaboard Slave States* and June Purcell Guild's *Black Laws of Virginia.*

The senior Styron, with his experience as an amateur genealogist, visited the Virginia State Library in Richmond and did some digging. He sent over a sheaf of photostats—articles and newspaper accounts published just after the uprising, most of them hysterical and inflammatory. These, Styron sensed, would not be of much use to him, but he was intrigued by a photostat of an ornately written five-thousand-word pamphlet entitled "The Confessions of Nat Turner," ostensibly taken down from Nat's lips in his jail cell while he awaited execution. The author of the pamphlet was a Southampton County lawyer named T. R. Gray, a shadowy figure whose reliability could not be known. Styron sensed, however, that at least some truth lay behind Gray's florid rhetoric.

Styron also wrote to Elizabeth McKee for help, asking that she purchase copies for him of Herbert Aptheker's *Negro Slave Revolts in the United States* and Ulrich B. Phillips's *Life and Labor in the Old South.* He worried a little about doing too much research and producing what amounted to a novel of manners about antebellum life in the Old Dominion. "I don't want to be known as the J. P. Marquand of Virginia or the Scott Fitzgerald of Lost Generation II," he told McKee, "but simply as a writer who is versatile enough to tackle anything."

Styron knew that it would be difficult to write about Nat Turner while living at the American Academy in Rome. He thought that he needed to spend a long period—several years, probably—reading about American slavery before he tried to write about it. He seems also to have sensed that he was not yet prepared, not intellectually mature enough, to confront the complex questions that a novel about a slave insurrection might bring out. He was certain, though, that he would not use the figure of Nat Turner to make an ideological statement. After he had read through the materials that his father and Saunders Redding had sent, he put down that resolution in a letter to Styron *père:* "I hope that when I'm through with Nat Turner (and God, I know it's going to be a long, hard job) he will not be either a Great Leader of the Masses—as the stupid, vicious Jackass of a Communist writer might make him out—or a perfectly satanic demagogue, as the surface historical facts present him, but a living human being of great power and great potential who somewhere, in his struggle for freedom and for immortality, lost his way."

Styron wrote to Hiram Haydn to get his reaction to this proposed novel. Haydn had never been in favor of Styron's writing about the Nat Turner Rebellion: he had discouraged him from tackling the subject when Styron was a student at the New School, and he still had misgivings. These he set down in a return letter to Styron: "I will repeat just what seems to me to be the central point: I would hate to see you get involved in subject matter as purple as your own imagination is. Purple, mind you, is a royal color, and what I am saying is intended to convey not a feeling that you are overly lush, but that the very richness and (in its exact sense) romantic coloring is not only the strength of your imag-inative gift and indeed of your vision, but also a potential danger. Just in so far as the decent recognizable every-day bread was present in *Lie Down in Darkness,* was the rich and wonderful jam that you spread on it really digestible."

Haydn's lack of encouragement, coupled with the difficulties of com-posing a historical novel about Southside Virginia while living in Italy, convinced Styron that he should postpone writing about Nat Turner. He would continue to read about slavery and plantation life, but for now he would write about something else.

17

❦

The
Long March

STYRON DECIDED to write about military service. It had been about a year earlier that Styron had reentered the Marine Corps. The memories from Camp Lejeune—the mortar explosions, the dead marines, the absurdly long march—were still fresh. He wanted to write about military life, in part because the two young American novelists against whom he was beginning to measure himself, Norman Mailer and James Jones, had already published important novels about warfare and the military—*The Naked and the Dead* and *From Here to Eternity.* Styron's wartime experiences had been relatively tame, but he knew that his time in the Marine Corps could still yield good material for fiction. The short mortar rounds and the long march at Lejeune were worth writing about; he decided now to transform them into fiction.

Styron's initial plan was to write a short story. He had an outlet in mind: a young writer named Vance Bourjaily had contacted him and described a new publication that he and the critic John W. Aldridge were to co-edit. This was *Discovery,* a periodical in paperback-book format that would feature fiction, poetry, and essays by young writers of talent. The journal would have no overt political stance and would resist what its editors, in their opening manifesto, called the tendency "to homogenize or otherwise adulterate the contents to meet the specifications of a particular style or school of writing, or to satisfy the demands of a pressure or special-interest group." (This turned out to be a matter of some importance for Styron because he would need to use obscenity—the word *fuck*—at the crucial point in his narrative.) *Discovery* would set no limits on form, approach, or length. Perhaps the most innovative thing about the journal was that it would be marketed as a thirty-five-cent paperback, on newsstands and drugstore bookracks, rather than as a conventional literary magazine sold from bookshops. In this way Bourjaily and Aldridge (and their publisher, Pocket Books) planned to tap into a distribution system that could reach a broad, nonacademic market. They hoped for a circulation as large as one hundred thousand and promised to pay their writers well.

Styron was pleased that he had been asked to contribute to the new journal: "In France, arse is longa and vita is brevis," he wrote to Bourjaily, "which, freely translated, means that there's plenty of tail around but it's not every day you get a chance to pick up a buck through *Discovery*." Styron probably felt that he could reach his natural audience— the readers of *Lie Down in Darkness*—through the journal. His decision to publish there also signaled the end, for the most part, of his efforts to write for conventional literary quarterlies. If he wanted to publish in a quarterly, he would aim for *The Paris Review,* assuming that it survived and prospered. Otherwise he would publish in periodicals that had substantial distribution and large readership.

That June, Styron began a manuscript based on his experiences at Camp Lejeune. Eventually this manuscript would become *The Long March.* At first Styron was not sure exactly what length or form the narrative would take but was conscious of what its themes would be—the absurdity of the soldier's life, the power of bureaucracy to influence human behavior, and the sinister dangers of a large military establishment. Years later Styron recalled that the writing went smoothly. "Through some stroke of luck," he remembered, "form and substance fused into a single harmonious whole and it all went down on paper with miraculous ease." Styron worked on the manuscript every afternoon, closeted in his hotel room. (He tried once or twice to write in Left Bank cafés, in the manner of Hemingway, but found that he could not concentrate.) In the two early, aborted versions of *Lie Down in Darkness,* Styron had struggled to find the right narrative voice, but with this story he had no such difficulty. He chose an omniscient narrative voice but filtered all action through the mind of a peripheral character, a Jamesian vessel of consciousness—Lieutenant Thomas Culver, a young attorney in civilian life who, like Styron, had been recalled into the Marine Corps for the Korean War.

Culver's perspective is maintained throughout: he is appalled by the idiocies of military life—the posturing and game-playing, the abuses of language, the carelessness and waste, and the mindlessness of the training. His ironic reactions, spoken to others or reported by the omniscient voice, are present in a minor key throughout the story. The chief object of Culver's interest is Captain Al Mannix, a rebellious Jewish reservist from Brooklyn who is outspokenly critical of the Marine Corps. Culver is the first of Styron's "square" observers: like Peter Leverett in *Set This House on Fire* and Stingo in *Sophie's Choice,* he is fascinated by rebellious behavior in others but does not himself yet have the courage to revolt. Because he is friendly with Mannix, Culver can function in the narrative as an intermediary, observing and interpreting Mannix's actions to the reader. Mannix talks to Culver, or talks *at* him, but Mannix never carries the narrative himself, nor does the reader have access to his thoughts.

In composing the story, Styron followed fairly closely his own training-camp experiences from the previous year. The narrative opens with the immediate aftermath of the mortar explosions: carnage is everywhere, mixed with half-eaten food and melting ice cream from a noontime chow line. Culver observes the damage and, badly shaken, returns to his unit, where his commander, Colonel Rocky Templeton, has decided to go ahead with a thirty-six-mile forced march for the next day. (Templeton is loosely modeled on Jungle Jim Masters.) The troops set out at dawn; as they march along, the reader enters more deeply into Culver's mind. Soon he and his men begin to tire. Flashbacks to civilian life and to earlier training-camp scenes creep into the narrative. There is a nightmarish, surrealistic quality to much of this part of the story, as if Culver is observing the march from a disembodied viewpoint, hovering above the weary, footsore men, watching impassively as they fall one by one beside the road and watching himself as he trudges doggedly ahead.

Styron's working title for his story was "Like Prisoners, Waking." The phrase, apparently an allusion to Beethoven's *Fidelio,* was meant to suggest that the marines had become prisoners, faceless zeroes dehumanized by military bureaucracy and discipline. But as he progressed, Styron found that Mannix had begun to push to the forefront of the narrative. "All my intentions to the contrary," Styron remembered, "I began to understand, as I wrote, that even in the midst of an ultimate process of dehumanization the human spirit cannot be utterly denied or downed." Mannix becomes the dominant character, stubborn and sweating, so rebellious that he eventually lashes out at Templeton. "*Fuck* you and your information!" he shouts, and for this act he is placed under arrest for gross insubordination. A court-martial is to follow, we understand, after the conclusion of the story.

As Styron worked on his manuscript through June and early July, it grew beyond the length of a normal short story. If he had been writing for a conventional periodical, he would have been required to bring the story to a quick conclusion, but because *Discovery* placed no length restrictions on its contributors, Styron could allow his tale to reach its natural length. The narrative, though more than twice as long as a conventional short story, is not loose or digressive; in fact it is one of the most economically written pieces of fiction that Styron ever produced.

The narrative covers a single twenty-four-hour period and is bound tightly together by image and symbol. Dominating the story is a sense of illogic and absurdity: Mannix wants to know *whom* to blame for the accident of the short mortar rounds, but there is no one who can or will assume guilt; responsibility is diffused and made impersonal by bureaucratic language and by the chain of command. Mannix knows this; he knows too that his impulsive rebellion against Templeton is misdirected. Templeton himself is not to blame for the pain and suffering of the men; both he and they are parts of a military apparatus that robs all men of individuality and identity. Even Mannix is implicated. He realizes in the end that he and Templeton were simply acting out roles that had been anticipated and prepared for within the Marine Corps system.

By July 15 Styron had nearly finished the manuscript. He wrote Bourjaily that the story would probably run a little under twenty thousand words and that it would be quite different from *Lie Down in Darkness.* "I'm pleased with it," Styron wrote in his letter, "and think it will turn out to be a strong pis of goots, as they say on 37th Street." Privately, though, he was uncertain about "Like Prisoners, Waking." It was an odd length and was written in an unusually spare style, more elliptical and suggestive than anything he had ever produced—partly, one suspects, in reaction to Haydn's letter about bread, jam, and the purple imagination. Styron therefore decided to try out the story on his *Paris Review* friends. He felt comfortable enough by now to read his work aloud to them, and he thought that most of them would be frank in their criticisms.

An impromptu reading was arranged. It was to take place in the Matthiessens' apartment: they had departed for Saint-Jean-de-Luz in the south of France, but Plimpton was apartment-sitting, and he served as host for the gathering. It was scheduled for the late afternoon; Plimpton issued invitations and supplied wine, cheese, and baguettes. In later years neither Styron nor Plimpton could recall exactly who came to the reading. Doc Humes and Mary Lee were certainly there, as were Billy and Jane du Bois. Probably there were others as well. Plimpton did remember that Styron went through a long preliminary round of throat-clearing before he began to read and that he was obviously nervous. Once under way, though, he read in a strong voice.

The people there had looked to the occasion more as a duty than as a pleasure, but as Styron read his way into the story they found themselves caught up in its momentum and intrigued by its eerie, dreamlike quality. Plimpton remembered that the sun set and the room grew cool, but no one stirred. "Part of the excitement," he recalled, "was that we were hearing something for the first time and exclusively—as if we were the first people into a great artist's studio to see a new work." Toward the end of the reading it became so dark that Humes had to light candles and place them on a table near Styron so that he could see to read. Plimpton recalled that the candles illuminated Styron's face and made it seem to float disembodied in the darkened studio. Hoarse by now, Styron read his final sentence and turned the last handwritten page facedown on the table. There was a long pause: then a voice from outside the circle of light said: "Well . . . *Mister* Styron!"

Forty years later, Plimpton could not recall who had uttered the words. He thought at one point that the speaker might have been James Baldwin, but Styron was certain that he and Baldwin did not meet until several years later. Plimpton was sure, though, that the speaker meant the words as "an accolade, a benediction." Others in the group quickly added their praise. Most of them had read *Lie Down in Darkness* and could see that Styron's new narrative was quite different from that novel. They were impressed by this versatility, but there was something else in the air as well, a mixture of admiration and envy. It was as if Styron had deliberately demonstrated his talent by turning out, under their very noses, this piece of excellent new writing. In the evenings he had eaten and imbibed and gossiped with them in the cafés and bistros, but in the afternoons, when no one ever saw him, he had put this arresting narrative down on paper. No one else was getting much work done— Paris was too distracting—but Styron had somehow found the energy to compose a substantial new work from start to finish, while joining in the obligatory expatriate activities almost every night. To the *Paris Review* crowd it was a notable display of self-discipline.

At about this time Plimpton asked Styron to write an opening statement, a credo of sorts, for the first issue of *The Paris Review*. Styron was a little surprised by the invitation: he had been content to be involved only peripherally with the journal and was hesitant about putting his ideas so visibly forward. He could see, though, that there was logic in Plimpton's request. He was the best-known member of the group: *Lie Down in Darkness* had been widely reviewed and discussed, and this new narrative, once it appeared in *Discovery,* would add to his visibility and reputation. Styron also felt that his ideas about the importance of creative work as opposed to criticism were worth putting into print. He agreed to write an opening salvo for the first issue and promised to have it finished before he left for Rome in the fall.

At this point there was also a small comic interlude. Styron had learned, from his agent for foreign rights, that the translation of *Lie Down in Darkness* into French had almost been completed. The novel would be titled *Un Lit de ténèbres* ("A Bed of Shadows") and would be issued soon by Editions Mondiales del Duca, a rising French house. The translator, however, had found it necessary to change Peyton's name throughout to Marjorie. Styron explained the problem in a letter to his father: " 'Peyton,' in French, read aloud, means the sound the intestines make after a large meal." He might have elaborated a bit more: the word *pe,* in French slang, means flatulence; and *-ton* is a fairly common diminutive ending. Thus Peyton's name, pronounced *pe-ton,* with the stress on the first syllable, would have suggested "small fart" to the average French reader. *Un Lit de ténèbres* was published in Paris in February 1953, to respectful reviews. The French as yet showed no special enthusiasm for Styron's work, but the translation did introduce him to

French readers and make him known to some important reviewers and critics.

Weary from his labor on "Like Prisoners, Waking," Styron decided to get away from Paris and take a trip to the south of France. He would travel with Doc Humes and with Mary Lee, who agreed to go along for part of the way. The mode of conveyance was to be Humes's rattletrap Volkswagen, a vehicle almost as eccentric as Humes himself. "It was blue and had a terrible odor," Plimpton remembered. "I don't know what had happened in there." The vehicle also had no brakes to speak of; one had to gear it down well in advance of a planned stop and had sometimes to open the door and drag one's foot on the pavement to bring it to a complete halt.

The trip commenced early in August, and at first it went well. Humes, Mary Lee, and Styron headed south, reaching the Rhone Valley and continuing on toward Saint-Tropez on the Côte d'Azur. By that time, however, Humes had begun to get on Styron's nerves. He was opinionated and overbearing, a nonstop talker and pontificator. "I couldn't get a word in edgewise," Styron remembered with a laugh. "Also, Doc was a psychopath." The car was jammed with luggage, and the strange odor was oppressive in the summer heat. By the time they reached Saint-Tropez, Mary Lee had dropped out and he and Humes were barely speaking to each other.

Fortunately they had a wonderful interlude by the sea there: they stayed with a movie actress from the early days of the French cinema, an older woman whom Humes had befriended in Paris. Her name was Marie-Thérèse Nénot, and she lived on a large estate overlooking the bay. Styron went skin-diving in the afternoons and acquired a tan. "I began to feel as healthy as Tarzan," he wrote to his father. He also betook himself to Mme. Nénot's kitchen and showed off his culinary skills: "I single-handed cooked a fried-chicken dinner for 18 count 'em 18 discriminating Frenchmen, all gourmets, and was applauded wildly: *quel poulet! formidable!*" After dinner each night their hostess, who spoke English well, told Styron and Humes romantic stories about her wartime experiences with the Free French in Algeria. She had fallen in love with an American naval officer who later, when invading France at Cap Myrtes, had been ordered to shell her estate—the very place where they sat—because the Germans were using it as a command post. The story was surely true, Styron thought, since parts of the estate were still in ruins from the bombardment.

Styron had brought the handwritten manuscript of "Like Prisoners, Waking" south with him on the trip; he had not yet managed to have it typed, and he was becoming nervous about making his August 15 deadline with *Discovery*. Humes, however, was resourceful. He located a young Danish typist in Saint-Tropez who had good English; she copied the text quickly for Styron, producing a ribbon and a carbon copy, and he mailed the ribbon copy off to Elizabeth McKee for submission to Bourjaily. Relieved of that worry, Styron resumed his journey with Humes. They headed west to Carcassone and spent a day touring that ancient fortified city. Then they continued on to Saint-Jean-de-Luz, a pleasant bathing and gambling resort on the Côte Basque, at the westernmost edge of the Pyrenees. The Shaws and the Matthiessens were already there and introduced them to a new couple, Art Buchwald and Ann McGarry, who were going to be married in October. Buchwald, a Marine Corps veteran and an alumnus of Southern Cal, was a columnist for the *International Herald-Tribune*. He was beginning to make a reputation for himself as a humorist, and his pieces were being syndicated in the United States.

One afternoon during the visit, Styron went to the bullfights in Bayonne with Shaw, Buchwald, Matthiessen, and Humes. Bullfighting was illegal in France if the bulls were to be killed, but in the southwest section of Gascony, just over the border from Spain, the prohibition was winked at if the bullfight promoters paid the fine in advance. Buchwald wrote up the event for the *Herald-Trib* in a mock-Hemingway *Death in the Afternoon* style, calling Matthiessen "the Old Lady" and letting him explain the fine points of the corrida to the others.

In Saint-Jean-de-Luz that week, Shaw played his customary role as generous host. He and Marian had rented a large house, which the young writers referred to as Le Château, and it became the focal point for the festivities. If the weather was good, the day began around one o'clock on the beach, where everyone gathered after ostensibly having spent the morning laboring on their writings. Someone would bring food, and the crowd would eat and swim and drink into the late afternoon. After breaking for showers and naps, they usually reassembled in the evening for dinner, either at Le Château or at a good restaurant. Shaw always picked up the check: *"L'addition, s'il vous plaît—à moi!"* he would say in fluent but Brooklyn-flavored French.

The trip back to Paris with Humes was as nerve-racking as Styron had feared, but he managed to endure it. He had thought that he might die in Humes's odoriferous vehicle—if not from asphyxiation, then from brake failure or from Humes's erratic driving—but he arrived safely back in the city in early August. Automobiles were not finished with him, though: one night, after a tour of the cafés, Matthiessen backed his little auto into Styron's leg as Styron stood behind the car. Styron was knocked to the sidewalk and his leg was so deeply bruised that he limped about for the remainder of his time in the city.

While he convalesced, Styron put his mind to writing the manifesto for the inaugural issue of *The Paris Review.* The first version of this statement does not survive, but apparently Styron had difficulty with it. He was uncomfortable composing in an oracular mode and felt that what he produced was stiff and truculent. Matthiessen, Plimpton, and John Train would later agree, but their criticisms would not reach Styron until he had left Paris and settled in Rome.

Other criticisms of his writing, however, did come to Styron. He had mailed a copy of the typescript of "Like Prisoners, Waking" to Hiram Haydn for his comments; now Haydn sent a letter with suggestions for a revised ending. Overall Haydn found the novella a "corking good job" and praised Styron for striking out in a new direction after *Lie Down in Darkness.* "It may interest you to know that I was constantly reminded of Conrad," said Haydn—a reaction that many subsequent readers of the narrative have had. Haydn had reservations, however, about the conclusion: "I was terribly bothered by a sense of the resolution not being achieved at the end. I reread the final scene with Culver looking down on Mannix sleeping three times trying to get more out of it than the sense of Culver's compassion and understanding. I didn't succeed, and hence I was left with a slightly unsatisfied feeling—one of irresolution. Can you clarify this?"

Haydn refers here to an ending for "Like Prisoners, Waking" that no longer survives in its entirety. Only a small fragment is present in the handwritten draft: in this extant bit, Culver and a jeep driver take Mannix to his room, put him in bed, and remove his shoes. Mannix falls asleep almost immediately, and Culver leaves to go to his own room. Haydn's letter suggests that, in the last few paragraphs of the novella, Culver returns and gazes compassionately at Mannix as he lies in exhausted slumber.

The matter is of some importance because Styron did rewrite the conclusion of the novella, and this ending—the published one—has been widely praised. In the new ending Mannix returns to his quarters, strips off his clothes, wraps a towel around his waist, and struggles down the hall toward the showers. Culver watches him as he inches his way along and sees him come face-to-face with a black maid who cleans their rooms. " 'Oh my, you poor man,' " she says. " 'Do it hurt?' " Mannix, who barely has the strength to reply, tries to take another step but falters. His towel falls to the floor, and he stands naked and helpless before the sympathetic woman. Culver senses that the two people, the Negro and the Jew, can communicate "across that chasm one unspoken moment of sympathy and understanding." " 'Deed it does,' " says Mannix ruefully. " 'Deed it does.' "—and there the novella ends.

The surviving holograph shows that Styron worked hard on this revised ending, composing it first in a short version and then rewriting it to introduce a longer, slower rhythm and a sense of anticipation as one approaches the last line. This revised ending he typed up himself and mailed to both Bourjaily and Haydn.

During his last few weeks in Paris, Styron attempted no new writing. Wanda Malinowska passed through on her way to Italy, and they saw some of the city together. Matthiessen and Plimpton also conducted an interview with him for *The Paris Review.* They had decided to publish an interview with a well-known writer in each issue of the journal. These interviews, which became one of the best-known features of the magazine, were not belletristic chitchat; they concentrated on the working methods of the writers—their ways of gathering material, their habits of composition, and their attitudes toward their craft. E. M. Forster, whom Plimpton had known at King's College, Cambridge, had agreed to be the first subject, and he had asked to see the questions in advance. Thus he had been able to think about his answers and essentially had dictated them to his interviewers. This established a precedent; from then on, the subjects were usually given their questions ahead of time. Interviewers usually worked in pairs ("like FBI agents," Malcolm Cowley later said). They took turns posing questions, and both scribbled down the answers, since tape recorders were not then readily portable or easy to use. Later the two transcripts were compared and conflated.

Styron was a natural subject for Plimpton and Matthiessen. He was immediately available, for one thing, and both of them knew his writing well. He had helped to found *The Paris Review* and was going to supply its opening statement of aims. Plimpton and Matthiessen arranged to interview him one morning about two weeks after he had returned to Paris from the southern tour with Humes. The three men met at Patricks, a café on the Boulevard Montparnasse. The hour was unconscionably early for Styron; in their headnote, Plimpton and Matthiessen record that he was "a little paler than is healthy in this quiet hour when the denizens of the quarter lie hiding." Styron shielded his eyes from the morning sun, they reported, and drank strong coffee during the first hour of the conversation.

Perhaps because of the early hour, Styron's responses were irritable and testy. "Do you enjoy writing?" he was asked. "I certainly don't," he replied. "I get a fine warm feeling when I'm doing well, but that pleasure is pretty much negated by the pain of getting started each day. Let's face it, writing is hell." He was asked about his composing habits: "What time of the day do you find best for working?" asked Plimpton. "The afternoon," answered Styron. "I like to stay up late at night and get drunk and sleep late. I wish I could break the habit but I can't. The afternoon is the only time I have left and I try to use it to the best advantage, with a hangover."

The interview proceeded, with Styron shifting now to cognac. There were questions about hypochondria, his roots in the South, his handling of time in *Lie Down in Darkness,* the models for his characters, his feelings about book critics, and his attitudes toward his fellow writers. What emerges is a picture of a sensitive, nervous young artist, uneasy in the role of interview subject but willing to state some opinions all the same. He is uncomfortable when asked about the influence of Joyce and Faulkner on his work. He is not willing to be seen as Faulkner's disciple or even as a particularly "southern" writer. He resents the tags of gloominess and morbidity that have been affixed to him and to other members of his generation: "The new writers haven't cornered any market on faithlessness and despair," he says. "Every age has its terrible aches and pains, its peculiar new horrors." Asked at the end of the interview for his thoughts on the writer engagé, Styron says:

> Most writers write simply out of some strong interior need. . . . A great writer, writing out of this need, will give substance to and perhaps even explain all the problems of the world without even knowing it, until a scholar comes along a hundred years after he's dead and

digs up some symbols. The purpose of a young writer is to write, and he shouldn't drink too much. He shouldn't think that after he's written one book he's God Almighty and air all his immature opinions in pompous interviews. Let's have another cognac and go up to Le Chapelain.

Styron was beginning to feel restless in Paris. He was learning that his periods of creativity—in this case the composition of "Like Prisoners, Waking"—were likely to be followed by stretches of enervation and depression. Such times were full of aimless worrying, jitteriness, insomnia, and increased drinking. Usually he was not good company during these periods.

Styron was ready now to move on to Rome. "Life in Paris has been fine," he reported to his friend John Marquand back in New York, "but has become monotonously the same during the past few weeks." Part of the trouble was that he was not writing anything. "With nothing to do now in Paris, and no project to concentrate on, the place has become something of a drag." Even with the *Paris Review* crowd to divert him he was bored. "Hell," he said in the letter, "the literary life is sure a pain in the ass, isn't it?"

Styron's time in Paris during the spring and summer of 1952 was important to him. For the first time in his life he had lived in a sophisticated city abroad; he had overcome his culture shock and learned to function on unfamiliar territory. He had seen, at first hand, the café life of the Left Bank and had enjoyed some of the upmarket pleasures of the Right Bank. He had completed a second work of fiction—not a full-length novel, but an innovative piece of respectable length that was scheduled to appear in a visible new outlet. He had also met the *Paris Review* crowd and won their respect. This group, which expanded over the next few years to include several other writers, was the only thing resembling a literary circle that Styron ever belonged to, and his friendships with most of its members lasted. Certainly he never felt constricted by this group, for it had no particular stance or policy, but he identified himself with *The Paris Review* and was always proud of the part he had played in its founding.

Styron's first exposure to French culture, it must be said, was relatively superficial. He saw Paris at her very best, in the spring and summer, at a period when the dollar was strong. He drank the wines and enjoyed the cuisine, walked the streets and saw the sights. He had not yet begun to study French thinking and writing: he had met no French intellectuals and had read very little in the way of contemporary French literature. His first exposure to France, however, did encourage him to press ahead and learn more about the culture—its customs, history, literature, and habits of mind. His own attitudes, then forming themselves, would eventually be shaped profoundly by French thinking and by a French reading public that would, a decade later, discover his work and begin to read it avidly.

18

Rome

TOWARD THE END of September, before leaving Paris, Styron showed "Like Prisoners, Waking" to Peter Matthiessen, who was now back in the city. Styron wanted to know what Matthiessen thought of the story; he also hoped that his friend might help him come up with a better title. Matthiessen had suggested the obvious title for *The Paris Review;* perhaps he could think of something as good for the novella. Matthiessen read the manuscript and praised it, especially its spare language and tight structure. And Matthiessen had a title that Styron liked: "The Long March."

Styron had booked a space on an overnight train to Rome; Matthiessen agreed to take him to the Gare de Lyon for the late-afternoon departure. The two men arrived at the station early and had drinks in a café there. They sat at the table for over an hour, discussing the novella. Matthiessen was still thinking about the title. The hour grew late, and the time of Styron's departure came near. At just that point Matthiessen suggested that Styron drop "The" from the title and simply call the novella "Long March." Styron liked the simplicity of the two-word title and decided, then and there, to use it for the *Discovery* text. He would write to Elizabeth McKee from Rome, he said, letting her know of the title change. Then Styron and Matthiessen looked at their watches and saw that Styron's train was about to pull out. They put some francs on the table, then hustled through the Gare de Lyon, getting Styron to the train just in time. Styron slept fitfully in his compartment that night: years later he remembered waking the next morning to see red-tiled roofs through the train windows. He was in Italy.

Styron settled in at the American Academy during the next two weeks. It was an impressive place. The Academy had been founded in 1894 by a group of prominent men who wished to make an American artistic and scholarly presence felt in Rome. They especially wanted young American classicists, archaeologists, architects, painters, and sculptors to be exposed to the influences of the city. Chief among the founders was Charles Follen McKim, senior partner of the New York architectural firm of McKim, Mead, and White. In 1914, backed by money from the financier J. P. Morgan and others, the Academy erected a large central building on the most elevated point of the Janiculum, the highest hill in Rome. This handsome, imposing structure was arranged around an open central courtyard. By the time Styron arrived in 1952, the Academy had expanded to take over three villas adjacent to it on the Janiculum—including the lovely Villa Aurelia, built during the seventeenth century for a Farnese cardinal.

During his first few weeks in Rome, Styron took walks around the city and went on expeditions organized by the Academy. He saw the standard sights: the Forum, the Vatican, the Pantheon, the Trevi Fountain, and the Palatine Hill. He also took an Academy-sponsored trip to Siena, Florence, Ravenna, Urbino, and Assisi. Everywhere in Rome he was conscious of the fountains and the baroque architecture of Borromini, Maderna, Bernini, and Pietro da Cortona. He could also see that Mussolini's unfinished plans for a *Roma monumentale del XX secolo* had left vulgar marks on the city. The Catholic Church was a dominating presence: priests, nuns, monks, and seminarians were everywhere, and the Academy-organized tours took him into more churches and cathedrals than he really wanted to visit. The weather was cool but still pleasant in October; sometimes he would sit at the cafés in the Piazza di Santa Maria, down the hill from the Academy, drinking Chianti or *birra,* studying his Italian phrase book and watching the native Romans. The only real irritation was the racket of the Vespa and Lambretta motorbikes that the young Italians piloted through the narrow streets.

Styron saw quickly that there was a clear division at the Academy between the artists and the scholars. That separation had existed from the earliest days of the institution—and persists, in fact, to the present day. Styron, as the only writer in residence, gravitated naturally to the painters, sculptors, and composers. They tended to be the looser and more relaxed group, easier to talk to and always ready to venture into the city on exploratory expeditions. Styron fit in well enough with these people. He felt free and unconnected—not a bad state, he thought, since he had no girlfriend. His relationship with Bobbie Taeusch had faded away: he and she had concluded that they were not meant to be married and had fallen out of touch, not even exchanging letters now. Perhaps he would meet someone new in Rome.

Styron's quarters at the Academy consisted of a small bedroom and a writing studio with a large window; he also had access to a general reading room, a library, and a billiard room, where he shot an occasional game of eight-ball. His meals were covered by his fellowship, but the food was bland and predictable. Styron quickly tired of it and got into the habit of taking his meals in Trastevere, a picturesque part of Rome down the hill from the Academy, filled with good trattorias and outdoor cafés. There he ate when it suited him and did not feel tied to the Academy's schedule. On most days he was satisfied enough with this state of affairs, though sometimes he found himself oddly homesick for America. "I'm really not much of a traveler," he confessed in a letter to John Marquand, "my baggage being my own neuroses and a hacking cough, which weigh me down too heavily, even if I were in the Garden of Eden."

One morning in late October, while on an Academy-sponsored trip to Florence, Styron was introduced to Robert White, a sculptor and painter who had just arrived in Italy. White, whom everyone called Bobby, was the grandson of the famous architect Stanford White. Bobby had won a fellowship to the Academy and was beginning a three-year stay in Italy. He was planning some figures in terra-cotta and was also beginning to work on a commission for a large stained-glass window. Bobby White and Styron hit it off, and White invited Styron to come along to a nearby café to meet his wife, Claire, a slim, dark-haired woman from the Limburg region of the Netherlands. Bobby and Claire had been staying with friends in Florence until they could find a place to live in Rome near the Academy. After two weeks of searching, Bobby had finally located an apartment—a new flat that was nondescript but comfortable. They were planning to move there very soon. The Whites already had two small children, a son named Sebastian and a daughter named Stephanie, and Claire was pregnant with their third child, Christian. In later years she remembered feeling very bulky as she sat in the café and greeted her husband's new friend.

Styron took an immediate liking to the Whites. Bobby, who was a little older than he, was garrulous and unpretentious. His talk was irreverent, his opinions delivered *con brio.* Claire was intelligent and lively, though just then she was weary from her pregnancy. She had a degree from Smith College, and was already beginning to write and publish poetry in English. She had read *Lie Down in Darkness* not long before and had been moved by the book; it pleased Styron when she told him so. He spent the rest of the afternoon with the Whites, going with them for lunch and a long session of talking and imbibing. It was soothing to be with them, drinking wine and listening to Bobby's funny monologues on the Italians and their ways.

A day or two later Styron found a note in his mailbox at the Academy. It was from Rose Burgunder, the graduate student he had met the previous fall in Louis Rubin's seminar at Johns Hopkins. She was in Rome and had received a letter from Rubin, telling her that Styron had won the Prix de Rome and was in the city for a year. She had been visiting the Academy with a friend and had noticed Styron's name on one of the mailboxes outside the director's office. On impulse she had scribbled a note to him, leaving her telephone number. Styron did not remember Rose by name. He hoped, though, that she might be the young woman he had chatted with after Rubin's class the previous October. He phoned her, making a date to meet two days later at the bar of the Hotel Excelsior, on the Via Veneto, not far from the Borghese Gardens. When Rose arrived at the bar (wearing a black velvet cape, lined in red, she later remembered) Styron was happy to see that she was indeed the good-looking young graduate student who had come to his reading the previous autumn. She was a small woman with wavy brunette hair, green eyes, and a quick, direct smile. She had been traveling in the south of Italy, and her skin had become darkly tanned. Her look was vaguely Mediterranean and a little exotic; he was immediately attracted to her.

Rose Burgunder was from an old German-Jewish family in Baltimore. Her ancestors had come to Maryland in the 1830s; her own family had been situated in Baltimore for more than three generations. Her father, B. B. Burgunder, had been a successful stockbroker in a Baltimore firm for most of his career. Her mother, Selma Kann, was from the family that owned Kann's, a department store at Seventh and Pennsylvania in Washington, D.C. Both sides of the family were active in civic work and liberal causes; Kann's, in fact, had been the first department store in Washington to integrate its sales force and to serve black people at its soda fountain and lunchroom. When Selma's father died, B. B. Burgunder had taken a leave of absence from his brokerage and assumed the top position at Kann's. He had liked the work so much that he had stayed on; he had also continued to invest in the stock market, on his own, with uncanny skill. He had died in 1948, leaving Rose's mother a well-to-do widow.

Rose's great passion was for modern poetry and criticism. She was a poet herself and had long been attracted to the verse of Donne and the other Metaphysical poets. Among the moderns she favored Yeats, Auden, Eliot, and Stevens; critics who interested her were I. A. Richards, William Empson, R. P. Blackmur, and Allen Tate. She had graduated from Wellesley in 1950 and had just finished an M.A. at Johns Hopkins, but she was not convinced that she wanted to take a Ph.D. and enter academe. She had decided to take time off for travel and study in Europe. That summer she had done some research at the British Museum and had spent time in London with the writer Angus Wilson and his friend Douglas Newton. In Rome she had met Newton's wife, the novelist Mary Lee Settle, and she and Settle had done some traveling together in southern Italy. Now Rose was living in Rome for a month or so, sharing an apartment with two young women who worked at the American embassy.

That afternoon at the Excelsior, Styron and Rose talked about the upcoming presidential election in the United States. He learned that she supported Adlai Stevenson, as he did, and that her opinion of Dwight D. Eisenhower was as low as his was. They chatted also with another young novelist who had come there with Styron for afternoon libations. This was Truman Capote, who had been in Italy since April, living in the village of Taormina in Sicily. Capote had made a name for himself in New York with several brilliant early stories in *Mademoiselle* and *Harper's Bazaar.* His first novel, *Other Voices, Other Rooms,* with the notorious photograph of him on the dust jacket, had been published four years earlier. (Rose had read it the previous year.) Now Capote had moved to Rome; he was living in a three-room apartment on the Via

Margutta with his companion, Jack Dunphy, and hoping for a screen-writing job to shore up his finances.

Capote was wearing a sailor suit with a little silver bosun's whistle attached above the breast pocket. He had brought along his mynah bird, Lola by name. She perched on his shoulder, gabbling and cursing in mixed Italian and English. Capote chatted with Styron and Rose well into the afternoon, during which time he told them that he had been written up in ten of the twelve departments of *Time* magazine—the exceptions being Sport and Medicine. With his clothes, exaggerated mannerisms, and mincing speech, Capote was a bizarre item. He was cheeky, too: toward the end of the session he looked admiringly at Rose, then turned to Styron and said: "You ought to marry that girl, you know."

Rose was much attracted to Styron on this first afternoon and was amused by his attire. He had on old khakis and a sport shirt of indeterminate color, a long black overcoat, faded blue espadrilles with holes in the toes, and no socks. "He looked a lot like a Bowery bum," Rose remembered with a laugh. But his conversation was quick and animated, and his comments about the Academy were very funny. He also brought out her protective instincts: he had visited Saint Peter's earlier that afternoon and had ascended, via a staircase, to a balcony along the inner perimeter of the dome. There he had become almost paralyzed by vertigo. He had had to be coaxed back down, step by step, by his companions. He tried to make a funny story of the experience to Rose, but she could see that he was still shaken by what had happened.

In the days that followed they saw more of each other. Rose knew from Louis Rubin that Styron had already won some notice as a writer, but she had not read *Lie Down in Darkness* and did not know how good it was. She had not actually been a student in Rubin's fiction seminar; she had attended Styron's reading only as a favor, to swell the audience to respectable size. Now she decided that she should read his book. She went to the library at the U.S. Information Service one afternoon, just before closing time, and asked for a copy of *Lie Down in Darkness*. The volume was fetched for her; it was wrapped in a protective cover that bore only the title. She stuffed the book into her bag and thanked the librarian, who was locking up. Back at her apartment that night, she curled up in bed, eager to begin the narrative. She read the first chapter, then sighed and shut the volume. "This is terrible!" she said to herself.

Alpheus Whitehurst Styron, the author's paternal grandfather. Alpheus was a pioneeer shipbuilder and steamboat operator in eastern North Carolina.

Marianna Clark Styron, the author's paternal grandmother, who told him stories of her two little slave girls, Drusilla and Lucinda.

Belle Abraham, William Styron's maternal grandmother, known as "Mother A" within the family.

Young William Styron
with his mother, Pauline,
who would die when
he was fourteen.

William Clark Styron, Sr.,
the author's father, at
about the age of thirty.

William Styron as a young
boy in Newport News, shortly
after his family moved to
Hilton Village, a government
housing development for
defense workers.

One of the May Day pageants at Billy Styron's elementary school.
He is the page boy in white tights, upper left.

Bill Styron as a freshman
at Davidson College.
"I was a rotten student,"
he later admitted.

William Blackburn, Styron's professor and mentor at Duke University, at a picnic
with a group of his students. Styron is in the very back row,
the fourth person to Blackburn's left.

Styron in his Marine
Corps uniform; the
cap was known as
a pisscutter.

Bill Styron with
Bobbie Taeusch,
his serious love
at Duke.

William Blackburn. His
pupils included the writers
Mac Hyman, Fred Chappell,
Reynolds Price, Anne Tyler,
and Josephine Humphries.

Styron, with ladle, dishing Marine Corps chow at Camp Lejeune.

Sigrid de Lima,
the writer to whom
Lie Down in Darkness
is dedicated.

Styron working on
Lie Down in Darkness
at a tilt-top desk that had
belonged to the radical
journalist Randolph Bourne.

Wanda Malinowska, whom
Styron knew in New York in
1950 and 1951. She would
become one of the models for
Sophie Zawistowska in
Sophie's Choice.

William Styron and Rose Burgunder in Italy, 1953.

Bobby and Claire White and children. Bobby, a sculptor and painter, was a partial model for Cass Kinsolving in *Set This House on Fire*.

William and Rose Styron at the Campidoglio in Rome on their wedding day, May 4, 1953.

MAILER
[Ca.17] March/1958

Bill,

I've been told by a reliable source[1] -- closer to you than one

might expect -- that you have been passing a few atrocious remarks[2]

about Adele. Normally, I would hesitate to believe the story,[3] but

my memory of slanderous remarks you've made about other women[4] leaves

me not at all in doubt. So I tell you this, Billy-boy. You have got

to learn to keep your mouth shut about my wife, for if you do not,

and I hear of it again,[I will invite you to a fight in which I

expect to stomp out of you a fat amount of your yellow and treacherous

shit.][5]

Norman

What you choose to do about this letter is of course your own

affair, but I suggest you do no more than button your lip. The

majority of things you do come back to me, and my patience with

your cowardly and infantile viciousness[6]--so demeaning and disgraceful

to your talent--is at an end.

1 (I suggest that this "reliable source" -- and I thought
you above this type of shady allusion, Norman -- is
either a person with a warped and perverted imagination
or simply an outrageous liar. I have no idea how close
he or she is to me but, as a curator of paradoxes, you
must be aware that closeness is no guarantee for the
preservation of decency, and the fact that you have
obviously not asked yourself whether this person simply
does not hate and envy me, or you, or both of us -- and
above all himself -- is one of the saddest parts of your
letter.

2 "Atrocious remarks". An unmitigated lie. Or, depending
on your definition of atrocious, simply a lie. You
force me to explain myself in some detail. I would be
less than frank if I told you that Adele was my favorite
person in the world. At the same time, I am honestly fond

The letter from Norman Mailer to Styron that began the rupture between the two writers.
Styron underlined several passages and annotated them, intending to send
the letter back to Mailer. Later he decided not to do so.

MAILER (below)

WILLIAM STYRON
ROXBURY, CONNECTICUT

3/17/58

Norman:

I don't know who your sick and pitiable "reliable source" is (how _much_ he must hate and envy me, or maybe you, but above all hate himself), but you might have him or her get in touch with me some day and repeat his allegations to my face. Your letter was so mean and contemptible, so revealing of some other attitude toward me aside from my alleged slander, but most importantly so utterly false, that it does not deserve even this much of a reply.

P.S.

I just got back from a few days in Florida, and found this billet-doux. So I invite you to get together with me face-to-face and repeat that my letter is mean, contemptible, and false — if you feel up to it. If you don't, recognize your reply for what it is — a crock of shit.

Mailer

This is the letter that Styron sent to Mailer instead. It dismisses Mailer's charges as "utterly false." Mailer penciled his reply at the bottom and returned the letter to Styron.

The author's proud father in 1960, just after the publication of *Set This House on Fire*.

REBEL MOTOR FREIGHT, INC.
PHONE: WH 8-1613
954 BARTON ST.   P. O. BOX 10106
MEMPHIS 6, TENNESSEE
★ OVER NIGHT SERVICE ★

Mrs. Nina Goolsby
Miss Press House. 1st place
general excellence
Welcome home, Bill F.
To Tell people every where -
Oxford, and all of us, are very
proud of W. F., one of us, The
Nobel Prize winning author,
(Picture of F. in Sweden, sitting
on sled with "little Swedish
lad" Old Miss Dry Cleaners;
Gathright-Reed Drug Co., A. H.
Avent Gin & warehouse
Miller's Café.
"Nobel Award for lit come to
Oxonian" next to School
Board Call for #625,000
building Program.
Jesse Phillips owner of
bookstore

MEMPHIS • HOLLY SPRINGS • ABBEVILLE • OXFORD
WH 8-1613   PH. 962   PH. 2604
    UNIVERSITY • WATER VALLEY • BATESVILLE
    OF MISSISSIPPI   PH. 777   PH. 9521
              GRENADA • COFFEEVILLEE
              PH. 1137-M

Styron wrote down these notes at William Faulkner's funeral, using a pad of paper that he found at the Faulkner house in Oxford, Mississippi.

Rose Styron on the porch of
their home in Vineyard Haven,
on Martha's Vineyard.

Styron recorded these annotations
on one of the endpapers of this
copy of William S. Drewry's
The Southampton Insurrection,
a major source of information
about the Nat Turner Rebellion.

The Masonic Temple in Woodbury, Connecticut.
Styron's daughter Polly, in the summer of 1962, told
her father that she had seen this building in a dream.
He used her vision for the opening sequence of
The Confessions of Nat Turner.

Styron with James Jones, who was perhaps his closest friend among fellow writers.

I stirred. "Izzy, he's awake!" "G'wan, yah mutha's mustache!" "Faaa-ck you!" "Blessing my resurrection, I realized that they *(children)* had covered me with sand, protectively, and that I lay as safe as a mummy beneath this *(fine)* enveloping overcoat. It was there that in my mind I inscribed the words: "Neath cold sand I dreamed of death but woke at dawn to see, in glory, the bright and morning star."

It was not judgment day but it was morning. Morning: excellent and fair.

#

Sunday. December 17th 1978
1:15 P.M. Grâce du Bon Dieu.

The final page of the manuscript of *Sophie's Choice*; it differs slightly from the published text.

Styron and Mailer after their reconciliation, with Mailer's wife, Norris Church.

William and Rose Styron and their children. Left to right: Polly, Susanna, Al, Tom. The dog is Aquinnah, Styron's companion on his walks.

William and Rose Styron around 1980.

"How could he write such awful prose?" At this point (she remembered) she leafed back to the title page and discovered the problem. She had the wrong book.

This was another novel, also called *Lie Down in Darkness,* a now for-gotten book by a writer named H. R. Hays, published in 1944. Rose was relieved: she hoped that Styron's *Lie Down in Darkness*—once she man-aged to get a copy—would be an improvement over this *Lie Down in Darkness.* The next day she asked Styron whether she might borrow his copy of the novel, and she read it over the next two evenings. She rec-ognized immediately that William Styron was immensely gifted as a writer, and this pleased her. There was much to like about him: he was easy to talk to, he was witty and ironic, he wrote well, and he was obvi-ously interested in her. "He was sexy and funny," she said many years later.

A few days after their initial meeting, Styron introduced Rose to the Whites. Soon the two couples thought of themselves as a foursome, op-erating outside the restrained circles of the Academy. Styron continued to hang around the Whites' apartment and occasionally made himself useful. Once he was able to provide antibiotics for the Whites' son, Se-bastian, who was quite ill with jaundice. Antibiotics were hard to get in Italy in the early 1950s; certainly they were not yet a part of normal medical treatment there. Knowing this, Styron had come prepared with a large bottle of Aureomycin in his suitcase and he gave the entire sup-ply to the Whites for Sebastian. He also coaxed the boy into taking the first pill or two. On another occasion, Claire developed an infection in her foot and had to have a minor but painful surgery performed. Dur-ing her convalescence, which was uncomfortable, Styron brought over his radio and spent a long time finding some Mozart for her. "There's nothing like Mozart when you have pain," he said.

Styron was seeing a great deal of Rose and found himself falling in love with her. He confided his feelings to the Whites—but in restrained language, as was his habit. Rose appealed to him in almost every way: she was frank and generous and daring; she was also maternal and didn't mind looking out for him, for he was suffering from bronchitis and other assorted aches and pains. "It was obvious that Rose was the person Bill needed," said Claire White years later. Rose was casual and slapdash in her approach to things: usually Styron liked this about her, though she could irritate him with her forgetfulness and lateness. There was another side to Rose, too, that drew him in a different way. She could be extraordinarily tough-minded and unyielding in argument; she was intelligent and articulate and had strong opinions about poetry and education and politics. Rose's surface lack of order could distract people from her underlying determination: she nearly always did what she wanted to do and did it in her own way.

Styron found himself powerfully drawn to this woman. He revealed a tiny corner of his feelings to his father in a letter: "I have met an absolutely beautiful girl, American, named Rose, with whom I get along right well," he said. He did not elaborate, mentioning only that Rose's apartment was on the other side of Rome. "This will obviously necessitate my buying a car *pronto,*" he told his father. In November he purchased a slightly used Austin convertible, green in color. He named it Warren C. Austin (after the inept American ambassador to the United Nations at the time) and, knowing almost nothing about automobiles, proceeded to drive it for two weeks with virtually no oil in the crankcase. The vehicle survived, though, and carried him across Rome nearly every day to visit Rose. "Roman traffic is really fierce," he reported in another letter to his father. "There's a law against using the horn, and to compensate for the silence you just *prod* the rear end of the car in front of you instead of blowing at him. It's great sport, but very nerve-wracking."

In late October Styron received a letter from John Train in Paris. Train, a Harvard friend of George Plimpton's, was serving as the nonfiction editor of *The Paris Review.* He had an M.A. in comparative literature, and his opinions about the validity and usefulness of literary criticism did not correspond to Styron's. Matthiessen and Plimpton, partly at Train's urging, had come to feel that Styron's manifesto for the first issue, which he had given them back in September, was too quarrelsome in tone. There was no point in taking literary critics to the pillory in this maiden issue. Someone had blue-penciled the typescript, producing a milder version, but Train wanted to ask Styron if he would simply rewrite the piece. "I think it might be more interesting if the whole thing were cast in the form of a letter to the other editors," said Train. "It will get away to some degree from those terrible manifestos found in vol. 1 no. 1 of all little magazines." Train laid out his objections, and those of the other two editors, and enclosed Styron's original typescript. That typescript has not survived—presumably Styron discarded it—but Train included quotations from it in his letter, and these passages show that it contained many of the arguments and much of the wording that eventually appeared in the published version.

Train asked Styron to rewrite and to make the points he had already made, but to use a different tone. Styron obliged. He took the suggestion in Train's letter and presented the statement in the form of a letter to the editors. His manner was now more relaxed: "It's inevitable that what Truth I mumble to you at Lipp's over a beer, or that Ideal we are perfectly agreed upon at the casual hour of 2 A.M. becomes powerfully open to criticism as soon as it's cast in a printed form," he wrote. The solution, he thought, was to avoid ringing assertions. "Let's by all means leave out the lordly tone and merely say: dear reader, THE PARIS REVIEW *hopes* to emphasize creative work—fiction and poetry—not to the exclusion of criticism, but with the aim in mind of merely removing criticism from the dominating place it holds in most literary magazines and putting it pretty much where it belongs, i.e., somewhere near the back of the book." The new journal, he believed, should open its pages to the best writers it could find, "the good writers and good poets, the non-drumbeaters and non-axe-grinders."

In this rewritten version, Styron did take issue with some of the book reviewers who had asserted that he and his contemporaries would not produce writing that would last. "Perhaps the critics are right," he said. "Who cares? The writer will be dead before anyone can judge him—but he *must* go on writing, reflecting disorder, defeat, despair, should that be all he sees at the moment, but ever searching for the elusive love, joy, and hope—qualities which, as in the act of life itself, are best when they have to be struggled for, and are not commonly come by with much ease, either by a critic's formula or by a critic's yearning."

Styron sent the letter to Train, and it was published without emendation. In later years Plimpton came to think that *The Paris Review* (which has lasted over forty years to date) could trace much of its success and longevity to the approach that Styron had sketched out in this letter. The magazine never did publish "learned articles on who influenced whom, or the higher significance of whatever," said Plimpton. It simply concentrated on "the prime matter"—the best writing, graphic art, and photography that it could find.

Very soon after mailing his letter to *The Paris Review,* Styron had his first meeting with Rose's mother, Selma Burgunder. Mrs. Burgunder was in Rome visiting the American ambassador, David Zellerbach, and his wife, who were family friends. Rose had set up this meeting and had urged Styron to spruce up. Styron put on his only suit, a double-breasted model that fitted him poorly in the shoulders and bagged in the seat. In a certain light, the suit had an azure sheen. Styron did not own a tie, so he borrowed one from Truman Capote. "The tie was awful," Rose remembered. It was gray, she recalled, and it had a bumpy, waffle-knit texture with red and white arrows worked into the weave. It also had a line of knitted red fringe along the bottom. (One almost suspects Capote of deliberate mischief in giving such a tie to the sartorially indifferent Styron.) Rose joked for years that this outfit, especially the tie, had much to do with her mother's initial reaction to Styron. The occasion did not go very well: Rose attempted lively conversation, Styron smoked and hacked and coughed and complained of his bronchitis, and Mrs. Burgunder listened, smiling politely from time to time.

A few days later there was a weekend expedition from the Academy to Ravello, a small town perched more than a thousand feet above the Gulf of Salerno, about forty kilometers south of Naples. The Gulf of Salerno region is among the most picturesque in Italy, and the road from Sorrento to Amalfi, along which one travels to reach Ravello, is famously beautiful. The road winds along the coast, halfway up the rugged cliffs that rise from the sea. Ravello (which would eventually be a most important place in Styron's life) is located on a hilltop some six or seven kilometers up the Dragone Valley. The town is known for its lush gardens and for the rugged landscape that surrounds it. Ravello is also remote enough to have escaped the ravages of war and the depredations of tourism. Many artists and writers have worked there. Wagner wrote the third act of *Parsifal* in the Palazzo Rufolo; the beautiful gardens there gave him the inspiration for the Home of the Flower Maidens in the opera. And E. M. Forster captured something of the mystery and spookiness of Ravello in his tale "The Story of a Panic," which is set in the town. Some parts of André Gide's *The Immoralist* occur in Ravello; both Virginia Woolf and D. H. Lawrence lived and wrote there, as did Paul Valéry, Graham Greene, and Tennessee Williams.

Styron decided that he wanted to see Ravello and asked Rose if she would come with him. In the early 1950s it was thought improper for her to go unattended, so Rose and her mother made the trip together. Styron went ahead with the group from the Academy; Rose and Mrs. Burgunder followed a little later. Mother and daughter checked into a suite at the Palumbo, then a modest hotel on an alleyway at the highest point of the town. Rose managed to spend most of the weekend with Styron; they were pleased to be together but a little irritated by the restrictions of convention. Everyone returned to Rome a few days later, and Mrs. Burgunder left for England, worried about Rose's developing attachment to this young writer, whom she was not yet sure she approved of as a suitor.

Through the last weeks of November and the early parts of December, Styron and Rose were almost constantly together. They spent time with the Whites but were just as often alone, happy in each other's company. He told her much about himself—about his upbringing in Newport News, his years at Christchurch and Davidson and Duke, his two stints in the Marine Corps, his relationships with Sigrid de Lima and Wanda Malinowska, and his years of work on *Lie Down in Darkness*. He spoke with great affection of his father and with bitterness toward his stepmother. He told Rose of his mother's death in 1939 but did not elaborate. He did not think that her passing had much affected him, he said. My God, it was the basis for his entire zeitgeist.

Rose told him her stories too during these weeks. She had been brought up in a secure, well-to-do family and had gone to the Friends School of Baltimore, a Quaker school near Johns Hopkins. Rose was in the third generation of her family to attend this school; she had taken much of her thinking, her approach to life, from her training there. She was the baby of her family and had been carefully protected, but she was adventurous, determined not to live a conventional life. Her father had left the family well fixed financially, and Rose now had money from her own trust fund. She was not wealthy, but she would not have to look for work unless she chose to. Her future was open.

One of the stories she told him, from her early childhood, revealed many things about her. During the summers of her sixth and seventh years she had gone to Atlantic City to stay with her grandmother, Gertrude Kann, and two of her great-aunts. Rose's parents and older brother and sister had traveled abroad during these summers, but Rose had been too young to go along, so she had been left with her grandmother. Gertrude Kann always spent part of the summer in Atlantic City, living in a suite at the Hotel President, a modest establishment, and passing her days by playing mah-jongg with her sisters in her sitting room. Rose was allowed to roam the tourist area by herself during the mornings. (Such freedom for a small child would be inconceivable today, but in the 1930s Atlantic City was considered a thoroughly safe place.) Rose loved these times. She would be given her money after breakfast and told to be back by lunch. She would then set out along the boardwalk, planning her activities. Sometimes she would wade in the sea; at other times she would wander through the arcades and tourist shops or go to a movie. Often she would watch the horses dive on the Steel Pier. She especially liked the open-air auction houses, where she listened to the chanting of the auctioneers and watched the tourists bid on the merchandise. She loved the independence of these mornings, she told Styron—the sense that she was on the loose, on her own, with money in her pocket and things to do.

Early in December, Styron asked Rose to marry him. They were in the elegant bar of the Hotel Flora, near the American embassy. He had no ring, he told her, but he would give her the engagement ring that his father had given his mother, as soon as it could be sent over from the States. Rose accepted, and they told the news to Bobby and Claire White the next day. About a week later, Rose received a telephone call from her mother, who was in London. Selma Burgunder was preparing to sail home to the States for Christmas and wanted to say good-bye. Toward the end of the call Rose said, "Mother, I have a surprise for you. Bill Styron and I are engaged." There was a long silence at the other end of the line. Finally Mrs. Burgunder said, "Well, good-bye," and hung up. Rose was stunned; she had not anticipated such a response. She and her mother had always been close. Selma Burgunder had supported her daughter in her desire to be a poet and had given her good counsel during earlier romances. The abrupt good-bye had been out of character.

Mrs. Burgunder was not the only person to have misgivings about the engagement. Some of Styron's friends were afraid that he was so taken by Rose's good looks and charm that he was rushing ahead too quickly.

Was he ready for marriage? Could he settle into domesticity? And a few of Rose's friends were fearful that she was ignoring the melancholy, crotchety side of Styron's personality, a side that might make him a difficult husband. Mary Lee Settle was forthright with Rose: "You leave that Bill Styron alone," she said. "He has mean little hands."

In an effort to banish such dissonance, Styron and Rose decided to go to Paris for Christmas. They had made friends with another couple, Frank and Ann Wigglesworth (he was a young composer on fellowship at the Academy). The Wigglesworths would accompany them on the journey, and, though it promised to be a cramped trip with four people in the Austin, they left in high spirits. They took the journey in stages, stopping overnight in Pisa and Imperia in Italy and in Avignon and Saulieu in France. In Paris they drank and caroused with the *Paris Review* crowd. The Matthiessens were there—Patsy was enduring a difficult pregnancy—and Plimpton and Train were still working on getting out the first issue of the journal. Doc Humes had decamped for New York, but his place had been taken by John Marquand, whose first novel, *The Second Happiest Day,* had been selected by the Book-of-the-Month Club. Rose was a great hit with this group, and she and Styron basked in the approval that comes to a newly engaged couple.

On Christmas night they flew across the Channel to London for three days of shopping and sightseeing. They returned to Paris in time for several New Year's Eve parties. Styron drank heavily at these gatherings, as did his friends, but they were all young and resilient and could absorb much alcohol at night and still function the next day. The only casualty was Peter Matthiessen, who was told a few weeks later by a Paris physician that he had to cease drinking for three months. He followed the orders of the *médecin* but was grumpy about it.

Near the end of the visit to Paris, something puzzling occurred. Styron received a letter from his father, telling him that a morose-looking private detective had shown up in Newport News and had been poking about, asking questions about the Styron family. Styron remembered years later that his father referred to the private eye as a "gumshoe." Styron also recalled that his father was frightened by the investigator, fearing that his son might be in serious trouble. Styron read this letter to Rose in the Matthiessens' apartment in Paris, and something clicked in her mind. She knew of two similar incidents, both involving people in whom her brother and sister had been romantically interested. Now she guessed (correctly, as it turned out) that her mother was having William Styron's background checked out. What were the politics of his family? What was their standing in Newport News? What situation would Rose be marrying into? Rose told Styron about her suspicions, and he became quite angry, assuming that he personally was being investigated. Why was her mother looking into his record? Did she have suspicions about his motives for wanting to marry Rose? These were not in fact Mrs. Burgunder's concerns, but at the time Styron thought that they were.

It is not difficult today to see things from Selma Burgunder's viewpoint. Rose was her baby, the pretty pet of the family and the child of her middle age. Mrs. Burgunder was widowed, and there was no father figure present. She knew nothing of William Styron really—only that he had written a novel, that he had a tendency toward bronchitis, and that he had execrable taste in neckties. And she had no knowledge at all of his family. Rose, she knew, could be romantic and impulsive. Mrs. Burgunder must have wanted to save her daughter from what might turn out to be an unwise marriage. Rose, however, could see none of this. Later, after Styron had become one of Mrs. Burgunder's favorites within the family, he and Rose could tease her about her precautions and smile at the thought of the lugubrious gumshoe snooping around in Newport News. But at the time both Rose and Styron were angry and hurt.

For the time being they decided to do nothing. They would return to Rome and discuss whether they should go on together. For the trip back Styron decided to avoid the Riviera route and take a northerly shortcut through Grenoble and Chambéry. The plan backfired, however, when the Austin became marooned in a snowstorm between Bardonnecchia and Turin and had to be pulled from a four-foot snowdrift by a team of farm horses. He tried to make a funny story out of it for his father: "I've never seen so much snow in all my life," he reported in a letter, "but five hours of pushing and shoveling, with hysterical Italians on all sides shrieking advice above the sound of the blizzard, restored color to my cheeks and tone to my muscles." In reality the ordeal left him and Rose exhausted and played out.

Back in Rome they talked for a long time about the situation. And there was a new wrinkle now: Elizabeth Buxton had written to Rose out of the blue, in care of the American embassy in Rome, warning her not to marry her stepson. He was a bad risk, she said. Both Styron and Rose were so upset by these incidents that they decided to break off their engagement. The opposition from both sides had interrupted their idyll and introduced self-doubt. Styron believed that he was being cast as a fortune hunter; he was also speechless with anger at his stepmother. Rose was terribly chagrined and was determined not to subject Styron to further humiliation. She later recalled that this painful conversation took place in the bedroom of her apartment in Rome, with her sitting on her bed and Styron pacing back and forth. When they said good-bye that day in January, both of them believed that their romance was over. Rose packed her bags and left for Florence, where she took a room in a *pensione* and tried to divert her mind by writing poetry, reading, and visiting the museums.

19

Marriage and Ravello

AFTER ROSE'S DEPARTURE, Styron hit rock bottom. He decided that the year, thus far at least, had been an utter waste. He had been ill for much of the fall and winter, and he was beginning to have pains in his legs that he thought might be evidence of blood clots. He had not written anything, partly because of his involvement with Rose but partly also because no idea for a novel had seized him and made him sit down at his desk. Throughout his career it would be this way with Styron: he had to see a novel whole in a burst of insight—had to know how it would begin and progress and almost where the last word would fall—before he could write. Probably he did not yet realize this about himself, but several false starts and aborted drafts over the decades that followed would teach him the lesson. What he really wanted to do now was to write about Nat Turner, but he knew that he was not prepared to do it. He therefore drifted and produced nothing of consequence.

One problem was "Long March." Haydn had praised the novella, but Styron did not want to issue it alone, in a slim volume. He wanted instead to follow *Lie Down in Darkness* with another full-length novel. He thought that he might write several short stories, publish them in periodicals, and then put them together in a collection of shorter fictional works, with "Long March" as the title piece. He had been working, in a desultory way, on a few short-story ideas, but none of these had panned out. He had also had some offers to write articles on the European scene for *Mademoiselle, Holiday,* and *Harper's Magazine.* These propositions had stirred his interest a little, but he did not really need the money, and no good article ideas had come to him. He described his state of mind in a letter to the critic Maxwell Geismar, whom he had met in New York in the fall of 1951: "I used to snicker when I read about the anguish writers had whenever they found themselves bone-dry, but I snicker no longer. It's hell the way these days go by with nothing accomplished and, seemingly, with nothing to anticipate in the future. I am as inspiration-less as a newt."

It had been an unproductive period as far as writing was concerned, but at least Styron had been reading. He usually began his days by reading in bed, and he often read again in the afternoons, sitting in the reading room of the Academy or, if the weather was good, moving outside to the gardens of the Villa Aurelia a half-block away. Some of this reading was light—magazines and newspapers—but most of it was not. At no time in his life did Styron read lightweight fiction or inconsequential journalism: as a man in his sixties he was hard-pressed to recall the title of a single detective novel or science-fiction yarn that he had ever read. (He did remember liking some of the psychological thrillers of Georges Simenon.) Virtually all of the books he read were serious and weighty, and he nearly always had two or three going at once. He read much fiction and poetry as a young man and a great many works of nonfiction as a mature writer—biographies, histories, cultural studies, memoirs, accounts of politics and warfare and religion.

During his year in Rome, despite the distractions of the city and the ups and downs of his love affair with Rose, he managed to read a great deal. He began to work his way through English translations of then current French literature—Sartre, Camus, de Beauvoir, and others of their generation. Camus spoke with special urgency to him; he never forgot the experience of reading *The Plague, The Rebel,* and *The Myth of Sisyphus* that fall and winter. He was strongly affected that year too by the works of the Swedish author Knut Hamsun, especially by the novel *Hunger,* a profoundly bleak document.

Styron used his time in Rome to double back and read (or reread) many nineteenth-century American authors—Whitman, Dickinson, Melville, and especially Hawthorne, whose late novel *The Marble Faun,* set in Rome, would have an influence on his own novel *Set This House on Fire,* which he would begin in 1954. Styron also reread some of the works of the generation just behind him, the generation of Fitzgerald, Faulkner, and Hemingway. Fitzgerald was in the literary news: Arthur Mizener had published a biography of him, entitled *The Far Side of Paradise,* in 1951; Malcolm Cowley had produced a new edition of *Tender Is the Night,* the Author's Final Version, that same year. Styron took time in Rome to reread Fitzgerald's writings, and perhaps as a result some clear echoes from both *The Great Gatsby* and *Tender Is the Night* are to be found in *Set This House on Fire.*

Styron went to see Bobby and Claire White at their apartment almost every day. Claire's baby had been born—a boy, named Christian—and Styron liked to watch Bobby play with him. John Marquand came to Rome in February, and he and Styron went out drinking a few times, but Styron's low spirits put a damper on the evenings. He spoke bitterly about being investigated and about having his motives for proposing to Rose come under scrutiny. The only good news Styron had was from Sigrid de Lima. She had won the Prix de Rome for 1953 and would come to Rome that summer. Her house at Valley Cottage had been a good incubator for young writers. Through Styron, Sigrid would meet the painter Stephen Greene, a fellow at the Academy, and would later marry him.

Styron's own marriage prospects, however, were not being advanced, so Claire White decided to take a hand in the matter. He had told her about his frustrations, and she had decided that something had to be done. Early in March, she got in touch with Rose in Florence and urged her to return to Rome. It was wrong for her and Bill to let other people get in the way of their love, Claire said. They must not let themselves be defeated by circumstance when their feelings for each other were so certain. Rose hesitated but finally decided to come back. She returned toward the middle of March. When she and Styron saw each other their emotions came rushing back, and they realized that they should not have parted. They became engaged again and were together constantly in the weeks that followed. Rose took a small basement apartment not far from the Academy, and Styron moved in with her. He announced that he and Rose would be wed in April or May and wrote home to Newport News, telling of his marriage plans and asking his father to send over Pauline's sapphire engagement ring. (Pauline had asked, before her death, that it be saved for her son.) Styron also told his father to send over several cans of black-eyed peas for the wedding dinner—this for luck, an old southern custom.

Not long after their reunion, Styron and Rose decided to take another trip to Ravello. They had been happy there in November; now they thought that they might spend the late spring and summer in the town, after they were married. It looked like a good place to write and a cheap place to live. One day in late March they drove down with Bobby and Claire White to scout for places to rent. To their surprise, they found the town nearly overrun by a Hollywood film crew. The movie being shot there was a comic mystery called *Beat the Devil*. It was directed by John Huston and starred Humphrey Bogart, Jennifer Jones, and Gina Lollobrigida, with Peter Lorre and Robert Morley playing the parts of inept swindlers. The original script had not suited Huston or Bogart, so Truman Capote had been brought down from Rome to write a new one.

The film was being made in a haphazard, ad-libbed fashion. Capote would write a scene each night, and Huston would shoot it the next day. Apparently no one but Capote (and perhaps not even he) knew how the story would turn out. His script was full of zany dialogue and absurd plot twists: the story line had something to do with uranium deposits in South Africa, but these were lost sight of for long stretches of the movie. The result was a film that had little success when it was released but that has since become a cult classic, largely owing to the performance of Robert Morley, who played what became his standard role—the sly, rotund, pompous, and thoroughly underhanded British buffoon. A very funny movie.

As the Styrons drove into the center of Ravello that day, Rose noticed long black cables snaking down from an abandoned villa on a hill above into the Duomo San Pantaleone, the beautiful eleventh-century church in the central square of the town. The cables had been laid by the movie crews, who were shooting scenes inside. As Rose watched, a flock of nuns made their way down the hill, tripping over the cables. That evening Styron and Rose saw Hollywood people everywhere in the town—in the hotels and restaurants and bars. Their movie-making paraphernalia and their show-biz dress and talk, juxtaposed against the lovely backdrop of Ravello, fixed some clear images in Styron's mind. He would create similar scenes for *Set This House on Fire* and would use the movie people as minor characters in the novel. Humphrey Bogart became the dissolute actor Carleton Burns, Jennifer Jones the self-absorbed actress Alice Adair, and La Lollobrigida the voluptuous Gloria Mangiamele. John Huston, who appears in the novel as the screenwriter and director Alonzo Cripps, is the only sympathetic character; he alone is given some perspective on the absurdity of the Hollywood enterprise.

Styron and Rose had hoped for a wedding in late April, but there was so much red tape that a date in early May was the best they could manage. Styron began writing to his friends, inviting them to attend the wedding. His letter to John Marquand included some snuffling and self-criticism: his nervous resources, he said, were "already depleted by a soggy, constant drunkenness brought on in part by the prospect of marriage, by insomnia, by clots, and by a general spiritual enervation resulting from the realization that already, going on 28, I am a wash-up as a writer and fit only to do the 'Recent & Readable' part of the book section in *Time.*" But all was not gloomy: at least the archaeologists had gone elsewhere. "Most of the creeps have crept away from the Academy for their spring bone-hunt," he told Marquand, "leaving it clean except for a couple of seedy art historians and myself, who is struggling manfully with his destiny."

Marquand responded with a long, funny cable: CITY ROCKED BY NEWS. YOUNG WOMEN LEAPING FROM BRIDGES, BUILDINGS . . . SEISMO-GRAPH AT FORDHAM SHATTERED INJURING TWO YOUNG JESUITS AND ONE LAY BROTHER. . . . LOOMIS IN STATE OF SEVERE SHOCK. . . . FAULKNER, SAD, SAYS "THE OLD PRIMEVAL LURE OF THE MAMMALIAN FLESH." Marquand promised to attend the ceremony, but it began to look as if Tom Guinzburg and the Matthiessens would not be able to come from Paris. Patsy had recently given birth to a boy and was not in condition to travel; Peter was reluctant to leave her and so cabled his regrets. Guinzburg, pleading other commitments, also begged off. At this point Irwin Shaw took charge. He and Marian had come to Rome for the spring and had taken a high-rise apartment in Parioli. Shaw was appalled that the *Paris Review* contingent would not be at the wedding: WHAT DO YOU MEAN YOU'RE NOT COMING TO BILL'S WEDDING? he cabled to Matthiessen and Guinzburg. DON'T YOU REALIZE A MAN ONLY GETS MARRIED TWO OR THREE TIMES IN HIS ENTIRE LIFE? That did the trick;

Matthiessen and Guinzburg booked tickets on a flight to Rome for the ceremony.

William Styron and Rose Burgunder were wed on the afternoon of Monday, May 4, 1953, at the Campidoglio. They were married in a small room with brocade-covered walls; a Signor Marconi, the matrimonial judge in Rome, performed the ceremony wearing a gold medal about his neck and a green-and-red sash around his middle. The bride and groom sat in high-backed gold chairs. In attendance were the Whites, the Shaws, the Wigglesworths, Matthiessen, Guinzburg, Marquand, and Rose's brother, Bernei, and his wife, Amelie. Bobby and Claire White were best man and matron of honor. Styron wore a new suit, single-breasted, and an appropriate necktie, selected by Rose. She wore a pale blue silk dress trimmed in black, with full skirts and a hooped petticoat beneath. Whenever she sat down in her gold chair during the ceremony, the front of the dress flew up and revealed her undergarments, making her laugh.

The Shaws had a reception afterward at their apartment in Parioli. There was champagne and a wedding cake in five separate sections, delivered by the baker on a brass window-display rack. The guest list for the wedding ceremony had been small, but Shaw had invited a great many other people to the reception, some of whom the newlyweds had never met. Lillian Hellman was among these guests. Styron and Rose, who did not know Miss Hellman, found themselves alone with her in the elevator ascending to the Shaws' apartment. "I remember all this rustling brown silk," said Rose, "with a little brown feathered hat, and a veil over her face—that was her style." No word was spoken during the trip up; only after they had been formally introduced at the reception would Hellman consent to speak.

Claire White had written a song for the occasion. She sang it in her clear, true voice, accompanied by Frank Wigglesworth on his recorder:

> "Roses bloom in wintertime,
>   Sweet williams grow in June;
>   Friends must part in course of time,
>   But not, but not,
>   But not the bride and groom."

"This sounds extremely corny," Styron wrote to his father, "but I assure you it couldn't have been more touching." Styron had become a husband. In the parlance of the time, he was now a man with responsibilities.

Shortly after the wedding Rose's brother, Bernei, called Selma Burgunder to tell her of the marriage. She accepted the news with equanimity and sent her blessings. She asked Bernei to tell her new son-in-law to treat himself to a wedding present of his choice—something elegant. This, she thought, would be more satisfactory than trying to select a gift herself that would suit him and mailing it over from the States. Styron decided to get a good wristwatch, a Patek Philippe. He and Rose picked it out one morning in May, a few days after the ceremony, in a jewelry store in Rome.

That same afternoon they took a drive to Anzio, a seaside town a few kilometers south of Rome. Irwin and Marian Shaw had invited them to make the trip. Irwin knew of a fine *ristorante* in Anzio and wanted to take Styron, Rose, and the Whites to luncheon there. It was a festive occasion: spring weather had arrived, and everyone's spirits were high. The meal was excellent, and they lingered at table until around three in the afternoon. Then they headed back to Rome. The Whites divided themselves between the two automobiles: Claire, Sebastian, and Christian went with the Shaws, and Bobby and Stephanie squeezed into the back of Styron's Austin. Rose rode up front in the passenger seat and, once they were out of Anzio, promptly fell asleep. Shaw, in his green convertible, drove on ahead and was soon lost sight of.

About halfway back to Rome, Styron hit a motorcyclist. He had been driving through a stretch of road that was bounded on either side by high terraces topped by hedges. Small side roads fed into the highway every few kilometers, but the openings for these roads were invisible from the main thoroughfare. A man on a Vespa popped out from a tributary road on the right. He was oblivious of Styron's onrushing vehicle. The front of the car struck him, and his body traveled along the hood and shattered the windshield. Somehow he was then flung forward and came to rest on the pavement in front of the automobile. His smashed motorbike was sent spinning forty yards down the road.

No one in Styron's car was injured. They all jumped out of the automobile and examined the man, who lay facedown and unconscious. Styron was horribly shaken: he assumed at first that the cyclist was dead, though it soon became apparent that the man was still breathing. The road had been deserted at the time of the accident, but within minutes a great number of Italians converged on the spot. They discussed the mishap in passionate language, paying no attention to the victim. Friends of the cyclist arrived and flopped him over; he revived slightly and mumbled a few words. He was covered with blood: Styron noticed that he was missing several fingers from one hand and that his left eye was gone. These lacunae, he assumed, had resulted from the collision, and he looked around queasily for the missing digits and the eyeball. Styron and Rose urged that an *ambulanza* be summoned, but the man's friends heaved him unceremoniously onto a farm truck and drove him off to a hospital. Styron and Rose followed and sat in the waiting room for two hours. At last a doctor emerged: *"Va bene,"* said the doctor. "He will recover." But what about the missing fingers and the empty left eye socket, Styron asked. *"Non si preoccupi,"* answered the doctor. "Do not worry. He lost those in his last accident."

The cyclist, as it turned out, had a history of violent mishaps. He had lost the fingers and the eye while experimenting with fireworks. He had ridden in front of Styron's car because he had not turned his head far enough to see the automobile with his remaining eye, the right one, and he had not been able to hear the approaching car because of the racket of his motorbike. Styron had already answered questions from the *polizia* and had given them his address at the Academy in Rome. He was now told that he could go. Eventually the Austin was repaired and made roadworthy again, but Styron was so badly undone by the accident that he refused to drive for several weeks. He was especially touchy and jittery during this period. ("Dat boy is an exposed noive," said Shaw to Bobby White.) Eventually Styron would write the accident into the beginning of *Set This House on Fire,* but for the present the mishap only seemed one more in a series of calamities that had befallen him during his time in Italy.

The experience had a final chapter so bizarre that no writer could possibly have put it into a novel. Later that spring Styron received a letter from a lawyer in Anzio telling him that he was to be sued by the motorcyclist. This was a nuisance action; the *avvocato* wanted to settle out of court for whatever could be extracted from Styron, whom he assumed to be a rich American. Styron was quite worried: he was covered by liability insurance but had no idea of how to defend himself in the

Italian courts and no confidence that justice would prevail. His only experiences with such matters—his efforts to get permission to marry Rose in a civil ceremony—had convinced him that the Italian bureaucracy was labyrinthine and supremely corrupt. Besides, there is a general rule in European driving (called *precedenza a destra* in Italy) that gives the right-of-way to any vehicle entering traffic from the right. Thus Styron was technically at fault for the accident.

Help was offered to Styron in his dilemma from an unlikely source. He had recently met an American named Don Allan, a foreign correspondent for *Newsweek* magazine who was living in Rome. Styron told Allan of his dilemma, and Allan assured Styron that he would take care of it. The rumor circulating about Allan was that his position with *Newsweek* was a cover and that he was in fact employed by the CIA. Allan spoke good Italian, and he claimed to have experience in assuming false identities. From a costume shop he rented an absurd getup that made him look like a prominent turn-of-the-century American lawyer—a frock coat, a dress shirt with a starched bosom, and a cravat with a stickpin. Rose swears to the truth of this tale: "He looked like a cross between William Jennings Bryan and Rudolph Valentino," she says.

Allan selected this costume with the motorcyclist's lawyer in mind: this, thought Allan, was what a member of the provincial Italian bar would expect a wealthy American attorney to look like. Attired in this rig, Allan went to the seedy office of the attorney and attempted to bluff him out of the suit, but the deception did not work. The lawsuit was pressed, and the motorcyclist was eventually awarded a settlement by Styron's insurance company. In *Set This House on Fire,* Styron uses the motorcyclist in a symbolic way: after the accident he goes into a coma, from which he awakes only at the very end of the book—a metaphor for the theme of death and rebirth in the novel. Styron could never have used the real story; it was too absurd, even for a work of fiction.

Once Styron had his nerve up to drive again, he and Rose, husband and wife, left for Ravello, where they planned to spend the summer. Pasquale Vuilleumier, the friendly and garrulous Swiss-Italian *padrone* of the Hotel Palumbo (who is fictionalized as Windgasser in *Set This House on Fire*) rented the Styrons a two-floor apartment in the Palazzo

Confalone, a rambling twelfth-century structure that he was then modernizing. The Styrons had a bedroom, a kitchen, a little sitting room, and a high-ceilinged living room. They also had access to a terrace with a spectacular view of the Gulf of Salerno. They sat there almost every night and watched the lantern-lit fishing boats venturing out into the clear waters of the gulf. The rate for these accommodations was low: one hundred American dollars per month in season and sixty dollars during the off season, with a native woman, named Anna, who cooked and cleaned for an additional twenty-five dollars a month. The movie people were still in Ravello, finishing the last few scenes of *Beat the Devil,* but by early June they had cleared out, and the Styrons had possession of the town.

The Whites had decided to live in Ravello for the summer as well. They took up residence in a small house that clung to the edge of a cliff, very near the Styrons' apartment. Bobby rigged up a makeshift studio for his sculpting on the roof of the house but found it difficult to work. Part of the trouble was Ravello itself. The town is famously daemon-haunted; both White and Styron testify to its bewitching spookiness and to the eerie effect on the creative spirit of the surrounding landscape, with its breathtakingly long views and stomach-clutching drops. The best known of these drop-offs is at the Villa Cimbrone, a small and gorgeous palazzo in which Greta Garbo lived for a time. And there are ghosts in Ravello, including one that resembles a small girl with a dog's face. (It sometimes still visits guests in the Hotel Palumbo.) Bobby eventually gave up his efforts to sculpt that summer and took to tramping about the mountains alone. He carried paints and small canvases in a backpack and spent his time doing landscapes.

Ravello was full of beautiful churches and artworks and ruins, but Styron found himself largely unmoved by them. Later he would admit that he possessed no special sensitivity to painting or sculpture and had only a passing interest in architecture. He thought that this might be typical of many creative people: they were knowledgeable about their own métiers and often responded intensely to one other art form (in his case it was music) but were indifferent to other genres. What fascinated Styron about Ravello were not the villas, churches, and artworks but the people and the surrounding landscape. He mentioned this in a letter to his boyhood friend Leon Edwards: "I have traveled happily all over Italy looking at churches and paintings," he wrote, but these, "distressingly enough, have not the powers to move me nearly so much as the marvelous black-eyed people and the fantastically beautiful hills, sky and sea." He also loved the local summertime fiestas, with their processions and drinking and fireworks.

Styron found life in Ravello soothing and lulling. His bronchitis disappeared, and he felt healthy. He liked the surrounding towns and hamlets and often took walks down the Dragone Valley to Atrani, a small fishing village on the water. This descent took him along a little stream that flowed through fragrant lemon and olive groves; sometimes he would also see herds of smelly goats, tended by local boys. It was all quite picturesque, though Styron could not help noticing the poverty of these rural people, so different from the comfort that visitors to Ravello enjoyed. Many of these contrasts would make their way into *Set This House on Fire.*

Various friends spent time with the Styrons that summer and fall. The Haydns came for three days, and William Blackburn passed through for a visit. Elizabeth McKee and her husband, Ted Purdy, who was an editor at Putnam's, came to Ravello for a week. The longest visit was by Peter and Patsy Matthiessen, who came with their new baby for almost a month. Peter began a short story in Ravello on that trip; eventually it grew into his novel *Partisans.* He made only a little progress on the narrative in Ravello, however, largely because he and Styron were enjoying each other's company so much. Matthiessen had recently completed his three-month abstention from drink and had resumed convivial imbibing; Styron introduced him to the Ravello rosé, a subtle vintage that carries unexpected alcoholic authority. Several years later Matthiessen recalled the visit in a letter to Styron:

> There was nary a night in that splendid month when, befuddled by the local grape, we were not locked in mortal combat over the chess board. As I recall, our ground rules specified that no more than three pieces could be maneuvered simultaneously, that the possession of three queens was unlawful, no matter how many pawns insinuated themselves through the confused defense, and that a player upsetting or vomiting upon the board more than once during the course of any one game was penalized one rook and two *coups de rouge.*

At some point in these bacchanals Matthiessen and Styron made up nicknames for each other. Matthiessen became Pete-man, Styron (for obscure reasons) became Porter—a name that Matthiessen still calls him today.

Styron was getting a little writing done, but he was easily distracted. He spent much of one week, for example, playing with an electric train set that belonged to an American living in the apartment above his. He worked for a time on a story set at Davidson College but abandoned it and began thinking again about doing some magazine articles. His and Rose's daily regimen was pleasant: writing in the morning followed by lunch at one or one-thirty, then by a siesta or perhaps a walk down the mountain for a swim in the ocean. Late afternoons were passed on the tennis courts (Rose was an excellent player), and dinner was around eight. Evenings were spent reading, smoking, drinking, and talking with guests.

Styron and Rose were adjusting to each other's ways. In most respects they made a smooth transition into married life, though she had some trouble getting used to his need to be alone for long periods. Sometimes she became frustrated by his unwillingness to do things on impulse—to accept a last-minute invitation or take a trip on a whim. For him even small activities had to be planned far in advance. From Styron's point of view, Rose's forgetfulness continued to be an irritation: she was casual and trusting with her valuables, often leaving her purse unattended in public places. Her wallet and passport were stolen during a trip to Rome; the thief took her money but returned the passport via the mails. "Italians are wonderful," Styron wrote to his father, "but not given to any excess of rectitude." More seriously, the engagement ring—Pauline's sapphire—was stolen from Rose's purse on the beach at Amalfi, a nearby tourist town. The ring was too large for her finger, and she had not yet had it sized. She was afraid to wear the ring into the water, fearing that it would slip off, so she got into the habit of leaving it in her purse. One day, while she and Styron swam, a thief rifled her pocketbook and took the ring. Styron was furious. The ring was never recovered; Rose never forgave herself.

In August, Styron began to write a novella about his experiences as a prison guard on Harts Island. This was an old project that he had thought about tackling as early as 1949, while he was living near the East Campus in Durham. He had been unable to get anywhere with the idea then, but now it jelled and he made some progress through August and September, producing almost nine thousand words. The narrative, which he was calling "Blankenship," focused on a young marine non-com, Gunner Joseph Blankenship, the captain of the guard at Hart's Island. Blankenship is the center of consciousness in the narrative, just as Thomas Culver had been in "Long March." The story gave Styron a chance to explore problems that he would address later in his career: the nature of authority and discipline, the effect of imprisonment on the incarcerated, and the corrupting influence of power on the captor.

The narrative opens with an emergency: two convicts have secretly built a boat and have escaped from the island. Toward the end of the first part of the story, Blankenship has a confrontation with a prisoner named McFee, an intelligent rebel who has liberated himself from military discipline simply by choosing to ignore it. Blankenship, normally an exemplary military man, loses control and strikes McFee with his billy club because McFee has called *him* a prisoner. McFee means to say that the Marine Corps is one vast system of incarceration, and that regulars like Blankenship are more thoroughly imprisoned by its rules and its mind-set than are the malefactors they guard. "You're the yardbird, Gunner," says McFee, just before Blankenship strikes him. "You're the yardbird, you son of a bitch."

Today it is impossible to know why Styron did not keep going with this narrative. Stylistically it is quite good, and it gathers considerable momentum toward the end of the surviving fragment. The only explanation for Styron's decision to abort is that "Blankenship" must have seemed quite similar to "Long March." "Blankenship" begins with an incident that disrupts the order of military life, just as "Long March" does, and like the earlier novella it is narrated from the point of view of a young military man in a position of authority. It also contains a rebel, McFee, who resembles Mannix in many ways. Perhaps Styron was afraid of repeating himself. This would not be the last time that self-criticism would cause him to abandon a manuscript.

Life in Ravello was so pleasant that the Styrons decided to stay there through the fall. After that, they were unsure where they would live. "That's the rub," Styron explained to his father in a letter. "If one is not tied down to a place or a job, as I am, it's a hell of a problem to decide whether to settle in Westport, Waukesha, or Woonsocket." One option was to become an expatriate. Certainly Styron could have done so: Irwin Shaw had shown him that an American author could conduct a successful literary career while living in Europe. The Continental ambience was attractive; the food and wine alone were almost enough to make one settle in France or Italy. And as Shaw had demonstrated, a writer could renew himself by changing his venue from time to time, moving from city to shore to mountains as the seasons changed. Styron seems to have sensed, however, that he needed to be in America if he were to keep working steadily. In almost two years of residence in Europe he had finished only one novella. The ease and sophistication of life on the Continent was so distracting that he found it difficult to keep focused on his projects. Styron seems to have recognized that he needed the irritations of American culture—its noise, commercialism, energy, and provincialism—to keep himself sharp.

He and Rose decided, in the fall of 1953, to return to the States. They would find an apartment in New York City and live there while they thought about a more permanent place to settle. They booked a December passage on the liner *Independence* and made the most of their last few weeks in Ravello. In the evenings now they discussed what they might do back in America and where they might live. "I am beginning to get distinct nervous twitches about coming back," Styron wrote to John Marquand. "Most of the time I am utterly unable to figure out a reason for returning, unless it's to get psychoanalyzed."

The Styrons sailed from Naples on December 13, and, after stops in Genoa, Cannes, and Gibraltar, docked in New York on December 22. There was a welcoming bash at a Manhattan restaurant with the Matthiessens, who had returned to America several months before on the *Andrea Doria* and were now living in East Hampton on Long Island. Peter was working there as a commercial fisherman and writing on days when the weather was too rough to go out. The Styrons spent Christmas with Rose's family in Baltimore; during that visit Styron and Mrs. Burgunder began to know and like each other. Selma Burgunder had read *Lie Down in Darkness* by now and had admired it greatly. She had begun collecting clippings and translations of Styron's work, a habit that she continued into her nineties. Styron and Rose had fun during the visit. She showed him around Baltimore, and they talked at length about what they would do during the next few years. The future looked promising, they thought.

20

New York and Roxbury

IN JANUARY 1954 the Styrons took a one-bedroom apartment in New York City at 231 East Seventy-sixth Street. They set about making it comfortable, painting the walls, installing a hi-fi, purchasing a stack of Mozart recordings, and laying in a supply of scotch. The music and alcohol should have eased the transition back into urban life for Styron, but to his surprise he found himself gripped by a severe case of reverse culture shock. He was in bed for ten days with heart palpitations and a buzzing noise in his ears that he thought might be symptomatic of a brain tumor, but he was told by a physician that he was only having trouble readjusting to the rigors of city living.

By February Styron was better, and he and Rose began to entertain. They had a party for Irwin Shaw, who had come over from Switzerland to collect a hundred-thousand-dollar check for the movie rights to *The Young Lions.* Some of the *Paris Review* crowd was reassembled for the fete: the Matthiessens came in from East Hampton, and John Marquand and Tom Guinzburg attended. Shaw brought along a large group of magazine, television, and movie people, more guests than the Styrons had counted on, so that their small apartment was crowded and their liquor supply overtaxed. Some of the guests behaved badly. Charles Addams, the *New Yorker* cartoonist, attempted humor by pouring salt into people's drinks. And Norman Mailer, who had not met Shaw until that night, confronted him on the issue of Communism, which he thought Shaw had skirted in *The Young Lions.* Imitating Tarzan, Mailer said to Shaw: "You—physical courage. Me—moral courage." Shaw was not pleased.

Styron saw a good deal of Mailer during the spring and summer of 1954. Mailer and his friends had established a salon of sorts at the White Horse Tavern on the corner of Hudson and West Eleventh in the Village; the idea was to meet there on Sunday afternoons for drinks, discussions, and literary gossip. Styron and Rose went once or twice, but they usually stayed clear of Mailer when he was in a crowd. Styron and Mailer got along better when they were away from other people. In one conversation they discovered that both of their fathers were inordinately proud of their sons, so when W. C. Styron visited New York that summer, Mailer set up a meeting between Styron *père* and his own father, Barney Mailer. Though of entirely different backgrounds and temperaments, the two got along well and spent a pleasant afternoon together at a restaurant called the Captain's Table, boasting about their writer sons.

Styron saw Hiram Haydn from time to time that spring and, through him, learned that J. Saunders Redding from Hampton Institute would be visiting New York for a few days in midsummer. Styron wanted to take Redding out for dinner, to renew their acquaintance and talk about Nat Turner. Styron was told by friends, however, that it would be hard to find a restaurant that would seat a black man and a white man together—or, if they were seated, their order would never be taken. Styron spent a frustrating afternoon on the telephone, trying to find a restaurant that would agree ahead of time to serve him and Redding. At last he thought of Vincent Montemora, the former husband of his old girlfriend Wanda Malinowska. Montemora, whom Styron had met at Wanda's when children were passing back and forth, operated a popular restaurant called Ricky's. Montemora agreed to help out: he told his maître d' ahead of time to expect Styron and Redding and to seat and serve them promptly. Styron and Redding discussed the situation openly at dinner that night. It had surprised Styron to learn that such covert Jim Crowism existed in New York City in 1954, but Redding, who had encountered similar problems many times in the North, was not surprised at all.

Styron had decided not to salvage the "Blankenship" manuscript, the novella about prison life on Hart's Island that he had begun in Ravello the previous fall. He now wanted to write a full-length novel, set mostly in Ravello and Rome. The narrative, he thought, would involve American expatriates in postwar Italy and France. By mid-March he had begun this new manuscript, and he sent a report on it to Bobby and Claire White, who were in Rome for a second year at the Academy. One recognizes the beginnings of *Set This House on Fire* in the description:

> I have begun Novel No. 2, which will be laid in Ravello and Rome mainly, with maybe a side-glimpse at Paris and New York. It's going to be about two young guys who were friends—a good guy and a perfect bastard, and it ends up with the good guy pushing the perfect bastard off the drop at the Villa Cimbrone. Also the bastard rapes one of the local girls in Scala (the girl whom the guy who is good is in love with). It is very complicated and very tragic and I will work on it for probably ten years and it will sell exactly 726 copies.

Styron and Rose had become friendly with a young woman who lived in an apartment upstairs in their building; she worked in an office all day and let Styron use her apartment as a workplace in the afternoons. He labored on the novel through March and April, producing a beginning episode of around twenty-five hundred words. In May, however, he became dissatisfied with this writing and decided to begin the novel again. He did save the false start: today it is among his papers at the Library of Congress. It is an intriguing fragment, for one can see in it the seeds from which *Set This House on Fire* would grow.

This false start, like the published version of *Set This House on Fire,* is narrated by a character named Peter Leverett. Peter begins by describing two ocean voyages—the first a pleasant trip to Europe that he made a few years after the end of World War II and the second a return to the United States several years later, shortly after the cataclysmic events that occurred in Sambuco (as Styron was calling Ravello). Peter recalls that during the first voyage to Europe, he was idealistic and vaguely romantic: he wanted to help rehabilitate Italy and hoped to find romance and love in a foreign setting. By the return voyage, however, much has changed. Peter is now nervous, jangled, and talky. He is panicked and shattered, "not nearly so much alive as one quivering, bottled-up scream." Certainly Peter has reason to feel unhinged—Styron's letter to the Whites shows that he has just murdered a former friend—but his narrative voice in this false start is so very different from his voice in the published novel that any reader familiar with *Set This House on Fire* will be puzzled. In the novel, Peter is quiet and withdrawn, a meticulous observer given to laconic understatement. In this aborted opening, by contrast, he is terribly unsettled and shaky—"removed the width of a hair from lunacy," he tells us. He sounds, in fact, very much like Cass Kinsolving, the angst-ridden painter who is the central figure of the published novel and who, in that novel, does kill Mason Flagg, Peter's onetime friend.

Therein lies one key for understanding *Set This House on Fire*. The false start, together with Styron's letter to the Whites, suggests that at this early point the character of Cass Kinsolving had not yet fully emerged in Styron's consciousness and had not become distinct from Peter Leverett. Cass is mentioned briefly in the surviving fragment, where he is called Ben Kinsolving, but he does not yet figure prominently in the narrative. Styron at this point seems to have conceived of his novel only as a moral face-off between Peter (the "good guy" in the letter) and Mason (the "perfect bastard").

What is fascinating to observe in the subsequent drafts, all of which survive, is the way in which the character of Cass Kinsolving is spun off from the original conception of Peter Leverett. In the rewritten version Peter acquires a meditative calm and a tendency to reserve judgment; Cass appropriates the neuroticism and fondness for abyss-peering of the first Peter. The novel, as a consequence, becomes a more complex three-way confrontation among Peter, Mason, and Cass. The point is worth mentioning because in the published novel Peter and Cass, while initially distinct from each other, do eventually merge into one narrative consciousness—one man, really—a blending that Styron surely planned and one that seems to have had its origins in his first attempt to write the book.

Styron aborted this first opening for *Set This House on Fire* in part because he was dissatisfied with Peter's character, but there was an even greater problem that spring: intolerable noise. As soon as the weather turned warm in late April, a wrecking crew set up across the street from the Styrons' apartment and began to demolish the building just opposite them. The noise was deafening. Styron had attempted to resume his habit of staying up at night and sleeping the next day until noon, but the din from across the street now made this impossible. Forty years later, Rose Styron could still remember how her husband would be routed from bed promptly every day at 7:30 A.M. by the shattering noise of jackhammers and a wrecking ball. Styron would emerge from the bedroom, livid with anger, and would spend the first half hour of the morning cursing. Because the noise continued all day, Styron found it impossible to write in the afternoons. He tried to readjust his schedule and compose in the evenings, but this threw him off-rhythm and prevented him from working in the upstairs apartment of their friend, who was home from her job by the time the demolition crew quit for the day. The racket was so loud that the Styrons shut their windows and drew down their shades against the noise. In the June and July heat this turned the apartment into an oven. "We had painted the walls of the apartment a pinkish color," Rose recalled. "I remember thinking that the walls were whale-belly pink and that we were trapped together in the belly of the whale."

To escape from the noise and heat, the Styrons visited friends outside the city whenever they could. In mid-May they spent several days with the Matthiessens in Springs, Long Island, an isolated part of East Hampton, and reveled in the quiet and privacy there, taking walks on the beach, staying up late, and sleeping well into the morning. It was on that visit that they conceived their first child. Several weeks later Rose told her husband that she was pregnant.

The noise from across the street continued through the summer and into the early fall. The Styrons had hoped for some respite once the building had been completely torn down, but on the day after its demolition was finished, a fresh crew of workmen moved in and began erecting the replacement building. The noise from this crew was almost as loud as that from the previous one, and Styron despaired of being able to push ahead with his novel.

The situation lasted until early October, when the Styrons were invited by Elizabeth McKee, his literary agent, to spend a long weekend with her and her husband in their cottage in Roxbury, Connecticut. The Styrons went and had a wonderful visit, absorbing the rusticity and quiet and going on treks through the woods around the town. That very weekend they began to talk about what it might be like to live there.

Roxbury is a small, picturesque village located in the rolling hills of western Connecticut, not far from Waterbury. It is surrounded by other New England towns—Southbury, New Milford, Woodbury, and Bridgewater. The most illustrious sons of the region were Ethan Allen,

Seth Warner, and Remember Baker—all of whom fought with the Green Mountain Boys just before and during the Revolutionary War. Roxbury was first settled in 1713 and by 1796 had grown to a town of almost one thousand inhabitants. Initially the Roxbury economy was based on agriculture, but by the late nineteenth century the town had become a center for iron, garnet, and silica mining. The deposits had been mined out by the 1950s, however, and Roxbury had again become a quiet backwater. Many of the inhabitants were members of old families that had lived in the town for generations—clans with such names as Hurlbut, Bronson, Squire, Warner, Hodge, and Canfield. Other citizens of Roxbury and the surrounding towns were more recent arrivals: among these were several artists and writers, including Alexander Calder, Arthur Miller, Peter Blume, Yves Tanguy, Robert Anderson, Van Wyck Brooks, and Malcolm Cowley. Roxbury itself was charming, with its saltbox houses and old families; but the chief attraction for the Styrons was the surrounding countryside with its gentle hills, stone fences, picturesque rivers, and deep woods. After the noise and oppressiveness of the city, the quiet of Roxbury was immensely soothing to them.

The Styrons never spent another night in their apartment in New York. They stayed at Elizabeth McKee's cottage through the weekend, then on Monday morning found a local real estate agent and began looking at property. They were lucky: the second or third place they looked at appealed to them immediately. It was a large two-story frame house erected originally in the mid-1800s, with a guest house that had originally been a small barn. These two structures were set on a property of fourteen acres that included a stream and a spring-fed swimming pond. The place was situated on a back road and was bordered on both sides by working farms. It seemed ideal.

The recent history of the house interested them. The previous owner had been a physician named Dubrowsky, a Russian émigré who had fled from the Bolsheviks in 1916. He had established a practice in Roxbury and for many years had been head of a group known as the Russian Red Cross, an operation that helped exiles from Soviet Russia to resettle in the United States. Many of these Russians had passed through the Roxbury house, visiting or living there temporarily until places could be found for them elsewhere. Some of Dubrowsky's books and papers were still in the house; in looking through them later Styron found a photograph of the exiled revolutionary Alexander Kerensky wearing an old-fashioned bathing suit and seated beside their swimming pond.

Dubrowsky had died several years earlier, and his widow had moved to France. The property had been for sale for quite some time, and the price had been lowered. The big house was not yet habitable—"It was just a broken-down old hulk," Styron remembered—but the guest house was furnished and livable, with a kitchen and two bathrooms, two bedrooms, and a large main room with a big stone fireplace. Styron and Rose decided that they could live in the guest house while the big house was being renovated. They knew that they were being impulsive, but they were captivated by the beauty of the Connecticut countryside in autumn, and they were desperate to escape from New York.

They decided to purchase the place. For the down payment Styron contributed what remained of his royalties from *Lie Down in Darkness* and Rose cashed some bonds. By the end of October they found themselves established as property owners and citizens of Roxbury. Probably Styron did not know it at the time, but this would remain his principal residence for the next forty-three years—until the present day, in fact. Rose, prescient, sensed that the move was permanent. "We know we'll be here forever," she wrote in a letter to the Whites.

The decision to settle in Roxbury was based on a series of choices that Styron made at about this time. He made some of these choices consciously, others instinctively. The first decision was not to live in New York City. The noise and stress of urban life, which he had not especially minded as a bachelor, now seemed intolerable. He and Rose would miss the restaurants, museums, concerts, and other diversions; but they both sensed that if they were to get on with their lives they would need to be away from those distractions. Styron felt no compulsion to be around other writers, nor did he need to be in day-to-day contact with publishers, magazine editors, or literary agents. He had already begun to realize that his own rhythm of composition was going to be slow and that he would not do much in the way of magazine fiction or book reviewing or odd-job journalism during his career. What he would aim for was a short shelf of novels, probably no more than four or five, each one serious and weighty, and no one of them repetitive of the others. For that long-term work he needed a setting like Roxbury, with its isolation and quiet, so similar in many ways to Valley

Cottage, where he had broken through on the creation of *Lie Down in Darkness*. New York was only a little over two hours away from Roxbury by automobile; he and Rose could come in for the occasional concert or dinner whenever they wanted to.

He also decided not to live in the South. Styron had no strong ties now to Newport News or Durham, the only two southern cities in which he had ever lived. Both places were heavily industrialized; neither possessed much charm or tradition, and there was no other location in the South that attracted him strongly. Styron knew that if he wished to, he could easily settle in the South and become a member of what was then being called the southern gothic school of letters. He could assume a position as the heir of William Faulkner, with whose work his own was compared, and could continue to write novels in the manner of *Lie Down in Darkness* about the decadence of modern southern life.

This arrangement might have been comfortable. Styron could have become an ex officio member of the academic circuit that had by then formed, in triangular fashion, among Vanderbilt, Chapel Hill, and Louisiana State University. Proximity to that triangle would put him in the way of semesters of guest teaching, occasional speaking engagements, and participation in summer conferences and workshops. These things were attractive, but Styron was canny enough to see that such a situation would not be good for his writing. It would be too easy to stagnate, to become a parochial writer and settle for a limited audience and small reputation. The designation "heir of Faulkner" was like a ready-to-wear suit that might fit him fairly well just now, off the rack. Inevitably, though, it would bind and chafe as he developed into a mature writer.

He also decided not to enter academe, even in a temporary or tangential way. Many of his fellow writers, in order to pick up needed money, served periodic stints as visiting teachers or writers in residence at colleges and universities. These were normally one- or two-year appointments, though some writers became full-time faculty members and held tenured positions. These jobs usually involved the teaching of creative writing classes, similar to the ones Styron had taken from William Blackburn at Duke. The teaching itself was not onerous; probably Styron would have been good at it. But he seems to have known that he could not tolerate the academic environment with its intrigues and jealousies and petty feuds. He also sensed that even intermittent exposure to the typical English department might give him what the French call *une déformation professionelle*—a skewed notion of the purposes of his fiction and its status vis-à-vis literary criticism. Styron had no desire to chronicle the world of academe in his fiction or to adopt the attitudes of English professors toward imaginative writing. He decided to stay clear of pedagogical appointments.

Yet another decision which he and Rose were making more or less unconsciously was to get on with the having of their children. Certainly they could have waited; she was only twenty-six and he twenty-nine. But Rose was already pregnant, and she and he had decided that they wanted a large family. He was especially conscious of the problems of growing up as an only child and wanted his own children to have brothers and sisters. To some degree this was an uninformed, romanticized notion. Styron had no real experience with large families and could not anticipate the tumult and noise and jockeying for position that would come with a brood of energetic young children. Rose, though not as yet a mother, understood a little more clearly what a large family would mean. She was the youngest of three children, and she knew something about the demands that offspring can put on a marriage. The challenge for both of them during the next several years would be to create and maintain a protected territory, a quiet path through each day, so that he could pursue the life of the imagination and still be the father of a large family. Neither of them fully realized that this task lay ahead, however, or how difficult it would be.

What made these decisions about place and manner of living possible, initially, was Rose's money. The income from her trust fund was not great, but it was enough to keep them in relative comfort. Styron did not need to take an academic job or accept freelance writing assignments; he could concentrate wholly on his novel. He could bring in money, if he needed it, by having his agent negotiate a series of advances on each succeeding book, but he was not required to arrange things in this way and so did not find himself facing deadlines that might cause his pen to run dry. Instead he could think and write at his own pace, free for the most part from serious financial pressure.

The decision during these years to rely on Rose's income was made easier by the fact that she was casual about money. She was not impressed by it and was not a woman who would use it to gain leverage within the marriage. As far as she was concerned, the money was there;

the only thing that interested her was how to use it to advance the family and create time for her and her husband to do what they wanted to do. Her own writing career, she thought, would probably have to wait for the time being: she was composing some poetry and publishing it in *The Yale Review* and *The American Scholar,* but she was thinking mostly now of her pregnancy and of what the birth of this child would mean to them.

Styron, for his part, could have allowed his wife's money to unman him and to undermine his position in the marriage—rather as Dick Diver in *Tender Is the Night* is finally overwhelmed by the wealth that his wife, Nicole, has inherited. But Styron too was largely indifferent to money and was ruthless enough, in the way that committed artists must be, to accept the fact of Rose's inheritance as a given and proceed from there. Her financial resources were part of the donnée of the situation. He had written his first novel on short funds; now he would write his second in easier circumstances.

These decisions, however, had hidden drawbacks that Styron became acutely aware of as time went on. By settling in Roxbury he did remove himself from the irritations of life in New York, but he also let himself in for long stretches of solitude and loneliness. Especially during the lengthy Connecticut winters he often found himself at loose ends, lacking stimulation and energy. And the absence of financial pressure removed a goad that many writers use unconsciously in order to produce. Freedom from debt can bring a sense of release, but it can also produce an odd kind of enervation, an absence of motive, a tendency toward inanition. It leaves the way open for two occupational hazards of the literary profession—writer's block and alcoholism. If there are no deadlines and no immediate financial pressures, then it does not really matter whether the novel is ever finished, nor does it matter how early in the day the first drink is taken.

Styron's solution was consciously to develop for himself a style of living—a loose regimen, really—within which he could function productively. This regimen was at once unconventional and practical; it allowed time for idling and rebelliousness when he was away from his worktable, but it demanded, at its center, a quiet and uncompromised period of four or five hours every day for writing. This would remain his habit for the next thirty years.

Styron's day began with a deliberate affront to convention: he slept always until noon. Then he often stayed in bed another hour or more, reading and thinking. He bathed and shaved and had a late lunch with Rose around one-thirty. He ran family errands or dealt with the mail for an hour or two after lunch, trying not to think yet about the writing that he wanted to do that day. Throughout his career Styron had to creep up on the act of composition. He was always nervous and apprehensive about his writing; some days he almost had to trick himself into taking up his pencils and legal pads.

Music provided a way of easing into his fictional world. He would sit in the living room of the little house and listen to Mozart or Brahms, allowing the music to quiet his mind and put him almost into a trance. He would think only a little about the writing to be done that day; he would not focus sharply on it yet. Around four o'clock in the afternoon he would mount the stairs to the loft room where he kept his worktable and stay there for the next four or five hours. As always, he would pace and write, pace and write, sitting and daydreaming at intervals, then writing again. His rate of composition remained as deliberate as ever: often he produced no more than two or three hundred words during a sitting, though his usual rate was between five and seven hundred words a day. These pages would be finished drafts and would normally go into the book unchanged. Styron was not Anthony Trollope, who composed each morning for exactly an hour, with his pocket watch sitting open beside him. Styron was, however, methodical and steady. He knew that if he produced a little every day, and if that little satisfied him, then he would eventually complete his novel.

Between eight and nine o'clock in the evening Styron would emerge from his workroom and begin the second part of his regimen. Music had aroused his creative impulses and helped him enter the world of his imagination; alcohol now provided him with a soothing way out of that realm, a transition back into everyday life. He would drink one or two stiff scotches, his first alcohol of the day, and then sit down to dinner with Rose at about nine-thirty—they having kept the European habit of late dining. He would eat only five or six dishes, Rose remembered. He asked her always to prepare one or another of them—spaghetti carbonara, fried chicken, roast beef, mixed grill, and one or two more. Even food, during this period of his life, had to be predictable.

He and she would talk during the meal about the events of her day, which would have been a full one. They had begun an extensive renovation of the main house by now: a new staircase was being erected in the front hall; the living room was being expanded, and two small rooms were being combined to form a big kitchen across the back of the house. The bedrooms upstairs would eventually be redone and two bathrooms would be installed, but these renovations would have to be done piecemeal as money came in. It would be four years before they could begin to live in the big house.

Rose dealt with the workmen during the day; each night over dinner she would discuss questions about the renovation with her husband or tell him of her decisions about the positioning of walls and doors. After the table was cleared they would walk over and check on the progress that the carpenters and plumbers had made. They would discuss trips to New York or upcoming weekend visits from their friends. Every night or two Styron would read aloud to Rose the most recent pages from the manuscript of his novel. These were times she looked forward to, and she learned to be forthright in stating her opinions about his writing. She was reading manuscripts regularly for *The Paris Review* and typing the text of *Set This House on Fire* from Styron's handwritten drafts. This secondary literary labor sometimes left her worn-out in the evenings. Because she was an early riser, Rose would retire at around eleven o'clock, but Styron would stay awake for another three or four hours, drinking and reading and smoking and listening to music. He would go to bed between two and three o'clock in the morning, sleep until noon, and begin his regimen again.

At some time during these years, Styron wrote a quotation from Flaubert on a piece of cardboard and tacked it on the doorframe outside his second-floor workroom. It read: "Be regular and orderly in your life, like a good bourgeois, so that you may be violent and original in your work." The quotation was apt: Styron needed the regularity of his peculiar schedule to bring him each day to his worktable. Though self-disciplined and ambitious, he knew that he could be distracted and thrown off course if he was not careful to order his pleasures and confine his drinking and socializing to particular periods of the day and week. Rose seems to have understood his needs from the first, and she worked over the years to be sure that they were met. She was careful to protect the habits and the space that he required in order to write.

21

❦

Mailer
and Others

STYRON HAD STARTED again on his novel soon after he and Rose had settled into the little house in Roxbury. He had chosen his title, *Set This House on Fire,* from one of John Donne's epistles to the Earle of Carlile. Styron had a clear vision of his narrator now: Peter Leverett was to be calm and objective, perceptive and sympathetic, with a strain of introspection but with little of the dramatic torment he had possessed in his first incarnation.

Peter's name provides a key to his character: the word *leveret,* which enters English from the Old French *levrete,* means a young hare in its first year of life. Thus Peter Leverett is Peter Rabbit, naive and inexperienced, ready to learn lessons about evil and good, sin and expiation. For students of the *Oxford English Dictionary,* the word *leveret* has two other meanings as well, both of which also fit Peter. The first of these is "a pet, a mistress." Peter is Mason Flagg's pet in the novel, and Mason takes the same kinds of mental and emotional liberties with Peter that one might take with a kept woman. The final definition in the *OED* is even more appropriate: a *leveret* is "a spiritless person." Surely the lexicographer meant "spiritless" to suggest "colorless" or "dull," but within the context of the novel the word "spiritless" has a different connotation. Peter has lost touch with his own spirit and with God. His recovery from this malaise—which, Styron suggests, is the existential dilemma of twentieth-century man—is a dominant concern in the narrative. Like John Donne in his epistle, Peter must beg God to set this house on fire, to rescue him from despair and enflame his spirit anew, to turn him back from melancholy and make him whole again.

Once Styron had made his decisions about Peter's narration, he progressed steadily on *Set This House on Fire* during the fall and early winter of 1954–55. He discarded the notion of beginning *Set This House on Fire* on an ocean liner, but he kept the travel motif in his new opening, beginning with a description of Sambuco/Ravello ostensibly taken from a tourist guidebook. The new first section of *Set This House on Fire* also incorporated a fictionalized version of the accident in which Styron had hit the motorcyclist—a character whom he named Luciano di Lieto in the novel and who would stay in a coma until the very end of the narrative. The main figures in the book would be three American men in their late twenties or early thirties—Peter Leverett, Cass Kinsolving, and Mason Flagg.

Set This House on Fire, however, would not be primarily a novel of character. Its dominant theme was to be a condemnation of postwar American culture—its vulgarity, commercialism, and insularity. Much of the novel is set in Europe, but it is an American story all the same; its expatriate characters are alienated from a homeland that has become, in Styron's view, morally shallow and ethically corrupt. As it grew under Styron's hand, *Set This House on Fire* became a jeremiad, a didactic novel meant to shame his country into greater cultural sophistication and a stronger awareness of its own past.

Styron was about to face some decisions about his career. In the spring of 1954, Hiram Haydn had been offered the position of editor in chief at Random House by Bennett Cerf and Donald Klopfer, the founders and owners of the firm. Haydn's first impulse, he later said, was to stay with Bobbs-Merrill: he was putting its nonfiction list into good shape and was having some success with fiction as well. But he had never felt comfortable with the midwestern mentality of the house, or with David Laurance Chambers, and the inefficiency of having to deal long-distance from New York with the Bobbs-Merrill bureaucracy in Indianapolis was beginning to wear on him. The Random House offer was exceptionally good—more than double his Bobbs-Merrill salary, plus generous benefits. Perhaps more important, Haydn would be joining a much more successful and energetic book-publishing firm than Bobbs-Merrill. During the summer of 1954 Haydn therefore decided to come to Random House. He assumed his new position in January 1955.

Random House had its beginnings in the firm of Boni & Liveright and its reprint line, the Modern Library. One of the most flamboyant American publishers of his time, Horace Liveright had built a strong trade list by 1925. His stable of authors included Eugene O'Neill, Robinson Jeffers, and Sherwood Anderson, and he had just published Theodore Dreiser's *An American Tragedy*. Later in 1925 Liveright would issue a book of short stories entitled *In Our Time* by a then unknown expatriate author named Ernest Hemingway; he would also bring out, in 1926 and 1927, the first two novels of an obscure Mississippi writer named William Faulkner. Liveright had good publishing instincts but was bored by the workaday chores of his business. For stimulation he gambled on best-sellers and Broadway shows and frequently overextended the resources of his house. Even a lucky string of best-sellers by such authors as Gertrude Atherton, Hendrik Van Loon, Samuel Hopkins Adams, and Anita Loos had not kept his operation comfortably afloat, and for cash he had resorted to selling off partnerships to well-to-do young men who wanted to make a start in publishing.

One of these apprentices was Bennett Cerf, a personable New Yorker of Jewish background who had finished his degree at Columbia University in 1919. Cerf worked for two years with Liveright in his brownstone offices on West Forty-eighth Street, but he had larger plans and wanted to found his own publishing house. His chance came in 1925, when Liveright, financially pressed as usual, offered to sell him the Modern Library list, stock, and imprint for two hundred thousand dollars. The Modern Library, a successful reprint line patterned on the Everyman's Library in England, should have been Liveright's safety net, providing steady and dependable venture capital that he could use to back his best-sellers and Broadway productions. But Liveright found reprint publishing overly predictable and decided, unwisely, to let the Modern Library go. Cerf teamed with his Columbia University classmate Donald Klopfer, raised the necessary funds, and purchased the Modern Library from Liveright in the summer of 1925. Liveright continued his speculative ventures and eventually brought his firm to the edge of insolvency. He was forced out of the business in 1929 and saw it go into bankruptcy in 1933, not long before he died.

This background is important because Cerf and Klopfer vowed not to commit the errors that Liveright had made. Their careful business practices eventually provided strong financial underpinnings for their publishing house. Cerf and Klopfer began slowly, rehabilitating the Modern Library list and building a dependable distribution system throughout the country. Their first efforts at original publishing were small collectors' editions, and in 1927 they secured American distribution rights for the de luxe editions of two small British operations—the Nonesuch Press and the Golden Cockerel Press. By 1933, now calling their enterprise Random House, Cerf and Klopfer felt ready to publish a few original trade books; they took over Eugene O'Neill and Robinson Jeffers from the ruins of the Liveright collapse, and in that same year Cerf traveled to Paris and acquired American rights for *Ulysses* from James Joyce. In a deliberate move, Cerf had a copy of the book seized by U.S. customs agents and won the ensuing obscenity trial, which was highly publicized. Cerf and Klopfer soon began publishing important British authors, including Stephen Spender, W. H. Auden, and Robert Graves; they added translations of books by Marcel Proust and André Malraux. American authors in their stable included Gertrude Stein, Moss Hart, and William Saroyan; Cerf and Klopfer took on William Faulkner as one of their authors in 1936, when they brought Hal Smith and Robert Haas, Faulkner's previous publishers, into their firm.

By 1954, when they made their offer to Haydn, Bennett Cerf and Donald Klopfer had become visible and successful as literary publishers. Not forgetting Liveright's errors, they had kept the Modern Library list in trim, issuing reprints of recent strong sellers and tapping into the college textbook market with their Modern Library Classics. Cerf himself had become a public personality, appearing on radio talk shows and lecture tours and becoming a fixture on the television program *What's My Line?* He also wrote a column for the *Saturday Review* called "Trade Winds." The firm itself was housed in one of the most handsome buildings in central Manhattan—a beautiful 1885 neo–Italian Renaissance mansion designed by Stanford White and situated at 457 Madison Avenue, behind Saint Patrick's Cathedral. Thus in the fall of 1954 Haydn was joining a financially secure house founded on sound business philosophy and with a good recent record in literary publishing.

For Styron this move would be of central importance to his development as a writer. The careers of many American authors are littered
with publishing failures and insolvencies; each time their firms have
gone under, these authors have scrambled to find new imprints willing
to take them on. (Dreiser is a good example, as is Sherwood Anderson.)
Late in their careers these same authors have often had to rescue old
copyrights still held by their earlier firms and have had to work free
from the entanglements of previous contracts. Almost none of these
difficulties has troubled Styron during his career. His single problem in
1954 was that Bobbs-Merrill held the publishing rights to *Lie Down in
Darkness.* Bobbs-Merrill wanted to keep Styron on their list, but he
could see that the Indianapolis firm was not especially well suited to
publish his work. The decision for Styron was therefore relatively easy.
His loyalty had always been to Haydn, not to Bobbs-Merrill (to which
Haydn, after all, had jumped from Crown). Styron was committed by
contract to Bobbs-Merrill for his novel in progress, but he was relatively
sure that Bobbs-Merrill would not try to hold him. He allowed himself
to be extricated from his agreement by Elizabeth McKee and signed
with Random House early in 1955, with a two-book contract and an
advance of fifteen thousand dollars on his new novel.

One of the things Styron liked about Random House was that it was
situated at the nexus of the New York publishing and entertainment
worlds. His association with the firm gave him a chance to meet people
outside the world of belles lettres. Styron made light of these new associations in a letter to John Marquand, but one still senses a certain pleasure in the report: "Being now in the Random House fold I am great
pals with not only old Ben Cerf but *his* pals, too: old Arlene Francis and
old Buddy Schulberg and old Mossy Hart and swell old Colesy Porter
and Dickie Rodgers and sweet, wry-witted bespectacled Stevie Allen.
We all get together up at Ben's place in Mt. Kisco and go swimming and
play charades and that sort of thing. . . . Who wants a Nobel prize when
you can pal around with people like Gore Vidal and Peter Viertel and
Niven Busch and 'Gadge' Kazan and Edmund Purdom? I have taken to
smoking black Brazilian cigars, so that my lips have become wet and lu-
bricious."

One opportunity Styron did not make light of was the chance to
meet William Faulkner, now his fellow author at Random House. In
January 1955, not long after Haydn had joined on, Styron went to

lunch with Haydn and Faulkner, who was in New York attending to some details involving the publication of his second Snopes novel, *The Town*. Styron remembered the luncheon as pleasant and relaxed: Faulkner was quiet and allowed Styron and Haydn to carry the conversation, but he listened and smiled at some funny stories that Haydn told about Truman Capote. Faulkner had been asked by *Sports Illustrated* to write about the Kentucky Derby, and the magazine had agreed to have him driven all the way to Louisville in a chauffeured limousine. "He thought that would be a right nice experience," Styron reported in a letter to William Blackburn.

Faulkner said nothing at the luncheon about having read Styron's work. By 1955 Faulkner had become wary about commenting on the writings of his contemporaries or on the work of young authors. He had been burned eight years before, when some idle remarks made in a University of Mississippi classroom about Ernest Hemingway ("He has no courage, has never climbed out on a limb. . . .") were printed and found their way onto the national wire services. Since then Faulkner had been careful when asked to rank himself among living American writers and had refused to mention younger authors whose work he thought had promise. (He usually dodged these questions, insisting that he read only the old masters now—Shakespeare, Cervantes, Balzac, Flaubert, Tolstoy, Melville.) Faulkner did break his rule for Styron, however. Two years later, in a seminar at the University of Virginia, when asked to name younger novelists whose work interested him, Faulkner mentioned only Styron. The remark was published in 1959 in *Faulkner in the University,* the printed transcripts of his classroom question-and-answer sessions at Virginia.

Random House wanted to put Styron's name before the reading public again. Part of the new arrangement with him was to publish a separate edition of "Long March" (now retitled *The Long March* by Styron) in the Modern Library paperback series. The anticipation of proceeds from this edition, combined with the advance on *Set This House on Fire* and with continuing royalties from *Lie Down in Darkness,* gave Styron a welcome feeling of solvency. The new money made it possible for Styron to begin helping his father financially. There had never been any feeling between the two men that Styron owed money to his father or that he was obliged to pay back, dollar for dollar, the funds that had been sent to him during the writing of *Lie Down in Darkness.* There was certainly an unspoken understanding, though, that the senior Styron could call on his son for help if he needed it. In the fall of 1957, W. C. Styron had a minor surgery that, with some other bills, put a strain on his resources. His son was able to ease the pinch and continued to do so throughout the next ten or fifteen years. Eventually W. C. Styron came to depend on his son for considerable financial support, especially during the last years of his life.

The Styrons' first child, a girl, had been born on February 25, 1955, at Mount Sinai Hospital in New York City. They had named her Susanna Margaret—Susanna from the figure of that name in Wallace Stevens's "Peter Quince at the Clavier" (Rose had written her M.A. thesis on Stevens), and Margaret for Styron's mother, Pauline Margaret Abraham. Styron found himself fascinated by the baby that spring; often he was drawn away from his writing table to study her moods and movements.

Styron was keeping in touch with his friends: Random House had published Mac Hyman's comic novel, *No Time for Sergeants,* the previous fall with great success, and Hyman was now enjoying the fruits of his labors. "The old gold-mine is perking along very fine," he wrote to Styron. "Have so far sold TV rights, pocketbook rights, play rights, and keep getting offers in from the movies that would knock your eyes out—or at least did mine, being as I have never thought in such sums, even in jokes." John Marquand, who was still living in Europe, was at work on a novella. Peter Matthiessen had published his second novel, *Partisans,* with Viking in the fall of 1955. Not long after the book appeared, Styron promised Matthiessen that he would write down his reactions to the novel. In December of that year he did so, setting out his evaluation in a Christmas letter. The remarks are interesting not only for what they say about Matthiessen's early work but for what they reveal about Styron's own attitudes toward imaginative writing. Styron praised Matthiessen's fusion of style and narrative power and complimented his "Dostoievski-like glimmerings of characterization—characterization *cum* scene." Then Styron turned to the shortcomings he saw in the novel:

> I think or had the feeling that in every single scene a fine, pure imagination was at work but at the same time I felt terribly let down that

this same imagination did not let itself go, prolong itself, take advantage of itself and fill out the crannies and corners. . . . There's a *hurried* quality, as if it were written by a man of enormous talent out of necessity and in great haste, who for some reason or another failed to realize the richness, the pregnancy, of his most promising and exciting scenes. . . . Such is my faith in your imagination, which you really *haven't* let loose—that if you were to sit down and, say, over a period of two or three or even four years really suffer over a scene and *let* it loose, you would make us all look like Harold Bell Wright. Shit you not.

Matthiessen recalled later that he appreciated Styron's bluntness without necessarily agreeing with what he said. "It's almost impossible to get honest criticism from a fellow writer," Matthiessen added. "This was honest criticism." Matthiessen would supply the same to Styron a few years later.

The Matthiessens and the Styrons visited one another often during the 1950s. Matthiessen came to know Styron well, and a considerable affection grew up between the two men. When they visited they usually stayed up late, drinking and talking. Matthiessen remembers today that Styron paced and smoked and drank scotch, and that the alcohol relaxed him and helped him overcome his instincts for privacy and self-concealment. "He was a good drinker," Matthiessen recalls. "I remember those times, at three or four in the morning, with Mozart going full bore. Those were the times when he was the most lucid. You saw his intellect best when he drank; you could see how unusual his mind was."

By the summer of 1956 the Styrons felt at home in Roxbury, though they had still not met many of the artists and writers in the area. One of these as yet unencountered neighbors was the dramatist Arthur Miller, who in late June married Marilyn Monroe in a ceremony in Roxbury. Styron reported to Marquand that the marriage brought "to these tranquil glens and glades a gawking procession of sportshirted, Pontiac-ensconced, yowling cretins such as you would never have imagined, and leaving dead around an oak tree not ½-mile from this house the lady correspondent from *Paris-Match,* who cracked up chasing the couple." The Roxbury locals, according to Styron, enjoyed the excitement: "The real estate agent who sold us our place, and who also doubles as town constable, told us with Rotarian pride that land values hereabouts have skyrocketed since the event. I wouldn't be surprised."

Styron did not yet know Arthur Miller (in later years they became good friends), so he had to content himself with only a glimpse of the playwright's famous wife. One afternoon, as he drove past Miller's property, he saw out of the corner of his eye the fleeting image of Marilyn Monroe in her bathrobe, setting out empty milk bottles on the back stoop.

In the fall of 1956 Norman Mailer moved to the area and rented a house in Bridgewater, a few miles away from the Styrons. Mailer and his wife, Adele Morales, had become weary of New York; Mailer had been struggling with his writing and wrangling with his publishers. He believed (as Styron had) that the quiet, isolated Connecticut countryside would help him get on more successfully with his career. Mailer also needed to escape from the Beat atmosphere of drinking and drugs in New York.

Mailer and Adele had been drawn to the Roxbury area by their friends John and Leslie Aldridge, who had moved there a few months before and were living in the house that Arthur Miller and Marilyn Monroe had inhabited, very briefly, just after their marriage. John W. Aldridge, Jr., was then a youngish literary critic whose first book, *After the Lost Generation,* had contained some of the first serious commentary on the fiction of Mailer, Shaw, Vidal, Capote, and several other writers. *Lie Down in Darkness* had been published too late to be treated in Aldridge's book, but Aldridge had liked Styron's novel and had reviewed it favorably in *The New York Times Book Review.* Aldridge's opinions were delivered with a ponderous authority beyond his years (he was only thirty-four that fall), and he thought of himself as potentially the critical arbiter of his generation in America. His wife, Leslie, was none other than Leslie Blatt, the young woman who had caused such a stir at Duke with Clay Felker during Styron's second stint there. Her marriage to Felker had not lasted, and she had wed Aldridge not long before they moved to Roxbury.

The Mailers and Aldridges saw a good deal of one another during the two years that they lived in the Roxbury area. The Styrons, however, visited with these two couples only now and then: they had a different circle of friends that included Lew and Jay Allen, Al and Ses Hine, Van Wyck Brooks and Malcolm Cowley and their wives, Hiram Haydn and his wife, Mary, and various members of the *Paris Review* crowd. The

Styrons did socialize occasionally with the Mailers and Aldridges, though, and Styron came to know Mailer much better than he had earlier.

Mailer was not easy to be intimate with during these years. At his best he was raffish, funny, and charming, but he could also be belligerent and confrontational. In part this was a holdover from his city-boy upbringing in Brooklyn, but it was also his natural style. Styron, whose tendencies were toward withdrawal and privacy, found himself put off by Mailer's probing, disputatious ways; Mailer, for his part, remembered being frustrated with Styron's taciturnity and his tendency to stick to superficialities in conversation.

Aldridge functioned as an intermediary between the two men, but both writers were impatient with Aldridge's manner and his notion of himself as the critical guru of their group. Aldridge would sometimes say that Roxbury was destined to be the "New Athens" of its time: he delivered this opinion as if it were a joke, but more than one observer thought he was serious. Rose remembered that Aldridge came to a dinner party one evening with a tape recorder under his arm; he set up the machine in the center of the table and recorded the conversation of the writers present that night. Another time, at Aldridge's home, Aldridge hid the tape recorder under the sofa and had Mailer, Styron, and their wives give readings from erotic books. Rose thought the exercise silly and began to laugh; her mirth spoiled whatever mood Aldridge was trying to create, and he gave up the effort, dragging the tape recorder from its hiding place and grumpily storing it away. Rose remembered other bits about Aldridge: he was a handsome man but was overly fond of his profile and always contrived to sit sideways to the company, even while eating dinner.

Evenings with the Mailers and the Aldridges were intense and stimulating but not especially pleasant. All three men were ambitious and competitive; all three women were good-looking and sexy. Rose's style was natural and unadorned, but she had by now blossomed into a healthy, womanly vitality, and her self-confidence was strong. Leslie was still pretty and was as trim and flirtatious as ever. Adele, whom Mailer called his "Indian," was Spanish-Peruvian—dark, sensual, and Latin in temperament. Her relationship with Mailer was strained and violent, and they often clashed. Adele had begun to paint seriously, partly at Mailer's urging. He and she were sexually adventurous, and their behavior was the subject of gossip.

Mailer himself still showed signs of strain from the drugs and alcohol of the Beat scene. He had given up cigarettes, though, and was boxing seriously. Sometimes he invited visitors to spar with him in a ring he had set up in a barn on his property. Mailer had also become interested in the teachings of Wilhelm Reich, a refugee from Freudian thinking who preached the therapeutic value of the orgasm. Reich's signature device was the orgone box, a contraption into which one climbed and sat, meditating, in order to absorb unseen psychic energy. This energy would be released later in cataclysmic orgasms. Mailer built a box for himself that resembled an orgone box, though he purposely did not follow all of Reich's specifications. He kept the box in the barn and would sit in it when he wanted to meditate.

Styron liked Mailer's magnetism; he also liked the way Mailer drew energy from confrontations with critics and the reading public. He was more doubtful about Mailer's involvement with the hip scene—with its drugs and violence and sex and nervous jazz. Much of that fascination was put on view in the summer of 1957 in Mailer's now famous essay "The White Negro," published in *Partisan Review.* Mailer had come to Styron's house one afternoon early that summer and read the essay aloud to him. Years later Styron would remember that Mailer called the essay "the most difficult thing I've ever written . . . like coughing up blood." Styron could not agree with the premise of "The White Negro" but was fascinated by it nonetheless. He also could not share Mailer's interest in the Beats and their free-form music and writing. Most of the poetry and prose of the movement bored him (he was particularly contemptuous of the writings of Jack Kerouac), and he could not stomach the jazz. This music was too aimless and jangled for him, and he was irritated by the pseudointellectual gravity of those who talked and wrote about it.

In retrospect one can see that Styron and Mailer had little common ground in the mid-fifties. Styron produced his best work by operating within formal boundaries and testing them with verbal inventiveness and technical experimentation. Mailer did his best writing in a headlong, improvisational style that showed the daring and violent energy of his mind. The two writers were going in different directions with their careers and lives; both thought of themselves as potentially important authors, but both wondered privately whether they could organize their lives successfully enough to put their best efforts down on paper. Both also were nervously eyeing a third writer who they feared was by far the best of their generation—James Jones.

Jones, like Styron and Mailer, was struggling to fulfill the promise that he had shown in an excellent first novel. He had labored since 1951 on a successor to *From Here to Eternity,* and by the fall of 1956 he had finished a draft of *Some Came Running,* an autobiographical novel about a World War II veteran who returns to his hometown. Soon after handing the manuscript over to his editors at Scribner's in December 1956, Jones met Gloria Mosolino, a beautiful, free-spirited blonde who had once acted as Marilyn Monroe's double in the movies. They were immediately attracted to each other; three weeks after they met they were talking of marriage. Jones extricated himself from his entanglement with Lowney Handy, the older woman who had sponsored him during his apprenticeship, and on February 27, 1957, he and Gloria were married.

Mailer and Jones had developed a friendship, but it was short-circuited now by the inability of their wives to get along with each other. The alliance began to cool late in 1957, at about the same time, ironically, that a strong and enduring relationship was developing between the Styrons and the Joneses. This foursome hit it off well from the beginning, Styron making contact with Jones's gentle, vulnerable side and Rose finding herself captured by Gloria's earthy good humor and sassiness. Mailer had placed value on his friendship with Jones; now he saw Jones moving away from him and toward Styron.

Much was happening in the Styrons' lives during this period. Rose had become pregnant again in the early summer of 1957 and was expecting their second child in March 1958. Susanna had already brought much noise and disorder to the house, and Styron had sometimes found it difficult to stick to his regimen. He knew that another baby would complicate his problems further. The renovations on the big house were moving ahead, but more slowly than Styron and Rose would have liked. At least his literary career appeared to be maintaining its momentum: he was always spoken of as a promising writer, and *Lie Down in Dark-*

ness continued to draw praise. Still, he felt pressure to get on with *Set This House on Fire.*

Perhaps most exciting to Styron that year was the likelihood that one of his narratives would be adapted for television. Some good original drama was being written for television during this period, but television was becoming so popular that its executives were starting also to acquire adaptation rights for works of drama and fiction. CBS had purchased television rights to *The Long March* for thirty-five hundred dollars in the fall of 1958 for its program *Playhouse 90,* a popular drama series. Now there was talk among Styron and his friends about who would play the leading roles. Burt Lancaster, perhaps, and Marlon Brando? Or maybe Kirk Douglas?

In the actual broadcast the roles were played by Sterling Hayden (as Colonel Templeton) and Jack Carson (as Mannix). Hayden gave a good performance, but Carson blew some of his lines—a disaster on live television. The script, too, was a great disappointment. Styron had let himself have high hopes for the adaptation, but when he watched the finished product in March 1959, he found the dialogue and direction "catastrophically bad." The script had gone to the *Playhouse 90* sponsors and to the Marine Corps for approval before performance. Apparently as a result the ending of *The Long March* had undergone a complete overhaul. A court-martial scene was added in which Mannix was convicted and made to see the error of his ways; the final message of the program, Styron felt, was that the Marine Corps was "still pretty much tops any way you look at it." He vented his irritation in a long letter to the editor in *The New Republic* for April 6, but the tone of the letter was more resigned than angry. This was Styron's first lesson in what could happen to literary creations when they went from print to screen.

Set This House on Fire was moving along fairly well, but the talk about the television production of *The Long March* sometimes made him fear that novels were becoming obsolete. He could see that the largest audiences in the years to come would surely be reached on television and movie screens. "The absurd thing is to find oneself 'creating' in a form which is practically dead," he grumbled to Leon Edwards in a letter. "No one reads the god damn things any more, and the only way you can achieve fortune & fame is to get into the loathsome movies."

At this point, roughly halfway through *Set This House on Fire,* Styron hit a snag. He wanted this novel to be an advance over *Lie Down in*

Darkness, not only in theme but in technique as well. As was often to be the case with Styron during his career, he had decided to be innovative with narration. Specifically he had decided to write the second half of *Set This House on Fire* simultaneously in the first person and the third person, two points of view that are normally irreconcilable. "I had never seen this welding of two points of view attempted in a work of fiction before," he later said. "I had never seen a narrator who, beginning in the first person, could, convincingly, end up in the third person, the story so merging and mingling that one might accept without hesitation the fact that the narrator himself knew the uttermost nuances of another man's thought."

The two points of view that Styron merged in Part II of *Set This House on Fire* were Peter Leverett's and Cass Kinsolving's. This fusing is appropriate, since, as we have seen, Peter and Cass began life as the same character—the original Peter Leverett of the 1954 false start. Cass was split off from Peter, taking as his dominant characteristics the parts of Peter's original personality that Styron had decided were not appropriate for a narrator. Part I of *Set This House on Fire,* which Styron had now finished, had been told in Peter's voice. Now in Part II Styron would begin to let Cass's voice and perspective take over—without shifting from Peter's first-person narration.

In the early sections of Part II, Styron allows Cass to tell long sections of the story in his own voice. This is accomplished by having Peter quote Cass directly. We hear Cass's voice and become accustomed to it, learning to allow for his exaggerations and self-interrogations. Then, before we grow weary of listening to Cass, who is too garrulous and digressive to be a good narrator, Styron shifts back to Peter's voice—but retains Cass's point of view. It is a daring bit of legerdemain: Styron has granted Peter access to Cass's mind, thus keeping the advantages of first-person narration (intimacy and verisimilitude) but casting his story into something resembling third-person limited omniscience, as defined and practiced by Henry James. So smoothly is the transition made in the published book that one never questions it. *Set This House on Fire,* in its second half, is thus told with a peculiar double-voiced technique, ideal for a novel in which the two major characters, Peter and Cass, merge finally into one consciousness, the better to examine the moral implications of what happened to them in Sambuco.

This narrative transition is carried off with apparent ease in the book, but the surviving manuscripts of the novel show that Styron had enormous difficulty working it out on paper. Preserved with the holograph draft of *Set This House on Fire* at the Library of Congress are fully five hundred leaves of discards and fragments, almost all from the second half of the novel. These manuscript leaves would constitute, in length, a respectable-sized novel by themselves. They are evidence of the great difficulty that Styron had in bringing off his experiment with narration.

An enormous, brooding energy is stored in these drafts, constricted and tightly wound, as if Styron were struggling to release his imaginative powers. He tried to explain the problem in a letter to Leon Edwards: "Writing a long novel, as I am doing, has an overpowering effect on the psyche. There's so *much* of it, there are so many things to keep straight, so much that you want to put into it but for artistic considerations can't, so much that's almost bound to fall short of your lofty aims that, if you're at all serious, you end up existing in a perpetual state of sweat and melancholy and quasi-alcoholism." In a letter to his father he was more direct about writing the novel: "It is the most difficult thing I have ever had to do in my life," he said.

Evidence of Styron's problems can be seen on a single sheet of legal-pad paper bearing private notes that he wrote to himself while he composed the manuscript. Styron had kept two or three such sheets with the manuscript of *Lie Down in Darkness*, but the notes for that novel are set down randomly on these pages, written higgledy-piggledy in a comfortably jumbled mess. The notes for *Set This House on Fire* are quite different. The single sheet is covered front and back and edge to edge with minuscule handwriting, perfectly aligned, and the notes themselves are cramped and cryptic. The edges of the sheet are smudged and tattered from handling, as if Styron held this particular sheet in his hands every day, thumbing its edges and worrying about whether he was managing to fit everything—every idea and point—into his narrative. Beside each of the notes is an asterisk, placed there by Styron, one assumes, when he was satisfied that the idea or reference had been incorporated into his story.

At some point during the composition of *Set This House on Fire,* Styron felt so blocked that he used amphetamines. "I took little green pills called Dexies," he recalled, "and I liked them." Styron found that the drugs liberated his pencil and gave him access to surrealistic visions and to deep levels of his subconscious mind. Unfortunately, the pills also gave him terrible insomnia, and he had to stop using them after a week or two.

By February 1958 the strain of this effort had begun to take its toll. Styron was having severe pains in his intestinal tract and, fearing ulcers or cancer, underwent a series of tests. He described the results in a letter to Leon Edwards:

> Outside of what a series of barium X-rays proved to be a case of "duodenitis" (I cannot find this term in Merck's manual), I am doing O.K., for a writer. I have just this day passed page 850 on my accursed manuscript, and the end is still not in sight. I will not bore you with a description of the agonies this book has caused me. I have heard it said that out of suffering great things come, and I certainly hope so, since to me at least it would be a colossal irony if all that came out of it was an exacerbated duodenum. I am taking probanthine, also Alka-Seltzer and several other panaceas, and they all seem to help some, but probably the major effect of this disease (which in turn, I'm sure, is caused by the wretched novel) has been to curtail my drinking which—since booze is such a remarkable tranquillizer—is a curse.

In the midst of these difficulties Rose went into labor. She was taken to Mount Sinai Hospital again and gave birth to their second child, another girl, on March 13, 1958. They named her Paola Clark, using the Italian spelling for her first name, and calling her Polly. (Paola was an echo of Pauline Styron's name, and Clark was William Styron's own middle name.) While Rose was recuperating in the hospital, Styron drove back to Roxbury to do some chores and check the mail. In his postbox he found this letter from Norman Mailer:

> Bill,
>
> I've been told by a reliable source—closer to you than one might expect—that you have been passing a few atrocious remarks about Adele. Normally, I would hesitate to believe the story, but my memory of slanderous remarks you've made about other women leaves me not at all in doubt. So I tell you this, Billy-boy. You have got to learn to keep your mouth shut about my wife, for if you do not, and I hear of it again, I will invite you to a fight in which I expect to stomp out of you a fat amount of your yellow and treacherous shit.
>
> Norman

Styron was astonished by the letter. His first impulse was to confront Mailer face-to-face, but he found that Mailer had left on a trip to Florida. His next instinct was to deny the allegations point by point: he went through the letter, affixing superscript numerals to the various charges and writing numbered annotations at the bottom of the page and on the back of the letter. Mailer's source, Styron suggested in these annotations, was someone with a "warped and perverted imagination." The accusation that he had passed "atrocious remarks" about Adele, he said, was an "unmitigated lie." Mailer had written that, under normal circumstances, he would hesitate to believe the gossip about Styron's behavior; Styron answered: "The venomous tone of your letter leads me to believe that, quite to the contrary, you wish to believe it more than anything in the world." Styron's last annotation was an attempt to go beyond the specifics of the letter: "Your delicate style, which would be degrading to you even if I were guilty of the monstrous things you allege against me, leaves me in little doubt that something is, and must have been, *eating* you that has nothing to do with the 'viciousness' you so meanly and falsely saddle me with."

Styron, however, did not send the annotated letter back to Mailer. Instead he took it with him the next day when he visited Rose in her hospital room. Jim and Gloria Jones had come to visit Rose that day; they were sailing for Europe soon and wanted to say good-bye. Styron showed Mailer's letter to Rose and the Joneses, and the four of them tried to puzzle out Mailer's motives for writing it. Jones agreed with Styron that something other than an alleged slander of Adele lay behind the letter. He also doubted that Styron's point-by-point refutation would do much to help the situation.

The Joneses had brought several bottles of champagne for bon voyage libations; these were consumed, and the mood in the hospital room became festive and giddy. Running beneath the hilarity, however, was an undercurrent of apprehension and sadness. Jones was leaving America at least in part because he could not endure the New York literary establishment. In his personal style and tastes he did not fit in with the uptown intelligentsia, and he had no more use for the hip scene in the Village than Styron did. His novel *Some Came Running* had been savaged by New York reviewers that January, and he had begun to believe that he would never make much headway with the eastern critics. Sty-

ron and Rose knew that this upcoming trip to Europe might turn out
to be more or less permanent for the Joneses—a prediction that in fact
did come true. They settled in Paris and stayed for sixteen years, returning to the States permanently only in 1974, when Jones's health
was failing and he was trying to finish his last novel, *Whistle,* before he
died.

Rose did not foresee all of this exactly, but she sensed some of it, and
it made her uncharacteristically mournful. She was also upset over
Mailer's letter to her husband. She allowed herself to be plied with the
champagne and became woozy in her hospital bed. Several hours later,
after everyone had left, she nursed Polly and tried to think about the
consequences of the Joneses' departure and of Mailer's break with her
husband. After a few minutes she noticed that Polly had passed out.
Some of the alcohol from the champagne had apparently made its way
into her milk, and Polly had become drunk. As a consequence Rose was
not allowed to nurse the child for the next two days—a prohibition that,
she later remembered, deepened her postdelivery blues and made her
weep more freely than she thought herself capable of.

Back in Roxbury two days later, Styron decided not to send the annotated letter back to Mailer. Instead he sat down and wrote a single
paragraph on a sheet of his own personal stationery. This he sent out in
the next morning's post:

3/17/58

Norman:

I don't know who your sick and pitiable "reliable source" is (how
much he must hate and envy me, or maybe you, but above all hate
himself), but you might have him or her get in touch with me some
day and repeat his allegations to my face. Your letter was so mean and
contemptible, so revealing of some other attitude toward me aside
from my alleged slander, but most importantly so utterly false, that it
does not deserve even this much of a reply.

B.S.

Mailer's answer was direct and crude. Beneath Styron's paragraph he
scrawled two sentences, then sent the sheet of stationery back to
Styron:

I just got back from a few days in Florida, and found this billet-doux.
So I invite you to get together with me face-to-face and repeat that my

letter is mean, contemptible, and false—if you feel up to it. If you don't, recognize your reply for what it is—a crock of shit.

Mailer

This was the last private communication that would pass between the two writers for almost twenty-five years. Their dispute would become one of the most celebrated literary feuds of their generation.

22

Completion

B Y THE FALL OF 1958 Mailer had folded his tents and returned to New York. Styron had come to believe that Mailer had decided ahead of time to break with him and that the issue of gossip about Adele had been a pretext. Styron was satisfied to let the matter lie: he felt no need to be in contact with Mailer and could see that their lives would take different courses. Mailer, however, wanted the rupture to be public. In fact he had decided to break off, or at least to test, his relations with the writers in his generation with whom he felt in competition. In the fall of 1959 Mailer published a wide-ranging miscellany with Putnam's entitled *Advertisements for Myself.* The collection contained essays and reviews and interviews; it also included a good deal of previously unpublished writing, together with an account of Mailer's difficulties in getting his novel *The Deer Park* into print and some passages from that novel that he had been required to tone down before publication.

The most talked-about item in *Advertisements,* though, was a previously unpublished piece entitled "Evaluations—Quick and Expensive Comments on the Talent in the Room." This was a series of short takes on the writing of Mailer's competitors. The piece contained praise for a few of Mailer's contemporaries, most notably for William Burroughs, but much of the space was given to criticisms of Styron, James Jones, Saul Bellow, J. D. Salinger, Vance Bourjaily, Gore Vidal, Calder Will-

ingham, Ralph Ellison, and James Baldwin. The remarks about Styron
were among the most damning:

> Styron wrote the prettiest novel of our generation. *Lie Down in
> Darkness* has beauty at its best, is almost never sentimental, even has
> whispers of near-genius as the work of a twenty-three-year-old. It
> would have been the best novel of our generation if it had not lacked
> three qualities: Styron was not near to creating a man who could
> move on his feet, his mind was uncorrupted by a new idea, and his
> book was without evil. There was only Styron's sense of the tragic:
> misunderstanding—and that is too small a window to look upon the
> world we have known.
>
> Since then only a remarkably good short novel, *The Long March,*
> has appeared by Styron. But he has been working hard over the years
> on a second novel, *Set This House on Fire,* and I hear it is done. If it
> is at all good, and I expect it is, the reception will be a study in the art
> of literary advancement. For Styron has spent years oiling every lit-
> erary lever and power which could help him on his way, and there are
> medals waiting for him in the mass-media. If he has written a book
> which expresses some real part of his complex and far from pleasant
> view of the American character, if this new novel should prove to
> have the bite of a strong and critical consciousness, then one can
> hardly deny him his avidity as a politician for it is not easy to work
> many years on a novel which has something hard and new to say
> without trying to shape the reception of it. But if Styron has com-
> promised his talent, and written what turns out to be the most suit-
> able big book of the last ten years, a *literary* work which will deal with
> secondhand experience and all-but-deep proliferation of the smoke
> of passion and the kiss of death, if he has done no more than fill a
> cornucopia of fangless perceptions which will please the conservative
> power and delight the liberal power, offend no one, and prove to be
> ambitious, traditional, innocuous, artful, and in the middle, breathy
> and self-indulgent in the beauty of its prose, evocative to the tender-
> hearted and the reviewers of books, then Styron will receive a rav-
> ingly good reception, for the mass-media is aching for such a novel
> like a tout for his horse. He will be made the most important writer
> of my generation. But how much more potent he will seem to us, his
> contemporaries and his competitors, if he has had the moral courage
> to write a book equal to his hatred and therefore able to turn the con-
> sciousness of our time, an achievement which is the primary measure
> of a writer's size.

Styron was irritated by the condescension and advice-giving inherent in the attack, but at least he found himself in good company among Mailer's other targets. He could see that Mailer, like Hemingway, conceived of novel-writing as a contest and took the notion of writing the Great American Novel with much competitive seriousness. For Mailer it was necessary that he antagonize his peers: he drew energy and motivation from these public challenges, in part because they placed pressure on him to deliver.

Styron thought of answering Mailer in print (he was urged to do so by some of his friends), but in the end he decided to keep silent. He had no desire to trade blows in the literary press with Mailer and suspected that he might be playing into Mailer's hands if he tried a counterattack. What he settled upon instead was a private gesture that only Mailer would recognize, but a gesture that would appear in a public place—the pages of *Set This House on Fire*. He began therefore to blend elements of Mailer's personality and behavior into the character of Mason Flagg, the corrupt, posturing villain of the novel.

Mason adopts many of Mailer's interests in contemporary art and hipster jazz, and he preaches the virtues of the Reichean orgone box. One also notes in Mason a leering interest in erotica and sexual experimentation and a pompous effort to link sex with violence. ("Sex is the last frontier," Mason intones, and then follows with a ponderous lecture on the "total exploration of sex, as Sade envisioned it.") Mason Flagg, as Styron surely knew, was fundamentally unlike Norman Mailer. Mason was a fraud with no talent; Mailer, though he could be obstreperous and offensive, was a serious and gifted writer. But Styron still wanted to say to Mailer, in the pages of *Set This House on Fire,* that he was wasting himself. The Beat scene and modern jazz and free sex and orgone boxes were, in Styron's estimation, surpassingly banal.

Styron also wanted to charge Mailer with betrayal. To do so, he put a direct quotation from Mailer's original letter to him into the mouth of Mason Flagg—early in the novel, on page 124, where he was sure Mailer would see it. Near the end of chapter II Mason is pursuing Francesca, an Italian peasant girl whom he has just raped. She has scratched his face and fled from his rented palazzo. Mason encounters Peter Leverett at the bottom of a flight of stairs and demands to know where Francesca has gone. "I swear to God," says Peter, "I just do not *know.*" Mason's response is vicious and deranged. "You're lying!" he screams. "You wait right there, Petesy boy, because when I come back I expect to stomp out of you a fat amount of your yellow and treacherous shit." Styron finished the chapter with these two paragraphs, meant especially for Mailer's eyes:

> Maybe you recollect that dream of betrayal which I described early in this story—of the murderous friend who came tapping at my window. Somehow when again I recall that dream and then remember Mason at this moment, I am made conscious of another vision—half-dream, half-fantasy—which has haunted me ever since I left Sambuco.
>
> It goes like this: I have taken a picture of a friend with one of those Polaroid cameras. While waiting for the required minute to elapse I have wandered into another room, and there I pull out the print all fresh and glossy. "Ha!" or "Well!" or "Look!" I call out expectantly to the other room. Yet as I bend down to examine the picture, I find there, not my friend at all but the face of some baleful and unearthly monster. And there is only silence from the other room.

Several of the other characters in the novel are based on people Styron knew or had come into contact with. The portrayal of Cass Kinsolving incorporates many of the mannerisms and much of the vocabulary of Bobby White, though Cass's self-questioning probably grows more out of Styron's own doubts and fears than it does from what Styron knew of Bobby's psyche. Poppy, Cass's childlike wife, has some superficial similarities to both Claire White and Rose. Mason is based in part on a student whom Styron had known at Christchurch, a boy who invented outlandish tales and bragged about his sexual adventures. And some of Mason's mannerisms are copied from an American named T. Rowland Slingluff whom Styron met in Ravello when he and Rose were living there. Mason's cock-and-bull story about serving as a spy in an Allied commando unit is based on a yarn that another Christchurch friend had told Styron during the summer of 1958. *Set This House on Fire,* then, is not exactly a roman à clef, but one can find some correspondences between certain of its characters and some of the people in Styron's life.

More important is the philosophical cast of the novel. Read today, almost forty years after its first publication, *Set This House on Fire* reveals itself to be a postwar European novel, permeated with the attitudes and thinking of what was then called Continental existentialism. The major characters, Peter and Cass, are grappling with life in an absurd universe filled with anguish and malevolence. Both men want to exercise free will, but both must first break away from the alluring figure of Mason, who promises money and ease and who represents what American culture of the 1950s was drifting toward. In literary terms *Set This House on Fire* is most closely akin to some of the novels of Albert Camus and to writings by Kierkegaard, Dostoevski, and Kafka. Styron's major characters, like most of Camus's, eventually right themselves and discover ways of continuing to live and function, even as they recognize the ultimate purposelessness of what they do. Through deliberate acts of will, both Peter and Cass rekindle their spirits and move away, at the end of the novel, from paralysis and despair.

Viewed in retrospect, *Set This House on Fire* is a probing critique of American society of the 1950s, summing up many of the apprehensions that Styron felt over the trends of postwar U.S. culture. It is a prophetic book, anticipating with considerable accuracy the banalities and self-indulgences of public behavior during the decades that would follow. *Set This House on Fire* is also a demanding novel that tests a reader's endurance and patience. Most of the action of the story is finished by the end of Book I; perhaps as a result the novel lacks narrative drive in its second half. Much of Book II is taken up with a meandering discussion between Peter and Cass about the morality and significance of what happened in Sambuco. One also encounters a character named Luigi, a garrulous Italian policeman who is an anarchist in politics but a humanist in general outlook. He speaks good sense but is too static and didactic for the benefit of the novel. There are long, meditative digressions—philosophical set pieces, almost—that retard the flow of the narrative. It is as if Styron was determined, in Part II of *Set This House on Fire,* to pursue and run to earth every question he had raised in Part I.

Hiram Haydn had done well at Random House after his arrival there in 1955, but Haydn wanted his own imprint. In the summer of 1958 he had begun talking with Pat Knopf (Alfred and Blanche Knopf's son) and with Simon Michael Bessie (a senior editor at Harper and Brothers) about founding a new publishing house, an independent operation of which they would be co-directors. Haydn was also distracted by his own literary ambitions. A better-than-average writer, he had been immersed in the composition of his novel *The Hand of Esau* during the gestation of *Set This House on Fire*. Styron turned in sections of manuscript to Haydn from time to time for commentary, but Haydn did not read them promptly. When he got around to looking at what Styron had written, his comments were superficial, and in conferences he seemed more interested in discussing his own work than Styron's.

Styron had already lost some of his faith in Haydn a year or so earlier when Haydn had turned down a chance to bring Vladimir Nabokov's *Lolita* to Random House. The novel had been published first in Paris by Olympia Press in 1955; two years later Styron had read a copy of that edition, lent to him by his friend Lew Allen. He and Allen had talked about publishing a private American edition of the book themselves, to challenge censorship restrictions, but they had been unable to swing the finances. Styron therefore gave the book to Bennett Cerf and urged him to publish it at Random House. Cerf read *Lolita,* thought it a masterpiece, and wanted to publish it.

Styron had also given a copy of *Lolita* to Haydn. He knew that Haydn was a broad-minded man, and he felt sure that Haydn would be eager to publish the book. Styron was shocked to learn, a week or so later, that Haydn had been repulsed by *Lolita* and had vetoed its publication by Random House. "That loathsome novel will be published over my dead body!" he said to Styron, telling him that he, Haydn, had a daughter the age of Lolita, and that Styron would understand his feelings when Susanna reached the age of twelve.

Haydn had missed the subtlety and playfulness of Nabokov's novel and had simply judged it dirty. Apparently he had been immune to Nabokov's probing satire and his manipulation of the reader's emotions and perceptions. Styron thought it a shame that Random House, the firm that had brought *Ulysses* to the United States in 1933, would now not risk publishing *Lolita*. Cerf had been in favor of taking the novel, but when he had brought in Haydn as editor in chief he had given him autonomy over the Random House list. Haydn had threatened to resign if Cerf overruled him on *Lolita;* Cerf had therefore passed on the novel. Eventually Nabokov published *Lolita* with Putnam's, and it became an enormous (and controversial) success.

Styron was not certain that he wanted to work with Haydn on *Set*

This House on Fire. Haydn's interest in him seemed to have diminished, perhaps because he was no longer a beginner. Haydn's energies were being absorbed instead by a group of young hopefuls whose first novels he was publishing with indifferent success. To Styron it seemed that Haydn was not capable of dealing with mature authors and was comfortable only with apprentices who depended on him emotionally.

Matters came to a head on March 15, 1959, when *The New York Times* reported that Haydn had resigned from Random House and that he, Knopf, and Bessie would begin a new firm, as yet unnamed, which would specialize at first in high-quality paperbacks. Styron, then entering the final push to finish *Set This House on Fire,* had to decide whether he would pull up stakes and follow Haydn once again to a new house—Haydn's fourth since Styron had met him in 1947—or stay behind with Random House. There seems to have been no question that Random House would be the publisher of *Set This House on Fire:* the novel was under contract there, and Styron had accepted a fifteen-thousand-dollar advance. But Haydn seems to have assumed that Styron would leave Cerf and Klopfer after *Set This House on Fire* appeared.

Styron was of a divided mind about the matter, and he mulled it over during the summer and fall of 1959. He felt indebted to Haydn for the faith he had shown in *Lie Down in Darkness,* and he had much personal affection for the man. On the other hand, Haydn had shown signs of diminished interest in Styron's work and had shown as well a tendency to jump from house to house during his career. There was no guarantee that this new publishing firm—which Haydn and his associates would name Atheneum—would be Haydn's last stop. (In fact it was not.) Would Styron be expected to follow Haydn to the next house after this one? Styron wanted a dependable, long-term relationship with a strong, financially secure publisher. Random House was such a firm; Haydn's new imprint, as yet, was not. Bennett Cerf had faith in Styron and wrote him a warm letter urging him to think carefully about his future. "We were proud to add you to the Random House list, and we will make every possible effort to keep you there," wrote Cerf. "In a single sentence, I would like to be your publisher for the rest of my life."

Styron decided in the fall of 1959 to stay with Random House. He did not tell Haydn immediately, in part because he feared a scene, for Haydn could be emotional. But Styron was certain that he would not leave Random House. He was hoping almost irrationally that *Set This House on Fire* would be a big success, that he would beat the second-novel jinx that had plagued both Jones and Mailer, and that he would immediately become one of the two or three brightest stars on the Random House list.

Styron's decision was made easier by the fact that there was an editor at Random House who had agreed to work with him on *Set This House on Fire*. This was Robert Loomis, his old friend from Duke. Loomis had come to Random House in 1957 after stints of manuscript reading and editing with Appleton-Century-Crofts and Rinehart. Styron and Loomis had kept up their friendship over the years; Styron had recently done duty as Loomis's best man. Loomis was soft-spoken and easy to get along with, and he was not inclined to intervene heavily in the compositional process. Loomis was almost exactly Styron's age, so the relationship would have no hint of paternalism. This suited Styron, who no longer felt the need of a fatherly editor to guide and advise him.

Styron found that he enjoyed working with Loomis. He would let Loomis know whenever a new section of the novel had been completed, and Loomis would come to Roxbury, where Styron would read the new pages aloud to him. Both men enjoyed these sessions—Styron because they were small ceremonies that marked off stages of progress on his novel, Loomis because he admired Styron's writing and enjoyed visiting with him. Loomis's method was to listen without interruption, then to offer comments about characters and motivations. Styron, he knew, was a skilled stylist who needed no line-by-line editing. What Styron wanted instead was his reaction to the sound of the narrative, to the voices in which it was told, and to the ideas that it embodied.

When Styron at last completed the manuscript in late 1959, he showed it to Peter Matthiessen, who praised the novel as "complex and powerful" and complimented Styron on its sophisticated structure and internal unity. Matthiessen thought, however, that the writing had flaws:

> I wonder . . . whether you don't underestimate the force of your own scenes by occasionally overstating, like a man running after a rolling cart to push it downhill faster. When, as in this case, a book and its scenes are moving rapidly and straight toward an inevitable terminal under their own considerable power, then the reader can only feel

badgered by gratuitous exposition and lily-gilding adjectives, not unlike a child who, once excitedly aloft on a swing, wants his benefactor
to keep his goddam mitts off him.

Loomis had already cautioned Styron about his tendency to over-
explain; Matthiessen's comments seemed to confirm what Loomis had
said. Styron therefore tried to work on the problem before the novel was
published. He cut fairly deeply in both typescript and galley proofs in
an effort to make Peter Leverett less garrulous. To some extent this difficulty was a holdover from the false start on the novel in 1954: Peter
was still showing vestiges of the behavior that Styron had transferred to
Cass Kinsolving. Styron's cuts were a final attempt to sever the two
characters from each other and to quicken the narrative pace.

Production of the novel proceeded smoothly, and advance copies
were ready by early April. When he saw a bound copy of *Set This House
on Fire,* he was stunned by its length. Even with the cuts, the novel
tipped in at 507 pages. To John Marquand he wrote: "I am being utterly
serious when I tell you that, hefting this mammoth excrescence of mine,
I have never been so utterly bereft and depressed in all my life. *Who,* in
God's name, is in this day and age going to sit down and read 507 pages
of haggard, neurotic outpouring when they can go see Tony Curtis or
learn to water-ski or fly to the Bahamas. . . . I have never been so dis-
consolate over anything in my life as the concrete proof, between hard
covers, of my own appalling logorrhea."

23

⟨◈⟩

Set This House
on Fire

R ANDOM HOUSE had budgeted twelve thousand dollars for pro-
motion of *Set This House on Fire,* a large amount in 1960. The
publicity arm of the firm now began to mount its campaign, sending
out advance copies and press releases. Random House also began to
offer the subsidiary rights before clothbound publication—a fairly new
practice on the New York literary marketplace at the time. A section of
Set This House on Fire was prepublished in *The Paris Review,* and two
more segments appeared in *Esquire.* The Book Find Club, which aimed
at highbrow readers, purchased book-club rights, and several paperback houses showed interest in doing a softcover edition. Formal publication was set, at Styron's request, for May 4, 1960, his and Rose's
seventh wedding anniversary.

By this time their family had again grown by one. Rose had become
pregnant during the winter of 1958, and on August 4, 1959, while the
family was vacationing on Martha's Vineyard, she had given birth to a
boy, whom they named Thomas Haydn Styron—the middle name from
Hiram Haydn. This new baby, a good-looking, demanding child, put
new strain on their family life and made Styron grumpy about the subject of fatherhood.

Styron felt unable to face the tensions that publication day would
bring. He also wanted to put some distance between himself and
Haydn so that he could break the news about his decision to stay with

Random House in a letter, not face-to-face. He and Rose decided to escape with the children to Europe. The plan was to go in February and stay for a few weeks in Paris, then progress by stages to Rome for an extended visit—perhaps for most of the summer. In this way Styron would be insulated from the reviews, which he was beginning to suspect would be less than favorable.

The Styrons sailed in mid-February 1960 for Paris. They spent much time there with Jim and Gloria Jones, who were then living in a small apartment at 17, Quai aux Fleurs. Gloria was pregnant after several miscarriages, and she and her husband had adapted as fully as they ever would to life in Paris. "They both speak an extraordinary brand of French, well-larded with shits and fucks," Styron wrote to John Marquand, "but they make themselves understood easily enough and they both know everyone in Paris." The Styrons had a dizzy time with the Joneses, finding it all "very alcoholic and exhausting," he reported to Elizabeth McKee. It was "tough on the liver and the estomac," he lamented.

While he was in the city, Styron went out of curiosity to a jazz-poetry session arranged by the Beat poet Gregory Corso. He sent this bulletin to Marquand:

> All the international hip set was there and afterwards I fell into company with Bill Burroughs. He is an absolutely astonishing personage, with the grim mad face of Savonarola and a hideously tailored 1925 shit-colored overcoat and scarf to match and a gray fedora pulled down tight around his ears. He reminded me of nothing so much as a mean old Lesbian and is a fantastic reactionary, very prim and tight-lipped and proper, who spoke of our present Republican administration as that "dirty group of Reds." . . . He is as mad as a hatter and after the jazz session a photographer from *Paris Presse* buttonholed Corso, Burroughs, and *myself* and took our picture (in front of a *charcuterie*), later captioned—so help me God—"Les 'Beats' à Paris."

During this visit Styron talked with Jim Jones about Mailer's remarks in *Advertisements for Myself.* Jones had made a joke of the book: he kept a copy on a sideboard near his bar, and whenever he and Gloria had a guest who was mentioned in *Advertisements,* that person was encouraged to write a scurrilous response inside. Styron obliged—as did other visitors over the years—but the copy was later stolen and has not resurfaced. Jones had already set down his own feelings about Mailer's attacks in a letter to Styron that January:

> When I read ADVERTISEMENTS I could not help feeling that he had taken an unfair advantage of everyone with that piece about us other writers of his generation. As he claimed in the introduction to it, it is like statements made during a gossipy evening of drinking and talk. That's all to the good, and I suppose he's as honest as he can be; at least it's an attempt to be completely honest. The unfair advantage comes in, to my mind, in the fact that he is—without mentioning it to a reader—giving the authenticity and authority of print to statements of ordinary gossiping talk.

The Styrons left Paris late in March and visited Geneva, Milan, and Florence in succession—"with double diaper changes at every railroad stop," Styron wrote in one letter. By early May they had arrived in Rome and settled into an apartment on the Via San Teodoro, near the Forum. The place was owned by a down-at-the-heels aristocrat named Prince Paolo di Borghese who made his living by renting the apartment to celebrities. (Previous tenants had included John Wayne, Rock Hudson, and Jayne Mansfield.) The appointments were too vulnerable for the rambunctious Styron children, whom their father had taken to calling "the little nose-pickers." Susanna, then five years old, made her presence felt by knocking over and smashing a five-hundred-dollar Della Robbia vase. She was forgiven, though, and she compensated for the breakage by beginning to speak Italian that spring, picking up the language almost effortlessly and pronouncing it with the local accent, as small children will do. Polly had not spoken at all until that same spring: now she began to babble constantly in English, speaking in sentences almost from the first. Tommy had become an agreeable, cheerful baby, and Styron began to rock him to sleep at night, singing Presbyterian hymns instead of lullabies.

In mid-May, Styron heard from his British publisher, Jamie Hamilton. *Set This House on Fire,* it appeared, was going to have to be bowdlerized if it was to appear in England. London publishers were then going through a period of harassment from the director of public prosecutions; several of them had been charged with printing obscene books during the 1950s, and most had knuckled under, withdrawing the offending volumes from the market and paying nominal fines. The publisher Frederic Warburg had not done so: he had challenged the existing laws in 1957, refusing to back down on a novel by Stanley Kauffmann entitled *The Philanderer.* Warburg had fought the case through a jury trial at the Old Bailey and had been acquitted, but the home secretary had continued to prosecute publishers, issuing summonses to three other houses soon after the Warburg trial. One of these houses, Hutchinson & Company, was found guilty of purveying salacious literature and was fined stiffly.

Publishers and authors mobilized their forces in 1959 and succeeded in having Parliament pass the Obscene Publications Act, a reasonably liberal statute. When Jamie Hamilton wrote to Styron in May 1960, however, this new law had yet to be tested in the courts. Hamilton was therefore extremely wary of publishing anything that might be labeled obscene and might land him and his firm in the Old Bailey. The situation was complicated by the fact that, under British law, the typesetter and the printer were equally liable with the publisher for prosecution if a book was judged to be pornographic. Hamilton reported to Styron that two British printers had already refused to typeset *Set This House on Fire* and that he was sure other printers would follow suit. He sent a list of offending words and terms to Styron and asked him for permission to expunge them from *Set This House on Fire.* The necessity for this sanitizing irritated Styron, but he had no choice if he wanted his novel to appear in England. He consented to the bleachings on condition that Hamilton see to them himself.

The offending words and phrases are not what one would expect. Some of them are predictable: the words *fuck* and *fucking* were altered, for example, and two references to masturbation were removed. A great many common profanities, however, were left unchanged in the text. What offended the British ear, according to Jamie Hamilton, were obscenities "complicated by a soupçon of blasphemy." Thus Cass Kinsolving's oaths "Triple bleeding God!" and "Bleeding Saviour!" and "Thrice-punctured Christ!" were either excised or softened. "I shit on Him because I do not believe!" became "He is a monster! He is the devil!" "Horseshit . . . triple bleeding horseshit" was cut from the text. And, in a comic touch, the southern vulgarism "grinning like a shit-eating dog" became "grinning like a big hairy dog."

Even with these expurgations, Jamie Hamilton could not persuade a British printer to compose the type for *Set This House on Fire*. As a consequence he had to have the novel printed in the Netherlands, via offset lithography, from a copy of the Random House text that had been expurgated by slice-and-paste methods. (Hamilton deserves credit for his persistence; he could easily have let the matter drop and declined to publish the novel at all.) This oddly manufactured edition eventually appeared in England in February 1961; its altered text, or an unrestored typesetting that descends from it, continues to be the version of *Set This House on Fire* that is read there today.

The American reviews of *Set This House on Fire* began to appear in June 1960. As Styron had feared, they were largely negative. This was not the novel that reviewers had expected from the author of *Lie Down in Darkness*. Though parts of it were laid in the South, it was manifestly not of the southern school. It belonged instead to another tradition, that of the expatriate novel, and it was colored throughout by a heavily Europeanized sensibility. *Set This House on Fire* was an attack, savage in some places, on the complacency of the Eisenhower era and the vacuity of American intellectual life. Such a novel was almost bound to take its knocks from the reviewers.

Certainly the book was not ignored. Styron was the subject of a cover story in the *Saturday Review* for June 4, and *Set This House on Fire* was treated at length in virtually every important literary organ in the country. Parts of most reviews were laudatory: Harvey Breit in *Partisan Review* called the novel "an immeasurable gain in maturity" over *Lie Down in Darkness,* and Granville Hicks in the *Saturday Review* found it "rich and deep," but even these reviewers criticized Styron's excesses of language and emotion. Orville Prescott, writing in the daily *New York Times,* found the novel "hollow and windy," and John K. Hutchens called it "overdone" in the *Herald-Tribune.* A few of the reviews were derisory: Arthur Mizener, writing for *The New York Times Book Review,* thought *Set This House on Fire* pretentious and found its scenes and characters "solemnly hopped up, emotionally and metaphysically." (The Mizener review particularly irritated Styron.) Phoebe Adams in the *Atlantic Monthly* wrote: "Mr. Styron is one of those novelists who assume that serious purpose constitutes a license to bore."

The killer among the reviews was the anonymous notice in *Time.* Under the heading "Empty Soul Blues," the reviewer placed Styron in the "Southern school of U.S. writers" but noted that "the passion seems to be draining out of this school: the magnolias are all too frequently stained with tired blood." The odor of *Set This House on Fire,* he said, was "more of the stage than the sulphur pit." The novel, in his opinion, was little more than "a 507-pp. crying jag."

Styron was floored by these notices. He had been prepared for mixed reviews but not for this kind of negativity. As the clippings came to him in batches in Rome, he could see that he had in no way fulfilled the promise that had been predicted for him—at least in the eyes of these book critics. He finally cabled Bob Loomis to send him no more reviews. It was a bitter time for him: he had retreated to Roxbury, where he had spent six years writing a serious, weighty novel. Now, if the reviews were to be believed, he had delivered a flatulent, pretentious flop. In his anger and disappointment Styron wondered whether Mailer's attack on him, which had called him a literary *flagorneur,* had queered the reception of *Set This House on Fire.* Perhaps Mailer was part of the problem, but Styron knew that some parts of his novel had in fact been overwrought, and that in the second half of the book he had demanded too much of his readers.

Toward the end of the summer, though, one late review of *Set This House on Fire*—an extended essay on the book, really—gave a lift to Styron's spirits. Charles A. Fenton, who had already written excellent books on Ernest Hemingway and Stephen Vincent Benét, published a long assessment of the novel in the Autumn 1960 *South Atlantic Quarterly* under the title "William Styron and the Age of the Slob." In part the review was a setup: Fenton was a visiting member of the English department at Duke, and the *South Atlantic Quarterly* was published at Duke, so his remarks were almost bound to be laudatory. (One suspects William Blackburn's hand here in arranging for the review.) The essay was so canny and perceptive, though, that one was tempted to ignore those circumstances. Fenton saw at once that *Set This House on Fire* was an ambitious performance: "What separates it from the machine-tooled facility of so many of our seminar-trained novelists," he wrote, "is the magnitude of its theme and the massiveness of its landscape." Fenton recognized the purpose of the novel without difficulty: "Styron's theme is nothing less than the stagnation and regeneration of the spirit," he said. He understood and discussed intelligently the experiments in point of view that Styron had attempted, and he analyzed accurately the various layers of time in the novel. Fenton saw that *Set This House on Fire* was an attempt to criticize American culture in the light of postwar European thinking. "What Styron has undertaken, and what he has in large part achieved," wrote Fenton, "is nothing less than a rendition of national mood."

Styron was so pleased by Fenton's review that he thought he might send him a note of thanks—a violation of protocol but one, he thought, for which he might be forgiven. At that point, however, a letter arrived from Bob Loomis telling him that Fenton had killed himself. The particulars of his death came to Styron later in a letter from Reynolds Price, a student of William Blackburn's who was now on the Duke faculty and who had known and liked Fenton. The story involved marital trouble and academic intrigue, and the details left Styron feeling "unaccountably wretched."

Styron was not in the best of condition in the weeks following the publication of *Set This House on Fire.* Away from Roxbury and without his customary regimen to give order to his days, he drank for long hours and gave himself over to idleness and brooding. This was a repetition of the slump that he had endured after finishing *Lie Down in Darkness,* though he probably did not recognize it as such. He admitted years later that while in Rome he was so unhappy that he allowed himself one or two fits of uncontrolled weeping.

Set This House on Fire, however, was a success in the eyes of Random House. Publishers know that book reviews have little effect on sales: this proved to be the case with Styron's novel. *Set This House on Fire* spent several weeks on the best-seller lists, rising as high as eighth place, and brought a $35,000 figure from New American Library for paperback rights—a healthy amount for 1960. The book sold over twenty-one thousand copies in hardback and, with subsidiary income, showed a respectable gross profit of almost $30,000 for Random House by the end of fiscal 1960–61. For Styron himself, *Set This House on Fire* was also successful financially: it more than earned out his $15,000 advance, and it brought him approximately $20,000 more in subsidiary income. None of this cheered him, however, and his mood remained bleak. He believed that he had failed spectacularly.

At this moment there appeared in Rome a man bearing news that would change Styron's literary career and show him a wholly different way of thinking about himself as a writer. This was Michel Mohrt, a representative of the prestigious publishing firm of Gallimard in Paris. Mohrt had come to deliver the personal regards of Gaston Gallimard, the patriarch of the house, and to urge Styron to allow Gallimard to publish the French translation of *Set This House on Fire.* The chief adviser to Gallimard on American literary matters in 1960 was Maurice-Edgar Coindreau, a professor at Princeton University who had translated into French many notable works of fiction by the generation of American writers just preceding Styron's. Coindreau had translated novels by Ernest Hemingway, John Dos Passos, Erskine Caldwell, John Steinbeck, and Flannery O'Connor, but his great discovery had been William Faulkner, whose genius he had recognized long before most American critics had begun to understand his work. Coindreau's brilliant translations of *The Sound and the Fury, As I Lay Dying, Light in August, The Wild Palms,* and other Faulkner novels—often prefaced by his explanatory remarks—introduced Faulkner's work to French readers and critics. Their recognition of his genius helped to spread his reputation in Europe and played a crucial role in bringing the Nobel Prize to him in 1950. Coindreau had continued to function as Gallimard's chief link to the contemporary American literary scene throughout the 1950s. Now he had discovered Styron's work and was keen to bring it to French readers, as he had done with Faulkner's.

Michel Mohrt, himself a well-known critic and translator, knocked on the door of Styron's apartment around three o'clock one afternoon in late May. Mohrt was a dapper man who wore a mustache: that afternoon, Styron later recalled, he sported suspenders and a derby hat. Mohrt introduced himself and explained his mission; then he handed Styron two letters. The first, written in English by Coindreau, was full of praise. It read in part: "Your new novel is one of the most powerful books I have read in years. It is not only beautifully put together with an uncanny sense of almost unbearable suspense, but the psychological analysis is as keen as it is fascinating. This book will stand as a masterpiece of modern American fiction."

Styron then turned to the second letter, written in French by Gaston Gallimard. Various French words stood out as he glanced through the letter: "*sincèrement,*" "*véritable enthousiasme,*" "*une oeuvre importante,*" "*admiration.*" Styron had been discussing the French translation of *Set*

This House on Fire in a desultory way with two Paris houses already—Robert Laffont and Plon—but he had made no firm commitment. Laffont had wanted to cut the novel for translation, and Plon had seemed only mildly enthusiastic about the book. (Del Duca, the house that had published the French translation of *Lie Down in Darkness* in 1953, had expressed no interest in *Set This House on Fire.*) Gaston Gallimard, by contrast, had sent a personal representative to Rome to court Styron. Mohrt took the Styrons and a group of their friends out to a festive dinner that night. Before the evening had ended Styron had decided to commit himself to the house of Gallimard. The two letters and the praise from Mohrt had lifted his spirits enormously. "It was like a shot of heroin," he later said. "It took a lot of the sting out of those American reviews."

If William Styron's literary career can be said to have had a turning point, this was that point. He was thirty-five years old. He had bottomed out that summer in Rome: drained by six years of solitary labor on *Set This House on Fire,* disappointed over the reviews of the novel, and unsure of his literary future, he had begun to question whether he should even continue as a writer. The praise from Coindreau and the invitation to publish with Gallimard had been timely and gratifying.

From that point on, his career would have a second and very lively dimension in France, and the great enthusiasm of the French for his work would spread over Europe and eventually into the Eastern bloc countries and the Soviet Union. Styron would learn to think of himself as more than a writer for American audiences, and his range as an artist would expand accordingly.

24

Reentry

THE STYRONS returned to Roxbury in the fall of 1960. Styron had decided to spend the next two years reading about American slavery, educating himself about the history and psychology of Negro bondage. He intended to tackle the Nat Turner novel; first, though, he needed to learn as much as he could about the South's peculiar institution.

Late that fall Styron learned from Robert Silvers (soon to become the editor of *The New York Review of Books*) that James Baldwin needed a place to stay. Baldwin was low on money; he wanted to get away from New York and work on the manuscript of a novel that he was calling "Another Country." Styron and Rose had met Baldwin a few times at literary gatherings in New York, and both had liked him. Styron had read Baldwin's first novel, *Go Tell It on the Mountain,* and knew some of Baldwin's stories and essays from *Partisan Review* and *The New Leader.* Styron's writing studio—the small house in which he and Rose had first lived—was not being used. Styron got in touch with Baldwin and offered this house to him for as long as he needed it. Baldwin accepted and moved in a few weeks later.

Initially Styron and Baldwin were a little wary of each other. Styron had never lived in close proximity with a black man, and Baldwin had never spent much time around a white southerner. After a few days of awkwardness, though, the two men settled into a comfortably open relationship that would ripen, over the next six months, into close friendship. They were an unlikely pair: Styron tall and pale and loose-jointed, given to introspection and abstraction, surrounded by his wife and children and house and possessions; Baldwin small, tightly wound, very dark, articulate and intense, an unattached homosexual without much more property than what he had brought in his suitcases. Yet the two men discovered a good deal in common and learned much from each other over the months that followed.

Styron remembered later that the weather that winter was severe and the snowfall heavy. The snowdrifts around the property became deep—over five feet in places—but Baldwin faithfully kept a path shoveled from the studio, where he was sleeping and writing, to the main house, where he spent his evenings with the Styrons. Every day around five o'clock, after he had finished his stint at the worktable, Baldwin would come over to the house for a drink. Styron would watch the top of Baldwin's black head moving along just above the snowdrifts that bordered the shoveled path. For Styron this was often the beginning of an absorbing, disturbing, revealing evening.

Almost the first thing that Styron and Baldwin discovered was that they had a common connection to slavery. Styron's grandmother had been a slave owner; Baldwin's grandfather and grandmother had both been slaves. The two men were a little surprised that their connection to slavery should be so close. Most members of their generation, if tied to slavery at all, were connected through a great-grandparent or some even more distant kin, but for Styron and Baldwin the connection was more recent and immediate. Styron told about his grandmother Marianna and her two little slave girls, Drusilla and Lucinda, whom she had loved and whose loss she had mourned. Later Styron remembered that Baldwin listened without flinching to the sentimental overtones of these stories. "Because he was wise," Styron recalled, "Jimmy understood the necessity of dealing with the preposterous paradoxes that had dwelled at the heart of the racial tragedy—the unrequited loves as well as the murderous furies." Baldwin in his turn told about his grandfather, who had been a slave in Virginia and whose anger over that fact had poisoned his life and the life of his son, Baldwin's father. Baldwin also talked about his grandmother, named Barbara, who had been born a slave in the Deep South and who spent her last years bedridden in the Baldwin apartment in Harlem. She had given birth to fourteen children, now scattered. Some of them, it was said, had been fathered by white men. Baldwin told his memories of sitting by her bed, and Styron found them oddly similar to his own recollections of Marianna Styron, beside whose bed he had sat as a boy on his visits to Little Washington.

Styron and Baldwin talked about many things but often found their conversations circling back to the subject of race, which intrigued them both. In Styron's recollection they did not quiz each other; they simply told their stories and brought out their memories, digressing at will, working back and forth over their childhoods and family histories and remembered experiences. Many times the two men sat up until dawn, drinking whiskey and smoking cigarettes until their voices were husky and weary. Sometimes they sang together: "After all," Baldwin later said, "we have the same songs."

Baldwin revealed much about himself during these evenings: "He was spellbinding," Styron remembered, "and he told me more about the frustrations and anguish of being a black man in America than I had known until then, or perhaps wanted to know. He told me exactly what it was like to be denied service, to be spat at, to be called 'nigger' and 'boy.' " For Styron much of this was revelatory. He knew a good deal in a disembodied way about the problems of the black man, but he had never had the hurt and resentment revealed to him so honestly and directly. He was fascinated by the psychology of blackness, as Baldwin revealed it, and was especially intrigued by Baldwin's view of the white man, which was permeated with both anger and love.

Styron told his own stories about black people, especially as he had known them during his early childhood. He told about seeing Daddy Grace and witnessing the processions and mass baptisms in Newport News and Hampton. He discovered that Baldwin had heard Daddy Grace preach in Harlem and that he remembered seeing Sweet Daddy's followers pin dollar bills to his robes as he bestowed his benedictions on them. Styron admitted to Baldwin his powerful curiosity about black people, his frustration at their tendency to hide their emotions, and his bafflement at their ability to disappear when white people moved too close.

Styron also admitted to Baldwin that he still harbored some skepticism about the intelligence of blacks. "Could a Negro *really* own a mind as subtle, as richly informed, as broadly inquiring and embracing as that of a white man?" Styron wondered. Baldwin listened to Styron's admission without visible emotion but, Styron later thought, with considerable amusement and magnanimity. By way of answer Baldwin simply put his own jewel-bright intelligence on display, making Styron marvel often at the suppleness and penetration of his thinking. "My God, what appalling arrogance and vanity!" Styron later wrote of his covert prejudices. And yet he was glad in retrospect that he had been honest with Baldwin, who, he came to believe, possessed "as marvelous an intelligence as I was ever likely to encounter."

Race was a personal issue for both men, but it was also an artistic challenge. Could a writer of one race imagine his way into the mind of someone from another race? Could a black man move into a white man's consciousness and understand his thinking? Could a white man get inside a black man's skull and do the same thing? Baldwin had already made the attempt: his second novel, *Giovanni's Room,* published in 1956, had been narrated in the first person by a young American white man. This character, who is called David, is living in Paris, where he becomes involved homosexually with Giovanni, an Italian barman in the Saint-Germain section of the city. David eventually betrays himself by leaving Giovanni and the world of emotion and commitment that Giovanni's "room" represents. David enters a loveless marriage to a safe, conventional woman. This was the great lament found in many of Baldwin's writings—that love is capable of transcending distrust and fear, but that most human beings cannot bring themselves to leap into the disorderly world of trust, sense, and emotion. As he writes in *Giovanni's Room,* "The great difficulty is to say Yes to life."

Styron read *Giovanni's Room* shortly after Baldwin came to live in Roxbury, and though he did not think the novel altogether successful he admired Baldwin's daring. It had taken nerve for Baldwin to write from the point of view of a white character and to describe the homosexual world so frankly. Styron talked much with Baldwin about his own similar problems in approaching Nat Turner. Styron admitted that he was reluctant to tell his story in Nat's voice; he frankly doubted his ability to enter into the consciousness of a black man, dead now for over one hundred years. Styron faced dauntingly high barriers of race and time: how could he travel imaginatively back through history and, simultaneously, move into the mind of a Negro slave born in 1800? Baldwin, though sympathetic, told Styron that he must take the chance. In later years Styron gave Baldwin credit for prodding him into making a crucial decision: he would write Nat Turner's story in the first person, using Nat's own voice. "I am certain that it was his encouragement—so strong that it was as if he were daring me not to—that caused me finally to impersonate a black man," Styron later said.

Baldwin left Roxbury in early June 1961. Styron was never sure what Baldwin himself took away from their period of communion, but he knew that many of his own attitudes had been altered. "I was by far the greater beneficiary," he later said of the friendship. "He revealed to me the core of his soul's savage distress and thus helped me shape and define my own work and its moral contours." This gift, given by a slave's grandson to the grandson of a slave owner, would be of immeasurable value to Styron.

In the spring of 1961, while Baldwin was still in Roxbury, Styron was invited by an editor at *Esquire* to become a regular contributor to the magazine. Styron liked the idea: he had written short pieces for *The Nation, Harper's Bazaar,* and *The New Republic* during the 1950s but for the most part had concentrated his energies on *Set This House on Fire.* Such single-minded preoccupation, he now thought, might not have been the best thing for him. Probably it would be a good idea with this next novel to break up the composition with occasional short pieces. Styron liked the fact that *Esquire* had a broad readership, and he was pleased that the editors had given him carte blanche to write on virtually any subject that interested him.

His first contribution, which appeared in *Esquire* that November, was a spoof review of *The Big Love,* a Hollywood tell-all book by Florence Aadland and Tedd Thomey. *The Big Love* bared the details of the tawdry romance between the aging screen star Errol Flynn and Aadland's fifteen-year-old daughter, Beverly. The book, which at its best reached an almost sublime level of banality, called forth a response in kind from Styron: "At certain rare moments," he wrote, "there will appear a work of such unusual and revealing luminosity of vision, of such striking originality, that its stature is almost indisputable; one feels that one may declare it a masterpiece without hesitation, or fear that the passing of time might in any way alter one's conviction. Such a book is *The Big Love.*" Styron's review, which he entitled "Mrs. Aadland's Little Girl, Beverly," is a compendium of clichés. *The Big Love,* Styron maintained, was a work of elevated moral seriousness, informed by "a sense of decency and high principles," moving toward "pathos," and verging near the end on "nightmare and hallucination." Styron pulled out the stops and gave play to his gift for parody, but despite this japery he found the book finally to be "at times, inexplicably touching" (though "flabbergastingly vulgar"). *The Big Love,* in part owing to Styron's review, became a cult book—admired by W. H. Auden, among others. It was later reissued in paperback, with Styron's review as an introduction.

The review brought a response from Florence Aadland, published under the title "From the Heart" in the letters column of the February 1962 issue of *Esquire:*

> I don't know how to begin to thank you. I am on cloud nine after reading William Styron's article in *Esquire*'s November issue. For him to find in our book the things that were truly in my heart, when I told Teddy Thomey the story of the "Big Love." Words fail me, I can only say thank you again.

Styron never knew how to take the letter. Was it meant seriously, or was Mrs. Aadland pulling his leg?

His next article for *Esquire* was of a very different character. While in Rome in the spring of 1960, he had joined several other writers in signing a public letter that dealt with the impending execution of Caryl Chessman, a convicted rapist who had been sentenced to death but who, through legal maneuvering and public self-advertisement, had managed to put himself in the headlines and delay his execution several times. Eventually Chessman did go to the gas chamber. Styron, however, remained uneasy over having signed the letter, realizing that he had developed no clear intellectual or moral position on the death penalty. He therefore resolved to read in the available literature on capital punishment and then set down his thoughts in an article for *Esquire.*

His reading included essays by Arthur Koestler and Jean-Paul Sartre, but the piece that seized his attention and almost by itself converted him into an opponent of the death penalty was Albert Camus's "Reflections on the Guillotine," an eloquent depiction of capital punishment as barbaric and inhumane. Styron agreed with Camus: the execution of criminals, no matter how heinous their crimes, finally damaged and corrupted society and served little purpose, other than to satisfy an unfocused craving for vengeance.

Among Styron's papers at the Library of Congress there survives an eight-page handwritten false start on the essay that he meant to send to *Esquire*. It is flat and static, a bit preachy and inclined to veer off into criticism of J. Edgar Hoover, who had recently been waging a public campaign in favor of the death penalty.* Styron must have realized that this first attempt was not up to par; it was overly abstract and had no story to tell. He therefore resolved to begin again, this time using a case study. In searching for an example, Styron came upon a small item on the back page of *The New York Times*. The item said simply that the execution date for a prisoner named Benjamin Reid, confined in the Connecticut state penitentiary, had been postponed. Knowing no more than this—knowing nothing of Reid's age, race, background, or crime—Styron decided that he would take this case as his example. This was an experiment, an attempt to see whether his principles would hold. "Going in blindly, so to speak, I became determined to deal with Benjamin Reid and his case as an unabashed advocate of abolition, regardless of what terrible things I might discover."

Styron traveled to Hartford and began to investigate. He found that Reid, a young black man, had murdered a middle-aged woman, also black, by beating her to death with a hammer. The motive had been robbery, though Reid had bungled the attempt, overlooking more than two thousand dollars that the woman was carrying. By studying the transcript of the trial, Styron learned that Reid was the product of an almost unimaginably bleak upbringing, that he was reported to be subliterate, and that he was thought to be mentally deficient. None of these factors had moved the jury: Reid had been convicted of first-degree murder and sentenced to the electric chair. He had been waiting on death row at the Connecticut state penitentiary at Wethersfield for over

---

*Styron and James Baldwin, in protest against Hoover's statements, had sent a public letter to the *New York Herald-Tribune* deploring his position. The letter appeared there, under the headline J. EDGAR HOOVER IS WRONG ABOUT DEATH PENALTY, in the issue for June 11, 1961. The text of the letter was clipped and placed in a file that the FBI began keeping on Styron at this time. A routing slip shows that the letter was seen by Hoover and then sent to his personal assistant, Clyde Tolson. The file was maintained until at least April 1970; the entries concern Styron's support of draft resisters during the Vietnam War, his activities at the 1968 Democratic Convention in Chicago, and his associations with people of leftist sympathies.

four years while his attorney, a public defender, had appealed his case.

All of this Styron set forth in an article entitled "The Death-in-Life of Benjamin Reid," which appeared in *Esquire* for February 1962. Styron did not extend much sympathy toward Reid, nor did he argue that Reid's case had been mishandled or that he should be pardoned. Styron addressed instead the irrationality of the death penalty in such a case as Reid's and, more generally, the corrupting influence of capital punishment on public morality. "It is the practice of capital punishment more than any other single factor that tends to blight our administration of justice and to cast over our prisons the shadow of interminable revenge and retribution," Styron wrote. "As for Ben Reid, in arbitrarily inflicting upon him the sentence of death, in denying him even the chance of rehabilitation that we have just as arbitrarily granted others, we have committed a manifest injustice; and the death penalty, once again, reveals its ignoble logic."

"The Death-in-Life of Benjamin Reid" is important in Styron's career for several reasons. As his first extended piece of writing on a social issue, it suggests that he was beginning to see that his name and pen might be turned to public topics and that he might bring about action and change. He was not yet engaged in any particular movement or cause, but he now saw that he could, from time to time, become active in public issues that mattered to him. If a magazine such as *Esquire* was open to him, then other outlets and readerships would be available as well. For a writer as protective of his privacy as Styron, this was an important shift in attitude.

Styron learned, over the next few months, that his essay on Ben Reid had made several things happen. A group of students and faculty from Trinity College in Hartford, galvanized by Styron's article, began to work in Reid's behalf for clemency. A Hartford lawyer named Robert Satter took up Reid's case; even Douglass Wright, the prosecuting attorney who had originally secured Reid's conviction, had come to believe that the death sentence was too harsh in Reid's case. At a hearing of the Connecticut Board of Pardons on June 25, 1962, testimony was offered in Reid's behalf by those interested in the case, including Satter and Wright, and by one of Reid's former teachers and his mother. Reid himself asked the board for clemency. (Among those present who advocated mercy were Styron; William Sloan Coffin, Jr., a chaplain at Yale who would later be a leader of antiwar protesters during the Vietnam era; and George F. Will, then a Trinity student, today a nationally syndicated columnist.) The attorney for the state of Connecticut made what amounted to a pro forma plea, leaving the way open for the board to grant clemency. After deliberating for several hours the board did so, commuting Reid's sentence to life imprisonment with the possibility of eventual parole.

Styron wrote an account of these happenings and published it as a follow-up article in the November 1962 *Esquire* under the title "The Aftermath of Benjamin Reid." In the conclusion of that article, Styron argued that the Connecticut laws on capital punishment needed to be changed. He suggested a "triple verdict" law—requiring proof of guilt, a determination of sanity, and an imposition of sentence—that would allow mitigating evidence to be presented for defendants. (This had not been possible for Reid.) Robert Satter, the Hartford attorney, eventually became a state legislator; he introduced and saw through to passage a bill very much along the lines that Styron had proposed. Styron never claimed, then or later, to have saved Benjamin Reid's life—too many others had been involved in the effort—but he was proud of the fact that the Connecticut statutes had been liberalized in part because of his writings. He was also glad that Ben Reid would have a second chance, though, as we shall see, Reid's rehabilitation would not be achieved quickly or, in the long run, without further failures.

The Benjamin Reid case almost surely had some effect on Styron's thinking as he prepared to write his novel about Nat Turner's Rebellion. The image of Reid, sitting alone in his cell on death row, meditating on his childhood and contemplating the murder that he had committed, seems to have fixed itself in Styron's mind as he looked for ways to frame his narrative on Nat Turner. Larger questions about slavery and imprisonment—about their effects on the captive and on the society that holds him in prison—these too must have occupied Styron as he searched for links between the antebellum South, remote and benighted, and his own times, contemporary but not necessarily more enlightened.

In February 1962, around the time that the first of the Benjamin Reid articles was appearing in *Esquire,* Maurice-Edgar Coindreau's translation of *Set This House on Fire* was published in France. Coindreau had chosen the title *La proie des flammes*—"The Prey of Flames," with the connotation for *flammes* of ardor or passion. Gallimard gave the book special treatment, issuing a limited advance edition of forty-two copies on fine linen paper (*sur vélin pur fil Lafuma Navarre*) and engaging the novelist Michel Butor to write a preface introducing Styron to French audiences. This preface, entitled "Oedipus Americanus," is an essay of around six thousand words. It is meandering and quirky but prepares the reader well for Styron's brooding, meditative narrative, which Butor calls "*une allégorie de la condition américaine.*" For Butor the novel was built on a foundation of Western myth and linked directly to Sophocles, Mozart, and Freud.

Styron went to Paris for publication day, hoping for an appreciative reception and a decent performance at the bookshops. He was unprepared for what in fact happened: raves from book reviewers and large and rapid sales. Gallimard orchestrated the publication of the novel skillfully; during its initial trade run, interviews with Styron appeared every few days in *Le Figaro Littéraire, Arts, Les Lettres Françaises, L'Express, Nouveau Candide, Les Nouvelles Littéraires,* and other newspapers and journals. Actual notices, nearly all quite laudatory, were published in *Le Monde, La Nouvelle Revue Française, Ésprit, Le Figaro Littéraire, Démocratie, La Revue des Langues Vivantes, Temps Modernes,* and other newspapers and magazines. Sales moved quickly past the 60,000 mark, a remarkably high figure for so demanding and lengthy a novel in a country the size of France. *Set This House on Fire* had sold only around 21,000 copies in the United States.

It is difficult today to say precisely what appealed to French readers about *La proie des flammes.* Certainly Coindreau's elegant translation was a factor, as was the well-known fascination of the French with writers from the American South. More important, though, was probably the existential mode of the novel and its sharp condemnation of the vulgarity of postwar culture, not only in America but in Europe as well. Styron had not expected such a reception for *La proie des flammes;* for the first week or so after publication he was caught flat-footed, surprised by the attention and apprehensive that it would all vanish as quickly as it had appeared. But as the days passed, it became clear that French readers had embraced him and his novel wholeheartedly. Styron gradually became comfortable with what was happening and began to crow a little in communications back home. To William Blackburn he sent this cable:

TRANSLATION SET THIS HOUSE BIGGEST SUCCESS IN FRANCE ANY AMERICAN NOVEL SINCE WAR RUNAWAY BEST SELLER MARVELOUS RE- VIEWS KINDLY ADVISE TIME MAGAZINE MIZENER PRESCOTT OTHER PA- TRIOTS BEST TO YOU=

BILL

To Bobby and Claire White he sent further details: "I have been feel- ing very good indeed," he reported, "being regarded in St. Germain des Près with the awe reserved, in America, only for dimwitted movie starlets, and even the fact that I fell drunkenly out of a taxi and broke my ankle disturbs me not a bit, the crutches actually enhancing my chic."

In the short run this attention from French readers and the Paris press was gratifying to Styron. It was welcome approval after the rough treatment given to *Set This House on Fire* in the United States and was the first wide praise he had received since *Lie Down in Darkness* had appeared eleven years before. In the long run the reception of *La proie des flammes* would be even more important, establishing a tie between Sty- ron and France that would color much of his subsequent writing and thinking. Everyday French life he had always found congenial. French attitudes toward food, drink, leisure, friendship, marriage, and litera- ture matched (and helped shape) his own. More important, he began to feel that he might eventually create for himself, in American society, a role not unlike the one played in French culture by such writers as Camus, Sartre, and Malraux. Styron thought that he might develop a public voice and might speak, through his fiction and other writings, to the significant issues of his time.

A suggestion that something of this nature might happen was wait- ing for Styron when he returned to Roxbury—an invitation to dinner at the White House. This was the famous occasion organized by John F. Kennedy and his wife, Jacqueline, for all winners of the Nobel Prize in the Western Hemisphere and for other Americans prominent in literature and the arts. Styron knew, of course, that being summoned to a public event of this kind was not terribly significant. A great many people had been invited, and the Kennedys were conscious of the publicity value of such an occasion. Still, in the optimistic early days of Kennedy's presidency, when JFK's charm and his wife's beauty and elegant style were so visible and refreshing after the dreary Eisenhower years, Styron allowed himself to hope for a period when serious artists and intellectuals might play an important role in American public life.

On Sunday, April 29, Styron and Rose attended the White House dinner in the company of James Baldwin, who had also been invited. Styron later said that he and Baldwin felt a little "like Huck and Jim." He set down his impressions of the affair a few days later in a long letter to Professor Blackburn. "The dinner was splendid, including the wine," Styron reported. Afterward, however, "there was a boring reading by Fredric March of a garbled and wretched piece of an unpublished Hemingway manuscript; it was done in semi-darkness, and most of the Nobel prize winners—many of whom are over 70—nodded off to sleep."

The lights eventually went up, and Styron thought that the evening was over, but as he moved toward the door he was stopped by an army major in full dress. " 'The President would like you and Mrs. Styron to join him upstairs in his private quarters,' " he said. A little mystified, Styron and Rose proceeded to the private elevator and ascended to the Kennedys' drawing room. The other guests summoned to this private audience were Diana and Lionel Trilling, Robert Frost, and Fredric March. By mistake Styron sat down in Kennedy's rocking chair, which JFK favored for his back trouble; when the president entered he took this faux pas with democratic good grace and sat down on the sofa next to Frost. Jackie Kennedy appeared, along with Pierre Salinger, Bobby and Ethel Kennedy, and some other members of the palace guard. Styron spent most of the next hour talking with Jackie about mutual friends and about Martha's Vineyard, where the Styrons were planning to spend the coming summer. She promised that she and her husband would sail over from the Kennedy compound at Hyannisport one day in July and would take him and Rose out on the presidential yacht.

Jackie Kennedy made good on her promise. She and her husband sailed to Martha's Vineyard on the fifteenth of July, a Sunday, and picked up the Styrons at the Edgartown dock. Also invited were John Marquand, who had known Jackie during his college years, and Marquand's wife, Sue. The party sailed on the *Patrick J,* the smaller sister ship of the *Honey Fitz,* on which the Kennedys were often photographed. Security was tight: several Secret Service men were on board, and two Coast Guard picketboats kept other craft at a distance.

Over Bloody Marys the Styrons and Kennedys discussed Virginia politics, and Styron helped Jackie repair a miniature Japanese camera that she was fiddling with. A phonograph in the corner played Chubby Checker records, for the dance craze that summer was the Twist. The Kennedys were affectionate—Jackie put her bare feet in her husband's lap and wiggled her toes. Lunch, Styron reported in a letter to his father, was disappointing, "dreary Navy officers' chow"—eggs in aspic, salad, and hot dogs, with beer that had somehow become frozen. After the meal Styron fell into a bookish conversation with Kennedy: "I don't think JFK has really much profound understanding of literature," Styron wrote to his father, "but his mind is wide-ranging and fantastically filled with facts, not a profound mind but an enormously sharp one, and when he asks you a question and you answer him you feel that he is listening to every word you say."

The question Kennedy asked Styron was the obvious one: what was he writing? Styron began to describe his novel about Nat Turner and noticed that Kennedy was listening carefully. He had never heard of the Southampton Rebellion. Kennedy's presidency had been marked by racial strife (the integration of the University of Mississippi had occurred the previous summer), and his curiosity was piqued by what Styron told him about Nat Turner's little-known slave revolt. Fearful of boring Kennedy with his own obsessions, Styron tried to cut the account short, but Kennedy held him to the narrative, probing for more detail and information. The conversation was brought to a halt only by a drizzling rain, which forced them all belowdecks.

As the afternoon drew to a close there occurred a potential contretemps: the skipper of the *Patrick J* headed for the private dock of the Edgartown Yacht Club—"membership composed of the blackest of black Wall Street Republicans," Styron explained in the letter to his father. " 'Better not put in there,' " Kennedy cautioned the captain. Then he turned to Styron to explain: " 'There's not a Democrat within three miles of *heah.*' " The yacht was redirected to the Edgartown public dock, and the Styrons and Marquands were put ashore. " 'I'll really be waiting to read that book of yours,' " Kennedy said to Styron as they shook hands.

Styron was flattered. He knew that Kennedy's interest was intermixed with any politician's desire to enlist allies among the intelligentsia. He also knew that Kennedy was sensitive about his limitations: he had been overpraised by the press for his Harvard education and for his supposed interest in literature and the arts and was now enduring a backlash of criticism, from Alfred Kazin and some others, who were pointing out that he was hardly an intellectual. Still Styron was pleased by Kennedy's curiosity about his book. What other recent American president would even have confessed to such an interest? Harry Truman?

That same summer of 1962 brought the death of William Faulkner. His passing on July 6 marked the end of a major period in American fiction: Fitzgerald, Wolfe, Hemingway, and now Faulkner were all dead, and their mantle was being passed to Styron's generation. Styron was asked by *Life* magazine, on short notice, to attend Faulkner's funeral in Oxford, Mississippi, and to write a valedictory piece on the novelist. Styron accepted the assignment and went in the company of Bennett Cerf and Donald Klopfer—Faulkner's publishers and his own at Random House. They traveled, in those days, by a series of one-hop flights from New York to Memphis, then took an automobile south to Oxford. Styron arrived weary but curious to see Faulkner's town, which had provided the backdrop for so much of his fiction.

The funeral service was to take place on the afternoon of July 7 at Faulkner's home, a large frame house that he had renovated himself and renamed Rowan Oak. Styron arrived around noon with Cerf and Klopfer, but at first he was denied admittance into the house by John Faulkner, the brother of the novelist, who had learned from Cerf that Styron was to write about the funeral for *Life*. Cerf, distressed, went upstairs and appealed to Faulkner's widow, Estelle, telling her that Styron was a great admirer of Faulkner's work and was certain to write a respectful account. Mrs. Faulkner recognized Styron's name—her husband had praised *Lie Down in Darkness* to her—and she directed that Styron be allowed to enter. Once inside, he waited in the downstairs rooms with the other guests. He found the Mississippi novelist and historian Shelby Foote in Faulkner's library, and they chatted about Faulkner's writing as they waited for the service to commence. The heat that day was fierce and smothering; electric fans whirred all over the house, and most of the men had taken off their coats. "You've got to walk through it gently," Foote said of the heat. "Don't make any superfluous moves."

The service was preceded by a buffet of good southern food: turkey and ham, stuffed tomatoes, loaves of fresh homemade bread and pitchers of strong iced tea. At two o'clock the men put their coats back on, and the service began. It was mercifully short; the heat was hard on everyone, including the Episcopal priest who conducted the ceremony. Afterward Styron, Cerf, and Klopfer drove their rented car in the funeral procession that moved down South Lamar Avenue and through the courthouse square that Faulkner had made famous in his novels. Styron had picked up a pad of paper imprinted with the name Rebel Motor Freight, a Memphis trucking company; now as he rode in the car with Cerf and Klopfer he took a few notes, setting down some details and the names of a few Oxford landmarks that he wanted to mention in his piece for *Life*. One fragmentary note seems to capture an emotion that arose unbidden: "Suddenly the *fact* of his death, for the first time, becomes briefly felt—almost unsupportable."

Styron attended the graveside service and saw where Faulkner would rest, between two oaks on a small hill. Then he and Cerf and Klopfer said farewell to the family and made their way out of town, driving north to Memphis, where they began the series of short, bumpy flights that took them back north.

Styron was under a short deadline to finish his manuscript for *Life*. The Martha's Vineyard airport was fogged in, and his plane had to land at an airport near Mount Kisco. From there he made his way to the Roxbury house, where he could be alone and compose without distraction. Though exhausted by travel, he immediately put in a concentrated stint of writing and produced a restrained, meditative tribute to Faulkner. The piece appeared in the July 20 issue of *Life* under the title "As He Lay Dead, a Bitter Grief." After finishing the manuscript and sending it to *Life* via special delivery, Styron returned to Martha's Vineyard. As soon as he arrived, he began drinking and sat up all night with Lillian Hellman, talking about Faulkner. Fagged out physically and emotionally, Styron turned to liquor for solace. It did its work, and by that night he had become thoroughly intoxicated—as drunk as he had ever been in his life.

He slept for much of the next day but found, when he awoke, that his body had not thrown off the effects of the drinking. For the rest of that day and most of the one following, he endured a punishing hangover. In later years Styron would recall the hangover ("I woke up into death," he said) and think of it as a signal that he would have to be more circumspect with alcohol. He had recently turned thirty-seven and could see that his health, though generally sound, would no longer tolerate such heavy drinking. He would have to monitor his intake more closely and keep liquor in its place. He had a novel to write: he must get himself into condition now for the work that lay ahead.

25

Preparations

INITIALLY STYRON had thought that he might write a screenplay about the Southampton Rebellion. He had been interested in writing for the stage or cinema since the early 1950s; now, as he told his father in a February 1961 letter, the Nat Turner material "seems to shape up much more as a movie than as a book." Styron was careful to explain his plans: "By movie I mean a good movie, not one of these Hollywood flashy colored numbers. . . . If done properly (meaning done as I see it in my mind's eye) it would make a violent, moving film." Styron's concern, he told his father, was to translate this historical incident into modern terms: "Very few 'historical' movies made in the U.S. have ever been good, because they tend to be cheap and romantic," he said. "The story of Nat, however, could be full of raw truth very meaningful to our time."

This early impulse to dramatize the Southampton Insurrection for the screen is important. Styron was intrigued by the possibilities of movies—by their visual dimension and their potential to reach large audiences—and he tried, at first, to conceive Nat Turner's story cinematically. He wanted his vision of the rebellion, then only beginning to take form, to reach a great many people. Any novel that he wrote, he suspected, would find a respectably large readership, but a work of serious fiction could not hope to reach the public in the same way that a movie would. Neither *Lie Down in Darkness* nor *Set This House on Fire* had sold especially well as trade editions; Styron had no reason to think, early in 1961, that a book about an obscure slave rebellion in Virginia would do significantly better. He wanted a large hearing for this story. American people needed to know the history of the Negro— a subject that for the most part did not then exist in the public consciousness. It is important to remember that during these years, many Americans thought that black people did not possess a separate history—or, if they did, that it was not worth studying.

Styron's idea of rendering the Nat Turner Rebellion in cinematic form did not last long. He never began a screenplay, never wrote even the beginnings of dialogue or continuity for such a film. On reflection he seems quickly to have realized that his métier was the novel and that he would need the medium of print to give full play to his gift for language. His early vision of Nat Turner's story as a movie is still important, though. It reveals his desire for an extraliterary audience and his wish to dramatize an incident of black history with contemporary resonances.

In the spring of 1961 Styron made a trip to Newport News with Rose and the children. They wanted to visit W. C. Styron, who doted on his grandchildren and liked to see them as frequently as he could. Tensions between Styron and Elizabeth Buxton had eased a little; the children acted as a solvent and a distraction, and Rose was good at keeping Elizabeth occupied in conversation. The immediate purpose of the trip for Styron, however, was to visit Southampton County. He explained his intentions to his father ahead of time in a letter:

> I have always wanted to trace the route of Nat's warpath—at least that part of it that can be traced—and, moreover, see whatever original houses and buildings are left standing, and in general get a "feel" of the exact landscape. Naturally I have a superficial sense of what it's like, having been through country like it many times when on our way to Washington, N.C., years ago; but the feeling tends to fade after some years, and I would like to re-experience the countryside, if only for a day.

Styron had written to the Virginia State Library in Richmond for materials and was following up other leads as well, but he felt the need of seeing Southampton County itself to get a sense of its terrain and atmosphere, and perhaps to find some vestiges of the rebellion. "If you are game for this," he wrote his father, "what I'd like to do is make a trip with you down there one day, starting early in the morning, and just snoop around for four or five hours. One or two of the houses he raided may be still there; certainly the sites are marked."

W. C. Styron prepared the way by contacting, through an in-law, a distant cousin by marriage who lived in Southampton County and who was willing to act as a guide. This man was a prosperous peanut and soybean farmer who was familiar with the layout of the county. Perhaps with the help of William S. Drewry's maps in *The Southampton Insurrection* (one of the books sent to Styron in Paris in 1952 by J. Saunders Redding) he could help them trace the path of the revolt. Styron was not approaching this trip as a historian might have done. He did not wish to do extensive research in the county courthouse records or to dig out old deeds or documents, nor did he truly need to see the few buildings that still stood from the time of the rebellion or to walk down the overgrown roadbeds that Nat Turner and his band had followed. Such activities were appropriate for the professional historian, he felt, but not for the imaginative artist. Too many facts might hobble his imagination and make his story too particular and localized—something he wanted to avoid.

With Rose and his father along for company, Styron made the hour-and-a-half drive to Southampton County from Newport News on a hot day in May 1961. First they visited the courthouse. Styron read through the bound trial transcripts there, but he found few clues in them. They were sketchy—only notes on the trials of the rebel slaves—and they revealed little. The most important thing they contained had been published already in Drewry's study: that some slaves in the county helped their masters hide or escape from Nat Turner's rebels, and at least two slaves testified in court against the captured insurrectionists.

After lunch, guided by the kinsman, they attempted to find some trace of the rebellion—a house still standing or a roadway yet in use—but they could not. In the afternoon they were joined by the county sheriff, who knew the local back roads well, but even he was of little help. They questioned residents of the county at gas stations and cross-roads stores, but no one seemed to know much. One person thought that Nat Turner might have been a Negro general during the Civil War. Another person, a young black man, believed that Nat Turner had been white. One of the idlers at a country store confused Nat Turner with a famous racehorse. Most people to whom they talked knew nothing at all of him or his rebellion.

Toward the end of the afternoon, hot and dispirited, Styron and the others were heading back toward Courtland, the county seat. As Styron gazed out of the car window, his eye was caught by the shape of a house standing about a quarter of a mile off the road, a frame structure sheltered by an enormous oak tree. Styron asked the sheriff, in whose cruiser they were now traveling, to stop and back up. Consulting his copy of the Drewry book, which he had brought with him, Styron recognized what he believed to be one of the houses that Nat Turner and his rebels had attacked. Styron believed that this was the Whitehead house, at which Nat had committed his only murder, killing young Margaret Whitehead with his sword and with a fence post.

As they approached the house, on foot now, Styron and the others could see that it was uninhabited. It was filled with shucked corn, used as fodder for hogs and cattle. Styron entered the front door and looked about. "The house had a faint yeasty fragrance, like flat beer," he later wrote. "Dust from the mountains of corn lay everywhere in the deserted rooms, years and decades of dust, dust an inch thick in some places, lying in a fine gray powder like sooty fallen snow. Off in some room amid the piles of corn I could hear a delicate scrabbling and a plaintive squeaking of mice." As the others chatted in the front yard, Styron mused on the rebellion and on Nat Turner's murder of Margaret Whitehead. Why had he killed only her? Why had he been unable to murder others? Had some instinct of humanity, of mercy, stayed his hand, once he began to see the terrible slaughter that he had unleashed? Styron did not know and could never know, but he was beginning to believe that Nat's murder of Margaret Whitehead somehow marked the apex of the rebellion, and that it might possibly become the climax of his novel.

As it turned out, Styron was not at the Whitehead house. He had instead found the Rebecca Vaughan house—also attacked by the rebels and also the scene of gruesome murders, though not the murder that so fascinated Styron. The Whitehead house also still stood, not far away, where it too was rotting and uninhabited. Styron's mistake was symbolic of his approach: he was not at the Whitehead house, but it did not matter. His instincts were correct, pushing him toward what was arguably the central event of the rebellion, the murder after which the enterprise fell into disarray and finally into defeat and failure.

Styron began writing his novel about Nat Turner a little over a year later, during the summer of 1962. He and his family were vacationing in the town of Vineyard Haven, on the island of Martha's Vineyard, and were living in a rented house on Hatch Road there. During the preceding winter and spring Styron had made several key decisions about the book, these having to do with its title, language, and mode of narration. The novel would be called *The Confessions of Nat Turner*—the same title that Thomas Gray had used for the 1831 pamphlet that Styron was using as one of his chief sources. The narration was indeed to be in the first person, from Nat Turner's point of view. Styron had decided to accept James Baldwin's challenge and to imagine his way back across time and into the consciousness of this rebel slave. Styron was also following Camus's example: the previous year he had read *The Stranger,* which is narrated by a condemned murderer as he sits in his jail cell awaiting execution. Styron would use the same setting, casting his novel in the retrospective mode, with Nat Turner contemplating his past as he waits in his jail cell in Jerusalem, Virginia, in October 1831, shortly before he is to be hanged.

The most important decision that faced Styron had to do with language. Would he use only words that Nat Turner could have known? Surely not: no matter how articulate Nat might have been or how much he might have read or heard, the range of his language would have been quite narrow. Styron could not limit the narrative by denying himself his own vocabulary and style. Still, this was to be a first-person narration by a slave who had never been far from the homes of his various owners in Southside Virginia. What should Styron do? What compromise about language could he strike?

Styron's decision was to blend his own voice with Nat Turner's. Nat would speak his lines of dialogue in the vocabulary and accent that would likely have been his in 1831. But Styron's own personal twentieth-century language and style would infiltrate and permeate the rest of the narrative, especially the interior, meditative sections that issue from Nat Turner's mind. Styron did place a few limitations on himself: he decided to avoid anachronisms and the modern vernacular and to cast the dialogue in a relatively formal nineteenth-century mode. Otherwise the vocabulary and perceptions granted to Nat would be

Styron's own. The narrative voice would not be limited by time or place: Nat Turner's language, and his world, would collide with Styron's on the printed page.

The Confessions of Nat Turner thus became a consciously literary construction. Styron's share of the central narrative voice in the published book is historically informed and modern, even engagé. Styron's own voice is never far from the surface of the narrative, but he weaves such a spell of realistic detail from the antebellum slave world that it is easy to forget that he is always present in the narration. Styron wanted his voice to be heard in conjunction with Nat Turner's and made no real effort to conceal it. Later, in an author's note that he published with the novel, he would call *The Confessions of Nat Turner* "a meditation on history"—a phrase that bears heavily on the matter of narrative voice. The phrase can be misleading if taken literally, and it caused Styron difficulty later with some critics of the novel. More nearly accurate is an earlier statement by Styron, made to a pair of interviewers in 1965 while the novel was still under composition. Asked to talk about the mixing of voices in the narrative, Styron explained, "This is a literary style." Then he added: "In reality it is a form of translation."

One other voice is present in the book as well—that of James Baldwin. One is on tenuous ground here: Styron has never said that Baldwin stood as a model for his fictional Nat Turner or even that Baldwin contributed, in some unspecified way, to the characterization of the protagonist. Nevertheless, one recognizes Baldwin's presence in Nat's thinking and speech—in his periods of "black-assed" melancholy and his contradictory attitudes toward white people. Nat's mingled respect and contempt for members of his own race—his frustration and exasperation with them, mixed with an impulsive and consuming love— seem to come from Baldwin. Likewise Nat's sexual ambivalence probably owes much to Baldwin's homosexuality.

Just before *The Confessions of Nat Turner* was published, Baldwin (who had read the novel in galleys) was asked by an interviewer for *Newsweek* whether he recognized himself in the narrator. "Baldwin grinned hugely when he heard this," reported the interviewer. " 'Yes, I think there's some of me in Nat Turner,' " he agreed. " 'If I were an actor, I could play the part.' " At the end of the *Newsweek* story Baldwin is given the final word on Styron's novel: "He has begun the common history—*ours,*" Baldwin says. The remark can be read as a tribute to Styron for his nerve in attempting, as a white man, to re-create black history. Thus interpreted, the comment has become attached to *The Confessions of Nat Turner* over the years and has appeared many times as a blurb on various editions. But Baldwin, who could be playful verbally, almost surely meant the comment to be taken by Styron in a more personal way. Baldwin was telling Styron that he recognized the intermingling of their consciousnesses and voices in the novel. *The Confessions of Nat Turner* was an attempt to represent the common history of black and white people, but on another and more private level it was "our" history, the history of two individual men—Baldwin's history and Styron's together.

In telling the story of Nat Turner's Rebellion, Styron was drawing on his own reading about the historical event. His principal source was Thomas Gray's pamphlet, "The Confessions of Nat Turner," published shortly after Nat's execution and based on interviews with him in his jail cell. Styron knew that Nat's voice in this testament had been filtered through Gray, an intermediary, but the account in the pamphlet was as close as anyone could ever get to Nat's own version of the events. Gray's ornate rhetoric was a distraction, but these "Confessions" still carried the ring of truth. Styron's other major source was Drewry's *The Southampton Insurrection*. This 1900 treatise, prepared as a doctoral dissertation at Johns Hopkins University, was based on research and interviews conducted by Drewry, a native of Southampton County, during the last years of the century. Drewry's own point of view colors the book strongly; he was an apologist for slavery and viewed the rebellion as an isolated incident caused by a madman. If one discounted this predisposition, however, Drewry had been an energetic historian, visiting the houses of those killed in the rebellion, talking with relatives only one or two generations removed from people who had lived through the event, and plotting out the path of Nat Turner's band as it went from farm to farm in search of victims. Drewry had published in the book his own photographs of buildings that still stood and of artifacts that still survived then, such as Nat Turner's Bible and his sword.

Drewry's book was of great value to Styron, and he read and annotated it carefully. The copy of the book that he used and marked is among his papers at Duke. Styron's marginal comments reveal both his

skepticism about Drewry's bias and his eye for details that might be incorporated into the narrative, such as the incident of the white women
who tortured Nat with their hatpins after his capture, or the fact that
the corpses of many of the victims were partially devoured by free-
ranging hogs.

One of Styron's annotations, on page 33 of his copy, is of particular
interest. It reads:

> Nat's wife: Fannie?
> "   son: Gilbert?

And on a blank page in the front of the volume he speculates on the fact
that none of the white women who fell into the hands of Nat Turner's
rebels was violated sexually: "No evidence of rape," Styron notes. "Perhaps Nat has seen his wife seduced by Travis. Is yet determined to pre-
clude rape in his campaign. 'We will not torment them with the scourge
+ fire, nor defile their women as they have done with ours.' (*Atlantic,* op.
cit.)." These annotations reveal, first, that Styron had read the account
entitled "Nat Turner's Insurrection" by the abolitionist Thomas Wentworth Higginson in the August 1861 *Atlantic Monthly*—a rendering as
highly colored, in its own way, as Drewry's would later be. (Styron had
a photostatic copy of Higginson's article; it is among his papers at
Duke.) This article contains the earliest mention of Nat Turner's wife,
though she is not given a name. Drewry too seems to have believed that
Nat Turner fathered children and mentions some of his descendants in
The Southampton Insurrection—hence Styron's speculations about a
wife and son. Whether Nat Turner actually had a slave wife or produced
issue has never been established. No document contemporaneous with
the rebellion mentions a wife or children; especially notable is the fact
that no wife or child is mentioned in the testimony set down by Thomas
Gray. What is important to realize is that Styron was aware, early on, of
the possibility of a wife and a child or children for Nat Turner, and that
he must therefore have chosen deliberately, for fictional purposes, to
make Nat unmarried and celibate.

Styron's annotations in his copy of *The Southampton Insurrection* reveal another quite important source—Frederick Law Olmsted's *A Journey in the Seaboard Slave States* (1856), an influential account of the
slave-owning South in the decade just before the Civil War. Best known
today as a landscape architect and as the principal designer of Central

Park in New York City, Olmsted made a lengthy trip through the South in 1852 and 1853, sending back his observations in a series of letters published in *The New York Times*. *A Journey in the Seaboard Slave States* is a revision and expansion of those letters. Olmsted, a native of Connecticut, was a firm opponent of slavery, but he kept an objective viewpoint in his book and has been applauded by modern historians for the dispassionate quality of his reporting. From Olmsted, Styron took much information about the nature and quality of life on an antebellum plantation, for owners and slaves alike. Details in Olmsted's book about food and dress, lower-class whites, animals and their treatment, and the plight of the free Negro all found their way into Styron's narrative. Styron also took verbatim from Olmsted part of a sermon by Bishop Meade, of the Church of England in Virginia, delivered to the slaves of the Commonwealth, urging them to obey their masters and serve willingly and cheerfully. Excerpts from this sermon, which Olmsted had reproduced in its entirety, were put by Styron into the mouth of young Richard Whitehead, a Methodist minister and the brother of Margaret Whitehead.

Styron used numerous other sources, many of which can be identified today. He possessed photostatic copies of Samuel Warner's *Authentic and Impartial Narrative of the Tragical Scene Which Was Witnessed in Southampton County . . .* (1831) and of an article entitled "The Light Dragoons" from the *Southern Historical Society Papers* (August 1899) that touches tangentially on the rebellion. He owned Herbert Aptheker's *Negro Slave Revolts in the United States* (1939) and June Purcell Guild's *Black Laws of Virginia* (1936). Other works in his library were Dwight Lowell Dumond's *Antislavery: The Crusade for Freedom in America* (1961), Oscar Handlin's *Race and Nationality in American Life* (1957), Miles Mark Fisher's *Negro Slave Songs in the United States* (1953), Eugene D. Genovese's *The Political Economy of Slavery* (1965), and reprints of Frederick Douglass's *Narrative of the Life of Frederick Douglass* (1845) and of Booker T. Washington's *Up from Slavery* (1901). Styron read several classic general accounts of slavery and southern life, including Ulrich B. Phillips's *Life and Labor in the Old South* (1929), an apologist treatment of the peculiar institution; W. J. Cash's *The Mind of the South,* a famous iconoclastic view; John Hope Franklin's *From Slavery to Freedom* (1947), a comprehensive textbook tracing the history of African Americans; and

Kenneth M. Stampp's *The Peculiar Institution: Slavery in the Ante-Bellum South* (1956), a methodical and impassioned rebuttal of Phillips. He also read Arna Bontemps's *Black Thunder,* a novel based on the Gabriel Prosser rebellion, and Harriet Beecher Stowe's *Dred: A Tale of the Great Dismal Swamp.* He remembered in later years being especially influenced by Stampp's arguments and by W.E.B. Du Bois's contention, in *The Souls of Black Folk* (1900), that "the color line" would be the central problem for the nation during the twentieth century. "I believed it when I wrote *Nat Turner* and I still believe it," he said in 1992.

Styron continued to read even after he had begun his manuscript, and in 1963 and 1964 he wrote lengthy reviews of reprints of three books on slavery for *The New York Review of Books.* These reissued books were Frank Tannenbaum's *Slave and Citizen: The Negro in the Americas* (1946), the first book to make close comparisons between slavery as practiced in America and in Latin America; Herbert Aptheker's *American Negro Slave Revolts* (1943), a work with a heavy Marxist bias; and Lewis H. Blair's *A Southern Prophecy* (1889), a powerfully hortatory book written by a former Confederate officer who had become an advocate of Negro equality.

One other book that influenced Styron strongly was Erik H. Erikson's *Young Man Luther: A Study in Psychoanalysis and History* (1958). The subtitle of this book suggests what Styron found fascinating about it—Erikson's effort to imagine his way back across history and into the mind of the young rebel Martin Luther. Of particular interest to Styron were Luther's asceticism, his difficult relationship with his father, and his mixture of love and contempt for the people he sought to save.

To trace with precision the impact of each of these books on *The Confessions of Nat Turner* is impossible. These titles represent only a part of Styron's reading and only some of the influences that worked on him. One can say, though, that these books constitute most of the best work that was available in the early 1960s on the subject of slavery. One can also say that nearly all of these works, like virtually all writings on American Negro slavery, are contentious and highly colored, permeated with their authors' personal, social, and political convictions. Perhaps no other subject in American history—unless it is the related subject of the Civil War—is so powerfully swept by currents of emotion and polemic. This was true in 1962 and remains true today. Styron was therefore strongly tested, as he negotiated his way through this material, to maintain his artistic equilibrium. He was working as a creator, not as a professional historian, and he was using these books to stimulate his imagination—the best of them enlarging his view of slave life, or adding to his store of knowledge about the prewar South, or helping him create images and sequences and dialogues in his mind.

It is important to realize that Styron was not Sinclair Lewis, who immersed himself in the subjects of his novels before beginning to write and who filled tablets and loose-leaf binders with extensive notes on his topics before he sat down to compose even the first word. Styron was not a social realist; he was not aiming to create a novel such as *Babbitt,* with its nervous overlay of slang and detail and its caricatures of American social types. Styron deliberately resisted the notion of doing extensive formal research into his subject, fearful that he might overburden his narrative with detail or become confused by the competition and jockeying of those who had written already about slavery. Styron wanted his imagination to remain free; he wanted to transcend the historical moment of 1831 and create a novel that combined the past and present in a single vision.

One work that did influence Styron deserves special mention—Stanley M. Elkins's *Slavery: A Problem in American Institutional and Intellectual Life.* First issued by the University of Chicago Press in 1959 and widely reprinted thereafter, this book was—and remains—one of the most controversial studies ever published about American Negro slavery. It is an audacious attempt, unlike anything that had appeared before it, to probe the psychology of slavery and to speculate about the long-term effects of the institution on the behavior of African Americans. By comparing slavery as it was practiced in the South to slavery as it existed in other parts of the Western Hemisphere—Brazil, especially, and the Caribbean—and by extrapolating certain generalizations about master-slave behavior from studies of the Nazi death camps, Elkins sought to explain what he saw as the psychological castration of the American Negro under slavery. That unmanning, together with other abuses inherent in the system, had undermined black social structure and cohesiveness. These tendencies had continued to operate in American society, as Elkins saw it, perpetuating cycles of poverty and defeatism in the lives of black people.

Elkins's book was almost immediately controversial in 1959, when first published, and it continued over the next few years to draw both fervent praise and angry criticism. What Styron seems to have found most stimulating in the book was its originality and suggestiveness, for Elkins was a skilled prose writer with a lucid and supple style. That Styron was entirely persuaded by Elkins's thesis is less certain; almost surely he was not wholly won over, since the rebel slaves in *The Confessions of Nat Turner* are hardly supine or psychologically unmanned. But Styron was intrigued by Elkins's effort to explore the psychology of slavery and by the points of comparison made between American slavery and the Holocaust. Styron continued to think about these matters, even after *The Confessions of Nat Turner* was completed. One sees evidence of his continued preoccupation with such questions in *Sophie's Choice,* the novel he would publish in 1979.

Two other writers, both older than Styron, colored his thinking about Nat Turner. These were his friends Robert Penn Warren and C. Vann Woodward. Both were southerners who had transplanted themselves to the North; they were colleagues at Yale University— Warren in the Department of English and Woodward in the Department of History. Styron had come to know both men relatively well by the early 1960s. Yale, in New Haven, is only a little distance from Roxbury, and Warren's home in Fairfield, Connecticut, was a short drive from the Styrons' house. Styron had long admired Warren's writing— his patterning of the opening pages of *Lie Down in Darkness* on the beginning of *All the King's Men* will be remembered. And Styron had come lately to respect the clearheaded observations in Woodward's books, especially in *The Strange Career of Jim Crow* (1955) and *The Burden of Southern History* (1960). In the latter book Woodward had praised Warren for basing some of his novels on historical events and figures. For Woodward the novelist could come closer than the formally trained historian to attaining what he called "the consciousness of the past in the present"—one of the goals of his own writings. These words touched a nerve in Styron; Woodward, he could see, understood what he wanted to do with Nat Turner's story.

Warren's fiction too was useful as a model, though Warren, in such novels as *At Heaven's Gate* and *World Enough and Time,* had changed the names of the historical figures on whom he partly based his characters. Styron made a different decision: he retained the names of Nat Turner and of the others, slaves and slave owners alike, who had participated in the events in Southampton County. Styron did this deliberately in order to bring the past into direct confrontation with the present. He meant to go Warren one better; he also wanted to write an unruly, uncooperative book. He decided to assert his right, as a novelist, to possess and transform the past. To have changed Nat Turner's name and the names of the others would have spared Styron much later criticism, but it would have skirted one of the central issues raised by his novel and would have robbed the book of much of the bite and energy that have kept it alive and controversial.

26

Composition

S TYRON WAS well prepared, in the summer of 1962, when he began to compose *The Confessions of Nat Turner*. He had chosen his title and narrative viewpoint and had made several key decisions about language. He had read widely, informing himself about the Southampton Rebellion and about slavery in the antebellum South. He had set up certain technical hurdles and challenges for himself, chiefly involving language and style. Now he needed a way into the narrative.

For the opening sequence he decided to use a dream that his daughter Polly, then four years old, had reported to him one morning earlier that summer. Polly had dreamed about a Masonic temple in the town of Woodbury, not far from Roxbury—a Greek Revival structure with Ionic columns. In Polly's dream the temple had had no doors or windows; its white walls had been solid and closed. Styron had already decided to begin his novel with a dream sequence in which Nat, sleeping, believes himself to be reclining in a skiff or canoe, floating down a broad estuary in Tidewater Virginia toward the sea. Now in the dream, as Styron created it on the manuscript page, Nat looks up and beholds, on a promontory above the sea, a strange building possessing an air of great mystery:

> It is square and formed of marble, like a temple, and is simply designed, possessing no columns or windows but rather, in place of

them, recesses whose purpose I cannot imagine, flowing in a series of arches around its two visible sides. The building has no door, at least there is no door that I can see. Likewise, just as this building possesses neither doors nor windows, it seems to have no purpose, resembling, as I say, a temple—yet a temple in which no one worships, or a sarcophagus in which no one lies buried, or a monument to something mysterious, ineffable, and without name.

The full dream sequence is one of the most evocative pieces of writing that Styron ever set down. It eases the reader into the narrative, lulling the senses just as the rocking of the small boat soothes Nat Turner in his dream. But abruptly the reader is made aware of Nat's actual state when Nat awakes and finds himself lying on a rough plank in a cold jail cell, his legs and arms in shackles. The mysterious white temple fades from his consciousness, and the narrative proper begins.

Styron made good progress with his manuscript that summer and kept his momentum through the fall and winter in Roxbury. He wrote the sections in which Thomas Gray visits Nat Turner in the jail cell, and he introduced the character Hark, Nat's chief accomplice in the rebellion. Styron now had caught the rhythm and timbre he wanted for the narration, and he allowed his voice to intermingle with Nat's in long, lyrical, meditative passages. Styron stayed reasonably close to the historical record—when any record existed—but as he composed he must have become aware for the first time of how truly sparse the primary data were. Almost nothing was known, for example, about the personalities of Thomas Gray, the lawyer who took down Nat's confession, or of Jeremiah Cobb, the judge who would condemn Nat to the gallows. Relying on his imagination, Styron made memorable characters of both men, turning Gray into a faintly repellent dandy and Cobb into a heavy-drinking misanthrope who despises the institution of slavery.

Styron made Nat Turner's mother into the family cook—an important, favored position on a plantation—and thus gave Nat access as a child to the language and books and habits of the white people in the big house. This decision was central to the plan of the novel, for Nat needed to observe and know the white world from within if he was to learn to hate it and later vow to destroy it. There was no historical evidence that Nat Turner's mother was a house slave or that Nat himself was a house servant. Even if he had been, he could not have worked in a house as large and elegant as the one Styron created in his novel, because (as we shall see) no such establishment existed in Southampton County in 1831.

These are only a few among many examples of the kinds of latitude that Styron allowed himself with the historical record, such as that record was. Styron wanted to write a novel with resonances beyond the specific incident of Nat Turner's Rebellion and the particular locale of Southampton County. The narrative, he felt, must expand to include the entire South and must encompass the entire institution of slavery, at all of its levels. The story also had to move forward through time to the present day. These were ambitious goals, Styron knew, and would be difficult to achieve. But what happened to Nat Turner in this novel had to be representative, in a larger sense, of what was happening in the present moment to the black man in America.

By the early summer of 1963 Styron had completed what he would later designate as Book I of *The Confessions of Nat Turner*—an extended, meditative prelude of some forty thousand words. Styron was satisfied with what he had produced. His problem was where next to proceed, what part of the story to reveal now.

That spring Styron and James Jones sat down together, at the request of *Esquire,* and tape-recorded a conversation. The Joneses were back in the States for a visit and were seeing a good deal of the Styrons, both in New York and in Roxbury, where they came for an extended stay. The friendship between the two couples had remained strong and active, with frequent visits back and forth and long, funny letters between Jones and Styron. Jones's excellent third novel, *The Thin Red Line,* had appeared in 1962, and he was working now on a detective story set on the island of Crete. He and Styron talked about their respective novels in progress in a rambling, chatty dialogue, and *Esquire* published an edited version in its July 1963 issue.

The conversation catches Styron at a moment when many ideas were revolving in his mind. He speaks of similarities between American Negro slavery and the Nazi death camps, for example, and makes connections between American blacks and new African nations. Styron also talks in the interview about the relationship between formal, recorded history and the novel that he is writing. When Jones asks Styron whether his novel will have a didactic historical purpose, Styron's answer is revealing: "Well, only by indirection," he says. "I don't want to grab the reader by the throat and say, 'Look, this is history you're reading.' Fact is, I consider this a very modern novel."

Three pages along in this same issue of *Esquire* there appeared a lengthy piece by Norman Mailer entitled "Some Children of the Goddess." Mailer's text was accompanied by a photograph that showed him leaning in the corner of a boxing ring. The picture was captioned "Norman Mailer vs. William Styron, James Jones, James Baldwin, Saul Bellow, Joseph Heller, John Updike, William Burroughs, J. D. Salinger, Philip Roth." The remarks that followed were a continuation of those in *Advertisements for Myself,* with Styron again taking heavy shots. Mailer called *Set This House on Fire* a novel of "hothouse beauty and butter bilge." It was "the book of a man whose soul had gotten fat," he said. Most explosive was a passage of gossipy revelation that bore directly on the friendship between Styron and Jones, who, to the *Esquire* reader, had been having a relaxed, friendly conversation just a few pages before. Here is what Mailer wrote:

> Styron was intensely competitive—all good young novelists are—but over the years envy began to eat into his character. Months before James Jones's *Some Came Running* was published (and it had the greatest advance publicity of any novel I remember—for publicity seemed to begin two years before publication), Styron obtained a copy of the galleys. There were long nights in Connecticut on "Styron's Acres" when he would entertain a group of us by reading absurd passages from Jones's worst prose. I would laugh along with the rest, but I was a touch sick with myself. I had love for Jones, as well as an oversized fear for the breadth of his talent, and I had enough envy in me to enjoy how very bad were the worst parts of *Some Came Running.*

Styron had learned ahead of time that these remarks were to appear in *Esquire.* He was friendly with Gay Talese, who wrote for the magazine; Talese telephoned Styron on June 6 to tell him that he had seen proofs of the July issue and that Mailer was going to publish the passage about "Styron's Acres" and the burlesque reading of *Some Came Running.* Styron sat down that day and wrote a long letter to Jones. Part of it reads as follows:

> The bulk of Mailer's hatred is reserved for me. An all-out, slavering attack on *Set This House on Fire;* but Talese said the thing that

bugged and horrified him the most was the personal venom, which has to do with both you and me. I am paraphrasing Talese's paraphrase of the article, but the gist is this: during the time Norman lived up here in Connecticut and we saw something of each other, I spent a great deal of time ridiculing *Some Came Running,* running the book down in general and poking fun at it. Well, maybe I did. I was quite nervous about you in those days—not knowing you, for one thing—and besides being exceedingly envious of someone who had muscled through with such prodigious energy that second-novel barrier. My wife Rose, the wife, who is so honest about such matters, is not at all sure: she distinctly recalls Mailer's hatred and envy of you (she has always been one of the greatest fans of *Running*) and remembers a two-hour argument with Mailer in the kitchen . . . in which she defended the book vainly against Mailer's snarls and sneers.

Jones's response was magnanimous. In a return letter to Styron he dismissed the incident as a "tempest teapot hardly worth pissing in to put the fire out."

Mailer was much in the public eye during these years. After a disastrous party at his brownstone in Brooklyn Heights on the night of November 19, 1960, he had stabbed his wife, Adele, in the abdomen and back. He had been arrested for assault, but Adele had not pressed the complaint, and the charges had been dismissed. This was only the most notorious incident of these years for Mailer: he was often visible in public, involving himself in New York City politics or making provocative statements to newspaper and television journalists.

Mailer was among the first of the writers of his generation to understand the symbiosis that exists between public figures and print and broadcast reporters. He learned to control that relationship, usually, and to draw stimulation from the clashes that resulted—with reviewers, journalists, feminists, politicians, and others. He had managed to turn himself into a celebrity and had become skillful at presenting himself, in various personae, to the press. The strain of this exposure, however, took a toll on him, distracting him from his writing and involving him in feuds with many people other than Styron and Jones.

Styron and Mailer were fairly often (and rather tensely) at the same parties, and they had friends in common. One of these was George Plimpton, who was now editing *The Paris Review* from his house on East Seventy-eighth Street. "What's Bill been up to?" Mailer would sometimes ask when he spoke with Plimpton. "Do you hear anything from Norman?" Styron would occasionally say. Plimpton thus became an intermediary of sorts, keeping the two men up-to-date on each other, rather as Maxwell Perkins had done with Fitzgerald and Hemingway during the 1930s. Plimpton attempted to keep things light and in perspective, observing Styron and Mailer (both of whom he liked), and wondering where their lives and careers were headed.

Styron tried to press on with *The Confessions of Nat Turner* that summer (they were renting in Edgartown rather than Vineyard Haven), but there was much to distract him. For one thing, he had stopped smoking. His consumption of cigarettes had risen to over two packs a day, and despite his using a cigarette holder that filtered out many impurities, he was dependent on nicotine. Often, toward the end of an evening of drinking and heavy smoking, he felt physically wretched.

Styron had known for a long time that he needed to give up tobacco, but his true wake-up call came from *The Consumers Union Report on Smoking and the Public Interest,* the first publication to present overwhelming evidence that smoking and lung cancer (among other diseases) were closely related. Styron reviewed this report in *The New York Review of Books* for December 26, 1963, commenting both on its persuasiveness and on the moral pliability of the tobacco lobby in Washington, which had tried to discount its findings. Styron's own experience during withdrawal from nicotine he found instructive: "After two or three days of great flaccidity of spirit, an aimless oral yearning, aching moments of hunger at the pit of the stomach, and an awful intermittent urge to burst into tears, the problem resolved itself, and in less than a week all craving vanished. Curiously, for the first time in my life, I developed a racking cough, but this, too, disappeared. A sense of smugness, a kind of fatness of soul, is the reward for such a struggle."*

Styron did not give up tobacco altogether. He began now to smoke cigars, one or two a day, and became something of an authority on their manufacture, procurement, and storage. He was especially happy in future years when he could manage to have a box of Cuban cigars smug-

---

*The phrase "fatness of soul" is an allusion to Mailer's "the book of a man whose soul has gotten fat" in the attack in *Esquire* cited earlier in this chapter.

gled to him by a friend. He usually smoked one cigar after lunch and another in the evening after dinner. He did not inhale, instead expelling the smoke through a string of plosive consonants: "Pffffpt!"

The irritation brought by Mailer's attack and the distraction caused by withdrawal from cigarettes seem to have combined during the summer of 1963 to short-circuit Styron's progress on *The Confessions of Nat Turner,* though he did get some other writing done. He added a few pages to the manuscript of his novel, but not many, and by the early fall he had stopped writing altogether. "I came to a dead halt," he later remembered. The problem was that he did not know what part of the story to tackle next.

Also most troubling, later that year, was the assassination of John F. Kennedy. Two weeks before Kennedy was shot, Styron and Rose had seen him in New York at a black-tie affair to which they had come late and dressed casually—in their "country duds," as Styron said in a letter to William Blackburn. Styron had thought Kennedy might not remember him and had tried to sidle past unobtrusively, but Kennedy had spotted him and Rose and greeted them warmly, almost effusively. "How did they get *you* here?" he said. "They had a hard enough time getting me here!" Styron was a little confused by the comment—was it meant as a compliment?—but soon enough Kennedy was asking about his novel. "How is that book of yours coming along?" he said. Styron was surprised that Kennedy had remembered their conversation from the day they went sailing, almost a year and a half earlier, but as it turned out Kennedy remembered the details quite well.

In the letter to Blackburn, Styron described what happened next: "And so we talked about it; he asked me something about historical sources, and what research I had used, and what approach I was going to use to tell the story, and of course that started me off, the flood-gates were opened, and we chattered happily about Negro slavery for a full ten minutes, the conversation finally getting around to the present revolt, just the three of us standing there amid a swirling mass of showgirls. It was all quite bizarre, but how much it tells about what kind of man Kennedy was! His eagerness, his honest curiosity, the real interest, the quality of *caring!*"

Toward the end of his letter to Blackburn, Styron summarized his feelings about Kennedy: "Anyway, he is gone, and I suspect that in the great sweep of history he will be measured as somewhat less than the colossus he has seemed to be as the result of his martyrdom. But no matter. No one we have had since Jefferson, certainly, would have literally homed in on a writer as he did that night, and cared and asked questions, and made a writer feel that writing and the republic of letters was an important part of the other Republic, and figured large in the scheme of things. He was, as my father said on the day of his death, better than America ever deserved. I do sorely miss him."

Styron was still struggling with the manuscript of his novel. Ten years later he described his difficulties to an interviewer:

I was frankly in despair because I didn't know how to go on. I had the vague idea: well maybe I'll now just start to describe the insurrection as it happened only a few days before. But that left me unhappy, and then a very funny thing occurred. Someone had brought up to my house in Connecticut a sixteen-millimeter print of the movie *Citizen Kane.* You know *Citizen Kane,* you know the story, and you know that it has to do with a sled, that on the sled is painted "Rosebud," a word which is so haunting. . . . I remember after seeing *Citizen Kane* and being so impressed by it, I remembered that "Rosebud" motif and suddenly it all became clear to me that what I had to do to fill this gap was to write about this man Nat—this now grown-up man, thirty-some years old—write about him as a boy, as a child. . . . It became a sort of plunge into memory and I distinctly remember starting off with an enormous sense of enthusiasm on this new part. . . . Once I was able to leap into an imaginative re-creation of his boyhood and his childhood, this would be the really major and most important part of my understanding of why he was a revolutionary.

One other occurrence that summer, by pure happenstance, gave Styron a body of immensely valuable material. While on a trip to Mexico for the Inter-American Foundation, Styron met a young woman named Magda Moyano, a cultural aide and translator. She was bilingual, speaking Spanish and English; her father was from Argentina, her mother from Fluvanna County, Virginia, on the James River above Richmond. Styron told Magda Moyano about his novel in progress on

Nat Turner, and she in turn told him of her ancestor John Hartwell Cocke, master of Bremo Plantation in Virginia.

John Hartwell Cocke (1780–1866) was an anomaly in Virginia history. Born into one of the most distinguished and public-minded of the old Virginia families, he broke with tradition and became a fierce opponent of slavery and an advocate of recolonization for blacks in Africa. He attacked tobacco growing as ruinous economically and socially, publishing his views in a book entitled *Tobacco, the Bane of Virginia Husbandry* (1860). He was in addition a fierce Christian and a devout believer in temperance, thrift, industry, and philanthropy. On one of his plantations, called Upper Bremo, he built one of the most handsome Greek Revival mansions in Virginia. He was a friend and correspondent of Thomas Jefferson, J. C. Cabell, and St. George Tucker, and he was active in Virginia politics and public life, serving in the legislature and helping to found the University of Virginia.

Cocke, like Jefferson, dreaded the legacy that chattel slavery was sure to visit on succeeding generations, but, also like Jefferson, he believed that manumission of slaves, before they had been educated, trained, and imbued with religious and temperate habits, would be dangerous and irresponsible. Cocke did free some of his own slaves and sent them as colonists to Liberia; others of his slave families he relocated on his two cotton plantations in Alabama, where they were allowed to work and buy their freedom. Slaves and their children at Bremo were taught reading and arithmetic; they were also given religious instruction and encouraged to avoid alcohol and gambling. For all these efforts, though, John Hartwell Cocke failed. There were too few others like him, and the problems he sought to remedy were too great. His angry fervor worked against him, alienating his fellow planters and opening rifts between him and his own children. He lived through the ravages of the Civil War, losing a son in the conflict, and died disappointed and embittered in 1866.

Magda Moyano knew a little of this history and told it to Styron. More important, she told him that a graduate student at the University of Virginia had recently finished a dissertation on John Hartwell Cocke. The Cocke family papers—a rich collection of letters, farming records, ledgers, and other items—had been donated to the Alderman Library at the university, and the dissertation had been based on these materials. Perhaps Styron could put his hands on a copy of the dissertation, once he returned to Connecticut?

Styron followed up on the suggestion. After he returned he got in touch with C. Vann Woodward and with his help traced the whereabouts of the young scholar from Virginia. He was M. Boyd Coyner, Jr., then teaching at Hampden-Sydney College, and his dissertation, over six hundred pages in length, was entitled "John Hartwell Cocke of Bremo: Agriculture and Slavery in the Ante-Bellum South." Coyner sent a copy of the dissertation to Styron, and Styron spent over two weeks reading it and absorbing its contents. Coyner's dissertation, never published, is a genuinely impressive work of scholarship. Based almost entirely on original letters, journals, and financial records, it gives a remarkably detailed picture of life on a large Virginia plantation during the first half of the nineteenth century. It also draws a compelling picture of Cocke as an agricultural reformer and an opponent of slavery.

Styron mined the dissertation for facts and other material. In 1963 there were not yet in print many studies of antebellum plantation life of such scope and depth. Coyner's dissertation was a trove of information for Styron, helping him create realistic portrayals in his novel of the everyday activities of his characters. Detailed accounts of farming methods, crops, marketing, slave life, and leisure activities were all of use to him in his writing.

Most important, though, was the figure of John Hartwell Cocke himself, who contributed a great deal to the portrayal of Samuel Turner in *The Confessions of Nat Turner.* Turner is Nat's most important master; his career (as Styron rendered it) follows a pattern quite similar to that of Cocke. Turner, like Cocke, is an opponent of slavery: in fact, Styron took passages directly from Cocke's letters on the subject of slavery (these passages quoted in Coyner's dissertation) and used them as letters written by Samuel Turner to Jefferson. Samuel Turner, however, is not nearly so fierce and uncompromising as was John Hartwell Cocke. Turner's idealism and his wish to dabble in the education and emancipation of his slaves wilts in the face of brutal economic realities during the 1820s, and he abandons Nat Turner, selling him to another owner after having promised him freedom. This act, as much as any other in the novel, embitters Nat and turns him toward rebellion and bloodshed. In these ways Samuel Turner was Styron's own creation, and a commentary on the shallow idealism of many twentieth-century friends of the Negro; but in his broad outlines Samuel Turner was John Hartwell Cocke.

In addition, Samuel Turner's Southampton County plantation in Styron's novel, as depicted in the later parts of the novel, was closely based on Bremo. Styron simply picked up John Hartwell Cocke's plantation from Fluvanna County and moved it—with its mansion, outbuildings, fields, livestock, slaves, and farming implements—to Southampton County. In 1831 there was no plantation in Southampton County that remotely resembled Bremo. A poor, backward region, Southampton County had within its boundaries no large and prosperous plantations, with stately mansions and grounds like those at Westover and Berkeley, just across the James River. Southampton County farms were much smaller and the houses and possessions of their owners more modest. Most of the slaveholders in the county had only a few field hands and worked side by side with them in the corn and cotton patches. Styron, however, wanted to make his novel a parable about slavery, and he needed to use images familiar from that historical period—the big plantation house with a formal parlor and dining room and a wide veranda, the well-dressed slave owners and their privileged house servants, the numerous and anonymous field hands and the extensive slave quarters. John Hartwell Cocke's Bremo was what Styron needed, so he transported it down the James River to the locale of his novel. This transplantation is indicative of Styron's working methods. As he progressed into his novel, he realized that the verifiable historical record of Nat Turner's Rebellion was far too thin for him to base his narrative entirely on it. He would have to draw on other material and other sources. In so doing Styron sought to broaden the scope and resonance of his book, making it relate to all of southern slavery and to other forms of imprisonment and oppression as well.

Now the novel was again in motion, and Styron worked steadily through the months that followed, creating an imagined version of Nat Turner's life as a child and young man. Nat became a complex character, part ascetic, part intellectual, part revolutionary. Styron drew heavily now on what he had read about American slavery and on what he knew of moral and psychological enslavement. He drew also on the Bible, making Nat Turner's mind resonate with passages from the fierce Old Testament prophets, after whom he patterns himself. Styron spent many afternoons in his studio reading the Old Testament, absorbing its language and rhythms, then weaving passages into his narrative.

Styron's momentum carried over into the next section of the novel—the account of the rebellion itself. Here he used Drewry's *The Southampton Insurrection,* with its maps tracing the route of Nat Turner's rebels and its testimony from descendants of the white families that had been attacked. Styron's greatest departure from the historical record in this section was to give Nat Turner a plan. No surviving evidence indicates that the historical Nat Turner had a clear strategy when he began his rebellion, that he contemplated anything other than random slaughter of white people. The path of the actual rebellion is illogical and aimless, suggesting that Nat and his followers had no ultimate destination in mind when they began. Styron's Nat Turner, by contrast, plans his route carefully over several years and has as his goal an escape with his band to the nearby Dismal Swamp, where he believes they can hide and live in a kind of freedom. Styron knew that such an aim was not unrealistic: many runaway slaves did live, sometimes for years, in the trackless Dismal Swamp, stealing out at night to raid farms for provisions and keeping in secret contact with sympathetic slaves. The point, an important one, was that Styron's Nat Turner should not be simply a bloodthirsty fanatic. Styron wished to humanize him and give him rational judgment. The failure of the rebellion, in fact, would be caused by Nat's humanity—his inability to kill, except in one instance, and his ultimate disenchantment with the bloodletting that he had ordained.

In these sections of the manuscript Styron took pains to describe the developing relationship between Nat Turner and Margaret Whitehead, the only person killed by the historical Nat. In Styron's imagination Margaret Whitehead became a southern belle, blond and flirtatious. She befriended Nat Turner and awakened in him complex and powerful emotions of love, hatred, sexual desire, admiration, resentment, contempt, protectiveness, and lust. She became the focus of his obsessions, racial and sexual—the being he could not possess and so had to destroy. Styron knew that the historical Nat Turner had admitted to killing Margaret Whitehead. Now, in the novel, her murder would become the climax of the narrative and the point at which the rebellion lost its momentum, beginning to spiral downward into disarray and eventual defeat.

• • •

The Styrons were on Martha's Vineyard again for the summer of 1964. They had been happy there during previous summers and had come especially to like the village of Vineyard Haven, which fronts on Vineyard Haven Harbor. The village itself was not much to see in 1964: a few ramshackle stores, a tacky souvenir shop or two, a post office, and one or two mediocre restaurants; but the Styrons liked the place. The movement and noise of the tourists were agreeable; most of them were day-trippers brought over by the ferryboats, which docked in the harbor. There was also good company in Vineyard Haven among the regular summer residents, many of whom were writers and artists with interests and political leanings that the Styrons found congenial.

The island itself was a good place to go exploring. It included barrier beaches, ponds, woodlands, moors, cliffs, hills, farmlands, and coastal plains. It was triangle-shaped, with Vineyard Haven Harbor at the northern point, Chappaquiddick Island at the eastern tip, and Gay Head at the western angle. Often the Styrons would take guests to the cliffs at Gay Head—brightly colored layers of stone and soil exposed in bands of red, purple, lavender, white, and yellow. The original inhabitants of the island, they learned, had been the Wampanoag Indians, whose presence was still evident in many of the place names: Mattakeset Bay, Lake Tashmoo, Menemsha Bight, Makonikey Head, Sengekontacket Pond.

The first white settlers on Martha's Vineyard grew vegetables and herded cattle and sheep; later, whaling became a major industry and dominated the economy from about 1770 to 1830. In the mid-1800s Martha's Vineyard became the site of some of the largest religious camp meetings in the country, attracting as many as twelve thousand visitors to single meetings during the 1860s and more than fifty thousand on some summer weekends later in the century. The Methodists made Martha's Vineyard a favored place; some families bought lots and built gingerbread-decorated frame cottages in an area called Wesleyan Grove—today the town of Oak Bluffs. By the early twentieth century Martha's Vineyard had become a summer vacation spot for many New Englanders. Large areas of Martha's Vineyard remained undeveloped, largely because the island was inaccessible by automobile. One went over either by ferryboat or, infrequently during the 1960s, by small airplane. Thus most of the tourists were walkers and bicyclists.

Life in Vineyard Haven was relaxed and casual. The pace and style

suited the Styrons: there was tennis for Rose in the mornings and afternoons, also swimming and sailing for the children at the Vineyard
Haven Yacht Club, an unpretentious establishment on the harbor. A
great deal of informal back-and-forth visiting took place, with cocktail
and dinner parties in the evenings, where writers, publishers, artists, editors, broadcast journalists, and others rubbed elbows.

Vineyard Haven provided peace and isolation for Styron. It was a
good place for him to work. Even with only makeshift studios rigged up
in rented houses, he had managed to get a good deal of writing done in
Vineyard Haven during the previous summers. The social life was
agreeable, Rose was happy, the children were occupied. Styron also
liked the smell of the salt water, the availability of fresh shellfish and
other seafood, and the swimming and sailing—all of which reminded
him of his years in Hilton Village and at Christchurch.

During the summer of 1964 the Styrons learned that a harbor-front
property in Vineyard Haven was for sale, not far from the rented house
on Hatch Road in which they were again staying. It was a big frame
house with several outbuildings and spacious front and side yards. The
property was owned by a well-to-do elderly woman who had decided
that she no longer wanted the worry of maintaining such an establishment. She had put it up for sale through a local realtor who had left the
intent-to-purchase papers with her in case a buyer might be willing to
sign, on impulse, while looking the place over.

As it turned out, the Styrons were seized by just that impulse. On
their first visit they were captured by the look and potential of the property. They liked the house, especially the broad front porch that faced
the harbor. There was a small guest house in the side yard that looked
as if it might be turned into a writing studio. The Vineyard Haven
Yacht Club was next door, with its tennis courts and swimming pier,
and the entire property was insulated from the main road by buffer
houses and lots. On this first visit, after looking over the house and yard
and the garage and plumbing, the Styrons put their heads together,
made up their minds, and signed the intent-to-purchase papers there
and then.

This was a fortunate move, because the realtor (who had thought the
asking price too low) was simultaneously offering the property at a
higher figure to another potential buyer. This client agreed to the higher
price. The realtor's mistake had been to leave the intent-to-purchase pa-

pers at the house a few days earlier. Now the elderly woman and both Styrons had signed them. The woman, who liked the Styrons and wanted them to have the property, and who was well-off herself and did not much care about the extra money being offered, refused to renege on her agreement. The issue appeared to be settled; the Styrons had purchased the place.

The realtor and his client, however, would not concede, and they persuaded a Massachusetts court to issue a restraining order that blocked the sale of the property. The Styrons were prevented from completing the purchase for two years. The woman who owned the property allowed them to move in, and they paid rent to her for the next two summers, but the case still had to be decided in court—giving the Styrons a feeling of impermanence and unease. They also could not begin repairs or renovations. Eventually the Styrons won the case and took possession fully in 1966, but not before the initial decision had been appealed by the realtor and his client.

Once the issue of ownership was settled, the Styrons began to feel like genuine residents of Vineyard Haven. It was a summertime community, but with much continuity and permanence. The same families returned year after year, each one following its own rhythm but all drawn to the island during the warm months. The Styrons began to fall into a cycle of their own: fall, winter, and early spring at Roxbury, late spring and summer at the Vineyard. Susanna and Polly were in the elementary grades now, and Tommy was in kindergarten. The two girls attended Rumsey Hall, a private school in Roxbury. Styron would go to the Vineyard in mid-May to open up the house; Rose and the children would follow in June, as soon as school ended, and would stay through August. Styron would often remain at Vineyard Haven after the others had returned to Roxbury; this was his favorite time of year on the island, when the tourists thinned out and the weather turned cool. These were good conditions for writing. He did some of his best work during September and often stayed until mid-October.

The Vineyard was good for Rose, too, allowing her freedom from the children's school schedules and time to think and write. She published her first collection of poetry, with Viking Press, in 1965, under her maiden name of Rose Burgunder. Its title, *From Summer to Summer,* captures the rhythm of the Styrons' family life. The months at Roxbury were times for work and duty, for following schedules and meeting deadlines. Summers at the Vineyard, though, were for loafing and dreaming. The family lived now "from summer to summer," anticipating the months at the Vineyard with great eagerness, talking of them during the winter evenings in Connecticut. The major part of the year, in Roxbury, was not unpleasant; they loved the countryside there, the big house, and the sense of busyness and purpose. Summers on the island, however, had an altogether different feel—relaxing and restorative. Rose caught this in one of her poems:

> A field of clouds,
> a wildflower sky;
> upside down
> goes summer by.
>
> My hammock rocks
> a leafy lake;
> I dive: the crystal
> ceilings break.
>
> A bird goes burrowing
> down in the air;
> an ant hangs high
> in my tangled hair.
>
> I'll skin-the-cat
> and cartwheels turn
> till proper Fall
> rights earth again.

Rose's poems in *From Summer to Summer* are remarkably personal and reveal much about the life of the family. Most of the poems are imagined from the point of view of a child—Susanna, Polly, or Tommy—or from the childlike part of Rose that she had kept alive. The verses are loose in rhythm with little enjambment and are carefully constructed in form, tied together with end-rhyme, internal rhyme, and near-rhyme. Read casually, they seem to celebrate summer, freshness, warmth, animals, and flowers. There is an undercurrent of melancholy, though, a sense of how rapidly youth passes and how quickly love can be lost. In many of the poems the poet wants to hide, to go to a private place, to be alone and dream. In "A Walk at Sunrise" the speaker escapes on a solitary trek, perhaps along the south shore of the island, where high cliffs tower above the sand:

> I'm older than these spiky cliffs
> and older than the sea,
> walking the silent sunrise beach
> there's no one old as me;
>
> no one to think of deaths to come
> nor watch our footsteps fading
> fast in the sands of morningtide
> where the wind and I go wading.

Many of the poems have a feel of morning about them—not surprising, since morning was when Rose wrote her poetry. She would almost always rise at six o'clock or earlier and go for a swim by herself in the chilly waters of the harbor. Then, with her hair wet, she would sit in her study and write for an hour or more. The household would begin to stir at eight o'clock or so, and by nine the telephone would be ringing, with invitations for tennis or afternoon cocktails, or with calls from mothers arranging playtimes with the Styron children.

The noise and energy created by her family blended well with the life Rose wanted to lead. She liked a crowded, busy schedule full of friends and shopping and picnics, food and laughter and spontaneity. But this intense activity, which flowed around and through the house all day, did not always sit well with her husband. Styron still maintained his dogged regimen, rising around noon, eating lunch, preparing to write, putting in his stint at the worktable, and tapering off with alcohol and a late dinner. The bruit of family life sometimes irritated him, especially when it encroached on his territory and upset his routine. What is more, many of the distractions on offer to Styron at the Vineyard were quite pleasant and tempting—invitations to go sailing, chances to talk with clever and accomplished people, visits from good friends and family. He often had to discipline himself to say no.

Rose was the person through whom most of the invitations came. She fielded telephone calls and met visitors, juggled schedules and kept the calendar more or less straight. She knew the kinds of parties and events that suited her husband and the kinds that did not. She learned to edit the invitations, refusing large, noisy parties or events at which he might be exposed to literary hangers-on, of whom there were a good many on the island. Inevitably, though, she made mistakes, accepting the wrong kinds of invitations, or inviting guests who turned out to be dull, or allowing the children to interrupt Styron as he worked. This ruffled and exasperated him, and he let her know it.

A strong tension developed between Styron and Rose over these issues, and the tension carried into their life in Roxbury. Her world, as always, was full of talk and laughter and children and pets and parties and tennis and conflict and noise. His world, by contrast, was patterned in its peculiar way—interior, contemplative, solitary. Neither could live the other's life, and neither was willing to compromise beyond a certain point, but each seemed to need the other to maintain balance.

Rose, like her husband, reserved a particular part of the day for writing—the early morning hours. She needed his resistance to certain kinds of social life to act as a brake on her natural openness and friendliness. He, on the other hand, needed color and distraction and disturbance to keep him from slipping too deeply into his introspective habits. Rose brought these things to him; she attracted people and invitations and fun, though keeping up with her could be exhausting. Most of the time she brought off her plans with deceptive ease: tennis was played, shopping was accomplished, flowers were delivered, luncheons were held, messages were passed on, conversations were completed, and dinner parties were attended.

Now and then, however, the whole edifice collapsed into a confusion of querulous guests, squabbling children, barking dogs, and forgotten engagements—all quite upsetting to someone of Styron's temperament. He liked the parties and attention, the music and drink, but wanted them in predictable increments and at prearranged times. She, by contrast, liked impulsive gifts and surprise visits and last-minute expeditions with the children. She liked to invent parts of her day as she went along. He wanted his day predictably structured; he disliked surprises; he detested the telephone. These tensions were at the heart of their marriage, dividing them (sometimes dangerously) but also binding them together in a strong, complex symbiosis.

27

The Confessions of Nat Turner

I N EARLY NOVEMBER 1963 Styron heard for the first time from
Willie Morris, a young Mississippian who was working at *Harper's
Magazine*. Morris had come to New York earlier that year after a stint
as editor of the *Texas Observer* in Austin. He would become editor in
chief of *Harper's* early in 1967 and would revitalize the magazine for a
time, putting it at the forefront of the New York periodical scene in the
late sixties. In this first letter, Morris asked Styron to contribute to a
special issue of *Harper's* that Morris was planning, an issue on the contemporary American South. Morris's idea was that Styron might want
to write about being an expatriated southerner, something he and Styron had in common.

The letter led to a personal meeting (C. Vann Woodward made the in-
troductions in his office at Yale), and that meeting led to a friendship.
Gregarious, bibulous, and prankish, Morris had a gift for fun and practical jokes that appealed to Styron. Morris also admired Styron's writing and told him so. Soon Morris and his wife, Celia, became members
of the Styrons' social circle, and the two couples visited back and forth.
Styron and Rose attended parties at the Morrises' farmhouse near
Brewster, New York, where the guests would include such couples as
the Woodwards, Robert Penn Warrens, Ralph Ellisons, Tom Wickers,
Larry L. Kings, Marshall Fradys, and others. The evenings were comfortably boozy, and those in attendance were relaxed and loquacious.

There was southern speechifying and burlesque sermonizing; sometimes the gatherings would also include ceremonies for bogus literary awards. One night, King remembered, Styron was given the Bull Connor Award for the best dog story; his prizes were a set of Boss Walloper work gloves, a tin of snuff, and a Mexican pornography magazine.

In the fall of 1964 Morris began to pull together the special *Harper's* issue, under the title "The South Today." He had managed to get contributions from Woodward, Louis E. Lomax, Walker Percy, Whitney Young, Leroi Jones, Louis Rubin, Arna Bontemps, Robert Coles, and several others. From Styron he expected an "Article on South for Travel Supplement," according to communications with Styron's literary agency. What he in fact received was much more—a searching, thoughtful composition entitled "This Quiet Dust." The issue appeared in April 1965, on the one-hundredth anniversary of the surrender at Appomattox. In the essay Styron tells of his trip to Southampton County, taken with Rose and his father in the spring of 1961, and weaves into the narrative an account of Nat Turner's Rebellion and its aftermath. Styron recalls his childhood experiences with Negroes in Tidewater Virginia and remembers the first mention of Nat Turner that he ever encountered—in the grammar-school history book, where the reference was brief and unsatisfactory. From that moment, he tells us, his fascination with Nat Turner could be dated, carrying him to the present time, when he was immersed in the composition of his novel.

In "This Quiet Dust" Styron speculates also on certain of the contradictions inherent in black-white relations in the South:

> No wonder the white man so often grows cranky, fanciful, freakish, loony, violent: how else respond to a paradox which requires, with the full majesty of law behind it, that he deny the very reality of a people whose multitude approaches and often exceeds his own; that he disclaim the existence of those whose human presence has marked every acre of the land, every hamlet and crossroad and city and town, and whose humanity, however inflexibly denied, is daily evidenced to him like a heartbeat in loyalty and wickedness, madness and hilarity and mayhem and pride and love? The Negro may feel that it is too late to be known, and that the desire to know him reeks of outrageous condescension. But to break down the old law, to come to *know* the Negro, has become the moral imperative of every white Southerner.

Styron concludes "This Quiet Dust" with speculations about the murder of Margaret Whitehead. "It is Nat's only murder," he writes. "Why, from this point on, does the momentum of the uprising diminish, the drive and tension sag? Why, from this moment in the *Confessions,* does one sense in Nat something dispirited, listless, as if all life and juice had been drained from him, so that never again through the course of the rebellion is he even on the scene when a murder is committed?" Styron cannot say, but it is clear that he has by now chosen this incident to be the pivotal point of his novel. It is clear too that Styron conceives of the book not simply as a historical retelling of the rebellion but as something more, a bringing together of events then and now. In the final lines of the essay, Styron imagines a fusion of past and present. "That day and this day," he writes, "seemed to meet and melt together, becoming almost one, and for a long moment indistinguishable."

B y way of setting his professional house in order before publishing his new novel, Styron had parted ways with his old agent for foreign rights. He had transferred this part of his literary business to a London-based agency, Hope Leresche & Steele, which claimed its descent through various partnerships from the firm of J. B. Pinker Associates, one of the first literary agencies ever established in England and the firm that had handled the work of Joseph Conrad, Stephen Crane, Henry James, and Arnold Bennett in the 1890s and early 1900s.

Hope Leresche, who headed the agency, was a tall, energetic Englishwoman, cheerful and confident in manner. She had made her reputation as a specialist in the international market. From her office in Chelsea she had been handling the work of James Jones and Irwin Shaw successfully, arranging for translations of their novels in Europe and South America and placing their shorter writings, from time to time, in British and Continental periodicals. (It was through Jones that Styron had met her, and on Jones's recommendation that he approached her to take him on as a client.) Hope Leresche's network of international contacts, built up over several decades, was impressively broad, and her knowledge of the British and Commonwealth markets was good. Styron had become one of her authors in May 1962, and she had begun immediately to examine the history and pattern of his works in translation. In his second letter to her, dated May 23, 1962, Styron had tried to help by filling her in on his international reputation, as accurately as he could then describe it:

> You get these queer cultural anomalies. In England I am doubtless best known for THE LONG MARCH, which is little-known in America and as yet unpublished (though forthcoming) in France, and at the same time vaguely recalled as the writer who wrote those dreary and cumbersome novels, LIE DOWN IN DARKNESS and SET THIS HOUSE ON FIRE. In America I am known as the writer of an early masterpiece, LIE DOWN IN DARKNESS, who badly betrayed his talent in a clumsy second work, SET THIS HOUSE ON FIRE. In France I am known as the authentic genius who created an incomparable *chef d'oeuvre*, SET THIS HOUSE ON FIRE, after an obscure and fledgling attempt called LIE DOWN IN DARKNESS.

Leresche set about marketing Styron's work in some of the countries in which it had yet to appear. In fairly short order she arranged for translations to be published in Czechoslovakia, Denmark, Switzerland, Hungary, Italy, Norway, Japan, Portugal, Mexico, the Netherlands, Poland, Romania, Sweden, and Yugoslavia. The contracts for these translations—many of them for *The Long March*—yielded small change, but they pleased Styron nonetheless. He wrote William Blackburn about these developments: "I think the average amount of money I get from any single country is about $250 gross (except for France) but it is agreeable to think of those gnarled peasants everywhere reading me, on top of quaint donkeys and between turns of the potter's wheel. My agent in London informs me that I am now in or about to be in 13 languages, including Dutch, Polish and, of all things, Serbo-Croatian, and my Tidewater mind reels." These contracts laid the groundwork for long-term relationships with many foreign houses and prepared the way for much bigger advances and agreements in future years, especially when Leresche's agency arranged for translations of *The Confessions of Nat Turner* and *Sophie's Choice*.

Hope Leresche also helped Styron change his publishing arrangements in England. Styron had been disappointed by the reviews and sales of his Hamish Hamilton editions; in September 1964 he learned that the Hamilton edition of *The Long March* was to be remaindered. This seems to have brought matters to a head, and on October 10, Sty-

ron wrote to Jamie Hamilton asking to be released from future commitments to the firm. Hamilton acquiesced, and by the new year Styron
was free to sign with another British publisher. He was guided to the
house of Jonathan Cape by Leresche, who had contacts there with a
young editorial director named Tom Maschler, who had taken over the
firm's literary list.

Maschler had read Styron's previous books and had admired them;
on a trip to the United States in the late summer of 1964 he met Styron
in Vineyard Haven and read the first seventy-odd pages of the Nat
Turner manuscript. Maschler was much taken by the writing: "Seriously, Bill," he said in a letter early that fall, "the seventy pages I read
were not only by far the best writing I saw on this last trip to America,
but I think were the most impressive work in progress I have ever seen."
Through Leresche, in February 1965, Maschler now received the first
two hundred pages of the typescript, which had been circulating to
American paperback houses. On the basis of this writing Cape signed
Styron, in March 1965, to a contract for *The Confessions of Nat Turner.*
The advance was for £2,500 against royalties that escalated from 12.5 to
15 percent. (The paperback rights were left unmarketed for the moment; eventually they went for £14,000 to Panther Books, which outbid
Penguin in the spring of 1968.) Cape also acquired the publication
rights and remaining unsold stock of Styron's previous books from
Hamish Hamilton. Thus all of Styron's British rights were brought
under one roof, in preparation for the appearance of his novel in England.

By the beginning of 1965 Styron felt confident of completing *The
Confessions of Nat Turner,* and Random House began arranging for
publication. It is instructive to trace out their plans, for by 1965 a great
many changes had taken place in the American literary marketplace.
Indeed Styron's career as a professional author is almost a textbook
case for the student of the American book trade in the second half of
the twentieth century. His major novels have been published at long intervals, and important changes in the book industry have occurred between them. Thus one can draw instructive contrasts between the
publication histories of these works.

Lie Down in Darkness, appearing in 1951, was published in a commercial atmosphere not appreciably different from the one that Edith Wharton, James Branch Cabell, and F. Scott Fitzgerald knew. Book publishing in 1951 was still thought of as a gentleman's profession, insulated from the coarser pressures of capitalism; subsidiary rights (paperback, book-club, radio, cinema, and stage) were usually not marketed until after the book had proved itself with a successful hardcover run; British and translation rights were often neglected by the originating houses.

By the time Styron published *Set This House on Fire* in 1960, however, American publishers had learned to plan in advance more carefully. Subsidiary rights for established authors, or for books that seemed certain of a large sale, were now marketed before hardcover publication; paperback and book-club editions were becoming much more important sources of extra income (or "flow-through," in publishing parlance); and even translation rights were growing in value as American popular and literary culture spread over the world during the decades after World War II. These various developments helped make *Set This House on Fire* a publishing success, even though its initial reception by American critics was mixed.

By the mid-1960s, the face of American book publishing had changed again. Random House had gone public in 1959, becoming the first major U.S. trade house to issue stock and pay profits to shareholders. In 1966 the firm was taken over by RCA, thus making it a significant part of a large media and communications conglomerate. This trend, played out for virtually all established American trade houses during the 1970s and 1980s, gave publishers access to much more capital than had previously been available; the consequence was a more commercial-minded approach to the book trade and a more pronounced risk-taking mentality. The publication of a major book such as *The Confessions of Nat Turner* was now orchestrated very carefully, and far in advance, so that its various incarnations—as hardcover, book-club edition, paperback, translation, and perhaps television or movie adaptation—would all energize each other and keep the title in the public eye for a long selling period. Publicity for literary novels, mostly a poky and haphazard business before 1945, had now become more sophisticated, especially after the advent of television with its power to create and cultivate celebrities.

These developments have opened up much wider and more varied markets to large trade houses and to the authors who publish with them. This has been especially true for mass-market and genre writers, but it has also been true for authors such as Styron. His desire to speak out on public and moral issues in his fiction has coincided with the coming of a much more efficient apparatus for conveying his words to readers, and this has given his name and voice a currency that he surely did not anticipate when he began writing in the 1940s.

One sees this pattern clearly in the publication history of *The Confessions of Nat Turner.* Book-club and paperback rights, for example, were marketed more than two years in advance of publication, and both were sold early for substantial figures. Styron's visibility from his appearances in *Esquire* and *Life,* together with the interest generated by "This Quiet Dust" in *Harper's,* created much anticipation for *The Confessions of Nat Turner.* The files of Random House and of Styron's American literary agency, Harold Matson, now among the publishing-history archives at the Butler Library, Columbia University, reveal that as early as the fall of 1964 there was already keen interest in paperback and book-club rights—this before Styron had come close to finishing the novel. Styron's work was being handled at the Harold Matson agency by Don Congdon, a savvy and energetic authors' representative who understood how various subsidiary rights could work, with a kind of synergy, to push all values higher and higher.

In January 1965 the paperback rights were put up for auction, still a relatively new strategy at that time. These rights went to New American Library for $100,000, then a substantial figure for rights to a novel. This amount set the standard for the negotiations that would follow, and these were kept simmering over the next fifteen months. In the spring of 1967, Random House and Congdon worked together to move toward closure on various arrangements. As a first step, formal publication of the novel was scheduled for early October. Then, in April, *Harper's* purchased North American first serial rights for Part II of the novel, entitled "Old Times Past," for its September issue. *Harper's* paid $7,500 for these serial rights and agreed, as a part of the arrangement, to allow *Life* to publish other excerpts from the novel in its October 13 issue. *Life* paid $5,000 for the portions of the novel it wanted to publish.

The Book-of-the-Month Club won the bidding for book-club rights, paying $150,000—a figure that topped Literary Guild's offer by $50,000. Literary Guild, not to be denied, paid $12,500 for follow-up book-club rights, agreeing not to issue its edition of the novel until five months after BOMC had published its edition. Thus there was a period, in 1968, when the two largest book clubs in the United States were both offering *The Confessions of Nat Turner* to members. Correspondence in the Random House files shows that copies of the manuscript and galleys of the novel were withheld from movie and theater people until the book-club and paperback rights had been sold. The large figures paid for those rights caused the price for the cinema rights to go higher. Shortly before publication day—now formally set for October 9, 1967—the movie rights were sold to the producer David Wolper for $800,000.

Thus *The Confessions of Nat Turner* generated, before publication, guarantees of over one million dollars. Styron had not dreamed that such figures could be reached. He found them both gratifying and daunting. Fortunately the bulk of this negotiating and selling took place well after he had finished composing the novel; only the paperback rights were sold while he was still writing the manuscript. But Styron was certainly aware of the early activity among book-club and movie people, and he could see that a considerable groundswell of interest in the novel was building. He knew now that he would have a great many readers and make a great deal of money.

The money was welcome. In the years since the publication of *Set This House on Fire,* Styron's income from his writing had increased steadily. His earnings were now counted on for the day-to-day expenses of maintaining the family; Rose's income went for extras—school tuitions for the children, for example, or travel and vacations. Inevitably this required her to cut into her capital, which made Styron's earnings that much more necessary if they were to continue to live and work as they wished to.

In January 1966, Rose became pregnant. She was quite pleased, as was Styron, though he wondered what effect the new baby would have on the family. He was much preoccupied with his novel and more prone than ever to arrange his days so as to avoid the noise and confusion created by his children. He knew what stresses a new infant would bring, but he knew also how much Rose wanted another child, and he was glad that he and she had brought another life into being. Despite his occasional irritation with his children he loved them and was immensely proud of them. All three were smart and talented, energetic and strong-minded, variously marked by their parents in looks and inclinations.

Rose's reaction to her pregnancy was a mixture of pleasure and apprehension. She had very much wanted another baby, but she had also begun to chafe at the demands of child-rearing and had recently been required to play a great many roles at once. For part of the day she had been a mother, a house manager, and a supply sergeant; for the other part of the day she had transformed herself variously into a literary critic, a hostess, and a dinner companion. She had no support system for her own writing, no one who seemed interested, and she sometimes felt frustrated and trapped in routine. Often she was so weary in the evenings that she had trouble making conversation at dinner. Sometimes she fell asleep at the table. Would the new baby, when it came, intensify these problems?

The pregnancy went smoothly, with no complications—something Rose had worried about. The baby, a girl, arrived on October 28, 1966. They named her Alexandra and called her Alex, then Al, perhaps choosing boys' nicknames because Tommy, then seven years old, had so badly wanted a brother. With the exception of Tommy and his father, the entire household at the time was female—mother, sisters, dogs, cats, birds, and even a pet boa constrictor. When Styron telephoned Tommy from the hospital and told him that he had yet another sister, Tommy cried out in piping tones, "Daddy! *Daddy,* no!" Styron wrote down the rest of the story many years later:

> I rather feared for his sanity when the next day, en route to his little workshop in the cellar, he asked me for the following items: rope, nails, a piece of lead, a sharp blade. I was certain he was building a torture device for his new baby sister. But in fact, after a long and sinister silence, he emerged with a wondrous artifact: a wooden bird with metal wings, a gift for Alexandra, and tribute to the fact that even he, after all his isolated maleness, wished to celebrate the arrival of another sister, my new daughter.

In spite of all else that was occurring in his life, Styron proceeded steadily with the manuscript of his novel, inscribing the pages that tell of the rebellion itself with its horrible savagery and bloodletting. These sections were written during the fall of 1966, in Roxbury. A great many years later Styron could still describe the headlong momentum that carried him forward: "I remember finishing *The Confessions of Nat Turner* with this kind of almost blind rush of creativity, with no rewriting at all—virtually the whole last one-fifth of that book was written in a kind of galloping rush."

Late on Sunday afternoon, January 22, 1967, sitting at his writing desk in the little house in Roxbury, Styron set down the last words of *The Confessions of Nat Turner* on the final leaf of the manuscript, numbered 647. He signed and dated the leaf at the bottom; he noted the time as 6:25 P.M. and recorded the weather as "Clear"—underscoring the word twice. Then he left his workroom and walked over to the main house, where Rose was standing at the kitchen stove preparing the children's supper. Susanna, Polly, and Tom were sitting at the table; Alex, only three months old, was strapped into a molded plastic baby-carrier on the kitchen counter with a pacifier in her mouth. Susanna later recalled what happened: her father shambled into the kitchen, surprising the children a little, because they were not accustomed to seeing him so early. These were normally his working hours. He slumped into a chair at the table, waved them all to silence, and announced, "Well, it's finished." As if on cue, at just that moment, like a tiny bottle of champagne, Alex expelled her pacifier with great force and a loud pop. The children and Rose all laughed, then shouted and cheered. Styron smiled. As a grown woman Susanna could still remember how relieved he looked.

Styron now reviewed his sources and read back through his manuscript one last time. He must have become fully aware then of how much he had drawn on his own imagination to fill out the meager historical record of Nat Turner's Rebellion and how much he had imported into the narrative from his broader knowledge of slavery. Perhaps as a consequence Styron decided that he needed to preface his novel with a statement in his own voice, a brief explanation of what he had attempted to do.

A marginal note on one of the early leaves of the manuscript reveals that Styron had an approximate model to work from: "MUST QUOTE: 1st part of 'Author's Note' from *Hadrian's Memoirs* for my own Author's Note." The reference is to the French author Marguerite Yourcenar's book *Mémoires d'Hadrien,* published originally in Paris in 1951 and translated and first published in the United States in 1963 as *Memoirs of Hadrian.* Styron had read the book while composing *The Confessions of Nat Turner.*

Memoirs of Hadrian is a philosophical meditation, written in the voice of the Roman emperor Hadrian during the weeks just before his death. It is an epistolary work, cast in the form of a letter to Marcus Aurelius, his adopted grandson. Hadrian (A.D. 76–138) was among the greatest of the Roman emperors, a successful warrior, a farsighted administrator, and a connoisseur of literature, music, and the arts. He is remembered today for having built the Pantheon in Rome and Hadrian's Wall in Britain.

Very little primary evidence survives from which to chronicle Hadrian's life. There is a garbled biography in the *Historia Augusta* that quotes a few passages from a lost autobiography; likewise there survives some administrative correspondence, together with fragments of a few discourses and reports. These were of limited utility to Yourcenar, but what she could draw upon to excellent effect was the rich historical record of Roman law, religion, and social life set down over the eighteen centuries that had intervened between Hadrian's time and her own.

In her author's note, placed at the back of *Memoirs of Hadrian,* Yourcenar reveals her methods: "History has its rules, though they are not always followed even by professional historians," she writes. "Poetry, too, has its laws. The two are not necessarily irreconcilable." Yourcenar tells the reader how she has rearranged details and adjusted the surviving records; she also describes how she has invented or fleshed out characters and how the "lack of authentic details" has prompted her to engage in "prudent filling in of such lacunae from information furnished by contemporary texts treating of analogous experiences or events."

Styron was surely struck by how similar Yourcenar's methods were to his own. Like him, she was working from a fragmentary, conjectural historical record. Like him, she had a rich tradition of historical and literary writing to draw upon. Also like him, she was traveling across boundaries of time—in her case fully eighteen hundred years. Her attempt as a woman to imagine Hadrian's erotic life was analogous to Styron's effort to imagine Nat Turner's negritude. Yourcenar's narrative, presented as a long letter dictated by Hadrian as he waits for death, was similar to Styron's own novel, narrated by Nat Turner from his jail cell as he awaits execution.

The lines in Yourcenar's author's note that almost certainly caught Styron's eye, and that he thought he might quote, were these two sentences: "A reconstruction of an historical figure and of the world of his time written in the first person borders on the domain of fiction, and sometimes of poetry; it can therefore dispense with formal statement of evidence for the historical facts concerned. Its human significance, however, is greatly enriched by close adherence to those facts." Yourcenar then supplies a detailed bibliographical note, occupying fully seventeen pages, in which she lists her sources and discusses how she has employed each one.

Styron thought for a time of using a similar strategy, discussing his few primary sources and giving an extended account of his other reading on the institution of slavery. Finally, though, he decided not to do this. He decided also not to quote Yourcenar. *Memoirs of Hadrian* was very close to a work of scholarship; *The Confessions of Nat Turner* was much more a work of the imagination. A long list of "works consulted" at the rear of his novel would give it the look of a Ph.D. dissertation and would destroy the elegiac note he had tried to strike at the end of the story. Some similar explanation at the front of the volume would start the reader on the wrong foot, suggesting that the novel was more a work of history than of fiction. Styron therefore decided not to list his sources and to include only a short, suggestive note at the beginning of his novel, mentioning Gray's "Confessions" as his primary source and describing, very briefly, the kinds of imaginative liberties he had taken for the rest of the narrative.

It is interesting to consider the effect that a detailed bibliographical account of sources would have had on the subsequent reception of *The Confessions of Nat Turner.* Once the historical accuracy of the novel began to be attacked, in late 1967 and 1968, Styron's impulse was not to talk about his reading and his sources. That has remained his strategy up to the present day. He has never compiled a list of his reading and has never described, in more than a general way, how he filled out the characterizations of such figures as Thomas Gray, Samuel Turner, and Jeremiah Cobb. He has presented himself as a novelist, a creator, and on that ground he has chosen to stand.

This decision was surely wise. A long bibliographical commentary published after the fact, subsequent to the appearance of the novel, would have dropped Styron directly into the morass of scholarship and opinion on the history of American slavery—a supremely contentious field. It would also have left him open to nitpicking and source-questioning and would have undermined his assertion of the primacy of the writer's imagination. It would have seemed a capitulation of sorts to his critics. There were disadvantages to this refusal to explain, however. Once *The Confessions of Nat Turner* began to be attacked, Styron's stubbornness about not discussing his sources made it seem to some observers as if he had done very little reading or study at all, that he had invented his novel more or less out of his head. Either way Styron lost. Perhaps he foresaw this: in any case he chose, in his Author's Note, not to say a great deal about sources. And once the book was in print and had come under fire, he decided to say only a little more. He would not backtrack and explain himself beyond a certain point.

Styron's own Author's Note, when he came to write it, caused him some difficulty. Several drafts of the statement survive with the manuscript of *The Confessions of Nat Turner,* all with adjustments in wording. Styron finally settled on this single paragraph:

> In August, 1831, in a remote region of southeastern Virginia, there took place the only effective, sustained revolt in the annals of American Negro slavery. The initial passage of this book, entitled "To the Public," is the preface to the single significant contemporary document concerning this insurrection—a brief pamphlet of some twenty pages called "The Confessions of Nat Turner," published in Richmond early in the next year, parts of which have been incorporated in this book. During the narrative that follows I have rarely departed from the *known* facts about Nat Turner and the revolt of which he was the leader. However, in those areas where there is little knowledge in regard to Nat, his early life, and the motivations for the revolt (and such knowledge is lacking most of the time), I have allowed myself the utmost freedom of imagination in reconstructing events—yet I trust remaining within the bounds of what meager enlightenment history has left us about the institution of slavery. The relativity of time allows us elastic definitions: the year 1831 was, simultaneously, a long time ago and only yesterday. Perhaps the reader will wish to draw a moral from this narrative, but it has been my own intention to try to re-create a man and his era, and to produce a work that is less

an "historical novel" in conventional terms than a meditation on history.

This Author's Note, which would later be the target of several attacks, can itself be read in several ways. Certainly it is Styron's effort to distance his narrative from the label "historical novel," his bid to circumvent the book's being grouped with such novels as Margaret Mitchell's *Gone With the Wind,* or, at a lower level, Hervey Allen's *Anthony Adverse* or James Boyd's *Drums.* Styron's note reveals that his major source has been Gray's "Confessions" and that he has consciously departed from the "*known* facts" about Nat Turner and the rebellion in relatively few instances.

But the note is also an assertion that, at base, *The Confessions of Nat Turner* is a work of the imagination, and that Styron has given himself great leeway to fill out the sparse record with his own conceptions of what might have happened. In his effort to do so, he has brought together past and present and produced, in his own phrase, a parable of sorts, a "meditation on history." This Author's Note seems now to have been an effort by Styron to describe, in just a few sentences, what he had done. But it is a statement that, in its elliptical character, is vulnerable to attack. Styron would learn this in the months after the publication of *The Confessions of Nat Turner,* though it would not necessarily make him regret having written the note.

Styron had the Author's Note typed, then reviewed the text once again. In late January he completed this work to his satisfaction and wrapped the manuscript for transport to Random House. He had stayed up late to complete the job; once it was finished he went up to the children's rooms and roused them all from their beds. He awakened Rose as well; it was nearly four o'clock in the morning. Everyone stumbled downstairs to the living room, where Styron lifted the three oldest children one by one onto the broad mantelpiece above the fireplace. The wrapped manuscript was displayed and admired; the ceremony of full completion was observed. The children smiled groggily and laughed, then went back upstairs to bed. Rose followed a short while later. This was the event that Styron chose later to mention to interviewers, many of whom included it in their stories when the first rush of publicity about *The Confessions of Nat Turner* was breaking. Susanna, however, always remembered the scene in the kitchen, on January 22, when Alex popped out her pacifier, as the real completion of the novel, the true end of her father's creative journey.

Random House prepared carefully for publication day. The initial plan was to have a first impression of 75,000 copies. Bound galleys with reproductions of the jacket art went out early to major periodicals and newspapers, and were sent as well to such writers as Wallace Stegner, John Cheever, Robert Lowell, and Robert Penn Warren. A limited signed edition of 500 copies in a special binding and slipcase was issued for friends and for collectors interested in Styron's work. Initial orders from bookstores were so heavy that three extra impressions had to be ordered before publication day. Fully 125,000 copies of the novel were in print when it was issued on October 9, 1967, and initial sales were so strong that another impression had to be ordered just two weeks later. The Book-of-the-Month Club was caught short of stock, with not enough copies in its warehouses to fill orders; Random House helped by lengthening its press runs and shipping trade sheets to BOMC, which sold them in its own bindings and jackets.

Bob Loomis had taken extra care with the text of the novel, engaging the best freelance proofreader in New York, a man with a reputation for nearly flawless work, to give Styron's novel an extra checking. But the man became so absorbed in the narrative that he lost his concentration and missed nearly forty typographical errors. Loomis was kept busy ordering corrections for each of the first five printings of the novel. Because the text of the book had been set in hot metal and cast in plates, these corrections were a fussy business. The printers had to chisel off the erroneous readings, set corrected readings, cast these in electrotype, mortise the new words onto the plates, and then get the plates back onto the presses. All of this activity caused a good deal of flurry, but it was the kind of flurry that publishers like to see.

The initial reviews were as good as Styron could have expected. The novel was written about nearly everywhere, from mainstream national journals to major quarterlies to academic periodicals to local newspapers. In all, nearly two hundred reviews and commentaries were published, including a long cover story in the October 16 *Newsweek* by Raymond Sokolov and a laudatory notice by an anonymous reviewer for *Time* who called the novel "a new peak in the literature of the

South." Many other major notices were favorable, or largely so, and some were raves. Alfred Kazin, writing in *Book World,* praised the novel as "a wonderfully evocative portrait of a gifted, proud, long-suppressed human being who began to live only when he was sentenced to die." Philip Rahv, in *The New York Review of Books,* called *The Confessions of Nat Turner* "a first-rate novel, the best that William Styron has written and the best by an American writer that has appeared in some years." Eliot Fremont-Smith, in the daily *New York Times,* praised the novel as "a dazzling shaft of light"; Edmund Fuller, in *The Wall Street Journal,* wrote that Styron had produced "the true American tragedy." Shaun O'Connell, reviewing in *The Nation,* called the novel "a stunningly beautiful embodiment of a noble man"; for John Thompson, in *Commentary,* Styron's book showed "an immense understanding of the human spirit and a fine novelist's ability to make us see." There were predictably favorable notices from Robert Penn Warren, C. Vann Woodward, Louis Rubin, and Arthur Schlesinger, Jr.; sympathetic personal portraits of Styron were published by his friends George Plimpton (in *The New York Times Book Review*) and John Marquand (in *Vogue*). Styron was pleased by positive reviews from John Hope Franklin and J. Saunders Redding. Probably he was pleased in a different way by George Steiner's analysis of the novel in *The New Yorker* as "a fiction of complex relationship, of the relationship between a present-day white man of deep Southern roots and the Negro in today's whirlwind."

But the reviews were not uniformly positive. Most visible was a front-page attack by Wilfrid Sheed in *The New York Times Book Review;* Sheed found Styron's novel marred by artificiality and dismissed it as "a kind of historical tone poem." Sheed scolded the author in the last two sentences of the review: "Styron has performed a signal, non-literary service in writing this book," said Sheed. "Now, I hope he will get back to work." Martin Duberman, in *The Village Voice,* faulted Styron for relying on the historical record and renouncing his "rich powers of invention"; Stanley Kauffmann, writing for *The Hudson Review,* likened the novel to the "bursting of one abscess in a large, poisoned body." June Meyer, a black critic writing in *The Nation,* called *The Confessions of Nat Turner* a "stunt," part of the "fantastic black-to-white 'dialog' miscarried by white-controlled media through the 'medium' of the now professional, white intermediary."

Styron was bothered by these criticisms. He was also troubled by reviewers and journalists (many of them favorably disposed toward him and his novel) who cast him as a spokesman for the white intelligentsia or as an oracle who was predicting future racial turmoil. He went to some lengths, in interviews and news stories, to disavow such a role and such intentions, but he was not wholly successful in doing so. Styron had not expected a fully favorable reaction, and most of the initial attacks did not surprise him. He had been toughened to bad reviews by the reception of *Set This House on Fire.* On balance he felt that he had received a decent press for *The Confessions of Nat Turner,* and certainly he was pleased by the performance of the novel at the bookshops. "It might go on + on forever, like Dr. Spock," he wrote to William Blackburn.

The tone and mood of that early reception was summed up for Styron by one day, November 21, 1967, about six weeks after the publication of his novel. On that day he was awarded an honorary degree at Wilberforce University, an all-black institution in Ohio, named after William Wilberforce, a prominent nineteenth-century British abolitionist. Styron recalled the occasion twenty-five years later: "In a sea of smiling black and brown people," he remembered, "I was greeted with good will, thanks, praise." In a brief speech at a convocation ceremony, he spoke of his southern upbringing and his efforts at "identification with the Negro people and the Negro spirit." He talked about the history of black people and lamented that so much of it had been suppressed and had passed into oblivion. "Such common history as the two races shared—shared in passion and heartbreak and hilarity and rage and hatred and love—this common history would not be allowed," he said. And he reviewed the terrible story of Nat Turner's Rebellion, seeing in it the lesson that "oppression is bound to breed hatred," and that "rampant hatred in return can only bring on catastrophe." Was there an answer? Styron could not give a simple one that afternoon. All that he could suggest, in closing his speech, was recourse to love and trust. "Love is perhaps now both too difficult and too easy, and in any event doubtless too late," he said, "but maybe when all is done it is love that is still our last, our only hope."

Many years later Styron described the reaction of the Wilberforce audience:

There was much applause. George Shirley, a Wilberforce alumnus who was a leading tenor with the Metropolitan Opera, gave a spine-chilling rendition of "The Battle Hymn of the Republic," in which the audience joined together, singing with great emotion. Standing in that auditorium, I was moved by a feeling of oneness with these people. I felt gratitude at their acceptance of me and, somehow more important, at my acceptance of them, as if my literary labors and my plunge into history had helped dissolve many of my preconceptions about race that had been my birthright as a Southerner and allowed me to better understand the forces that had shaped our common destiny. For me it was a moment of intense warmth and brotherhood.

At that moment at Wilberforce, it could not have occurred to Styron that in only a few months he would be the target of passionate attacks, that he would be called an enemy of the black man, and that his novel would be condemned as immoral and racist.

28

Aftermath

S TYRON WAS IN a fallow period for much of 1968, considering several ideas for his next novel and dealing still with the ongoing success of *The Confessions of Nat Turner.* Sales of the book were climbing toward 150,000 for the clothbound trade edition, and translation rights were selling rapidly, sometimes for substantial figures. The German hardback rights, for example, fetched $50,000, and even so seemingly minor a piece of the pie as Norwegian book-club rights brought $25,000. Styron continued to be interviewed regularly for national magazines and was invited to give on-campus readings at a great many colleges and universities, from the most prestigious to the most modest.

During the first half of 1968 Styron worked to support Eugene McCarthy in the Democratic primaries. Like many Democrats, Styron was disillusioned with Lyndon Johnson's inability to end the Vietnam War and was hopeful that McCarthy, if elected to the presidency, could extricate U.S. armed forces from Southeast Asia. Styron was attracted by McCarthy's low-key manner, and he watched with excitement as McCarthy's bid for the nomination gathered momentum, pleased by his strong showings in the early primaries and his popularity with young voters. Styron cosponsored a fund-raiser for McCarthy and even found himself working the telephones to organize support for his candidate.

There were other matters on Styron's mind, however. It now looked as if a considerable controversy was going to develop over *The Confes-*

sions of Nat Turner and that it would not die down soon. At various points in 1968 the novel was attacked in *The New Republic,* the *Saturday Review,* the *Journal of Negro History,* and the *Massachusetts Review.* The book was defended in *Partisan Review, The Yale Review, The Southern Review,* and the *Kenyon Review.* In April, Styron allowed himself to be drawn into printed debate with the Marxist/Communist historian Herbert Aptheker in *The Nation,* and he stated his position at length in interviews in *The New York Times, The Boston Globe,* the *Yale Alumni Magazine,* and the *Yale Literary Magazine.*

Styron was also hearing from Hollywood that the movie version of his novel was in trouble. The black actors Ossie Davis and Ruby Dee, husband and wife, were organizing Negro actors and screenwriters to demand a say in the casting and script of the film version of *The Confessions of Nat Turner.* They called their group the Black Anti-Defamation Association. This was a period of much contentiousness in Hollywood over the images of African Americans projected in American films; Davis, Dee, and their supporters wanted a decisive, heroic Nat Turner, not a brooding, vacillating figure. They did not want to see the cinematic Nat Turner fantasize sexually over a golden-haired white woman.

Styron also began to be distracted by one of the side effects of public fame: strange mail. Some of the letters he received were harmless enough—long, idiosyncratic missives from lonely, slightly unbalanced people. Other letters were merely irritating; they scolded him for the sexual frankness of his novel or solicited help in getting published or begged for money. Still other letters, though, were genuinely disturbing, with messages of hatred and even threats of violence. Some of these were from racial bigots, black and white, who were angry over Styron's portrayal of Nat Turner. Depending on the point of view, Styron had either vilified a Negro folk hero or had elevated a murderous black man to heroic stature. Other letters seemed not even to possess this logic, revealing hatred for Styron simply because he had become famous.

Most of these letters Styron ignored, but a few gave him real worry, less for himself than for Rose and the children. One evening at dinnertime Styron called Bob Loomis in New York, distraught because he feared that Rose had been abducted. There had been a threatening letter in the mail a few days earlier; now Rose, who had come to the city earlier that day, was missing. She had agreed to telephone him in Roxbury at an appointed time in the early afternoon, but she had not made the call. Styron, worried, had tried to reach her by phone for several hours, calling her hotel and contacting people whom she had been scheduled to see. He had had no success and, greatly upset, had driven from Roxbury into the city to look for her at her hotel. He could not find her there and now was calling Loomis from the hotel. Styron asked Loomis to bring a belt and a pair of socks when he came to the hotel; in his rush to leave Roxbury, Styron had forgotten both.

Rose turned up a short while later. She had been working with several Russian poets on poems of theirs that she was translating into English, and she had been unable to get to a telephone. This was normal for her, and ordinarily Styron would not have been worried. He was quite angry with her now, but both she and Loomis could see that his anger grew out of a genuine fear for her safety. The threatening letter had done its work. That evening Styron made Rose promise, over and over, to stay in close contact with him until the worst of the reactions to *Nat Turner* had died down.

On Sunday, March 31, Lyndon Johnson announced that he would not run for reelection. Styron's relief at that news, though, evaporated four days later when Martin Luther King, Jr., was shot and killed in Memphis, setting off racial violence in cities all over the country. Later that same month the Students for a Democratic Society (the SDS) occupied several buildings at Columbia and managed to shut down the university. There was civil unrest all over the country, on campuses and in cities, much of it reported nightly on the television. Styron followed these developments carefully; he realized that his own difficulties with *The Confessions of Nat Turner* were related to what was happening elsewhere.

The last half of 1968 surely must stand as the most crowded and turbulent period of Styron's life. Some of what happened to him was individual and personal, but much of it was tied to the violent spasms through which American society was then passing. Styron learned in May that he had been selected as one of four delegate challengers for Eugene McCarthy to the Democratic national convention that would take place that August in Chicago. He and three others would appear before the Credentials Committee at the convention to argue that Mc-

Carthy deserved thirteen delegates out of the Connecticut contingent of forty-four, rather than the nine he had been allotted.

Styron also learned in early May that *The Confessions of Nat Turner* had won the Pulitzer Prize for fiction, a welcome validation of his achievement from the literary establishment and the first major award he had won since the Prix de Rome in 1952. The difficulties continued in Hollywood, however, over the casting and script of *The Confessions of Nat Turner.* Late in May Styron flew to Seattle with Arthur Miller and Jules Feiffer to campaign for Eugene McCarthy in the Washington and Oregon primaries. Then Styron traveled to Los Angeles to debate his vision of Nat Turner's Rebellion with Ossie Davis at a left-liberal nightclub called Eugene West (the name taken from Eugene Mc-Carthy). James Baldwin served as the moderator for the debate, and he found the role uncomfortable. Styron recalled that Baldwin kept referring nervously throughout to "my friend Bill" on the one hand and "my friend Ossie" on the other, trying to establish some common ground between the two men but largely failing.

Also in May the British edition of *The Confessions of Nat Turner* was published in London by Jonathan Cape. Encouraged by Tom Maschler's enthusiasm for the novel, Styron had hoped for a good press, but only a few of the reviews were laudatory. One reviewer judged the novel "impressive though oppressive"; another called it a "thick, daunting read, with no moral." The best praise that the *Sunday Times* reviewer could muster was that the novel was "decently written" and "not to be sneezed at." Other reviewers were derogatory: Styron's narrative "tends to sag," wrote one; Nat Turner was "never a credible figure," said another; Nat was "an entirely synthetic and contrived character," wrote a third. The two most bruising notices appeared in the two most visible places. Stephen Vizinczey, in the daily *Times* for May 4, pulled out all stops: "I doubt that it is possible to write a more harebrained, insensitive, not to say impertinent book about human suffering," he said. And an anonymous reviewer in the May 9 *Times Literary Supplement* (all *TLS* reviews during these years were published anonymously) attacked Styron for using the Nat Turner persona to narrate the novel. Styron's sense of history, wrote the reviewer, was "at a freshman level" and his meditating "no more profound than that of most talented novelists, even great ones." This reviewer criticized Styron most severely for mixing his own voice with Nat Turner's: "One wonders in the end," wrote the reviewer, "whether [Nat Turner] is anyone, or whether perhaps the author hasn't rolled back the gravestone and found the body arising in his novel to be no more or less than William Styron himself."

Styron was stung by these reviews, and he let his anger show in a letter to Tom Maschler: "It is as always a matter of supreme indifference to me if I am read in England or not," he wrote. "England is the only country in the world whose shallowness and smallness of spirit—that sniggering refusal to face up to what is serious and good—makes me enormously proud to be an American." Maschler's reaction is not recorded. To his credit, though, he had already taken steps to have *The Confessions of Nat Turner* defended. At Maschler's suggestion, a long rebuttal of the major reviews was written by the novelist Carlos Fuentes, a Mexican who had been educated in part in the United States and who now lived in London. His views were set forth in a letter to *The Times Literary Supplement,* published in its May 16 issue. Fuentes and Styron had met in 1964 and were on friendly terms; each admired the other's writing (Fuentes wrote in both English and Spanish), and the two men had similar political interests and convictions. Perhaps because of his transnational background, Fuentes was able to move outside the question of race and address Styron's novel as something else—a radical experiment in language:

> By choosing the first person singular, Styron is by no means trying to supplant or reproduce Nat Turner, but creates a completely new figure within a completely new construction, and is doing so, not through traditional techniques (Styron is neither Somerset Maugham nor Irving Stone) but, quite simply, through a creation of language. . . . The real meaning of *The Confessions of Nat Turner* must be sought, I believe, in its approach to language as the first of all master-slave relationships. . . . Well before rising up in arms against a given social system, Nat Turner has been in rebellion against the language on which that system is based. . . . [Styron] comes from the present to meet a man from the past who comes to meet him, and he bears not the gifts of a facile, reasonable, and finally philanthropic characterization so as to save Nat Turner, but the real drama of a culture and a language (Styron's) that have become as insufficient as those of any oppressed chattel. Through his masterful use of the first person, Styron achieves an encounter of two alien-

ations: that of the book's subject and that of the book's author. Both Nat Turner and William Styron, one through need, the other through excess, are displaced persons.

It pleased Styron to be defended (and understood) in this way. Still, the reception of *The Confessions of Nat Turner* in "perfidious Albion," as he called it in another letter to Maschler, stuck in his craw, even though sales of the Cape edition were reasonably healthy—some twelve thousand copies purchased by mid-August and a few thousand more in the months that followed.

Styron probably consoled himself with the hope that the French reception would be better. Maurice-Edgar Coindreau was already at work on the translation and was in correspondence with Styron, who was helping by identifying passages in the novel taken from the Bible and by explaining the southernisms and dialect usages in the text. Coindreau hoped to be finished by September; the work of translating, he reported, was "very exciting for the mind." For Styron this must have been reassuring; perhaps the worst of the negative reaction to his novel was over.

On June 5 Robert Kennedy was shot in Los Angeles; he died on June 6. Kennedy had just won the California primary and appeared likely to take the Democratic presidential nomination over Hubert Humphrey and Eugene McCarthy (whose run was losing momentum). Like most Americans, Styron was stunned by Kennedy's death; suddenly civil anarchy seemed quite close. Styron was asked to be an honorary pallbearer for Kennedy and stood vigil for several hours over Kennedy's coffin a few nights later in New York, at Saint Patrick's Cathedral.

The Confessions of Nat Turner was about to be attacked again. In early August, the Boston publisher Beacon Press issued a small book entitled *William Styron's Nat Turner: Ten Black Writers Respond.* The volume, edited by the African American historian John Henrik Clarke, brought together ten attacks on Styron's novel written by black academics, intellectuals, novelists, and journalists. Some of the attacks had appeared elsewhere already; others were published in this volume for the first time. The contributors were Lerone Bennett, Jr., Alvin F. Poussaint, Vincent Harding, John Oliver Killens, John A. Williams, Ernest Kaiser, Loyle Hairston, Charles V. Hamilton, Mike Thelwell, and Clarke himself.

The essays in *Ten Black Writers* are short, angry, and unforgiving. The two most probing analyses, by Harding and Thelwell, question Styron's understanding of black religion, language, and psychology. "Whose mind has he entered save his own?" asks Harding. "The whitened appropriation of our history," he adds, is "a total negation of our power and our truth." Thelwell writes: "Nat sounds like nothing so much as a conscious parody of the prose voice of James Baldwin, the Negro Mr. Styron knows best, or Faulkner at his least inspired." For Thelwell, Styron's novel is based on a "Freud, moonlight, and magnolia view of history." The other attacks in *Ten Black Writers* are much more intemperate; several are pitched at a near-hysterical level. For Bennett, Styron is "playing the 'new history' game of reviving Big Black Sambo." Poussaint condemns Styron's "white supremacist attitudes" and his "unconscious white racism." Killens, whose contribution is entitled "The Confessions of Willie Styron," charges that Styron "has not been able to transcend his southern-peckerwood background"; he is "like a man who tries to sing the blues when he has not paid his dues." For Williams, Styron has given the history of black and white people "another shot of Whitey-Serum." To Kaiser, Styron's novel "is a meditation all right and that of an unreconstructed southern racist." Hairston attacks Styron for making Nat Turner a "rogue-nigger"; Styron's slave-rebel is "guilty of nothing but unwittingly exposing his author's moral senility." And Hamilton charges that Styron has "manipulated and toyed with" a figure from black history. "Nat Turner is our hero, unequivocally understood," writes Hamilton. "He is a man who had profound respect and love for his fellow blacks and who respected black womanhood and held utter contempt for those white slavemasters who violated the purity and beauty of our black women."

To anyone educated to observe basic standards of logic and decorum, *Ten Black Writers* is an appallingly poor performance. Many of the essays are based on shaky scholarship, and most are flawed by emotionalism, some of it theatrical. The contributors, individually and severally, cannot decide whether to judge Styron's novel as history or fiction; sometimes it is treated as both simultaneously, within the same essay and even within individual paragraphs. Much of the writing is turgid, dense, and clotted. And yet for any student of that historical moment, the summer of 1968, *Ten Black Writers* is a fascinating and troubling document, suggestive of much that would follow in American public discourse over the next thirty years. Certain themes sound throughout the volume: Nat Turner belongs to black history; he cannot be interpreted by a white man, especially by a white southerner. African American history has been manipulated and corrupted by white writers; often the worst offenders have been white liberals, such as Styron. Black history is the territory, the property, only of people who have lived the black experience.

The attacks on the novel itself in *Ten Black Writers* follow these same lines of argument. The contributors charge that Styron has weakened and emasculated Nat Turner by making him contemplative and ambivalent. Nat's masturbatory fantasies about white women, and particularly about Margaret Whitehead, are ill timed, damaging, and psychologically invalid. The historical Nat Turner, they argue, almost certainly had a black wife; Styron has ignored her and has made his character celibate, onanistic, and latently homosexual. Nat Turner's Rebellion, contrary to Styron's belief, was only one among many slave revolts in the antebellum South. Styron has failed to capture the idioms of slave speech, and he cannot hope to penetrate the African American psyche. Styron's message toward the end of his novel—that black and white people must attempt to love and trust one another—is inadequate and naive.

Ten Black Writers had a lively press. At least two black reviewers who had originally written admiring reviews of Styron's novel were now moved to recant. Several white critics—chief among them Eliot Fremont-Smith, in a two-part essay in the August 1 and 2 *New York Times*—reconsidered their earlier praise for the book. Styron was also defended. Martin Duberman published an energetic counterattack entitled "Historical Fictions" in the August 11 issue of *The New York Times Book Review.* For Duberman *Ten Black Writers* was "a depressing volume" and an undeserved "assault" on Styron. "Blacks are entitled to their version of Turner," Duberman writes, "but let them not pretend that those versions are incontestably validated by the historical evidence." He continues: "What makes Styron a better historian than any of his critics is that he will not bury unpleasant evidence or minimize the complexities of past experience in order to serve some presumed contemporary need."

The longest and most telling refutation of *Ten Black Writers* was published by Eugene D. Genovese, a Marxist historian then at the University of Rochester who had spent most of his professional career studying the history of American slavery. Genovese's defense, entitled "The Nat Turner Case," appeared in *The New York Review of Books* for September 12. The chief focus of Genovese's rebuttal was the need for African American intellectuals, who were pressured greatly by the black-power movements of the time, to resist the temptation to manufacture history suitable to ideological requirements. "Revolutionaries do not need Nat Turner as a saint," writes Genovese; "they do need the historical truth of the Nat Turner revolt, its strength and its weakness." Genovese denies the claim that Nat Turner had been known and admired by past generations of blacks. No evidence exists, he argues, that "slaves and postslavery blacks kept alive a politically relevant legend of Nat Turner or of any other Southern slave leader." For Genovese, Styron has been faithful to the larger demands of history. "The novel is historically sound," he insists. "Styron takes liberties with fact, as every novelist does, but he does not do violence to the historical record."

Genovese defends Styron also against specific charges. He addresses the claims that Styron has emasculated Nat Turner, that he has pictured slavery as benign, that he has made Nat aspire to whiteness, that he has misunderstood slave religion, and that he has projected his own sexual fears and fantasies onto the relationship between Nat Turner and Margaret Whitehead. Genovese fears the effect of black-power movements on Negro historians because such movements demand "conformity, myth-making, and historical fabrication." For him the danger is obvious: "Until a people can and will face its own past, it has no future."

Styron did not respond in print to *Ten Black Writers,* but he did correspond privately with some of his friends, and his irritation showed in his letters. To Chalmers Davidson, a professor who had taught him English and history at Davidson, he wrote, "I am much more impressed by the cowardly acquiescence on the part of certain white writers to the black outrage over my book than I am by the black protest itself, which is largely infantile and which will eventually pass away." Some of his friends set down their reactions to *Ten Black Writers* in letters to Styron. The historian Arthur M. Schlesinger, Jr., who had studied the Nat Turner Rebellion, wrote: "They so desperately miss the point of everything you were trying to do. And, in attacking you for supposedly creating your own Nat Turner, they ignore the fact that very little is known historically about Nat Turner, that he must therefore by definition be semi-mythic and that their Nat Turner is therefore just as much an imagined figure as yours." Schlesinger found some of the assertions of Styron's critics to be flimsy: "Turner's marriage is not, of course, a 'fact' in any sense acceptable to historians; all the references to Nat Turner's wife, so far as I know, come thirty years after his execution. So too the Aptheker idea of a long series of slave revolts is pure mythology."

Styron had little time to brood over *Ten Black Writers,* though, for he was scheduled to travel to Chicago for the Democratic convention in August. He arrived there on the Tuesday before the convention began and immediately appeared before the Credentials Committee with the other delegate challengers from Connecticut to argue for more representatives for Eugene McCarthy. From the glazed, inattentive expressions on the faces of the committee members, however, it quickly became obvious to Styron that his appeal would be futile. After Styron had made his statement, the chairman of the committee, Governor Richard J. Hughes of New Jersey, said: "Thank you, Mr. Michener." Styron and the other three delegate challengers were denied seats at the convention.

Styron, however, stayed in Chicago for the convention itself. He had never seen the workings of American politics up close, and he was appalled over the next several days by what he observed. Chicago was crowded with yippies and other young protesters, and Mayor Richard Daley's police were out in force. The protests escalated: someone threw a stink bomb into the lobby of Styron's hotel, the Conrad Hilton, and the management attempted to neutralize the stench with aerosol deodorants, to disastrous effect. The resulting smell—"the fetor of methane mingled with hair spray," as Styron described it—seemed somehow to typify for him the odor of the American political scene.

Styron visited the convention floor once but spent much of his time in the streets, where he witnessed several beatings of demonstrators by the police. He also participated in a sit-in in Grant Park, a gathering as peaceful as a "Presbyterian prayer meeting," he later wrote in a report he published in *The New York Review of Books.* The Chicago police, however, moved in on the demonstrators and routed them from the park with tear gas. Styron described what had happened this way:

> Suddenly they were here, coming over the brow of the slope fifty
> yards away, a truly stupefying sight—one hundred or more of the po-

lice in a phalanx abreast, clubs at the ready, in helmets and gas masks, just behind them a huge perambulating machine with nozzles, like the type used for spraying insecticide, disgorging clouds of yellowish gas, the whole advancing panoply illuminated by batteries of mobile floodlights. . . . I had a quick sense of the medieval in juxtaposition with the twenty-first century or, more exactly, a kind of science fiction fantasy, as if a band of primitive Christians on another planet had suddenly found themselves set upon by mechanized legions from Jupiter.

The next day, with his eyes watering from more tear gas he had caught on the street, Styron stumbled into the Haymarket bar at the intersection of Michigan Avenue and Balbo Street. There, sitting with the Chicago journalist Studs Terkel, he witnessed the largest confrontation of the convention, a pitched battle between thousands of antiwar demonstrators and hundreds of blue-clad policemen. The scene was surreal: the clashes and beatings appeared as if in mime, for all noise was shut out from the bar by the sound-resistant plate-glass windows that looked out onto the street. In queasy fascination Styron and Terkel watched a "dumbshow of cops clubbing people to the concrete, swirling squadrons of people in Panavision blue and polystyrene visors hurling back the crowds, chopping skulls and noses while above me on the invincible TV screen a girl with a fantastic body enacted a comic commercial for Bic ballpoint pens, and the bartender impassively mooned over his daiquiris (once pausing to inquire of a girl whether she was over twenty-one), and the Muzak in the background whispered 'Mood Indigo.' "

Suddenly there was a shattering explosion as half a dozen bystanders were pushed through one of the plate-glass windows by the crush outside. Several demonstrators ran through the bar into the lobby of the hotel, pursued by a wedge of policemen. Terkel seized Styron's arm and told him that they needed to get out. Terkel knew the layout of the building (Styron never asked him how) and led the way down a nearby flight of stairs, through the bowels of the hotel, then back upstairs and out a back entry into an alley. Together they made their way to a Chinese restaurant in a safe zone and called for scotch. Even Terkel, who thought he had witnessed most kinds of police violence during his years as a reporter, was shaken.

Styron left Chicago in a hurry the next day, oppressed by a sense of gloom. Rational political process had failed spectacularly. Hubert Humphrey had been nominated, but after the debacle in the Chicago streets the Democratic party would have great difficulty casting a reassuring gloss over his candidacy. Humphrey would run in November against Richard Nixon, whose nomination by the Republicans was assured. Styron returned to Vineyard Haven and wrote his report for the September 26 *New York Review*—a bitter essay that he entitled "In the Jungle." He believed that the American people had been misled and betrayed.

In September and October Styron and Rose sought escape in a trip to Russia that they had agreed to take months before. They attended an Afro-Asian authors' conference sponsored by the Soviet writers' union; they were the only Western authors who had been invited. While in Moscow, Styron persuaded the poet Yevgeny Yevtushenko to make a public protest against the recent Soviet invasion of Czechoslovakia. Styron and Rose then traveled to Tashkent, where they heard troubling accounts of severe mistreatment of dissident writers by the Soviet government. Styron spoke out against these evils, and his remarks were reported in the international press. As a consequence, publication of *The Confessions of Nat Turner* in Russian, which had been scheduled for the following year, was canceled. He and Rose also had trouble exiting the country; they were told that their papers were not in order and that they could not leave. Only by convincing the border official that Styron was a writer, and showing the official a copy of a magazine containing a Russian translation of *The Long* March, were they allowed to depart.

On his way back to the States, Styron stopped off in Paris to see Jim and Gloria Jones for a few days. If anyone could sympathize with Styron over rough treatment from critics, it was Jones. The Styrons and Joneses frequently vacationed together now, and in most years they managed to visit back and forth once or twice. Jones filled Styron in on the student riots that had taken place in Paris that spring. Jones was writing a novel about the riots; it would be published in 1971 under the title *The Merry Month of May.* The door at 10, Quai d'Orléans (their residence now) was always open to Styron: "We enjoy having your sour visage floating above the whiskey bottle," wrote Jones in one invitation. The Jones apartment during these years was often crowded with Americans visiting Paris—writers, movie people, and others whom Jim and

Gloria Jones had befriended over the years. There were spaghetti suppers and all-night poker games and much drinking and talking. Sometimes Jones and Styron, to escape the crowd in the apartment, would walk the streets or sit together in a café talking. When their speculations and ruminations became too heavy, they had a method of clearing the air. One of them would look at the other and, with sophomoric fatuousness, utter this line: "Well . . . what does it all mean?" Then, after a suitable pause, they would crack up in helpless laughter. "What does it all mean, Jim?" "What does it all mean, Bill?"

From time to time during 1968, Styron had appeared on college campuses to give readings from *The Confessions of Nat Turner* and to answer questions from audiences about how and why he had written the novel. In February, for example, he had spoken at Smith College, sharing the platform with three historians of slavery. That occasion, like most of the others early in the year, was lively but cordial, with a good exchange of opinions. By the summer of 1968, however, some of the campus appearances had become confrontational, especially during the question-and-answer sessions that followed the readings. One of the most heated of these exchanges took place at Harvard at a lecture in Emerson Hall, late in July. Styron was taunted by a dashiki-clad black man and then heckled by other blacks in the audience. Nothing was accomplished in the session, and Styron thought for a time of canceling further public appearances until the controversy over his novel died down. "I feel like a combination of Theodore Bilbo and Lester Maddox," he confessed in a letter to William Blackburn. He decided, however, to fulfill those commitments he had made, not wishing to hide from his attackers.

By far the most volatile of these confrontations took place later in the year, on the evening of November 6, at a meeting of the Southern Historical Association in New Orleans. Styron appeared there on a panel with Robert Penn Warren and Ralph Ellison. C. Vann Woodward was the moderator; the title of the session was "The Uses of History in Fiction." Each of the three novelists on the panel had at some point in his career used historical data and personages in his fiction; the announced purpose of the session was to discuss, in the abstract, the fluctuating boundaries between fact and invention—a matter of concern to historians and fiction writers alike. The real occasion for the event, though, was the controversy over Styron's novel, and those who attended the session at the Jung Hotel expected to see fireworks. The session was packed, with latecomers required to stand.

In his opening comment Woodward set the agenda: "An historian stands in no less need of imagination than the novelist," he said. "If anything he needs rather more." Each novelist then delivered a prepared statement—Warren first, then Ellison, then Styron. Warren stressed the ambiguity of both history and fiction and discussed the differences between historical and literary insight. Ellison focused on the similarities between history and fiction: "They're both artificial," he said; "both are forms of literature." When Styron's turn came he cited previous novelists who had departed from the historical record: Scott, Stendhal, Tolstoy, Pushkin, Faulkner, and Warren himself. Styron then quoted, at some length, the Hungarian Marxist critic Georg Lukács, whose book *The Historical Novel* he had discovered only after writing *The Confessions of Nat Turner.* For Lukács, " 'The deeper and more genuinely historical a writer's knowledge of a period, the more freely will he be able to move about inside his subject and the less tied will he feel to individual historical data.' " Lukács thought that the historical novelist should try to capture " 'the great collisions, the great crises and turning-points.' " That statement struck an answering chord with Styron: "A writer's responsibility is not to the dead baggage of facts," he said, "but to the unfettering and replenishing power of his own imagination." Woodward and the panelists offered further comments, most of them centering on *The Confessions of Nat Turner.* Ellison, surprisingly, said that he had not read the novel. "Our house burned down so I didn't get to read it at first, and after the controversy I deliberately did not read it." Styron did not believe Ellison; he felt that Ellison was simply avoiding the necessity of taking sides. He and Ellison had been friends before the incident; afterward the relationship cooled and was never reestablished.

Then followed the question-and-answer period. Questions were immediately directed at Styron by two black men in the audience. After a confusing exchange over whether Nat Turner had a slave wife, the confrontation became ugly. The second of the two questioners spoke up: "Seeing as though calling historians liars tonight has been quite popular, I can remember that the last time I called you a liar, it became very bitter. It seems as though we confront each other from the North to the South. I met you in Massachusetts this summer, and now all the way down in New Orleans I'm here to call you a liar again." Ralph Ellison interrupted: "Which one of us, please?" he said. "I'm primarily concerned with Styron," said the man, who missed Ellison's irony. "I met him this summer at Harvard," he added. The questioner then followed with a meandering diatribe aimed at Styron. Here are his remarks:

> I think possibly we need to take a look at the revolutionary black figure, Nat Turner, to see what he actually represents to black people. I think when we talk about slavery and revolution that it has to be looked at from a psychiatric or a psychological viewpoint. Okay, we take a look at the ten blacks who responded to your book on *The Confessions of Nat Turner*. In this group we have C. V. Hamilton, we have Alvin Poussaint. These men have really delved into the thing; they have looked at it from a psychological viewpoint.
>
> I heard Warren say a few minutes ago that fact can destroy, that fact can be deadly. I contend that imagination and lying can also be deadly and can also destroy. Now let's take a look at this a bit further. First of all we see two major bases from which this book was written. We see some religious ties with Nat Turner—that he was a preacher or something, who had some vision about killing white folk. Secondly, I remember your statement that the white woman was a higher symbol or goal for the black man or the black slave—something that he looked up to and wanted and desired. Okay, I remember asking you that question up North, and I want you to tell these Southern whites this same thing. I want to know this: if the white woman was the symbol for Nat Turner to look up to and this was why he wanted sexual relations, and had all these desires, then, since that black woman was below the white man, what kind of image was she?

When his attacker paused, Styron countered: "Indeed you have haunted me. You're my *bête noir*, I'm afraid. I recall you from Harvard Summer School with terror." People who were present at the session remember that there was an enormous release of tension in the room when Styron spoke the words "*bête noir*," followed by an outburst of relieved, almost hysterical laughter. Styron then tried to answer several of the questions posed to him but was interrupted. The exchanges continued in the same vein as before; much heat was generated but no light. "Listen to me, will you please?" Styron says at one point, but communication does not improve. The exchanges go on, now very confusingly. Finally Styron gives up: "We're at an impasse, my friend," he says. "You ought to stop lying," says the questioner.

After the conference Styron decided to withdraw from the public stage for a time. He had become a target for abuse; confrontations such as this one accomplished nothing. He had begun to suspect that his novel had simply become an excuse for histrionic displays by his African American critics and, further, that a good many of them had not actually read the book. Styron was depressed by other developments as well: Richard Nixon had defeated Hubert Humphrey by a small margin, and the country now faced four years with a Republican in the White House. The riots in Chicago that summer were continuing to have repercussions; Styron would himself become involved by serving as a witness for Abbie Hoffman in the trial of the Chicago 7. Sales for the trade edition of *The Confessions of Nat Turner* had topped out at a bit over 170,000, but that news brought little cheer. The movie version looked as if it would be badly compromised or abandoned; the mail still yielded threatening letters; he was unable to write or even to think much about his next novel. Styron must have felt that, on balance, he had paid a heavy price for this particular success.

29

Interlude

IN JANUARY 1969 excerpts from *Les Confessions de Nat Turner* began to be serialized in Paris in *L'Express*. The book version of Coindreau's translation was published in mid-February to extended, respectful coverage in *Le Magazine Littéraire, La Quinzaine Littéraire, Réalité, Le Figaro Littéraire, La Croix, Le Monde, Le Devoir, Lettres et Arts, La Nouvelle Revue Française,* and *Le Nouvel Observateur.* Styron had been unable to come to Paris for publication day, however, and as a consequence only one interview of substance had appeared in the Paris press. Sales were not as high as Gallimard had expected; the history of slavery might not have been a compelling subject for French readers, though the philosophical cast of *Les Confessions* should certainly have suited them.

Styron was preoccupied that winter and spring with his father's welfare. Elizabeth Buxton was entering the last stages of a terminal malignancy, and Styron was worried about the strain on his father. She died in late August 1969 of complications from cancer. Styron's father was left alone in the house on Chesapeake Avenue in Newport News. Styron worried about what would happen to him, how he would now organize his days and live out the remainder of his life.

The controversy over *The Confessions of Nat Turner* continued to simmer in 1969 and into the early 1970s, though by now most of the action had filtered down to academic forums. Two collections of materials—comprising original sources, reviews, interviews, and critical essays—had been published as textbooks, for the novel was being taught in college classrooms. And a historian named Henry Irving Tragle published a book in 1971 entitled *The Southampton Slave Revolt of 1831,* a collection of original materials from the rebellion that included court records, newspaper accounts, and other documents and retellings. Tragle worked hard to present his documents as sources that Styron should have consulted (indeed, Styron had used many of them but had not said so in interviews); but Tragle was not able to demonstrate that *The Confessions of Nat Turner* had seriously violated the historical record. His principal demonstration was that the historical record was thin and that the Nat Turner story had been adapted by many other writers for their own purposes, which included religious admonitions and temperance lectures. The court records from Southampton County, reproduced by Tragle, proved to be especially sketchy and elliptical. Repeatedly and ironically Tragle was thrown back for his most reliable information on the same two sources that Styron had used— Thomas Gray's original "Confessions" and William S. Drewry's *The Southampton Insurrection.*

A lengthy and adroit defense of Styron entitled "History, Politics, and Literature: The Myth of Nat Turner," by Seymour L. Gross and Eileen Bender, was published in the *American Quarterly* for October 1971. Another kind of validation had already come to Styron by then in the form of the 1970 Howells Medal, awarded by the American Academy of Arts and Letters every five years for the best work of fiction published by an American writer during the preceding half-decade. Styron received the award for *The Confessions of Nat Turner* on May 26, 1970; he was diplomatic in his acceptance speech:

> It seems to me that in honoring my work this award underscores some certainties about the nature of literature. One of these is that a novel worthy of the name is not, nor ever has been, valuable because of its opinions; a novel is speculative, composed of paradoxes and riddles; at its best it is magnificently unopinionated. . . . This award therefore implies an understanding that a novel can possess a significance apart from its subject matter and that the story of a nineteenth-century black slave may try to say at least as much about longing, loneliness, personal betrayal, madness, and the quest for God as it does about Negroes or the institution of slavery. It implies the un-

derstanding that fiction, which almost by definition is a kind of dream, often tells truths that are very difficult to bear, yet—again as in dreams—is able to liberate the mind through the catharsis of fantasy, enigma, and terror.

By the time he received the Howells Medal, Styron knew that there would be no movie version of *The Confessions of Nat Turner.* Twentieth Century–Fox had decided to cut its losses and abandon work on the script and locations. The official reason given was that the studio had lost money on several recent failures and now needed a sure bet at the box office to recoup its finances. Styron believed to the contrary that Twentieth Century–Fox had simply feared bad publicity over his novel. James Earl Jones had been scheduled to star as Nat Turner and Sidney Lumet to direct the movie, but the producer, David L. Wolper, had capitulated to black pressure groups and had agreed not to use Styron's novel as his only source. The title of the project had been changed from "The Confessions of Nat Turner" to "Nat Turner." Styron had begun as an adviser for the film but had withdrawn when Wolper made these decisions. Now Fox had decided to shelve the project. Privately Styron was not sorry. He was certain that any cinematic version of his book would have been heavily compromised.

Styron was heartened, on the other hand, by the reports he received from Hope Leresche about the performance of *The Confessions of Nat Turner* in other countries. Contracts for translations into Spanish, Portuguese, Hungarian, Slovene, Czech, Danish, Finnish, Italian, Japanese, Dutch, Polish, Romanian, and Swedish had been signed. The Norwegian book-club edition, which he had assumed was a small-scale publication, had sold fully 96,000 copies—a remarkably large number for a country the size of Norway. Similar reports came in from other foreign publishers.

At about this time Styron began a new novel. He had decided to tackle a subject that had been on his mind for many years—warfare and the military mentality. He had a title that he liked: *The Way of the Warrior,* an approximate translation of the Japanese term *Bushido,* meaning the code of the feudal samurai, which stressed unquestioning loyalty and valued honor above life. Styron meant to question the concept of *Bushido;* certainly such an examination was in order in the early 1970s, with American military involvement in Vietnam continuing to divide the country. Styron's view was not one-dimensional; he himself had mixed feelings about the military. On the one hand he detested the oppressiveness and banality of day-to-day life in the service, but on the other he recognized that there was a quasi-religious element in military life that could be seductive.

The major character in this novel needed to embody this ambivalence. He should be a model soldier, brave and patriotic, but also needed to be intelligent and perceptive enough to recognize the flaws and dangers in the system. To play this role Styron created Lieutenant Colonel Paul Marriott, a career officer in the Marine Corps. We see Marriott through the eyes of an unnamed narrator whom Styron based on himself. For a setting Styron relied on his own experiences at Camp Lejeune in the spring and summer of 1951, when he had been called up for the Korean War. The narrator is a young novelist who has just reported for duty; he is reading galley proofs of his first novel while in training camp, just as Styron had done. There he is introduced to Paul Marriott, a heavily decorated battalion commander and a consummate warrior but also a man who knows literature and speaks French fluently. From this improbable mixture of characteristics Styron meant to create a complex man who, as the Korean conflict progressed, would begin to doubt his government and lose faith in his mission. Certainly such a story would have resonances during the ongoing Vietnam War.

Styron made a good start on the novel, calling on his recollections of Camp Lejeune. He worked on the manuscript intermittently for the next year but was unable to bring the story entirely into focus or to decide exactly what his theme should be. The writing itself he found pleasurable enough, but he was bothered by his inability to conceptualize a metaphor, a central statement, that would drive the narrative.

In early April 1970 Styron learned that Benjamin Reid, whom he had helped to save from execution in 1962, had escaped from prison. Reid had been scheduled for parole, and Styron had agreed to have him come to Roxbury and live with his family while reacclimating himself to society. The plan was for Reid, after a few weeks, to enroll as a special student at Trinity College. He was to begin his classes that summer. Styron had kept in touch with Ben Reid, exchanging letters with him from time to time, and he had been impressed by Reid's ability to express his ideas and by his genuine contrition. Styron and the others who had helped rescue Reid eight years before had high hopes that he could be rehabilitated.

Then early in April, just a few days before his scheduled release, Reid walked off from a work detail and fled into the woods near the state prison in Somers, Connecticut, where he had been confined. Reid eluded capture and made his way across the state border to Longmeadow, a suburb of Springfield, Massachusetts. He broke off a radio antenna from a car and sharpened it to use as a weapon. Then he entered a house and forced a woman and her two children to go with him in her family car. He made the woman drive the automobile aimlessly for most of a day; then he told her to stop in a deserted lot in a state park. There he raped her. He then had her drive him to a bus station in Holyoke, where he boarded a bus to New York, but he was seen by a prison official and arrested.

Styron was horrified. He knew that Reid's illogical flight almost surely stemmed from his fear of reentering normal life outside the prison, but he was shocked nonetheless by the abduction and rape and felt much guilt for what had happened to the woman and her children. His guilt was complicated and intensified by the relief he felt over not having had Reid come to live in his own home.

Styron's first impulse was to write Ben Reid off, to let him be locked up for life and to forget him. But Robert Satter, the attorney who had argued in Reid's behalf in 1962, overcame his own disgust and sense of betrayal and once more gave Reid legal and moral support in his subsequent trial. Styron, after thought, did the same, finding himself unable to turn his back completely on Reid. For the abduction and rape Ben Reid received a sentence of ten to fifteen years in the Massachusetts state prison. Styron continued to write letters to him and to talk to him from time to time on the telephone. In these awkward conversations Reid spoke with great feeling of his regret and remorse, and Styron—despite many misgivings—believed him.*

---

*Styron has taken an interest also in other prisoners, helping them appeal their cases or fight against forced confessions. Among these men are William A. Maynard, a friend of James Baldwin's who was falsely accused of murder; James Blake, a career criminal who had considerable talent as a writer; Peter Reilly, a Connecticut teenager who was pressured into confessing to a murder that he could not have committed; Shabaka Sundiata Waglini, wrongly convicted of murder and an in-

Styron continued to work on *The Way of the Warrior* through 1970 and most of 1971. The opening sections of the novel were published in the September 1971 issue of *Esquire* as "Marriott the Marine," and *Esquire* agreed to publish an excerpt from the second part of the novel, once Styron completed it. At this point, however, Styron seems to have lost his direction on the narrative. A section of the manuscript—the only copy of this particular part—was stolen from him in the Port Authority Terminal in New York City as he waited to catch a bus back to Connecticut. It is symptomatic of Styron's dissatisfaction with what he had been writing that he was not particularly upset by the loss. Later he joked about it, imagining the look on the thief's face when he found the briefcase full only of penciled sheets of paper.

As a change of pace Styron decided to try his hand at writing for the stage. He was urged to do so by Robert Brustein, then the dean of the Yale drama school. Styron had by now become friendly with his neighbor Arthur Miller and went over to Miller's house from time to time to use his Thermo-fax machine. The two men talked sometimes about the differences between writing prose fiction and drama dialogue. Miller maintained that drama was a less constricted form: freed from the necessity of creating settings or describing action, the writer could simply listen to his characters and write down what they had to say.

Styron tried the drama form and at first did find it liberating. "What a thrill to be freed of those endless descriptions of sunsets!" he wrote to William Blackburn (echoing Somerset Maugham). He began writing a play and by the summer of 1972 had produced a complete script entitled *In the Clap Shack*. The story line was based on his experiences as a recruit at Parris Island in early 1945. The hero, Private Wallace Magruder, lands in the base urological ward and endures the nightmarish regimen that Styron had gone through. Eventually Magruder is told that he only has trench mouth and is set free, but not before he has

---

mate of death row in Florida; Eddie Bunker, a thief who taught himself to write in prison and then went on to a successful career as an actor, novelist, and screenwriter; Richard Lapointe, a mentally deficient man from whom a false confession was extracted; and Mumia Abu-Jamal, a newspaperman and radio journalist convicted of murder and sentenced to death in a trial badly flawed by errors in judicial procedure.

crossed the path of an inhumane, judgmental doctor, named Glanz, who pries with ill-concealed curiosity into his sexual past.

In the Clap Shack was staged by the Yale Repertory Theatre on December 15, 1972. The one significant review, by the theater critic Clive Barnes in the December 17 *New York Times,* was unfavorable. Styron had hoped to see the play performed in the city, perhaps in an Off-Broadway venue, but no one seemed interested in producing it. He therefore decided to publish *In the Clap Shack* in book form, and Random House issued an edition in June 1973. Though the play did not succeed onstage, it is an important piece of writing in Styron's oeuvre. The most significant of the characters is neither Magruder nor the nefarious Dr. Glanz but is instead Lorenzo Clark, a syphilitic black man incarcerated on the ward. In his bitter nihilism and sneering animosity toward whites, Clark functions as a commentary on what Styron believed might happen to the Negro in American society. Clark will not allow himself to be treated as a human being; he revels in paranoia and victimhood. He dies toward the end of the play, destroyed more by the toxin of hatred than by the spirochetes that have invaded his body.

Styron also tried collaborating with two of his friends. He and George Plimpton made a stab at writing a play together (neither can now remember what the script was to have been about), but they found that they did not work easily together. Plimpton came out to Roxbury one Saturday in November to begin the script; Styron made elaborate preparations, gathering yellow pads and sharpening pencils, but once they sat down to work Plimpton became impatient with Styron's ruminations about how each line of dialogue should read. Styron would not move on to the next line until the previous one suited him. The two men put a page or two down on a yellow pad, then Plimpton became distracted and wandered off to another part of the house. He turned on the television set and began watching a football game. That was the end of the collaboration.

Styron and John Marquand had better results. During the summer of 1973, at the Vineyard, they together wrote a screenplay entitled "Dead!" The collaboration went smoothly, and both men enjoyed the work. "It was like playing tennis with someone who has terrific strokes," Marquand remembered. "Your own game goes up a few notches." The script was based on the notorious murder of Albert Snyder, who was strangled in March 1927 by his wife, Ruth Snyder, and her lover, Judd Gray. Both Ruth Snyder and Judd Gray were convicted and sentenced to death; she became the first woman to die in the electric chair in the United States. A New York *Daily News* reporter covering the execution at Sing Sing prison strapped a small camera to his leg and contrived to photograph Ruth Snyder just as the switch was thrown. The photo appeared on the front page of the *Daily News* beneath the headline "Dead!"—with the exclamation point italicized. Hence the title of Styron and Marquand's screenplay. For background the two men relied on newspaper accounts of the court trials and on Judd Gray's death-house memoir, *Doomed Ship* (1928). They also used H. L. Mencken's "A Good Man Gone Wrong," a tongue-in-cheek review of *Doomed Ship* published in *The American Mercury* for February 1929.

"Dead!" is an exercise in black comedy. The banal dialogue between Ruth Snyder and Judd Gray is hilarious in a very dark way when juxtaposed against the plans for homicide that they are laying. "Momsie, you're bending me to your will!" cries Judd as Ruth works on him, persuading him to assist in the murder of her husband. "Did you get the red bandanas? And the Wop newspaper?" Ruth queries. "They're for our alibi. . . . It was the work of Italian anarchist burglars who broke into the house to steal my jewelry. They were big men with black mustachios like da Woppas—Sacco, Vanzetti—and they left a lot of telltale clues."

Acted and filmed in the proper manner, "Dead!" might have become a cult classic, either as a television production or a Hollywood film. But Styron and Marquand (quite surprisingly) did not know that the story of Ruth Snyder and Judd Gray had already been fictionalized by James M. Cain in his novel *The Postman Always Rings Twice,* nor did they know of the 1946 film version of that book, starring John Garfield and Lana Turner. Neither had ever read Cain's book or seen the movie. (The remake of *Postman* with Jack Nicholson and Jessica Lange would not appear until 1981.)

Styron's agent, Don Congdon, showed the script for "Dead!" to several production companies and got some nibbles but received no firm offers to produce. To help things along, Styron and Marquand published the script in *Esquire;* it appeared there in December 1973—and brought Styron a fan letter from Theodor Geisel (Dr. Seuss). Several television and movie production companies looked at "Dead!" over the next few years, often paying for fixed-time options on the script, but the

screenplay was never put into production. To judge from the correspondence in the files of Congdon's literary agency, many of these pro-
ducers did not recognize "Dead!" as black comedy. They wanted to take
it seriously.

In March 1973, Styron had a comic experience of a different kind.
He learned that he had been elected to an alumnus membership in the
Duke chapter of Phi Beta Kappa. This amused him, inasmuch as he
had hardly been a standout student at the university. The honor also
pleased him, though: he had begun to feel warmly toward Duke; and
the university, proud of his achievements, had begun to invite him
down from time to time to give lectures and participate in symposia.
The library asked him to begin placing his publications and literary papers in their rare books and manuscripts departments. The curators
John Sharpe and Mattie Russell mounted an extensive exhibition of his
manuscripts, proofs, first editions, translations, and other materials in
April 1976; Styron enjoyed the exhibit enough to visit it twice, the second time bringing Rose and Tommy down with him to see the cases of
Styroniana.

During these years Rose was changing her life. She was not entirely
fulfilled by her roles as wife, mother, and mistress of the house. Part of
the time she reveled in those duties, knowing that she was good at them,
but she also now began to seek other outlets for her energies and abili-
ties. One possible avenue was politics, but like her husband she was dis-
enchanted for the time being with the Democratic party. Nixon had
been reelected to the presidency in November 1972; the Watergate scandal had broken the following spring; Washington seemed corrupt beyond expression. Rose did not want to hold an elective office. She
needed freedom to move about and make things happen in her own
way.

Another outlet was poetry: she began now to devote more time to her
own writing and assembled a strong collection, entitled *Thieves' Afternoon,* which she published with Viking Press in 1973. The dedication
page reads "for Bill," and many of the poems seem addressed to him.
Thieves' Afternoon is divided into two sections; the poems in the first
section, entitled "Chansonnier," show tension, puzzlement, a desire to
reach the person to whom they are addressed:

I find
constantly your eyes,
seeing in their darkness now only
lightning, my own dreams.

Oh if I could
I'd catch their perilous light,
their schemes
and hold them,
keep us safe tonight,
abandoning the angelic orders.

In other poems the speaker is elusive:

Pursue me
if you've time
or the nonsense to care.
I won't count on your coming.

Others look back:

. . . for it is Rome and I am
radiant, twenty, fresh from luck,
your love, and once more
mistress of the dark.

The poems in the second section of *Thieves' Afternoon,* entitled "Islands of Childhood," are less introspective, more focused on nature and its power to sustain. Many of these poems seem to have been written in early hours on the Vineyard:

Stay as the morning, island,
a changing song and sky
a lover, a deceiver
and my life goes skimming by

in stormclouds and a turning wind
fresh rain and spits of foam
the bay a sudden topaz
and a rowboat coming home.

The forum that appealed most to Rose, however, was in the area of human rights. She had been translating the work of dissident Russian poets into English for publication; this had put her into contact with many of these literary rebels, whose writings had been suppressed in the Soviet Union. Some of these poets had also been imprisoned in the gulags. Rose responded deeply to their plight, finding herself consumed by a desire to help. She therefore began now to work for Amnesty International, becoming very quickly one of its most active members. Rose's talents—her great energy, her contacts, her ability to organize, and her nerve—served her well here. She thought nothing of putting some money in her pocket, packing a few clothes, and flying to Chile or South Africa or Northern Ireland. There, with other activists like herself, she confronted dictators and heads of secret police to demand information about political prisoners or to investigate acts of torture and murder. Her weapon was openness: most of these men feared exposure in the international press, for such exposure would make it difficult for leaders in other countries to deal with them.

Some of the work was genuinely dangerous. In January and February 1974, Rose and Susanna went to Santiago, Chile, to investigate reports of political imprisonments and torture by the men of General Augusto Pinochet, the dictator who had seized power the previous September from the government headed by Salvador Allende. Rose brought Susanna, then eighteen years old, because she spoke Spanish well and could act as a translator. Rose knew that violations of human rights were taking place in Chile but did not know how profound and violent they were. Once in Santiago she found out: through the underground church network known as the Vicaria, and from prisoners' wives who met with her, she collected evidence of numerous violations—information about the whereabouts and condition of prisoners, and details about tortures and murders. Each day she and Susanna went shopping and sightseeing, as cover, but Pinochet's police were not deceived. Men in blue taxicabs followed Rose and Susanna everywhere; soon the women came to recognize the faces of these men, for they made no particular effort to conceal what they were doing. Rose was warned by a Chilean priest that she and Susanna were under suspicion. Their hotel room was ransacked one afternoon while they were out. It was clear to Rose that Pinochet did not particularly care about his image in the international community and that he would not hesitate to detain her and Susanna, or do worse. The two women therefore took the lists of prisoners and the other documents that had been given to them, stitched them inside their underwear, and booked a flight to leave the country.

On the day they were to depart from Santiago, Rose was told at the hotel that their tickets had been changed to another airline. An excuse about overbooking was given. This made Rose suspicious. She and Susanna had been scheduled to make a stop in Lima; now they were told that the stop would not be necessary. Rose feared that something would happen to her and Susanna on the new flight; perhaps the plane would make an unannounced stop elsewhere in Chile, and they would be taken off, questioned, and searched. Rose therefore bribed a bellboy to fetch her original ticket from the hotel office. Then she wrote out a postcard to Teddy Kennedy, telling him to meet her at the terminal in New York, as they had planned. She gave the postcard to the desk clerk at the hotel, then watched from a distance as he read the message and conferred with the manager. The message was a fabrication: Rose hoped that the card would be passed along to Pinochet's men; perhaps the Kennedy name would make them reluctant to detain her and Susanna, if that was their aim. (Kennedy had been especially critical of the Pinochet regime, calling in Congress for cessation of U.S. foreign aid to Chile.) At the airport, with the documents still sewn inside their undergarments, they decided to get in line to be searched by a male guard, guessing that he would be less thorough in his attentions than the female guard in the other line. This proved to be true; the documents were not detected.

On the airplane Rose and Susanna took their assigned seats and noticed, sitting next to them, a man who they were sure had been following them earlier in the week. Rose feared that this man might attempt something—she was not sure what. All during the flight to Lima, she and Susanna chattered brightly, like tourists, about their shopping and sightseeing. Once they had landed at the Lima airport, the two women left the airplane and went into the ladies' room in the terminal, where they stayed until their airplane had departed. Then they located another flight heading for New York City and booked tickets on it immediately. The suspicious seatmate was not in evidence; they took off a few minutes later. They arrived in New York without incident, but their luggage, on the original plane, was never returned to them. After landing they unstitched the documents from their undergarments and turned them over to Amnesty, which processed them for a speech given to the United Nations Human Rights Commission a few days later.

Such tales of derring-do were fascinating to Styron, though they also made him uneasy. He feared that Rose, with her gutsy stubbornness, might someday bring real harm on herself. He also admired her nerve, however, and in some ways she began to play Maud Gonne to his W. B. Yeats. Rose's political convictions were very similar to Styron's—in fact, these beliefs were one of the strongest bonds between them—but he could not imagine playing as active a role in public as she did in her work for Amnesty. His weapon was his pen. He would turn it to many causes over the next two decades, but it would be his place now increasingly to stay in Roxbury or at the Vineyard while she traveled in her human rights work.

For Styron this was a distinct shift in his role within the family, and at first he did not particularly like it. Soon, though, he discovered compensations. He had always liked to fool around in the kitchen and fairly frequently had prepared a meal. He still had his knack for fried chicken, and he could bake a Southside Virginia ham to perfection. Now he began to study the culinary arts seriously and to bring off some quite ambitious dinners, sometimes only for himself and his family, sometimes for guests as well.

It was easier now to purchase good meats, vegetables, and other ingredients in and around Roxbury. When he and Rose had first moved there in the mid-1950s, the pickings at local grocery stores had been limited, but recently the shopkeepers had learned to stock venison and game birds and fresh seafood brought from the shore. Other ingredients Styron secured in bulk on his trips to New York. Once or twice a week now he would stage a meal. His children remember him as being something of a martinet in the kitchen, fussy about temperatures and spices and cooking times, but he let them help with the stirring and serving, and the results were good.

Styron came to know his children better during these years. The first three were older now, and he discovered much that he could talk with them about. Susanna was a typical senior child, adventurous and strong-willed. She had an affinity for languages and wrote well. She graduated from high school in the spring of 1971, at the age of sixteen. She took a year off from her schooling and traveled, then entered Yale in the fall of 1972. Polly was a good horsewoman, though sometimes this worried Styron; a few years earlier she had taken a nasty fall and had spent time in the hospital with a serious head injury. Her best talent was for the dance; tall and supple, she moved beautifully and was not averse to hard practice. Tom, now in his early teens, was independent and private; he liked electronic gadgets and complicated games; he would soon discover girls; like his mother he played a good game of tennis.

Perhaps the closest relationship that Styron developed during these years was with Alexandra, the youngest child. Rose was often traveling, the three older children were in school or pursuing their activities, and this left Styron and Al together in the house. Sometimes he was gruff with her when she was noisy or when she watched too much television, but she was a spunky child and barked back at him, asserting her point of view. It became a game for them to scare each other; sometimes Al would plot for half a day in order to pop out of a cupboard or closet at the right moment and spook the wits out of her father. In quieter moments he liked to read to her or occasionally to play board games. He also trained her, when she was still very young, to operate a complicated uncorking device that he kept to open bottles of wine at dinner parties. He taught her to read wine labels and to identify the various vintages stored in the cellar. She became his wine steward at parties, and she took the duty seriously. Friends remember that she would discharge her assignments with great gravity, fetching the right bottles from the basement, bringing them to the table, uncorking them, and serving the guests.

Styron's worries about his father had dissipated. After a proper period of mourning, his father had begun to move about in Newport News and Hampton, occupying himself by attending concerts and church functions and by doing genealogical research. At this point, romance reentered his life. He had been on a trip to Florida, attending a convention in Miami, and on impulse had telephoned Eunice Edmundson, the woman he had loved and lost so many years before, in 1914, when she had chosen to marry Greene Johnston, a man with better prospects. W. C. Styron had known of her whereabouts; she and Johnston had established themselves in Tallahassee, where he became a successful lawyer and state comptroller in the 1940s and 1950s. She had had a satisfying career as a high school English teacher. W. C. Styron had checked on her quietly from time to time in the intervening decades but had never contacted her. He knew that she and Johnston had had two children and had adopted another child, and that their marriage had been a good one. Johnston had died in 1966, and Eunice was now living as a widow.

W. C. Styron telephoned Eunice and paid her a visit. They spent a long afternoon talking about their lives since 1914. They continued to see each other in the months that followed and found themselves falling in love. This was a passionate affair that went far beyond smiles and hand-holding. The two old people soon decided to marry. Styron sent the details to William Blackburn: "My father," he wrote, "is planning at the age of 81 to take unto himself a wife. . . . She—who is 76—calls him 'Dynamite' and he refers to her as 'this girl I've been seeing.' " The two were wed in January 1971 in Goldsboro, North Carolina, Eunice's hometown. She had inherited a comfortable brick house in Goldsboro; they would stay and live there permanently. For William Styron these were good developments. He was immensely pleased to think that his father might find some love and contentment in what would probably be the last chapter of his life.

30

Sophie's Choice

B Y THE SUMMER OF 1973 Styron had all but ceased to work on *The Way of the Warrior.* He had lost the thread of the narrative and was finding it nearly impossible to make headway with the manuscript. He was at the Vineyard with his family; it was a fine, busy time for Rose and the children, but he was introspective and fractious, troubled about his difficulties in writing and inclined to avoid everyone but his closest friends.

One morning early that summer, however, Styron literally awoke to a vision. He had been dreaming over the past several nights of Sophie, the Polish Catholic survivor of Auschwitz whom he had known briefly in Brooklyn in the summer of 1949. As he later described it, he woke that morning and lay in bed, staring at the door of a closet in his and Rose's bedroom. He saw the word "Sophie" on the door. He was still partly dreaming, perhaps, but his mind felt preternaturally alert. It came to him then that he must write a novel about this woman. "Sophie imposed herself upon me," he later said.

The metaphor that came to Styron that morning, and which he followed throughout the composition of the narrative, was taken from two books: Olga Lengyel's *Five Chimneys* and Hannah Arendt's *Eichmann in Jerusalem.* Olga Lengyel's book he had read many years before, not long after returning to Duke from the Marines. Olga Lengyel was a Hungarian who had been sent to Auschwitz along with her two

children, a boy and a girl, and her mother. Her book, issued in 1947 by
Ziff-Davis, was one of the first accounts of the Nazi death camps to be
published in the United States. In the book she told of how she had unwittingly sent her son to his death. She had thought that she would
save him from hard labor if she understated his age to the guards on the
train platform at Auschwitz. In doing so, however, she caused him to
be sent directly to the gas chambers, as all very young children were. He
had gone with her mother, who was also chosen for execution. Later her
daughter died in the camp as well. The book she wrote from these experiences, eerily unemotional in tone, affected Styron deeply when he
read it in 1947. Like most Americans at that time, he was only beginning to learn about the horrors of the extermination camps. He remembered years later that he had been unable to sleep for several nights
after reading *Five Chimneys.* The memory of the book had stayed with
him over the next twenty-five years.

The other book on which he drew for this metaphor was Hannah
Arendt's *Eichmann in Jerusalem,* an account of the trial of Adolf Eichmann and a controversial exploration of the behavior of the inmates at
Auschwitz and the other camps. From Arendt's book Styron recollected a story of a Gypsy woman who had been forced, on the platform
at Auschwitz, to choose which one of her two children would live and
which one would die. "That struck me between the eyes," Styron said.
"I suddenly realized that this had to be the metaphor for the most horrible, tyrannical despotism in history, that this was a new form of evil,
an evil so total that it could cause a woman to murder one of her own
children."

Styron decided that morning to put aside *The Way of the Warrior*
and to begin this new novel. Soon a working title came to him: "Sophie's Choice, A Memory." The title alludes to several choices Sophie
must make in the story—for or against anti-Semitism, for or against the
resistance movement, and eventually for her own life or her death. The
central choice, which Sophie makes at Auschwitz between her two children, would symbolize the haphazard cruelty of the death camps and
would be revealed, Styron thought, only with great difficulty by his central character, after the narrative had progressed quite far.

Styron now had several choices to make himself. The first was how
to narrate his novel. The natural decision was to create a quasi-
autobiographical character, patterned on himself when he had lived in

Flatbush in 1949. This fictional second self, he decided, would resemble him in many ways and would narrate the novel in retrospect, as an older writer, taking a long view back across his literary career. What would he call this character? What would his name be? Styron wanted a name similar to his own but could think of nothing satisfactory, so for the time being he left the narrator unnamed. Several days later, having already set down twenty or thirty pages of manuscript, Styron was pacing on the front lawn at his Vineyard Haven home, revolving some possibilities for names in his mind. Polly, then fifteen, asked him what he was thinking about, and he told her that he needed a name for his narrator. "What did they call you when you were young?" she asked. Styron said that most people had called him Billy. At Christchurch he had been Sty. At Davidson, though, some of his friends had called him Stinky. "Call him Stingo," said Polly, who had had a friend at camp one summer with that nickname. Styron liked the suggestion. He thought about it for the rest of that day and slept on it that night. In the morning he decided that he still liked it. During his work stint that afternoon, he added a page to the manuscript (beginning with the words "Call me Stingo," in the Melvillian manner) and gave his narrator a name and a little more background. Then he pushed on.

The early parts of the novel were amusing to write. Styron gave play to his gift for irony, and he enjoyed recalling his time as a bored employee of McGraw-Hill, which he at first called McGee-Dale in the manuscript. He also invented a name for Edward Aswell, calling him Carl Asbury initially, but later he shifted to The Weasel, a near anagram of Aswell's surname. At about this point Styron decided to drop the McGee-Dale subterfuge and to call McGraw-Hill by its actual name. The firm, he thought, could probably stand a little direct criticism.

Styron's narrative technique began to take on complexity as it developed in the early sections of the manuscript. In Stingo one begins to see a blending of two voices in a single narrator, a figure who can be seen simultaneously as Styron and not-Styron. Stingo seems to exist in a parallel but independent universe—one that mirrors our own very closely but not identically. Stingo's voice is reflective, relaxed, digressive, self-possessed, humorous, meditative, informed, and engaged. It is also more transparently autobiographical and didactic than any voice Styron had ever written in.

The character can be seen as a culmination of several other charac-

ters from Styron's earlier writings. Stingo, who assesses dull manuscripts at a New York publishing house and inhabits a dreary cell in a
rooming house at night, is a successful reimagining of the weak Marcus
Bonner character from "Inheritance of Night," the aborted first version
of *Lie Down in Darkness.* Stingo also resembles Lieutenant Thomas
Culver from *The Long March:* he is an observer of someone who has
faced a moral dilemma and made a choice, though he hesitates to make
choices and take action himself. The older Stingo resembles Nat Turner
as well; he reviews the past, reconsiders his behavior, and ruminates on
its moral implications.

Of all the correspondences with Styron's earlier characters, however,
the one with Peter Leverett from *Set This House on Fire* is closest.
Stingo, like Peter, is an observer, given to introspection and self-doubt
but acutely alive to those around him. The methods of narration in the
two novels are very similar. Stingo, like Peter, begins his narrative in
the conventional first-person mode but quickly becomes fascinated by
the mysterious Sophie Zawistowska, just as Peter becomes intrigued
by Cass Kinsolving. Stingo carries the narrative in the earliest parts of
the book, just as Peter does, but in the later sections of both novels Styron begins to merge the voices and consciousnesses of his two major
characters. In *Sophie's Choice,* Sophie begins to tell her story in her own
voice and accent, just as Cass does in *Set This House on Fire.* But Styron cannot permit her to carry the narrative for very many pages: for all
its charm her broken English is a distraction, and Styron cannot give
her the vocabulary he gave to Nat Turner. So Stingo resumes the narrative in the first person, but like Peter Leverett he is now granted powers
of insight and can tell the reader what Sophie is thinking. Stingo is always careful, though, to document himself, telling us that he knows
what he knows because Sophie revealed it to him. One never asks,
"How does Stingo know this?" Styron explained the technique this way:
"If each voice is convincing in its own mode, then you can start fluidly
interchanging them. . . . There's no strain on the reader's imagination,
and because you're still using the first-person narrator, the Stingo voice,
you get an added dimension—authenticity."

This retrospective quasi-autobiographical voice, Styron discovered,
had some useful advantages. He could, for example, answer critics of
The Confessions of Nat Turner in the pages of *Sophie's Choice,* but he
could let Stingo offer the response. The older Stingo is the author of a

novel, entitled *These Blazing Leaves,* about Nat Turner's slave rebellion in Virginia in 1831. Stingo has been attacked by black critics for daring to take on the voice of a slave and for having had that slave fantasize about a white woman. Using Stingo's fictional voice Styron could respond to his critics, in the pages of *Sophie's Choice,* more acerbically than he might have done otherwise. "What the hell," muses the older Stingo at one point; "once a racist exploiter always a racist exploiter." He was also free to reminisce about the creation of *Lie Down in Darkness,* here called *Inheritance of Night,* and to do so with the advantage of fictional license. Allusions to his real life in *Sophie's Choice* were quite conscious on Styron's part; they were efforts to connect his novel in a postmodernist way (though he would resist that term) to his previous writings and career, and to his public persona.

An important advantage of the Stingo voice was that Styron could use it to document his sources in this novel in a way that he had not been able to do in *The Confessions of Nat Turner.* In recounting Sophie's story and in attempting, as an older man, to learn what had happened to her, Stingo has read widely in the literature of the Holocaust. Thus in the narrative he can give authors and titles and can discuss his sources—the memoirs of Rudolf Höss, for example, or the fiction of Tadeusz Borowski, or the writings of Bruno Bettelheim and George Steiner, Olga Lengyel and Hannah Arendt, Simone Weil and Richard L. Rubenstein, Jean-François Steiner, Eugen Kogon, André Schwarz-Bart, and Elie Wiesel. With this method, Styron avoided including a statement about his sources; he did not even need to write an Author's Note such as the one he had prepared for *The Confessions of Nat Turner.* Instead he could document within the text itself. Throughout the composition of *Sophie's Choice* Styron continued to read accounts of death-camp survivors and historical analyses of Hitler's final solution. The books stacked beside his manuscript in Vineyard Haven in September 1973 give some idea of the range of that reading: in addition to Lengyel's *Five Chimneys* there was André Schwarz-Bart's *The Last of the Just,* Ota Kraus and Erich Kulka's *The Death Factory,* Leon Poliakov's *Harvest of Hate,* and Primo Levi's *If This Is a Man.*

In the spring of 1974 Styron learned that *Lie Down in Darkness* had been chosen as one of the books on the reading list in English for the prestigious national *Agrégation* in France, a comprehensive examination taken by all candidates for teaching positions in French universities. Styron was the only living author on the list and only one of three American writers—the other two being Hawthorne and Poe. (The British authors were Shakespeare, Ben Jonson, John Donne, James Thomson, and Thomas Carlyle.) As a consequence of his selection, Styron was invited to come to France in April and tour several universities where he would give readings and meet with students.

Styron decided that this was a good opportunity to see the death camp at Auschwitz. As with *The Confessions of Nat Turner,* he wanted to visit the locale about which he would write. He made the trip in late March, traveling first to Warsaw and Crakow, then to Auschwitz by train, for he wished to arrive there just as Sophie would have. "I spent a long day there," Styron remembered. "A horrible visit, beyond anything believable. Several days later in the plane from Warsaw to Vienna I was still in a state of complete emotional shock, as in a coma."

At a bookshop near the ruins of the camp he purchased two volumes in English, both published by the museum at Auschwitz. These books would prove useful to him, and he read and annotated them extensively. The first was entitled *Amidst a Nightmare of Crime: Notes of Prisoners of Sonderkommando Found at Auschwitz* (1973), a collection of notes that had been kept by Auschwitz prisoners and had been found when the camp was liberated. From this volume Styron learned details, many of them inexpressibly horrible, about daily prison life at Auschwitz. The notes also revealed a great deal about the functioning of the gas chambers and the crematoria. The other volume, titled *KL Auschwitz Seen by the SS* (1972), was a collection of three memoirs written by the Germans Rudolf Höss, Pery Broad, and Johann Paul Kremer. Of these the account by Höss was of greatest interest to Styron, and he read it with sick fascination, remarking especially the peculiar turn of mind in Höss that made him seek sympathy for his own great administrative problems in operating the extermination center. Höss's memoir gave Styron information about the many non-Jewish prisoners at Auschwitz—the Poles, Hungarians, Czechs, Ukrainians, Russians, and Gypsies. The book also helped Styron form a conception of Höss, who would appear in *Sophie's Choice* as a character.

After his visit to Auschwitz, Styron went to France and made his tour of the universities at Nantes, Paris, Rennes, and Bordeaux. The attention he received was gratifying but the pace was exhausting, and he was glad when the tour was completed. Back in Roxbury that spring and later in June at the Vineyard, Styron could not stop thinking about his trip to Auschwitz. The result was a short, evocative essay that he wrote and published under the title "Auschwitz's Message" on the op-ed page of *The New York Times* for June 25, 1974. The essay begins this way:

> Springtime at Auschwitz. The phrase itself has the echo of a bad and tasteless joke, but spring still arrives in the depths of southern Poland, even at Auschwitz. Just beyond the once electrified fences, still standing, the forsythia puts forth its yellow buds in gently rolling pastures where sheep now graze. The early songbirds chatter even here, on the nearly unending grounds of this Godforsaken place in the remote hinterland of the country. At Birkenau, that sector of the Auschwitz complex that was the extermination camp for millions, one is staggered by the sheer vastness of the enterprise stretching out acre upon acre in all directions. The wooden barracks were long ago destroyed, but dozens of the hideous brick stablelike buildings that accommodated the numberless damned are still here, sturdily impervious, made to endure a thousand years.

The description continues. Styron is surprised to learn that there is a small hotel for tourists who visit Auschwitz. "What does the guest really order for breakfast?" he wonders. "A room with *which* view does one request?"

Styron used this essay to reflect on issues of anti-Semitism and Christian guilt. He also discussed those victims at the death camps who were not Jewish. "Of many origins but mainly Slavs—Poles, Russians, Slovaks, other—they came from a despised people who almost certainly were fated to be butchered with the same genocidal ruthlessness as were the Jews had Hitler won the war." Thus Styron cannot accept anti-Semitism as the only explanation for the death camps. "Its threat to humanity transcended even this," he writes. "If it was anti-Semitic it was also anti-Christian. And it attempted to be more final than that, for its ultimate depravity lay in the fact that it was anti-human. Anti-life."

Styron knew that he was on dangerous ground here. He was a southern-born Gentile, with no firsthand knowledge of the death camps, venturing to write about a historical event that he had learned about primarily from his reading. Rose was Jewish, but her upbringing had not been orthodox, and her Jewishness was not a major influence on her. Styron knew Jews for whom the Holocaust was an almost-consuming interest. He knew that he could not write from their perspective; he must use his own. He knew too that some critics—George Steiner and Elie Wiesel primarily—had argued that the Holocaust was so terrible that it could not be written about: the only appropriate response was silence. Styron, however, could not wholly accept this view. He did decide not to take his narrative into the actual death camp— Sophie was never put there in his story—but he wrote by inference about what had happened behind the fences. Undoubtedly influenced by his experiences with critics of *The Confessions of Nat Turner*, Styron believed that he had to continue to move across cultural lines and to address difficult historical and moral questions, whatever price he might pay. The central evil of the twentieth century, his century, was the Nazi final solution. For Styron it was a phenomenon that moved beyond anti-Semitism and embodied crucial issues: the nature of evil, the question of guilt, and the difficulty of expiation. He would write about these issues—but his central character would be Sophie, a Polish Catholic, not a Jew.*

As he resumed work now on *Sophie's Choice,* Styron found himself creating an odd mixture in his novel. Outwardly and for long stretches it was a sexual comedy about Stingo's search for coital initiation. Stingo's solitary onanism and his frustrating encounters with Leslie Lapidus, a quintessential cock-tease, and Mary Alice Grimball, who masturbates him freely but will not allow him to touch her, are broadly humorous and almost caricature-like. But interspersed between these scenes are others of much greater intensity involving Sophie and her Jewish lover, Nathan Landau. He is a complex and sometimes confusing character, alternately charming and manic. (He reminds one of Mason Flagg in *Set This House on Fire.*) As the narrative progresses both he and Sophie reveal their secrets, bit by bit, as they move toward their deaths. *Sophie's Choice* is also a philosophical meditation on the final solution by the mature Stingo, who has attempted, from his alien background, to penetrate its mystery. Finally he fails to do so: the phenomenon is too large and all-encompassing, but in helping Sophie tell her story he has at least preserved her words "as a reminder of some fragile yet perdurable hope."

---

*For a good discussion of this aspect of the novel, including a foreword by Styron and an interview with him in the back matter of the volume, see Rhoda Sirlin, *William Styron's* Sophie's Choice: *Crime and Self-Punishment* (Ann Arbor: UMI Research Press, 1990).

As he moved toward the halfway point of his narrative, Styron found that writing Sophie's story was becoming more difficult, not least because she was not telling him the truth. In that peculiarly private relationship that develops between an author and a character, Styron had found himself listening to Sophie as she spoke, almost as if she had an independent existence. She had revealed herself to him only in small glimpses. She had told him that her father, the austere Professor Zbigniew Bieganski, a scholar of the law at the Jagiellonian University of Cracow, had been an opponent of anti-Semitism and of Hitler's final solution. She had said that her father had defended the Jews passionately in his speeches and writings, but somehow this did not ring true. "This woman is lying to me," Styron later remembered thinking. His sense of his task with Sophie now became more complex. He needed to remove the layers of her personality and behavior in order to discover the truth about her father—that he was a virulent anti-Semite who tried to court favor with the occupying Nazis. They ignored him and eventually had him shot. This disclosure would lead to the central moment of the book, when Sophie reveals to Stingo how she was made to send her own daughter to the death chambers at Auschwitz.

On whom is Sophie Zawistowska based? As with Peyton Loftis in *Lie Down in Darkness,* Sophie is based on several women. Her physical looks and the fact that she is a Polish Catholic come from the real Sophie whom Styron had known in Brooklyn in the summer of 1949. Her personality, however, seems drawn in part from Wanda Malinowska, the woman with whom Styron had been involved in New York in 1949, while he was living on West Eighty-eighth Street, and whom he had continued to run into in Europe from time to time in the years that followed. Sophie's beauty and sexual allure are reminiscent of Wanda, as is her tendency toward self-destructiveness. Wanda's father, Bronislaw Malinowski, had been much like Sophie's father—remote, austere, scholarly, misogynistic—and she, like Sophie, had suffered from his disapproval and his inability to love her.

Sophie's gentleness and her great sensitivity to music are reminiscent of Bobbie Taeusch, Styron's first serious love, with whom he spent much time during his months at McGraw-Hill and the New School in 1947 and 1948. Bobbie said years later that the music echoing through *Sophie's Choice*—by Mozart, Brahms, Beethoven, and others—is precisely the music that she and Styron listened to during those months, before she decided that she was not ready for marriage.

Sophie's speech—the particular rhythms of her voice, and her inflections—come from another woman. This was Joanna Rostropowicz Clark, a native of Poland whom Styron met on the Vineyard in the summer of 1973. Joanna had lived through World War II in Cracow; as a young girl she had known members of the Armia Krajowa, the "Home Armies," who had conducted guerrilla and terrorist attacks on the occupying Germans. Joanna told Styron the story of a young soldier in the Armia whom she had known only by his first name, Ryszard. She had been told that he carried out assassinations of targeted Nazis; one day he disappeared, and she assumed that he had been captured and executed. In the novel Ryszard becomes a similar figure, called Jozef, whom Sophie knows briefly in Warsaw. As Styron listened to Joanna's stories, he absorbed her way of speaking and her pronunciations. These he gave to Sophie Zawistowska in his novel. He also picked up some of Sophie's rhythms and usages from the writer David Halberstam's wife, Elzbieta Czyzewska, an actress.

Styron pressed on with the manuscript of *Sophie's Choice* through 1975 and 1976. This was a particularly good time for him, and his periods of composition were stimulating and satisfying. So fertile was he that he managed to write a lengthy short story between stints on the novel. This was "Shadrach," the tale of an aged former slave who travels all the way from Alabama back to Virginia, to the banks of the James River, in order to die on the farm on which he was born. The narrative is based on a true story, told to Styron by a boyhood friend he ran into and chatted with on a trip to Newport News. The friend presented the story only as a curiosity, but Styron immediately saw its fictional possibilities. At first he thought it might function as a side incident in *Sophie's Choice,* but as he worked with the material it grew into a full-length story, an unsentimental parable about poverty, kindness, and the love that can sometimes be possible between black and white people. Styron sent "Shadrach" to *Esquire,* where it was published in November 1978. Then he returned to the manuscript of *Sophie's Choice.*

During these years Styron began walking in the afternoons. In part he did this for his health: he had turned fifty in June 1975, and he knew that he would have to pay better attention now to his heart and lungs. But he began his habit of walking also to be alone and to think. He found it a satisfying way to arrange his day; the walk became the beginning of his period of composition. His only company on his treks was usually an intelligent, affectionate dog named Aquinnah, a mixed Labrador and golden retriever. During the first ten minutes or so of his walks he often found himself grumpy and out of sorts, his mind cluttered by mundane concerns—his bank balance, a dental appointment, a leaky faucet, a bad review of one of his novels. Then (as he described it in an unpublished manuscript) his mind would begin to clear:

> Without fail there comes a transitional moment—somewhat blurred, like that drowsy junction between wakefulness and sleep—when I begin to think of my work, when the tiny worries and injustices that have besieged me start to evaporate, replaced by a delicious, isolated contemplation of whatever is in the offing, later that day, at the table at which I write. Ideas, conceits, characters, even whole sentences and parts of paragraphs come pouring in on me in a happy flood until I am in a state close to hypnosis, quite oblivious of the woods or the fields or the beach where I am trudging, and finally as heedless of the rhythmic motion of my feet as if I were paddling through air like some great liberated goose or swan.

Family life and social duties during this period were demanding for Styron, and he had to work hard to protect his time for the novel. There was much to keep up with: Susanna was now at Yale, Polly at Brown University, Tom at the Taft School, and Al in grade school at Rumsey Hall. Rose continued her travels and her work with Amnesty. Summers at the Vineyard were satisfying and restorative, and Styron developed close relationships there. Among his friends were Art Buchwald, who had become a kind of resident guru on the island, and Lillian Hellman, who was the high priestess. Styron also came to know and like his next-door neighbors in Vineyard Haven, Sheldon and Lucy Hackney. Sheldon Hackney was a historian of the South, a former student of C. Vann Woodward's, and he and Styron had long talks about slavery and Nat Turner. Later Sheldon would become president of the University of Pennsylvania and would settle with his wife in Philadelphia. Lucy Hackney, a lawyer and activist, began her work then with young women who needed to be represented and defended in the city's legal system. Lucy became Rose's close friend: both women were excellent tennis players and often joined in mixed doubles with Buchwald and the CBS journalist Mike Wallace, another good friend.

Lucy Hackney's mother was Virginia Foster Durr, one of the earliest civil rights activists in Montgomery, Alabama, and an important figure in the history of the movement for Negro rights. She and Styron developed an elaborate relationship, affectionate in a courtly way, such as one often finds between senior southern women and younger southern men. At the same time Styron maintained a similar friendship with a much more difficult southern grande dame who was his Vineyard Haven neighbor on the opposite side of his property—Lillian Hellman, who qualified as a southerner by virtue of her upbringing in New Orleans. This friendship was not always smooth. Hellman was jealous of Styron's attentions to Virginia Durr and would not attend parties if she knew that Mrs. Durr would be there. (It did not help that both women had impeccable liberal credentials.) Hellman could be fractious about trivial matters: one June she disagreed vehemently with Styron over the proper way to carve and serve Virginia ham—she said hot, he said cold—and she became so incensed that she refused to speak to him for the rest of the summer. In some ways this was a relief: with Hellman on one side and Mrs. Durr on the other, Styron sometimes found himself literally caught in the middle.

The 1970s brought losses and deaths. Hiram Haydn and Bennett Cerf both died during the decade. Leon Edwards, the boyhood friend who had become a surgeon, died in a crash of his private airplane. William Blackburn, with whom Styron had stayed in close touch, died in 1972. The seventeen-year-old daughter of Bobby and Claire White, whose name was Natalie, died in a car wreck in 1975. The Styrons set off eight acres of their property in Roxbury as a memorial to her, and Rose wrote a long poem in her memory. Bobby White made a sculpture of a stone boat for the site, which had been a favorite place to play for Natalie and Polly, who had been close friends.

The death that affected Styron most profoundly was that of James Jones, who succumbed to congestive heart failure on May 8, 1977, at the age of fifty-five. Jim and Gloria Jones had abandoned their Paris apartment and returned to the States; in the mid-1970s they settled at Sagaponack on Long Island, quite close to Peter Matthiessen. Willie Morris, who had resigned from the editorship of *Harper's* after a dispute with its owners, lived in nearby Bridgehampton. Jones was struggling to finish *Whistle,* the last volume of his trilogy on World War II. He almost completed the manuscript but died short of his goal. Jones designated Styron and Morris to finish the book for him and tried, on his deathbed, to give them directions for its completion. Styron and Morris attempted to finish the book but gave up the task, realizing that they could never reproduce Jones's idiom. Morris supplied summaries of the final three and a half chapters, and the novel appeared in 1978. Styron was hit hard by Jones's death. His friend had been too young to die; he had come cruelly close to finishing his trilogy, only to have that satisfaction denied him.

W. C. Styron and Eunice, his third wife, had flourished during their first three years together in Goldsboro, but her health began to fail in 1975, and she died in 1977. By then the senior Styron had himself become infirm and was no longer able to take care of himself. Styron decided to bring him to Connecticut. Styron and Willie Morris flew down to Goldsboro and brought the old man back north, where he was placed in a nursing home near Roxbury. There Styron, Rose, and the children could visit him. His mind became increasingly dim in the months that followed until he had difficulty identifying those who came to see him. He would drift in and out of consciousness, sometimes not even recognizing his son.

All during these months Styron was writing steadily on *Sophie's Choice,* moving toward its conclusion, which he could visualize clearly. In August 1978, a few thousand words short of the end, he visited his father in the nursing home and told him that the novel was almost finished. "I've dedicated this book to you," Styron said. "It's in honor of you." Styron was not sure that his father had heard or understood, but then the old man roused himself and seemed to smile. "Wonderful," he said, "wonderful," in a soft, wheezy voice. These were the last words that Styron exchanged with his father. Not long after, on August 10, 1978, W. C. Styron died. His son's grief was deep and persistent. His father had been a support and a guide for him, especially during the years of his boyhood and young manhood, and he had admired his father's honesty and steadfastness. Stingo's father in *Sophie's Choice* is Styron's portrait of his own father, his final tribute to the example W. C. Styron had set of loyalty and love.

On Sunday, December 17, Styron wrote down the last words of the manuscript of *Sophie's Choice*. He noted the time, 1:15 P.M., and added these words: "Grâce du Bon Dieu."

Prepublication momentum for *Sophie's Choice* was building. Two sections from the novel had been published in *Esquire,* one entitled "The Seduction of Leslie" in September 1976 and a second called "My Life as a Publisher" in March 1978. These are the humorous early parts of the book in which Stingo labors at McGraw-Hill, as his creator had done, and pursues the elusive Jewish American princess Leslie Lapidus. These early prepublished sections had stimulated interest in the subsidiary rights for *Sophie's Choice*. Book-club rights went to the Book-of-the-Month Club for $305,000. Paperback rights were auctioned (by this time a standard practice) and went finally to Bantam for $1.575 million. Negotiations for the film rights were labyrinthine; for a time it looked as if no sale would be made, but eventually the director Alan J. Pakula, in partnership with a real estate investor named Keith Barish, acquired the movie rights for $650,000. Styron was pleased; *Sophie's Choice,* he could see, would have a wide audience and be a considerable financial success. Styron had high hopes for the movie. Pakula was a director of ambition and talent who had been much praised for his movies *To Kill a Mockingbird, The Parallax View, Klute,* and *All the President's Men.* Pakula was entirely taken by *Sophie's Choice* and believed in its possibilities for the screen. "I was knocked out by the book," he told a *New York Times* reporter. "I have rarely felt this kind of passion for anything in my life."

Styron's friend Philip Roth, after reading of the movie sale in *The New York Times,* was moved to send a postcard to Styron. "Your name, your face, and your new tax problem are everywhere," wrote Roth. It was a problem that Styron was glad to have. He and Rose had continued to divide the family's financial responsibilities, he providing the running expenses and she using her money for large purchases and for extras. But these practices had diminished her capital, and eventually would consume it altogether. Styron was therefore happy to see that *Sophie's Choice* would provide new income, although, as he was fond of saying, it had taken him seven years to write the book and would take him several years more to collect his royalties and his percentages of the subsidiary monies. In the end, he calculated, his average yearly income would be about that of a successful physician.

The passage of *Sophie's Choice* from manuscript to print was smooth. The typescript setting copy and the proofs for the novel show little in the way of cutting, revision, or adjustment. This reflects Styron's confidence during the composition of the novel—unusual among his works in that there seem to have been no major hiatuses in its creation. The writing of *Sophie's Choice* for him was a five-year period of almost uninterrupted creative involvement, often challenging but always intensely stimulating. This helps to explain the emptiness that Styron began to feel as he approached publication day. He was nervous as well, not sure what to expect from critics and readers.

Sophie's Choice was formally published on June 11, 1979, Styron's fifty-fourth birthday. Initial reviews were mixed. Many of them were long and halting, heavy with speculation, as if *Sophie's Choice* were too complex and multifaceted a piece of fiction to be managed in one reading. John Gardner's front-page review for *The New York Times Book Review* was a disappointment; Gardner assessed *Sophie's Choice* only within the boundaries of what he called the southern gothic tradition and found it wanting. "Though I am profoundly moved by *Sophie's Choice* and consider the novel an immensely important work," wrote Gardner, "I am not persuaded by it." Gardner's mixed notice was counterbalanced by Christopher Lehmann-Haupt's praise in the daily *Times* ("a stunning achievement") and Larzer Ziff's in *Commonweal* ("his narrative mastery continues to be astounding"). Paul Fussell, in *The Washington Post,* put *Sophie's Choice* "on that small shelf reserved for American masterpieces." Robert Alter, writing in the *Saturday Review,* gave some praise but criticized the "overwrought quality" of the prose and showed some squeamishness about Stingo's sexual candor. The anonymous reviewer for *Time* called the novel a "sprawling, uneven yet brave attempt to render the unimaginable horror of the Nazi death camps." And Robert Towers, in *The New York Review of Books,* found *Sophie's Choice* overly self-conscious and was troubled by the difficulty of unraveling "author from narrator, Styron from Stingo." Benjamin DeMott's review in the *Atlantic Monthly,* though filled with demurs, finally offered this praise: "The overall scale and tone, the willingness to ask some height of the reader, the quality of the book's ambition to be adequate to a major moral challenge, stand forth, well before the end, as thoroughly admirable." Styron had anticipated adverse reactions from some Jewish critics who, he assumed, would take him to task for universalizing the Holocaust and writing about it from the perspective of a southern white Gentile. In the event, though, no organized attack emerged. Styron received some criticism later, in the 1980s, for choosing Sophie as his heroine and for trespassing into Jewish territory, but the tone of this writing never approached the shrillness and anger found in *Ten Black Writers Respond.*

Public recognition for Styron's achievement in *Sophie's Choice* came in February 1980 when the novel won the American Book Award for fiction, the first time that the prize was given. Styron, Philip Roth, and Norman Mailer had announced in March that they would refuse to participate in the American Book Awards; they disapproved of the nominating process, the elaborateness of the planned awards ceremony, and the "public-relations" aura of the event. These features were changed or toned down considerably, largely as a result of pressure from Styron, Roth, and Mailer—and from some forty other former winners and judges of the National Book Awards, which the American Book Awards were designed to replace. Styron decided, in consequence, to allow *Sophie's Choice* to stand for the award, and it won.

Three weeks after its publication, *Sophie's Choice* was in the number two spot on the *New York Times* best-seller list. "I only have to dislodge a moronic thriller by someone named Ludlum to reign supreme (at least for a while)," Styron wrote to his friend Sadri Khan, a longtime sponsor of *The Paris Review.* The novel did reach the number one spot a short while later and stayed there for several weeks. Clothbound sales for Random House remained vigorous throughout 1979 and into 1980, and a great many more copies were distributed through the Book-of-the-Month Club. The Bantam paperback edition appeared in 1980 and sold in large numbers over the next three years. The novel continues to be read today in a Vintage edition published by Random House. English-language sales in all editions have gone well beyond the two-million mark.

Tessa Sayle, who had taken over Hope Leresche's London literary agency, arranged for translations of *Sophie's Choice* into German, Spanish, Italian, Portuguese, Dutch, Swedish, Norwegian, Finnish, Danish, Czech, and several other languages. Most of those negotiations went smoothly; the only one to present difficulty was with Gallimard in Paris. For a time it looked as if *Sophie's Choice* would be published in France by du Seuil, a competing house, but a personal appeal to Styron by Françoise Gallimard, granddaughter of the founder of the house, kept the novel on the Gallimard list. Maurice-Edgar Coindreau was now in retirement, so Styron acquired a new and quite talented translator for this novel, a man named Maurice Rambaud who already had experience as a translator of books by Peter Matthiessen, Nelson Algren, John Barth, John Updike, and Donald Barthelme. The Gallimard edition appeared in 1981.

The immense success of *Sophie's Choice* changed Styron's life, though not necessarily in ways that he welcomed. He was visible everywhere now and was under heavy and constant pressure to give interviews, make speaking appearances, and lend his name to causes. His mail was full of oddities, including a remarkably tasteless request by a businessman who wanted to name a kosher delicatessen "Sophie's Choice" and an offer from an importunate would-be novelist to come and paint Styron's house in return for writing lessons. As always, some of the mail was disturbing, and Styron occasionally let this anger him. Across the top of an angry, taunting letter he scrawled, in blue ink: "The tone of your letter indicates that you are an asshole. Do not write me any more letters." Thus purged, Styron decided not to return the missive to the man who had written it. He knew that it was unwise to bait such people; he and his family might be vulnerable, in both Roxbury and Vineyard Haven, to vandalism, harassment, or worse.

This should have been a period of great triumph and satisfaction for Styron, and in most ways it was, but there was an undertone of melancholy to many of his days. It was as if a significant chapter of his life were now closed. The two questions that confronted him were how to deal with his fame and what to write next.

31

Breakdown

The years 1981 and 1982 brought many good things to Styron. In France he saw François Mitterrand elected president and was invited to the inauguration ceremonies in July 1981, shortly after *Le Choix de Sophie* was published by Gallimard. The reception of the novel in France was enthusiastic, with extended coverage in *Les Nouvelles Littéraires, Le Monde, L'Express, Le Pèlerin, Le Nouvel Observateur, Révolution, La Nouvelle Révue Francaise, Le Nouvelliste, Le Magazine Littéraire, Le Point,* and other publications.

Styron and Mitterrand became friendly in the years that followed, and Mitterrand systematically read his way through Styron's works in their French translations. When he was in Paris, Styron was often invited to public occasions by Mitterrand and to small luncheons at the presidential palace. One of Styron's favorite moments from the friendship occurred at a reception in Paris in the summer of 1988 when Mitterrand broke off an inconsequential conversation with George and Barbara Bush and took Styron aside to talk about literature. Later in the afternoon Styron heard Mitterrand recommend to George Bush that he read *The Confessions of Nat Turner*. Mitterrand praised the novel to Bush, searching in English for the right words to describe it. Finally he resorted to his own language: "Styron's novel is *très dur,*" he said, choosing the French adjective that means hard, or difficult, but also carries connotations of intellectual challenge and durability.

Styron occupied himself in late 1981 and early 1982 by collecting the best of his essays, reviews, and occasional pieces into a volume called *This Quiet Dust and Other Writings*. This is a carefully arranged collection, bringing together the best of Styron's nonfiction about such subjects as the South, slavery, smoking, his literary forebears, the Nazi death camps, the environment, the death penalty, and military life. The volume also includes several portraits of his friends and a group of short memoirs. Styron tied the collection together with freshly written connective statements, including a small essay on the military mentality and an account of Benjamin Reid's escape from prison and subsequent recapture.

It was the Ben Reid experience that helped bring about an end to the estrangement between Norman Mailer and Styron. Mailer had adopted as a protégé a convicted thief and murderer named Jack Abbott, who had spent twenty-four of his thirty-eight years in penal institutions of one kind or another. Abbott had written a book called *In the Belly of the Beast* about life in prison; Mailer helped him have the book published and helped further by having Abbott assigned to a work-release program. Mailer's efforts turned out badly: not long after leaving prison, Abbott began an altercation in a New York bistro with a waiter named Richard Adan, an aspiring actor and playwright. Abbott went into an alley nearby with Adan; there he stabbed and killed him. Abbott was arrested and put back in prison; Mailer took heavy criticism in the press for his role in having Abbott released into society. Styron, at a symposium sponsored by the Fortune Society, a prisoner advocacy group, was asked to comment on the matter, and he defended Mailer. Later he defended him at a PEN conference as well. "My heart goes out to him," said Styron. "I have an Abbott in my life"—meaning, of course, Ben Reid. Mailer learned of Styron's statements and, after a pause, typed this short letter to him:

Dear Bill,
I thought I'd wait a month before writing to see if I still feel the same, and I do. So I just wanted to say that it was gracious of you and generous and kind of gutty to speak up the way you did about the Abbott business.
See you anon.

Cheers,
Norman

In this way the rift between the two men began to be healed. They saw each other from time to time now; often they found themselves supporting the same causes and signing the same public letters. Both admired François Mitterrand, and both had been present at his inauguration. Styron and Mailer, in fact, had gone about together in Paris for several days before the ceremonies and had enjoyed each other's company. There seemed no reason to continue the estrangement: there was no issue of competition; Styron and Mailer had writing to do in the years to come; there was no time for feuding. The two men did not become close friends and are not today, but they are on cordial terms. Styron praises Mailer's writing, especially his nonfiction, which he sees as spontaneous and daring. Mailer says, "I have a lot of respect for the way Bill has run his life."

These years also saw the completion and successful release of Alan Pakula's film of *Sophie's Choice*. Pakula cast Meryl Streep in the role of Sophie; Kevin Kline played Nathan; Peter MacNicol was Stingo. Pakula himself wrote the screenplay, adhering to Styron's novel with much fidelity. Pakula gave a copy of the script to Styron, who read and annotated it. "Is suicide pact adequately prepared?" he wrote on the first page. "Fine condensing," he wrote further on. And throughout the script he suggested music that might play on the sound track. "Allegro 4th mvt. Royal Fireworks," he noted on page 21. "Marriage of Figaro on radio here," he penciled seventeen pages along. Beyond these suggestions Styron played no part in translating *Sophie's Choice* to the screen. He visited the film set once or twice and was dazzled by Meryl Streep's rendering of a Polish accent. Otherwise he stayed away from Pakula and the actors. Very good movie.

The movie, which premiered in December 1982, was a considerable success. Streep's performance was brilliant and won her an Academy Award that spring. Kline was passionate and intense, MacNicol boyish and winning. The film was much praised for its visual and musical qualities and for its mood of restrained sorrow. The scene on the platform at Auschwitz, where Sophie must choose which of her children is to die, is wrenching to the heart. "I read that scene once only for the film," Streep recalled many years later. "I couldn't read it again. Every time I even thought about it, I had to put it out of my mind, like Sophie. I still can't think about that scene." Styron was enthusiastic about Streep's work: "I think Meryl's performance is the best performance I've ever seen by an actress in the movies," he told an interviewer. With Pakula's adaptation he was equally satisfied: "I felt there'd been no violation whatsoever of my work," he said.

Certainly these successes should have buoyed Styron's spirits, but he was troubled during this period by his inability to get rolling on another novel. *Sophie's Choice* was now behind him, gone from his worktable, and the image of Sophie was no longer his alone. Polly Styron, always attuned to her father's moods, sensed an emptiness in him. In a letter that she sent to him at about this time she wrote, "I sense your nights at home alone, now you are no longer living in chambers of Sophie. . . . I've so much I'd like to say to you, stuff about things and stuff about nothing—it doesn't matter what. But stupid me, I get intimidated by the shadows in your voice." Polly was prescient. As her father approached his sixtieth birthday he began a physical, emotional, and creative decline that eventually rendered him almost helpless and brought him near death.

Styron had begun work in 1981 on a new version of *The Way of the Warrior.* The old version, the one on which he had been laboring when Sophie's story seized on his imagination, did not now figure in his plans. This old version—which is represented by "Marriott, the Marine," published in *Esquire* in September 1971—had never pleased Styron entirely. Now he felt that he had lost the thread of Marriott's story (if indeed he had ever known it), and he resolved to begin anew. He still wanted to write about World War II, wanted to measure himself against Jones and Mailer, but he needed a new story to tell. The obvious course was to continue to write in Stingo's voice. Styron had found it comfortable to narrate *Sophie's Choice* from Stingo's retrospective, quasi-autobiographical viewpoint. Now he would double back and tell Stingo's story before he had met Sophie, while he was still a young second lieutenant in the Marines, heading into his first experience of combat, just at the end of the war.

This new novel, though, would be about more than its historical moment. Styron believed that the worst of the political looniness of postwar American life, then resurrecting itself in the early years of the Reagan administration, had its origins at the end of World War II. What Styron wanted to do in this new version of *The Way of the War-*

rior was to create a character, superficially attractive, who would embody much of this right-wing ideology. The character would be Doug Stiles, a Marine Corps second lieutenant and Stingo's comrade, a handsome and winning figure, brave and eager for battle. Stiles was to have been based, in broad outline, on William F. Buckley, Jr., the conservative journalist and television interviewer. Stiles was to have had Buckley's Anglo-Saxon good looks, some of his gestures and mannerisms, and his distinctive smile. Buckley was a figure whose ideology Styron found repellent but whose public persona he thought oddly attractive. As a mature man Styron could resist the Buckley manner, but he knew that Stingo, barely twenty-one in the narrative, would find Stiles seductive. From that conflict between the older Stingo and his younger self Styron would generate tension in his story.

Stiles was to die in this version of *The Way of the Warrior*. He was to be virtually the last American GI to be killed in the war—shot in a mop-up operation on Okinawa just before the atomic bomb was dropped on Nagasaki. Stingo, who would have accompanied Stiles on this operation and would have seen him die, was to have lost his reason after Stiles's death and to have landed in a military psychiatric ward. From that point on Styron was unsure what direction the narrative would take, but he felt that the plot would reveal itself further as he went along.

Styron made some progress with this manuscript and worked on it sporadically over the next three years. He hit on the device of using an old war diary that Stingo had kept in order to capture, in his hero's youthful voice, his naiveté and trepidation about battle. The mechanics of the manuscript felt right, and Styron pushed ahead with it, producing an opening sequence that he titled "Love Day" and published in the August 1985 issue of *Esquire*. "Love Day" was announced as the beginning of a new novel. Styron put down a good bit more of the story on paper. Two sections in particular, neither ever published, stand out from the surviving drafts. One is a sequence about Stingo's troubled erotic fantasies while in the war zone; the other is a description of his demented attempt at suicide by drowning, just after Stiles's death.

By the summer of 1985, however, Styron had begun to lose his way with this novel. He was on the Vineyard, where he had usually written well, but now his narrative began to elude his grasp. He seemed unable to keep his focus on the main story and found himself wandering off in episodes that were tangential to the central plot. Typically he would begin an episode, write on it for several days, and then recognize that he was creating a sideshow, a diversion, rather than advancing his story. This was a new problem for Styron, something that had almost never happened during the composition of a manuscript. He had weathered several periods of writer's block during his career and had run up against problems of form and structure more than once, but he had never lost control of a narrative in quite this way.

There were other signs during the summer of 1985 that all was not right with Styron. Shortly after his sixtieth birthday, as if on cue, his body rebelled and became intolerant of alcohol. For most of his adult life he had used drink as a soothing agent and, often in company with music, as a way of reaching visions and dreams from his subconscious mind. Since the memorable hangover after William Faulkner's funeral, he had usually watched his intake and paced himself fairly carefully, but he had still abused alcohol, by his own admission. Now alcohol turned abruptly against him and began to torment him. Whiskey, and even wine and beer, produced violent pains in the prostate area and brought severe urinary discomfort. Styron went to a specialist and learned, not to his surprise, that he would have to stop drinking for the time being and that he should probably curtail his intake, by a significant increment, from then on.

For Styron this was a shock. He recognized that drink had become habitual to him: it was a "soothing, often sublime agent," a "friend" and an "invaluable senior partner of my intellect," he later said. Alcohol had protected him for many years, masking much anxiety that was latent in his personality. He did not consider himself an alcoholic, either then or later; he never wrote under the influence of drink, but alcohol was still an invariable part of his evening regimen and a dependable defense against many interior fears. Without it he felt unprotected and—his own word—"unhelmed." Perhaps as a consequence Styron's hypochondria, for years a low-grade component of his makeup, now flared up alarmingly. He had always admitted that he was hypochondriacal and usually had been able to joke about it. Now, however, he felt himself in the grip of a constant physical malaise, beset by aches and gripes that he could not identify. The beautiful Vineyard weather was no solace: "I felt ill at ease," he later said, "as if something was stealing up on me."

One especially troubling feature of Styron's discomfort was a rupturing of his sleep patterns. He now found it quite difficult to drop off at night and was apt to wake up at around three o'clock in the morning and find it impossible to sleep again. He began taking a tranquilizer called Ativan, prescribed to him by a doctor on the Vineyard who assured him that it was as safe as aspirin and that he could take it in doses as large as he wished. Not long afterward Styron shifted to a stronger sedative, a tiny gray-green oval-shaped pill with the chemical tag triazolam—known also by the trade name of Halcion. What Styron did not know, and what most American physicians then were not yet fully aware of, was that Ativan and especially Halcion often have dangerous side effects. They can bring on attacks of acute depression; they can also awaken powerful urges toward suicide.

Styron recognized later that in the summer of 1985 he was entering a downward-spiraling period of depression. This disease is an old one in human history: it has gone by many names and has been anatomized by many students of the mind and body. Among its older names are melancholia and neurasthenia; William James, who suffered from it, called it a "psychical neuralgia" and a "pathological melancholy." The disease was known to Hippocrates and Plato, to Saint Paul, to René Descartes and Robert Burton, to Philippe Pinel, to Emil Kraepelin and Sigmund Freud, and to almost countless artists and writers, from Virgil to Shakespeare to Samuel Johnson to Vincent van Gogh to Virginia Woolf. Its etiology is mysterious and never precisely the same in two individuals. Its only unfailing characteristic is that it is democratic, striking young and old, fit and infirm, wealthy and poor, talented and dull, famous and obscure—moving across class and gender lines with ease. Its most common forms are a bipolar dysthymia known as manic-depressive syndrome and a unipolar dysthymia, or simple depressive syndrome, which is the more common of the two and is the form of the disease that struck Styron.

He was already exhibiting (or would do so shortly) most of the standard symptoms of depression: a jumbled memory, an overreliance on habit and routine, a disturbance of the circadian rhythms, a tendency toward hypochondria, a diminished libido, an exaggerated dependency on others, a pessimism bordering on nihilism, and (perhaps most debilitating) an acute self-loathing. Styron was unusual in at least one respect, however. For him the most agonizing part of the day was the early to mid-afternoon. Most depressives cannot function in the morning, often finding it nearly impossible to rise and make basic decisions about the day. As the morning progresses, though, the grip of the disease loosens, and most sufferers are able to function with some normalcy in the afternoons and evenings. For Styron it was the opposite: he found himself functional in the mornings but increasingly debilitated in the afternoons, stumbling through a murky drizzle of anxiety and fear, often able only to lie in bed and stare at the ceiling. He persisted quite stubbornly, however, in trying to follow the normal patterns of his life—a feature that would mark his behavior until he entered the worst phases of the disease. He took his daily walks, tried to eat (though food had lost its savor), and continued to try to write, though with less and less success.

In the second week of September he flew from the Vineyard to New York for a dinner party in honor of Gabriel García Márquez, but he unwisely downed a scotch on the short flight, then had another at the party, and almost immediately found himself in a ghastly state of illness, unable to eat or even speak. A week later he kept a prearranged date to speak at Connecticut College in New London, but he became terribly anxious before his speech (which he had not prepared well), and he gave a muddled and embarrassing performance.

Styron knew by now that he was ill but still hoped that his troubles might be bodily. At a fellow writer's suggestion he went to a well-known physician, who recommended an entire physical workup, a battery of diagnostic tests designed to identify any latent cause of distress. Styron's last several weeks at the Vineyard that year were spent undergoing these examinations, which included several fasts, a period of wearing a heart monitor on his belt, and a colonoscopy, which he said he would "not have wished on Adolf Eichmann." In an understandable way Styron hoped that these tests would reveal something wrong with him, but even as he went through them, he later said, he was almost sure that his difficulties lay elsewhere. In the meantime he continued to be morose and, with alarming rapidity, to lose weight—between twenty and twenty-five pounds over a period of about six weeks.

One of his last acts on the Vineyard late that September was to follow the progress of Hurricane Gloria. The Vineyard itself was under no threat from the storm, but Styron seemed nonetheless unable to take his eyes from the TV screen, where computer-generated satellite images of the eye of the hurricane were displayed every few minutes. Two years later Styron could still remember staring at the weather maps with sick fascination. In its shape the hurricane seemed to resemble a monstrous, pulsating amoeba, advancing inexorably on the Outer Banks of North Carolina.

By early October Styron had returned to Roxbury. Normally this was a time of year he enjoyed, taking pleasure in the beautiful New England autumn, but this year, unaccountably, his house and his surroundings seemed threatening. "There was a strange characteristic that the light itself had," he recalled. "The afternoon light had a touch of menace about it. There was a sense of alienation and creepiness about the house, too." Styron also became conscious at about this time of an odd little imp, a doppelgänger, who would drift in every afternoon and roost on his shoulder, observing his anxiety with unnerving calmness. And Rose was not there to help; she had flown to Budapest for a human rights conference. He felt so terrified by his daemons that he telephoned her there and begged her to return immediately, which she did.

Styron now began to suspect that he was suffering from clinical depression. He located a few books on the subject and began to educate himself, recognizing some of his own symptoms and ailments in the literature. Art Buchwald had gone through a period of depression on the Vineyard earlier that summer; he had largely recovered by now and was urging Styron to seek treatment from a psychiatrist. Mike Wallace, who had himself endured a siege of depression not long before, told Styron also that he should get psychiatric help.

Wallace put Styron in touch with a New York psychiatrist of good reputation, and Styron made an appointment to see this man. In the meanwhile, though, it was necessary for him to go to Paris to receive an award—an impressive one, the Prix Mondial Cino del Duca, given each year to a scientist or artist whose work reflects high humanistic values. Styron was determined to make the trip for several reasons: he had agreed to be present many months before and now felt that he could not cancel out; the prize carried a substantial cash award, which he wanted to donate to a cause as a part of a larger philanthropic gift he had pledged; and it would give him a chance to see Paris, his favorite city, and escape the Roxbury house, which had now become oppressive to him. His willingness to make the trip was also characteristic of an almost unceasing restlessness that afflicted him during the entire course of his illness—an unusual characteristic for depressives, many of whom are inactive and nearly catatonic in advanced stages of the disease. For Styron it was the opposite: he doggedly kept to his routines, going to social events at which, as often as not, he would stand mute; making agreed-upon appearances and giving readings at which he would usually do poorly; and, against all logic, continuing to try to write—now a great torture for him, since words, if they appeared at all, came only in a trickle.

The trip to Paris was nightmarish. The October weather, normally bright and pleasant in the city, was cold and wet, and it rained for most of his time there. He could do little more on his first day after arriving than lie in a hotel bed with Rose, clinging to her and saying over and over, "I'm sick, I'm sick." The awards ceremony the next day turned sour: in his muddled state Styron had forgotten that he needed to attend a luncheon in his honor just after receiving the medal and had made an engagement to have lunch with Françoise Gallimard, his French publisher. At first, with demented insistence, he announced to his hosts that he must keep his appointment with Françoise Gallimard. Then, having realized his gaffe, and at the urging of both Françoise and Rose, he began to apologize, insisting that it was all an unfortunate *malentendu* and hearing himself utter a sentence that he had not until then been able to bring himself to say: "I'm sick," he blurted out, *"un problème psychiatrique."*

Styron stumbled through the rest of his visit to Paris, managing to keep his other engagements but thinking only of escape from his beloved city so that he could fly home and consult the New York psychiatrist. On his last evening in Paris, heading back to his hotel in a taxi, he happened to look out of the window and spot, through a downpour of rain, the dimly lighted sign of the Hôtel Washington—the modest establishment where he had spent his first few nights in Paris in April 1952. He had not set eyes on the place in the intervening years. Somehow the conjunction of events—his illness, his confusion, his desire to flee the city—made him believe that he had come full circle and would never see Paris again.

Styron and Rose returned to New York, and Styron went to the psychiatrist in Manhattan. He turned out to be a somber, dour figure whose manner unnerved Styron. This psychiatrist did, however, take him off Halcion and Inderal (a medication prescribed to him by a rural

Connecticut GP for stage fright) and substituted Ludiomil, an antidepressant. Back in Roxbury, Styron found the results of his full diagnostic workup waiting. Not surprisingly there was nothing physically wrong with him. "I was as healthy as a pig," he later said. At first this news gave him a boost, but in a few days he had settled back into his daily cycle of depression, and the afternoons had become nearly intolerable.

Polly, now married, lived with her husband, Rob Faust, in nearby Warren, Connecticut. She began to drive over almost every day and help her mother care for her father. Styron, Polly, and Rose would take walks in the afternoons during which he would babble uncontrollably about his symptoms. Rose and Polly would try to steer the talk in other directions but with little success. By this time Styron had also developed an almost infantile attachment to Rose and became anxious if she was even briefly out of his sight. He accompanied her everywhere, when she went shopping or ran errands or kept social engagements, or even as she moved from room to room in the house.

By early November the Ludiomil prescribed by the New York psychiatrist had begun to have an anticholinergic effect on Styron, interfering with his ability to urinate. He had decided that he could not commute twice a week to New York to see this psychiatrist and had switched to a psychiatrist in New Haven. This physician, the sixth that Styron had consulted since early that summer, prescribed Nardil to counteract depression and Xanax to combat anxiety. (These were the fifth and sixth drugs he had taken.) Styron began to see this man now twice each week; he was usually driven to and from his appointments by Rose or Polly.

That Thanksgiving, as had been their custom for many years, Styron and Rose went to the Vineyard for a late-in-the-year reunion of their summer crowd—the Hackneys and Buchwalds and Wallaces and a few others. The idea of suicide had now begun to appear unbidden in Styron's thinking from time to time: on the ferryboat to Vineyard Haven he had fantasies about slipping over the rail and allowing himself to drown. The weather was cold and rainy, and once they got to the house he spent most of his time in bed. He did take a walk with Rose around West Chop, and as they talked he spoke to her obliquely of suicide, confessing that he was coming to understand why depressives might want to seek oblivion. Rose was alarmed but took care not to show it. After they returned to Roxbury, though, she secretly searched the house for weapons or other means of self-destruction. She found a pistol that had belonged to James Jones, which Gloria had given to Styron as a memento. Rose took the pistol and hid it; a few days later, when Styron was in New Haven seeing his psychiatrist, she threw it in the Shepaug River.

Styron should by now probably have been in a hospital, but his psychiatrist kept advising him not to commit himself—because of the public stigma, he said. Styron later came to feel that he should have insisted then on hospitalization—the stigma meant nothing to him—but at this point he was unable to stand up for himself and so accepted the doctor's judgment. Two engagements followed just after Thanksgiving, a speaking appearance in New York and a dinner a few days later with Rose and two friends at a good Italian restaurant in Manhattan. Both occasions, however, went badly: Styron misplaced his anti-anxiety pills before the reading, precipitating a mad search for them by Bob Loomis, who finally delivered them moments before Styron was to go onstage. The dinner was no better, with Styron sitting mute at the table. He left at one point to go to the men's room and, on his way back to the table, groaned aloud, "I'm dying . . ." to a startled stranger whom he passed on the stairs. Months later, when he recollected the incident, it mystified him that he could have behaved in such a way.

The bouts of anxiety were now beginning earlier in the day. Styron's voice had become a raspy wheeze and his gait had deteriorated to a bent shuffle. The Nardil he was taking had blocked his ability to dream—one of its common side effects—and his few hours of sleep each night were antiseptic and bare. In this dilemma Styron called his friend Ed Bunker, an ex-convict and writer in San Diego in whose work he had taken an interest. Bunker had gone through depression himself and had seen its effects on other convicts during his years of imprisonment. He put Styron in touch with the head of a suicide prevention center in southern California. Both this man and Bunker suggested that Styron try methadone, but Styron was afraid to use it. He was so near his final crisis by now that no new drug would likely have helped him.

On the night of Wednesday, December 11, during an informal dinner with some friends at the Roxbury house, Styron came to the decision that he would end his life. Like many incipient suicides he became methodical: he excused himself from the table and went upstairs, where he retrieved from its hiding place a notebook to which he had committed, over the years, certain private thoughts that he did not wish to be seen by anyone but himself. He carried this journal to the kitchen, wrapped it in paper towels, secured it with Scotch tape, and put it into an empty raisin-bran box, which he then pushed far down into the garbage pail on the back stoop of the house. Late that night and again the next day, Styron tried to compose a suicide letter, but in an irony that he could not then appreciate he found the task beyond him. "I couldn't manage the sheer dirgelike solemnity of it," he later remembered. He wanted to write a document of eloquence and dignity, but what he produced seemed pompous and offensive. He made two tries but tore them both up. In extremis, words had failed him. He would have to exit in silence.

Late on Thursday morning, December 12, he visited Lincoln Cornell, his family lawyer in Roxbury, and gave him a written set of revisions for his will. Cornell, recognizing that Styron looked and talked as if he was under great stress, decided to stall. It would take him a few days to have a new will typed up, he said. Could Styron return next Tuesday to sign the revised document? Styron agreed. A short while later Cornell telephoned Rose and told her about the incident. She knew now that she would have to watch her husband very carefully until he could be put where he could not harm himself.

Two years later Styron recalled his search for a location and a means to take his own life. The attic, with its stout rafters, became a place where he might hang himself. The small garage on their property might serve as a chamber for asphyxiation from car exhaust. He knew of a steep cliff with a two-hundred-foot drop near which he often walked; perhaps he could summon the nerve to throw himself over the edge to his death.

That night, after Rose had fallen asleep, Styron wandered aimlessly about the house. He was cold—the furnace had broken down earlier that day—and he had on a heavy jacket. His anxiety had lifted a little, as it often did late at night. Someone had given him a videocassette of a recent movie, *The Bostonians,* with Christopher Reeve, and to divert his mind he decided to put it into the player in the large back room of the house. A young actress named Madeleine Potter, who has the role of the ingenue in *The Bostonians,* had played the part of Ruth Snyder in an Off-Broadway stage production that December of "Dead!"—the drama that he and John Marquand had collaborated on several years earlier. Styron had liked her acting in "Dead!" Now he sat and tried to concentrate on her performance in the movie, simply to occupy his attention and stop the grinding of his brain.

About twenty minutes into the film there is a scene in which Christopher Reeve and Madeleine Potter walk through Harvard Yard. In the background one hears an orchestra and chorus, in Harvard Chapel, rehearsing the "Alto Rhapsody" by Brahms. The familiar music took Styron by surprise and pierced straight to his heart: as he sat before the television set in the cold house, he experienced a rush of memory. The "Alto Rhapsody" had been his mother's favorite musical work; as a child he had heard her sing it many times, without accompaniment, as she moved about the house or worked in her flower beds. The music was on the sound track of the movie only briefly, but it acted as a signal for Styron, almost as if his mother were reaching out to him, reminding him of what she had endured and lost. As he later described it, Styron came at that moment to realize that he could not abandon life. Too much good had happened to him, in this house and in this room. He could not inflict the burden of his suicide on his wife and children and on others who had loved him and believed in him. He left his chair, rushed upstairs, and shook Rose awake. "Help me," he said.

Rose sat with Styron until morning, when he drifted into a light sleep. She then called Polly and Rob, both of whom drove over early that afternoon. A few days later, in a quiet hour, Polly put down in her private journal what she had seen and heard:

> When I went upstairs to his room he was lying there, with his long grey hair all tangled and wild. I took his hand, which was trembling. "I'm a goner, darling," he said, first thing. His eyes had a startled look, and he seemed to be not quite there. His cool, trembling hands kept fumbling over mine. "The agony's too great now, darling. I'm sorry. I'm a goner."

Styron spoke obsessively to Polly of his wrongdoings and his self-loathing. "You'll hate me, you'll hate me," he whispered to her. He begged her to remember that despite his failings he had been a good man. Then he clutched at her awkwardly, holding her head to his breast and continuing to speak:

> "I love you so much. And the other children. And your mother. I always loved her. I loved her with a passion. She's a saint. I love her so

much. I love you people so much. Please tell the others how much I love them. You remember everything I'm saying now. You promise? . . . Try not to hate me. Try to forgive me."

Rose, downstairs, had reached the New Haven psychiatrist on the telephone and had persuaded him to have Styron admitted to the unit for affective illness at Yale–New Haven Hospital. This was Friday: Styron could enter on the following day, Saturday, December 14. Rose got Styron into a hot bath now and stayed with him, swabbing his face and body. Polly and Rob hid his barbiturates and poured out all liquor in the house. Styron became quieter as the afternoon went on, and they all had dinner together on trays in the bedroom. The knowledge that he was to be hospitalized the next day had a calming effect on Styron, and he eventually dropped off to sleep. The next day at around noon, Polly drove her father and mother to the hospital in New Haven. Styron went through the check-in procedures, then was taken away. "I can remember the strange, almost surreal sensation of watching, up ahead of me, my once imposing father shuffle down the sterile hospital hallway toward the locked door of the mental ward," Polly wrote in her journal. None of them knew at that point what the next few weeks would bring, or when he would be able to leave the ward.

Styron was now safe from himself, but he still had some difficult hours ahead. Almost immediately after being put in his hospital room, he underwent a panic attack. His heart began to pound wildly, his sight became blurred, and he felt disoriented and light-headed. Such attacks are common among persons who are first being confined in hospitals, asylums, and prisons. Styron did not realize this, though, and in his stricken state he believed that he was dying. Curiously he was resigned and a little relieved, knowing that death would finally free him from pain. He became methodical, just as he had been a few days before. He remembered that he had not signed his revised will, so he took a sheet of his stationery and a pen and stamps from his suitcase (Rose had packed these for him), and he wrote a letter in shaky handwriting to Lincoln Cornell, affirming that the notes he had given Cornell represented his final wishes and that his signature on this letter should stand in lieu of his signature on the will. Then he wrote a second letter, a brief one, saying good-bye to Peter Matthiessen. He and Matthiessen had seen a good deal of each other over the past few years. Matthiessen had become a disciple of Zen Buddhism, and Styron had come to admire the serenity and repose that Matthiessen had achieved.

Dear Peter:

I've gone through a rough time. I hope you'll remember me with love and tenderness. I wish I'd taken your way to peace and goodness. Please remember me with a little of that Zen goodness, too. I've always loved you and Maria.

Love
Porter

Styron addressed envelopes for these two letters, affixed stamps, and walked down the hall to put the envelopes into the outgoing mail basket at the nurses' station. Then he returned to his room and prepared to write a third and last letter, this one to Rose and the children. He would leave this letter on his bedside table, he thought; there was no need to mail it. A nurse, however, had been alarmed by Styron's looks when he had carried the first two letters down the hall, and she had followed him back to his room. Now she took his pulse. "You're having a panic attack," she said. "But it's all right; it's very common." She explained to Styron what was happening to him and told him that the symptoms would subside in a few minutes. Yes, he was safe. No, he would not die. Later Styron remembered feeling foolish. His little imp, his doppelgänger, came to sit now on his shoulder and to talk to him. "Look at the fuss you are making," it said. Just before supper that evening Styron remembered the two letters he had written to Cornell and Matthiessen. He tried to retrieve them but found that the mail had gone out.

That Monday, December 16, Styron began his treatment. There were some bad times for him before he began to improve. His sleep was still poor; the nurses reported that he slept like a dog, twitching and growling. He began to suffer in the night from auditory hallucinations: he would be awakened by the sensation, quite terrifying, that a huge bird had swooped down and screamed into his ear. In more lucid moments he examined his insurance policy and decided that it would never cover all of his expenses, for at this point he anticipated an incarceration that would go on for years, perhaps for the rest of his life. He telephoned Rose in Roxbury one morning and told her with great earnestness that she must divorce him. Otherwise he would bleed the family dry and have to be sent to the state asylum as a pauper.

Styron was still confused mentally. Though much of his anxiety had dissipated—along with the worst of his suicidal urges—he found that he could not read normally or focus his mind on one topic. He was given a test soon after he arrived in the hospital: he was asked to read a short paragraph and then, without looking at it, to summarize its contents. Even this small task was beyond him. For the present his brain had almost no power of retentiveness.

Styron did not undergo a full psychiatric analysis in the hospital, either then or later. After the first week, though, he did attend group therapy and art therapy sessions. At first he sat through these numbly, but as he rested and began to recover he began to be irritated by the sessions—a good sign. He developed a strong distaste for the smug young therapist who supervised the group sessions and who often reduced the women patients to tears. He also rebelled in the art classes, which he later called "organized infantilism"—though despite himself he came to like the cheerful young woman who ran them. There were many dead hours during his days at the hospital, but Styron did not mind the boredom as much as he normally might have. His body was freeing itself from the pharmaceuticals he had been taking, and his mind was resting and healing itself. He was released too from any sense of having to fulfill difficult responsibilities. There were no appearances to make or readings to give, no social occasions, no writing that had to be done.

One of Styron's clearest memories from his weeks in the Yale Hospital was of killing time by watching television, something he had almost never done. He sat through talk shows and sitcoms, took in *Dallas* and *Knots Landing,* and even tuned in to a few games of professional football—a sport that he normally loathed. He also listened to music, something that he had not done in recent years except on long drives in his automobile. These activities calmed his mind and allowed him to rest, especially during his first two weeks in the hospital.

On Christmas Day Styron's entire family came to visit him—Rose, Susanna and Polly and their husbands, Tom and Al—all of whom had come for the holidays. They brought food, gifts, energy, and chatter to the room. Susanna had spliced together a videotape incorporating scenes from old home movies and family trips and weddings. This was shown and laughed at, though her purpose in making the tape, as they all knew, was more than to provide humor. The celebration left Styron exhausted but feeling more nearly whole than he had in many months.

In January he began to read again with comprehension. Almost his first wish was to learn as much as he could about his illness and about what had happened to him. He was given several good books on depression to read, including *Mood Disorders,* by Peter C. Whybrow, Hagop S. Akiskal, and William T. McKinney, Jr. He also read Sigmund Freud's classic essay "Mourning and Melancholia." From these writings and others he learned that there might have been a genetic component to his disease. Suicide and depression run in families, sometimes appearing with baleful predictability from one generation to the next. Styron was unsure whether there was a genetic marker in his own background but suspected that there might be. Two of his father's brothers had been confined in asylums in North Carolina for long periods. His own father had suffered depressive episodes: he had been hospitalized for three weeks after his wife's death in 1939, and Styron suspected that there might have been other depressive periods of which he had not been informed. He also began to suspect that he had himself suffered through unrecognized periods of depression during his own life.

In these books and in other writings, Styron learned that persons who have suffered traumatic losses in childhood are particularly vulnerable to depression as adults. Especially devastating is the loss of a parent when one is between the ages of one and five or between the ages of ten and fourteen. Styron had first become aware of his mother's illness when he was ten, and she had died a few weeks after he turned fourteen. Adolescents of these ages are unable to understand death or to express grief as adults do, and they often carry with them through life a sense of unresolved or incomplete mourning. Frequently they develop elaborate strategies to conceal their emotions as adults; often they find it difficult to express love openly for others, though they feel love and attachment quite deeply. Much of this was a revelation to Styron. He had for so long professed not to have been much changed by his mother's death that he had come to believe it. He now began to think that her passing had probably affected him more deeply than he had ever known. He was reluctant, then and later, to place all of the responsibility for his depression on this childhood loss, but he knew that it must have been important, perhaps central, in the constellation of factors that had laid him low. As he rested in his hospital room he began to turn over in his mind how he might someday express these things, for he knew that one way of emotional purgation for him had always been the calmness that came when he rendered experience into art.

As his health improved, Styron began to see visitors. Vann Wood-ward, the Hackneys, Arthur Miller, John Marquand, and others came to see him. Bob Loomis visited, as did Peter and Maria Matthiessen. Rose came almost every day, often with Polly. Through January, Styron gained strength and confidence; Polly happily noted a return of his old temper and willfulness in her journal.

By February 8, 1986, Styron was ready to return to Roxbury. Late that afternoon Rose came to drive him home. After he had finished sup-per that night he sat in a Jacuzzi that she had just had installed. The warm, swirling water soothed and lulled him. He went to bed and im-mediately fell asleep. That night he had his first dream in months, a romp of a dream that went on and on. Almost two years later he could still describe the dream: "It was safaris and war, but jolly," he said, "and I was in and out of teepees, and I was running around in stockades, and I was up and down hills. There was music; it was the most astounding dream; it went on for eight or nine hours." Styron's imagination was be-ginning to function again. In the weeks to come he would reassemble his life, arranging it differently now but still building it around family and work. He knew things now that he wanted to write about. He was in no particular hurry to do so, but there were things that he wished eventually to say.

32

❧❦

"A Tidewater Morning"

THE FIRST THING that Styron decided to write was a fictionalized account of his mother's death. He began work on it late in the summer of 1986. He had included a little about her final illness in *Sophie's Choice,* but he had never allowed himself to remember and contemplate her last days. He had been away from the house for most of that period, staying with neighbors, but he had witnessed some of his mother's pain and had watched his father suffer during her final few weeks.

His story, which he called "A Tidewater Morning," was more than a simple recollection of Pauline Styron's death. It was also a meditation on rebellion and resistance to tyranny—political, religious, and individual. Styron brought several elements from the past together in the story. He reached back into his own life and remembered a boyhood experience—his afternoon paper route during the spring of 1940—and merged it with his mother's death, which had occurred in June 1939. He then took the writer's liberty of superimposing these two memories further back, onto the events of the very early fall of 1938, when Adolf Hitler threatened Czechoslovakia and caused the British prime minister, Neville Chamberlain, to back down. In these political maneuverings the stage was set for World War II.

"A Tidewater Morning," published in the August 1987 issue of *Esquire,* is acutely personal. In it Styron draws heavily on his memories of

Hilton Village and of the house on Hopkins Street where he and his parents lived. There is much atmosphere from the late 1930s in the story—mention of popular radio shows and brand-name products and movie stars of the time, and of FDR and the Depression. The atmosphere of Newport News is also captured, with its intense heat, its bustling war industry, its black people and working-class fathers and footloose children. Styron's purpose is more than to recapture that time and place, though: he also places a rebellious act by his autobiographical hero, a thirteen-year-old boy named Paul Whitehurst, alongside a similar act by the boy's father, Jefferson Whitehurst. Paul rebels against the mean-spirited bullying of Mr. Quigley, the beer-hall owner who bosses the paperboys in their work; Paul's father rebels against the saccharine, avuncular words of the neighborhood Presbyterian minister who offers the comfort of conventional religion to him just after his wife has died. These two acts of private resistance are themselves set against the larger backdrop of Hitler's aggression against the Czechs and Chamberlain's capitulation—this accomplished through the headlines on the newspapers that Paul delivers. Styron's story says that people must learn to resist tyranny in all of its forms—large and small, cruel and benign—and at all levels.

One other theme emerges from the story. At important moments in the narrative, Paul—who is a sensitive young artist-figure—deliberately lifts himself above the stress and pain that threaten to envelop him and creates an abstraction of what he is experiencing, the better to understand and bear it. That was just what William Styron was doing as he wrote this story. Fearful mysteries of grief, remorse, memory, and guilt could be faced and brought under control, he knew, by the power of art. The writer could confront and master his past through a willed act of the imagination, and he could place his own private losses in context by seeing them against larger historical movements. This, Styron seems to be saying, is the only way finally to address the almost intolerable ambiguities and injustices of one's private experience, and of the times through which one has lived.

"A Tidewater Morning" is a long story, almost the length of a novella. It is carefully crafted and luminously written. To have produced such a story so soon after his illness was a sign of Styron's return to health and balance. He had decided to arrange his life differently; he arose now in the mornings around nine o'clock, tended to personal and family business before noon, ate lunch around one, took his walk, and wrote (as always) in the afternoon. In a move that perhaps had private meaning for him, he ceased now to work in the little house that had been his writing studio since 1954. Instead he took over Polly's old bedroom upstairs in the main house and fitted it out to be his study, using for his writing surface a tilt-top table similar to the one he had used for *Lie Down in Darkness.* At this table he put in his daily stints of composition, just above the noise and movement of family life, no longer so solitary and removed. He began to socialize and to accept speaking and reading engagements again. He regulated his intake of alcohol quite carefully: one beer most days with lunch and a glass or two of wine with dinner—never more. He no longer drank whiskey; he knew that his body would not tolerate it.

Styron thought for a time of extending "A Tidewater Morning" into a novel. He believed that he might follow out the life of Paul's father, Jefferson Whitehurst, who was based on his own father. The incident that Styron had thought of fictionalizing was his father's enduring love for Eunice Edmundson and their reunion and marriage. Jefferson Whitehurst, he thought, might have a similar love with a similar denouement; he might also, along the way, witness events that would change him—the lynching of a Negro man, for example, which one of W. C. Styron's brothers had seen in rural North Carolina in the 1890s. The mechanism that Styron devised for this proposed novel was to have Paul Whitehurst discover, after his father's death, a box of letters that he had written to his former love over a period of fifty years—letters that he had never mailed. These letters would be reproduced from time to time in the novel so that Paul's voice would alternate with his father's. Styron finally decided, however, that he would leave "A Tidewater Morning" as it stood. He had written it originally as a short story, and it had a wholeness and integrity in that form that it might lose if made into the opening of a novel.

What Styron decided to do instead was to begin a different novel, this one based quite closely on his sufferings from depression. He never gave this novel a title, but he worked on it steadily for about three months, producing almost one hundred yellow leaves of manuscript. The writing is heavily autobiographical, opening with its narrator-protagonist, a fiction writer, in a mental ward where he has been hospitalized for depression. This narrator, whose name is Paul Whitehurst (the name of the boy in "A Tidewater Morning,") is patterned on Styron. Paul's wife, called Francesca, is based on Rose; of her Paul writes, "She was the first beautiful woman I wanted to love for her beauty alone." Paul describes the first hours of his hospitalization and tells of a panic attack he experienced in his room. He then doubles back to tell about the melancholia that has afflicted him and the drugs that he has been given to combat it. He tries to lull himself to sleep at night with this litany: "Nardil Desyrel and Xanax . . . Wynken Blynken and Nod . . . Hart Schaffner and Marx . . . Sage Rosemary and Thyme . . . Surely Goodness and Mercy . . ."

Parts of this manuscript are quite good, especially some of the scenes in the hospital, but Styron was working quite close to his own experience, and much of what he wrote is introspective and static. Passages early in the fragment show that he was uncomfortable with self-revelation. "It is easy to become beset by hesitations when thinking of setting down a personal chronicle of one's own mental illness," he says. "It is not something that one longs to write about." Further along he adds, in unusually stiff language: "One of the chief hesitations in my own case lies in the certain foreknowledge that if my account is to serve any worthwhile purpose I must be prepared to exhibit more of myself than either my sense of propriety or instinct for privacy would ordinarily allow me to do." Perhaps this discomfort is what caused Styron to abandon the manuscript.

He thought for several months about other ways of making fiction from his experience with depression, but no good ideas came to him. He had almost decided not to use the material at all when a series of happenings that seem, in retrospect, largely accidental persuaded him to treat the experience in a personal memoir. Styron had not planned to write this account. He had published a few short memoirs of personal experiences from time to time, but they had usually been humorous or ironic. He had never written at length in the autobiographical or confessional mode, and certainly not about an experience as personal as a mental breakdown. Since his depression, though, he had come to have great sympathy for other writers and artists who had succumbed to the disease and had taken their own lives. One of these victims was the Italian writer Primo Levi, a survivor of Auschwitz who had written eloquently of his experiences and had seemed to have overcome his past. On April 11, 1987, however, Levi threw himself down the stairwell of his apartment building in Turin and died of massive injuries from the fall. In late November 1988, New York University held a conference on Levi's life and work. The event was covered by *The New York Times;* an account of the proceedings appeared in the Arts section for Saturday, November 26. According to the report, many of the speakers at the conference were puzzled and dismayed by Levi's suicide. Alfred Kazin was quoted as saying, "It is difficult for me to credit a will to blackness and self-destruction in a writer so happy and full of new projects." Other conference participants wanted to deny that Levi had killed himself, or, if he had, to search for a ready-to-hand explanation for his despair—his mother's lingering illness, for example, or an irrational and uncontrollable impulse of some kind. At the root of these efforts seemed to be a sense of shame over Levi's act, as if he had revealed a weakness in character by his suicide.

Styron read the account with some irritation and found himself moved to respond. The next day, November 27, he wrote a short essay that was printed in the op-ed section of the *Times* for Monday, December 19. Entitled "Why Primo Need Not Have Died," Styron's piece was an argument that no stigma should be attached to Levi's decision to end his life. "The vast majority of those who do away with themselves," wrote Styron, "do not do it because of any frailty, and rarely out of impulse, but because they are in the grip of an illness that causes almost unimaginable pain." Styron then revealed that, three years before, he had undergone a period of serious depression. "I never attempted suicide," he wrote, "but the possibility had become more real and the desire more greedy as each wintry day passed and the illness became more smotheringly intense." Levi's mental agony, Styron thought, was beyond the understanding of most people. "This horror," he said, "is virtually indescribable since it bears no relation to normal experience." Styron ended the essay with a plea that depression be rid of its taint and that sufferers from the disorder be identified and hospitalized more readily. Perhaps in this way Primo Levi might have been saved.

To Styron's surprise this short essay brought numerous letters to the *Times,* three of which were published in the issue for January 4, 1989. The essay also brought him an invitation to appear that May at a Johns Hopkins symposium on affective disorders and another invitation to speak to the first meeting of the American Suicide Foundation in New York. One of those present at this meeting was Tina Brown, then the editor of *Vanity Fair*. She heard Styron describe what he had gone through, making his same points: that depression was a disease, not a failure of character, and that hospitalization and rest had saved him. A few days later she got in touch with Styron and asked him to write a longer account of his experiences. *Vanity Fair* would publish the manuscript, she said, and he should not worry about its length.

Styron decided to undertake the assignment, partly at Tina Brown's urging but also because he could see that most victims of depression were unable to express what they were enduring. Even he himself, with his command of the rhythms and metaphors of language, had felt stymied and choked when he had tried, during his illness, to anatomize his suffering for others. He would now attempt to become a voice for fellow sufferers from this disease, and he would reveal—in a good cause, he hoped—some of his own private pain.

That summer at the Vineyard, Styron began to set down an extended essay on his period of madness. The narrative gained momentum as he progressed with it, and he put all of his verbal power into play to evoke the experience of the disease. Depression, he wrote, is characterized by a "dank joylessness" and a "visceral queasiness." It is "painful and elusive," "malefic" and "stifling." One's thought processes are "engulfed by a toxic and unnameable tide." The atmosphere of the ailment is "unmodulated, its light a brown out." "This leaden and poisonous mood," he wrote, is "the color of verdigris," causing in the brain an "insidious meltdown." One lives in a "storm of murk," a "gray drizzle of horror," a "poisonous fogbank."

This essay, which Styron would entitle "Darkness Visible," is in part about language itself. In it Styron laments the fact that we have become saddled with the word "depression" to describe this most deranging of afflictions. "Depression," he says, is "a true wimp of a word for such a major illness." "The word," he continues, "has slithered innocuously through the language like a slug, leaving little trace of its intrinsic malevolence and preventing, by its very insipidity, a general awareness of the horrible intensity of the disease when out of control." A better word, much more apt, might be "brainstorm," for that is what the experience most nearly resembles. *Earthquake of the brain*

"Darkness Visible" is not a day-by-day or week-by-week account of Styron's breakdown and recovery, nor is it a fully revealing confession. Part of its effectiveness is that it is a shaped tale of selected incident and a meditation on the larger problems of depressive mental disorder. Styron does not attempt, for example, a full analysis of the pharmaceuticals that he took, nor does he mention each doctor who treated him. All physicians are subsumed in the figure of "Dr. Gold," who is based for the most part on the New Haven psychiatrist but who stands also for the medical profession at large. A good deal of Styron's treatment at Yale Hospital is also telescoped and summarized rather than particularized. Styron meant not so much to write a diary of his illness as to reflect on its sources and characteristics. Much is held back, much only suggested.

"Darkness Visible" appeared in *Vanity Fair* in December 1989, and the response to the piece was immediate and strong. Both the magazine and Styron himself received a flow of mail that did not slow for several months. Styron's impression, often confirmed by the letters, was that copies of the essay had been passed from hand to hand and read by as many as four or five persons. This pleased him; it was the strongest response he had ever received for an essay published in a magazine. Many of these letter writers thanked Styron for having described, in such evocative language, what they themselves had experienced but had been unable to recount. Many depressives had passed "Darkness Visible" along to their families and friends in an effort to educate them and make them begin to understand the illness. Styron said later that he was overwhelmed by the volume and character of these letters. He was accustomed to mail from readers of his fiction—some of it adoring, some abusive, some intelligent, some obtuse. What he had not felt before was such a strong sense of shared experience. The letters were often testamentary and frequently quite heartfelt. Styron had not dreamed that he would ever touch such a nerve.

"Darkness Visible," in its *Vanity Fair* text, had totaled almost fifteen thousand words, but even with that generous allowance of space Styron was aware of having left out some things that he could have said. In discussions with Robert Loomis early in 1990 he decided that he would expand the essay a little, adding some four thousand words to cover his experiences in Paris when he received the Del Duca prize. Then Random House would publish the longer text as a small book. In part Styron decided to do this in order to round out the story of his illness; in part he also wished to see his essay have a more permanent form and availability.

There was one other motive as well: in the spring of 1988 Styron had undergone a recurrence of depression, triggered by the drug Halcion. He was physically uncomfortable early that spring because of a calcium deposit in his upper spine that was pressing on a nerve and deadening his writing arm. The discomfort in his shoulder, quite intense, had made it difficult for him to fall asleep, and he had asked a physician to prescribe a sleeping pill. The doctor had given him a mild sedative, and this had helped him to become drowsy at night. In April, Styron and Rose made a trip together to Santa Monica, California, to see Susanna and her family and to fulfill a speaking engagement that he had accepted at Claremont Graduate School. His supply of sleeping pills had run out; Rose had some Halcion with her, which she had been taking to help her fall asleep, with no bad side effects. Styron took some of the Halcion and almost immediately began to experience a return of anxiety and dread such as he had not felt in three years. Worse, he began to fantasize greedily about death. "There, in that sunny landscape," he later wrote, "I was all but totally consumed by thoughts of suicide that were like a form of lust." While visiting Susanna at her home on the shore he sat up late one night, "thinking only of walking out into the ocean and being engulfed by the waves." Later, at Claremont, his thoughts became more specific: "I kept constant schemes in mind to have my wife lured away so I could secrete myself in a closet and end it all with a plastic bag."

Styron and Rose returned east, where he underwent surgery on his shoulder. During his convalescence, the dalliance with suicide continued. It was only during a consultation with a staff psychiatrist, to whom he reported that he was taking Halcion, that Styron learned of the evil side effects of the drug. He was immediately given another sleeping pill, and a few days later the murky depression lifted.

To the book version of *Darkness Visible* Styron added an indictment of Halcion, though he did not include an account of his experience with the drug. But he did eventually publish that story in an essay entitled "Prozac Days, Halcion Nights" that appeared in *The Nation* in January 1993. The essay, only in part a personal memoir, was intended primarily as an attack on the Upjohn pharmaceutical company, makers of Halcion, for resisting its banning in this country. The essay also criticized the Federal Food and Drug Administration for countenancing Upjohn's behavior and running interference between the company and the press.

Darkness Visible appeared as a book in 1990. It was reviewed in most major literary publications in the United States and in dozens of newspapers and other magazines, almost uniformly with high praise. The book appeared on the *New York Times* list of best-sellers, rising to the top position and remaining on the list, a little lower down, for several weeks. Styron was written about by newspaper columnists and appeared on national talk shows and on a CBS documentary on depression. Invitations to speak and read came in a constant stream; Styron turned down many of these, fearing that he would become a "guru of depression," but he felt duty-bound to make some appearances, often speaking to groups of physicians or to organizations for the prevention of suicide. His personal mail became enormous for a time, and the flow continues, only somewhat more slowly, to this day. Styron tried then and still tries to answer as many of these letters as he can. Sometimes he telephones the writer of a letter. He has saved all of this mail; it fills a white bureau in his workroom in Roxbury.

Coda

William Styron has continued to write and publish since the appearance of *Darkness Visible* in 1990. In 1993 he published *A Tidewater Morning: Three Tales from Youth,* a carefully crafted trio of long stories—"Love Day," "Shadrach," and "A Tidewater Morning." The Styrons divide each year, as always, between Roxbury and Vineyard Haven. Rose Styron continues her work for Amnesty International and other human rights organizations. In 1995 she and Craig Dripps published *By Vineyard Light,* a collection of her poems and his photographs. The Styron children, the three oldest now married, are pursuing careers in cinema, writing, dance, and psychology. William and Rose Styron are grandparents. Styron takes his daily walks and still sets a good pace. At seventy-two he remains innovative and productive.

SOURCES AND NOTES

The major collection of Styron's papers is in the Manuscript Department, W. R. Perkins Library, Duke University. Besides the holograph of *Sophie's Choice* and other manuscripts, typescripts, proofs, and published texts, this collection includes three large scrapbooks of memorabilia compiled by Styron's father; Styron's letters to his father; an extensive collection of Styron's letters to others and of correspondence sent to him; the letters sent by Styron to Elmer Holmes; the Wanamaker Diary for 1940; a copy of "The Genesis of William Styron," the account written by W. C. Styron, Sr., for Bobbs-Merrill in 1951; a long correspondence between Styron and the writer Don Harington; and the letters sent by Styron to Leon and Marianne Edwards. Styron's letters to William Blackburn and to Reynolds Price are filed separately in the Blackburn and Price papers at Duke. Unless otherwise indicated, letters are quoted from the originals in the Duke archive or from copies of other letters—these copies in the biographer's possession. All such materials will eventually become part of the Duke collection.

A second important collection of Styron's papers is in the Manuscripts Division, Library of Congress. It includes holograph manuscripts of *Lie Down in Darkness, The Long March, Set This House on Fire,* and *The Confessions of Nat Turner,* together with some typescript and proof material. Also at the Library of Congress are the false starts on "Blankenship" and *Set This House on Fire,* and the manuscripts of several shorter items. The papers of *Harper's Magazine* at the Library of Congress contain important information about Styron's appearances there during Willie Morris's editorship.

Styron's publishers and literary agents have been most helpful to me in the writing of this biography. I am grateful to them for granting access to their records. The Bobbs-Merrill papers are at the Lilly Library, Indiana University; the Random House and Harold Matson papers (which include the correspondence with Styron's first agent, Elizabeth McKee) are at the Butler Library, Columbia University; the Jonathan Cape papers are in the publishing history collections at the University of Reading; the Gallimard records are at that firm's headquarters on the rue Sébastien-Bottin in Paris. Copies of the Styron records from the files of the Hope Leresche and Tessa Sayle literary agencies (London) are in the biographer's possession, kindly provided by these firms.

Many of the comments by Styron are taken from a series of three lengthy oral history interviews that I conducted with him at Thanksgiving 1986, on 12 August 1987, and on 1 December 1987. Transcriptions and tapes of these interviews are in the Oral History Collections at the Butler Library, Columbia University; copies are in the Duke archive. For the present these materials are closed but eventually will be open to those who study Styron's life and career. The transcripts are cited here as Oral History I, II, and III, followed by page numbers.

Citations from Styron's nonfiction collection, *This Quiet Dust,* are from the expanded edition published by Vintage Books in January 1993. This volume includes six items not published in the 1982 first edition, and it substitutes a later memoir of James Jones for the one in the 1982 edition. The pagination for the two editions differs. The citations here are from the Vintage text, which is currently in print, though the quotations can easily be traced in the first edition by essay and section titles, which are always supplied.

The initial reviews for *Lie Down in Darkness, Set This House on Fire, The Confessions of Nat Turner,* and *Sophie's Choice* are not cited in the notes by title and date of review; that information is readily available in Jackson Bryer, with Mary Beth Hatem, *William Styron: A Reference Guide* (Boston: G. K. Hall, 1978). This annotated secondary bibliography is essential to anyone who wishes to study Styron's career and the reception of his writings. Also quite useful is Philip W. Leon, *William Styron: An Annotated Bibliography of Criticism* (Westport, Conn.:

Greenwood Press, 1978). A record through 1977 of Styron's own publications is James L. W. West III, *William Styron: A Descriptive Bibliography* (Boston: G. K. Hall, 1977).

Additional information may be found in Arthur D. Casciato and James L. W. West III, eds., *Critical Essays on William Styron* (Boston: G. K. Hall, 1982), and in James L. W. West III, ed., *Conversations with William Styron* (Jackson: University Press of Mississippi, 1985). These volumes are cited as *Critical Essays* and *Conversations.*

The following abbreviations are used throughout the Notes.

WS	William Styron
WCS	William C. Styron, Sr.
WB	William Blackburn
JJ	James Jones
PM	Peter Matthiessen
JPM	John P. Marquand, Jr.
JLWW	James L. W. West III
LDID	*Lie Down in Darkness* (1951)
LM	*The Long March* (1953)
STHOF	*Set This House on Fire* (1960)
NT	*The Confessions of Nat Turner* (1967)
SC	*Sophie's Choice* (1979)
TQD	*This Quiet Dust* (1982; 1993)
DV	*Darkness Visible* (1990)

1. Ancestors

The best account of Styron's childhood is "The Genesis of William Styron," a typescript prepared by his father for Bobbs-Merrill before publication of LDID. Copies of the typescript are in Styron's papers at Duke and in the Bobbs-Merrill papers, Lilly Library, Indiana University.

For the Styron and Clark families: Dora Adele Padgett, *The Styron (Styring) Family in America* (Washington, D.C.: privately published, 1966); Harold K. Styring, *Earls without Coronets (The Styr Dynasty)* (Sheffield: Hartley & Son, 1965); Ronald Tree, *A History of Barbados* (London: Rupert Hart-Davis, 1972); Karl Watson, *The Civilised Island of*

Barbados (Barbados: privately published, 1979); Ben B. Salter, *Portsmouth Island: Short Stories and History* (privately published, 1972); James Edward White III, *The Gilgoes of Portsmouth Island and Related Families* (New Bern, N.C.: Eastern North Carolina Genealogical Society, 1979)—see the chapter on the Styron family; U.S. Census Records, Manufacturing Schedules, and Slave Schedules for Beaufort and Hyde Counties, 1820–1880, 1900–1920 (the records for 1890 were burned); *Branson's Business Directory,* edns. of 1872ff.; Registry and Deed Books, Beaufort County Courthouse, Washington, N.C., esp. Bk. 22A: 548–49, and Bk. 71: 521–23; fire maps, BHM Regional Library, Washington, N.C.; Louis H. Manarin, *North Carolina Troops, 1861–1865, A Roster* (Raleigh: State Dept. of Archives and History, 1966–87); Confederate Veterans Records, National Archives, Washington, D.C.; *Washington Daily News,* esp. "Greater Washington Edition" of 11 Aug. 1914, obituary for Alpheus Styron, 5 Nov. 1920, for Marianna Clark Styron, 14 Feb. 1938; Clark family wills (transcripts), Genealogy Folder, Styron papers, Duke; William N. Still, "The Shipbuilding Industry in Washington, North Carolina," in Joseph F. Steelman, ed., *Of Tar Heel Towns, Shipbuilders, Reconstructionists and Alliancemen: Papers in North Carolina History* (Greenville: East Carolina University, 1981): 26–50; Marilu Burch Smallwood, *Some Colonial and Revolutionary Families of North Carolina* (Macon, Ga.: Southern Press, 1964)—esp. useful for the Clark family; *Washington, North Carolina, Metropolis of the Pamlico* (Richmond: Central Publishing Co., 1915); Ursula Fogleman Loy and Pauline Marion Worthy, eds., *Washington and the Pamlico* (Washington, N.C.: Washington-Beaufort Bicentennial Commission, 1976); C. Wingate Reed, *Beaufort County: Two Centuries of Its History* (privately published, 1962); *Washington Gazette,* files for 1889 esp.; headstones in the Styron family plot, Live Oaks Cemetery, Washington, N.C.; North Carolina State Univ. archives and alumni records, and *The Agromeck* (A&M yearbook), vol. 8, 1910; *Catalog of the North Carolina College of Agriculture and Mechanic Arts, 1906–1907* (Raleigh: Uzzell and Co., 1907)—for W. C. Styron's curriculum.

For the Abraham family: Evelyn Abraham, *Over the Mountains* (Uniontown, Pa.: privately published, 1936)—a biographical account of the original Enoch Abraham; extensive Abraham family papers and photographs in the possession of Susannah Benson (Willow Street, Pa.); additional family papers held by Lenore Abraham (Uniontown, Pa.) and by Dee and Arthur Sloughfy (Smithfield, Pa.), esp. the obituary clipping (ca. 1 Sept. 1911) "E. H. Abraham Dies after a Long Illness"; *Alumni Directory, University of Pittsburgh, 1787–1916,* vol. 2; Muriel Sheppard, *Cloud by Day*

(Chapel Hill: University of North Carolina Press, 1947)—an account of coke mining in and around Uniontown; Richard Robbins, "Pulitzer Prize Winner Shaped by a Uniontown He Barely Knew," *Tribune-Review* (Greensburg, Pa.), 19 June 1994, 4–6; WS, " 'A Horrid Little Racist,' " *New York Times Magazine,* 8 Oct. 1995, 80–81.

For background on the Duke family see Nannie May Tilley, *The Bright-Tobacco Industry, 1860–1929* (Chapel Hill: University of North Carolina Press, 1948); Robert F. Durden, *The Dukes of Durham, 1865–1929* (Durham: Duke University Press, 1975).

Quotations: p. 11—"that sometime between . . ." WCS to Eunice Edmundson, 19 Oct. 1914; p. 16—"Pauline, you sinner . . ." Vehna Sharp to Pauline Abraham, 15 Nov. 1908; p. 17—"How's your voice? . . ." "Gwen" to Pauline Abraham, n.d. [1907]; p. 17—"Are you never . . ." "Gwen" to Pauline Abraham, 17 Nov. 1910.

2. Youth

Sources for information about Styron's childhood include WCS, "The Genesis of William Styron"; Scrapbook I at Duke; WS's grade-school records, Microfilm Dept., Newport News Public Schools; scrapbooks at Hilton Village Elementary School. See also *Hilton Village after Fifty Years* (Newport News: Dept. of City Planning, 1968); Ruth Hanners Chambers, *Hilton Village, 1918–1968* (Newport News: Woman's Club of Hilton Village, 1967); and "Hilton, Once Muddy Woodland Spot, Now Thriving Center," *Newport News Daily Press,* 26 Apr. 1936. For the May Day pageants: "Colorful May Celebration Is Held at Hilton," *Newport News Times-Herald,* 23 May 1931; "Colorful May Day Fete Is Held by Hilton Students," *Newport News Times-Herald,* 21 May 1932.

3. Newport News

For Newport News: Parke Rouse, Jr., *Endless Harbor: The Story of Newport News* (Newport News: Newport News Historical Committee [1969]); Rouse, *The Good Old Days in Hampton and Newport News* (Richmond: Dietz Press, 1986); Alexander Crosby Brown, ed., *Newport News' 325 Years* (Newport News: Newport News Golden Anniversary Corporation, 1946); Annie Lash Jester, *Newport News, Virginia, 1607–1960* (Newport News: City of Newport News, 1961); *Commemorating the Fiftieth Anniversary of* the *James River Country Club* (Newport News: James River Country Club, 1982); J. Edward Peeples, *Centennial History of First Presbyterian Church, Newport News, Virginia, 1883–1983* (Bryn Mawr, Pa.: Dorrance and Co., 1983). Thomas Wolfe wrote of his experiences as a worker in Newport News in "The Face of War," *From Death to Morning* (New York: Scribner's, 1935).

For African American culture in Newport News: Raymond Wolters, *The New Negro on Campus* (Princeton: Princeton University Press, 1975), chap. 6; *The Hampton Album* (photographs), intro. Lincoln Kirstein (New York: Museum of Modern Art, 1966); Arthur Huff Fauset, *Black Gods of the Metropolis: Negro Religious Cults of the Urban North* (1944; repr. Philadelphia: University of Pennsylvania Press, 1971); Robert Taylor, "In Search of Daddy Grace," *Boston Globe,* 11 May 1969 (magazine section): 35–41; "Solomon Lightfoot Michaux," *Dictionary of American Negro Biography* (New York: Norton, 1982); clipping and photograph files, Newport News Public Library, West Branch (30th St.), Newport News, Va.

Quotations: p. 31—"Essentially the city . . ." "A Voice from the South," TQD, 56; p. 32—"Certainly no landscape . . ." "The Service," TQD, 208; p. 34—"These last . . ." and "They were poor . . ." WS, *Inheritance of Night: Early Drafts of "Lie Down in Darkness"* (Durham: Duke University Press, 1993), 130–31; p. 35—"Even now I marvel . . ." unpublished graduation address, Christopher Newport College, May 1973, 14–15; p. 37—"confused and blurred . . ." "This Quiet Dust," TQD, 10; pp. 37, 38—"To my bemused . . ." and "My awareness of Negroes . . ." and "rootless and synthetic town . . ." "A Voice from the South," TQD, 55–58.

4. Pauline's Death

Issues of *The Sponge* for 1938–39 survive, but the issue containing "Typhoon and the Tor Bay" remains unlocated. The letters to Elmer Holmes, from both WS and his mother, are in the Styron papers at Duke. The obituary for Pauline Styron is in WCS's Scrapbook I, at Duke. The death certificate for Pauline Styron, completed and signed by Dr. Russell Buxton, who performed surgery on her, is in the Commonwealth of Virginia Division of Vital Records, doc. 16874. Styron's recollections of the James River plantations are taken from "Children of a Brief Sunshine," *Architectural Digest,* March 1984, 32ff.

Quotations: p. 44—"the South of pine forests . . ." "A Voice from the South," TQD, 59; p. 47—"I wrote an imitation Conrad thing . . ." from

"William Styron," *Writers at Work: "The Paris Review" Interviews,* ed. Malcolm Cowley (New York: Viking, 1958), 270; p. 50—"I was not mature enough . . ." and "They considered . . ." Oral History I, 25.

5. Fourteenth Year

Sources are the Morrison High School 1940 yearbook (*The Warwick*) and the 1939–40 school newspaper (*The Sponge*); also Margaret T. Peters, *A Guidebook to Virginia's Historical Markers* (Charlottesville: University Press of Virginia, 1985), entry U-122. The Wanamaker diary is in the Styron papers at Duke.

6. Christchurch

Sources are the Christchurch school archives and alumni records; issues of the school newspaper (*The Stingaree*) and the 1941 and 1942 yearbooks (*The Log*); Willis H. Wills (former teacher at Christchurch) to JLWW, 9 July 1987.

Quotations: p. 65—"While my Ivy League friends . . ." "Christchurch," TQD, 312; p. 75—"Haarmann's methodical brain . . ." WS, *A Chance in a Million,* facsimile edn. (State College, Pa.: Press de la Warr, 1993)—the MS is at Duke; pp. 76, 78—"I'll never forget . . ." and "Christchurch may not have been . . ." "Christchurch," TDQ, 309–10, 312.

7. Davidson

Davidson College archives and alumni records; issues of the 1942–43 college newspaper (*The Davidsonian*) and the 1943 yearbook (*Quips and Cranks*). Styron's academic transcripts from the Davidson registrar's office. Styron's copy of *The Wildcat Handbook* for 1942 is among his papers at Duke (and bears his marginalia). The accounts of hot-boxing and of WS's first sexual experience are from Oral History I: 27, and II: 67–71. The freshman themes are in the Davidson College Library; Styron's difficulties with the Court of Control are recorded in the issues of the *Davidsonian* for 8 Oct. and 5 Nov. 1942; the account of the readings at Sigma Upsilon is in the *Davidsonian,* 10 Dec. 1942. On Davidson's fraternities: Chalmers G. Davidson to JLWW, 1 Feb. 1990.

Quotations: pp. 83, 87—"I mean really unmanly . . ." and "My memory of these two old fossils . . ." WS to Chalmers Davidson, 4 Nov. 1958; pp. 86, 87—"as wicked and exciting . . ." and "the most miserable freshman . . ." typed transcript of Styron's remarks at a Davidson College Convocation, 18 Apr. 1986, Alumni Office, Davidson; p. 89—"The exodus . . ." "Writer Tells of Confusion in Migration," *Davidsonian,* 25 Feb. 1943, 1; p. 89—"Although the large majority . . ." "Birdmen Get Fine Welcome by Local Mob," *Davidsonian,* 11 Mar. 1943, 1; p. 91—"People are being drafted . . ." WS to WCS, dated 29 Mar. 1943 in WCS's hand.

8. Duke and William Blackburn

Styron's academic transcripts are preserved at the Duke University registrar's office. Other information has been taken from his file in the Duke alumni office. His disciplinary record in the V-12 unit is a part of his Marine Corps file, USMC Records, St. Louis, Mo. Information about Duke during World War II has been drawn from photographs in the Duke archives and from runs of the student newspaper (*The Duke Chronicle*) and the yearbook (*Chanticleer*) in the Duke archives, which also holds the issues of the *Archive* that print Styron's early literary efforts. A useful volume has been James G. Schneider, *The Navy V-12 Program* (Boston: Houghton Mifflin, 1987).

For the history of Duke, see Earl W. Porter, *Trinity and Duke, 1892–1924* (Durham: Duke University Press, 1964); Robert F. Durden, *The Launching of Duke University, 1924–1949* (Durham: Duke University Press, 1993); and Jeanne E. Stevens, "The Impacts of World War II on Duke University," senior honors thesis, Dept. of History, Duke University, April 1991. On Blackburn, see John V. Blalock, "A Day in the Life of a University Professor," *Durham Morning Herald,* 23 Feb. 1947. The account of Styron's debate with his math teacher is taken from a letter that he wrote to her on 9 August 1965, facsimiled as Keepsake No. 1, University of North Carolina at Charlotte Library Assoc., 1987. The story of Styron's identifying himself as Ben Franklin is from James L. W. West III, " 'Blankenship': An Introduction," *Papers on Language and Literature* 23 (Fall 1987), 426. The typescript of the second theme for Blackburn is among Styron's papers at Duke; the poetic effort by "Martin Kostler" is identified in Styron's hand as his own work on a clipping pasted in WCS, Scrapbook I.

Quotations: pp. 93, 94—"appeared to regard . . ." and "Dark as they were . . ." untitled memoir in *Duke Encounters* (Durham: Duke University

Office of Publications, 1977); other recollections of Blackburn are from "William Blackburn," TQD, 275–78; p. 99—"one-man rampage . . ." "On William Blackburn and Creative Imagination," *Duke Dialogue,* 13 Dec. 1991, 4; "Hemingway, Wolfe . . ." WS to WCS, 23 Nov. 1943; p. 100—"I think he's . . ." WS to WCS, 28 Sept. 1943; p. 100—comments on Thomas Wolfe are from " 'O Lost!' Etc.," TQD, 73–86; p. 101—"My work, while far . . ." WS to WCS, 18 Jan. 1944; p. 101—"I take great pride . . ." quoted by WS in a letter to WCS, 12 Mar. 1944; p. 102—"I am continually . . ." WS to WCS, 15 Sept. 1943; p. 104—"erotic ice age" preface to *Inheritance of Night: Early Drafts of "Lie Down in Darkness":* viii; p. 106—"He gazed . . ." "Autumn," *Archive,* Feb. 1945; p. 106—" 'This day is so strange . . .' " "Sun on the River," *Archive,* Sept. 1944. "The Long Dark Road," *Archive,* March 1944, has been reprinted in *One and Twenty: Duke Narrative and Verse, 1924–1945,* selected by William Blackburn (Durham: Duke University Press, 1945), and in *William Styron's "The Confessions of Nat Turner": A Critical Handbook,* ed. Melvin J. Friedman and Irving Malin (Belmont, Calif.: Wadsworth, 1970).

9. Marines, First Stint

The details of Styron's tenure in the Clap Shack are drawn from the medical records in his Marine Corps service file; from his account in Oral History II, 10–16; and from "A Case of the Great Pox," *The New Yorker,* 18 Sept. 1995, 62–75. A few details are taken from Styron's play *In the Clap Shack* (New York: Random House, 1973).

Quotations: p. 110—"the boys pulling . . ." WS to WCS, 31 Dec. 1944; p. 110—"the remorseless . . ." "A Farewell to Arms," TQD: 227; p. 111— "Bill sang it . . ." Robert C. Snider to JLWW, 8 Aug. 1989; pp. 111, 112— "They sizzle . . ." and "He carried in his dungaree . . ." "A Farewell to Arms," TQD, 229–30; p. 114, 116—"charnel-house atmosphere . . ." and "with no more ceremony . . ." "My Generation," *Esquire,* Oct. 1968, 123–24; p. 116—"Cruel bastards!" and "Ignoramuses!" Oral History II, 14–15; p. 117—"Last night when . . ." WS to WCS, dated "Saturday" by WS [9 Dec. 1944?]; p. 119—"hotshot Stanford . . ." Oral History II, 17; p. 119—"frog-faced fellow . . ." and "Did you ever put . . ." WS to Robert C. Snider, 29 Jan. 1958; p. 120—"You can figure . . ." and "the class just ahead . . ." "My Generation," 123; p. 121—"He was a great . . ." Oral History II, 18–19; p. 122—"I recall . . ." WS to Snider, 29 Jan. 1958; p. 124— "I remember being given . . ." from the intro. to "Blankenship," *Papers on*

Language and Literature, 427; pp. 124–25—descriptions of Harts Island are from the text of "Blankenship," 430–48 (the surviving typescript is at the Library of Congress); p. 126—"Billy *thinks* he can write . . ." Mary Wakefield Buxton, "One Woman's Opinion," *Southside Sentinel* (Urbanna, Va.), 18 Feb. 1993, 2; p. 127—"training manuals . . ." "MacArthur," TQD, 214; p. 127—"It is for me . . ." "A Farewell to Arms," TQD, 228; p. 128— "In many ways . . ." intro. to "The Service," TQD, 209.

10. After the War

A few details of the trip to Trieste are taken from Styron's "A Moment in Trieste," *American Vanguard,* ed. Don M. Wolfe (Ithaca, N.Y.: Cornell University Press, 1948). Information about Bread Loaf is from Theodore Morrison, *Bread Loaf Writers' Conference: The First Thirty Years (1926–1955)* (Middlebury, Vt.: Middlebury College Press, 1976). Some information about Styron's relationship with Blackburn is from "Professor, Novelist Talk about Success," *Charlotte Observer,* 27 Jan. 1952; the picture of Blackburn as a teacher is partly from Virginia G. Ficke (former student) to JLWW, 1 Feb. 1989. For descriptions of Hiram Haydn, see the tributes to him in "Hiram Haydn (1907–1973)," *American Scholar* 43 (Summer 1974), 371–82. A good source of information about the Rhodes Scholar program is Lord Godfrey Elton, *The First Fifty Years of the Rhodes Trust and the Rhodes Scholarships, 1903–1953* (Oxford: Basil Blackwell, 1956). Styron recalled his Rhodes Scholar interview in "Almost a Rhodes Scholar," TQD, 317–22; other information about the experience is from WS to WCS, 15 Dec. 1946. Styron's correspondence with the *Virginia Quarterly Review* is at the Alderman Library, University of Virginia. The letter to him from John Selby, dated 6 February 1946, is in WCS, Scrapbook I at Duke.

Quotations: p. 140—"I've come to the stage . . ." WS to WCS, 21 Oct. 1946; pp. 140–41—"There is, I think . . ." WS to WCS, 2 Mar. 1947.

11. McGraw-Hill

Both false starts on LDID are facsimiled in *Inheritance of Night: Early Drafts of "Lie Down in Darkness."* On the New School, see Peter M. Rutkoff and William B. Scott, *New School: A History of the New School for Social Research* (New York: Free Press, 1986). Financial details of the legacy left to WS and his father are from WS to WCS, 28 Oct. 1947. "A Moment in Trieste," which appeared in the 1949 volume of *American Vanguard,* was cited in the previous chapter; "The Enormous Window" appeared in the next volume of *American Vanguard,* ed. Charles I. Glicksberg (New York: Cambridge Publishing Co., 1950).

Quotations: pp. 143, 144—"The work is about the same . . ." and "I have often thought . . ." WS to WCS, 24 July 1947; p. 144—"I don't think I'm a complete sybarite . . ." WS to WCS, 20 Aug. 1947; p. 144—"The doctor informs me . . ." WS to WCS, dated "Saturday" in WS's hand; pp. 144–46— "The gist of her letter . . ." WS to Mary Wakefield Buxton, 16 Feb. 1983; p. 146—"When I left . . ." WS, "Recollections," *Hartford Courant Magazine,* 3 Jan. 1982, 4; p. 146—"Aswell obviously . . ." WS to WCS, 10 Oct. 1947; p. 149—"[He] liked them . . ." WS to WCS, 5 Jan. 1948; p. 150—"I'm very glad . . ." WS to WCS, 28 Oct. 1947; p. 154—"No work since . . ." *"Lie Down in Darkness"* TQD, 325; pp. 156,158—"I can't tell you . . ." and "New York is beginning to wear . . ." WS to WCS, dated "Wednesday Night" in WS's hand.

12. Durham and Flatbush

Styron's correspondence with Elizabeth McKee, and with subsequent literary agents, is in the Harold Matson papers, Manuscripts Division, Butler Library, Columbia University; McKee and her partner, Elizabeth McIntosh, merged their agency with the Matson agency, and the papers of the two firms are filed together. Mozart's Piano Concerto no. 20: William Canine to JLWW, 1 Aug. 1985; Brice's parties, Lewis Leary to JLWW, 21 Apr. 1985. The typescript of "The Brothers," 8 pages, together with the cover sheet listing magazines to which it was submitted, is among Styron's papers at Duke. Information about the progress of the novel is taken from the facsimile edition of *Inheritance of Night.* Recollections of the period in Flatbush are from Michel Braudeau, "Why I Wrote *Sophie's Choice"* (interview), *L'Express,* 28 Feb. 1981, 76; trans. *Conversations,* 243–55.

Quotations: pp. 160, 161—"only a small part . . ." and "I'm twenty-three years old . . ." WS to McKee, 9 Sept. 1948; p. 161—"The story, in short . . ." WS to McKee, 12 Oct. 1948; p. 164—"The novel is coming along . . ." WS to WCS, dated 7 Oct. 1948 by WCS; p. 164—"I write and write . . ." WS to WCS, 10 Nov. 1948; p. 165—"That was quite a letter . . ." Hiram Haydn to WS, 23 Mar. 1949; p. 166—"very profound and stoical . . ." WS to WCS, dated "Sunday" in WS's hand; p. 166—"That will cut down . . ." WS to WCS, 16 Apr. 1949; pp. 167, 170—"The house where I live . . ." and "a handyman's job . . ." WS to WCS, 6 June 1949.

13. Valley Cottage and West Eighty-eighth Street

The alternate titles for LDID are inscribed on a sheet of notes kept with the MS of the novel at the Library of Congress. For Styron's fried chicken recipe, see "Southern Fried Chicken (with Giblet Gravy)," *The Artists' and Writers' Cookbook,* ed. Beryl Barr and Barbara Turner Sachs (Sausalito, Calif.: Contact Editions, 1961), 87–92. Joe Gould is the subject of Joseph Mitchell, *Joe Gould's Secret* (New York: Viking, 1965). Haydn's account of his dealings with Bobbs-Merrill is given in some detail in his memoir, *Words and Faces* (New York: Harcourt Brace Jovanovich, 1974), 63–80, et passim. Styron's eye-test score is recorded in his medical record in his Marine Corps file. His letters to William Canine are in Special Collections at the Fishburn Library, Hollins College. For Styron's further thoughts on Douglas MacArthur, see "MacArthur" TQD, 210–20.

Quotations: p. 172—"It just wouldn't come . . ." John J. Geoghegan III, "William Styron at Home," *Connecticut,* April 1982, 33; p. 178—"I'm hard at work . . ." WS to WCS, 31 July 1949; p. 178—"ocean of trees . . ." WS to WCS, 4 July 1949; p. 178—"I've begun to wonder . . ." WS to WCS, 31 July 1949; p. 179—"Sigrid and I were down . . ." WS to WCS, undated [Oct. 1949]; p. 179—"For private and gratuitous . . ." WS to WCS, 1 Sept. 1949; pp. 179–80—"I've learned to write . . ." WS to WCS, 12 Dec. 1949; p. 180— "The cocktail party . . ." WS to WCS, 11 Feb. 1950; p. 180—"the 'G.A.N.,' . . ." WS to WCS, 11 Feb. 1950; p. 180—"well along into . . ." WS to WCS, 15 May 1950; p. 181—"I think I'm all set . . ." WS to WCS, 8 July 1950; p. 185— "I almost faint . . ." WS to William Canine, 27 Jan. 1951; p. 185—"I don't know . . ." WS to WCS, 6 Dec. 1950; pp. 185–86— "So close to the end . . ." WS to Canine, 27 Jan. 1951; p. 186—"It was a great shock . . ." WS to WCS, 6 Feb. 1951; p. 188—"Flanked by . . ." WS, "Marriott, the Marine," *Esquire,* Sept. 1971, 102.

14. Marines, Second Stint

Herman Ziegner's report on LDID, together with internal documents relating to its expurgation, are in the Bobbs-Merrill files, Lilly Library; the memo quoted in this chapter is dated 7 May 1951. Styron's recollections of the matter are published in " 'I'll Have to Ask Indianapolis,' " *Traces* (Indiana Historical Society), Spring 1995, 5–12. In that same issue of *Traces,* see J. Kent Calder, "David Laurance Chambers, Hiram Haydn, and *Lie Down in Darkness,*" 14–23; see further Arthur D. Casciato, "His Editor's

Hand: Hiram Haydn's Changes in *Lie Down in Darkness*," *Studies in Bibliography* 33 (1980), 263–73; repr. *Critical Essays:* 36–46; and Haydn's own comments in *Words and Faces,* p. 49, et passim. Styron had the opportunity to restore the cut passages for the Vintage Uniform Edition of his writings but chose to let the text stand as originally published.

On Jones's success, see A. B. C. Whipple, "James Jones and His Angel," *Life,* 7 May 1951, 142–57; Styron remembers reading *From Here to Eternity* at Valley Cottage in "A Literary Friendship," *Esquire,* April 1989. On Charlie Sullivan's record in Korea, see H. D. Quigg, "Sacramentan Leads the Band; Machine Gun His Baton," *Sacramento Bee,* 7 Feb. 1951, 3. Details of the short mortar rounds at Lejeune are from "Shells Fall Short, Kill 8 Marines," *New York Times,* 21 June 1951, 1; and from two brief follow-up stories in the *Times* for 22 and 23 June. C. P. Kimbal's report on WS's eyesight is in the medical history portion of Styron's Marine Corps file, entry dated 26 June 1951. Details of "Anna's" suicide are from interviews with Newport News residents and from coverage in the *Daily Press* and *Times-Herald,* 29 and 30 July 1951.

Quotations: p. 190—"I've forgotten . . ." WS to Tom Peyton, 24 Apr. 1951; p. 191—"Of course you must know . . ." WS to WCS, 1 June 1951; p. 192— "Bill, you certainly know . . ." Haydn to WS, 24 May 1951; p.193—"I think that Mr. Styron . . ." from Haydn to WS, 18 June 1951; p. 193—"Jack Aldridge had gone . . ." Didi Parker to WS, 29 May 1951; p. 195—"If the lunatic fringe . . ." WS to Tom Peyton, 9 May 1951; pp. 196–97—"We marched and marched . . ." WS to Sigrid de Lima [postmarked 22 June 1951]; p. 199—"I owe that guy . . ." Oral History II, 26.

15. *Lie Down in Darkness*

Hiram Haydn's memories of John Maloney, whose talent he especially admired, are in *Words and Faces,* 38–41. Some of Marquand's recollections of Styron during this period are from John Phillips [Marquand, Jr.], "Styron Unlocked," *Vogue,* Dec. 1967, 269. The letters to Styron from Elizabeth Buxton Styron, Tris Blackburn, Ashbel Brice, and friends from Newport News are in the Duke collection. Styron's statements about himself are from "William Styron," *New York Herald-Tribune Book Review,* 7 Oct. 1951, 26; "The Author," *Saturday Review of Literature,* 15 Sept. 1951, 12; and "This Week's Personality," unlocated clipping in WCS, Scrapbook I, Duke. Details about subsidiary rights to LDID are from the Bobbs-Merrill papers, Lilly Library, and the Random House and Harold Matson files,

Butler Library. Particulars of the Prix de Rome are from Mary T. Williams (of the American Academy in Rome) to WS, 27 Feb. 1952, and from WS to WCS, 22 Feb. 1952. Bryan Forbes has given an account of his trip with Styron in chap. 23 of *A Divided Life: Memoirs* (London: Heinemann, 1992), 231–41. Details of the trip to Denmark are from WS to WCS, 1 May 1952.

Quotations: p. 205—"Truly I'm proud . . ." Blackburn to WS, 2 Sept. 1951; pp. 207–8—"The Oliviers . . ." WS to Edith Crow, 11 Jan. 1952; p. 210—"I'm of course looking . . ." WS to WCS, 12 Feb. 1952; pp. 210, 211—"Lena sang . . ." and "The British are admirable . . ." WS to Edith Crow, 13 Mar. [1952]; p. 212—"groaning, crashing sea . . ." WS to WCS, 30 Mar. 1952.

16. Paris, 1952

For Styron's memories of his time in Paris in 1952, see his article *"The Paris Review,"* Harper's Bazaar, Aug. 1953, 122–23, 173; and his introduction to *Best Short Stories from "The Paris Review"* (New York: Dutton, 1959). His recollection of the party hosted by Darryl Zanuck, and several other details in this chapter, are from Michael Shnayerson, *Irwin Shaw, A Biography* (New York: Putnam's, 1989), 211, et passim; and Shnayerson, "Higher Matthiessen," *Vanity Fair,* December 1991. The scene at the Blue Mill Tavern is taken from Styron's "The Distant Shaw," *Vanity Fair,* Aug. 1989, 48, 53. William Pène du Bois's story of Styron's lunchtime visits is from "The Paris Review Sketchbook," *Paris Review* 79 (1981), 338, a useful compendium of recollections by the founders of the journal and by others associated with it during its early years. Also helpful are Christopher Sawyer-Lauçanno, *The Continual Pilgrimage: American Writers in Paris, 1944–1960* (New York: Grove Press, 1992); and Craig Lambert, *"The Paris Review,* Interviewed," *Harvard Magazine,* Nov.–Dec. 1993, 68–73.

Quotations: p. 217—"I was wrong . . ." WS to McKee, 27 May 1952; pp. 219–20—"Paris is just about all . . ." WS to WCS, 1 May 1952; p. 220— "I would be perfectly . . ." WS to McKee, 20 Apr. 1952; p. 220—"people whom I haven't . . ." WS to McKee, 14 May 1952; p. 221—"I've finally pretty much decided . . ." WS to WCS, 1 May 1952; p. 222—"I don't want to be . . ." WS to McKee, 14 May 1952; p. 222—"I hope that when I'm through . . ." WS to WCS, 20 May 1952; p. 222—"I will repeat . . ." Haydn to WS, 15 May 1952.

17. *The Long March*

The manifesto for *Discovery* is in the first number of the journal (Feb. 1953). The holograph of LM is at the Library of Congress; the typescript, and Styron's letters to Bourjaily, are at the University of Florida Library, to which Bourjaily donated the files of the journal. Plimpton's account of the reading of LM was first published in *Colony News* (MacDowell Colony, Peterborough, N.H.) 18 (Fall/Winter 1988), 2–4; repr. *The Best of Plimpton* (New York: Atlantic Monthly Press, 1990), 212–19. Styron's *Paris Review* interview first appeared in the Spring 1954 number of the journal and is collected in *Writers at Work: "The Paris Review" Interviews,* ed. Malcolm Cowley (New York: Viking, 1958), 267–82. Buchwald's column is "The Brave Bulls and the Cowardly Fan," *New York Herald-Tribune* (American edn.), 4 Sept. 1952.

Quotations: p. 225—"In France . . ." WS to Bourjaily, 13 June 1952; pp. 225, 227—"Through some stroke . . ." and "All my intentions . . ." *"The Long March,"* TQD, 333–35; p. 227—"I'm pleased with it . . ." WS to Bourjaily, 15 July 1952; p. 229—" ' "Peyton," in French . . .' " WS to WCS, 18 July 1952; p. 230—"I couldn't get . . ." Oral History II: 60; p. 230—"I began to feel . . ." WS to WCS, 9 Sept. 1952; p. 232—"corking good job . . ." Haydn to WS, 27 Aug. 1952; p. 233—"like FBI agents . . ." Cowley's intro. to *Writers at Work,* 5; p. 235—"Life in Paris . . ." WS to JPM, 17 Sept. 1952.

18. Rome

The farewell meeting between Styron and Matthiessen in Paris is described in WS's letter to Elizabeth McKee, 8 Oct. 1952. Background on the fellows at the American Academy is taken from *American Academy in Rome: Report, 1951–55* (New York: American Academy, 1955). Styron's recollections of Truman Capote are from "In Celebration of Capote," *Vanity Fair,* Dec. 1984, 120, 122. Other information from Gerald Clarke, *Capote: A Biography* (London: Hamish Hamilton, 1988). Some details of the Styrons' first meeting in Rome are from Elizabeth Maker, "Could Styrons Build Romance in a Day?" *Litchfield County Times,* 12 May 1995. Information about the Austin convertible is from WS to Leon and Marianne Edwards, 10 Dec. 1952. Styron's "Letter to an Editor" is in the inaugural issue of *The Paris Review* (Spring 1953), 9–13.

Quotations: p. 239—"I'm really not much . . ." WS to JPM, 8 Oct. 1952; p. 244—"I have met . . ." WS to WCS, 27 Oct. 1952; p. 244—"Roman traffic . . ." WS to WCS, 5 Dec. 1952; pp. 244–45—"I think it might be . . ." John Train to WS, 27 Oct. 1952; p. 245—"learned articles . . ." Plimpton, "The Paris Review Sketchbook," 312; p. 250—"I've never seen so much snow . . ." WS to WCS, 8 Jan. 1953.

19. Marriage and Ravello

The text of "Blankenship" appears in *Papers on Language and Literature* 23 (Fall 1987). Styron's correspondence with Maxwell Geismar is in Geismar's papers, Boston University Library. Styron's letter to his father announcing his wedding plans is dated 24 Apr. 1953. Shaw's cable was quoted first in "The Paris Review Sketchbook," 333; it is also quoted in Shnayerson, *Irwin Shaw,* which is the source for Rose Styron's memory of Lillian Hellman (p. 220).

Quotations: p. 253—"I used to snicker . . ." WS to Geismar, 24 March 1953; p. 256—"already depleted . . ." WS to JPM, 17 Apr. 1953; p. 256—"CITY ROCKED BY NEWS . . ." JPM to WS, n.d. [April 1953]; p. 257—"This sounds . . ." WS to WCS, 6 May 1953; pp. 261–62—"I have traveled . . ." WS to Leon and Marianne Edwards, 10 Dec. 1952; p. 262—"There was nary a night . . ." PM to WS, 20 Dec. [1955]; p. 263—"Italians are wonderful . . ." WS to WCS, 11 Oct. 1953; p. 264—"That's the rub . . ." WS to WCS, 6 July 1953; p. 265—"I am beginning to get . . ." WS to JPM, 11 Nov. 1953.

20. New York and Roxbury

Styron describes his reacclimation to urban life and gives an account of the party for Irwin Shaw in a letter to Bobby and Claire White, 15 Mar. 1954. The exchange between Mailer and Shaw is taken from Shnayerson, *Irwin Shaw,* 194. The aborted start on STHOF was first published, with editorial commentary by Arthur D. Casciato, as "The Discarded Opening for *Set This House on Fire*," *Mississippi Quarterly* 34 (Winter 1980–81), 38–50; repr. *Critical Essays,* 146–54. Styron's comment about his house in Roxbury is taken from Frederick Ungheuen with Lewis and Ethel Hurlbut, *Roxbury Remembered* (Oxford, Conn.: Connecticut Heritage Press, 1989), 210.

Quotations: p. 268—"I have begun Novel No. 2 . . ." WS to the Whites, 15 Mar. 1954.

21. Mailer and Others

Accounts by various observers of the period during which Mailer lived in Connecticut are given in Peter Manso, *Mailer: His Life and Times* (New York: Simon & Schuster, 1985), 228–49, et passim. For a fictionalized version, see Edwin Gilbert's novel *Connecticut Circle* (New York: Putnam's, 1972). See also Leslie Aldridge Westoff, "Faulkner Flirtation," *New York Times Magazine,* 10 May 1987, 69ff. Haydn's account of his move to Random House is in *Words and Faces,* 77–106. For the history of Random House, see *At Random: The Reminiscences of Bennett Cerf* (New York: Random House, 1977); see also Charles A. Madison, *Book Publishing in America* (New York: McGraw-Hill, 1966), 356–60, 507–10. Faulkner's "Kentucky: May: Saturday" appeared in *Sports Illustrated* for 16 May 1955; repr. in *Essays, Speeches, and Public Letters,* ed. James B. Meriwether (New York: Random House, 1965). Faulkner's remarks about Hemingway are in *Lion in the Garden: Interviews with William Faulkner, 1926–1962,* ed. James B. Meriwether and Michael Millgate (New York: Random House, 1968), 58. Information about paperback sales for LDID and financial arrangements with Random House is taken from the Harold Matson files, Butler Library.

Adele Mailer's recently published memoir, *The Last Party: Scenes from My Life with Norman Mailer* (New York: Barricade, 1997), has this to say: "Finally the tension between Styron and Norman exploded, with Styron employing one of his sneaky tactics. He'd been saying that I was a lesbian, and the rumor got back to Norman . . . . Norman, in his drunken camaraderie with Styron, probably bragged about the few times we'd indulged in threesomes" (p. 261).

Quotations: p. 282—"Being now in the Random House fold . . ." WS to JPM, 4 July 1956; p. 283—"He thought that would be . . ." WS to WB, 20 Apr. 1955; p. 284—"The old gold-mine . . ." Hyman to WS, 13 Jan. 1955; pp. 284–85—"I think or had the feeling . . ." WS to PM, 16 Dec. 1955; p. 285—"to these tranquil glens . . ." WS to JPM, 4 July 1956; p. 290—"The absurd thing . . ." WS to Leon Edwards, 12 Feb. 1957; p. 291—"I had never seen . . ." "William Styron Writes PW about His New Novel," *Publishers Weekly,* 30 May 1960, 54; p. 292—"Writing a long novel . . ." WS to Leon Edwards, 29 Aug. 1957; p. 292—"It is the most difficult . . ." WS to WCS, 9 Nov. 1957; p. 293—"Outside of what . . ." WS to Leon Edwards, 3 Feb. 1958; p. 293—"I've been told . . ." Mailer to WS, n.d., dated March 1958 in WS's hand; p. 295—"I don't know . . ." WS to Mailer, 17 Mar. 1958.

22. Completion

For details about Styron's revisions in the typescript and galley proofs of STHOF, see James L. W. West III, "Styron's Revised Opening for *Set This House on Fire,*" *Belgian Essays on Language and Literature* 2 (1991), 153–62. Styron's recollections about Haydn and *Lolita* are from "The Book on Lolita," *New Yorker,* 4 Sept. 1995, 33. The founding of Atheneum is announced in "3 Book Executives Forming Own Firm," *New York Times,* 15 Mar. 1959. Haydn's comments about Styron's decision to stay at Random House are in *Words and Faces,* 285.

Quotations: p. 303—"We were proud . . ." Cerf to WS, 17 Mar. 1959; pp. 304–5—"I wonder . . ." PM to WS, 14 Sept. 1959; p. 305—"I am being utterly serious . . ." WS to JPM, 4 Apr. 1960.

23. *Set This House on Fire*

Details about the Rome apartment are from WS's letter to JPM, 4 Apr. 1960. The necessity for expurgation of the British STHOF is taken up in Jamie Hamilton's letter to WS, 12 May 1960; see also James L. W. West III, "The Scholarly Editor as Biographer," *Studies in the Novel,* 27 (Fall 1995), 295–303; and West, *William Styron: A Descriptive Bibliography,* 78–79. A good account of the legal problems faced by British publishers during this period can be found in Frederic Warburg's *All Authors Are Equal* (New York: St. Martin's, 1973), chap. 12. Fenton's essay on STHOF is reprinted in *Critical Essays,* 86–92. The details of Fenton's death are given in Reynolds Price's letter to WS, 20 Sept. 1960. Information about the budget and sales performance of STHOF is from the Random House files, Butler Library. For an account of Coindreau's career, see *The Time of William Faulkner,* ed. and trans. George McMillan Reeves (Columbia: Univ. of South Carolina Press, 1971). Negotiations with Laffont and Plon for a French translation of STHOF are covered in WS's letter to Maria Horch (literary agent), 12 Mar. 1960, Matson files, Butler Library.

Quotations: p. 307—"They both speak . . ." WS to JPM, 4 Apr. 1960; p. 307—"very alcoholic . . ." WS to McKee, 29 Feb. 1960; p. 307—"All the international hip set . . ." WS to JPM, 4 Apr. 1960; p. 307—"When I read . . ." JJ to WS, 8 Jan. 1960, in the Jones papers at the Harry Ransom Humanities Research Center, University of Texas, Austin; p. 308—"with double diaper changes . . ." WS to Leon and Marianne Edwards, 4 Apr. 1960; p. 308—"the little nose-pickers . . ." WS to Leon Edwards, 22 Apr.

1960; p. 312—"unaccountably wretched . . ." WS to Reynolds Price, 10 Oct. 1960; p. 313—"Your new novel . . ." Coindreau to WS, 21 May 1960; p. 313—*"sincèrement . . ."* Gaston Gallimard to WS, 20 May 1960.

24. Reentry

Styron's recollections of Baldwin's stay in Roxbury were published as "Jimmy in the House," *New York Times Book Review,* 20 Dec. 1987, 30; repr. in *James Baldwin: The Legacy,* ed. Quincy Troupe (New York: Simon and Schuster, 1989). The quotation from Baldwin ("After all, we have the same songs") is from Raymond A. Sokolov, "Into the Mind of Nat Turner," *Newsweek,* 16 Oct. 1967, 67. See also James Campbell, *Talking at the Gates: A Life of James Baldwin* (New York: Viking, 1991); and David Leeming, *James Baldwin: A Biography* (New York: Knopf, 1994). For Diana Trilling's account of the after-dinner audience with the Kennedys, see "A Visit to Camelot," *The New Yorker,* 2 June 1997, 54–65.

"Mrs. Aadland's Little Girl, Beverly" is reprinted as *The Big Love* in TQD, 193–99; the two essays on Benjamin Reid, together with additional commentary, appear in the section "Victims" of TQD; and the tribute to Faulkner is included in the "Portraits and Farewells" section. The notes taken by Styron at Faulkner's funeral are among Styron's papers at the Library of Congress. On the change in Connecticut law, see Robert Satter to WS, 10 June 1963, in Styron's papers at Duke.

An English translation of Michel Butor's preface to the French edition of STHOF is published in *Critical Essays,* 135–45. Useful bibliographical listings of reviews and commentary on Styron in France have appeared in *Configuration Critique de William Styron,* ed. Melvin J. Friedman and August J. Nigro (Paris: Minard—Lettres Modernes, 1967), and in *Delta,* no. 23 (janvier 1986), a special Styron issue. See also the essays by Friedman and by Valarie Arms in the section "Styron *en France*" in *Critical Essays,* 289–315. The publication histories of Styron's French editions through *Les Confessions de Nat Turner* are detailed in *William Styron: A Descriptive Bibliography,* section B. For information about the White House dinner, see Dorothy McCardle, "Kennedys Salute Nobel Winners," *Washington Post,* 30 Apr. 1962, B5. Styron set down a description of his afternoon of sailing with the Kennedys in a letter to his father dated 21 July 1962; he has also published two accounts: "The Short, Classy Voyage of JFK," *Esquire,* Dec. 1983; and "Havanas in Camelot," *Vanity Fair,* July 1996. See also Styron's

" 'John Fitzgerald Kennedy . . . As We Remember Him,' " *High Fidelity,* Jan. 1966, 38, 40.

Quotations: p. 325—"TRANSLATION SET . . ." WS to WB, n.d. [Feb. 1962]; p. 325—"I have been feeling . . ." WS to Bobby and Claire White, n.d. [Feb. 1962]; p. 326—"like Huck and Jim . . ." WS to WB, 2 May 1962; p. 327— "dreary Navy officers' chow . . ." WS to WCS, 21 July 1962.

25. Preparations

A good summary of the events of Nat Turner's Rebellion can be found in Thomas C. Parramore, *Southampton County, Virginia* (Charlottesville: University Press of Virginia, 1978). For the period after the rebellion, see Daniel W. Crofts, *Old Southampton: Politics and Society in a Virginia County, 1834–1869* (Charlottesville: University Press of Virginia, 1992). Two useful overviews of the history of slavery are John B. Boles, *Black Southerners, 1619–1869* (Lexington: University of Kentucky Press, 1983); and Peter J. Parish, *Slavery: History and Historians* (New York: Harper & Row, 1989). The account of Styron's trip to Southampton County is based on "This Quiet Dust," TQD, 9–30; the quotation ("The house had . . .") is from p. 29. For an examination of Styron's use of the Drewry and Olmsted books, see Arthur D. Casciato and James L. W. West III, "William Styron and *The Southampton Insurrection,*" *American Literature* 52 (January 1981), 564–77; repr. *Critical Essays,* 213–25. Styron's reading on slavery and slave rebellions has been documented from interviews (esp. those in *Conversations,* 40–113), from inspection of Styron's library in Roxbury, from interviews with him, and from letters contemporaneous with the period during which *Nat Turner* was being written (see, e.g., WS to Don Harington, 12 Sept. 1966, at Duke).

Quotations: pp. 331, 332, 333—"seems to shape up . . ." and "I have always wanted . . ." and "If you are game . . ." WS to WCS, 24 Feb. 1961; p. 336— "This is a literary style . . ." Robert Canzoneri and Page Stegner, "An Interview with William Styron," *Per/Se,* Summer 1966, repr. *Conversations,* 66–79—the interview was conducted in September 1965; p. 336—"Baldwin grinned hugely . . ." Sokolov, "Into the Mind of Nat Turner," 67–69; p. 340—"I believed it when . . ." Bahgat Elnadi and Adel Rifaat, "Interview: William Styron," *UNESCO Courier,* April 1992, 10; p. 342—"the consciousness of the past in the present . . ." Woodward, *The Burden of Southern History* (Baton Rouge: L.S.U. Press, 1960), 35.

26. Composition

The conversation with Jones in *Esquire,* "Two Writers Talk It Over," is reprinted in *Conversations,* 40–48. For comments by Mailer and Styron on the feud, see Myrick Land, *The Fine Art of Literary Mayhem* (New York: Holt, Rinehart & Winston, 1963). Styron's review of the report on smoking is reprinted in the section entitled "The Habit" in TQD. The copy of M. Boyd Coyner's dissertation used by Styron is in his papers at Duke. See also *"Dear Master": Letters of a Slave Family,* ed. Randall M. Miller (Ithaca: Cornell University Press, 1978); these are letters written to John Hartwell Cocke by the Skipwiths, a family of slaves whom he set free and sent to Liberia, where they made a new start.

Quotations: pp. 347–48—"The bulk of Mailer's hatred . . ." WS to JJ, 6 June 1963, Jones papers, Texas; "tempest teapot . . ." JJ to WS, 1 Aug. 1963, in *To Reach Eternity: The Letters of James Jones* (New York: Random House, 1989), 304; p. 350—"I came to a dead halt . . ." Ben Forkner and Gilbert Schricke "An Interview with William Styron," *Southern Review* 10 (Oct. 1974); repr. *Conversations,* 190–202 (the quotation is from p. 195); pp. 350, 351— "And so we talked . . ." and "Anyway, he is gone . . ." WS to WB, 18 Dec. 1963; p. 351—"I was frankly in despair . . ." Forkner and Schricke, 196.

27. The Confessions of Nat Turner

Willie Morris's letters to Styron are among Styron's papers at Duke; the first letter is dated 6 Nov. 1963. Styron's letters to Morris are among Morris's papers at the University of Mississippi. Morris's recollections of Styron are found in *New York Days* (Boston: Little, Brown, 1993)—the source for Larry L. King's account of the dog-story prizes (p. 111).

Information about Styron's dealings with the Hope Leresche agency is taken from his file there, which contains contracts, royalty statements, originals of his letters, and copies of letters sent to him. The originals of most of Leresche's letters are among Styron's papers at Duke, as are the originals of letters to Styron from the firm of Hamish Hamilton. The Jonathan Cape correspondence is in the publishing history archives at the University of Reading, England; some of the firm's correspondence with Styron survives in his papers at Duke. For an account of Maschler's rise in the firm of Cape, see Michael S. Howard, *Jonathan Cape, Publisher* (London: Cape, 1971).

Details of the negotiations for subsidiary rights to NT are taken especially from Maschler to Leresche, 25 Feb. 1965; WS to Leresche, 21 Jan. 1965; WS to WB, 30 Mar. 1965; WS to Leresche, 21 Feb. 1967 (Book-of-the-Month-Club sale); Loomis to Don Congdon, 19 Sept. 1967 (Literary Guild); Willie Morris to Congdon, 7 Apr. 1967 (*Harper's* excerpt); copies of contracts in the Random House and Hope Leresche files; and Paul Nathan, "Rights and Permissions," *Publishers Weekly,* 9 Mar. 1967, 47.

James Baldwin wrote a review of *The Confessions of Nat Turner* entitled "A Praying Time" but did not publish it. The review, which survives among Baldwin's papers, is mentioned by David Leeming in *James Baldwin: A Biography,* 285. Styron began a review of Baldwin's *The Fire Next Time* but did not complete it; the unfinished MS is in Box 8 of his papers at the Library of Congress.

The relevant edition of Yourcenar's *Memoirs of Hadrian,* trans. Grace Frick, was published by Farrar Straus, 1963; the quotations in this chapter are from pp. 299 and 312. Styron's memories of the occasion at Wilberforce are from "Nat Turner Revisited," *American Heritage,* Oct. 1992; reprinted as an afterword to the current Vintage printing of NT and, in abbreviated form, in the current Modern Library edition of the novel. The holograph of Styron's speech at Wilberforce is at the Harry Ransom Humanities Research Center, University of Texas, Austin; the typescript is at the Library of Congress. See also Dave Arnett, "Novelist Says 'Love' May Be Path to Racial Peace," *The Sun* (Springfield, Ohio), 22 Nov. 1967.

Quotations: p. 365—"You get these queer . . ." WS to Leresche, 23 May 1962; p. 365—"I think the average . . ." WS to WB, 3 Oct. 1962; p. 366—"Seriously, Bill . . ." Maschler to WS, 9 Sept. 1964; p. 370—"I rather feared . . ." WS, intro. to *Fathers and Daughters,* photographs by Mariana Cook (San Francisco: Chronicle Books, 1994); p. 371—"I remember finishing . . ." Paul Mandelbaum, "William Styron: A Profile," *Poets and Writers Magazine* 23 (Nov./Dec. 1995), 61; p. 378—"It might go on . . ." WS to WB, 1 Feb. 1968.

28. Aftermath

Information about translations of NT is from the Hope Leresche files; see esp. Leresche to WS, 25 Nov. 1967. Styron saved some of the mail generated by NT; it is among his papers at Duke in the files for 1968 and 1969. Information about the debate at Eugene West is from Julie Adams to WS,

28 May 1968. A comprehensive, annotated listing of the documents published during the controversy over NT is available in Bryer, *William Styron: A Reference Guide,* 61–103. "In the Jungle" appears as "Chicago: 1968" in TQD, 255–63. Styron's recollections of his conversations with James Jones appeared in a eulogy published in *New York,* 6 June 1977, and are included in the 1982 edition of TQD, 267–70. A longer piece on Jones (the introduction to a 1989 edition of Jones's letters) is substituted in the 1993 Vintage TQD, 289–98. For Styron's remarks about Soviet oppression of writers, see Alden Whitman, "Styron Discloses Protest in Soviet," *New York Times,* 1 Nov. 1968, 21. An account of Styron's appearance at Smith College is given in Frank Bailinson, "Styron Answers 'Turner' Critics," *New York Times,* 11 Feb. 1968, 59. A transcription of the session at the Southern Historical Association appeared as "The Uses of History in Fiction," *Southern Literary Journal* 1 (Spring 1969), 57–90; repr. *Conversations,* 114–44.

Quotations: p. 384—"It is as always . . ." WS to Maschler, 10 May 1968, Cape files, Reading; p. 385—"perfidious Albion . . ." WS to Maschler, 21 May 1965; p. 385—"very exciting for the mind . . ." Coindreau to WS, 4 Sept. 1968; p. 388—"I am much more impressed . . ." WS to Chalmers Davidson, 22 Aug. 1968, Davidson College Library; pp. 388–89—"They so desperately miss . . ." Schlesinger to WS, 16 July 1968; p. 391—"We enjoy having your sour visage . . ." JJ to WS, 4 Nov. 1965; p. 392—"I feel like a combination . . ." WS to WB, 15 Mar. 1968.

29. Interlude

The two collections of materials relating to the NT controversy are *William Styron's "The Confessions of Nat Turner": A Critical Handbook,* ed. Melvin J. Friedman and Irving Malin (Belmont, Calif.: Wadsworth, 1970); and *The Nat Turner Rebellion: The Historical Event and the Modern Controversy,* ed. John B. Duff and Peter M. Mitchell (New York: Harper & Row, 1971). The article by Gross and Bender was reprinted in the 1st ed. of *The Achievement of William Styron,* ed. Robert K. Morris and Irving Malin (Athens: University of Georgia Press, 1975). Styron's acceptance speech for the Howells Medal is given in *Critical Essays,* 226–27.

Information on the aborted film version of NT is summarized in A. H. Weiler, "Styron Charges 'Black Pressure' on Turner Film," *New York Times,* 28 Jan. 1970, 48; see also Steven V. Roberts, "Over the 'Nat Turner' Screenplay Subsides [*sic*]," *New York Times,* 31 Mar. 1969, 28; and Tom

Wicker, "In the Nation: What Sense in Censorship?" *New York Times,* 3 Apr. 1969, 42. Information about Benjamin Reid's escape is from a lengthy memorandum, Robert Satter to Styron (and others), 13 Jan. 1971, Styron papers, Duke; and from "Aftermath of 'Aftermath'," TQD, 147–52.

For a discussion between Arthur Miller and WS about differences between writing drama dialogue and prose fiction, see "Conversation: Arthur Miller and William Styron," *Audience* (Nov.–Dec. 1971), 4–21, repr. *Conversations,* 162–89. The fan letter to WS from Theodor Geisel is dated 3 Dec. 1973, Styron papers, Duke. For a good picture of Rose's activities during these years, see the photo-essay by Jane Howard, "Rose Styron," *Vogue,* May 1968.

Quotations: p. 401—"What a thrill . . ." WS to WB, 3 Oct. 1971; p. 410—"My father is planning . . ." WS to WB, 3 Dec. 1970.

30. *Sophie's Choice*

Styron's remarks about *Five Chimneys* and *Eichmann in Jerusalem* are from "A Wheel of Evil Come Full Circle: The Making of *Sophie's Choice,*" *Sewanee Review,* 105 (July–Sept. 1997), 395–400, originally an address delivered at the Holocaust Museum in Washington, D.C. A list of the books stacked beside the MS of *Sophie's Choice* was made by the biographer on his first visit to Styron, September 1973. For information about the *Agrégation* examination, see Gilbert Schricke and Ben Forkner (of the Université de Nantes) to WS, 11 Jan. 1974, Styron papers, Duke. A useful interview with Styron by Schricke and Forkner appeared in the *Southern Review* 10 (Oct. 1974), 923–34; repr. *Conversations,* 190–202. The books acquired by Styron at Auschwitz and annotated by him are in a private collection. "Auschwitz's Message" appears as "Auschwitz" in TQD, 336–39.

The unpublished essay on walking is among the most recent group of papers deposited by Styron at Duke. On Styron's friendship with Hellman, see his sketch "Lillian Hellman," in *Double Exposure,* photographs by Roddy McDowall (New York: Delacorte, 1966), 190–93; see also his statement at her funeral, *Vineyard Gazette,* 6 July 1984. On Mrs. Durr, see Styron's "Virginia Foster Durr," *Esquire,* June 1987, 161. Styron described the day he told his father of the dedication to *Sophie's Choice* in Paul Mandelbaum, "William Styron: A Profile," 59. Information about the sale of film rights to *Sophie's Choice* is from "Pakula Will Film 'Sophie's Choice,' " *New York Times,* 29 May 1979, C10; and Aljean Harmetz, " 'Sophie' Film Deal Was

Dream," *New York Times,* 24 July 1979. John Gardner qualified his criticisms of *Sophie's Choice* in a headnote to a reprinting of his review; see *Critical Essays,* 245–47. The dispute over the American Book Awards is covered in Michiko Kakutani, "Mailer, Styron and Roth Shun American Book Awards," *New York Times,* 21 Mar. 1980, C28.

Quotations: p. 411—"Sophie imposed herself . . ." Michel Braudeau, "Why I Wrote *Sophie's Choice,*" *Conversations,* 246; p. 412—"That struck me . . ." Stephen Lewis, "William Styron," *Art out of Agony: The Holocaust Theme in Literature, Sculpture and Film* (Toronto: CBC Enterprises, 1984) repr. *Conversations,* 258; p. 414—"If each voice . . ." taped interview with JLWW, 18 Sept. 1988, Vineyard Haven; p. 416—"I spent a long day . . ." Braudeau, *Conversations,* 253; p. 424—"Your name . . ." Roth to WS, n.d. [ca. 29 May 1979]; p. 426—"I only have . . ." WS to Sadri Khan, 5 July 1979.

31. Breakdown

The account of Styron's descent into depression, and of his recovery, is based primarily on the third Oral History interview, conducted with him on 1 December 1987, before he wrote *Darkness Visible.* A few details and quotations are taken from the text of *Darkness Visible* and from subsequent conversations with Rose and Polly Styron.

Styron's report on Mitterrand's inauguration was published as "A Leader Who Prefers Writers to Politicians," *Boston Globe,* 26 July 1981. Styron's defense of Mailer was reported in *The Times* (London), 23 Jan. 1982, 3. Styron's marked copy of the screenplay for *Sophie's Choice* is among his papers at Duke. Copies of the pages from Polly Styron's journal quoted here are also in the Duke collection. The letter to Peter Matthiessen is in Matthiessen's possession. For Styron's comments on daytime TV, see Roderick Townley, "First, Let's Ban All Morning Programs" (interview), *TV Guide,* 4 Mar. 1989, 13–14. A good account of Ed Bunker's career is Richard Stratton's "The Resurrection of Edward Bunker," *Prison Life,* Sept.–Oct. 1995, 45ff.

Quotations: p. 429—"Dear Bill . . ." Mailer to WS, 31 Mar. 1982; p. 430—"I have a lot of respect . . ." Mailer in interview, 18 Sept. 1988; p. 430—"I read that scene . . ." Meryl Streep quoted in a press release for "William Styron: The Way of the Writer," documentary film for the WNET *American Masters* series, January 1997; pp. 430–31—"I think Meryl's . . ." Michiko Kakutani, "William Styron on His Life and Work," *New York*

Times Book Review, 12 Dec. 1982, 3; p. 431—"I sense your nights . . ." Polly Styron to WS, dated only 2 May in Polly's hand.

32. "A Tidewater Morning"

The holograph draft of Styron's attempt to write a novel about his depression is among his papers at Duke. For the account of the conference on Primo Levi that triggered Styron's op-ed essay, see Stewart Kellerman, "Shadow of Auschwitz on Primo Levi's Life," *New York Times,* 26 Nov. 1988. The quotations from Styron concerning his trip to Santa Monica are from "Prozac Days, Halcion Nights," *Nation,* Jan. 1993.

ACKNOWLEDGMENTS

My greatest debt is to William Styron, who submitted to my interviews with amused tolerance, gave me access to the documents I wished to see, and never asked about what I was writing. I thank him for his trust. I also thank Rose Styron, who made me welcome always, answered my questions, and told me many of the stories that appear in this book. After the manuscript of this biography was complete, both William and Rose Styron read it and pointed out errors of fact. At William Styron's suggestion, one incident, in which he had played a minor role, but which reflected unfavorably on a fellow writer, was omitted.

I owe special thanks to John L. Sharpe III and the late Mattie Russell, both of the William R. Perkins Library, Duke University. Through their efforts, Styron's papers began to come to Duke in the early 1970s; I have been the greatest beneficiary of their foresight. I am also grateful to Robert L. Byrd, director of the Special Collections Library at Duke, for his cheerful assistance and his energetic work in building the Styron collection to its present strength. My sincere thanks also to these members of the Manuscript Department staff at Duke: Linda M. McCurdy, William R. Erwin, Ellen G. Gartrell, and Patricia Webb.

I owe debts to many other archivists and librarians, including Alice L. Birney at the Library of Congress; William Cagle at the Lilly Library, Indiana University; Bernard Crystal at the Butler Library, Columbia University; Mary Kayaselcuk at the War Memorial Museum, Newport

News; Rebecca Abromitis at the University of Pittsburgh Library; Maurice S. Toler at North Carolina State University; Thomas M. Verich at the University of Mississippi; Sarah A. Polirer at Harvard University; Cathy Henderson at the Harry Ransom Humanities Research Center, University of Texas at Austin; the staff at the Outer Banks History Center, Manteo, N.C.; and Charles Mann and Sandra Stelts at Pennsylvania State University.

For grants, fellowships, and residencies that enabled me to write various parts of this biography during the twelve years of its making, I thank the J. S. Guggenheim Foundation, the Fulbright Commission, the National Endowment for the Humanities, the American Council of Learned Societies, the American Academy in Rome, and the Hambidge Center. At Pennsylvania State University I am grateful to the College of the Liberal Arts, the Institute for the Arts and Humanistic Studies, and the Department of English. I wish to thank these administrators, colleagues, and friends: Robert Edwards, Christopher Clausen, Robert Secor, Don Bialostosky, Susan Welch, Stanley Weintraub, Nancy Tichler, Evelyn Hovanec, Shirley Rader, Sue Reighard, Bonnie Farmer, Art Casciato, George Core, Rhoda Sirlin, Fred Hobson, and Tom Riggio. Special thanks to Robert Loomis and Georges Borchardt, and to Barbé Hammer. Much gratitude to these research assistants: LaVerne Kennevan Maginnis, Robert Myers, Tracy Simmons Bitonti, Flora Buckalew, Suzanne Marcum, John Hruschka, and Christopher Weinmann.

The following persons kindly granted interviews and supplied information: Lenore Abraham, Susannah Benson, William Bowman, the late Ashbel Brice, Charles Buxton, Mary Wakefield Buxton, Russell Buxton, Audrey Downes Cacioppa, William Canine, Jean Cash, Carroll Chowning, Joanna Clark, Gavin Cologne-Brookes, the late Lucille C. Coltrane, Robert Coltrane, Joel Connaroe, Don Congdon, William Coyle, the late William P. Cumming, Guy Davenport, James Davenport, Sigrid de Lima, Hugh Dischinger, Robert Durden, Virginia Foster Durr, Clay Felker, Virginia G. Ficke, Charles Forbes, Kennedy Forbes, Emily Lankes Fournier, Gilbert Francis, Marjorie Styron Franklin, the late Melvin Friedman, Françoise Gallimard, Clarence Gohdes, Yannick Guillou, Lucy Hackney, Sheldon Hackney, Edgar Hatcher, Wilson C. Hayes, Howard Hoffman, Josephine Humphreys, Gloria Jones, Claude R. Kirk, Margaret Lambeth, Michelle Lapautre,

Lewis Leary, Dorothy Groome Lee, the late Hope Leresche, Norman Mailer, Wanda Malinowska (Shortall), Jean Campbell Maclay, James McGee, Elizabeth McKee, the late John P. Marquand, Jr., Thomas Maschler, Peter Matthiessen, William Mayo, Michael Mewshaw, Variety Moszynski, Willie Morris, Gordon B. Neavill, Dorothy Parker, Claire Patry, Marena Brickell Handy Pemberton, Thomas Peyton, George Plimpton, Reynolds Price, Maurice Rambaud, Linda Rogers, Parke Rouse, Jr., Judith Ruderman, the late Tessa Sayle, Arthur M. Schlesinger, Jr., JoAnne Sharpe, Greig Campbell Sheldon, Dee and Arthur Sloughfy, the late Shaw Smith, Robert C. Snider, W. Lashlie Spiegel, William N. Still, Jr., Alexandra Styron, Polly Styron, Susanna Styron, Thomas Styron, the late W. C. Styron, Sr., Charles Sullivan, Louise Todd, Barbara Taeusch Tufty, Katherine E. Walker, the late Robert Penn Warren, Alexander D. Watson, Willis H. Wills, Robert and Claire White, Langley Wood, C. Vann Woodward, Katherine Zeno. My apologies to anyone whose name I have inadvertently omitted.

I send affectionate regards to Pierre and Christiane Michel at the Université de Liège, where I began composing this book. Sincere thanks to my family: to my mother, Kate B. West, and my father, the late James L. W. West, Jr.; to my children—Emily, Jim, Tom, and Will; and finally to Melinda.

—J.L.W.W. III

INDEX

Aadland, Beverly, 319
Aadland, Florence, 319–20
Abbott, Jack, 429
Abraham, Annabelle Rush (Belle),
    14, 16, 18–19, 147–48
Abraham, Clyde, 14, 15, 18–19, 20,
    57
Abraham, Enoch, 13
Abraham, Enoch Hamilton,
    13–14, 16
Abraham, Harold, 14, 15
Abraham, Jean Hamilton, 13
Abraham, Juddy, 46
Abraham, Mary Wynne, 13
Abraham, Noah, 13
Abraham, Pauline Margaret, *see*
    Styron, Pauline Margaret
    Abraham
Abu Jamal, Mumia, 401*n*
Adams, Milton, 57, 60
Adams, Phoebe, 310
Adams, Raymond, 57
Adan, Richard, 429
Addams, Charles, 266
Advertisements for Myself (Mailer),
    297–99, 307–8, 347

"Aftermath of Benjamin Reid,
    The" (Styron), 323
After the Lost Generation
    (Aldridge), 193, 286
Aldridge, John W., Jr., 193, 207,
    224–25, 286, 287
Aldridge, Leslie Blatt, 135–36, 286,
    287
Allan, Don, 260
Allen, Jay, 286
Allen, Lew, 286, 302
All the King's Men (Warren), 154,
    160, 342
Alter, Robert, 425
American Academy in Rome, 222,
    238–39, 240, 242, 256
American Academy of Arts and
    Letters, 209, 397–98
American Book Awards, 426
American Mercury, 164, 403
American Scholar, 148, 181, 203,
    221, 275
Amnesty International, 406–8, 456
Anderson, Sherwood, 280, 282
"Anna" (model for WS's charac-
    ter), 176–78, 199–201

Appleton, John, 207
Aptheker, Herbert, 222, 339, 340, 381, 389
Archive, 105–7, 129, 136, 137, 162, 166
Arendt, Hannah, 411, 412, 415
Arnold, Matthew, 98, 151
"As He Lay Dead, a Bitter Grief" (Styron), 329
As I Lay Dying (Faulkner), 172, 174
Aswell, Edward C., 145, 146, 193
Atlantic Monthly, 203, 310, 338, 425
Auden, W. H., 209, 320
Auschwitz, 169, 411–12, 416, 417, 419, 430, 450
"Autumn" (Styron), 105, 106
Avakian, Aram (Al), 215
Ayers, E. W., 9

Baldwin, James, 228, 298, 315–19, 326, 335, 336–37, 347, 383, 400*n*
Barish, Keith, 424
Barnes, Clive, 402
Barth, John, 208
Baum, Paull F., 98, 135
Beacon Press, 384
Beats, 286, 288, 307
Beat the Devil (movie), 255–56, 261
Bellow, Saul, 297, 347
Bender, Eileen, 397
Bennett, Jack, 74, 77
Bennett, Lerone, Jr., 385, 386
Bessie, Simon Michael, 301–2, 303
"Betty," WS's affair with, 202–3, 210
Big Love, The (Aadland and Thomey), 319–20)
Black Anti-Defamation Association, 381
Blackburn, William, 96–99, 101–2, 103, 105, 106, 108, 129,

133–38, 141, 148–49, 158, 179, 186, 262, 273, 312, 422
marital problems of, 134, 160, 166, 176
WS's career aided by, 136–37, 150, 311
WS's correspondence with, 205–6, 283, 325, 326, 350–51, 365, 378, 392, 401, 410
blacks, 15, 23–24, 41, 52, 70, 84–85, 267, 315–19, 382
Confessions of Nat Turner as viewed by, 381, 383, 385–89, 392–95, 398
as mystery to WS, 35–38, 51–52, 75, 85, 317
in Newport News, 23, 31, 35–38, 45, 49, 317
in WS's work, 106, 157, 402, 449; *see also Confessions of Nat Turner, The*
see also slavery, slaves
Blair, Lewis H., 340
Blake, James, 400*n*
Blanchard, Gunner Joseph, 103
"Blankenship" (Styron), 264, 267–68
Bobbs-Merrill, 181, 191–92, 193, 201, 208, 221, 279–80, 282
Bogart, Humphrey, 255–56
Bontemps, Arna, 340, 363
Book Find Club, 306
Book-of-the-Month Club (BOMC), 368–69, 376, 424, 426
Book World, 377
Bostonians, The (movie), 440–41
Bourjaily, Vance, 224–25, 227, 231, 233, 297
Bourke-White, Margaret, 96
Bourne, Randolph, 178–79
Bowman, Bill (Mick), 65, 66, 70, 73, 74, 76, 77
Branscomb, Harvie, 138–39

Bread Loaf Writers' conference, 130, 132–33, 134
Breit, Harvey, 203, 310
Brice, Ashbel, 135, 159–62, 166, 206
Brooks, Van Wyck, 209, 271, 286
"Brothers, The" (Styron), 163–64
Brown, Alexander C., 205
Brown, Sir Thomas, 186
Brown, Tina, 451–52
Brown, William Cabell, 63
Brustein, Robert, 401
Bryan, Colgate, 66
Buchwald, Art, 231, 421, 422, 436
Buckley, William F., Jr., 432
Bunker, Eddie, 401n, 439
Burgunder, Amelie, 257
Burgunder, B. B., 240–41, 247
Burgunder, Bernei, 257, 258
Burgunder, Rose, see Styron, Rose Burgunder
Burgunder, Selma Kann, 241, 246–50, 258, 265
Burnside, Ambrose, 7
Burroughs, William, 297, 307, 347
Bush, George, 428
Butler, Benjamin F. (Spoon), 28
Butor, Michel, 324
Buxton, Helen, 59, 152
Buxton, Joseph T., 20, 58–59, 60, 71, 72
Buxton, Russell, 41, 58–59, 73
By Vineyard Light (Rose Styron and Craig Dripps), 456

Cain, James M., 403
Caldwell, Erskine, 163
Cameron, Joseph, 64–65, 70
Campbell, Greig, 24
Camp Lejeune, N.C., 119–20, 121, 127, 186, 188–201, 206, 224, 225, 399
Camus, Albert, 253, 301, 320–21, 325, 335

Canby, Vincent, 67
Canfield, Cass, 210–11
Canfield, Michael, 210–11
Canine, Bill, 159–60, 162, 185–86
Capote, Truman, 241–42, 246, 255, 283, 286
Captain's Beach (de Lima), 166, 180
Carlyle, Thomas, 98, 118
Carson, Jack, 290
Cather, Willa, 40
Cerf, Bennett, 207, 279–82, 302, 303, 328, 329, 422
Chambers, David Laurance, 181, 191, 279
"Chance in a Million, A" (Styron), 75–76
Chappell, Rebecca, 69
Chaucer, Geoffrey, 135
Cheney, Tris, 134, 160, 176, 206
Chesapeake & Ohio (C&O), 23, 29–30, 33
Chessman, Caryl, 320
Chowning, Carroll, 76, 77
Chowning, Randolph, 65, 70–71
Christmas Carol, A (Dickens), 25
Civil War, U.S., 5, 6–7, 13, 28–29, 30, 44–45
Clap Shack, 112–16, 119, 121, 127, 199
Clark, Caleb F., 6–7, 8
Clark, Joanna Rostropowicz, 420
Clark, John Henrik, 385
Clift, Montgomery, 207
Cobb, Jeremiah, 345, 373
Cochran, Jimmy, 25
Cocke, John Hartwell, 352–54
Coffin, William Sloan, Jr., 322–23
Coindreau, Maurice-Edgar, 313, 323–24, 385, 396, 427
Collier's, 160
Collins, Lewis (Zeke), 65–66
Commentary, 377
Commonweal, 425

Community Concert Association, 42–43
concentration camps, 169, 346, 411–12, 416, 417, 419, 430, 450
Cone, Bonnie, 100
Confederates, Confederacy, 5, 6–7, 28–29
"Confessions of Nat Turner, The" (Gray), 221–22, 335, 337, 338, 373, 375, 397
Confessions of Nat Turner, The (Styron), 323, 327–28, 331–47, 349–55, 363, 364, 366–89, 391–98, 414–15, 416, 418, 428
  Author's Note to, 371–75
  foreign editions of, 365, 380, 383–85, 391, 396, 398
  names in, 7, 342–43
  publishing arrangements for, 366–69
  research for, 220–23, 315, 332–34, 337–43, 351–55
  reviews of, 376–78, 381, 383–87, 396
  voice in, 318–19, 335–36, 383–84
Congdon, Don, 368, 403, 404
Conrad, Joseph, 47, 150, 162, 232
Cooks Corners, 70, 76
Cornell, Lincoln, 440, 442, 443
Corso, Gregory, 307
Cowley, Malcolm, 144, 156–57, 203–4, 207, 209, 233, 254, 271, 286
Coyner, M. Boyd, Jr., 353
Crow, Arthur, 45–46
Crow, Edith Abraham, 14–16, 20, 45, 207–8, 210, 211
Crown Publishers, 137, 140, 149, 156, 160, 181
Culver, R. O., 125–26
Cumming, William P., 80, 87, 89
Cunningham, John R., 85
Czyzewska, Elzbieta, 420

Darkness Visible (Styron), 453–56
"Darkness Visible" (Styron), 452–53
Davenport, Guy, 135, 159–60
Davenport, Jimmy, 65, 70–71, 74
Davidson, Chalmers, 87, 388
Davidson, William Lee, 79
Davidson College, 77, 79–92, 94, 95
Davis, Jefferson, 33
Davis, Ossie, 381, 383
Davis, Robert Gorham, 203
"Dead!" (Styron and Marquand), 402–4, 440–41
"Death-in-Life of Benjamin Reid, The" (Styron), 322
death penalty, 320–23, 403
Dee, Ruby, 381
Deer Park, The (Mailer), 297
de Lima, Agnes, 166–67, 170, 172, 178–81, 183
de Lima, Sigrid, 166–67, 170, 172, 178–81, 183, 186, 196–97, 247, 254
Democratic Convention (1968), 321*n*, 382–83, 389–91
Democrats, Democratic party, 325–28, 380, 382–83, 385, 389–91, 395, 404
DeMott, Benjamin, 425
Denmark, 3, 212–13
Depression, Great, 22, 31, 32, 63, 448
"Deputy Sheriff" (story), 84
Diamond, Lou, 111
Dickens, Charles, 25
Dietrich, Marlene, 207–8
Dischinger, Hugh, 65, 77
Discovery, 224–25, 227, 229, 231, 237
Donne, John, 278, 279
dramatics, 67–68, 82
Dreiser, Theodore, 280, 282

Drewry, William S., 221, 333, 334, 337–38, 355, 397
Dripps, Craig, 456
Duberman, Martin, 377, 387
du Bois, Jane, 215, 219, 228
Du Bois, W.E.B., 340
du Bois, William Pène, 215, 216–17, 219
"Ducks, The" (Styron), 136
Duke, Benjamin N., 9
Duke, James Buchanan (Buck), 9, 14, 93
Duke, Washington, 93
Duke University, 91–108, 129–30, 133–37, 139–41, 286, 404
   V-12 program at, 94–95, 100, 102–3, 105, 107–8, 115, 130
   writing and literature studies at, 96–99, 101, 105–7, 129–30, 133–37, 139–40
Duke University Press, 159, 160
du Maurier, Daphne, 212
Dunphy, Jack, 242
Durham, N. C., 93–108, 129–30, 133–37, 139–41, 158–66, 273
Durr, Virginia Foster, 422

Eastern State Sanitarium, 177, 199, 200
Edwards, Holland, 61–62
Edwards, Leon, 25, 56, 61–62, 126, 261–62, 290, 292, 293, 422
Eichmann in Jerusalem (Arendt), 411, 412
Eisenhower, Dwight D., 241, 310
Elkins, Stanley M., 341–42
Ellison, Ralph, 298, 392–94
England, 3–4, 209–12, 308–10, 364–66, 383–85
"Enormous Window, The" (Styron), 149
Erikson, Erik H., 340

Esquire, 68, 135, 164, 306, 319–23, 346–48, 368, 401, 403, 420, 424, 431, 432, 447–48

Faulkner, Estelle, 328
Faulkner, John, 328
Faulkner, William, 27, 144, 151, 154, 156–57, 160, 172, 174–75, 193, 203, 204, 209, 234, 254, 273, 280–83, 313, 328–29, 433
Faust, Paola Clark Styron (Polly) (daughter), 293, 295, 307, 308, 332, 344, 358, 359, 370, 371, 375, 408–9, 421, 422, 449
   WS's depression and, 431, 438, 441–42, 444, 446
Faust, Rob, 438, 442
Feiffer, Jules, 383
Felker, Clay, 135–36, 286
Fenton, Charles A., 311–12
Fitzgerald, F. Scott, 157, 192, 254, 275
Five Chimneys (Lengyel), 169, 411–12, 415
Flaubert, Gustave, 277
Flynn, Errol, 319
Foote, Shelby, 329
Forbes, Bryan, 211–12
Forster, E. M., 233, 246
Franklin, John Hope, 339, 377
fraternities, 82–83, 91, 94, 404
Fremont-Smith, Eliot, 377, 387
Frick, Henry Clay, 14
From Here to Eternity (Jones), 192, 193, 208, 209, 224, 289
From Summer to Summer (Burgunder), 358–60
Frost, Robert, 133, 326
Fuentes, Carlos, 384–85
Fuller, Edmund, 377
Fussell, Paul, 425

Gallimard, 313–14, 426–27
Gallimard, Françoise, 426–27, 437

Gallimard, Gaston, 313, 314, 324
García Márquez, Gabriel, 435
Gardner, John, 425
Garrett, Bertha (Buffa), 129
Geisel, Theodor, 403
Geismar, Maxwell, 203, 253
Genovese, Eugene D., 339, 387–88
Germany, Nazi, 54, 75–76, 82, 169, 230
"Get All You Can" (Styron), 88
Ghost Train, The (Ridley), 67–68
GI Bill, 147, 148, 150
Gide, André, 246–47
Giovanni's Room (Baldwin), 318
Gohdes, Clarence, 98, 139–40
Goldwyn, Sam, Jr., 218
Gould, Joe, 182
Grace, Charles Emmanuel (Daddy Grace), 36–37, 317
Gray, Judd, 403
Gray, T. R., 222, 335, 337, 338, 345, 373, 375, 397
Great Gatsby, The (Fitzgerald), 157, 254
Groome, Dorothy (Nutt), 69, 70
Gross, Seymour L., 397
Guild, June Purcell, 221, 339
Guinzberg, Thomas, 215, 216–17, 256–57, 266

Haas, Robert, 281
Hackney, Lucy, 421–22, 446
Hackney, Sheldon, 421, 446
Hadrian, 372–73
Hairston, Loyle, 385, 386
Hall, Donald, 217
Hamilton, Charles V., 385, 386, 394
Hamilton, Jamie, 308–10, 366
Hamilton, Jean, see Abraham, Jean Hamilton
Hamish Hamilton, 209, 210, 365–66
Hampden-Sydney College, 61, 77

Hampton Institute, 35–36, 43, 75, 221
Hamsun, Knut, 253
Handy, Lowney, 192–93, 289
Harding, Vincent, 385, 386
Harper & Brothers, 145, 301
Harper's Bazaar, 160, 164, 241, 319
Harper's Magazine, 253, 362, 363–64, 368
Harrison, Thomas P., 11
Hart, Moss, 281, 282
Harts Island prison, 124–26, 164, 263
Harvard University, 392, 394
Hatcher, Ed, 147
Hawthorne, Nathaniel, 253–54
Hayden, Sterling, 290
Haydn, Hiram, 137, 140, 148–49, 150, 153, 180, 184, 222–23, 227–28, 232–33, 262, 267, 286, 306–7, 422
    Lie Down in Darkness and, 137, 152, 158, 164, 165, 179, 181, 185, 186, 191–92, 193
    at Random House, 179–83, 301–3
Haydn, Mary, 184, 262, 286
Hayes, Buddy, 21, 25, 47
Hayes, Sally Cox, 21, 25, 46–47, 52
Hays, H. R., 243
Hayton, Lennie, 210
Hayward, Frances Taylor (Fan Tay), 69
Heller, Joseph, 347
Hellman, Lillian, 257, 329, 421, 422
Hemingway, Ernest, 136, 192, 225, 231, 254, 280, 283, 299, 311, 326
Herald-Tribune (Paris), 220
Herald-Tribune Book Review, 203, 206
Hersey, John, 207, 209
Hicks, Granville, 310

Higginson, Thomas Wentworth, 338
Hilton Village, Va., 22–26, 33, 34, 40–43, 46–47, 52, 54, 56–57, 72, 106, 448
Historical Novel, The (Lukács), 393
Hitler, Adolf, 82, 148
Hoffman, Howard, 181–83, 187
Hoke, Robert F., 6
Holmes, Elmer, 47–48, 56, 72, 74, 75, 77
Holmes, Lynwood R., 47
Hoover, J. Edgar, 321
Horne, Lena, 210
Höss, Rudolf, 415, 416
Housman, A. E., 110–11
Howard, Ebenezer, 22
Hubbell, J. B., 98
Hudson Review, 377
Hughes, Richard J., 389
Humes, Harold L. (Doc), 215, 216, 228, 230–32, 235, 249
Humphrey, Hubert, 385, 391, 395
Huntington, Archer M. 33
Huntington, Collis, P., 29–30, 33
Huston, John, 218, 255, 256
Hutchens, John K., 310
Hyman, Gwen, 152–54
Hyman, Mac, 135, 152–54, 284

In the Belly of the Beast (Abbott), 429
In the Clap Shack (Styron), 401–2

Jackson, Harlan, 70
James, Henry, 150, 291
James, William, 434
James River, 22, 23, 25–30, 33, 41, 50, 51, 106, 215
James River Country Club, 33–34
Janeway, Elizabeth, 203
Japan, in World War II, 76–77, 82, 111–12, 120, 123
Jeffers, Robinson, 280, 281

Jefferson, Thomas, 352, 353
"John Hartwell Cocke of Bremo" (Coyner), 352–53
Johnson, Lyndon B., 380, 382
Johnston, Greene S. III, 11, 409–10
Jonathan Cape, 366, 383, 385
Jones, Gloria Mosolino, 289, 294–95, 307, 346, 391–92, 422, 439
Jones, Howard Mumford, 203
Jones, James, 192–93, 207, 208, 224, 289, 294–95, 297, 304, 307–8, 346–48, 364, 391–92, 422–23, 439
Jones, James Earl, 398
Jones, Jennifer, 255, 256
Journey in the Seaboard Slave States, A (Olmstead), 221, 338–39
Joyce, James, 174, 191–92, 234, 281

Kaiser, Ernest, 385, 386
Kann, Gertrude, 248
Kauffmann, Stanley, 309, 377
Kazin, Alfred, 328, 377, 451
Kennedy, Edward (Ted), 407
Kennedy, Jacqueline, 325–28
Kennedy, John F., 325–28, 350–51
Kennedy, Robert F., 326, 385
Khan, Sadri, 426
Killens, John Oliver, 385, 386
Kimbal, C. P., 198
King, Larry L., 362, 363
King, Martin Luther, Jr., 382
Kline, Kevin, 430
Klopfer, Donald, 279–81, 303, 328, 329
Knopf, Pat, 301–2, 303
Koestler, Arthur, 320
Korean War, 182, 185–88, 194–95, 198, 399
Kuhn, Ed, 193
Kurnitz, Harry, 218

labor, labor unions, 14–15, 31–32
Lanier, Sidney, 11
Lapointe, Richard, 401n
Laurents, Arthur, 210
Leary, Lewis, 98, 159–60
Lee, Mary (Moose), 215, 228, 230
Lee, Robert E., 6, 51
Lehmann-Haupt, Christopher, 425
Leigh, Vivien, 207–8
Leighton, Claire, 136
Lengyel, Olga, 169, 411–12, 415
Leresche, Hope, 364–66, 398, 426
Lerman, Leo, 207–8
Lerner, Max, 203
Leschetizky, Theodor, 16
Levi, Primo, 450–51
Lewis, Sinclair, 341
Library of Congress, 268, 292, 321
Lie Down in Darkness (Hays), 242–43
Lie Down in Darkness (Styron), 24, 36, 100n, 137, 151–58, 164–65, 172–86, 201–11, 220, 223, 228, 234, 240, 242–43, 252, 265, 272, 273, 283, 290–91, 292, 298, 310, 328, 331–32, 365, 366–67, 414, 415–16, 419, 449
    "Anna" and, 176–78, 199–201
    literary influences on, 154–57, 160, 164, 172, 174–76, 342
    reviews of, 203–5, 211, 216, 229, 286, 289–90
    sexually explicit language in, 191–92, 193
    translations of, 209, 229–30, 314
    voice in, 172–74, 225
Life, 192, 328–29, 368
Lilly, Henry T., 87
Limouze, Sandy, 159–60
Literary Guild, 368–69
Liveright, Horace, 280
Lolita (Nabokov), 302

Lollobrigida, Gina, 255, 256
"Long Dark Road, The" (Styron), 106, 136–37
Long March, The (Styron), 122, 126, 197, 224–33, 235, 237, 264, 283, 290, 298, 365, 414
Look Homeward, Angel (Wolfe), 100
Loomis, Robert, 135, 159–60, 166, 170, 381–82, 439, 446
    as WS's editor, 135, 304, 305, 311, 312, 376, 453
Lorimer, Graeme, 133
Lorre, Peter, 255
"Love Day" (Styron), 432, 456
Lowry, Malcolm, 162, 174, 176
Lukács, Georg, 393
Lumet, Sidney, 398
Luther, Martin, 340

Maas, Peter, 135
MacArthur, Douglas, 187–88
McCarthy, Eugene, 380, 382–83, 385, 389
McClellan, George B., 28
McCoy, Joe, 81
McCullers, Carson, 164
McGarry, Ann, 231
McGraw-Hill, 137, 142–47, 193
MacGregor, Martha, 203
Machell, Roger, 210
McIntosh, Mavis, 181
McKee, Elizabeth, 160–61, 163–64, 181, 187, 217, 220, 222, 231, 237, 262, 270, 271, 282, 307
McKim, Charles Follen, 238
MacNicol, Peter, 430
Mademoiselle, 207, 241, 253
Magruder, John Bankhead, 28
Mailer, Adele Morales, 286–89, 293–95, 297, 348
Mailer, Barney, 267
Mailer, Norman, 207, 224, 266–67, 286–89, 304, 307–8, 426

WS's feud with, 293–300, 311, 347–50, 429–30
Malinowski, Bronislaw, 183–84, 419
Maloney, John, 202
Marble Faun, The (Hawthorne), 253–54
March, Fredric, 326
Marine Corps, 290
  long march in, 196–97, 199, 224
  mortar accident in, 195, 197, 199, 224
  WS in, xi, 80, 90–91, 94–96, 100, 102–3, 105, 107–28, 182, 185–201, 224
  in WS's work, 399, 401–2, 430–31; *see also Long March, The*
Marquand, John P., Jr., 207, 235, 239, 249, 254, 256, 257, 265, 266, 282, 284, 285, 305, 307, 327, 328, 377, 402–4, 440–41, 446
Marquand, Sue, 327, 328
"Marriott the Marine" (Styron), 401, 431
Martha's Vineyard, xi, 306, 326–30, 335, 349, 356–59, 366, 391, 411, 421–22, 432–36, 438, 456
Maschler, Tom, 366, 383, 384
Masson, Elise, 183–84
Masters, James M., 195–96, 197, 226
Matthiessen, Patsy Southgate, 214–15, 217, 231, 249, 256, 262, 265, 266, 270
Matthiessen, Peter, 214–17, 231–35, 237, 244, 249, 256–57, 262–63, 265, 266, 270, 284–85, 304–5, 422, 442–43, 446
Memoirs of Hadrian (Yourcenar), 371–73
Mencken, H. L., 403

Menin, Alice M., 24–25
Meyer, June, 377
Michaux, Solomon Lightfoot, 36
Miller, Arthur, 285–86, 383, 401, 446
Mitterrand, François, 428, 430
Mizener, Arthur, 254, 310
Mohrt, Michel, 313–14
"Moment in Trieste, A" (Styron), 149
Monroe, Marilyn, 285, 286, 289
Montemora, Vincent (Nicky), 184, 267
Montemora, Wanda Malinowska, 183–85, 187, 247, 267, 419
Mordecai, Ellen, 159–60
Morgenstern, William, 41–42
Morley, Robert, 255
Morris, Celia, 362
Morris, Willie, 362, 363, 422–23
movies, 56, 68, 70, 73, 207, 284, 331, 332, 351, 403
  Confessions of Nat Turner and, 369, 381, 383, 398
  see also specific movies
Moyano, Magda, 351–52
Mozart, Wolfgang Amadeus, 162, 243
"Mrs. Aadland's Little Girl, Beverly" (Styron), 319–20
music, 24, 82, 183, 226, 243, 276, 288, 419–20, 441, 444
  black, 36, 74–75
  in Newport News, 36, 42–43
  Pauline's education in, 15–17
Mussolini, Benito, 148, 238
My Cousin Rachel (du Maurier), 212

Nabokov, Vladimir, 302
Nation, 203, 377, 381, 454
National Book Award, 209, 426
Nénot, Marie-Thérèse, 230
New American Library, 312, 368

New Leader, 203, 315
Newport, Christopher, 28
Newport News, Va., 11, 12, 17–23,
    26–38, 42–43, 56–62, 71, 92,
    122, 126, 130, 273, 332
  blacks in, 23, 31, 35–38, 45, 49,
    317
  defense industry in, 30–31, 32,
    54
  World War I and, 17–19, 30–31
  in WS's work, 33, 34, 155, 175,
    176, 204–5, 448
Newport News Shipbuilding and
    Drydock Company, 11, 12, 14,
    19, 20, 22, 30–32, 49, 54, 56,
    57, 61, 89–90
New Republic, 148, 203, 290, 319,
    381
New School for Social Research,
    148–49, 153, 164, 166, 168,
    181
New Statesman and Nation, 211
Newsweek, 203–4, 205, 260,
    336–37, 376
Newton, Douglas, 241
New York City, 317
  Flatbush neighborhood in,
    167–71
  WS in, 61–62, 73–74, 124, 129,
    140, 142–58, 164, 166–71,
    180–88, 201–10, 265–70, 283,
    284, 350, 382, 385, 401, 435,
    437–38
New York *Daily News,* 403
New Yorker, 160, 164, 204, 218, 377
New York *Herald-Tribune,* 310,
    321*n*
New York Post, 203
New York Review of Books, 340,
    349, 377, 388, 389–90, 391,
    425
New York Times, 67, 203, 212, 310,
    321, 339, 377, 381, 387, 402,
    417, 425, 426, 451, 455

New York Times Book Review, 203,
    286, 310, 377, 387, 424, 425
Nixon, Richard M., 391, 395, 404
No Time for Sergeants (Hyman),
    153, 284

O'Connell, Shaun, 377
O'Connor, Flannery, 160
"October Sorrow" (Styron), 106
Olivier, Laurence, 207–8
Olmsted, Frederick Law, 221,
    338–39
Omnibook Best-Seller Magazine,
    209
One and Twenty (anthology),
    136–37
O'Neill, Eugene, 280, 281
Osbourne, Dick, 25
Oxford University, 138, 139

Pakula, Alan J., 424, 430, 431
Paris, 42, 210, 212–38, 249–50, 295,
    307–8, 324–25, 396, 428, 430,
    436–37, 453
Paris Review, 215–17, 225, 229,
    232–35, 237, 244–46, 249, 306,
    348
Parker, Dorothy, 146, 160, 193
Partisan Review, 288, 310, 315, 381
Partisans (Matthiessen), 262, 284
Patton, Frances Gray, 133
Payne, John, 95–96
Pearl Harbor, bombing of, 76–77,
    120
PEN Club, 207
Peninsular Campaign (1861), 28,
    55
Penn, William, 12
Perkins, Maxwell, 145, 192, 349
Perry, Bliss, 161
Peyton, Tom, 65, 66, 69, 74, 77,
    155, 176, 190, 195
Phillips, Ulrich B., 222, 339, 340
Pinochet, Augusto, 406, 407

Plimpton, George, 211, 215–17, 219, 228, 229, 230, 232–35, 244, 245, 249, 348–49, 377, 402
poetry, 110–11
    Rose's interest in, 241, 244, 275, 284, 358–60, 382, 404–6, 422, 456
    of WS, 48, 88, 105, 106
Poole, William, 142
Porter, Chet, 74
Postman Always Rings Twice, The (Cain), 403
Potter, Madeleine, 440–41
Poussaint, Alvin F., 385, 386, 394
Presbyterianism, 34–35, 75, 77, 79, 85
Prescott, Orville, 310
Price, Reynolds, 312
Prix de Rome, 209, 210, 216, 240, 254
"Prozac Days, Halcion Nights" (Styron), 454–55
Purdy, Ted, 262

Rahv, Philip, 377
Rambaud, Maurice, 427
Random House, 135, 279–84, 301–7, 310, 312, 328, 366–69, 375, 376, 426, 453
Ravello, 246–47, 255, 260–65, 267–68, 300
Redding, J. Saunders, 221, 222, 267, 333, 377
Reeve, Christopher, 440, 441
"Reflections on the Guillotine" (Camus), 320–31
Reich, Wilhelm, 288
Reid, Benjamin, 321–23, 399–400, 429
Republicans, Republican party, x, xi, 327, 391, 395, 404
Ridley, Arnold, 67–68
Rinehart, 136–37, 140, 142

Robert Laffont, 314
Robinson, Edward G., 68
Rome, 209, 210, 222, 237–60, 268, 307, 308, 311–14, 320
Roth, Philip, 347, 424, 426
Roxbury, Conn., x, 270–79, 285–96, 304, 315–19, 329, 342, 346, 358, 359, 370, 371, 381–82, 422, 436–42, 446, 456
Roy, Carl, 25
Rubin, Louis D., Jr., 208, 240, 242, 363, 377
Russell, Mattie, 404

Salinger, J. D., 209, 297, 347
Salter, George, 201
Sanders, Manly C. (Slimy), 82
Santayana, George, 117
Sartre, Jean-Paul, 320, 325
Satter, Robert, 322, 323, 400
Saturday Review, 209, 281, 310, 381, 425
Saturday Review of Literature, 203, 206
Sayle, Tessa, 426
Schlesinger, Arthur, Jr., 377, 388–89
Schnabel, Lois, 133
Scribner's, 166, 180, 192, 289
Selby, John, 136–37, 140, 142
Set This House on Fire (Styron), 226, 253–56, 259, 260, 262, 268–69, 277, 278–79, 283, 290–92, 298–314, 331–32, 347, 365, 367, 369, 414, 418
    foreign editions of, 308–10, 313–14, 323–25
    Mailer-WS feud and, 299–300, 311
    philosophical cast of, 300–301
    reviews of, 307, 310–12, 314, 378
Settle, Mary Lee, 241, 249
Seward, John (Bubba), 129
"Shadrach" (Styron), 420, 456

Shakespeare, William, 66
Sharpe, John, 404
Shaw, Irwin, 217–18, 231, 256, 257, 258, 264–67, 286, 364
Shaw, Marian, 218, 231, 256, 257, 258
Sheed, Wilfrid, 377
Shirley, George, 379
Silvers, Robert, 315
Simenon, Georges, 253
Simpson, Louis, 193
Skinner, Thérèse, 42
Skinner, Tom, 42
slavery, slaves, 4, 5, 7, 23, 29, 44, 51–52, 315–19, 331–47, 421
    insurrections of, 55–56, 220–23, 327, 331–34, 337; see also Confessions of Nat Turner, The
Slavery (Elkins), 341–42
Slingluff, T. Rowland, 300
Sloane, William, 133
Smith, Constance, 211–12
Smith, Hal, 281
Smith, John, 29
Smith, Pershing G., 130
Smith, Shaw, 82
Smith, William, 63–64, 68–69, 72
Snider, Bob, 110–11, 112, 119, 122, 123
Snitger, Bill, 159
Snyder, Albert, 402–3
Snyder, Ruth, 402–3
Sokolov, Raymond, 376
Some Came Running (Jones), 289, 294, 347, 348
"Some Children of the Goddess" (Mailer), 347
Sophie (Flatbush boarder), 169, 411, 419
Sophie's Choice (movie), 424, 430–31
Sophie's Choice (Styron), 137, 226, 342, 411–20, 423–27, 430–31, 447

foreign editions of, 365, 426–27, 428
models for characters in, 169, 185, 419–20
reviews of, 425–26, 428
Sound and the Fury, The (Faulkner), 151, 156–57, 174–75, 203, 313
Southampton Insurrection, The (Drewry), 221, 333, 334, 337–38, 355, 397
Southern, Terry, 215
Soviet Union, 82, 314, 391, 406
Stampp, Kenneth M., 340
Stegner, Wallace, 133
Steiner, George, 377
Stevens, Wallace, 284
Stevenson, Adlai, 241
Stireing, John, 3, 4
Stiron, Benjamin F., 5
Stiron, George, 4, 5
Stiron, Mary Salter, 5
"Story About Christmas, A" (Styron), 106
Stranger, The (Camus), 335
Streep, Meryl, 430–31
Styr clan, 3–4
Styring, Adonijah, 4–5
Styring, Cason, 4–5
Styring, Elizabeth, 4–5
Styring, George, Jr., see Stiron, George
Styring, George, Sr., 3–5
Styring, Henry, 4–5
Styring, John, 4–5
Styring, Joyce, 5
Styring, Mary Cason, 4
Styron, Alexandra (Alex; Al) (daughter), 370, 371, 375–76, 409, 421
Styron, Alpheus Whitehurst (grandfather), 5–10, 14, 44, 93
Styron, David (great-uncle), 6

Styron, Elizabeth Buxton (stepmother), 58–59, 60, 71–73, 90,
122, 126, 130, 152, 176, 247,
251, 332, 396
   WS's correspondence with, 115,
   118, 144–45, 205
Styron, Eunice Edmundson Johnston (stepmother), 11–12,
409–10, 423, 449
Styron, Hugh (cousin), 59–60
Styron, Marianna Clark (grandmother), 7–8, 44–45, 51, 316,
317
Styron, Paola Clark, see Faust,
Paola Clark Styron
Styron, Pauline Margaret Abraham (mother), 12–23, 39–49,
254, 284, 441
   breast cancer of, 39–41, 45, 46,
   52, 58, 73, 445
   death of, 40–41, 52–53, 57, 71,
   72, 92, 247, 445, 447
   marriages of, 19–20, 248
   travels of, 16, 17, 42, 43–46
Styron, Rebecca Whitehurst (great-
grandmother), 5
Styron, Rose Burgunder (wife), x,
208, 263–78, 300, 315, 326,
332–34, 348, 350, 357–62,
381–82, 391, 404–9, 436–44, 454
   family background of, 240–41,
   247–48
   in France, 249–50, 307–8, 437
   in Italy, 240–44, 246–58, 260,
   263–65, 307, 308
   poetry interests of, 241, 244, 275,
   284, 358–60, 382, 404–6, 422,
   456
   pregnancies and childbirths of,
   270, 274, 284, 289, 293, 294,
   295, 306, 369–70
   in Roxbury, x, 270–78, 286, 287,
   289, 316, 370, 371, 375,
   438–43, 446

   trust fund of, 247, 272, 274–75,
   369, 424
   WS's marriage to, 208, 248–51,
   254–58
Styron, Susanna Margaret (daughter), 284, 289, 302, 308, 358,
359, 371, 375–76, 406–8, 421,
444, 454
Styron, Thomas Haydn (son), 306,
307, 308, 332, 358, 359, 370,
371, 375, 404, 409, 421
Styron, Thomas Wahab (great-
grandfather), 5
Styron, William Clark, Jr.:
   accent of, 153, 168
   Anglophobia of, 211, 384, 385
   authority resented by, 67, 68, 71,
   72, 207
   awards and honors of, 26, 209,
   210, 216, 240, 383, 397–98,
   404, 426, 436–37
   birth of, 20
   childhood of, 20–26, 29, 31–46
   dating and romances of, 60,
   69–70, 73, 74, 78, 102, 104–5,
   122–23, 129, 179, 180, 183–85,
   202–3, 210; see also Taeusch,
   Barbara
   depression and melancholy of,
   186–87, 215, 235, 249, 254,
   312, 395, 431–45, 449–55
   diary of, 56, 58, 59, 61, 62
   drinking of, 60, 70, 71, 76, 77,
   86, 91, 102, 121, 126, 130, 139,
   144, 145, 166, 179, 210, 215,
   218, 234, 235, 249, 254, 256
   driving of, ix-xi, 59, 244, 258–60
   drug use of, 292–93, 434,
   437–38, 439, 454
   early writing efforts of, 47, 48,
   67, 75–76, 80–81, 88–89, 91,
   97, 105–7, 136–37, 149
   education of, xi, 12, 21–22,
   24–25, 29, 47, 50, 54–56,

Styron, William Clark, Jr. *(cont'd)*
    60–108, 129–30, 133–41, 148–49
  family background of, 3–17
  as father, 284, 289, 306, 369–70,
    408–9, 421
  finances of, 142, 147–50, 170–71,
    181, 202, 209, 272, 274–75,
    282, 283–84, 290, 303, 312,
    365, 366
  guilt of, 40–41, 53
  health problems of, 20–21, 26,
    102, 112–16, 144–45, 232,
    243, 246, 252, 266, 293, 433,
    454
  interviews of, 203, 206, 233–35,
    324, 336, 351, 375
  jobs of, 23, 56, 57–58, 130–32,
    137, 142–47
  lawsuit of, 259–60
  magazine work of, 160–61,
    163–64, 253, 319–23, 328–29,
    346–48, 363–64, 368, 401, 431,
    432, 447–48
  in Marine Corps, xi, 80, 90–91,
    94–96, 100, 102–3, 105,
    107–28, 182, 185–201, 224
  physical appearance of, 20, 24,
    25, 47, 50, 54, 67, 70, 91, 104,
    127, 132, 179, 242, 246, 257,
    316
  politics of, 206, 207, 241,
    320–23, 380, 382–83, 389–91,
    395, 408, 431–32
  reading of, 21, 22, 25, 47, 65, 67,
    99–100, 144, 154, 180, 207,
    253–54, 445
  religious experience of, 34–35,
    74–75, 87–88, 91
  sexual experience of, 86–87, 91,
    104, 114–15, 116, 166, 168
  travels of, xii, 43–46, 48–49, 52,
    61–62, 73–74, 130–34, 137–39,
    209–65, 307–14, 324–25,
    332–34, 351–52, 383, 428

  vision problem of, 90, 110, 119,
    127, 186, 198–99
  writing ambition of, 96, 105,
    126, 130, 132–33, 139, 141,
    149–50, 157, 206
  writing habits of, 183, 272, 275,
    276
  writing problems of, 157–58,
    163–68, 170, 252–53, 268,
    269–70, 431–33
Styron, William Clark, Sr. (father),
    xi–xii, 10–12, 14, 19–22,
    39–46, 56–62, 90, 126, 267,
    332–34, 351, 409–10, 445, 449
  death of, xii, 423–24
  Elizabeth Buxton and, 58–59,
    60, 71–73, 152, 176, 396
  marriages of, 12, 19–20, 71–73,
    248, 410
  at Newport News shipyards, 11,
    12, 14, 19, 20, 22, 30, 31, 49,
    56, 57
  stress of, 49, 56–57
  WS's correspondence with, 91,
    100, 101, 102, 115–18, 140–41,
    143, 144, 146–51, 156, 158,
    164, 166, 167, 170, 178–81,
    185, 186, 187, 191, 199–201,
    211, 219–22, 229, 244, 249,
    254–55, 257, 264, 292, 327,
    331, 332–33
  WS's relationship with, 12,
    41–42, 60, 61, 73, 85–86, 130,
    150, 158, 170, 188, 190–91,
    205, 247, 283–84
Sullivan, Charles H., 121–22, 123,
    194–95
"Sun on the River" (Styron), 106–7
Swados, Harvey, 203
Swan, Annie, 23–24

Taeusch, Barbara (Bobbie), 105,
    108, 122–23, 124, 129, 140,
    144, 147, 149, 239, 419–20

Talese, Gay, 347–48
Tannenbaum, Frank, 340
Tate, Allen, 209
Tender Is the Night (Fitzgerald), 157, 254, 275
Tennyson, Alfred, Lord, 12
Terkel, Studs, 390
"Terrible Case of Theodore Twaddle's Hiccups, The" (Styron), 88
Thelwell, Mike, 385, 386
Thieves' Afternoon (Rose Styron), 404–5
"This Is My Daughter" (Styron), 136
"This Quiet Dust" (Styron), 363–64, 368
This Quiet Dust and Other Writings (Styron), 429
Thomey, Tedd, 319–20
Thompson, John, 377
Tidewater Morning, A (Styron), 456
"Tidewater Morning, A" (Styron), 16, 35, 447–50, 456
Time, 204, 205, 242, 311, 376–77
Times Literary Supplement, 211, 383–85
Towers, Robert, 425
Tragle, Henry Irving, 397
Train, John, 217, 232, 244–45, 249
Truman, Harry S., 187, 188
Turner, Nat, 55, 183, 220–23, 252, 267, 315, 318–19, 327, 331–43, 363, 364, 421
Turner, Samuel, 353, 373
Tyler, Charles, 85

Ulysses (Joyce), 174, 191–92, 281, 302
Under the Volcano (Lowry), 162, 174, 176
Uniontown, Pa., 12–17, 20, 45–46
Untermeyer, Louis, 133

Urbana, Va., 63, 69, 70, 76
Urb girls, the, 69, 76

Vanity Fair, 452, 453
Vargas, Alberto, 68
Vaughan, Rebecca, 334
Veterans Administration (VA), 147, 148, 162
Vidal, Gore, 207, 282, 286, 297
Vietnam War, 30, 321*n,* 322–23, 380, 398–99
Viking Press, 284, 358, 404
Virginia, University of, 61, 77, 91, 283, 352
Virginia State Library, 221, 332–33
Vizinczey, Stephen, 383
Voorhees, Peyton, 155, 176
Vuilleumier, Pasquale, 260–61

Waglini, Shabaka Sundiata, 400*n*-401*n*
Walker, Herman, 81
Wallace, Mike, 422, 436
Warburg, Frederic, 309
Warren, Robert Penn, 154, 155, 160, 342–43, 377, 392–94
Washington, Booker T., 35
Washington, N.C. (Little Washington), 6, 8–10, 21, 41, 43–45
Washington and Lee University, 51, 61, 77
Watson, Aleck, 23, 25, 47
Waugh, Evelyn, 162
Way of the Warrior, The (Styron's incomplete novel), 398–99, 401, 411, 412, 431–33
Welch, Arthur, 52
Welch, Frances, 52
West Durham Literary Society, 158, 185, 206
"Where the Spirit Is" (Styron), 97, 105–6
Whistle (Jones), 295, 423
White, Christian, 240, 254, 258

White, Claire, 239–40, 243, 247, 248, 254, 255, 257, 258, 261, 268–69, 300, 325, 422
White, Natalie, 422
White, Newman Ivey, 98
White, Robert, 239–40, 243, 247, 248, 254, 255, 257, 258, 259, 261, 268–69, 300, 325, 422
White, Sebastian, 240, 243, 258
White, Stanford, 239, 281
White, Stephanie, 240, 258
Whitehead, Margaret, 334, 339, 355, 364, 387, 388
Whitehead, Richard, 339
"White Negro, The" (Mailer), 288
Whittlesey House, 142–47, 160, 193
"Why Primo Need Not Have Died" (Styron), 451
Wigglesworth, Ann, 249, 257
Wigglesworth, Frank, 249, 257
Will, George F., 323
Williams, John A., 385, 386
Williams, Tennessee, 207–8, 247
"William Styron and the Age of the Slob" (Fenton), 311–12
William Styron's Nat Turner (anthology), 385–89, 426
Willingham, Calder, 212, 297–98

Wilson, Angus, 241
Wolfe, Thomas, 27, 40, 100, 117, 145, 175, 192
Wolper, David, 369, 398
Wood, Langley, 65, 77
Woodward, C. Vann, 342, 353, 362, 363, 377, 392, 393, 421, 446
World War I, 15, 17–19, 30–31
World War II, 54, 68, 75–77, 80, 82, 88–92, 107–23, 182, 199, 230, 431–32
Wright, Douglass, 322
Wright, James, 74–75
Wright, Naomi, 74
Wyman, Jane, 95–96
Wynne, Thomas, 12–13

Yale Repertory Theatre, 402
Yale Review, 275, 381
Yevtushenko, Yevgeny, 391
Young Lions, The (Shaw), 266, 267
Young Man Luther (Erikson), 340
Yourcenar, Marguerite, 372–73

Zanuck, Darryl, 218
Zellerbach, David, 246
Ziegner, Herman, 191
Ziff, Larzer, 425

ABOUT THE AUTHOR

JAMES L. W. WEST III, a native of Virginia, is Distinguished Professor of English at Pennsylvania State University, where he is a Fellow in the Institute for the Arts and Humanistic Studies. He has been awarded fellowships by the J. S. Guggenheim Foundation, the National Endowment for the Humanities, and the National Humanities Center; he has also held Fulbright appointments to England and Belgium and has been a visiting scholar at the American Academy in Rome. His previous books include studies of F. Scott Fitzgerald and of the profession of authorship in America. He has published scholarly editions of writings by Theodore Dreiser and other authors, and he is general editor of the Cambridge Edition of the Works of F. Scott Fitzgerald.

ABOUT THE TYPE

This book was set in Times Roman, designed by Stanley Morison specifically for *The Times* of London. The typeface was introduced in the newspaper in 1932. Times Roman had its greatest success in the United States as a book and commercial typeface, rather than one used in newspapers.